Cyber Security and Global Information Assurance:
Threat Analysis and Response Solutions

Kenneth J. Knapp
U.S. Air Force Academy, Colorado, USA

INFORMATION SCIENCE REFERENCE

Hershey · New York

Director of Editorial Content: Kristin Klinger
Senior Managing Editor: Jamie Snavely
Managing Editor: Jeff Ash
Assistant Managing Editor: Carole Coulson
Typesetter: Chris Hrobak
Cover Design: Lisa Tosheff
Printed at: Yurchak Printing Inc.

Published in the United States of America by
        Information Science Reference (an imprint of IGI Global)
        701 E. Chocolate Avenue, Suite 200
        Hershey PA 17033
        Tel: 717-533-8845
        Fax: 717-533-8661
        E-mail: cust@igi-global.com
        Web site: http://www.igi-global.com/reference

and in the United Kingdom by
        Information Science Reference (an imprint of IGI Global)
        3 Henrietta Street
        Covent Garden
        London WC2E 8LU
        Tel: 44 20 7240 0856
        Fax: 44 20 7379 0609
        Web site: http://www.eurospanbookstore.com

Library of Congress Cataloging-in-Publication Data

Cyber-security and global information assurance : threat analysis and response solutions / Kenneth J. Knapp, editor.
        p. cm.
Includes bibliographical references and index.

Summary: "This book provides a valuable resource by addressing the most pressing issues facing cyber-security from both a national and global perspective"--Provided by publisher.

ISBN 978-1-60566-326-5 (hardcover) -- ISBN 978-1-60566-327-2 (ebook) 1. Information technology--Security measures. 2. Computer security--Management. 3. Cyberspace--Security measures. 4. Data protection. 5. Computer networks--Security measures. I. Knapp, Kenneth J.

QA76.9.A25C918 2009
  005.8--dc22

                                2008052439

British Cataloguing in Publication Data
A Cataloguing in Publication record for this book is available from the British Library.

All work contributed to this book is new, previously-unpublished material. The views expressed in this book are those of the authors, but not necessarily of the publisher.

Cyber Security and Global Information Assurance: Threat Analysis and Response Solution is part of the IGI Global series named *Advances in Information Security and Privacy (AISP)* Series, ISBN: Pending

Advances in Information Security and Privacy (AISP) Series

Editor-in-Chief: Hamid Nemati, The University of North Carolina, USA
ISBN: Pending

Cyber Security and Global Information Assurance: Threat Analysis and Response Solutions

Edited By: Kenneth J. Knapp, U.S. Air Force Academy, USA

~ Information Science Reference
~ Copyright 2009
~ Pages: 381
~ Our Price: $195.00
~ H/C (ISBN: 978-1-60566-326-5)

Cyber Security and Global Information Assurance: Threat Analysis and Response Solutions provides a valuable resource for academicians and practitioners by addressing the most pressing issues facing cyber-security from both a national and global perspective. This reference source takes a holistic approach to cyber security and information assurance by treating both the technical as well as managerial sides of the field.

As information technology and the Internet become more and more ubiquitous and pervasive in our daily lives, there is an essential need for a more thorough understanding of information security and privacy issues and concerns. The **Advances in Information Security and Privacy (AISP) Book Series** will create and foster a forum where research in the theory and practice of information security and privacy is advanced. It seeks to publish high quality books dealing with a wide range of issues, ranging from technical, legal, regulatory, organizational, managerial, cultural, ethical and human aspects of information security and privacy. It will do so through a balanced mix of theoretical and empirical research contributions. AISP aims to provide researchers from all disciplines with comprehensive publications that best address the current state of security and privacy within technology and worldwide organizations. Because of the growing importance of this field, the series will serve to launch new developments with international importance and practical implication.

Order Online at ww.igi-global.com or call 717-533-8845 x100 – Mon-Fri 8:30 AM - 5:00 PM (EST) or Fax 24 Hours a Day 717-533-8661

John Bell, *United Stated Air Force, USA*
Bart Hubbs, *Hospital Corporation of American, USA*
Shane Balfe, *Royal Holloway, University of London, UK*
Paul Powenski, *BT/INS International Network Services, UK*
Matt B. Palmer, *Michigan State University, USA*
Pat P. Rieder, *United States Air Force Academy, USA*
Doug Patton, *United States Air Force Academy, USA*

Table of Contents

Foreword xvi

Preface xviii

Acknowledgment xxii

Section I
Risk and Threat Assessment

Chapter I
Dynamic Modeling of the Cyber Security Threat Problem: The Black Market for
Vulnerabilities 1
Jaziar Radianti, University of Agder, Norway
Jose J. Gonzalez, University of Agder and Gjøvik University College, Norway

Chapter II
An Attack Graph Based Approach for Threat Identification of an Enterprise Network 23
Somak Bhattacharya, Indian Institute of Technology, Kharagpur, India
Samresh Malhotra, Indian Institute of Technology, Kharagpur, India
S. K. Ghosh, Indian Institute of Technology, Kharagpur, India

Chapter III
Insider Threat Prevention, Detection and Mitigation 48
Robert F. Mills, Air Force Institute of Technology, USA
Gilbert L. Peterson, Air Force Institute of Technology, USA
Michael R. Grimaila, Air Force Institute of Technology, USA

Chapter IV
An Autocorrelation Methodology for the Assessment of Security Assurance 75
Richard T. Gordon, Bridging The Gap, Inc., USA
Allison S. Gehrke, University of Colorado, Denver, USA

Chapter V
Security Implications for Management from the Onset of Information Terrorism 97
Ken Webb, Webb Knowledge Services, Australia

Section II
Organizational and Human Security

Chapter VI
The Adoption of Information Security Management Standards: A Literature Review 119
Yves Barlette, GSCM-Montpellier Business School, France
Vladislav V. Fomin, Vytautas Magnus University, Lithuania

Chapter VII
Data Smog, Techno Creep and the Hobbling of the Cognitive Dimension 141
Peter R. Marksteiner, United States Air Force, USA

Chapter VIII
Balancing the Public Policy Drivers in the Tension between Privacy and Security 164
John W. Bagby, The Pennsylvania State University, USA

Chapter IX
Human Factors in Security: The Role of Information Security Professionals within
Organizations 184
Indira R. Guzman, TUI University, USA
Kathryn Stam, SUNY Institute of Technology, USA
Shaveta Hans, TUI University, USA
Carole Angolano, TUI University, USA

Chapter X
Diagnosing Misfits, Inducing Requirements, and Delineating Transformations within
Computer Network Operations Organizations 201
Nikolaos Bekatoros HN, Naval Postgraduate School, USA
Jack L. Koons III, Naval Postgraduate School, USA
Mark E. Nissen, Naval Postgraduate School, USA

Chapter XI
An Approach to Managing Identity Fraud 233
Rodger Jamieson, The University of New South Wales, Australia
Stephen Smith, The University of New South Wales, Australia
Greg Stephens, The University of New South Wales, Australia
Donald Winchester, The University of New South Wales, Australia

Section III
Emergency Response Planning

Chapter XII
A Repeatable Collaboration Process for Incident Response Planning 250
Alanah Davis, University of Nebraska at Omaha, USA
Gert-Jan de Vreede, University of Nebraska at Omaha, USA
Leah R. Pietron, University of Nebraska at Omaha, USA

Chapter XIII
Pandemic Influenza, Worker Absenteeism and Impacts on Critical Infrastructures:
Freight Transportation as an Illustration 265
    Dean A. Jones, Sandia National Laboratories, USA
    Linda K. Nozick, Cornell University, USA
    Mark A. Turnquist, Cornell University, USA
    William J. Sawaya, Texas A&M University, USA

Chapter XIV
Information Sharing: A Study of Information Attributes and their Relative Significance During
Catastrophic Events 283
    Preeti Singh, University at Buffalo, The State University of New York, USA
    Pranav Singh, University at Buffalo, The State University of New York, USA
    Insu Park, University at Buffalo, The State University of New York, USA
    JinKyu Lee, Oklahoma State University, USA
    H. Raghav Rao, University at Buffalo, The State University of New York, USA

Chapter XV
An Overview of the Community Cyber Security Maturity Model 306
    Gregory B. White, The University of Texas at San Antonio, USA
    Mark L. Huson, The University of Texas at San Antonio, USA

Section IV
Security Technologies

Chapter XVI
Server Hardening Model Development: A Methodology-Based Approach to Increased
System Security 319
    Doug White, Roger Williams University, USA
    Alan Rea, Western Michigan University, USA

Chapter XVII
Trusted Computing: Evolution and Direction..343
    Jeff Teo, Montreat College, USA

Chapter XVIII
Introduction, Classification and Implementation of Honeypots 371
    Miguel Jose Hernandez y Lopez, Universidad de Buenos Aires, Argentina
    Carlos Francisco Lerma Resendez, Universidad Autónoma de Tamaulipas, Mexico

Compilation of References 383

About the Contributors 420

Index..430

Detailed Table of Contents

Foreword...xvi

Preface.. xviii

Acknowledgment...xxii

Section I
Risk and Threat Assessment

Chapter I

Dynamic Modeling of the Cyber Security Threat Problem: The Black Market for
Vulnerabilities... 1

Jaziar Radianti, University of Agder, Norway
Jose J. Gonzalez, University of Agder and Gjøvik University College, Norway

This chapter discusses the possible growth of black markets (BMs) for software vulnerabilities and factors affecting their spread. The authors conduct a disguised observation of online BM trading sites to identify causal models of the ongoing viability of BMs. Results are expressed as a system dynamic model and suggest that without interventions, the number and size of BMs is likely to increase. A simulation scenario with a policy to halt BM operations results in temporary decrease of the market. Combining the policy with efforts to build distrust among BM participants may cause them to leave the forum and inhibit the imitation process to establish similar forums.

Chapter II

An Attack Graph Based Approach for Threat Identification of an Enterprise Network....................... 23

Somak Bhattacharya, Indian Institute of Technology, Kharagpur, India
Samresh Malhotra, Indian Institute of Technology, Kharagpur, India
S. K. Ghosh, Indian Institute of Technology, Kharagpur, India

As networks continue to grow in size and complexity, automatic assessment of the security vulnerability becomes increasingly important. The typical means by which an attacker breaks into a network is through a series of exploits, where each exploit in the series satisfies the pre-condition for subsequent exploits and makes a causal relationship among them. Such a series of exploits constitutes an attack path where the set of all possible attack paths form an attack graph. Attack graphs reveal the threat by enumerating all possible sequences of exploits that can compromise a given critical resource. The contribution of this chapter is to identify the most probable attack path based on the attack surface measures of the individual hosts for a given network and subsequently to identify the minimum securing options. As a whole, the chapter deals with the identification of probable attack path and risk mitigation that can significantly help improve the overall security of an enterprise network.

Chapter III

Insider Threat Prevention, Detection and Mitigation...48
    Robert F. Mills, Air Force Institute of Technology, USA
    Gilbert L. Peterson, Air Force Institute of Technology, USA
    Michael R. Grimaila, Air Force Institute of Technology, USA

This chapter introduces the insider threat and discusses methods for preventing, detecting, and responding to the threat. Trusted insiders present one of the most significant risks to an organization. They possess elevated privileges when compared to external users, have knowledge about technical and non-technical control measures, and potentially can bypass security measures designed to prevent, detect, or react to unauthorized access. The authors define the insider threat and summarize various case studies of insider attacks in order to highlight the severity of the problem. Best practices for preventing, detecting, and mitigating insider attacks are provided.

Chapter IV

An Autocorrelation Methodology for the Assessment of Security Assurance......................................75
    Richard T. Gordon, Bridging The Gap, Inc., USA
    Allison S. Gehrke, University of Colorado, Denver, USA

This chapter describes a methodology for assessing security infrastructure effectiveness utilizing formal mathematical models. The goal of this methodology is to determine the relatedness of effects on security operations from independent security events and from security event categories, identify opportunities for increased efficiency in the security infrastructure yielding time savings in the security operations and identify combinations of security events which compromise the security infrastructure. The authors focus on evaluating and describing a novel security assurance measure that governments and corporations can use to evaluate the strength and readiness of their security infrastructure.

Chapter V

Security Implications for Management from the Onset of Information Terrorism..................................97
    Ken Webb, Webb Knowledge Services, Australia

In this chapter, the author presents the results of a qualitative study and argues that a heightened risk for management has emerged from a new security environment that is increasingly spawning asymmetric forms of Information Warfare. This chapter defines for readers what the threat of Information Terrorism is and the new security environment that it has created. Security implications for management have subsequently evolved, as managers are now required to think about the philosophical considerations emerging from this increasing threat.

Section II
Organizational and Human Security

Chapter VI

The Adoption of Information Security Management Standards: A Literature Review 119

Yves Barlette, GSCM-Montpellier Business School, France

Vladislav V. Fomin, Vytautas Magnus University, Lithuania

This chapter discusses major information security management standards, particularly the ISO/IEC 27001 and 27002 standards. A literature review was conducted in order to understand the reasons for the low level of adoption of information security standards by companies, and to identify the drivers and the success factors in implementation of these standards. Based on the findings of the literature review, the authors provide recommendations on how to successfully implement and stimulate diffusion of information security standards.

Chapter VII

Data Smog, Techno Creep and the Hobbling of the Cognitive Dimension 141

Peter R. Marksteiner, United States Air Force, USA

The overabundance of information, relentless stream of interruptions, and potent distractive quality of the Internet can draw knowledge workers away from productive cognitive engagement. Information overload is an increasingly familiar phenomenon, but evolving United States military doctrine provides a new analytical approach and a unifying taxonomy organizational leaders and academicians may find useful. Using military doctrine and thinking to underscore the potential seriousness of this evolving threat should inspire organizational leaders to recognize the criticality of its impact and motivate them to help clear the data smog, reduce information overload, and communicate for effect.

Chapter VIII

Balancing the Public Policy Drivers in the Tension between Privacy and Security 164

John W. Bagby, The Pennsylvania State University, USA

The public expects that technologies used in electronic commerce and government will enhance security while preserving privacy. This chapter posits that personally identifiable information is a form of property that flows along an "information supply chain" from collection, through archival and analysis and ultimately to its use in decision-making. The conceptual framework for balancing privacy and security developed here provides a foundation to develop and implement public policies that safeguard individual rights, the economy, critical infrastructures and national security. The illusive resolution of the practical antithesis between privacy and security is explored by developing some tradeoff relationships using exemplars from various fields that identify this quandary while recognizing how privacy and security sometimes harmonize.

Chapter IX

Human Factors in Security: The Role of Information Security Professionals within Organizations 184

Indira R. Guzman, TUI University, USA

Kathryn Stam, SUNY Institute of Technology, USA

Shaveta Hans, TUI University, USA

Carole Angolano, TUI University, USA

This chapter contributes to a better understanding of role conflict, skill expectations, and the value of information technology (IT) security professionals in organizations. Previous literature has focused primarily on the role of information professionals in general but has not evaluated the specific role expectations and skills required by IT security professionals in today's organizations. The authors take into consideration the internal and external factors that affect the security infrastructure of an organization and therefore influence the role expectations and skills required by those who are in charge of security. The authors describe the factors discussed in the literature and support them with quotes gathered from interviews conducted with information security professionals in small organizations in central New York. They present a set of common themes that expand the understanding of this role and provide practical recommendations that would facilitate the management of these professionals within organizations.

Chapter X

Diagnosing Misfits, Inducing Requirements, and Delineating Transformations within
Computer Network Operations Organizations 201
  Nikolaos Bekatoros HN, Naval Postgraduate School, USA
  Jack L. Koons III, Naval Postgraduate School, USA
  Mark E. Nissen, Naval Postgraduate School, USA

In this chapter, the authors use Contingency Theory research to inform leaders and policy makers regarding how to bring their Computer Networked Operations (CNO) organizations and approaches into better fit, and hence to improve performance. The authors identify a candidate set of organizational structures that offer potential to fit the U. S. Department of Defense better as it strives, and struggles, to address the technological advances and risks associated with CNO. Using the Organization Consultant expert system to model and diagnose key problems, the authors propose a superior organizational structure for CNO that can also be applied to organizations in the international environment. Results elucidate important insights into CNO organization and management, suitable for immediate policy and operational implementation, and expand the growing empirical basis to guide continued research

Chapter XI

An Approach to Managing Identity Fraud 233
  Rodger Jamieson, The University of New South Wales, Australia
  Stephen Smith, The University of New South Wales, Australia
  Greg Stephens, The University of New South Wales, Australia
  Donald Winchester, The University of New South Wales, Australia

This chapter outlines components of a strategy for government and a conceptual identity fraud management framework for organizations. Identity crime, related cybercrimes and information systems security breaches are insidious motivators for governments and organizations to protect and secure their systems, databases and other assets against intrusion and loss. Model components used to develop the identity fraud framework were selected from the cost of identity fraud, identity risk management, identity fraud profiling, and fraud risk management literature.

Section III
Emergency Response Planning

Chapter XII

A Repeatable Collaboration Process for Incident Response Planning...250

Alanah Davis, University of Nebraska at Omaha, USA

Gert-Jan de Vreede, University of Nebraska at Omaha, USA

Leah R. Pietron, University of Nebraska at Omaha, USA

This chapter presents a repeatable collaboration process as an approach for developing a comprehensive Incident Response Plan for an organization or team. This chapter discusses the background of incident response planning as well as Collaboration Engineering, which is an approach to design repeatable collaborative work practices. A collaboration process for incident response planning is presented that was designed using Collaboration Engineering principles, followed by a discussion of the application process in three cases. The presented process is applicable across organizations in various sectors and domains, and consist of codified 'best facilitation practices' that can be easily transferred to and adopted by security managers.

Chapter XIII

Pandemic Influenza, Worker Absenteeism and Impacts on Critical Infrastructures:

Freight Transportation as an Illustration 265

Dean A. Jones, Sandia National Laboratories, USA

Linda K. Nozick, Cornell University, USA

Mark A. Turnquist, Cornell University, USA

William J. Sawaya, Texas A&M University, USA

A pandemic influenza outbreak could cause serious disruption to operations of several critical infrastructures as a result of worker absenteeism. This paper focuses on freight transportation services, particularly rail and port operations, as an illustration of analyzing performance of critical infrastructures under reduced labor availability. Using current data on performance of specific rail and port facilities, the authors reach some conclusions about the likelihood of severe operational disruption under varying assumptions about the absentee rate. Other infrastructures that are more dependent on information technology and less labor-intensive than transportation might respond to large-scale worker absenteeism in different ways, but the general character of this analysis can be adapted for application in other infrastructures such as the cyber infrastructure.

Chapter XIV

Information Sharing: A Study of Information Attributes and their Relative Significance During

Catastrophic Events 283

Preeti Singh, University at Buffalo, The State University of New York, USA

Pranav Singh, University at Buffalo, The State University of New York, USA

Insu Park, University at Buffalo, The State University of New York, USA

JinKyu Lee, Oklahoma State University, USA

H. Raghav Rao, University at Buffalo, The State University of New York, USA

We live in a digital era where the global community relies on Information Systems to conduct all kinds of operations, including averting or responding to unanticipated risks and disasters. This chapter focuses on Information Sharing within a disaster context. To study the relative significance of various information dimensions in different disaster situations, content analyses are conducted. The results are used to develop a prioritization framework for different disaster response activities, thus to increase the mitigation efficiency. The authors also explore roles played by existing organizations and technologies across the globe that are actively involved in Information Sharing to mitigate the impact of disasters and extreme events.

Chapter XV

An Overview of the Community Cyber Security Maturity Model 306

    Gregory B. White, The University of Texas at San Antonio, USA

    Mark L. Huson, The University of Texas at San Antonio, USA

The protection of cyberspace is essential to ensure that the critical infrastructures a nation relies on are not corrupted or disrupted. Government efforts generally focus on securing cyberspace at the national level. In the United States, states and communities have not seen the same concentrated effort and are now the weak link in the security chain. Until recently, there has been no program for states and communities to follow in order to establish a viable security program. The authors develop the Community Cyber Security Maturity Model to provide a framework for communities to prepare, prevent, detect, respond, and recover from potential cyber attacks. This model has a broad applicability and can be adapted to nations and organizations as well.

Section IV

Security Technologies

Chapter XVI

Server Hardening Model Development: A Methodology-Based Approach to Increased

System Security 319

    Doug White, Roger Williams University, USA

    Alan Rea, Western Michigan University, USA

The authors present essential server security components and develop a set of logical steps to build hardened servers. The authors outline techniques to examine servers in both the Linux/UNIX and the Windows Environment for security flaws from both the internal and external perspectives. The chapter builds a complete model covering tactics, and techniques that system administrators can use to harden a server against compromise and attack. The authors build a model to assist those who want to implement and maintain secure, hardened servers not only for today's intense demands but also for the foreseeable future as more servers come online to support new Internet-enabled services.

Chapter XVII

Trusted Computing: Evolution and Direction 343

    Jeff Teo, Montreat College, USA

To effectively combat cyber threats, our network defenses must be equipped to thwart dangerous attacks. However, our software-dominated defenses are woefully inadequate. The Trusted Computing Group has embarked on a mission to use an open standards-based interoperability framework utilizing both hardware and software implementations to defend against computer attacks. Specifically, this group uses trusted hardware called the trusted platform module (TPM) in conjunction with TPM-enhanced software to provide better protection against such attacks. This chapter will detail a brief history of trusted computing, the goals of the Trusted Computing Group and the workings of trusted platforms.

Chapter XVIII
Introduction, Classification and Implementation of Honeypots 371
    Miguel Jose Hernandez y Lopez, Universidad de Buenos Aires, Argentina
    Carlos Francisco Lerma Resendez, Universidad Autónoma de Tamaulipas, Mexico

This chapter discusses the basic aspects of Honeypots, how they are implemented in modern computer networks, as well as their practical uses and implementation in educational environments. This chapter covers the most important points regarding the characteristics of Honeypots and Honeynets. The implementation of Honeypots provides an answer to a common question posted by the field of information security and forensics: How to dissect the elements that make up an attack against a computer system. The chapter summarizes the different features and capabilities of Honeypots once they are set up in a production environment.

Compilation of References 383

About the Contributors 420

Index 430

Foreword

The modern era can be characterized by increasing rates of change within every dimension of the environments in which we operate. Global economic and political conditions, technological infrastructure, and socio-cultural developments all contribute to an increasingly turbulent and dynamic environment for those who design and manage information systems for use in business, government, military, and other domains. Even weather patterns and events seem to change more rapidly in recent years! As our institutions (economic, political, military, legal, social) become increasingly global and inter-connected, as we rely more and more on automated control systems to provide our needs for energy, food, and services, and as we establish Internet-based mechanisms for coordinating this global interaction, we introduce greater vulnerability to ourselves as individuals, for companies, and for our governments, including their military organizations. This increased dependence on cyberspace also inflates our vulnerability – isolation is no longer an option. Perhaps no aspect of this phenomenon is as alarming and challenging as the need to understand the various risks to the security of our information systems and the methods for addressing them.

These risks arise from a plethora of sources and motivations. Some are natural; in recent years we have seen significant weather events (Asian Tsunami, Hurricane Katrina, major earthquakes, etc.) that threaten organizations and their physical resources, including information servers. Some risks are from intentional human activity, and the world is now full of new, more sophisticated hackers, spies, terrorists, and criminal organizations that are committed to coordinated global attacks on our information assets in order to achieve their many goals. Some wish to inflict damage and loss for political reasons or for military purposes, some are seeking "trade secrets" and proprietary corporate information, and others are seeking financial information with which to conduct fraud, identity theft, and other criminal acts. Another category of risks has arisen from new classes of increasingly-devious and effective malware capable of penetrating even the most recent perimeter defenses. These include not only viruses, worms, and trojans, but now also rootkits, distributed botnet attacks, and a new scary sophisticated category called the "Storm" class of malware, which includes programs which are self-propagating, coordinated, reusable, and self-defending peer-to-peer tools that use decentralized command and control and seem to use intelligence to dynamically defend themselves from users and software.

Perhaps the greatest threat of all is the insider threat – the organizational member who is a "trusted agent" inside the firewall. This employee or other constituent with a valid username and password regularly interacts with the information assets of the organization, and can initiate great harm to the confidentiality, integrity, or availability of the information system through deliberate activities (consider the disgruntled employee or the counter-spy). Or they may introduce risk via passive noncompliance with security policies, laziness, sloppiness, poor training, or lack of motivation to vigorously protect the integrity and privacy of the sensitive information of the organization and its partners, clients, customers, and others. I call this problem the "endpoint security problem" because the individual employee is the endpoint of the information system and its network – the employee has direct or indirect access to the entire network from his or her endpoint and can inflict great harm (and has!). The insider threat has repeatedly been called the greatest threat to the system, and yet this is often overlooked in a rush to protect the perimeter with ever-increasingly sophisticated perimeter controls (intrusion detection systems, firewalls, etc.). Greater emphasis on hiring, training, and motivating employees to act securely will generate great payoff for the organizations that pursue this strategy. Mechanisms to support this goal are paramount to the future security of our information assets.

Developing and testing creative solutions and managerial strategies to identify these threats, analyze them, defend against them, and also to recover, repair, and control the damage caused by them is a critical management imperative. Leaders in government and industry must actively and aggressively support the ongoing design and implementation of effective, appropriate solutions (technologies, policies, legal strategies, training, etc.) that can be targeted to these diverse threats to our information assets and to the smooth functions of individuals, teams, organizations, and societies in our global network of systems. New methods of analysis (e.g. threat graphs, evolving standards, government actions) and new solutions (e.g. honeynets, firewall designs, improved training and monitoring) will be required to keep up with the ever-changing threat environment. Research in this area is critical for our protection in this new age of global inter-connectivity and interdependence. We need to continually seek new and better solutions because the enemy is constantly improving the attack vectors. The alternative is not acceptable. The costs are too high. We must prevail.

Merrill Warkentin
Mississippi State University

Merrill Wakentin *is Professor of MIS at Mississippi State University. He has published several books and over 150 research manuscripts, primarily in computer security management, eCommerce, and virtual collaborative teams, in books, Proceedings, and in leading academic journals. He is also an Associate Editor of Management Information Systems Quarterly (for security manuscripts), Information Resources Management Journal, and Journal of Information Systems Security. Professor Warkentin is Guest Editing the special issue of the European Journal of Information Systems on Computer Security and has chaired several global conferences on computer security. He has Chaired the Workshop on Information Security and Privacy (WISP) twice and the Information Security Track at DSI. He has served as Associate Editor for the Information Security tracks of AMCIS and ICIS several times, and will co-Chair the IFIP Workshop on Information Security in 2009. At Mississippi State, Dr. Warkentin directs research projects and doctoral student dissertations in the various areas of computer security and assurance research, including behavorial and policy studies, design of password systems, and managerial controls for computer security management. He serves as a member of the research staff of the Center for Computer Security Research. He has also served as a consultant to numerous organizations and has served as National Distingushed Lecturer for the Association for Computing Machinery (ACM). His PhD in MIS is from the University of Nebraska-Lincoln. He can reached at mwarkentin@acm.org and his website in www.MISProfessor.com.*

Preface

In the 2003 publication, *The National Strategy to Secure Cyberspace*, the United States Government acknowledged, "our economy and national security is now fully dependent on information technology and the information infrastructure" (U. S. Government, 2003, p. 9). The candid use of the word "fully" is no overstatement. If the Internet infrastructure were significantly compromised, critical systems supporting supply chains, financial markets and telecommunications, for example, could simultaneously be severely handicapped or completely cease from functioning.

Particularly since the turn of the century, modern society's dependence on cyber and information related technologies for daily living has increased at an astonishing rate. Entire cultures of what many call 'developed nations' such as the United States are engulfed in a cyber technology way of life that takes for granted the availability and integrity of information systems and the Internet. Additionally, in some "developing" nations, the outsourcing of knowledge work from developed nations has created high-technology subcultures in the developing world. While a global digital divide certainly exists between nations with ready access to cyberspace and those without such access, overall, an increasing global economic dependency on cyberspace is undeniable. Some argue, such as James Lewis in testimony to the U. S. Congress, "Cyber security is now one of the most important national security challenges facing the U. S. This is not some hypothetical catastrophe. We are under attack and taking damage." Indeed, the cyber security situation facing the U. S. has gotten worse in the past decade, while cyberspace now supplies the foundation of much of the nation's economic activity (Lewis, 2008).

This book addresses the growing societal dependence on information technologies by providing a literature resource for academics and practitioners alike that speaks to the pressing issues facing cyber security from both national and global perspectives. Book chapters cover critical topics to include information security standards, information overload, cyber privacy issues, information terrorism, the cyber security black market, threat assessment for enterprise networks, an analysis of critical transportation infrastructures with cyberspace implications, information sharing during catastrophic events, as well as chapters discussing trusted computing, honeypots and server hardening. The underlying premise of the book stresses the global nature of cyber security problems; in doing so, each chapter provides an analysis of specific threats facing society with proposed solutions. Ultimately, we hope this book will facilitate international cooperation to help build a more secure future in cyberspace.

Before continuing, it is worthwhile to review the term *security* and offer a formal definition to help explain why books such as this are valuable. Security is the condition of being protected, which includes freedom from apprehension and the confidence of safety; hence, assurance. We can think of security as that which makes safe or protects (Webster's Revised Unabridged Dictionary, 2008). Regarding information or cyber security, both practitioners and academics often stress the importance of three desirable aspects of security: Confidentially, Integrity and Availability. This CIA triad serves as a limited, but useful framework for thinking about and understanding security and how data and cyber-based systems need protecting (Whitman & Mattord, 2004). Security becomes especially critical in hazardous environments when the risk of danger and the consequence from damaging incidents are high. This is the reason why cyber security has become so critical in recent times. We have become progressively dependent on cyberspace for daily living yet the cyber environment is full of serious dangers.

Now that we have briefly framed the term security, we may ask, what aspect of security is most important to enhance our understanding and lower risks? In his edited book titled, *Information Security Management: Global Challenges in New Millennium*, Dhillon argues that the management of information security should be broader in scope than just focusing on the technological means to achieve proper security (2001). This indeed is the case with the current text: fully grasping today's challenges requires a broad view of cyber security that includes both technical and managerial dimensions. To this end, each chapter offers a valuable perspective of cyber security and information assurance. If read from cover to cover, the reader will gain a holistic understanding and systems view of cyber security challenges. While the book is not encyclopedic in scope, it offers a broad view of security challenges through 18 chapters, each dedicated to a different but important topic in the cyber security domain. Each chapter was double blind reviewed. Authors went through a process of submitting a proposal, completing a manuscript, and then revising the manuscript while responding to comments from at least three external reviewers. Finally, each author of an accepted manuscript worked with me to produce a publishable chapter. This process has been immensely valuable to me as the editor. I thoroughly enjoyed working with each author and found the publication process to be professionally satisfying. In reviewing each chapter as the editor, I found myself enlightened and better educated about this dynamic, complex and critical field. It is my hope that readers will share a similar experience.

I divided the book into four major sections, each containing at least three chapters. Together, the four sections present a broad and global picture of major cyber security challenges. The first section offers chapters on the theme of *Risk and Threat Assessment*. The second section focuses on *Organizational and Human Security*. The third presents topics covering *Emergency Response Planning*. Finally, the fourth section covers important *Security Technologies*.

The book begins with a section on *Risk and Threat Assessment*. I placed this section first because of my belief that understanding risk and the threat environment is a foremost step in addressing security. In Chapter I, Jaziar Radianti and Jose J. Gonzalez discuss their observations of the black market for software vulnerabilities and the factors affecting its spread. They illustrate a system dynamic model and suggest that, without interventions, the number and size of black markets will likely increase. In Chapter II, Somak Bhattacharya, Samresh Malhotra, and S. K. Ghosh provide an attack graph approach to network threat identification. The chapter deals with identifying probable attack graph and risk mitigation in order to improve enterprise security. Chapter III introduces the insider threat and methods for preventing, detecting, and responding to this threat. In their work, Robert F. Mills, Gilbert L. Peterson, and Michael R. Grimaila define the insider threat and offer best practices for mitigating this serious problem. Chapter IV describes a method for assessing security infrastructure effectiveness utilizing formal mathematical models. Here, Richard T. Gordon and Allison S. Gehrke discuss a novel security measure that organizations can use to evaluate the strength of their security infrastructure. In the final chapter of this section, Chapter V, Ken Webb argues that a heightened risk for management has emerged from a new security environment that is producing asymmetric forms of information warfare. This chapter aims to provide guidance for future thinking to inform readers about information terrorism and the security implications for management.

The second section covers the important area of *Organizational and Human Security*. While sometimes described as the "soft" or non-technical side of security, this area is often at the very core of many security problems and incidents. In Chapter VI, Yves Barlette and Vladislav V. Fomin discuss major management standards, particularly ISO/IEC 27001 and 27002. Based on the findings of their literature review, the authors recommend how to successfully implement and diffuse information security standards in organizations. Chapter VII covers the important topic of information overload. Peter R. Marksteiner uses military doctrine to underscore the seriousness of the overload threat. The chapter provides a detailed discussion explaining the problem and suggests improvements concerning organizational communication effectiveness. In Chapter VIII, John W. Bagby posits that personally identifiable information flows along an "information supply chain" and offers a useful conceptual framework for balancing privacy and security. In Chapter IX, Indira R. Guzman, Kathryn Stam, Shaveta Hans, and Carole Angolano focus on the role of information security professionals in organizations. They explicitly focus on the specific roles, expectations and skills required by IT security professionals based in part on interviews conducted with security professionals. In Chapter X, the authors Nikolaos Bekatoros, Jack L. Koons III, and Mark E. Nissen discuss improving the structural fit of organizations involved in computer network operations (CNO). The authors use contingency theory research to inform leaders and policy makers on how to bring CNO organizations into a better fit in order to improve organizational performance. In Chapter XI, Rodger Jamieson, Stephen Smith, Greg Stephens, and Donald Winchester offer a strategy for government and a useful framework for identify fraud management. The authors based this framework on a literature review of related fields and organized the framework into anticipatory, reactionary and remediation phases.

The third section of the book deals with the emerging area of *Emergency Response Planning*. In light of serious external threats from terrorism and natural disasters, organizations must ensure that proper planning occurs to ensure continuity in the event of a disaster. In Chapter XII, Alanah Davis, Gert-Jan de Vreede, and Leah R. Pietron present a repeatable collaboration process as an approach for developing an incident response plan for organizations. The authors use collaboration engineering principles and present a process that consists of codified facilitation practices that can be transferred to and adopted by security managers in various types of organizations. Next, Chapter XIII deals with the possibility of a pandemic influenza, worker absenteeism and its impacts on the critical infrastructure of freight transportation as an illustration of how other infrastructures can be impacted. In this work, Dean A. Jones, Linda K. Nozick, Mark A. Turnquist, and William J. Sawaya then address the relevant question of how does this idea extend to other infrastructures, particularly those that are more information-oriented and less labor-intensive than transportation. Chapter XIV focuses on information sharing and information attributes within a disaster context. The authors Preeti Singh, Pranav Singh, Insu Park, JinKyu Lee, and H. Raghav Rao use content analysis to develop a prioritization framework for different disaster response activities. In Chapter XV, Gregory B. White and Mark L. Huson develop the community cyber security maturity model to provide a framework for states and communities to help prepare, prevent, detect, respond, and recover from potential cyber attacks. This model has broad applicability and can be adapted to nations and communities.

The fourth and final section offers chapters focusing on three vital security-related technologies. In Chapter XVI, Doug White and Alan Rea present essential server security components and develop a set of logical steps to build hardened servers. This chapter presents a complete model that includes advice on tools, tactics, and techniques that system administrators can use to harden a server against compromise and attack. In Chapter XVII, Jeff Teo provides an overview and direction of trusted computing and the goals of the Trusted Computing Group. This group uses trusted hardware in conjunction with enhanced software to provide better protection against cyber attacks. Chapter XVIII, the final chapter of the book, comes from Miguel Jose Hernandez y Lopez and Carlos Francisco Lerma Resendez. They discuss the basic aspects of Honeypots and how they are implemented in modern computer networks. The authors provide readers with the most important points regarding the characteristics of Honeypots and Honeynets, which are highly useful platforms in supporting security education and forensics.

It is my hope that after reading this book in part or in its entirety, readers will feel more knowledgeable and enlightened about the scope of challenges facing global cyber security. Considering the types of cyber threats facing our world, books such as this can make an important contribution by enhancing our understanding concerning the problems we are facing and solutions we should contemplate. I would enjoy hearing from readers about your opinions and experiences with this book. Feel free to contact me at knappkj@gmail.com.

With warm regards,
Kenneth J. Knapp, Editor
United States Air Force Academy, Colorado
November 2008

DISCLAIMER

Opinions, conclusions and recommendations expressed or implied within this book are solely those of the authors and do not necessarily represent the views of US Air Force Academy, USAF, the DoD or any other U. S. government agency.

REFERENCES

Dhillon, G. (2001). *Information Security Management: Global Challenges in the New Millennium.* Hershey, PA: Idea Group Publishing.

Lewis, J. A. (2008). *Cybersecurity Recommendations for the Next Administration Testimony by James A. Lewis, Center for Strategic and International Studies, September 16, 2008.* Washington D.C.: Subcommittee on Emerging Threats, Cybersecurity, and Science and Technology.

security. (n.d.). *Webster's Revised Unabridged Dictionary.* Retrieved September 17, 2008, from Dictionary.com website: http://dictionary.reference.com/browse/security

U. S. Government. (2003, February). *National Strategy to Secure Cyberspace.* Retrieved May, 2004, from http://www.whitehouse.gov/pcipb

Whitman, M. E., & Mattord, H. J. (2004). *Management of Information Security.* Cambridge, MA: Course Technology - Thompson Learning.

Acknowledgment

Research projects such as this book require a team of supporters and this one is no exception. First, I am grateful for the outstanding assistance from IGI Global. They provided me with responsive, courteous and expert guidance throughout this project. I am equally grateful to the members of the Editorial Advisory Board, most of whom reviewed several manuscripts that prospective authors submitted for consideration. Additionally, I am appreciative to the external reviewers for their quality and timely reviews. Several individuals contributed significantly to this project to include Hamid R. Nemati for initially contacting me and supporting this project as well as Merrill Warkentin for graciously writing the Forward to this book. I am most thankful to the contributing authors of accepted manuscripts for their professionalism and patience during the review and publication process.

A prominent acknowledgement goes to the Department of Management at the United States Air Force Academy. Specifically, I would like to recognize two fantastic bosses, Brigadier General Rita A. Jordan and Colonel Andrew P. Armacost, as well as my faculty colleagues for the friendship, support and confidence place in me over the years. No doubt, this was the best assignment of my Air Force career. Moreover, I am thankful to Harold Webb and the Information and Technology Management department at the University of Tampa for bringing me on their team.

I would like to single out both Thomas E. Marshall and R. Kelly Rainer, Jr. from Auburn University. They encouraged and supported me in great ways since starting my doctoral program in 2003 to this current project. I have benefitted mightily from their solid counsel and friendship.

These acknowledgements give me the opportunity to publically thank Dorsey W. Morrow and the (ISC)^2 organization, who provided me with several outstanding opportunities to explore the social and human dimensions of information security. Most of my publications in academic journals have resulted from data involving (ISC)^2 and the certified security professionals associated with this fine organization. Without such previous support, this current project would never have been feasible.

Finally and most essential, I acknowledge my eternal indebtedness to my wife and children for supporting me during this project. My family is what makes life worth living.

Section I
Risk and Threat Assessment

Chapter I
Dynamic Modeling of the Cyber Security Threat Problem:
The Black Market for Vulnerabilities

Jaziar Radianti
University of Agder, Norway

Jose J. Gonzalez
University of Agder and Gjøvik University College, Norway

ABSTRACT

This chapter discusses the possible growth of black markets (BMs) for software vulnerabilities and factors affecting their spread. It is difficult to collect statistics about BMs for vulnerabilities and their associated transactions, as they are hidden from general view. We conduct a disguised observation of online BM trading sites to identify causal models of the ongoing viability of BMs. Our observation results are expressed as a system dynamic model. We implement simulations to observe the effects of possible actions to disrupt BMs. The results suggest that without interventions the number and size of BMs is likely to increase. A simulation scenario with a policy to halt BM operations results in temporary decrease of the market. The intervention ultimately meets policy resistance, failing to neutralize a reinforcing feedback. Combining the policy with efforts to build distrust among BM participants may cause them to leave the forum and inhibit the imitation process to establish similar forums.

INTRODUCTION

Cyber security is a challenging problem for various computer network users and administrators, both in public and private sectors. The defense capability of cyberspace users commonly lags behind that of malicious attackers who are quick in discover-ing holes, weaknesses, flaws and vulnerabilities in hardware and software systems. Escalating costs of computer incidents increasingly puts the security of computer networks at risk. Failures in securing cyberspace are partially rooted in the software vulnerability problem. One emerging issue as a result of the undiscovered ubiquitous flaws in software is the black market (BM) presence which allows people to trade exploits for vulnerabilities. The objectives of this chapter are threefold: first, to address general knowledge on discussions surrounding vulnerability discovery and the black market for vulnerabilities; second, to briefly illustrate our disguised observation in online BMs; third, to build a simple system dynamics model about how BMs spread.

This chapter is divided into several sub-sections. We start the discussion with the problem background, followed by a description of the black market terms and the complexities to keep software secure. Next, we cover the history and background surrounding the vulnerability discovery and the development of the market for software vulnerabilities, whether legal or illegal. In other words, we describe the process from non-profit-based vulnerability discovery process to profit-seeking discovery process. The legitimate market discussion in theory and practice is embedded to further show the connection with the underground trading problems. The subsequent sub-section deals with the dynamic model of BMs. We have used system dynamics (SD) models to map the causal structure of vulnerability trading. SD modeling supports iterative development, allowing us to refine and incrementally validate the model's structure and dynamic behavior as empirical data emerge. For this chapter we present a simple, observation-based model to illustrate how the black markets may spread. In the last sub-section, we discuss future trends and draw conclusions.

BACKGROUND

The vulnerability black market (VBM) discussions surfaced almost as the same time as the increasing public debates on the emergence of legitimate markets where vulnerability researchers can sell vulnerability information. The existence of black hat hackers has long been known; however, a recent trend is that they are becoming profit-seeking (Itzhak, 2006). In the past, they searched vulnerabilities mainly to improve their opportunity for financial gain through successful exploitation. Lately the black hat hackers are developing easy-to-use attack tools and selling them underground. However, most of the research on VBMs is scattered, with limited systematic studies.

Several security company's reports, such as from IBM ISS X-Force (2007), PandaLabs (2007), and Symantec (2008) note the growth of malicious attacks, some of which may be the result of the limited circulation of zero-day vulnerability information. Symantec has been observing the black market forums operating in underground economy. According to Symantec's report, the forums are likely to be used by criminals and criminal organizations to trade various goods and services for identity theft purposes. Therefore, Symantec's report considers the emergence of black markets for zero-day vulnerabilities as a serious threat. However, it is premature to connect an increase in malicious attacks solely to the presence of VBM's. The IBM report links underground sales and markets for Web-browser exploits to the obvious growth in targeted attacks against specific customers and sites. PandaLab's report even reveals the price of malware kits sold underground. These data indicate indirectly that there are software developers and black hat attackers exchanging information about targets and tools. Such information exchange would be the core of a VBM. Basic questions emerge: Is the number of black markets increasing and how the do the black markets spread?

BLACK MARKET FOR VULNERABILITIES: DEFINITION, ISSUES AND PROBLEMS

In this sub-section, the goals are threefold. First, to clarify the idea of some essential terms, such as "the market", "the black market" and "the vulnerability black markets". These terms will be discussed elsewhere in the chapter. Second, to present the discussion regarding the history of the vulnerability discovery and disclosure. Third, to see how the BMs for vulnerabilities issue is connected to these various discussions.

Terms

The "*market*" term is mostly used by economists. The everyday, traditional notion of a market is a specific place where certain type of commodities are bought and sold. However, new emerging markets in recent days have more advanced properties than merely being a place for goods exchange. The economist Coase (1988, p. 7) criticizes that modern microeconomics textbooks deal with market prices determination but lack deep analysis of the market itself. Social institutions and factors affecting the exchange are completely neglected. The market structure concept introduced by economists is intriguing because it has little to do with social institutions, and instead refers to the notion of numbers of firms, access to the market and product differentiation.

We now present varying definitions of a market. Gravelle & Rees (1981), for example, propose that "*a market exists whenever two or more individuals are prepared to enter into exchange transaction, regardless of time or place*". Perloff (2007, p. 5) defines **market** as "*a social arrangement that allows or facilitates buyers and sellers to discover information and carry out a voluntary exchange of goods or services*". A market is an exchange mechanism that allows buyers to trade with sellers. Parkin et al. (2005, p. 44) propose an almost similar definition, that a market is "*any arrangement that enables buyers and sellers to get information and to do business with each other*". In orderly markets, enterprising individuals and firms benefit from goods and services transactions. However, Parkin et al. also underline the importance of the property rights as a prereq-

uisite of markets to operate properly. Property rights regulate the ownership, use and disposal of resources, goods, and services. Therefore, contemporary economics differentiates between private goods and public goods. Private goods have the following properties: *excludability* and *rivalry*. Property rights are applicable for private goods, but not for public goods since they have non-rivalry and non-excludability characteristics. Markets coordinate individual decisions through the *price* mechanism.

Mostly, market definitions are associated with the physical facility. Coase (1988) argues that markets require more than physical facilities for conducting buying and selling. However, for this statement, Coase points out the importance of the legal rules governing right and duties of those who conduct the transaction, and introduce "transaction costs" term. Coase (1988, p. 30) contends that without considering transaction costs it is impossible to understand properly the working of the economic system and have a rational basis for establishing economic policy.

For this chapter, we extend the market discussion. We refer to the emergence of online commerce, which covers virtual marketplace, virtual trading, even virtual commodity in which buyers and sellers do not physically interact, since all transactions are conducted via the Internet. Hence, all sellers and buyers are not only physically dispersed but also virtually scattered. Regarding this fast changing phenomenon, Kahin and Varian (2000) note that actually, the economics of electronic commerce on the World Wide Web was beginning to take shape around mid of 1990's. The increasing popularity of Internet usage does not only transform the way information is accessed and used in business, but also the nature of existing economic relationships and business models. Kahin and Varian (2000) point out that cookies and clicks, animation, linked words, pop-up windows and hyperlinks was among the advanced features of Internet's commercial strategy to attract costumers and shape decisions.

To observe the shifting toward the information-based "new economy", DeLong and Froomkin (2000) utilize three pillars of market systems in traditional economy, i.e., most goods have *excludability*, *rivalry* and *transparency* properties. *Excludability* prevents people who have not paid for them from enjoying their benefits and are depletable or reduce the amount available to others. *Rivalry* prevents simultaneous good consumption by other consumers. *Transparency* deals with the ability of individuals to see clearly what they need and what is for sale, before taking a purchase decision. Information-based goods do not possess these properties and require different pricing and resource allocation. The absence of *excludability*, e.g., television broadcast, does not reduce the availability of programs for others; it does not prevent others from enjoying it. *Non-rivalry* goods allow two to consume as cheaply as one. For example, the cost to produce an extra copy of software is almost zero. This situation creates a dilemma when a producer charges a price above the marginal cost. In addition, information goods are no longer *transparent*.

Furthermore, DeLong and Froomkin (2000) examine various pricing policies and virtual business practices such as the market for software (shareware, public beta), shop-bots, online auctions, meta-auction sites, and bidding services. DeLong and Froomkin suggest that the *non-ex-cludability*, *non-rivalry* and *non-transparency* characteristics of information goods may affect the structure of the New Economy; economists need to answer some challenges in this era. From the aforementioned description, we learn that the nature of the market has changed in the "new economy" and possess following attributes: the information-based market precludes the traditional characteristics of market systems, and operates as an online economy.

We return to the issue of a market definition for our case. Based upon previous discussion, we propose to define a market as:

a place and social arrangement for conducting buying and selling regardless of the physical or virtual nature of the marketplace

Next, we shift our focus to the black market term. The actual origin of the "black market" or "underground market" term is not quite clear, although it seems that the "black" term attached to the market is to indicate illegal activities occurring under the condition of great secrecy (Clinard, 1969, p. 2). According to available literature (Boulding, 1947; Clinard, 1969), the black market (BM) emerges because of government regulations for applying ceiling prices (due to scarcity problems of certain products such as food, gas or other luxury goods). The violations arise as over-ceiling, evasive price violation or rationing violations. The Merriam-Webster Dictionary defines a black market as "an illicit trade in goods or commodities in violation of official regulations". The actors in the market tend to avoid identification by the public. The term of "black market" originally appears in the Second World War especially in the United States, when drastic regulations were issued, making it illegal to charge more than a certain ceiling price for nearly all commodities (Clinard, 1969).

A BM not only emerges in wartime, as numerous prohibited goods are traded at any time (such as drugs, pornography, gambling, etc). Today, illicit trading in the black market still develops because of tight governmental regulations on various ranges of lucrative commodities. Basically, a BM operates outside the law and is driven by the opportunity for profit and the needs of consumers. BM covers a wide range of activities and commodities, from heavy industrial materials to items such as clothing, gasoline, shoes, sugar, cigarettes and alcoholic beverages. Therefore, the BM term also refers to goods trading that involves tax avoidance so that the customers find certain products less expensive in such a market (Bajada & Schneider, 2005; Ray, 1981). Some legitimate profitable and highly regulated businesses are becoming opportunities for the proliferation of the BMs. The banned products in BMs can be smuggled or produced illegally, and the sellers yield profits based solely on demand. In brief, nearly all BM traits and activities deal with intricate, criminal and disobedient behaviors that might be considered as "crimes".

Beyond the traditional definition of market where buyers and sellers may have contact physically, nowadays innumerable virtual markets have developed to be marketplaces for various illegal commodity trading. The mixture of the popularity of Internet trading and the effortless creation of markets triggers the market for vulnerabilities' exploits and pushes the market growth further. Perhaps there are similarities between wartime and today's BMs: both may disregard the law, constitute illegal activities and be a place of commodity trading for malicious purposes. The trading is conducted in the "dark", and avoids the open view of authorities.

Having described various discussions previously, we turn next to the nature of our endeavor, to define what BM is. We define black market as:

an arena or any arrangement for conducting illegal trading which takes place hidden from public eyes. The trading covers all motives such as to avoid government regulations, to trade prohibited commodities, or to trade commodities that may be utilized for malicious or criminal purpose.

We are moving into the discussion about the black market for vulnerabilities. It is important first to clarify the definition of the vulnerability term, since in the computer security field the term covers diverse aspects of software, hardware and network. We skip the discussion on the various software vulnerability problems and vulnerability taxonomy. For a detailed discussion of this topic see Du & A.P Mathur (1998), Landwehr, Bull, Mc. Dermott & Choi (1994), Seacord & Householder (2005). For the sake of brevity, in this chapter we define vulnerability as:

bugs and flaws (caused by programming errors) that give rise to exploit techniques or particular attack patterns.

The vulnerability black markets relate to the current discussion of the emergence of the market for vulnerabilities of zero days exploits. The discussion becomes a part of a broader discussion of various types of legitimate markets that established to provide monetary rewards for vulnerability information. Based on previous explanations, we define the vulnerability black market (VBM) as:

an arena or any arrangement for illegal selling and buying activities to trade vulnerability exploits and malware or any products taking malicious advantage of the weaknesses in software and computer networks.

Related Works

Recently, two empirical works were published relating to the underground market, from Franklin et al. (2007) and Zhuge et al. (2007). Based on the collected information, they examine the size of the underground black markets. Zhuge et al. focus on the aspects of the underground market that are visible as part of the World Wide Web. They examine the relationship between individual actors within the market and also study the size of the actual market. Zhuge et al. use a combined method to automatically browse the Web and analyze all content that may contain malicious sites on the Chinese Web.

Franklin et al. investigate a large number of underground Internet Relay Chat (IRC) channels, and examine the advertisements of black market trading. The data was taken from archived IRC logs that contain 13 million messages. Their main focus is to find an underground economy which specializes in activities such as credit card fraud, identity theft, spamming, phishing, online credential theft and sale of compromised hosts.

Franklin, Zhuge and their co-authors are also concerned with the market mechanism, as we are. However, we also focus on how the black markets actually develop over time, by observing some key variables such as membership development, buying, selling, trading activities, and also threads development in the VBM forum.

Complexities to Keep Secure Software

For our present purpose, we have divided the actors related to the vulnerability into four categories, i.e., software vendors, malicious attackers, security researchers and software users. This framework also incorporates the major issues related to the actors' interest when encountering vulnerabilities, some possible motives behind their stance and some problems that may arise for conducting or disobeying their role. Within the framework presented in Table 1, we can look more specifically at the different issues related to the vulnerability from the perspective of different actors:

Malicious attackers refer to virus and exploit writers and malware creators; attackers who continuously search for diverse methods and tools to attack the software weaknesses. People are aware that the motivation for finding the weaknesses in software is not only for notoriety or adventure, but also for more commercial motives, mainly for financial advantage.

The ideal situation when encountering the software vulnerabilities is that the non-malicious parties play their role, as they should be:

Software vendors are supposed to develop more secure software and patch vulnerabilities as well as offer good protection to clients. Good quality software is important to build credibility and reputation among clients. But since software production is also clearly a profit-oriented business, the conjunctions of both motives sometimes create problems. One well-known problem is the dilemma between adequate software testing and market pressure to have more sophisticated software versions and to compete with other vendors in developing more attractive software products. In addition, a reward dilemma surfaces due to an ethical consideration or appropriateness to give monetary reward to security researchers who discover vulnerabilities.

Security researchers are also key actors in the effort of securing software vulnerabilities, because of their skill to find any unrecognized flaws in the software. Vulnerability discovery has been a long time part of their interests, but the motives behind these efforts are various (such as gaining/improving reputation). A broader goal of announcing publicly the vulnerability may be driven by the more altruistic motive to enhance users' awareness on possible exploitation of newly known vulnerabilities. Recently, the researchers'

Table 1. Vulnerabilities from the perspective of different actors

Issues	Different Actors			
	Malicious Attackers	**Software Vendors**	**Security Researchers**	**Software Users**
Interest	attack	secure software	flaws discovery	defense
Motive	- notoriety - adventure - financial gain	- credibility - profit	- altruistic - reputation - monetary reward	- protection - risk security mitigation
Problems	- searching opportunities - develop exploits	- buggy software - reward dilemma - market pressure	- reward maximization - channeling	- updates negligence

motive for the discovery effort is also driven by economic consideration.

Software users (including computer administrators) may defend their computer with new updates to mitigate security risks. Imbalance of this system happens because each actor plays inappropriately leading to more complex relationships and further software vulnerability problems: users do not patch, vendors produce buggy software, or software vendors do not reward security researchers, while security researchers (who can be black hat and white hat hackers) eventually trade their findings (they may sell to the security companies or to malicious individuals or even criminals). In addition, it is unclear how to channel the vulnerability discoveries and there are some disagreements among non end-user actors regarding how

to disclose vulnerabilities. These problems also involve the reward maximization issue whether to further engage in illicit trading. Researchers with altruistic and voluntary motives may be blamed for supporting the "full-disclosure" style because the discovery process creates unintended problems. The main intention to announce publicly the software flaw is to press vendors, but as an unintended effect, malicious actors might work faster to develop attack tools.

TRACING THE HISTORY OF VULNERABILITY DISCOVERY

We cannot neglect the history and problems surrounding vulnerability discovery and disclosure

Figure 1. Timeline of vulnerability discovery initiatives and approaches

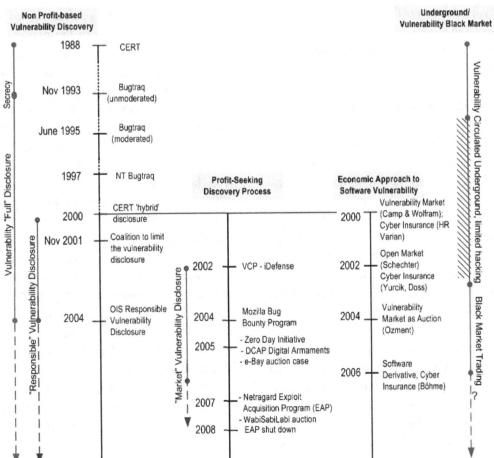

policy, as well as the current discussion and development of legitimate markets, to understand the underlying factors influencing the emergence of the black market for vulnerabilities. Has the black market for vulnerabilities existed before the vulnerability disclosure and the emergence of the legitimate market, or did the black market surface because of the legitimate market? Is the legitimate market formed to attract hackers and security researchers or to contain the black market?

In the literature related to the vulnerability markets, vulnerability discovery and vulnerability disclosure, the main debates regarding the vulnerability disclosure models can be split into three: *vulnerability secrecy/non-disclosure* (to suppress publication entirely until patches or updates are available), *vulnerability disclosure* (to publish full details) and *responsible disclosure* (to conceal some details). This sub-section also briefly reviews the emerging profit motive vulnerability discovery. The history of the vulnerability discovery is shown in Figure 1. The sources utilized in the diagram are cited throughout the description of this section.

Vulnerability Secrecy Period

Some groups have being practicing "security through obscurity", relying on flaws not known and attackers being unlikely to find them. Small groups of interested parties were unwilling to disclose them to the masses. As these bugs were slowly found by others or passed on to vendors, they eventually got fixed. This "security through obscurity" approach didn't lead to secure software. Before the disclosure policy was introduced, the software companies were inclined to take no notice of the vulnerability reported by security researchers and trusted the vulnerability secrecy. Furthermore, it was considered to be an 'illegal action' if security researchers disclosed vulnerabilities (Schneier, 2007).

CERT (*Computer Emergency Response Team*) was established by DARPA (*The Defense Advance*

Research Projects Agency) in 1988 to coordinate and respond to internet attacks, including vulnerability reports (Schneier, 2000b). Over the years, CERT has acted as a central agency for reporting of vulnerabilities. Researchers are supposed to report discovered vulnerabilities to CERT. CERT will verify the vulnerability and silently inform the vendor and make public the details (and the fix) once patches are available. In sum, people were keeping software vulnerabilities secret.

Vulnerability concealment has been criticized for causing a significant delay between vulnerability finding and patch development. Secrecy prevents people from accurately assessing their own risk. Secrecy precludes public debate about security and hinders security education that leads to improvement.

Vulnerability Disclosure Period

The full-disclosure movement started because of the dissatisfaction with the previous "slow" process. CERT obtained a great number of vulnerability reports, but it was very slow in verifying them; also the vendors were slow to fix the vulnerabilities after the notification and, to worsen matters, CERT was slow to publish reports even after the patches were released (Schneier, 2000b). Well-known security mailing lists such as Bugtraq (begun in 1993) and NT Bugtraq (begun in 1997) became a shared forum for people believing that the only way to improve security was to publicize the problems (Rauch, 1999; Schneier, 2000b, 2007). In this approach, vulnerabilities and solutions are disclosed and discussed openly. In essence, full-disclosure is the practice of making the details of security vulnerabilities public. Since 1995, the growth of people participating in "full disclosure" has increased significantly (Rauch, 1999).

The proponents of this idea believe that the policy will force vendors to be more responsive in fixing vulnerabilities and security will improve (Rauch, 1999). Full disclosure proponents argue that public scrutiny is the only reliable way to improve security (Levy, 2001; Schneier, 2000a, 2000b, 2001, 2007). Keeping software vulnerabilities secret was intended to protect the information out of hands of the hackers. But hackers have proven to be skillful at discovering unknown vulnerabilities, and full disclosure is the only reason why vendors regularly patch their systems.

Critics of the full-disclosure movement especially point out that hackers at the same time can use these mailing lists to learn about vulnerabilities and write attack programs (called "exploits"). Before public vulnerability disclosure, the actors exploiting the vulnerability would only be the ones who discovered it, and they could only compromise a finite number of machines. If they did use automated exploits or used a worm, the chances of being discovered were high and their zero-day backdoor became publicly known and subsequently patched. However, after the vulnerability is publicly disclosed, the world learns about

the flaw, and the number of computer victims will increase significantly (Grimes, 2005). The debates between proponents and opponents of full disclosure can be summarized as follows:

Responsible Disclosure Period

Accordingly, software companies and some security researchers proposed "responsible disclosure". This movement appeared because a number of security researchers considered that the negative effects of full disclosure were greater than the positive impacts. The basic idea is that the threat of publishing the vulnerability is almost as good as actually publishing it. A responsible researcher would quietly notify the vulnerability to the software vendor and provide a deadline to work on patching, before the vulnerability is disclosed. CERT/CC (2000) introduced a new vulnerability disclosure policy, although the information security community still has doubts about this proposal (CyberEye, 2001). All vulnerabilities reported will be disclosed to the public 45 days after the initial report, regardless of the existence or availability of patches or workarounds from affected vendors.

In addition, pressure came from a coalition of well-known software developers and some security companies established to push a standard policy of limiting public disclosure of security vulnerability (Middleton, 2001), and a number of guidelines are currently available to govern the relationship between the vendors and the vulnerability reporter. Software vendors and security research firms have begun to jointly develop a unified framework for vulnerability disclosure under OIS Guidelines (*Organization for Internet Safety*) (2004). Some issues that may appear from responsible disclosure have been also discussed by Cavusoglu et.al (2005). Presently full disclosure and responsible disclosure are practiced simultaneously.

Table 2. Summary of the reasons of proponents and opponents of the full disclosure (FD)

Disagree	Agree
• Nobody except researchers need to know the details of flaws	• FD helps the good guys more than the bad guys
• FD results in information anarchy	• Effective security cannot be based on obscurity
• Good guys who publish virus code may also have malicious intentions	• Making vulnerabilities public is an important tool in forcing vendors to improve their products
• Safer if researchers keep details about vulnerabilities and stop arming hackers with offensive tools	• If an exploit is known and not shared, the vendor might be slower to fix the hole
• The risk associated with the publishing information outstrip its benefit • FD serves to arm hackers with tools to break systems	• Sharing information security with other professionals is an absolute necessity

Emergence of Theories and Practices "Legitimate" Market

This sub-section describes the current theoretical markets proposal and expansion of the vulnerability markets. The objective is to understand the black market issue under the current development.

In line with the vulnerability disclosure debates and the emergence of the economics of information security in early 2000s, a new "stream", the so-called "Market" approach surfaces, both at the theoretical and practical level. Economics of information security is becoming a thriving and fast moving discipline that merges the economic considerations and economic theories into the computer security field. Anderson (2001), one among the originators, argues that most security problems cannot be solved by technical means only; instead, microeconomics terms are more able to explain security problems (Anderson & Moore, 2006). Schneier advocates that economics has appropriate theories to deal with computer security issues (Schneier, 2006).

On the theoretical level, economics of vulnerabilities is becoming one fast-developed subject among other concentrations in the field of economics of information security. The initial thoughts on the economics of vulnerabilities concerns measuring software security through market mechanisms. Camp and Wolfram (2004), propose a market through which vulnerability findings could be traded; such markets have worked previously to create incentives for the reduction of negative externalities like environment pollutants. Schechter (2002) proposes creating markets for reports of previously undiscovered vulnerabilities, while Ozment (2004) suggests a vulnerability market as an auction. Böhme (2006) adds possible market forms, i.e., vulnerability brokers, exploit derivatives and cyber-insurance in the vulnerability market discussion. His objectives are to compare the best vulnerability market type to trade security-related information and to

find which type serves best to counter security market failures. However, Kannan and Telang (2005) criticize that the business models of these organizations are not socially optimal and Rescola (2005) finds no support for the usefulness of vulnerability finding and disclosure.

On a practical level, the 'legitimate' market for vulnerabilities is developing as well. Apparently, this is also a period of "commercialization" of vulnerability research. Sutton and Nagle (2006) wrote a paper based on the model that already exists in various markets rather than a theoretical model and classifies the current vulnerability market divisions as government market, open market, underground market, auction market and vendor market. iDefense announced the VCP (*Vulnerability Contributor Program*) in one security mailing list in 2002, offering rewards for verified vulnerability information. In 2004, Mozilla Foundation offered payment to those who find critical security flaws in its product, including the Firefox Web browser (Lemos, 2004), TippingPoint announced the ZDI (*Zero Day Initiative*) in 2005 (Evers, 2007) and Digital Armaments creates DACP (*Digital Armaments Contribution Program*) at the end of 2005. In 2007, two new marketplaces emerged: Netragard with EAP (Exploits Acquisition Program), and Wabisabi Labi as an auction site. The latter company claims only to provide a market place (and not to buy the vulnerabilities). The company acts as a mediator to bridge sellers and buyers in four schemes: *traditional auction* (the winner is the best bidder), *Dutch auction* (allow more than one winner), *buy now* (allow the bidders buy immediately) and *buy exclusively* (allow the buyer to buy the item, and close the auction). Unfortunately, EAP from Netragard only had a short lifespan. In March 2008 (after it had operated for approximately fourteen months), the program was shut down.

Concerning those market places, Ozment and Schechter (2006) criticize the obscurity of the price of vulnerabilities that hinders development toward an open market. The weakness of all market-based approaches is that they may increase the number of identified vulnerabilities by compensating people who would otherwise not search for flaws.

A Summary of the Vulnerability Discovery Discussion

We return to the initial question about the historical order of black markets, disclosure movement and legitimate markets. The previous historical depiction shows that the underground movement may already have existed before the vulnerability disclosure policy. Some full disclosure proponents who disagree with the opponent of this movement, point out that vulnerabilities have been known by attackers and circulated quietly in the hacker underground for months or years before the vendor ever found out. Therefore faster vulnerability publication is considered a better action (Schneier, 2000b). This situation indicates that the security community was already aware that an underground movement existed before the full disclosure movement. However, the emergence of the BMs may be a new phenomenon, and be driven by economic motives.

If we observe carefully, as full disclosure is implemented, there is an indication that the information from full disclosure discussions in the mailing lists may also be traded among the underground actors looking to break into machines (Rauch, 1999). Furthermore, Rauch concludes that full disclosure results in a grey market economy in exploits. This market broadens the options for independent "vulnerability researchers" to sell their findings to security companies or spyware manufacturers, whichever bid higher.

Regarding the question of whether the legal market's (LM) motivation is to attract the security researcher from BM, we found claims that part of the justification of the market establishment is to give better rewards to security researchers. However, some critics of current market practice point out the inability of legitimate markets to

acquire critical vulnerabilities (Evers, 2007). Malicious actors want to keep those vulnerabilities for themselves and use them to exploit systems in the wild, and it is doubtful that the underground hackers are motivated to sell vulnerabilities to the security company if they earn more by holding the vulnerability information private.

THE DYNAMIC MODEL OF THE BMs

The Basic Modeling Approach and Observation

Our motivation for investigating these problems using system dynamic modeling is to ascertain future trends. System dynamics (SD) is a methodology for modeling and simulating dynamic, non-linear systems describing real world issues. SD captures non-linearity and time delays in complex systems, as well as feedback loops and their interactions. Outputs of SD modeling include causal maps, causal map analysis, 'dynamic stories' that visualize the behavior of complex security systems, leading to team/organizational learning and to policies to manage complex systems. Sterman (2000) wraps up in a brief statement that system dynamics is a method to enhance learning in complex systems.

Indeed, the markets for software vulnerabilities are far too complex to be captured in a simple model. Therefore, we target a particular problem relating to BMs rather than attempting to capture all issues surrounding BMs in their full complexity

Our belief of the existence of the BMs or underground markets does not only rely on news and reports, but it is also grounded in our disguised observation of twelve websites comprising tangible BM forums. A limitation of our observations is that we have only been able to examine black markets that are trading exploits and malware, and not direct trading of the vulnerability information.

Certainly, we noticed that the BMs do not only trade exploits and malware, but also other illegal items such as stolen personal information and credit card trading, bank logins, compromised hosting sites, etc.

We could measure the "growth" of the BMs from a macro perspective, i.e., the number of underground websites with black market forums. We could also observe them from a micro perspective, i.e., the development of the individual BM grows especially in trading advertising volume and the membership. In this chapter, we will mainly focus on the macro perspective. The purpose of the modeling in this chapter is to answer the questions: What factors affect the spread of the black markets and what is the possible future growth of the markets?

Methods

We began our data collection by observing the contributions and discussions on hacker websites that feature an explicit Black Market (BM), marketplace or trading forum. Once sites were identified, we visited them and observed the activities related to zero-day exploit and other vulnerability-related attack tools. We could observe the market's dynamic from message boards or IRC networks. Both of these mediums are usually accessible to visitors. In this research mode, quiet observation without participating or interfering with the actors is a viable technique for data capture. Data was retrieved from the site's public interface, without other access to the server functions. Most of observed BM forums require registration with a valid email address. During this study, we registered on boards with an anonymous email address, disguising our identity so that we could explore all message board areas.

We found 12 BM forums that we coded as W1…W12. Then, we identified an additional five emerging BM forums. In Figure 2, we coded those new forums as N1 … N5. We didn't use them in our analysis because of their short historical

records. Nevertheless, this indicates that more forums are appearing. Unlike other studies, such as conducted by Zhuge et al. (2007) that search malicious websites using automatic techniques, our searching was performed manually. We coded, categorized the information and analyzed all postings in each forum. Based on the available forums, we note that BMs develop over time. We could trace the starting time of each forum from the first posting, mostly performed by the webmasters who set the rules for the forum. Among those twelve forums, we are only able to trace ten forums with first posting history.

Our observation of BM sites indicates common traits across the different BMs in various websites:

- The most basic characteristic of the forum is that their presence is typically combined with intermittent downtime. The consequences of this behavior are that there is a period where many people join the market and cause peaks in buying-selling-trading activities. There are periods when marketplaces become unavailable. However, the reason for the accessibility problem is not only triggered by the forum availability, but also by the forum rules.

- The availability of the *forum rules* are a part of the BM's characteristics. There are differences between large forums and smaller forums. We differentiate the forum size from *a number of participants in the website* (less or over 15,000 registrants), *the continuity of new advertisement in the forum over time* (sometime only a few advertisements in small forums over several months) and *forum's sustainability* (the ability to sustain the forums. Small forums tend to frequently be shut down). Large forums have tighter rules and easily exclude or "ban" participants who do not follow the rules of the forum. Some forums even create "criteria" for potential participants intending to enter the BM forum.

- Furthermore, big BM forums develop verification procedures to be passed before new participants can trade in the forum. On the other hand, small forums have less stringent rules and allow people to freely enter the market. But not many visitors are interested in posting or trading in small forums and, thus, small forums tend to stagnate over time.

- The observed markets do not conduct direct vulnerability information trading, but mostly exploits, malware and other malicious tools. Usually security companies or vendors would learn about unknown vulnerabilities when they are exploited. For example, an exploit circulating in the black market might be detected when it is used against a system.

Reference Mode

Reference behavior modes should be provided before starting the modeling process (1980; Richardson & Pugh, 1981), that is, a plot of the behavior of key variables of the system over time. The reference behavior modes capture historical data, mental models and policy behavior. As previously mentioned, the modeling approach aims at finding the answer as to which factors affect the spread of the black markets and what is the possible future growth of the markets. Confidence on such answers depends on the SD model being

Figure 2. Observed BMs development based on first posting history in BM Forum (source: Observation from BMs Forum)

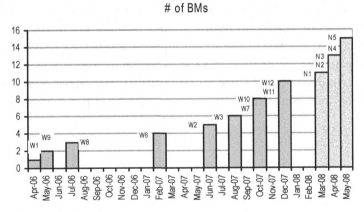

Figure 3. Reference mode

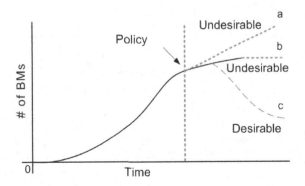

able to reproduce the reference behavior modes for the right reasons.

On a macro scale, we hypothesized that BMs would increase over time across the Internet, although in a micro or individual scale, they might fluctuate due to the unstable capability of some individual forums to maintain the websites. Figure 2 demonstrates the development of observed BMs and shows an increasing trend. Labels such as W1, W2... and W12 indicate the emergence of BM forums. These statistics are limited to the BMs that we could examine. Perhaps, the number of BMs forums with various trading styles are numerous and scattered in various online underground websites. Automatic searching approach in Chinese websites alone done by Zhuge et al. (2007) who identified 2,149 malicious websites. However, the study does not mention a number of specific black markets among this function since it focuses on how these malicious websites try to redirect the visitors to the Web-based Trojans.

Building upon Figure 2, we hypothesize the reference mode of BM future behavior (Figure 3, path a) as a consequence of two conditions: with or without specific policy. The curve shows unexpected BM's growth due to the absence of any policy intervention to diminish the BMs' spread.

However, when discretionary operations to "disrupt" underground market are carried out, there are still two possible results, desirable and undesirable. Undesirable development is represented by the S-shaped and sustained growth curve (path b). This situation may happen because of individual website's protection mechanisms. In avoidance of repressive actions toward underground markets or risks of being a hacked or attack target, individual website may be hidden temporarily, the website redirected to a new place, the hosting place changed or a new site re-established.

Desirable advancement occurs when policy intervention causes the market to gradually collapse over time. Effective policy intervention will hopefully reduce the activities. The situation is illustrated by the curve c, with collapse and decay. Indeed, there are natural reasons for BMs decay. A weak BM forum leads participants to doubt the "safety" of their underground transaction. An unpopular websites cause BMs arena less attractive. Too few visitors or participants restrain the potential sellers or buyers enter the market. Or a BM could decay simply because the participants distrust the forum. However, the fraction may be small compared with the development itself.

Figure 4. The flow of vulnerabilities

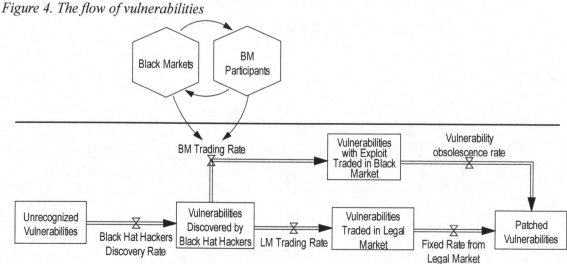

Therefore, the focus on policy intervention to produce desired results is important.

Simple Dynamic Model of BM Spreads

In previous work (Radianti & Gonzalez, 2007) we have already identified the flow of vulnerabilities from unrecognized vulnerabilities, discovered and traded to patched vulnerabilities, as illustrated in Figure 4. However, the model for this chapter will focus on the development of black market sites and BM participants' growth (two hexagons) that furthermore may affect the vulnerability with exploit trading. Note that in the model description, rectangles represent stocks of variables (e.g. of vulnerabilities); double line arrows with valves and cloud symbols represent flows; thinner arrows indicate causal influences; arrows with minus signs indicate inverse causal influence.

Vulnerability exploits and malware trading is facilitated by the availability of BMs, as well as the availability of the participants. We capture

these two important factors into two sub-models, illustrated in Figure 5 and 6. The following dynamic story behind this model building is developed based on the aforementioned observation on underground websites.

The stock of "Black Markets" increases by establishment of BM instances and decreases by stagnation and disappearance instances. The latter process is represented by "BM Decay Rate". A possible cause of stagnation would be that the forum didn't attract enough participants, that visitors did not conduct trade or posting advertisements or frequent forum downtime. Additional reasons could be inability of the webmasters to promote the sites to acquire more potential visitors and gain trust from the participants. We found examples of such cases in forum W3 (gone and reborn as a new forum without BM features), W10 (BM is available but with only 3 postings within 6 months) and W8 (it slowly develops in the beginning and stagnates).

Furthermore, we identify three aspects influencing BMs establishment: BM existence, opportunity and process grasp. We captured those

Figure 5. BM establishment sub model

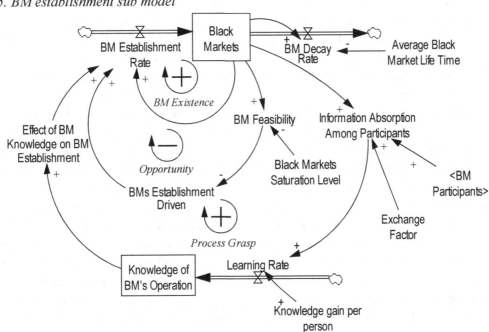

three factors in two reinforcing loops (marked with positive sign) and one balancing loop (negative sign) as shown in Figure 5. The balancing loop counteracts black market growth and it can even suppress growth if the balancing loop is stronger than the reinforcing loops.

Process Grasp loop: We assume that learning occurs among underground actors, triggering duplication processes to imitate the previously available BM forums. Available markets provide a chance for underground actors to learn the BM market process, mechanism and operations. We did observe that some administrators/moderators of certain BM forums were participants in the W1 forum, one of the oldest and biggest BMs. Imitation process manifested in how the newer forum reproduce similar rule and verification process. The *Process Grasp* loop captures this procedure imitation. The more the participants have direct and indirect contacts, the more the participants learn about the BM operation. Accumulated knowledge will motivate some underground activists to extend their hacker website by opening a market forum.

Opportunity loop: Online BMs may be triggered by many reasons and this opens opportunities for establishment of new BM instances. For some underground actors the available markets may not fulfill their expectations. For example, a BM specializes in trading specific malware, i.e. specialized on various types of packers and binders. A packer is a "compression tool" to take known Trojan executables and compress them so that they are unrecognizable to anti virus software. Binders are programs that allow hackers to "bind" two or more executables together resulting in one single .exe file. The inserting Trojan executables files are commonly passed as email attachments. Some sites permit participants to buy-sell trade various personal identities, hacked credit cards, including CVV2 information. In other forums, similar commodities are prohibited. Some sites mostly focus on zero-day exploits and malware trading. Another BM applies very restricted

rules and tight verification procedures, otherwise disobedient participants cannot advertise in the forum.

All diverse needs and demands of the underground community that are not fulfilled by existing BMs, either because they are too restricted or too specialized, create opportunities for other types of BMs, i.e., with less tight regulations, allowing credit cards trading besides exploits and malware. We capture the "space" for creating BMs by a concept of "BM Feasibility". BM Feasibility is the ratio of existing "Black Markets" to "Black Markets Saturation Level". If the ratio is still low, i.e., space is still available and it is still possible to attract underground actors to enter BMs, the "BMs Establishment Driven" will be high. As the markets grow, near to the saturation level, or even experiences double or triple growth, fewer actors try to open new forums.

BM Existence loop: BM existence also reinforces BM establishment. We could trace new BM forums based on links or advertising in other BM websites. This is only an example for how the existing black market could serve as a reinforcing agent to spread more BM forums.

Now we shift our focus to the BM Participants Sub-model illustrated in Figure 6. BM participants play an important role to expand the BMs: They serve as agents who keep the BM forum alive with postings, discussions and advertising for buying and selling exploits, malware and other malicious tools. They may transfer insights about black market operation from big and well-known forums to smaller, emergent forums. As shown in Figure 4, the BM Participants (Figure 6) sub-model contains a feedback to the BM sub-model (to reinforce the BM establishment). On the other hand, the BM sub-model also provides a link to the BM Participants sub model (served as attractiveness for visitors to enter the BM). The stock of "BM Participants" increases by the inflow of "Entering BM" and decreases by the outflow "Leaving BM". Three main feedback loops capture the dynamics of BM Participants: *BM*

Doorway loop (reinforcing, positive), *Elimination* loop (reinforcing, positive) and *Restraining* loop (balancing, negative).

BM Doorway loop: This external reinforcing loop adds to the flow of new participants entering the BM. There are two possibilities for how visitors may become BM participants. First, they may have direct information contact from colleagues or friends, simply because they belong to an underground community with higher likelihood to access the development of BMs. Second, they may search the Internet, find the site and become intrigued enough to join the forum. Therefore, the "New Participants" variable in this model is affected by the development of active BM participants, "Potential Website Visitors" and "Contact rate". However, we need to differentiate the contact rate in this sub-model and in the previous sub-model that is captured by "Information Absorption among Participants" and "Exchange Factor". The latter is connected to the process of grasping the BM idea. The former is related to the willingness and possibility of visitors to be in a BM forum. The concept describes the possibility

and intensity of contacts involving the ordinary websites visitors and underground community.

Restraining loop: This loop captures the internal process of how the administrator maintains the forum. Our observations indicate that there are differences between small forums and big forums, and between new and old forums, in regulating the BM participants. A new and small forum tends to be less regulated, and on the other hand, bigger forums often apply quite strict regulations and treatment to the BM participants. Apparently, there are in many cases criteria to be met by the participants before they are allowed to enter the forum, such as: they're willing to be verified by moderator or administrator; they won't annoy the forum and flame other members, or other behavior that could reduce the forum's credibility; and, they won't trade prohibited items in the BM forums. One forum operates with several stages before excluding the participants, such as: first warning, second warning, currently banned and banned status. Another forum will simply put a "banned" label to the participants, and block them from further posting. If they post advertisements,

Figure 6. BM participants sub model

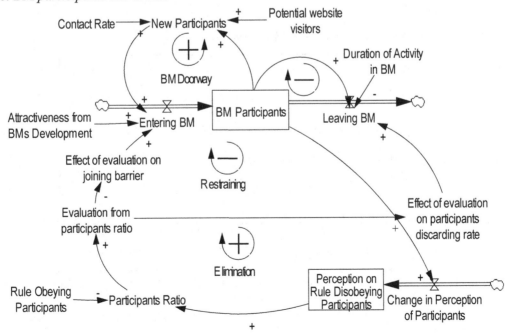

17

the administrator may remove the texts or lock the advertisement thread.

From the aforementioned description, we capture that the BM administrator has a perception from existing BM participants, that some of them may disobey the forum rules. To capture this situation, we create a variable called "BM Participants Ratio" to represent a comparison between a perception of rule disobeying participants and rule obeying participants. Again, there is a delay to recognize whether the ratio increases via an evaluation process. The state of the ratio affects two things in managing the BM participants: the joining barrier and the participant discarding rate.

The doorway to the BM is represented by a non-linear table function. If the ratio is very low, the doorway is highly open. In other words, there will be fewer barriers to enter the market. But if the ratio of disobeying participants increases, the doorway will be tighter, and only a small fraction of potential visitors will be allowed to join the BM.

Elimination loop: a similar evaluation affects the participant discarding rate. Low ratio of disobeying participants will slow down the

participant discarding rate, and higher ration of disobeying participants will increase their elimination from the forum.

Simulation

The SD approach uses computer-aided modeling. Several software tools are available for performing SD simulations. We use the Vensim software for our simulation, which is arguably the most popular one in the SD field.

For our initial simulation runs we examined three scenarios within a 200 weeks time horizon (Figure 7). The first scenario ('Base Run') represents the absence of policy intervention concerning the BMs' presence. We assume that initially one BM is present. Assuming that all structures and feedback loops in the model (Figure 5 and 6) have captured the essential connection among the main important factors affecting the BM spread, the base run simulation (number 1) demonstrates that the number of BMs is likely to increase over time.

The second scenario we call "BM Life Time". An example of an action to shorten BM life time was an investigation that targets underground

Figure 7. Simulation results of black markets development

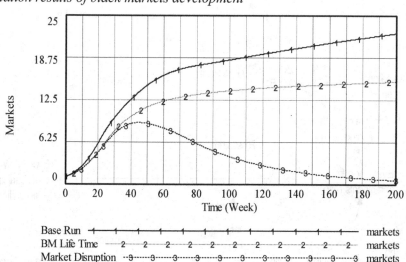

hacker organizations, such as implemented by U.S. Secret Service, called "Operation Firewall" (Francis, 2005). The operation, conducted in the late of 2004, intended to disrupt the organized online criminal activity that was threatening the financial infrastructure in the US. To capture such countermeasure policy against underground operations, we used a parameter called "Average BM Life Time". We can modify the value for this parameter, i.e., by putting smaller values, to observe the dynamic of the BMs over time.

In this second scenario, we could observe that the BM's growth is slower and flattens out. As previously explained, the intended operation to disrupt the underground sites' life may actually only provide short-term downtime of the website. In the case of Operation Firewall, some people were arrested because of alleged involvement in global organized cyber crime. Also two well-known examples where the black markets were shut down from a similar operation are the cases of shadowcrew.com and carderplanet.com. However, it is still a big question if the old websites are totally gone or if in the long-run certain websites do reappear with different names. Often BM sites are only temporarily down and reactivate after less pressure toward underground online trading.

The third scenario we call "Market Disruption". It intends to capture a suggestion (Franklin et al., 2007) to disrupt the market by creating distrust surrounding the BM participants so that they will leave the markets through defamation, or by undercutting the website participants' verification system. The previous assumption in the second simulation is also applied in the third scenario. We assume smaller values for the "Exchange Factors" in the model as well as for "Average BM Life Time". The simulation shows the growth and collapse of the BM number. In this simulation, the knowledge accumulation does not happen because the distrust among participants reduces learning exchange and market growth. The BMs also decline quicker in this scenario because of faster BM decay rate.

LEARNING FROM MODEL AND FUTURE TRENDS

Developing a model is a method to capture reality. Performing a simulation is a risk free method to learn about the implications of various decisions. The reliability of the conclusions derived from the simulation results depends on how well the model represents the structure of reality, the robustness of the model and the underlying assumptions behind the model. By making the assumptions of our models explicit and presenting the simulation of potentially interesting scenarios, we hope to initiate a fruitful discussion among experts and to get constructive feedback to further improve our models and hopefully to increase understanding of how BMs perform.

The model structure presented in the previous section suggests that imitation processes may happen among the underground actors and may push further development of the black market. Initiatives to temporarily disrupt the markets may be not yield a sustainable effect to stop the BM operation, since the participants are too many to be caught and the possibilities to create similar forum are so wide.

Our observation and simulation suggest several possible future trends regarding the BM issue:

- The number of black markets for trading vulnerabilities zero day exploits, malware and other commodities for malicious purposes are likely to grow over time.
- As a consequence, theoretically the proliferation of cyber-attacks linked to the BMs spread is likely to increase as well.
- Various possible underground contacts are actually one critical point that affects the black market growth, more than the existence of the BM sites itself. Because once malicious actors learn about the success of BM operation, the Internet provides immense possibilities to develop similar forums.

- Apparently, underground actors benefit from BMs' development since it extends the possibility to reach wider potential buyers and sellers. The ground for this is our observation where BM participants do not enter only one BM, but they also try to advertise the same products to multiple BM forums.

CONCLUSION

Cyber threats are a complex problem to solve, especially if they involve hidden malicious activities. The malicious actors may operate across a nation's border in performing illicit efforts. To keep the computer system safe from any harmful activities, all parties who deal in cyber space should be aware that any form of intangible threats may endanger these attempts.

Our initial questions for the modeling effort are to answer whether the numbers of BMs increase and how the black markets spread. Our observation on BMs strengthens the hypotheses that BMs tend to increase. Recognizing the factors affecting BMs' establishment is important to understand the dominant traits and characters that reinforce the BM's growth. We find some possible factors affecting the spread: the existence of markets itself (create attractiveness for malicious actors to enter the forum) and the existence of the transmission agents, i.e., BM participants who may imitate similar forums in different websites.

We believe there are many feedback loops that govern the behavior of BM systems. The use of an SD modeling technique is helpful to elaborate the problem and build an understanding about intertwined factors affecting the BM problem. We expect our approach will elicit an exchange with readers and experts, as to the underlying structural assumption of the model and plausibility of its behavior over time.

REFERENCES

Anderson, R. (2001). *Why information security is hard, an economic perspective.* Paper presented at the 17th Annual Computer Security Applications Conference.

Anderson, R., & Moore, T. (2006). The economics of information security. *Science, 314,* 610-613.

Bajada, C., & Schneider, F. (2005). *Size, causes and consequences of the underground economy: An International Perspective.* Ashgate: Aldershot.

Boulding, K. E. (1947). A note on the theory of the black market. *The Canadian Journal of Economics and Political Science / Revue canadienne d'Economique et de Science politique, 13*(1), 115-118.

Böhme, R. (2006). *A comparison of market approaches to software vulnerability disclosure.* Paper presented at the International Conference, ETRICS 2006, LNCS 3995 Freiburg, Germany.

Camp, L. J., & Wolfram, C. (2004). Pricing security, a market in vulnerabilities. In L. J. Camp & S. Lewis (Eds.), *Economics of Information Security.* Boston: Kluwer Academic Publishers.

Cavusoglu, H., Cavusoglu, H., & Raghunathan, S. (2005). *Emerging issues in responsible vulnerability disclosure.* Paper presented at the 4th Workshop of Economic and Information Security (WEIS), Cambridge, MA, USA.

CERT/CC. (2000). Vulnerability disclosure policy. *CERT Coordination Center.* Retrieved June 10, 2007.

Clinard, M. B. (1969). *The Black market: a study of white collar crime.* Montclair, New Jersey: Patterson Smith.

Coase, R. H. (1988). *The Firm, the market and the law.* Chicago: The University of Chicago.

CyberEye. (2001). *CERT's full-disclosure policy is responsible, but mistrust remains.* Retrieved April, 15, 2007, from http://www.gcn.com/state/vol7_no1/tech-report/946-1.html

DeLong, J. B., & Froomkin, A. M (2000). Speculative microeconomics for tomorrow's Economy. In H. R. Varian (Ed.), *Internet publishing & beyond: The economics of digital information & intellectual.* Cambridge, MA, USA: MIT Press.

Du, W., & Mathur, A. P. (1998). *Categorization of software errors that led to security breaches.* Paper presented at the 21st National Information Systems Security Conference, Crystal City, Virginia, VA.

Evers, J. (2007). *Offering a bounty for security bugs* [Electronic Version], 2007. Retrieved from http://news.com.com/Offering+a+bounty+for+security+bugs/2100-7350_3-5802411.html?tag=sas.email

Francis, B. (2005). *Know thy hacker.* Retrieved April 28, 2007, from http://www.infoworld.com/article/05/01/28/05OPsecadvise_1.html

Franklin, J., Paxson, V., Perrig, A., & Savage, S. (2007). *An inquiry into the nature and causes of the wealth of internet miscreants.* Paper presented at the 14 th ACM Conference on Computer and Communications Security (CCS), Alexandria, VA, USA.

Gravelle, H., & Rees, R. (1981). *Microeconomics.* London: Longman.

Grimes, R. A. (2005). *The full disclosure debate.* Retrieved June 19, 2007, from http://www.infoworld.com/article/05/09/30/40OPsecadvise_1.html

IBM. (2007). *IBM internet security systems X-Force 2006 trend statistics* [Electronic Version]. Retrieved January, from http://www.iss.net/documents/whitepapers/X_Force_Exec_Brief.pdf

Kannan, K., & Telang, R. (2005). Market for software vulnerabilities? Think again. *Management Science, 51*(5), 726-740.

Landwehr, C. E., Bull, A. R., Mc. Dermott, J. P., & Choi, W. S. (1994). A taxonomy of computer program security flaws, with examples. *ACM Computing Surveys, 26*(3).

Lemos, R. (2004). *Mozilla puts bounty on bugs.* Retrieved June 10, 2007, from http://news.com.com/Mozilla+puts+bounty+on+bugs/2100-1002_3-5293659.html

Levy, E. (2001). *Full disclosure is a necessary evil.* Retrieved June 10, 2007, from http://www.securityfocus.com/news/238

Middleton, J. (2001). *Coalition condemns full disclosure.* Retrieved April 10 2007, from http://www.vnunet.com/vnunet/news/2116546/coalition-condemns-full-disclosure

OIS. (2004). *Guidelines for security vulnerability reporting and response* [Electronic Version], 2007, from http://www.oisafety.org/guidelines/

Ozment, A. (2004). *Bug auctions: vulnerability market reconsidered.* Paper presented at the Workshop of Economics and Information Security (WEIS), Minneapolis, MN.

Ozment, A., & Schechter, S. (2006). *Milk or wine: does software security improve with age?* Paper presented at the The Fifteenth Usenix Security Symposium. July 31 - August 4 2006, Vancouver, BC, Canada.

PandaLabs. (2007). *Quarterly report PandaLabs* [Electronic Version]. Retrieved July 15, 2007, from http://www.pandasecurity.com/

Parkin, M., Powell, M., & Matthews, K. *Economics.* (2005). Harlow, England: Pearson Addison Wesley.

Perloff, J. M. (2007). *Microeconomics* (Fourth Edition ed.). Boston: Pearson, Addison Wesley.

Radianti, J., & Gonzalez, J. J. (2007). *A preliminary model of the vulnerability black market.* Paper presented at the the 25th International System Dynamics Conference Boston, USA.

Randers, J. (1980). *Elements of the system dynamics method.* Cambridge, Massachusetts: The MIT Press.

Rauch, J. (1999). *The Future of vulnerability disclosure?* Retrieved June 19, 2007, from http://www.usenix.org/publications/login/1999-11/features/disclosure.html

Ray, S. K. (1981). *Economics of the black market.* Boulder, Colorado: Westview Press.

Rescola, E. (2004). *Is finding security holes a good idea?* Paper presented at the The Third Workshop on the Economics of Information Security, Minneapolis.

Richardson, G. P., & Alexander L. Pugh III. (1981). *Introduction to system dynamics modeling.* Portland, Oregon: Productivity Press.

Schechter, S. (2002). *How to buy better testing: using competition to get the most security and robustness for your dollar.* Paper presented at the Infrastructures Security Conference, Bristol, UK.

Schneier, B. (2000a). *Full disclosure and the window of exposure.* Crypto-Gram Newsletter Retrieved March 10, 2006, from http://www.schneier.com/crypto-gram-0009.html#1

Schneier, B. (2000b). *Publicizing vulnerabilities.* Retrieved April 10, 2007, from http://www.schneier.com/crypto-gram-0002.html

Schneier, B. (2001). *Bug secrecy vs. full disclosure.* Retrieved April 10, 2007, from http://news.zdnet.com/2100-9595_22-531066.html

Schneier, B. (2006). *Economics and information security.* Retrieved December 12, 2006, from http://www.schneier.com/blog/archives/2006/06/economics_and_i_1.html

Schneier, B. (2007). *Schneier: full disclosure of security vulnerabilities a 'damned good idea'.* Retrieved June 19, 2007, from http://www.schneier.com/essay-146.html

Seacord, R. C., & Householder, A. D. (2005). *A structured approach to classifying security vulnerabilities.* Retrieved December 22, 2005, from http://www.sei.cmu.edu/pub/documents/05.reports/pdf/05tn003.pdf

Sterman, J. D. (2000). *Business dynamics: systems thinking and modeling for a complex world.* Boston: Irwin/McGraw-Hill.

Sutton, M., & Nagle, F. (2006). *Emerging economic models for vulnerability research.* Paper presented at the The Fifth Workshop on the Economics of Information Security (WEIS), Robinson College, University of Cambridge, England.

Symantec. (2008). *Symantec Global Internet Threat Report: Trend for July - Dec 07,* [Electronic Version]. Retrieved January, from http://eval.symantec.com/mktginfo/enterprise/white_papers/b-whitepaper_internet_security_threat_report_xiii_04-2008.en-us.pdf

Varian, H. R. (Ed). (2000). *Internet publishing & beyond: the economics of digital information & intellectual....* Cambridge, MA, USA: MIT Press.

Zhuge, J., Holz, T., Song, C., Guo, J., Han, X., & Zou, W. (2007). *Studying malicious websites and the underground economy on the Chinese website* [Electronic Version]. Honeyblog. Retrieved February 25, 2008, from http://honeyblog.org/archives/2007/12/summary.html

Chapter II
An Attack Graph Based Approach for Threat Identification of an Enterprise Network

Somak Bhattacharya
Indian Institute of Technology, Kharagpur, India

Samresh Malhotra
Indian Institute of Technology, Kharagpur, India

S. K. Ghosh
Indian Institute of Technology, Kharagpur, India

ABSTRACT

As networks continue to grow in size and complexity, automatic assessment of the security vulnerability becomes increasingly important. The typical means by which an attacker breaks into a network is through a series of exploits, where each exploit in the series satisfies the pre-condition for subsequent exploits and makes a causal relationship among them. Such a series of exploits constitutes an attack path where the set of all possible attack paths form an attack graph. Attack graphs reveal the threat by enumerating all possible sequences of exploits that can be followed to compromise a given critical resource. The contribution of this chapter is to identify the most probable attack path based on the attack surface measures of the individual hosts for a given network and also identify the minimum possible network securing options for a given attack graph in an automated fashion. The identified network securing options are exhaustive and the proposed approach aims at detecting cycles in forward reachable attack graphs. As a whole, the chapter deals with identification of probable attack path and risk mitigation which may facilitate in improving the overall security of an enterprise network.

INTRODUCTION

With the increased reliance and dependence on networks, the threats that an enterprise faces, both external as well as internal, has also increased phenomenally. A security administrator is always faced with the challenge of identifying these threats, and in retrospect, securing the organization's network. The classical approach of identifying the vulnerabilities of individual hosts using commercially available tools, like the *Retina* and *Nessus,* does not take into account vulnerability interactions. These vulnerability interrelationships are very important to get a holistic view of network security from the security administrator's point of view. The vulnerability interactions are best captured by an attack graph, which helps in identifying all the possible ways in which an attacker can reach a critical resource on the network.

The attack graph generation is a first step towards threat identification of an enterprise network. There are two basic approaches of generating an attack graph, namely the state based approach (Ammann et al., 2002; Philips et al., 1998) and host based approach (Ammann et al., 2005; Ingols et al., 2006). Several previous approaches (Ammann et al., 2002; Li et al., 2006) have used the combination of a forward and backward chaining algorithm to identify an attack graph. The state based approach gives information at a more granular level whereas its representation soon becomes very large and complex even for a moderate size network (Sheyner et al., 2002). On the other hand, in a host based attack graph each node will be identified as a network entity and the edges will be privileges obtained after applying exploits among them. The host based approach gives a compact representation which may be useful for a visual representation and handle scalability at the cost of abstracting several low level details related to exploit correlation, vulnerability and attacker privileges. For example, obtaining *user* level privilege on a host, say *host 1,*

and escalation of that privilege to the *super user* level can be treated as two distinguished states in a state based approach. On the other hand, a host based approach combines all such individual privileges and retains the highest level privilege as a graph edge. Availability of the low level details in a state based attack graph makes it convenient for proper risk management.

The proposed approach uses the state based forward chaining algorithm (Ammann et al., 2002) to generate an attack graph with necessary exploits. The necessary exploits are the set of exploits, subset of which will be actually used by the attacker to obtain the goal. Therefore, the forward reachable attack graph may contain redundancies. The run time complexity of such forward chaining algorithm can be represented by the polynomial $O(|A|^2. E)$ (Ammann et al., 2002), where A is the number of network conditions and E is the number of exploits. Each vertex in the generated attack graph is used to represent network state and the corresponding exploits, the edges are used to represent the causal relationship among network states and exploits. The proposed approach in Ammann et al. (2002) does a backward search to generate attack graph with sufficient exploits from the forward reachable attack graph. Our proposed approach differs from Ammann et al. (2002) in that it works in two dimensions. On one hand it identifies the most probable attack path(s) based on the attack surface measure of the individual hosts, independent of the vulnerabilities or the exploits that may exist and on the other hand that for identifying the actual exploit correlation for risk mitigation rather than generating an attack graph it uses a forward reachable graph and thus identifies all the possible network securing options.

The rest of the chapter is organized as follows. Section 2 presents a detailed literature survey on previous approaches. Section 3 describes the proposed approach. Section 4 presents a case study in support of the model's efficiency and finally the conclusion is drawn in section 5.

BACKGROUND

The initial effort of generating an attack graph was first carried out using the *red team* approach, but this manual effort was tedious, error-prone, and impractical for even a moderate size network. Philips and Swiler (1998) developed a tool for generating the attack graph. It constructs the attack graph by forward exploration starting from an initial state using attacker's profile, configuration information of networked host and a database containing template of actions. The work by Sheyner et al. (2002) have used BDD (Binary Decision Diagram) based model checker NuSMV (a new symbolic model checker) to compute multi-stage, multihost attack paths in a form of scenario graph. Amman et al. (2002) shows how assumption of monotonocity helps to address scalability problem of attack graph. Bhattacharya et al. (2007) proposes an artificial intelligence based search approach to generate attack graph. Jajodia et al. (2005) describes the "Topological Vulnerability Analysis" (TVA) which implements an integrated, topological approach to network vulnerability analysis using the underlying algorithm of Ammann et.al (2002). Noel et al. (2005) and Wang et al. (2006) use the exploit-dependency representation of TVA (Jajodia et al., 2005) and represent it into symbolic equation. Analysis of this equation recommends the least cost change to be done in terms of minimal independent set of security conditions in order to guarantee the safety of critical network resources. Noel et al. (2004) describes various approaches to collapse parts of exploit-dependency attack graphs generated by the TVA (Jajodia et al., 2005) system to make visual understanding easier and interactive. Ammann et al. (2005) describes an algorithm for computing suboptimal attack path among each and every pair of hosts in the network to find out maximum privilege that can be gained on each host by an attacker. Ou et al. (2006) uses a monotonic logic-based approach called Mul-VAL to produce a counter-example for a given

security policy over an enterprise network. Li et al. (2006) describes a process to model system vulnerabilities and possible exploitations in homogeneous cluster environments using exploitation graphs or e-graphs. Bhattacharya et al. (2008) proposes risk identification through integration of attacker's profile and publicly available data sources. Dantu et al. (2004; 2005) formulated a Bayesian network based mechanism to estimate the risk level of critical resources that may be compromised based on attacker's behavior. A number of previous approaches by Ning et al. (2003; 2004) have used attack graph to integrate or correlate alerts generated by reactive security devices like Intrusion Detection System (IDS), to identify multistage attack scenarios. Current intrusion detection methods may be able to identify individual stages of an attack with more or less accuracy and completeness, the recognition of a sophisticated multi-stage attack involving a complex set of steps under the control of a master hacker remains difficult. The correlation of stages separated by a significant amount of time is also difficult to model.

The attack surface measurement is relatively a new research area for risk assessment and management. It was Howard et al (2003; 2005) who first laid the grounds for the measurement of the attack surface. As proposed by Manadhata et al. (2006) the attack surface is a measure of a systems security in quantifiable terms. The attack surface is measured in terms of system resources along the three dimensions of the *methods*, *channels* and the *un-trusted data items* that an attacker may use to attack the system. Each resource in turn has an *attackability* measure and the resource's contribution to the attack surface depends on its *attackability*. Higher the *attackability*, the higher the contribution towards the attack surface measure. Manadhata et al. (2006) later improved on the proposed technique and suggested an *entry/exit point framework* to identify resources contributing to a system's attack surface. They also suggested a notion of *attackability* that is a cost benefit ratio in terms of the *damage potential* of a resource and the *effort* that the attacker has to spend in order to acquire that resource. As has been mentioned earlier, the attack surface is defined along the dimensions of the *methods, channels* and the *data items,* collectively referred to as the *system resources.* Only those resources that an attacker may utilize, contribute towards the attack surface measure. Therefore, given two systems, the security administrator can decide as to which system is more secure based on the comparison of their attack surface measure.

PROPOSED APPROACH: THREAT IDENTIFICATION AND ATTACK PATH PREDICTION

In an attack graph generation process, the forward chaining approaches suffer from circular dependencies or cycles among the exploits and their pre-conditions and post-conditions. Though the recent approach (Ingols et al., 2006) is able to generate the attack graph in linear time of the size of network, Ingols (2006) has admitted that their proposed multiple-perquisite (MP) graph contains a large number of cycles due to back edges, makes it difficult to identify the coherent layout of exploits for risk mitigation. Actually, the resolution of cycles represents an attacker's thought who will not execute the same set of exploits repeatedly for already obtained privileges. The cycles and other redundancies are common in real networks, and are violations of monotonicity (Ammann et al, 2002) that must be resolved. Indeed, in the real world, attackers themselves would try to avoid such redundancies (Noel et al., 2005). To overcome this redundancy problem (Lippmann et al., 2005), the proposed approach initially detects and removes cycle from a forward reachable attack graph and thereafter executes a backward search algorithm to identify non-redundant exploit sequences as attack path.

The attack graphs and the attack paths show sequence of exploits, which may be useful for applications that focus on the attacks themselves. The network administrators are usually less interested about exploit sequences rather they are more eager to identify the best possible / most probable ways to secure their network. This necessitates identification of best possible network hardening options from a generated attack graph or attack path. To achieve this objective, the proposed work identifies the network securing options using the generated attack paths and applying the boolean minimization logic onto it. The proposed exhaustive risk management methodology can be classified as:

- Detection and removal of cycles from a forward reachable attack graph.
- Identifying all the attack paths from the forward reachable directed acyclic attack graph.
- Identifying the minimum possible network securing options for risk mitigation.
- Identifying the most probable attack path based on the attack surface measure.

Detection and Removal of Cycles

The generation of cycle is an inevitable part of a forward reachable algorithm (Philips et al., 1998) due to the fact that a single network condition can contribute both as a pre-condition and post-condition for a single exploit. Such cycles in attack graph is treated as redundant or useless edges. There is no reason to cycle among exploits whose post-conditions have already been satisfied (Noel et al., 2005). Little attention has been paid in most of the previous approaches (Ammann et al, 2002; Ingols et al., 2006; Li et al., 2006; Sheyner et al., 2002) to remove and detect cycles from a forward reachable attack graph. The method proposed by Noel et al (2005) and Wang et al (2006) is not very clear as to how using number of vertices in shortest path can help them to detect and remove cycles from a forward reachable graph.

The standard *depth first search (DFS)* marks nodes as they are encountered over a graph. If a previously marked node is seen again, then a cycle exists and the same is detected. This approach does not work on a graph, because a graph node can have multiple parents.

For example, application of standard *depth first search* (DFS) (Mendelson et al., 1997) algorithm starting from node 1 on both figures 1(a) and 1(b) falsely identify that either of the edge (3, 2) or edge (2, 3) are redundant and part of a cycle. Actually, in Figure 1(a), removal of edge (2, 3) would lose the attack path (1, 2, 3, 4) and in Figure 1(b) none of the edges are redundant. The elimination of any edge from Figure 1(b) removes attack path (1, 2, 3, 4) or (1, 3, 2, 5).

To determine if an edge *(u, v)* is *useless* or *redundant* and contributes to cycle in an attack graph, vertex *u* can be removed from the graph and it can be tested if **goal** vertex can still be derived from vertex *v*. This can be done by a *depth first search* (DFS) from *v*. If **goal** vertex is reachable, the edge is not redundant as there is an alternate path for *v* which does not involve *u* to reach the **goal**. On the other hand, inability of reaching **goal** implies existence of an edge from vertex *v* to *u* towards **goal**. The edge has been temporarily deleted along with removal of vertex *u* from the graph. The proof of existence for both the edges *(u, v)* and *(v, u)* indicates the presence of cycle in the graph and declares edge *(u, v)* as redundant. The proposed method finally removes

those *redundant* or *useless* edges for eliminating cycles from the graph. For example, application of the proposed methodology on Figure 1(a) identifies and removes edge (3, 2) (as shown in figure 1(c)) as it does not contribute to any of the attack path. On the other hand, on figure 1(b) no such modification is necessary as edges (2, 3) and (3, 2) contributes to two different attack paths and does not form cycle.

Each instance the approach takes any two vertexes as source and destination from the graph to identify cycles. Hence, the algorithm for finding all *useless* or *redundant* edges in an attack graph is at most quadratic in the size of the attack graph (in terms of number of vertex in the attack graph).

Identification of Attack Paths

The detection and removal of cycles from forward reachable attack graph generates an acyclic directed attack graph with necessary exploits that will be required by the attacker to reach the **goal**. Most of the previous approaches try to produce an attack graph from this forward reachable graph using backward search methodology (Ammann et al., 2002; Jajodia et al., 2005; Ou et al., 2006). However, for an organizational network this attack graph eventually becomes very large and complex. It also becomes difficult for the security administrator to interpret (Ingols et al., 2006) the same and make any meaningful interpretation out of it. The recent approach (Ingols 2006) reports that even after 99% reduction in the size

Figure 1. Attack graph with cycles

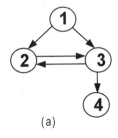

(a)

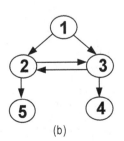

(b)

of the generated attack graph (on a network of 16 hosts), the graph contains 80 nodes and 190 edges and becomes too complicated to interpret and comprehend.

From a system administrator's perspective, identifying the sequence of exploits that a potential attacker may use to reach the goal (attack path) is more important than the attack graph itself. Identifying all the attack paths from an attack graph is a cumbersome process and needs certain level of manual expertise as no automated process to extract attack path from an attack graph has been proposed. There are also certain alternate research efforts using search based methodology like *prolog* (Boddy et al., 2005; Ou et al., 2006) to find an attack path. Such approaches are not exhaustive in nature and only able to find out the minimal level attack path. Once the administrator has invalidated the minimal level path, the algorithm goes in search for other paths. Removing single exploit from an attack path disables all other attack paths which use that removed exploit and thus the search algorithm is not able to find

out those paths. To overcome the aforementioned difficulties, the proposed *GenerateAttackPath* algorithm in Figure 2 generates the entire exploit dependent attack paths from the forward reachable acyclic directed graph in an exhaustive manner. The outcome of the algorithm shows all possible ways that an attacker can take to reach a goal.

In *GenerateAttackPath* algorithm (refer figure 2), the model extends the meaning of terminology *exploit set* as a collection of exploits and initial network conditions. For example, if there is an exploit E_1 whose pre-conditions are satisfied by three exploits namely E_2, E_3, and E_4, then these three exploits can be represented as an *exploit set* using $\{E_2, E_3, E_4\}$.

The *GenerateAttackPath* algorithm uses two simple basic data structures namely *stack* and *queue*. The *stack* and *queues* are used to account the exploit sets that belong to a single attack path and exploit sets that are applied at a particular level of attack graph respectively. The *queues*, for each level of *stack* are identified as *queue$_i$* where *i* belong to stack pointer *sp*. The state based

Figure 2. Attack path generation algorithm

```
1. GenerateAttackPath (Graph g, Goal)
2. Input: as Directed Acyclic Forward Reachable Graph
3. Output: Generated Attack Paths
4.
5. Initialize stack pointer sp=0.
6. do
7.    Find all exploit set that satisfy the Goal.
8.    Enqueue Queue_sp with the chosen exploit set.
9.    Chose one of the exploit set from Queue_sp.
10.   Push it at Stack_sp and dqueue from Queue_sp.
11.   Update the Goal with chosen exploit set and go to step 7.
12.   Update stack pointer as sp=sp+1.
13. while (all preconditions of exploit set belongs to initial condition)
14. Read the stack form the top and get the attack path.
15. do
16.   if (Queue_sp is empty)
17.     Delete Queue_sp.
18.     Delete the stack top exploit set and update sp=sp-1.
19.     if (sp==-1)
20.        Go to Step 9.
21.     endif
22.   endif
23. while (not found an non empty Queue_sp)
24. goto Step 9.
25. END GenerateAttackPath
```

forward reachable attack graph (Ammann et al., 2002) represents each *pre* and *post -conditions* and *exploits* as graph *vertex* and their causal relationship as *edges*. The basic loop of the proposed algorithm (figure 2, line number 6-13) visits each *vertex* in the forward reachable attack graph and identifies all of its predecessor vertex (along each edge of the attack graph only once) and put them in the *queue* for future reference.

A single exploit may appear several times within a single attack path which is quite trivial, as the post-condition of a single exploit can be used as many of its successor exploit's pre-conditions. So the algorithm outputs an attack path which has been represented in a *transitively reduced[1]* (Deo 1974) exploit dependent form. For example, in figure 3(a) exploit E_1 satisfies the pre-conditions for exploit E_2 and exploit E_1 and E_2 jointly satisfy the pre-condition(s) for exploit E_3. In contrast, figure 3(b) shows the equivalent transitively reduced graph without any loss of generality. The running time for standard *transitive reduction* algorithm is $O(|V|+|E|)$ where $|V|$ and $|E|$ are the number of vertices and edges of the graph. The underlying philosophy of this reduction is that once an exploit within an attack path has been successful, its ef-

fect can be used repeatedly without representing it visually every time.

The backward traversal nature of the *GenerateAttackPath* algorithm and appearance of multiple exploits with same post-conditions raises a new sort of problem. For example the exploit dependency graph in figure 4 depicts that exploit E_4's pre-condition can either be satisfied by exploit set $\{E_1, E_3\}$ or $\{E_2, E_3\}$ and exploit E_3's pre-condition is also satisfied either by exploit E_1 or by E_2 individually. In the first iteration of the *GenerateAttackPath* algorithm in Figure 2, exploit set $\{E_1, E_3\}$ is chosen and in the next iteration exploit E_3's pre-condition can be chosen out of exploit E_1 and E_2. Selection of exploit E_2 will report that the attack path consists of $\{E_2\} \rightarrow \{E_1, E_3\} \rightarrow \{E_4\}$. Though the generated path is a valid one but it violates the principle of monotonicity (Ammann et al, 2002). The monotonicity assumption states that an exploit will never get executed for a privilege which has already been obtained. The generated attack path violates this by using exploit E_1 and E_2 for obtaining the same privilege within a single attack path. Actually, these two exploits contribute to two different paths over the graph. In an attack graph generation problem several attributes can be satisfied by multiple exploits, each of which will lead to a separate attack path. On the other hand, during a single attack path generation the exploit set for a particular attribute will remain same. To solve this problem, once an attack path is generated, a list of attributes and corresponding exploits is kept during read of the attack path from the stack top (Figure 2, line number 14]. Thus for attack path $\{E_2\} \rightarrow \{E_1, E_3\} \rightarrow \{E_4\}$, once exploit E_1 has been met, it reports a violation of the monotonicity constraint as the corresponding attribute has already been satisfied by exploit E_2 and hence corresponding path is rejected. Furthermore, the attack path with smallest value of *stack pointer (sp)* essentially identifies the minimum level attack path.

Figure 3. Transitive reduction of directed graph

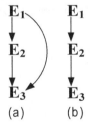

Figure 4. Exploit dependent attack graph

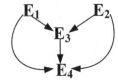

Identification of Network Securing Options

Once the attack paths have been generated by *GenerateAttackPath*, identification of network securing options can be initiated. Previous approaches have addressed this problem by computing minimal critical set of exploits (Ammann et al., 2002; Jha et al., 2002; Sheyner et al., 2002). However, such solutions are not directly enforceable, because some of the vulnerabilities or attributes are logical consequences of other exploits or vulnerabilities, and the consequences cannot be removed without first removing the reasons. For example, success of an *ssh* related exploit depends upon two primary pre-conditions, existence of the vulnerable version of the *ssh* daemon in the victim host and attacker having *ssh* access privilege on the source host. However, the later condition may depend on some other vulnerability and its corresponding exploit(s) to get that privilege. A critical vulnerability or an exploit is not under the direct control of an administrator, therefore the exploits dependencies are found in a recursive manner until all of its pre-conditions belong to the initial condition set. The initial conditions represent the entire network configuration in its initial stage, which is under the direct control of the administrator. For example, running of *ftp* service on *host1* can be considered as initial network condition. Proper control on such initial

network conditions prevents attacker to execute necessary exploits.

Once the attack paths have been identified, a linear scan on it helps to identify the network conditions that belong to the initial network condition in linear time. The attacker's privilege on his own system is excluded from this consideration as it is out of the control of system administrator. Removing any of the initial conditions from an attack path will be sufficient to prevent an attacker from following that path. On the other hand, to make the network secure exhaustively, each such attack paths should be prevented which yields the **goal** as a *sum of product (SOP)* or *disjunctive normal form (DNF)* (Mendelson et al., 1997). For example, if a network contains three attack paths to its critical resource namely A_1, A_2, A_3 with initial conditions as C_1 (for A_1), C_2, C_3 (for A_2), C_2, C_4 (for A_3) then the *Goal* can be represented as *goal* $= C_1 + C_2 C_3 + C_2 . C_4$. The *DNF* is then converted into a *canonical conjunctive normal form (CCNF)* (Mendelson et al., 1997) where each *maxterm* in the *CCNF* represents a particular combination of initial network condition state (in the form of either condition *exist* or *not exist*) for which the *goal* is not achievable. The entire network securing option identification methodology has been described as *NetworkHardening* algorithm in figure 5.

In worst case, the number of generated *maxterm* within a *CCNF* from a *DNF* is exponential

Figure 5. Network securing option identification algorithm

```
1. NetworkHardening (Attack Paths)
2. Input: Generated Attack Paths
3. Output: Network hardening options
4.
5. for each identified attack path do
6.    Read each attack path and identify the preconditions belongs to
7.       initial conditions.
8.    Represent the condition as "AND" form.
9. endfor
10. Represent the entire goal condition as disjunctive normal form (DNF).
11. Solve the disjunctive normal form DNF using Boolean Minimization
12. Logic to identify minimum cover.
13. END
```

(Mendelson et al., 1997). Though all of these *maxterm* provides an exhaustive network securing options, some of them are redundant, hence not desirable. As a result, there is a need to identify *maxterm* that correspond to the minimum network changes to be done as well as exhaustive in nature. Noel et al. (2005) and Wang et al. (2006) have proposed the comparison of taking two maxterms at a time. To overcome the tedious *maxterm*s comparisons, existing boolean logic minimizer *Quine–Mccluskey²* algorithm is used to find out a minimal cover from the *CCNF* in an automated fashion. The minimum cover generation problem is a *NP-hard* problem, so the *Quine–Mccluskey* algorithm also grows exponentially as $3^n/n$ where *n* is the number of initial conditions. To deal with such situations, non-optimal heuristic methods like *espresso logic minimizer³* can be used to obtain the approximate minimal cover. The basic steps of *Quine–Mccluskey* algorithm can be described as follows:

- **Find prime implicant:** Categorize the *maxterm* into groups based on number of 1's within it in a tabular form known as *maxterm* table.
- **Find essential prime implicant:** Compare each *maxterm* with its adjacent group's *maxterm* and keep continuing when none of the *maxterm* can be further combined (Boolean Multiplication) and identify the prime implicant. Two *maxterm* can be called as adjacent if there is a single bit difference among two *maxterm* and combination of these two *maxterm* removes the differentiating bit from the resultant. For example *maxterm* (X+Y+Z') and (X+Y+Z) are adjacent to each other and combination of these *maxterm* results as (X+Y).
- **Select a minimal set of remaining prime implicant that covers the on-set of the function:** In some cases, the essential prime implicant do not cover all minterms, in which case additional procedures for *max-*

term table reduction can be employed. The simplest "additional procedure" is trial and error, but a more systematic way is *Petrick's Method⁴*.

In the following case study, we show how the algorithm is implemented over a *DNF* representation to identify minimum cover efficiently. The effectiveness of the proposed exhaustive risk identification approach has been validated by applying it on a test networks in the case study (refer to section 4).

Identification of the Most Probable Attack Path

In this section, we explain how we can identify the most probable / critical attack paths for a given network. The approach in this section digresses from the conventional approach of the attack graphs as the proposed model is organized around the hosts rather than the vulnerabilities or the exploits with the attack surface measure (Howard et al., 2005; Howard et al., 2003; Manadhata et al., 2006) being the centre piece of the proposed approach. Therefore, the attack surface measurement is described first before making its use in the methodology proper.

As proposed by Manadhata et al. (2006), the attack surface is a measure of a systems security in quantifiable terms and is used to compare similar software systems or the systems having similar functionality. Manadhata et al. have described an *"entry/exit point framework"* to measure the attack surface of a given system. The attack surface is measured in terms of system resources along the three dimensions of the *methods*, *channels* and the *un-trusted data items* that an attacker may use to attack the system. Each resource in turn has an *attackability* measure, which is the cost benefit ratio of the *damage potential* of the resource and the *effort* that the attacker has to spend in order to acquire that resource. More specifically *damage potential* is an indication of the degree of damage that the attacker may cause by acquiring the resource, whereas the *effort* is an indication of the work that the attacker will have to put in to acquire the resource. Therefore, each resource's contribution to the attack surface depends on its *attackability*. Higher the *attackability* of a resource, the higher its contribution towards the attack surface measure. For example, given a system, its attack surface measurement with respect to the *methods* dimension is done by, first listing out all the methods that can be invoked by the attacker to send/receive data from the system. In the next step, the *attackability* measurement of each of the methods is carried out. Once the *attackability* measure of each of the methods has been calculated as a final step the summation of the individual *attackability* measures is carried out to get the total attackability along the method dimension. Similar calculation is carried out to measure the *attackability* along the channel as well as the data dimensions. Thus, finally the attack surface is calculated. Attack surface is represented as a triple <*SA, CA, DA*> where *SA* is the sum total of the *attackability* of the *system attack class* (contribution coming from the attackability of the methods), whereas *CA* and *DA* are sum total of the *attackability* of the *channel* and the *data attack classes* respectively. A detailed example for attack surface measurement can be found in Manadhata et al. (2006) for two *FTPD* applications.

The proposed approach is based on the attack surface measurement and the following assumptions:

- The network environment is such, that the *method attackability* poses a more serious threat than the *channel* and the *data attackability*.
- The enterprise network comprises of similar software systems.

Therefore, given the attack surface measure in the form of triple <*SA, CA, DA*> we will only be dealing with the quantity *SA* that is the *system attackability* arising because of the *attackability* of the *methods dimension*. Thus given the network each host will have its attack surface measure indicating its *methods attackability*. The second assumption although not restrictive, allows us to compare the attack surface measures of the hosts with ease.

Malhotra et al. (2008) explained that one can discover attack paths independent of the vulnerabilities and the exploits therefore the proposed methodology is based around the hosts. As explained earlier for a host based approach, the vertices/nodes of the attack graph represent the hosts forming part of the network and the logical connectivity/access level that a host has on the other is represented by means of directed edges. Therefore, in the proposed methodology for a given attack graph $G(V,E)$ with host set V and a set of edges E, a directed edge from host $u \in V$ to host $v \in V$, is denoted as edge $(u \rightarrow v) \in E$. In turn the edge $(u \rightarrow v) \in E$ represents the access level that u has on v. The access levels form part of the access level set, *Acc*. It is likely that between any two given hosts a number of access levels may be available but it will be the highest level of access that will interest us. In Ammann et al. (2002) it has been shown that during the course of formulation of the access graph, between any two hosts, the edge with the highest available access level will only be retained and rest all will be eliminated. Finally the graph $G(V,E)$ will be an access graph based on the attack surface measure and the access levels between the hosts.

While generating the access graph we make use of an *access control matrix (ACM) model* (Boddy et al., 2005) which is a matrix A_{pq} whose cell entries contain the access levels available to a subject over an object. In our context the subjects as well as the objects are the hosts forming the network, and each cell entry contains the access level that the host u has on host v, $\forall (u, v) \in V$. As a first step towards obtaining an optimal attack path, we *relax* the access control matrix and prefer to retain only the highest access level between the hosts. This is for the reason that given *root* and *guest* level access from *u* to *v,* an attacker, making use of *root* access level can mount a more powerful attack than using the *guest* access level. In order to quantify the access level, we attach a metric to each access level. For this, we make use of a function *wt: acc → N* which maps each access level $acc_i \in Acc$ to a numeric value *N*. At present we consider the set *Acc* as follows:

Acc = {root, authenticated, anonymous = unauthenticated = guest}

The numeric values are assigned in accordance with the total ordering of the access levels, TO_{acc}, such that the following holds:

$$\forall \, acc_i, \, acc_j \in Acc, \, (acc_i \, TO_{acc} \, acc_j) \Rightarrow (wt \, (acc_i) \leq wt \, (acc_j)$$

The algorithm *RelaxMatrix* as shown in figure 6, takes as its input the matrix A_{pq} (directed network graph with all the available access rights between the hosts) and produces another matrix

Figure 6. Algorithm RelaxMatrix

```
1. RelaxMatrix(A_pq, Acc) /*Produces a weighted
2.              attack graph with highest
3.              access level between
4.              hosts in the form of
5.              adjacency matrix*/
6. Input: Access Control Matrix, A_pq ;
7.     Set of access rights, Acc;
8. Output: Relaxed Access Control Matrix, RelA_pq
9.     with access rights replaced by their
10.     numeric values
11.
12. BEGIN RelaxMatrix
13. for i ← 1 to p
14.   for j ← 1 to q
15.     do
16.         for each acc_i ∈ Acc
17.           if acc_m ≤ acc_n
18.               acc = acc_n
19.         else
20.             acc = acc_m
21.         wt: acc → N
20.     RelA[i][j] = N
21. return RelA_pq
22. END RelaxMatrix
```

$RelA_{pq}$ which is *relaxed,* that is to say a matrix that retains only the highest access level between the hosts, as its output. The matrix so obtained can also be termed as a *weighted adjacency matrix (RelA$_{pq}$)* and it represents a weighted access graph with highest access level between the logically connected hosts. Taking this matrix as one of the inputs, we find *an* optimal path that an attacker may take to reach his goal node.

In order to find as to how the attack will perpetrate through the network the penetration tester must designate the source and the goal nodes. The source node is representative of the attacker and the goal node is the target node that the attacker wants to compromise. If the attacker is a node other than the nodes in the network then the attacker node requires to be added to the network and its connectivity with the nodes on which it has access need to be updated in the weighted adjacency matrix, produced as a result of the algorithm *RelaxMatrix*. The adjacency matrix is updated by adding a row and a column for the attacker node, *'s'* (indicating source), and a numeric entry of unity is made in all the cells against the row for *'s'*, for the nodes that are reachable from *'s'*. In case the attacker node is from among the nodes that form part of the network then the weighted adjacency matrix produced by the algorithm *RelaxMatrix* can be used as such.

The other important input for the attack path generation is the set of attack surface measures

Figure 7. Algorithm GenAccessGraph

```
1. GenAccessGraph(RelA_pq,ASA) /*Produces a
2.              weighted attack
3.              graph G (V, E)*/
4. Input: A relaxed access control matrix, RelA_pq ;
5.     An array containing the attack surface
6.     measure of each individual host forming
7.     the network, ASA;
8.
9. BEGIN GenAccessGraph
10. for i ← 1 to p
11.   NodeWt = ASA_i /*Assign node weight*/
12.     for j ← 1 to q
13.       if RelA[i][j] ≠ 0 /*create edge from I to j*/
14.           wt (i → j) = RelA_ij
15. END GenAccessGraph
```

ASA of the individual hosts that form part of the network. $ASA = \{SA_1, SA_2 .... SA_n\} \mid SA_i = Attack$ *surface measure of the ith host*

The attack surface measures can be kept pre-calculated using the methodology explained earlier and as described in Ingols et al. (2006). Thus, given the matrix $RelA_{pq}$, with the attacker node '*s*' added to it and the set of the individual attack surface measure of the nodes *ASA* generating the attack graph is trivial. The algorithm *GenAccessGraph*, for generating the attack graph $G(V, E)$ where *V* is the set of vertices and *E* the set of edges, is as given in figure 7.

Figure 8. Algorithm FindPath

```
 1. FindPath(G,s,g)  /*Finds an optimal attack
 2.          path*/
 3. Input: Access Graph, G (V, E); Single source
 4.    vertex (attacker node), s ; Goal node g;
 5. Output: An optimal path to reach the goal
 6.    node
 7.
 8. BEGIN FindPath
 9. /* Initialising the graph*/
10. for each host u Є V[G] – {s}
11.    do color[u] ← white
12. color[s] ← grey
13. wt[s] ← 0
14. PUSH(S,s) /*Pushing the source node into
15.       the stack.*/
16. v = s
17. while (v ≠ g)
18.    if (Adj[v] != ф && Neighbor(v))
19.      v = FindNext(G,v)
20.      if (Adj[v] == NULL || ! Neighbor(v))
21.         then color[v] ← black
22.            x = v;
23.            v =S[TOP(S)]
24.         wt[x] = wt[x] – wt[v] – wt(v → x)
25.         else
26.         color[v] = grey
27.            PUSH(S,v)
28. else
29.      color[v] = black
30.         POP(S)
31.         v =S[TOP(S)]
32.         if (v = s && Adj[v] = black)
33.         print ("Path is not available")
34.            exit (0);
35. print ("Reverse path from goal to source as:")
36. while(stack != NULL)
37.    node = POP(S)
38.    print(node)
39. END FindPath
```

Having generated the access graph $G(V, E)$ and given a distinguished source vertex (attacker node) '*s*', the algorithm *FindPath* of figure 8, finds an optimal attack path from the source to the goal node, '*g*'. The algorithm makes use of a *stack* to store the nodes that are discovered on the path from the source to the goal node. The algorithm carries out graph coloring in order to avoid the nodes which do not lead to the goal node. We refer to such nodes as *"no go"* nodes. The algorithm starts by initializing the graph. All nodes are colored white other than the source node which is colored grey (lines 12 – 15 of figure 8).

As the algorithm progresses towards discovering a path from the source node to the goal node it keeps on coloring the discovered nodes grey, before pushing them into the stack (line 27- 28 of figure 8). This is done with the purpose of avoiding cycles in the graph. In case the discovered node does not has any path leading to the goal node it is colored black (line 30 of figure 8), to avoid it in any subsequent path tracing. Once a node is colored black it is popped out of the stack and the algorithm *backtracks* to the previous node in order to trace an alternate path. The back tracking

Figure 9. Algorithm FindNext

```
 1. FindNext(G,v) /*Finds the next node which acts
 2.          as pivot*/
 3. Input: Access Graph, G (V,E); Node whose
 4.    successor is to be selected,v;
 5. Output: Next suitable network node in the path
 6.    to goal node, next;
 7.
 8. BEGIN FindNext
 9. wt = 0
10. prev = 0
11. next = 0
12. for i = 1 to G[V]
13.    do if RelA[v][i] ≥ 1
14.    then wt[i] = wt[i] + wt[u] + wt(u → i)
15.         if wt ≤ wt [i]
16.      then prev = next
17.         next = i
18.    if (prev ! = 0)
19.         then wt(prev) =wt – wt[u] –
                  wt (u → prev)
20.      wt = wt[i]
21. return next
22. END FindNext
```

is done sequentially for the reasons that even the attacker would not start afresh every time and would like to maximize the benefit of an already exploited host.

In order to discover the nodes on the attack path the algorithm makes use of another routine *FindNext* as shown at figure 9. The *FindNext* algorithm carries out a breadth first search every time it is invoked (line 20 of figure 8), to systematically explore the edges of the graph *G (V, E)* and *"discover"* every host that is reachable from the host discovered in the previous call (source node *'s'* for the first invocation). The nodes that are found available as a result of this search are the ones from which the attacker will select a potential victim (lines 9 to 14 of figure 9). The selected node acts as a *pivot* for selecting the subsequent victim hosts. This process of finding the subsequent node is carried out every time the algorithm *FindNext* is called, and the node found in previous call acts as a stepping stone on the attack path to the goal node. The decision for selection of potential victim is done using *greedy choice*. This is shown in lines 12 to 20 of figure 9. The greedy choice of victim node is not only based on nodes weight (attack surface measure) $wt(v)$, but also the weights of the source node $wt(u)$ and the edge weight $wt(u \rightarrow v)$ between them. The node and edge weight resulting in the highest sum is selected as the victim node on the attack path to the goal node.

The algorithm *FindPath* of figure 8 therefore either reports the nodes discovered on the attack path or incase the path is not available, it reports same. Once the attack path has been discovered the next logical step is to carry out threat management. Although, at the moment we are not getting into the exact details of threat management, it will certainly be addressed as future work, but at the same time a broad overview is given here. Having discovered the probable attack path it is at this stage that the penetration tester will require to carry out a vulnerability scan of the nodes that form part of the attack path. One must note that

it is only the select nodes, falling on the attack path that need to be scanned and not all the nodes forming the network. Once the vulnerabilities have been identified it will be logical to patch those vulnerabilities for which the exploits give maximal privilege level to the attacker. A similar approach is also followed in Ammann et al. (2002). Having done so the penetration tester can re-run the algorithm and thus identify other paths that lead to the designated goal machine. Thus, a repeated application of the algorithm coupled with the threat management after every run will help identify the other sub optimal choices as well, that an attacker may make to reach up to the goal node.

One must also make note of the fact that the path optimization problem in this case is NP-Complete (Cormen et al., 2006). However, an analysis of the *FindPath* algorithm shows that the while loop at line number 18, in worst case will be executed V times. The *FindNext* function will also be executed V times in the worst case. This can be the case when the depth of the network is only up to one level and all nodes $v \in V$ are accessible from the source node *'s'*. Thus in worst case the complexity of our algorithm is of the order $O\ (V^2)$ which is better than that of Ammann et al. (2005.

CASE STUDY

The opted test network in this case study has been used by several previous research (Ammann et.al, 2002; Jajodia et al., 2005; Sheyner et al., 2002) efforts to validate their approach.

Test Network

The example network is shown in figure 10. There are two hosts on the internal network, *Host1* and *Host2*, and the firewall separating the internal network from external network. The attacker's host is *Host0* on the external network.

Figure 10. Network diagram for case study

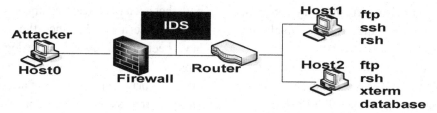

Table 1. Host configuration

Host	Services	Vulnerabilities	OS
Host1	WuFTPD, SSH, RSH	sshd buffer overflow, ftp .rhost overwrite	Linux
Host2	ProFTPD, RSH, XTERM, DATABASE,	ftp.rhost overwrite, local xterm buffer overflow	Linux

Table 2. Connection description

Relation	Host0	Host1	Host2
Host0	Local host	FTP, SSH	FTP
Host1	Any	Local host	FTP
Host2	any	FTP	Local host

The host information on the internal network is shown in table 1. The firewall allows the inbound *ftp* and the *ssh* packets to communicate with the *Host1* and *Host2*, but interdicts other packets. In the internal network, connection relation won't be controlled by firewall, so it can be assumed that the internal host can make connection with any remote server. The connection relation among each host is described in table 2. There are four possible atomic attacks which can be denoted as follows: *sshd_ bof()*, *ftp_rhosts()*, *rlogin()* and *local_bof()*. The details of these exploits are described in Jha et al (2002) as follows:

- *sshd_bof*: This attack exploits a remote buffer overflow vulnerability in *ssh* daemon. A successful execution of the attack immediately gives a root shell on the victim machine to the remote user. It has detectable and stealthy variants.

- *ftp_rhosts*: Using an *ftp* vulnerability, the intruder creates an *.rhosts* file in the *ftp home* directory, creating a remote login trust relationship between his machine and the target machine. This attack is stealthy.

- *rlogin*: Using an existing remote login trust relationship between two machines, the intruder logs into from one machine to another and get a user shell without supplying a password. This attack is detectable.

- *local_bof*: Exploiting buffer overflow vulnerability on a *setuid root* file, gives attacker root privilege on a local machine. This attack is stealthy.

The intruder launches his attack starting from a single computer *Host0* which lies outside the firewall. The **attacker**'s eventual *Goal* is to disrupt the functioning of the database server on *Host2* for which he needs *root* privilege on *Host2*.

Experimentation: Threat Identification and Attack Path Prediction

The following section describes the outcome of the proposed algorithms on the test network.

Detection and Removal of Cycles

The forward reachable exploit dependent attack graph is shown in figure 11 that has been generated using the proposed algorithm of Ammann et al. (2002). In figure 12 and 13 the numbers *0, 1, 2* represent *Host0, Host1* and *Host2* respectively of figure 10. The *root(2)* in figure 11 (black bold dotted circle) represents attacker's objective. The figure 11 contain 2 cycles in the form of

Cycle 1: (user 1) →rlogin(1,2) →(user2) →ftp_ rhosts(2,1) →(trust2,1) →rlogin(2,1) →(user1)

Cycle 2: (user1) →rlogin(1,2) →(user2) → sshd_bof(2,1) →(user1)

Execution of the cycle identification procedure (refer section 2) on the forward reachable **attack graph** results the redundant edges as shown in figure 11 with dotted lines.

Identification of Possible Attack Paths from Forward Reachable Directed Acyclic Attack Graph

Once the cycles are resolved, the generated attack graph becomes a *directed acyclic graph (DAG)*. Applying the *GenerateAttackPath* algorithm on the resulting graph identifies three transitive reduced attack paths as follows:

Attack Path 1: {ftp_rhosts(0,2)}→{rlogin(0,2)}→ {local_bof(2,2)}

Attack Path 2: {sshd_bof(0,1)}→{ftp_ rhosts(1,2)}→{rlogin(1,2)}→ {local_bof(2,2)}

Attack Path 3: {ftp_rhosts{0,1)}→{rlogin(0,1)}→ {ftp_rhosts(1,2)}→{rlogin(1,2)}→{local_ bof(2,2)}

Figure 12 depicts the execution traces for the *stack* and *queues* of *GenerateAttackPath* algo-

Figure 11. Attack graph with useless or redundant edges

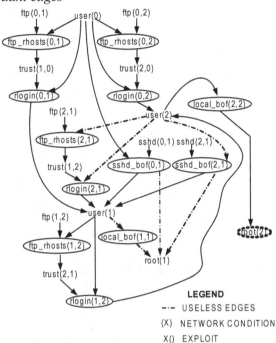

rithm for attack path 2. Figure 12 shows (in black ark lines) the exploit set, being transferred from *queue* to *stack* in each iteration of the proposed algorithm (figure 2, line number 3.5). The stack will continue to grow until all the preconditions of current exploit set belong to the initial condition set. The *stack* and *queue* traces (refer figure 12) reveal that subsequence of exploits *{B,4,D,E}→{6,8}→{3}→{1}* or *{rlogin(0,1)}→ {ftp_rhosts(1,2),sshd_bof(0,1)}→{rlogin(1,2)} →{local_bof(2,2)}*, will also be generated as an attack path. In order to be consistent with the monotonicity approach this attack path is not taken into account as *(user 1)* attribute is being satisfied by both the exploits *rlogin(0,1)* and *sshd_bof(0,1)* during a single attack path generation.

This is evident from figure 13 that how output of *GenerateAttackPath* is scalable, non-redundant, and easier to interpret compared to the attack graph generated by model checker approach (Ammann et al, 2002).

The attack graph in figure 13(a) also contains redundant edges (shown in black bold line). For

Figure 12. Execution traces for attack path identification in case study

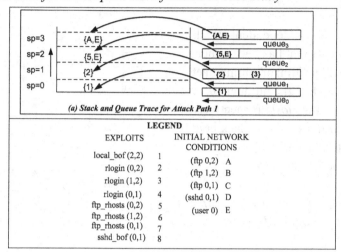

Figure 13. Comparisons between two attack graph/path generation approaches

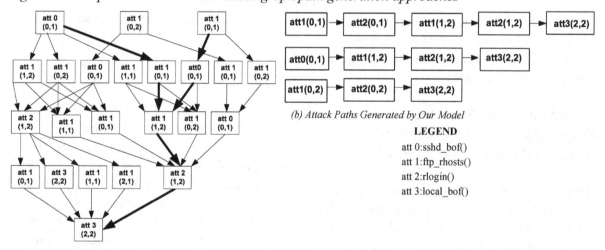

example, the only difference between two attack paths shown in figure 13(a) (*in black bold line*) is the order of occurrence between two exploits namely, *att0(0,1)* or *sshd_bof(0,1)* and *att1(0,1)* or *ftp_rhosts(0,1)* from *Host0* to *Host1*. However, none of these two exploit depends on each other by their pre or post-conditions under given network specification. Hence in reality they can be executed in any order. The attack path *att0(0,1)*→ *att1(1,2)*→*att2(1,2)*→*att3(2,2)* also appears twice in the graph.

Identification of the Minimum Possible Network Securing Options

Once the attack paths have been generated, the attack goal can be represented as

$$goal = A + BC + BD$$

where *A*, *B*, *C* and *D* signify the initial conditions *(ftp 0,2)*, *(ftp 1,2)*, *(ftp 0,1)*, and *(sshd 0,1)* as shown in figure 12. Initial condition *(user 0)*, the **attacker**'s privilege on his own system, has not been taken into account as it is outside the control of the administrator. The equivalent *canonical conjunctive normal form (CCNF)* of equation 1 can be realized from the truth table (shown in table 3) where each *maxterm* correspond to a *0-value* row as goal or *A+BC+BD*. The *CCNF* equivalent of equation 1 is shown in equation 2.

$goal = (A+B+C+D) . (A+B+C+D').$
$+B+C'+D) . (A+B+C'+D') . (A+B'+C+D)$

The equation 2 identifies the different possible combination of initial conditions to be removed for which **goal** is not attainable. Due to *maxterm* representation, each of the non-prime literals indicates the network conditions to be removed. Moreover, a closer look on each of the *maxterm* of equation 2 reveals that there are certain *maxterm* whose all the non-prime literals belongs to another *maxterm*. To avoid such redundancy, *Quine-Mccluskey* on *equation 2* identifies the prime implicant as shown in table 4.

Table 3. Truth table for equation 1

A	B	C	D	Goal (A+BC+BD)
0	0	0	0	0
0	0	0	1	0
0	0	1	0	0
0	0	1	1	0
0	1	0	0	0
0	1	0	1	1
0	1	1	0	1
0	1	1	1	1
1	0	0	0	1
1	0	0	1	1
1	0	1	0	1
1	0	1	1	1
1	1	0	0	1
1	1	0	1	1
1	1	1	0	1
1	1	1	1	1

Table 4. Finding prime implicant

Number of 1's	Maxterm	0-cube	Size 2 implicant	Size 4 implicant
0	M0	0000	M(0,1) 000_	
	M1	0001	M(0,2) 00_0*	
	M2	0010	M(0,4) 0_00*	
1	M4	0100	-----------------	M(0,1,2,3)
2	M3	0011	M(2,3) 001_	00__*

Table 5. Essential prime implicant

Prime Implicant Chart	0	1	2	3	4
M(0,1,2,3) (A+B)	X	X	X	X	
M(0,2) (A+B+D)	X		X		
M(0,4)* (A+C+D)	X				X

The *maxterm* with "*" in table 4 identifies the prime implicant which cannot be further combined with other *maxterm*. For example *maxterm M (0,2), M (0,4)* and *M (0,1,2,3)* (table 4, column 4] are being identified as prime implicant in table 4. The prime implicant in table 5 helps to identify essential prime implicant for equation 2. Each "X" in table 5 identifies the combined *maxterm* (column wise like *M(0,1,2,3)* or *A+B*] and their corresponding coverage over the actual *maxterm* (row wise like *0*] of the given *goal*. For example, *maxterm* 4 can only be covered by *M(0,4)*, hence it is an essential prime implicant and marked as "*" in table 5. Apart from that, the term *M(0,1,2,3)* covers all the *maxterm* which is covered by *M(0,2)* as shown in table 5. Hence, non-availability of the **goal** is represented in equation 3 and equation 4 as:

goal =M (0,1,2,3) . M (0,4)

Or,

goal = (A+B) . (A+C+D)

Analysis of equation 4 shows that administrator needs to opt any of the following options to secure the network.

Option 1: Stop *ftp* (0,2) and *ftp* (1,2) implies stop *ftp* service between *Host0* and *Host2*, *Host1* and *Host2,* or,

Option 2: Stop *ftp* (0,2), *ftp* (0,1), and *ssh (0,1)* implies stop *ftp* service between *Host0* and *Host2*, *Host0* and *Host1* and Stop *ssh* service between *Host0* and *Host1.*

The immediate advantage of using *Quine-Mccluskey* method over manual comparison method proposed by Noel et al. (2005) and Wang et al. (2006) is reduction in the number of comparisons of *maxterm* while identifying prime implicant in table 4. For example *maxterm* M1 (0001) needs to be compared only with *maxterm* M0 (0000) and M3 (0011) for possible identification of size-2 implicant, as rest of the *maxterm* belong to the same group of *maxterm* M1.

Identification of Most Probable Attack Path Based on the Attack Surface Measure

Having explained the aforementioned, we now show how to identify the most probable attack path in a network. We will make use of a hypothetical network and for the purpose of the case study, we will make use of the network at figure 10.

As a first case, we consider a hypothetical network of figure 14 comprising of five nodes A to E excluding the attacker. The attack surface measures for the nodes are given as per table 6.

Note that these are hypothetical figures and as per the assumption mentioned earlier, only the *system attackability (SA)* measure has been listed while the others have been omitted. The attack surface measures represent the node weights for the respective nodes.

In order to model the trust between the hosts the access control matrix given as per table 7 is made use of. As described earlier a total ordering of the access rights *Acc* is assumed, thus the following holds:

root > authenticated > anonymous = unauthenticated = guest

Therefore, the access level of *root* is greater than that of *authenticated*, and that of *authenticated* is greater than *anonymous/unauthenticated/ guest*. Here a limited, ordered set of access rights has been considered, however, for the example

Figure 14. Network configuration for Example 1

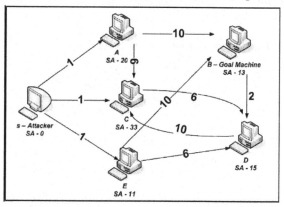

Table 6. Attack surface measures

Node	Attack Surface Measure		
	System Attackability	Channel Attackability	Data Attackability
A	20	NA	NA
B	13	NA	NA
C	33	NA	NA
D	15	NA	NA
E	11	NA	NA

considered here it is adequate. Thus this is just a guideline and it is advised to the general reader that in a similar manner one can decide on the access levels that need to be considered to best fit a network.

As a next step, the access control matrix is *relaxed* by applying the algorithm *RelaxMatrix*. The algorithm maps the access levels to their respective numeric values. The mapping here has been done as per table 8. These values are not standardized but then they serve the purpose well. The conversion of the qualitative aspects to the quantitative values has been carried out based on the experience and the pragmatic judgment. Since security is not an either-or property there are no fixed conversion rules for mapping the qualitative aspects of security to the quantitative values. It is suggested that other security administrators may customize the mapping values to better fit their specific organization environment in synchronization with the access levels that they consider for their network.

The algorithm results into a *weighted adjacency matrix* given in table 9 retaining only the highest access level between the hosts, with access levels replaced by their numeric values.

Table 7. Access control matrix (note: auth = authenticated)

	A	B	C	D	E
A	-	root, auth, guest	auth, anonymous	-	-
B	-	-	-	guest	-
C	-	-	-	auth	-
D	-	-	root	-	-
E	-	root, guest	-	auth	-

Table 8. Access level mapping table

Access Level	Value
Root	10
authenticated	6
anonymous/ unauthenticated/guest	2

Table 9. Weighted adjacency matrix

	A	B	C	D	E
A	-	10	6	-	-
B	-	-	-	2	-
C	-	-	-	6	-
D	-	-	10	-	-
E	-	10	-	6	-

Table 10. Updated weighted adjacency matrix

	s	A	B	C	D	E
S	0	1	0	1	0	1
A	0	0	10	6	0	0
B	0	0	0	0	2	0
C	0	0	0	0	6	0
D	0	0	0	10	0	0
E	0	0	10	0	6	0

Next the attacker node '*s*' is added to the adjacency matrix of table 9. A numeric value of one is assigned for the edges to the nodes accessible from the source node. In this example it is assumed that the nodes that are accessible from the attacker node, '*s*' are nodes A, C and E. Therefore, the matrix is modified suitably to show the connectivity of '*s*' to other nodes. The updated matrix is as shown in table 10. The weighted network graph of figure 14 is thus based on the data of table 6 and table 10. The edge weights are shown along the edges in bold and the attack surface measure is shown at the bottom of each host as *SA*.

In this example, we have considered node B as the **goal** node. The algorithm *FindPath* starts by first pushing the source node into the *stack*. There after a greedy choice is made from among the nodes that are connected to the source node, resulting into maximum sum of the edge weight and the node weight. As a result an initial choice of node C is made. As soon as it is discovered it is colored grey. Since the adjacency of the node is not null and there are neighbors (node D) which are not colored black, node C is pushed into the stack. The node C, now acts as the pivot, using which the attacker selects the next subsequent node. The next greedy choice is node D. However, its adjacency has only node C which has already been discovered and colored grey. Thus, a check on node's color helps avoid a cycle. In addition, since no other path exists to the goal node from D, node D is colored black and the algorithm backtracks. The backtracking is done sequentially, one node at a time and node C is popped out of the stack. It once again acts as the pivot. Since the neighboring node reachable as per the adjacency of C are all colored black, the backtracking continues. Node C is also colored black and the attacker returns to his own node, *'s',* and the same is popped out of the stack. The algorithm now searches for an alternate path avoiding the nodes colored black. As a result the next node that is selected is A, as the next potential victim, as it has the second largest measure for the attack surface from among the nodes directly accessible from *'s'*. The algorithm once again proceeds in a similar manner as has been explained previously. Once A has been selected it is pushed into the stack and *FindNext* returns C as the next greedy choice, but since it is already colored black (a *"no go"* node), the algorithm looks for an alternate path, which in this example returns B, which is also the goal node. At this stage, having reached the goal node the algorithm stops its search and returns the nodes falling and forming part of the attack path thus tracing the attack path. Therefore the attack path is *s*(Attacker)→A→B.

Let us consider the test network of figure 10 consists of two *ftp* servers. We consider the ProFTPD 1.2.10 and Wu-FTPD 2.6.2 for which the attack surface measures are available from Manadhata et al. (2006). The values of table 11 have been calculated from Manadhata et al. (2006). The data provided by Manadhata et al. (2006) shows that the attack surface measure of the WuFTPD is higher than that of ProFTPD when compared along the *method* dimension. The *attackability* along the *method* dimension is as

Table 11. Attack surface measures

Application	Measure along Method Dimension
ProFTPD 1.2.10	312.99
WuFTPD 2.6.2	392.33

given in table 11. The network setting considered for the example is given as per figure 10. It is assumed that there exists an authenticated access from WuFTPD to ProFTPD. This connectivity is shown in the form of a dotted line. For this example, we consider that the aim of the attacker is to compromise the ProFTPD.

The relaxed access control matrix including the attacker node is summarized in table 12. Mapping to the numeric values is done based on table 8.

Since we are looking at the network from a penetration tester perspective, it is assumed that the attacker has similar accessibility to both the ftp servers and for this very reason we are not concerned at the moment by the presence/absence of the firewall and the IDS. It must also be understood that the attacker in most of the cases will never be aware of the complete network topology and once he has been able to gain an initial access into the network will use classical tools to find out the accessible nodes. Here, we have considered that both the ftp servers are equally accessible to the attacker.

Application of the algorithm to the network shows that even though a direct path to the ProFTPD is available to the attacker, the attacker will first attack the node with higher attack surface. Therefore, the WuFTPD which has a higher attack surface measure as compared to the ProFTPD, will be the first host on the attack path. Since

Table 12. Relaxed access control matrix

	s	WuFTPD	ProFTPD
s	0	1	1
WuFTPD	0	0	6
ProFTPD	0	0	0

authenticated access is available from WuFTPD to ProFTPD, the attacker next makes use of this existing path to attack the ProFTPD and reach the goal node. However, in case this access was not available then, as per the algorithm the attacker would have had to back track. In that case the only option left open would have been to attack the ProFTPD through the direct path. In the present settings the application of the algorithm lists out the attack path as follows: *Attacker → WuFTPD → ProFTPD.*

Measuring Effectiveness of Attack Path

In this section, we show the effectiveness of the attack path with respect to the example network of the case study. The national vulnerability database (NVD[5]) reveals that the number of critical vulnerabilities reported for WuFTPD is five, of which four vulnerabilities allow the attacker to compromise the basic tenets of *confidentiality, integrity* and *authenticity (CIA)* on the victim host. In contrast, ProFTPD has only one and it does not allow a complete compromise of the three security tenets of *CIA*. Table 13 gives the details of the vulnerabilities. Note that only the critical vulnerabilities have been listed. The vulnerability score has been calculated on a scale of 10.0. The calculation is based on the technical report on *Common Vulnerability Scoring System version 2.0* (Mell et al., 2007). A vulnerability score of 7.0 or more is categorized as critical.

Taking a probabilistic approach one can assess that the probability of attacking the WuFTPD is certainly more than that of the ProFTPD. We assign probabilities based on the data from table 13. This is shown in figure 15. The probabilities attached to each path are shown in italics.

The probabilities have been assigned proportionate to the number of critical vulnerabilities reported for each of the *ftp* servers. Therefore the probability of attacker attacking the WuFTPD is 5/6 = 0.8 and that of attacking the ProFTPD is 1/6

Table 13. Vulnerability listing of WuFTPD and ProFTPD

Application	CVE ID No.	Severity	Allows violation of CIA
WuFTPD	CVE-2004-0148	7.2	Yes
	CVE-2004-0185	10.0	Yes
	CVE-2003-1329	7.8	No
	CVE-2003-1327	9.3	Yes
	CVE-2003-0466	10.0	Yes
ProFTPD	CVE-2005-4816	7.5	No

Figure 15. Probability analysis

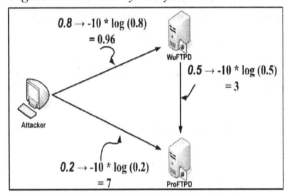

= 0.2. The probability of attacking the ProFTPD from WuFTPD has been considered as 0.5 for the reason that although the same set of exploits is available to the attacker, the access available is that of an authenticated user. Therefore, attacking the ProFTPD from WuFTPD rather than attacking directly has a higher probability. Once the probabilities have been assigned a normalization by taking the log values of the probabilities and multiplying by a factor of (– 10) is carried out. Resulting values are shown in figure 15. This normalization in turn reduces the maximization problem to a minimization problem. The problem can now be viewed as that of finding the shortest path to the **goal** node. It is verified that application of Dijkstra single source shortest path algorithm results in the same attack path as discovered by the proposed methodology.

Attack Path: Attacker → WuFTPD → ProFT-PD

We also checked our proposed algorithm against the other host based technique as proposed in Ammann et al.(2005). In order to apply the algorithm to our test case we have assumed that a vulnerability score of 7.0 or more allows root level access to the attacker. As a result root level access is available to the attacker on both the WuFTPd as well as the ProFTPD. The access level between the WuFTPD and the ProFTPD also gets upgraded to root from authenticated access. As a result two attack paths are available as follows of which the first one confirms to the attack path proposed by the algorithm.

Attack Path 1: Attacker → WuFTPD → ProFT-PD

Attack Path 2: Attacker → ProFTPD

One must note that the path identification is not the end of the matter. The final goal is to mitigate the risk and secure the network once the path is identified. The reader must understand that once the risk mitigation is carried by plugging the security holes / vulnerabilities on a node falling on the attack path, the figures as given in table 13 will need to be updated. In addition, this will have a corresponding effect on the probability calculation. Therefore, the process of path identification is not an isolated process; it has to follow hand in hand with the risk mitigation as well. Thus, this iterative process will lead to overall improvement of **security** of the network as a whole.

FUTURE RESEARCH & CONCLUSION

The attack graph provides a global view of the system security against an attacker's objective. However, the proposed approach goes beyond the generation of attack path or attack graph and focuses on identification of possible risk management measures using the attack graph in a proactive manner. This chapter deals with risk management through threat identification and attack path prediction approach. The work demonstrates how attack paths can be generated from a forward reachable exploit dependent attack graph in an exhaustive manner. The approach also addresses the issue of the cyclic dependencies of attack graph and proposes the detection and removal of the same. The generated attack paths are then used to represent the attack goal in terms of initial network security conditions. Application of *Boolean* logic minimizer helps to identify minimum possible network securing options in an automated manner. The identified network hardening options are exhaustive and minimum.

It further extends towards the identification of the most probable attack path independent of the vulnerabilities or the exploits through usage of a new metric attack surface measurement. The proposed methodology achieves the aim of identifying the most probable attack path in polynomial time complexity, given the attack surface measures of the hosts forming the network. If applied iteratively with threat management at every stage, the penetration tester/security administrator can identify other sub-optimal attack paths as well, thus securing the network as a whole. Thus, the proposed methodology can be adopted for efficient risk mitigation over an organizational network.

The chapter proposes a risk management approach for local area networks by applying available theoretical models and practical technologies. The major objective of this work is to propose a proactive risk mitigation methodology through correlation of individual vulnerabilities over the network. The efficiency of the proposed approach can further be improved in different ways, leaving much opportunity for future work.

The proposed approach has been applied for a wired network. However, with increasing proliferation of wireless technology, multi-stage threats becomes prevalent in such network. **Threat** analysis in wireless networks is also gaining significant interest among research communities. Efforts can be directed to apply the proposed work on such network. Determining reachability between all hosts in large network with many firewalls is a computationally complex task. Firewalls can contain hundreds to thousands of access control rules and *network address translation* (NAT) rules. Better algorithms for computation of host reachability in organizational network can be explored..

An extension of vulnerability analysis is the attack surface measurement which helps to quantify the system **security.** Similar systems can be made directly comparable through the usage of attack surface metric. In the future, there are additional research opportunities of applying formal methods of risk management in order to reduce the attack surface of the more vulnerable systems on the attack path.

REFERENCES

Ammann, P., Pamula, J., Ritchey, R., & Street, J. (2005). A host based approach to network attack chaining analysis. In *21st Annual Computer Security Applications Conference (ACSAC '05)* (pp. 72-84). IEEE Computer Society, Washington, DC, USA.

Ammann, P., Wijesekera, D., & Kaushik, S. (2002). Scalable, graph-based network vulnerability analysis. In *9th ACM Conference on Computer and Communications Security (CCS)* (pp. 217-224). ACM Press, New York, NY.

Bhattacharya, S., & Ghosh, S. K. (2007). An Artificial Intelligence Based Approach for Risk Management Using Attack Graph. In *International Conference on Computational Intelligence and Security (CIS 2007)* (pp. 794-798). Harbin, China.

Bhattacharya, S., & Ghosh, S. K. (2008), A Decision Model based Security Risk Management Approach. In *International MultiConference of Engineers and Computer Scientists 2008 (IMECS 2008)* (pp. 1194-1200). Hong Kong.

Boddy, M. S., Gohde, J., Haigh, T., & Harp, S. A. (2005). Course of Action Generation for Cyber Security Using Classical Planning. In *International Conference on Automated Planning and Scheduling (ICAPS '05)* (pp. 12-21). California, USA.

Cormen, T. H., Leiserson, C. E., Rivest, R. L., & Stein, C. (2006). *Introduction to Algorithms.* India: Prentice Hall.

Deo, N. (1974). *Graph Theory with Applications to Engineering and Computer Science.* NJ, USA: Prentice-Hall.

Dantu, R., & Kolan, P. (2005). Risk Management Using Behavior Based Bayesian Networks. In *IEEE International Conference on Intelligence and Security Informatics (ISI '05)* (pp. 115-126). IEEE Computer Society, Washington, DC, USA.

Dantu, R., Loper, K., & Kolan, P. (2004). Risk Management using Behavior based Attack Graphs. In *Information Technology: Coding and Computing (ITCC '04)* (pp. 445-449). IEEE Computer Society, Washington, DC, USA.

Howard, M., Pincus, J., & Wing, J.M. (2005). Measuring Relative Attack Surfaces. *Computer Security in the 21st Century.* USA: Springer.

Howard, M., Pincus, J., & Wing, J. M. (2003). Measuring Relative Attack Surfaces. In *Workshop on Advanced Developments in Software and System Security.*

Ingols, K., Lippmann, R., & Piowarski, K. (2006). Practical Attack Graph Generation for Network Defense. In *22nd Annual Computer Security Applications Conference (ACSAC' 06)* (pp. 121-130). IEEE Computer Society, Washington, DC, USA.

Jajodia, S., Noel, S., & O'Berry, B. (2005). Topological Analysis of Network Attack Vulnerability. In V. Kumar, J. Srivastava, & A. Lazarevic (Ed.), *Managing Cyber Threats: Issues, Approaches and Challenges.* Springer.

Jha, S., Sheyner, O., & Wing, J. (2002). Two Formal Analyses of Attack Graphs. In *15th IEEE Computer Security Foundations Workshop (CSFW '02)* (pp.49-63). IEEE Computer Society, Washington, DC, USA.

Li, W., & Vaughn, R. B. (2006). Cluster Security Research Involving the Modeling of Network Exploitations Using Exploitation Graphs. In *6th IEEE International Symposium on Cluster Computing and the Grid (CCGRID'06)* (pp.26). IEEE Computer Society, Washington, DC, USA.

Lippmann, R. P., & Ingols, K. W. (2005). *An annotated review of past papers on attack graphs* (Tech Rep. No. ESC-TR-2005-054). MIT Lincoln Laboratory, Lexington, MA, 2005. web: www. ll.mit.edu/IST/pubs/0502_Lippmann.pdf.

Malhotra, S., Bhattacharya, S., & Ghosh, S. K. (2008). A Scalable Approach to Attack Path Prediction based on the Attack Surface Measures. In *6th International Conference on Informatics and Systems (INFOS 2008)* (pp. 27-37). Cairo, Egypt.

Manadhata, P., Wing, J. M., Fynn, M., & McQueen, M. (2006). Measuring the Attack Surfaces of Two FTP Daemons. In *2nd ACM workshop on Quality of Protection* (pp. 3-10). Alexandria, Virginia, USA.

Mell, P., Scarfone, K., & Romanosky, S. (2007). *A Complete Guide to the Common Vulnerability Scoring System Version 2.0.* Retrieved June, 2007, from http://www.first.org/cvss/cvss-guide.html

Mendelson, E. (Ed.) (1997). *Introduction to Mathematical Logic.* Chapman & Hall.

Ning, P., Xu, D., Healey, C., & Amant, R. S. (2004). Building Attack Scenarios through Integration of Complementary Alert Correlation Methods. In *11th Annual Network and Distributed System Security Symposium (NDSS '04)* (pp.97-111). San Diego, California, USA.

Ning, P., & Xu, D. (2003). Learning Attack Strategies from Intrusion Alerts. In *10th ACM Conference on Computer and Communications Security (CCS '03)* (pp.200-209). ACM Press, New York.

Noel, S., & Jajodia, S. (2004). Managing attack graph complexity through visual hierarchical aggregation. In *ACM workshop on Visualization and data mining for computer security (VizSEC/DMSEC '04)* (pp.109-118). ACM Press, New York, NY.

Noel, S., Jajodia, S., O'Berry, B., & Jacobs, M. (2005). Efficient minimum-cost network hardening via exploit dependency graphs. In *19th Annual Computer Security Applications Conference (ACSAC '03)* (pp.86-95). IEEE Computer Society, Washington, DC, USA.

Ou, X., Boyer, W. F., & McQueen, M. A.(2006). A Scalable Approach to Attack Graph Generation. In *13th ACM conference on Computer and Communications Security (CCS '06)* (pp.336-345). New York: ACM Press.

Phillips, C., & Swiler, L. P. (1998). A graph-based system for network-vulnerability analysis. In *Workshop on New Security paradigms (NSPW '98)* (pp.71-79). ACM Press, New York, NY.

Sheyner, O., Haines, J., Jha, S., Lippmann, R., & Wing, J. M. (2002). Automated generation and analysis of attack graphs. In *IEEE Symposium on Security and Privacy* (pp.273-284). IEEE Computer Society, Washington, DC, USA.

Wang, L., Noel, S., & Jajodia, S. (2006). Minimum-cost network hardening using attack graphs. *Computer Communications, 29*(18), 3812-3824.

ENDNOTES

[1]   http://www.algorithmic-solutions.info/
        leda_guide/graph_algorithms/transitive_
        closure.html

[2]   http://www.mrc.uidaho.edu/mrc/people/
        jff/349/lect.09

[3]   http://www.eecs.berkeley.edu/~brayton/
        courses/219b/ppslides/2-espresso.ppt

[4]   http://www.mrc.uidaho.edu/mrc/people/
        jff/349/lect.10

[5]   http://nvd.nist.gov/

Chapter III
Insider Threat Prevention, Detection and Mitigation

Robert F. Mills
Air Force Institute of Technology, USA

Gilbert L. Peterson
Air Force Institute of Technology, USA

Michael R. Grimaila
Air Force Institute of Technology, USA

ABSTRACT

The purpose of this chapter is to introduce the insider threat and discuss methods for preventing, detecting, and responding to the threat. Trusted insiders present one of the most significant risks to an organization. They possess elevated privileges when compared to external users, have knowledge about technical and non-technical control measures, and potentially can bypass security measures designed to prevent, detect, or react to unauthorized access. In this chapter, we define the insider threat and summarize various case studies of insider attacks in order to highlight the severity of the problem. We then discuss best practices for preventing, detecting, and mitigating insider attacks, to include application of risk management principles specific to the insider threat. Finally, we provide a survey of ongoing research into detecting irregular activities that are potentially harmful to an organization.

INTRODUCTION

Organizations have long relied on security controls (e.g., combinations of policies, processes, and technologies) to reduce their exposure to harmful acts by individuals within, and outside, its perimeter to an acceptable level. As organizations have embedded more information technology into their core processes, risk mitigation has shifted from a primarily physical control issue to an electronic one. While many organizations spend a significant amount of resources on mitigating risks originating from outside the organizational perimeter, few explicitly consider the threats originating from trusted insiders. This is despite the fact that insider activities can result in significant losses in revenue, intellectual property, and reputation if the organization fails to prevent, detect, and mitigate insider threats.

Damage from insider activity, regardless of the intent, can be very significant, and perhaps even crippling. Insiders may disrupt internal network operations, corrupt databases and file servers, or deny the use of information systems and their data to authorized users. Staggering amounts of information can be stolen, lost, deleted, or corrupted literally at the press of a button. For example, an individual who mistakenly thought she was going to be fired deleted files from a computer system valued at $2.5 million (Kamm, 2008). Malicious insiders may even collude with outside parties to receive technical assistance or to help identify useful information (USDOJ/OIG, 2003). The fallout from such activities may in turn result in significant losses in corporate revenue and reputation. Unfortunately, when addressing security risks, many focus on the problem of pe-

rimeter security where we have seen tremendous advances in security technology, with countless dollars invested in perimeter security, encryption, antivirus systems, and content filtering, all of which aim to keep outsiders from harming the organization. Ironically, most security professionals would agree the insider poses the greatest risk to information systems and is the most difficult to detect (Denning, 1987; Insider Threat IPT, 2000; CSO, 2007).

Figure 1 illustrates the various factors involved in mitigating the insider threat. The figure is not all-inclusive but addresses the main points covered in this chapter. First, we have a notional organization with information systems (IS) and services that are of *high*, *medium*, and *low* values of importance to the organization. The organization employs security mechanisms to protect and monitor IS usage, such as firewalls, intrusion detection and prevention systems, auditing and authentication systems. The organization has vulnerabilities that

Figure 1. Defining the insider threat problem

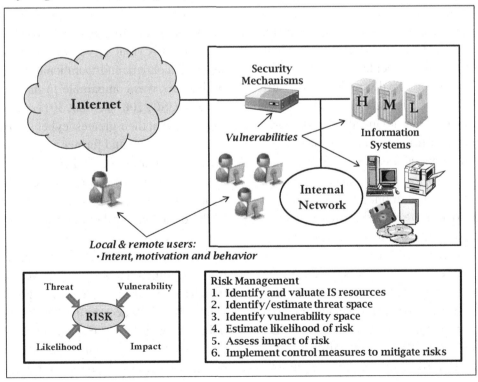

arise from gaps in security policies and inherent flaws in the IS and security mechanisms. Finally, the organization has people—insiders—who represent potential threats to the organization by virtue of the access and trust granted to them. Some insiders are benign while others act with malicious intent and motivation. Insider behavior produces observables which should monitored by the organization to ensure compliance with established policies.

All organizations are subject to risks, which are the potential for negative consequences to their mission, resulting from vulnerabilities that are present in their operational environment. The risk associated with any given organizational resource can be expressed as a function of the threats to which the resource is exposed, the vulnerabilities present in the resource or its environment, and the likelihood the threats will exploit the resource's vulnerabilities. If the risk materializes, the risk will result in a negative consequence (impact) to the organization. To mitigate the insider threat risk (or a subset of those risks that have been deemed more critical), the organization should employ a risk management process that explicitly identifies these risks (e.g., risk assessment), evaluates cost-benefit tradeoffs in selecting controls which mitigate the risk to an acceptable level (e.g., risk mitigation), and periodically reviews to assure that any changes within the organization which significantly change the organization's risk profile are accounted for in a timely and efficient manner (e.g., evaluation and assessment). Risk management enables organizations to implement control measures, within operational and organization constraints, to mitigate the risks to an acceptable level usually through a combination of prevention, deterrence, detection and response.

In this chapter, we will address these issues in more detail. First, we examine the prevalence of insider attacks, discuss the importance of recognizing insider threats, and motivate why organizations should actively take steps to mitigate it. We then discuss the different types of insider threats.

Because our emphasis is primarily on malicious actors, we provide a discussion of the behavioral and motivational factors that identify and explain why people perform actions that are harmful to the organization. We then discuss the application of standard risk management principles to the insider threat problem, which then leads into a discussion of "best practices" for mitigating the threat. Finally, we address the problem of collecting, monitoring and analyzing observable behavior for predicting and detecting irregular activity. This is an especially difficult problem because overt behavior must be used to infer what someone's internal motivation and intent are, and two people exhibiting the same behavior may very well have different intentions. We conclude with a brief discussion of ongoing research in the area of detecting irregular activity.

BACKGROUND

The need for effective insider threat detection, prevention, and mitigation is driven by the growing number, and magnitude, of reported losses resulting from insider incidents. Consider the results of a 2007 E-Crime survey that showed that the reported economic and operational damage caused by insiders was comparable to that of external attacks (CSO, 2007). About 30% of respondents indicated that their greatest cyber security threat was from current and former employees, service providers, contractors, and consultants. Further, 34% of 671 completed surveys stated that insider attacks resulted in the most cost and/or damage to the organization. Despite these findings, the E-Crime survey showed that organizations are reducing their efforts at mitigating the insider threat! Compared to the previous year, organizations have decreased employee background checks from 73% to 57%, account/password management policies from 91% to 84%, employee monitoring from 59% to 42%, and employee security awareness training from 68% to 38%. While this appears counter intuitive based upon the magnitude of damage attributed to insiders, it stems from the difficulty in justifying expenditures to mitigate low-probability, high-impact risks which are characteristics of insider risk. A cost-benefit analysis is often used to justify resource allocations, but obtaining accurate estimates of metrics are often difficult and if the data is inexact can undermine the quality of the resource allocation decisions (Kohlenberg, 2008).

Other studies that further document the insider problem. The Computer Security Institute, in conjunction with the Federal Bureau of Investigation (FBI), conducts an annual computer crime and security survey, and theft of intellectual property and proprietary information is among the top causes of financial loss (Richardson, 2007). The Computer Emergency Response Team (CERT) Coordination Center at Carnegie Mellon University and the United States Secret Service National Threat Assessment Center have also conducted several studies of incidents involving insider attacks in the government sector (Kowalski et al., 2008a), critical infrastructures (Keeney et al., 2005), information technology sector (Kowalski et al., 2008b), and banking/finance sector (Randazzo, et al., 2004). The results of these surveys underscore that the insider threat problem is real and pervasive.

Some key findings from the Secret Service/ Carnegie Mellon report on the insider activity in the government sector (Kowalski et al., 2008a) indicated that insiders did not share common demographic characteristics. Current employees caused the vast majority (90%) of the incidents, and most (58%) were people in administrative and positions requiring limited technical skill. In contrast, the report on the IT sector showed that current and former employees committed illicit activities in roughly equal numbers, with most holding technical positions (Kowalski et al., 2008b).

One of the challenges in deriving these statistics is that many incidents go unreported. In the 2007 CSI/FBI study, only 29% (up from 25 percent from the previous year) reported incidents to law enforcement (Richardson, 2007). Similarly, the 2007 E-Crime survey results indicated that fully two-thirds of the cyber crimes committed (whether from insiders or outsiders) are dealt with internally and not reported to law enforcement (CSO, 2007). Reasons for not reporting incidents include loss of reputation, negative publicity, increased liability, inability to identify the perpetrator, and belief that the harm caused is not sufficient enough to report (Randazzo, 2004; CSO, 2007). Organizations are reluctant to report any computer intrusions, so it is reasonable to assume the insider threat is under-reported. Unfortunately, the full impact of the insider threat problem will remain unknown unless organizations report the crimes to law enforcement and researchers can analyze all of the available case data for insider attacks.

Defending against the insider threat is extremely difficult because, by definition, the people who commit the harmful acts (intentional or not) have been granted certain authority and trust and generally have superior knowledge of the organization's inner workings. Insiders come in many forms, as do the actions they take, and in most cases, those actions or behavior are part of their normal duties and indistinguishable from normal activity. While insider threat mitigation is a complex, challenging task, it can be approached in a straightforward manner, using risk management to guide the process. Studies have shown that insider attacks are typically planned and that others (coworkers, colleagues, supervisors, or even people outside the organization) may have knowledge of the insiders' intentions and/or ongoing activities. There is, therefore, a window of opportunity during which managers can intervene and prevent the attack—or at least limit the amount of damage done by the attack. However, with the focus on lean management, managers and supervisors have less time and are likely to overlook any warnings signs. What is required is an automated way to generate leads so that managers can focus 80% of their time on the 20% that appear more likely to be suspect (assuming the organization has managers who look at the insider threat seriously to begin with).

DEFINING THE INSIDER THREAT

One of the reasons why mitigating the insider threat has been difficult is because there are various definitions used, and the definition tends to depend on the perspective of the one defining the problem. In this section, we will provide an in-depth discussion of the different types of insiders, both based on behavior and relationship to the organization. We then define the insider threat, with our emphasis being on those who have malicious intent.

Who is an Insider?

Sociological definitions for *insider* include "a person who is a member of a group, organization, society, etc.; a person belonging to a limited circle of persons who...share private knowledge; a person who has some special advantage or influence; or a person in possession of corporate information not generally available to the public" (Dictionary.com, 2008). Someone who formerly met one of these conditions could also be considered an insider because of their knowledge of the organization's practices and functions.

In the context of an information system (IS), which is our focus here, an insider is someone who has been authorized access to an organization's IS resources. This includes employees of the organization, contractors, employees of other organizations with which there is an established trust relationship, and possibly someone from outside the organization such as the user of the organization's public web site. The point is that an insider is someone with access to the computer system. Some authors suggest that the term insider could also be used to refer to system components

(hosts) or applications/software, since an active process running on a computer executes functions for which it has been granted some specified level of access (Maybury, 2006). Still others suggest that the developers, vendors, and suppliers of systems and software are also insiders. Finally, insiders could include overlooked personnel such as maintenance and custodians (Brackney & Anderson, 2004).

As we can see, *insider* can mean many different things to different people. In fact, some might even use the term insider when in fact they are referring to insiders with malicious intent. For our purposes, we will use the first definition given before—namely, an insider is someone with authorized access to an organization's IS. By *access*, we refer to the ability to connect to and interact with the IS. Historically, this assumed physical access—that is, you had to physically be sitting at the terminal in order to use the system. However, with the rate at which information systems have been networked, largely through the Internet, virtual private networks, and extranets, physical access is less of a factor. An employee or contractor who connects through a virtual private network connection is still an insider, even though they may be several time zones away and never set foot inside the facility.

Closely related to access is *authority*. We have used the word access to refer to the ability to connect, whereas authority refers to procedural controls and permissions to regulate what the insider can actually do. This includes user permissions such as the ability to read and write information, execute queries against a database, archive information, and delete information. Authority is more in the realm of policy and procedure, and limits are imposed based on the level of trust extended, need-to-know, and job function.

Finally, the insider has some *intent* or need to use the organization's resources. In the most general sense, the insider's intent may be malicious or benign. The decision to use the IS resource may be voluntary or required as part of the individual's assigned job duties. Related to this is the notion that the insider has some knowledge of the organization and its information resources, such as how information is organized in the system, or the type of technology used.

Insider Threat

A *threat* is "an expression of an intention to inflict pain, injury, evil; or an indication of impending danger or harm; or one that is regarded as a possible danger" (American Heritage, 2008). Previously, we stated that an insider refers to an individual who has trusted access to an organization's information resources, to include the computing network and data stores, or knowledge about the organization that was gained through a trust relationship with the organization (e.g., a utility repairman who installs a new power distribution unit in the data center and sees a diagram depicting the security architecture of the organization). The insider threat is the threat that an insider would use or misuse his privileges or inside knowledge to the detriment of the organization. This definition encompasses both the malicious and unintentional insider threat and does not specify severity, intention, or what constitutes an insider threat.

As with the case of the term *insider*, there are different definitions of *insider threat*. In many instances, the term *insider threat* describes agents of an *insider attack*. Schultz (2002) defines an insider attack as a "deliberate misuse by those who are authorized to use computers and networks" (p. 526). Theoharidou et al. (2005) define an insider threats "originating from people who have been given access rights to an IS and misuse their privileges, thus violating the IS security policy of the organisation" (p. 473). Stanton et al. (2004) define insider threats as "intentionally disruptive, unethical, or illegal behavior enacted by individuals who possess substantial internal access to the organization's information assets" (p. 125). There are other definitions appearing in the literature, which convey similar concepts of

trust, privileged access, and abuse or unauthorized use of the organization's resources.

A common theme in these definitions is the concept of trust. Trust is often multivariate and is commonly considered to be a combination of benevolence, competence, and integrity (McKnight et al., 1998). Benevolence is the belief that an individual will act in the best interest of the organization's interest. Competence is the belief that an individual can carry out their duties in an adequate manner. Integrity is the belief that the individual will act in an honest manner and keep promises. Alternative theories exist including the theory of reasoned action that includes the very important, in terms of insiders, concept of intent (Fishbein & Ajzen, 1975). Insiders themselves are trusted and expected to work toward the benefit of the organization, an external focus. It is when their personal intentions are at odds with the organization that they become a threat.

There are many examples of insider threat actions: deleting critical information; leaking information outside the organization to a competitor, foreign country, the news media or public; or snooping for information restricted to specific people for the performance of their assigned duties. These insider "incidents" may or may not be malicious or intentional, but rather could result from accidents, carelessness, or unintended acts. Further, it is very difficult to distinguish between proper and improper or suspicious behavior, because in many cases the insider threat ultimately boils down to people performing authorized tasks (Anderson, 2000).

Categorizing Insiders

There are many ways to categorize the insider threat. Categorization of insider attributes is required to effectively prevent, detect, and mitigate insider threats and attacks. As with the preceding definitions, the method of categorization will depend on the one who is defining and solving the problem. These methods tend to categorize insider threats based on organizational affiliation, access and permission levels, behavioral intent and motivation, and technical proficiency.

Organizational Affiliation

As noted previously, the term "insider" often refers to members of the organization, or employees of a business. These insiders have knowledge of the internal workings of the organization, its rules, and/or the locations where critical information is stored. Employees may work directly for the organization, or they could be contractors working in the facility.

Former employees are also a type of insider. They may have less access than before, but they still have knowledge of the organization. They may also have social connections to current insiders. A 2007 survey on loss of proprietary information reported that former employees represented the greatest threat to proprietary information and intellectual property (Trends, 2007).

Depending on the trust relationships the organization has, insiders could also include employees of other organizations, such as business partners, allies, or coalition members. In network security, a risk accepted by one is a risk shared by all.

Information service providers are a form of insider. They may not be part of the organization, but like contractors, they have legitimate access to the information systems and the information that resides on them as part of their contracted service.

Access and Permission Levels

Insiders can be categorized based on their position within the organization, their level of trust, or job function. Insiders span the spectrum ranging from administrative clerks to mid-level managers to the chief executive officer, commanding general, or company president. Insiders include general users of the IS, first line help desk personnel, and system administrators. The level of access

and permissions granted are factors to consider because of the potential harm from willful or accidental acts. Insiders range from those with limited or no access to sensitive information (based on need-to-know) to those with extensive access, which may even include access to the organization's security program.

Technical Proficiency

Insiders have various levels of technical knowledge, skill, and ability. Technical proficiency is tightly coupled with competence and is part of the trust given to insiders. Technical proficiency can extend from barely being able to work on the problem through being able to circumvent IS security policies and systems.

A system administrator with knowledge and access privileges can cause great harm, but one insider threat study found that 87% of insider attacks in the banking and finance sector required little or no technical expertise (Randazzo et al., 2004). In fact, 43% of those attacks occurred while the perpetrator had logged in under their own credentials, and only 23% of the malicious insiders were IT workers.

While companies have benefited greatly from advances in IT, so has the threat. The proliferation of network connections, encryption, "thumb drives" and CD burners has increased the ease with which insiders can both conduct and conceal their activities (NIPC, 2004). Instead of tediously photocopying hundreds of pages of documents that are awkward and bulky, inside attackers can quickly copy the data to a small medium that can be easily hidden in a pocket or briefcase. In some cases, the information is encrypted and transmitted via e-mail.

Behavioral Intent and Motivation

The majority of insiders are everyday users of the information systems and simply doing their jobs. When these people do cause harm to the organization, it is unintentional and through ignorance, carelessness, or mistakes. In some cases, people may be duped (using social engineering methods) into violating company policy because they want to be helpful.

More harmful is disdain for security practices. Some insiders may not have malicious intent, but they are also not acting in a positive manner to prevent information security breaches. Finally, there is the malicious insider who uses and abuses inherent trust and privileges to intentionally harm the organization. Examples include sabotage, destruction, theft, embezzlement, espionage, etc.

Behavioral Motivational Typology

The concept of insider motivation is most complex when dealing with a malicious insider. In the case of a benign insider, the intent is benevolent, and the outcome is just unfortunate. While we recognize the threat of accidents and careless individuals, we will focus on the malicious insider hereafter. However, for simplicity, we will use the terms *insider* and *insider threat* interchangeably. The exploration of motive predominantly affects response and mitigation of the threat.

The study of motive is one of behavioral motivational typology (Turvey, 1999). The focus in behavioral motivational typology can be one of classifying offenders, to one of classifying offensive behaviors (Casey, 2004). We focus on offensive behaviors as they lead into deductive reasoning into insider threat mitigation.

Casey (2004) describes six categories of motives: power reassurance (compensatory), power assertive (entitlement), anger retaliatory (anger or displaced), anger excitation (sadistic), opportunistic, and profit oriented. Many of the identified motives in insider threat related work conform to this typology.

Power reassurance includes low-aggression behaviors that promote or restore the self-confidence of individual. This includes insider attacks that cause mischief or test their skills (Jarvis, 2001).

Power assertive refers to the use of moderate to high-aggression behaviors to promote or restore the self-worth of the individual. This would include a need for recognition and a desire be seen as irreplaceable (Shaw et al., 1998). Kowalski et al. (2008b) describe a case where an employee used a contractor badge to gain access to a company's network operations center and offsite storage facility. Using that unauthorized access, the employee stole the backup tapes and caused system failures. Because he had the backup tapes, the employee had hoped to be in a position to "save the day."

Anger retaliatory is the one of the two most commonly associated behavior motivations in insider threat research. This includes revenge, retaliation, ideology, and sabotage (Denning, 1999). In May 2000, Timothy Lloyd became the first American sent to prison under new laws for deleting critical organizational files (Koenig, 2004). Lloyd sought revenge against his company after being demoted. The prosecution was able to prove guilt after forensic analysis of a hard drive found in Lloyd's garage revealed "time bomb" code used to delete the files. His malicious actions cost his organization, Omega Engineering, an estimated $10 million dollars in damage.

Anger excitation is not often associated with the insider threat because it is a high-aggression personal attack through which the attacker gains pleasure (such as sadism). This is not to say that anger excitation cannot be a motive for a malicious insider, but it has not been recognized as such. It may be reasonable to assume that a malicious insider would use the IS to defame or misrepresent other individuals and gain pleasure from their anguish, for example.

Opportunistic malicious insider threat behavior occurs when a moral conundrum arises between pursuing selfish and selfless actions. Often this behavior occurs when an opportunity for satisfaction occurs associated with low probability of discovery. An example would be Melvyn Spillman who was found guilty in 2002 of using his computer network privileges to redirect more than $4.9 million dollars into his personal banking account. His extravagant spending went unnoticed, and in the three-year period prior to his arrest, he sponsored a Formula 1 racing car despite having an annual salary of only $33,000. Replacement parts alone for the racing car totaled over $250,000 in a single quarter (Cole, 2006).

The remaining most common motive for malicious insiders is that of *profit*. Profit motives are associated with money (Denning, 1999; Herbig & Wiskoff, 2002), and greed (Shaw et al., 1998). Profit motive is often associated with power reassurance ("my beliefs are right, yours are not"). Another common manifestation of profit is the modus operandi of espionage. In espionage, individuals view selling secrets as a business affair rather than an act of betrayal or treason.

Espionage is possibly the most serious form of the insider threat. Two notable examples are Robert Hanssen and Aldrich Ames. Former FBI agent Hanssen provided highly classified documents and details about US intelligence sources and capabilities to Russia. Because he was an authorized user, his activities did not raise suspicion. He used a variety of methods to steal information, and on many occasions simply walked out of his FBI office classified documents and digital media in his briefcase. Hanssen committed espionage for more than 15 years before being caught, despite the fact that there were a number of indicators that something was amiss (USDOJ/OIG, 2003; Coe, 2004). While profit was certainly a factor, he also exhibited power assertive behaviors.

Between 1986 and 1994, former Central Intelligence Agency (CIA) officer Aldrich Ames provided classified human source information to the Soviet Union in exchange for over $2.5 million. Despite an openly extravagant lifestyle, his activities went unchallenged for eight years (Wise, 1995). While this is not strictly a case of abuse of the organization's IT systems, it highlights our contention that mitigating the insider threat is a multidisciplinary problem requiring people, process and technology.

COUNTERING THE THREAT: RISK MANAGEMENT

Security management is an organizational function concerned with the administration of people, policies, and programs with the objective of assuring continuity of operations while maintaining strategic alignment with mission and operational requirements (Cazemier et al., 2000). Risk management is an analytical methodology used to evaluate tradeoffs in protection strategies when mitigating risks subject to organizational constraints (Finne, 2000; Gordon et al., 2002; Stoneburner et al., 2002). The primary function of risk management is to assign protective measures to assure the ability of the organization to conduct its mission. Risk management is comprised of three subordinate processes as shown in Figure 2: risk assessment, risk mitigation, and the evaluation and assessment process (Stoneburner et al., 2002). Collectively these processes enable management to identify and evaluate the risks present within their organization so that they can make informed security resourcing decisions.

In order to make the risk management process effective, one must develop a holistic understanding of the organization's mission and be able to quantify how value is derived by the organization conducting its mission. This is essential because while determining the Total Cost of Ownership (TCO) of a control measure is straightforward, determining the criticality of a resource is ultimately dependent upon the value it provides in supporting the organizational mission. The goal is to make informed decisions when strik-

Figure 2. Risk management components

ing a balance between the costs of protective measures (prevention, deterrence, detection, and response) and the benefits provided by protecting the organizational mission. These decisions can only be made after the value that an information resource provides to the organization has been established.

Risk Assessment

The risk assessment process, the first step of risk management, is used to characterize and document the nature and magnitude of risks that are present within the organization. Risk assessment requires the identification of critical organizational resources (e.g., information, people, processes, and technologies); estimation of the value they contribute in accomplishing the organizational mission; enumeration of vulnerabilities that place the resources at risk; identification of threats which may exploit these vulnerabilities; and an estimation of the likelihood that each threat will intersect with a corresponding vulnerability resulting in a loss. Collectively, this information provides the ability to "rack and stack" risks according to their severity.

The risk assessment process, as defined by the National Institute of Standards and Technology (NIST) Special Publication 800-30 "Risk Management Guide for Information Technology Systems," is shown in Figure 3 (Stoneburner et al., 2002). While the purpose of the NIST guide is to assess system risk, the scope can be extended to assess overall mission risk. In the following discussion, we summarize the nine steps identified by NIST in light of their application to insider risk assessment.

In the first step, *System Characterization*, the scope of the risk assessment is determined and any required information is collected. This step is

Figure 3. Risk assessment process (Stoneburner et al., 2002)

Input	Risk Assessment Activities	Output
• Hardware & software • System interfaces • Data & information • People • Mission	**Step 1** **System Characterization**	• System boundary • System functions • System/data criticality • System/data sensitivity
• History of system attack • Data from intelligence sources	**Step 2** **Threat Identification**	• Threat statement
• Prior assessments • Audit comments • Security requirements • Security test results	**Step 3** **Vulnerability Identification**	• List of potential vulnerabilities
• Current controls • Planned controls	**Step 4** **Control Analysis**	• List of current and planned controls
• Threat-source motivation • Threat capacity • Nature of vulnerability • Current controls	**Step 5** **Likelihood Determination**	• Likelihood rating
• Mission impact analysis • Asset criticality assessment • Data criticality & sensitivity	**Step 6** **Impact Analysis** **(integrity, availability, confidentiality)**	• Impact rating
• Likelihood of exploitation • Magnitude of impact • Adequacy of controls	**Step 7** **Risk Determination**	• Risks and associated risk levels
	Step 8 **Control Recommendations**	• Recommended controls
	Step 9 **Results Documentation**	• Risk assessment report

one of the most difficult steps in the risk assessment process, because it requires the assessor to (1) develop a holistic view of the organizational mission, (2) understand how value is derived by the organization's existence, and (3) document how resources support the organizational mission. Information is collected from multiple sources including knowledgeable individuals using interviews and questionnaires; by reviewing relevant documents; and by direct observation of organizational operations. Unfortunately, the time, effort and resources to undertake this step may be seen as too costly, resulting in no formal risk assessment being conducted. Worse, the assessment may be performed without the quality of information necessary to ensure an accurate result.

The second step, *Threat Identification*, requires the identification and characterization of threat sources that may potentially exploit vulnerabilities (accidentally or intentionally) present within the organization. In this step, threat sources are enumerated; threat actor motivations, resources and capabilities are considered; and historical data is analyzed to determine the likelihood of threats exploiting organizational vulnerabilities resulting in an adverse mission impact. This is perhaps the most important step for addressing the insider threat. If the organization does not explicitly consider the activities of trusted insiders, it will miss a significant source of threat source by assuming all threats originate only from outside the organizational perimeter. This problem is perpetuated by the lack of historical data available that can help organizations in understanding the prevalence of insider threats.

The third step, *Vulnerability Identification*, requires the identification and characterization of vulnerabilities present within the organization. A vulnerability is "a flaw or weakness in system security procedures, design, implementation, or internal controls that could be exercised (accidentally triggered or intentionally exploited) and result in a security breach or a violation of the system's security policy" (Stoneburner et al., 2002, p. 15). In this step, vulnerability sources are discovered by reviewing traditional vulnerability repository listings, conducting security testing and auditing, reviewing security requirement checklists that are used to mitigate known vulnerabilities, critically examining past security incidents, and linking each of the threat sources previously identified to their appropriate vulnerabilities. It is important to note that this leads to the identification and subsequent accounting only for known vulnerabilities; yet undiscovered vulnerabilities are unaccounted for since they, by definition, are unknown. Organizations that fail to explicitly consider the access and capabilities possessed by trusted insiders miss a significant number of vulnerabilities that may endanger the organization's mission. A useful exercise to reveal insider vulnerabilities is to brainstorm scenarios where any given individual inside the organization could exploit their knowledge, access, and position to harm the organization. Unfortunately, this is a resource-intensive exercise that few organizations choose to undertake. Instead, many organizations simply "bury their head in the sand" and assume employees will not exploit their trust relationship. Typically, it is not until the organization itself (or another organization of interest) is victim of an insider attack that it begins to seriously address the insider threat.

The fourth step, *Control Analysis*, requires the identification and characterization of existing (or planned) controls that are designed to reduce the (or eliminate) the likelihood that a threat will exploit a known vulnerability. Controls may be categorized in a variety of ways including technical or non-technical; preventative, detective, corrective, or reactive; or as static or dynamic in nature. Controls vary in their costs, effectiveness, their impact to organizational operations, and their practicality. For example, the United States implements an interlocking, mutually supporting series of controls (e.g., need-to-know, background investigations, polygraphs, access control measures, adjudication) to reduce vulnerabilities which may result in the compromise of Sensitive Compartmented Information (SCI) (DCID 1/19, 1995; DCID 6/4, 1998). Compartmentalization is used to limit the number or individuals who can access SCI by requiring individuals to not only possess a clearance at a level commensurate with the SCI, but they must have a "need-to-know" the information that is approved by the source of the information. While the strategy may be financially expensive, the process significantly reduces the vulnerability of the breach of SCI. One of the difficulties in this step is the quantification of how much a given control will reduce the likelihood of any given threat from exploiting a known vulnerability. This is not unique to dealing with insider threats as it is present in all risk assessments. Another significant problem is identifying combinations of controls that are ineffective, incompatible, or act to increase the risk of a compromise.

The fifth step, *Likelihood Determination*, requires estimating the probability that a given threat will intersect with a matching vulnerability resulting in a loss to the organization. Quantifying the likelihood is a function of the threat source motivation and resources, the nature of the vulnerability, and the existence of existing controls designed to reduce the probability. Estimation of this quantity can be determined using historical data, subject matter experts, and modeling techniques. Unfortunately, since the likelihood is a function of all of the elements discussed previously, estimating insider risk is especially problematic. A qualitative assessment using three categories (e.g., Low, Medium, and High) is often used to estimate the likelihood that a risk will materialize in a given timeframe. While this reduces the burden of estimating the likelihood accurately, it simultaneously limits the granularity of the analyses and degrades the ability to resolve fine differences between controls in the risk mitigation process.

The sixth step, *Impact Analysis*, requires the estimation of the impact (loss) to the organization should a given risk materialize (e.g., a threat intersects with its matching vulnerability). Estimation of impact can be expressed in terms of how a loss or degradation of the confidentiality, integrity, or availability of a resource would negatively affect the organizational mission. In some organizations, the information may already exist in the form of a business or mission impact assessment that prioritizes the impact associated with a compromise of an information asset in terms of the organization's mission. In any case, accurately estimating the impact is very important because is directly affects the rank ordering of risks, which is the overall output of the risk assessment process. One difficulty in impact analysis is that while some impacts are tangible (e.g., lost revenue, system downtime), others are less tangible (e.g., loss of consumer confidence, damage to reputation). As a result, impact may again be expressed using qualitative categories (e.g., Low, Medium, and High) rather than quantitative values or ranges. Similar to likelihood estimation, this reduces the burden of estimating the impact accurately but greatly limits the granularity of analysis, which in turn degrades the ability to discriminate between alternate control choices in the risk mitigation process.

The seventh step, *Risk Determination*, combines the information from the previous steps to assess the overall risks present. Mathematically, the probability of a given threat intersecting with a given vulnerability times the impact (loss) to the organization yields the expected loss, per unit time, resulting from that risk in the current environment. A rank ordering of the risks provides an order listing of risks from most to least severe. To visualize risks, a risk matrix is constructed as shown in Figure 4. Each possible risk is annotated in the risk matrix based upon its threat likelihood and impact pair and the overall risk level is determined as a Low, Medium, High, and Critical risk.

Figure 4. Example risk level matrix

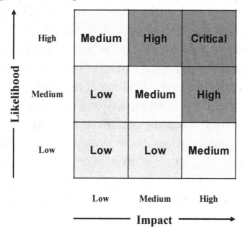

Risk Mitigation

Risk mitigation, the second step of risk management, is the analytical process that involves prioritizing, evaluating, and implementing controls to mitigate risks to an "acceptable level". There is no universal acceptable level of risk, because different organizations may have different tolerance levels based upon their risk preference, historical events, resources, and/or other priorities. What is acceptable for one organization may be completely unacceptable for another organization.

In general, the risk mitigation process does not differ substantially when dealing with traditional and insider risks. The risk mitigation process, as defined by the National Institute of Standards and Technology Special Publication 800-30 "Risk Management Guide for Information Technology Systems," is comprised of the following seven steps (Stoneburner et al., 2002):

1. Prioritize Actions
2. Evaluate Recommended Control Options
3. Conduct Cost-Benefit Analysis
4. Select Control
5. Assign Responsibility
6. Develop a Safeguard Implementation Plan
7. Implement Selected Control(s)

The eighth step, *Control Recommendations*, involves the identifying controls that can be used to mitigate (or eliminate) the identified risks. The purpose of this step is to make recommendations and enumerate alternatives to reduce the risks to an acceptable level. Factors considered should include the following: the effectiveness of controls; legal or regulatory requirements; organizational policy; the operational impact of the controls; and the safety and reliability of controls. Recommendations then feed into the risk mitigation process where the recommended controls are evaluated and prioritized, and a cost-benefit analysis is conducted.

The ninth step, *Results Documentation*, involves the documentation of all of the information collected and analyzed in the preceding steps. In this step, a formal risk assessment report is created in order to document all of the threats, vulnerabilities, probabilities, and recommended controls. This documentation is important because it informs stakeholders, provides justification for resourcing decisions, documents the effort and commitment that management exerts in dealing with risks, and significantly reduces the burden when conducting subsequent risk assessments. It is important to note that risk assessment is not a one-time activity, and should be performed periodically or whenever a significant change to the environment occurs.

One of the greatest challenges when dealing with insider risk mitigation is that organizations who have not yet experienced a successful insider attack may falsely believe that they are immune, or invulnerable, to an insider attack and may fail to consider insider threats in their established risk assessment processes. As a result, the organization may never discover serious insider vulnerabilities until they materialize in a successful attack. Worse, the organization may be subject to continuing information exfiltration, corruption, or disruption without implementing detective measures that would reveal the source is a trusted insider.

Evaluation and Assessment

The final step of the overall risk management process is Evaluation and Assessment. This step allows for continuous process improvement so that any changes in the operational environment and organization's risk profile are accounted for in a timely and efficient manner.

In summary, risk management requires the evaluation of risk tradeoffs by accounting for the potential impact to resources, the cost and effectiveness of control measures, and any constraints present in the environment. The quality of risk mitigation correlates directly with the quality, accuracy, and scope of the risk assessment conducted within the organization. The diligent recognition and quantification of the risks posed by insider threats as discussed previously is one of the most challenging aspects when conducting risk management. Underestimating the insider threat will prevent the organization from allocating sufficient resources for mitigating the insider threat, thereby placing the organization at increased risk. Conversely, overestimating the insider threat will result in wasted effort and resources that could be used to mitigate other risks.

BEST PRACTICES FOR MITIGATING THE INSIDER THREAT

As with any other security challenge, countering the insider threat involves prevention, detection, and response (or remediation). Security is a complex system that is primarily concerned with the interrelationships between people, organizational policy and process, and materiel assets (i.e., surveillance, alarm and auditing systems). Because of this interrelationship, a security strategy that employs defense-in-depth principles will offer the most robustness, since it relies on more than just a few mechanisms or focusing on only one area. Based on a review of the literature, we suggest a number of best practices for preventing and de-

tecting malicious insider activity, as summarized to follow. The degree to which these practices are implemented will depend on the results of a risk management study that evaluates the potential threats, likelihood of those threats taking place, and impact of a successful attack.

Promote Effective Management. Management practices that foster employee satisfaction and loyalty prevent insider incidents (Shaw et al., 1998). People who are content and believe they are valued by the organization are less likely to cause harm than someone who feels undervalued or threatened. Managers and supervisors play a pivotal role to addressing the insider threat problem, because they are directly responsible for monitoring the performance and behavior of their employees. However, with the focus on lean management, managers and supervisors have less time and are likely to overlook these warnings signs. The human resources staff also plays a significant role in insider threat mitigation. Well-documented processes should be developed and followed when indoctrinating new employees, and access should be terminated for employees who have left the organization. Background checks should be conducted for people working in sensitive positions (such as auditors, systems administrators, and other users with privileged access).

Establish an Actionable Security Policy. Establishing a good security policy is a fundamental part of any robust security program (Pipkin, 2001). The organization's business processes and importance of those processes as articulated by senior leaders will help determine the specific policies required. Ideally, security policies should be clear, concise, understandable, current, accessible, realistic, enduring in nature, and technology-independent. The policies should provide guidance and have executive management support. Further, they articulate the repercussions of failing to adhere to the security policies. For these reasons, it is essential to make everyone aware of the policies and obtain their acknowledgement that they will comply with the policies *before* allowing access to the organization's information systems and network.

Audit User Access and Activity. Just because an organization has established policies and requires employees to acknowledge that they will comply with the policies does not mean those policies are being followed. It has been the authors' personal experience that in many organizations employees do not follow established policies. For this reason, periodic and random should be performed to ensure compliance. Maintaining access logs and reviewing the actions of individuals provides evidence and accountability. Good managers and managerial strategies that foster good security practice, periodically conduct audits and take punitive actions against willful violators are imperative. In many insider cases, there were policy violations that were present and ignored. Willful violations of security policy are often leading indicators of an insider attack (Coe, 2004; Cole, 2006; USDOJ/OIG, 2003; Wise, 1995). Auditing also provides a measure of deterrence. Unfortunately, it is not possible or feasible to audit every action taken by every user. Even if it were possible, it would be very difficult to determine the intent behind the activity, and most of the logging entries would be routine activity.

Create a Security-Minded Culture. Security awareness training for all employees is important because people (supervisors, co-workers and subordinates) are the first line of defense against insider attacks. Kowalski et al. (2008b) note that 76% of documented insider attacks in the IT and telecommunications sector involved a degree of planning. Fifty-five percent of those cases involved behavior that was irregular or otherwise inappropriate (system misuse, tardiness, absenteeism, workplace aggression), and in 97% of those cases, others within the organization were aware of the insider's behavior (Kowalski et al., 2008b). There is a window of opportunity during which people can intervene and prevent the attack, or limit the amount of damage done by the attack.

Organizations should therefore strive to create a security-minded culture in which *everyone* understands their roles and responsibilities with respect to security.

Enforce Strict Account Management Policies. Organizations should limit user access to areas for which they have a need-to-know. Role-based access control ensures that employees will only have access to information and facilities that are required to do their assigned duties. Ensuring good access controls means setting an access controls that adhere to the *principle of least privilege*, which states that someone should have the minimum level of privilege to complete a task. For example, posting a document on a server does not require full system access. Another important is *separation of duties*, also known as *two-person integrity*. Requiring two people to authorize a specific action (such as transferring a large sum of money from one account to another) makes it much less likely that a single insider could perform a malicious act. Separation of duties may be difficult to achieve given personnel availability. In this case, rotation of duties may provide the additional checks and balances to detect irregularities and deter malicious activity. Finally, shared accounts should be avoided because they do not provide the ability to trace actions to a specific user. There have been documented cases where someone with access to a shared account was terminated; although their personal account was deactivated, the individual still had access to the shared account (Kowalski et al., 2008b).

Establish Business Continuity Plans. Regardless of how well an organization attempts to prevent an insider attack, there is still a chance that an insider will be successful. Organizations should therefore plan for such contingencies and have business continuity plans in place to remediate denial of access and data loss. This requires documenting the critical information requirements for the organization and understanding how that information is used. Knowing what to protect (and why) is critical. A workable system backup and recovery process is a key element of the business continuity plan. This includes regular backups and storage of the backup media at a secure, off-site location. Multiple backups will provide additional security, with different people being responsible for safeguarding the media (Capelli et al., 2005).

Pay Extra Attention to System Administrators. System administrators are perhaps the most worrisome insider threat. With carte blanche, they can access all files, delete applications and data, circumvent internal controls, erase or modify audit logs, and reconfigure the systems for which they are responsible. In many cases, they are also responsible for the backup/recovery systems.

Guard Against Remote Attacks. Remote access methods, such as virtual private networks and web-based e-mail, introduce risk. While at work, individuals may be less willing to engage in unauthorized activity for fear of observation by co-workers. However, this inhibition may be reduced when logging into the organization's systems from home or some other location. An organization that provides remote access capability should limit that access to those systems and services that are less critical to the overall business functions. Additional monitoring of the remote access channels should also be employed (Capelli et al., 2005).

DETECTION MEASURES

Should prevention fail, organizations must be able to detect malicious insider activity. Ideally, detection will occur immediately when the activity takes place. Further, the detection system should also be fine-grained to allow detection of genuinely suspicious activity while ignoring legitimate activities. An exceptionally skilled insider's actions may be very difficult to distinguish from normal, authorized and benign activity. Einstein commented, "Not everything that can be counted counts, and not everything that counts

can be counted." For example, an auditing system could be used to generate warnings based on file access or network activity in real time. Depending on the alarm criteria, administrators may very quickly be overwhelmed with alerts of benign activity (Type I errors), and yet the system may actually fail to identify activities that are indeed malicious because those actions are commonly performed.

The simple fact that no two people are alike makes it difficult to introduce sound prediction strategies, and as a result, few exist. Research has shown that malicious insiders do not share a common profile. They come from all occupations and have different skill sets (Keeney et al., 2005; Kowalski et al., 2008a; Kowalski et al., 2008b; Randazzo et al., 2004). Studies of espionage and "white collar" crime cases have not shown a correlation between personal attributes such as age, gender or level of education with an inclination or desire to do harm to the organization (Herbig & Wiskoff, 2002). Because we are dealing with social/psychological factors that are internal and unique for each individual, we must focus on behaviors and actions rather than the individual characteristics or attributes of the employees. When dealing with complex systems, we often want to know what is happening inside the system, but we cannot directly measure it. Instead, we must determine what things are measureable and then infer what we cannot measure directly. This is certainly true when attempting to characterize and mitigate the insider threat. It is impossible to determine what is going on inside people's minds, so we can only observe their behavior in an attempt to guess or predict whether they are in fact doing something that is harmful to the organization.

Observables

The quality of any insider threat detection and response methodology is therefore strongly dependent upon the ability to collect and process a relevant subset of all possible *observables*. According to Merriam-Webster, an observable is something that is "capable of being observed." The American Heritage Dictionary extends this idea by defining an observable as "a physical property, such as weight or temperature, that can be observed or measured directly, as distinguished from a quantity, such as work or entropy, that must be derived from observed quantities." For our purposes, an observable is anything that can be affected by the behavior of the insider and can be sensed, collected, processed and stored within the given environment.

As shown in Figure 5, there are many observables associated with detecting potential insider threat activity. The observables shown were determined as part of a research challenge workshop sponsored by the United States Intelligence Community (RAND, 2004; Maybury, 2005). The study team, consisting of researchers from government, industry and academia, analyzed dozens of espionage cases as detailed in a 2002 espionage report by Herbig & Wiskoff (2002).

The team especially focused on a subset of high profile cases involving Aldrich Ames, Robert Hanssen and Ana Belen Montes. Ames (CIA) and Hanssen (FBI) were briefly discussed earlier, and Montes was a Defense Intelligence Agency (DIA) analyst who was convicted in 2002 of spying for Cuba. The study team found that with these three individuals, two had passed counterintelligence polygraph examinations, and the range of technical skill varied. Further, while each person was extremely careful to avoid detection, in each case there were opportunities to "observe individual incidents and/or to detect anomalous behavior from correlated observables" (Maybury, 2005, p. 2). This is very important, because a detection strategy that focuses strictly on cyber activities (e.g., system usage monitoring) will have limited effectiveness, especially if the perpetrator has the ability to conceal the suspicious activity.

In the majority of documented insider threat cases, other people were aware of irregular activity. A management tool is therefore needed to gather as much of the information shown in Figure 5 as possible for correlation and analysis. The tool would combine these observables to provide timely alerts and warnings for management (Hanssen spied for 15 years even though there were indicators throughout that period). This is not to say that an automated insider threat detector can (or should) be built. Ultimately, managers, security officials and human resource management personnel will need to consider all factors to develop a representation for the "whole person." For example, someone who is having financial difficulties and verbally attacks a coworker may simply be going through a very stressful situation (such as divorce or death of a close family member). In some cases, just simply identifying someone who is "at risk" may be enough to prevent or deter any further problems.

Another important issue to consider when selecting observables for insider threat mitigation is privacy. Collecting the observables shown in Figure 5 certainly has a "Big Brother" aspect and may pose legal challenges. However, many employees of government agencies and their contractors routinely undergo extensive background investigations for security clearances, and these observables are indeed being collected.

The Detection Process

The detection algorithm is the heart of any detection system. Many of the concepts developed for traditional intrusion detection systems (IDS) apply to the problem of detecting undesirable insider activity. In fact, one could argue that insider threat detection is a specialized subset of intrusion detection. However, as discussed previously, the insider threat often requires the selection of observables that are outside the realm of traditional IDS methods. Despite this limitation, the more salient elements of intrusion detection provide a foundation for understanding the process of insider threat detection.

Figure 5. Taxonomy of insider threat observables (after Brackney & Anderson, 2004)

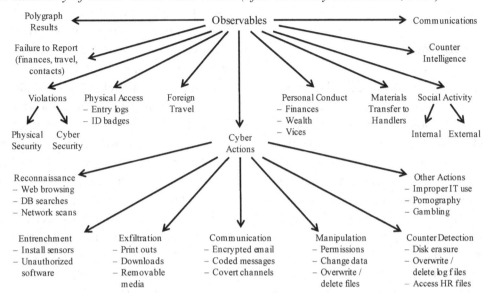

An IDS is typically focused on the collection and analysis of pattern-sequenced or time-sequenced observable events. The system monitors observables such as system logs, resource consumption and network activity to classify observed behavior into classes of acceptable and unacceptable behavior. Detection can be based on adherence to known unacceptable patterns (signature detection), deviations from acceptable usage (anomaly detection), or some combination of the two methods. A detection threshold is established under which the system will not generate an alarm. When the threshold is met or exceeded, an alert is generated and investigated. Performance of the IDS is measured in terms of its ability to correctly identify suspicious behavior (probability of detection) while avoiding false positives (false alarms). How an organization handles the investigation (and remediation) of the alert is critical to the success of the whole process of the detection system and should be factored into the risk management process.

Detecting undesirable insider activity is similar in that it consists of sensing and collecting observables in the environment, processing the observables using some detection algorithm, and the dissemination and response to alerts generated by the algorithm. Unlike traditional IDS, however, the observables present in insider threat detection include not only those from the network and host domains, but also elements from the human behavior domain (e.g., conduct, mood, demeanor, stress, etc.) and the physical domain (e.g., working hours, physical access control logs, etc.). Further, since insiders have internal access to the information infrastructure of an organization, the location of critical observables for intrusion detection may not be sufficient for the detection of insider behavior.

Note that some observables may be collected, but might not be useful for detection. Instead, these observables may be used to support a forensic analysis for post-incident attribution and correlation purposes. A key challenge in configuring an IDS is that as number of sensors increases, it becomes increasingly difficult and expensive to manage the data collection, storage and analysis. The organization must balance the benefits provided by the IDS and its total cost of ownership. The problem is only worse for the insider threat, which is by nature a low-probability, high-impact threat.

Security Auditing

Information system auditing can play a vital role when attempting to detect insider threats (Anderson, 1980). However, research has shown that to be effective it requires that organizations customize their audit policies and implement an audit review program. For example, one study focused on Windows XP logs and their usefulness when it comes to insider threat detection (Levoy, 2006). Levoy et al. (2006) examined various auditing templates to determine the most effective configuration for detecting an insider on a Windows XP system. Eighteen unique malicious user scenarios were generated, and their effectiveness was measured against all possible permutations (262,144) of system security policy settings. A utility function was created that accounted for the costs related to store and analyze the data necessary which allowed the optimal system security policy setting to detect all 18 malicious scenarios at a minimal cost.

By evaluating the various scenarios, it was determined that the default system audit settings are not as effective at insider detection as customized settings. The research also demonstrated that when conducting insider threat detection through auditing and log analysis, organizations must strike a balance between the costs and benefits associated with this detection method. While increasing auditing and logging of events improves the chances of identifying malicious behavior, it also leads to increased costs because of the amount of data to be collected, analyzed and reviewed. Conversely, when decreasing the number of auditable events, the amount of data is reduced, but the probability of detecting malicious behavior also drops. While this research focused on the Windows XP operating system, the proposed method could be applied to other logging environments.

Organizations that are committed to conducting insider threat detection should therefore configure their auditing policies to reflect their security requirements. Organizations will then improve the likelihood of detecting undesirable or unauthorized activity. For example, auditing and logging may reveal unauthorized activity when reviewing logs for remote access, file access, system configuration changes, database or application usage, and electronic mail (Carroll, 2006). A side benefit of auditing is that it forces the organization to understand clearly its audit policies and organizational user activity. In order to best utilize log auditing to its fullest benefit, it is necessary for an organization to understand the threats and attacks that exist for its set of resources (Anderson, 1980).

Data Mining

User profiling has been suggested as a method for improving the detection of insider misuse (Anderson, 1999). Behavior profiles can be established using the observables discussed earlier, such as files and processes normally accessed, periods of system usage, and keystroke patterns for example. Anomalies are detected by comparing old profiles with current activity. This may be successful if there is sufficient historical data to compare, but the amount of history that needs to be stored could be overwhelming. One way to reduce the amount of data required is to perform data mining and generate knowledge from the data. Data mining has proven successful in identifying fraud, terrorists, new marketing strategies, health epidemics, and patent developments (Cerrito, 2004; Clark, 2002; D'Amico, 2002; Lok, 2004; Robb, 2004; USDOJ, 2004).

The principle behind data mining is to search a data store and identify patterns (temporal, spatial, or contextual). There are two forms of data mining: structured data mining is performed on data that has been formatted and organized in a database structure, while unstructured data mining (or text mining), is used for data contained in documents, presentations, emails, and web pages. Structured data mining can best be used for identifying potential insider abuse from observables such as file access, user logins, and keystroke patterns (Anderson, 1999). The difficulty with this is that this data is often not collected (or is very difficult to collect), and the environment may not be modifiable to provide the attribution and timing information needed.

An alternative means to detect insiders is to consider whether a person's interests match with the people they contact. By analyzing the content of a person's email and web sites visited, a profile is created to describe the individual's interests. Textual clustering and data mining using Probabilistic Latent Semantic Indexing (Okolica, et al., 2008) and Author-Topic (Rosen-Zvi et al., 2004) can be used to generate links among documents, topics of interest, and people. From these links, an interest profile for an individual can be generated. This profile can be matched to an "insider model" profile, or more feasibly be used to develop social networks connecting individuals with similar interests. If two people have a high probability of being interested in the same topic, the probability that they know each other is much higher than the pure random chance of them knowing each other. If given this high probability, they do not exchange any emails, it may be suggestive of a clandestine link. In addition, the person may warrant additional attention if the category matches one that is "dangerous." On a more positive note, this technique can also be employed to build collaborative teams by finding people across many different divisions of an organization based on their interest in a particular topic.

In addition to clustering to develop social networks, other tools and techniques exist that build and analyze social networks. These techniques use a number of techniques to identify relationships and have extended from using web and available mailing lists into sources for social networking sites. For example, ReferralWeb (Kautz et al.,

1997) uses the co-occurrence of names in close proximity in World Wide Web documents to build a social network. The research of Adamic & Adar (2003) functions similarly, having been used on mailing lists and the homepages of students at Stanford and MIT. The idea is that when people create homepages, they link to their friends' homepages (and ask their friends to link to theirs). Culotta et al., (2004) extracted names from email messages, then found the person's "web presence" (a personal homepage for example) and used that to describe the person and to find friends of that person. After the social network was created, they used graph-partitioning algorithms to find highly connected components. While their dataset was small (53 email correspondents), their results were promising. However, the drawback of the approach was the lack of web presence for many of the correspondents (31 of 53).

More recently, research focuses on social networking site data sources that include much more detail and connections among individuals. This includes the use of the (now defunct) buddyzoo. com website, that allowed users to compare their AOL Instant Messenger buddy lists with others (Hogg & Adamic, 2004). The Text REtrieval Conference (TREC) Blog-Track 2006 database (MacDonald & Ounis, 2006), and Facebook (Golder, et al., 2007) have also been used in social network analysis. Research on social networks often makes use of visualization (Heer & Boyd, 2005; Paolillo & Wright, 2005), and importance metrics (Shi et al., 2008) derived from direct links between individuals to identify highly connected individuals, fringe groups, and individuals.

Information Fusion

As previously discussed, selecting the observables to use for detecting insider attacks is driven primarily by the detection algorithm used. Information fusion takes an alternate approach by collecting all available observables and using continually refining the detection model as a larger history of observables is collected and stored. Fusing works by collecting data from multiple sensors and storing them in such a way that the detection algorithm can analyze the data to determine any indication of malicious insider activity.

Not only does fusing rely on real-time data, it also takes integration further by suggesting the use of *honeytokens*. Based on the idea of *honeypot* networks used to entice malicious attackers, the honeytoken is "a semi-valuable piece of information whose use can be readily tracked" (Maybury et al., 2005, p. 3). Honeytokens provide an additional data point from which to track and identify insider activity. Fusing also implements event proximity with regard to time, and observable ordering to create a simulated timeline of events. Additionally, the data fusion engine will associate activities by internet protocol (IP) address, username, and other identifiers to assist in identifying malicious activity. A consequence of the collection of a wide collection of observables is potential increase in false alarms.

A benefit of fusing is that using information from heterogeneous sources may provide more accurate and timely indications and warning of insider attacks (Maybury, 2006). As shown in Figure 5, many observables can be collected and exploited to detect undesirable activity. Relying solely on cyber observables (while perhaps easier to collect) presents a small picture of the spectrum of human behavior that might indicate malicious intent and activity.

Drawbacks of fusion include the amount of data that must be collected, stored, and analyzed; the human interaction necessary during model refinement; and the computational resources necessary to make the detection algorithm useful in an operational setting. Ideally, the application of additional domain knowledge can provide more accurate contextual information. Another significant issue with fusion is the temporal nature of the observables. Personnel background checks, foreign travel, and the other non-cyber actions have a much different timeline than, say,

file access and web browsing. Fusing data under these conditions is challenging.

Attack / Protection Tree Modeling

Attack trees have been successfully used to identify the threats and risks to systems (Edge, 2007; Mauw et al., 2005; Schneier, 1999). Protection trees are used, in conjunction with attack trees, to evaluate trade-offs in the risk mitigation process (Bistarelli et al., 2006; Edge et al., 2006; Edge et al., 2007a; Edge et al., 2007b). While the focus of attack and protection trees is generally on the determination of overall system risk, the methodology is equally applicable to the insider threat domain. Attack trees formally represent all attack vectors and help determine which events must occur for the attack to be successful.

The calculation of metrics, such as the impact to a system if an action is accomplished, can be used to determine the risk level of each node (Edge, 2007). Although the values of the leaf nodes may be dynamic, attack trees still provide a viable method for determining risk. Defining attack trees is an iterative process requiring domain expertise. Applying attack tree methods to the insider threat requires a certain level of domain expertise to build the tree.

Systems Dynamics Modeling

It is clear that technology alone cannot solve the insider threat problem. Furthermore, organizational policies and security processes, while necessary and useful, are also insufficient in themselves. What is still not well understood is the human behavioral aspect to the problem. Martinez-Moyano et al. (2006, 2008) have developed a behavioral theory insider threat mitigation based on judgment and decision theory and system dynamics. Simulation is then used to predict behavior and shed insight into how potential inside attackers might be deterred or dissuaded. System dynamics presents a method for analyzing and managing complex systems that exhibit positive and negative feedback components. Feedback refers to a situation where some variable, event or parameter affects another variable, which in turn affects the first. It is not possible to study the linkages independently, and the system must be studied as a whole.

A system dynamics model for the insider threat is shown in Figure 6. The arcs represent influences (positive or negative) between two entities. A positive (+) sign on the arrow denotes that an increase in value at the source also results in an increase at the measure at the destination, while a negative sign denotes an inverse relationship. For example, consider the loop R1. An increase in detection capability drives an increase in detected precursors of undesired activity. As the number of detected precursors increase, the perceived risk increases, which then drives additional investments in security measures. Conversely, poor detection technology will decrease the number of detected precursors, which in turn decreases the organization's perceived risk, which may even lead to decisions that further diminish the detection capability. This false sense of security is known as the detection trap.

Demonstrating the complexity of the problem, consider the impact of the detection cycle on managerial trust (loop R2). As the organization detects more events, trust decreases, which in turn increases the perceived risk, which in turn will result in additional investments in detection technology. If the detected precursors decrease over time, managerial trust is positively reinforced which in turn drives down investments, and another negative cycle results, known as the trust trap.

Finally, loop R3 shows the unobserved emboldening trap. If the detection capability is lacking, then a portion of the insider activities will go unnoticed. The insider's perceived risk of being caught decreases, which results in an increased willingness to test the system, generating additional precursor events. If nothing changes in the other loops (R1 and R2), the insider becomes more willing to test the system and perhaps launch a more harmful attack.

This approach represents a significant step in addressing the insider threat because it allows study of the human as a complex system. A limitation of this approach is that the system dynamics model must be developed for specific threats, such as long-term fraud, sabotage, theft, and other threats. The risk management process described earlier would need to be applied for the various motivational factors (power assertive, greed, opportunistic, etc.) to be more useful.

Figure 6. Using system dynamics to model the insider threat (after Martinez-Moyano et al., 2006)

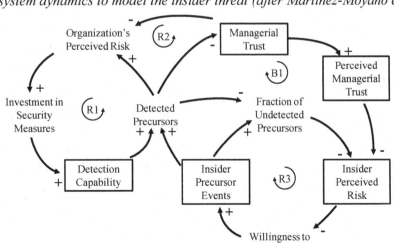

CONCLUSION

In this chapter, we identified the threats that trusted insiders pose to modern organizations. The primary difficulty in dealing with insider threats is that by definition insiders are trusted, so they possess elevated privileges and insider knowledge when compared to external users. While there are common motivational factors, such as greed and revenge, people who have been caught performing malicious acts do not fit a standard profile. Our intent was not to provide an exhaustive reference on the subject, but to provide a foundation for understanding characteristics of the insider threat.

The insider threat is a complex, challenging problem, but it can be approached in a straightforward manner using a combination of technology and standard security management practices, such as risk management, management oversight, policies, and procedures. The insider threat cannot be solved through technology alone, because security is at its very core, a people problem.

We reviewed some of the more popular trends in technology, processes, and behavioral profiling that we identified in research to enhance the identification and to mitigate the insider threat. Despite the work that has been completed in the area, further research is needed to develop a better understanding of the observables created by insiders, more accurately quantify threats, and develop cost effective methods for insider threat detection, prevention, and mitigation.

REFERENCES

Adamic, L., & Adar, E. (2003). Friends and Neighbors on the Web. *Social Networks, 25*(3), 211-230.

American Heritage (2008). *The American Heritage Dictionary of the English Language*. Fourth Edition. Retrieved April 03, 2008, from Dictionary.com website: http://dictionary.reference.com/browse/threat.

Anderson, J. P. (1980). *Computer Security Threat Monitoring and Surveillance*. Contract 79F296400," Fort Washington, PA: James P. Anderson Co. Retrieved January 12, 2008 from http://csrc.nist.gov/publications/history/ande80.pdf.

Anderson, R. H. (1999). *Research and Development Initiatives Focused on Preventing, Detecting, and Responding to Insider Misuse of Critical Defense Information Systems*. Retrieved April 11, 2008 from http://www.rand.org/publications/CF/CF151/CF151.pdf.

Anderson, R., et al. (2000). *Research on Mitigating the Insider Threat to Information Systems*. Retrieved April 3, 2008, Web site: http://www.rand.org/publications/CF/CF163/.

Bistarelli, S., Fioravanti, F., & Peretti, P. (2006). Defense Trees for Economic Evaluation of Security Investments. *Proceedings of the First International Conference on Availability, Reliability and Security (ARES'06)*. Vienna, Austria, 2006.

Brackney, R., & Anderson, R. (2004). *Understanding the Insider Threat*. CF-196. Santa Monica CA: RAND Corporation, March 2004.

Capelli, D., Moore, A., & Shimeall, T. (2005). *Common Sense Guide to Prevention and Detection of Insider Threats*. United States Computer Emergency Response Team. Retrieved June 11, 2008 from http://www.us-cert.gov/reading_room/prevent_detect_insiderthreat0504.pdf.

Carroll, M. D. (2006). Information Security: Examining and Managing the Insider Threat. *Proceedings of the 3rd Annual Conference on Information Security Curriculum Development* Kennesaw, GA: ACM, 2006.

Casey, E. (2004). *Digital Evidence and Computer Crime*. London: Academic Press.

Cazemier, J. A., Overbeek, P. L., & Peters, L. M. (2000). Security Management. *IT Infrastructure Library (ITIL) Series*, Stationery Office, UK.

Cerrito, P. (2004). Inside Text Mining. *Health Management Technology*, March 2004.

Clark, K. (2002). From Data to Decisions. *Chain Store Age, 78*, 62.

Coe, K. (2004). Behind the Firewall - The Insider Threat. *eWeek.com*, March 5, 2004. Retrieved January 12, 2008 from http://www.eweek.com/article2/0,1759,1543223,00.asp.

Cole, E. (2006). *Insider Threat: Protecting the Enterprise from Sabotage, Spying and Theft*. Rockland, MA: Syngress Publishing.

Culotta, A., Bekkerman, R., & McCallum, A. (2004). Extracting social networks and contact information from email and the Web. *First Conference on Email and Anti-Spam (CEAS)*. Mountain View, CA.

D'Amico, E. (2002). Sorting out the Facts. *Chemical Week, 164*, 22. 16 October 2002.

DCID 1/19 (1995). Director of Central Intelligence Directive No. 1/19: Security Policy for Sensitive Compartmented Information and Security Policy Manual. *Director of Central Intelligence*, March 1, 1995.

DCID 6/4 (1998). Director of Central Intelligence Directive No. 6/4: Personnel Security Standards and Procedures Governing Eligibility for Access to Sensitive Compartmented Information. *Director of Central Intelligence*, July 2, 1998.

Denning, D. (1987). An intrusion-detection model. *IEEE Transactions on Software Engineering, SE-13*(2), 222-232.

Denning, D. (1999). *Information Warfare and Security*. New York: Addison-Wesley.

Dictionary.com (2008). *Dictionary.com Unabridged* (v 1.1). Retrieved April 3, 2008, from Dictionary.com website: http://dictionary.reference.com/browse/insider.

Drucker, P. E. (1995). The Post Capitalistic Executive. In P. E. Drucker (Ed.), *Management in a Time of Great Change*. New York: Penguin.

CSO (2007). *2007 E-Crime Watch Survey – Survey Results. CSO magazine*, U.S. Secret Service, CERT® Program, Microsoft Corp. Retrieved March 30, 2008 from http://www.cert.org/archive/pdf/ecrimesummary07.pdf.

Edge, K., Dalton, G., Raines, R., & Mills, R. (2006). Using Attack and Protection Trees to Analyze Threats and Defenses to Homeland Security. *Proceedings of the 2006 Military Communications Conference (MILCOM)*, Washington, D.C.

Edge, K. (2007). *A Framework for Analyzing and Mitigating the Vulnerabilities of Complex Systems via Attack and Protection Trees*. Doctor of Philosophy. Graduate School of Engineering and Management, Air Force Institute of Technology, Wright-Patterson AFB, OH.

Edge, K., Raines, R., Grimaila, M.R., Baldwin, R., Reuter, C., & Bennington, B. (2007a). Analyzing Security Measures for Mobile Ad Hoc Networks Using Attack and Protection Trees. *Proceedings of the 2007 International Conference on Information Warfare and Security (ICIW 2007)*. Naval Postgraduate School, Monterey, CA; March 8-9, 2007.

Edge, K., Raines, R., Grimaila, M.R., Baldwin, R., Reuter, C., & Bennington, B. (2007b). The Use of Attack and Protection Trees to Analyze Security for an Online Banking System. *Proceedings of the Fortieth Annual Hawaii International Conference on System Sciences (HICSS)*.

Finne, T. (2000). Information systems risk management: Key concepts and business processes. *Computers and Security, 19*(3), 234-242.

Fishbein, M., & Ajzen, I. (1975). *Beliefs, Attitude, Intention and Behavior: An Introduction to Theory and Research*. Reading, MA: Addison-Wesley.

Golder, S. A., Wilkinson, D., & Huberman, B. A. (2007). Rhythms of social interaction: Messaging within a massive online network. In C. Steinfield, B. Pentland, M. Ackerman, & N. Contractor (Eds.), *Proceedings of Third International Conference on Communities and Technologies* (pp. 41-66).

Gordon, L. A., & Loeb, M. P. (November 2002). The Economics of Information Security Investment. *ACM Transactions on Information and System Security*, 5(4), 438-457.

Heer, J., & Boyd, D. (2005). Vizster: Visualizing online social networks. *Proceedings of Symposium on Information Visualization*, (pp. 33-40).

Herbig, K., & Wiskoff, M. (2002). *Espionage Against the United States by American Citizens 1947-2001*. Defense Personnel Security Research Center PERSEREC-TR 02-5. Retrieved December 19, 2007 from http://www.ncix.gov/archives/docs/espionageAgainstUSbyCitizens.pdf.

Hogg, T., & Adamic, L. (2004). Enhancing reputation mechanisms via online social networks. *Proceedings of the 5th ACM Conference on Electronic Commerce*, (pp. 237-237).

Insider Threat IPT (2000). *DoD Insider Threat Mitigation: Final Report of the Insider Threat Integrated Process Team*. Department of Defense, April 24, 2000, Retrieved on March 15, 2008 from https://acc.dau.mil/CommunityBrowser.aspx?id=37478.

Kamm, G. (2008). Disgruntled Worker Accused of Deleting $2.5 Million of Files. *First Coast News*, January 23, 2008, Retrieved from http://www.firstcoastnews.com/news/local/news-article.aspx?storyid=100625.

Kautz, H., Selman, B., & Shah, M. (1997). Referral Web: Combining Social Networks and Collaborative Filtering. *Communications of the ACM, 40*(3), 63-65.

Keeney, M., et al. (2005). *Insider Threat Study: Computer System Sabotage in Critical Infrastructure Sectors*. Technical Report, U.S. Secret Service and Software Engineering Institute, Carnegie Mellon University, May 2005. Retrieved January 5, 2008 from http://secretservice.tpaq.treasury.gov/ntac/its_report_050516.pdf.

Koenig, R. (2004). Beware of Insider Threats to Your Security. *CyberDefense Magazine*. August 2004. Retrieved on January 11, 2008 from http://www.viack.com/download/200408/cdm.pdf.

Kohlenberg, T. (2008). *Intrusion Detection FAQ: How to Make the Business Case for an Intrusion Detection System SANS Institute*. Retrieved March 12, 2008 from http://www.sans.org/resources/id-faq/business_case_ids.php.

Kowalski, E., et al. (2008a). *Insider Threat Study: Illicit Cyber Activity in the Government Sector*. Technical Report, U.S. Secret Service and Software Engineering Institute, Carnegie Mellon University, January 2008. Retrieved February 11, 2008 from http://secretservice.tpaq.treasury.gov/ntac/final_government_sector2008_0109.pdf.

Kowalski, E., et al. (2008b). *Insider Threat Study: Illicit Cyber Activity in the Information Technology and Telecommunications Sector*. Technical Report, U.S. Secret Service and Software Engineering Institute, Carnegie Mellon University, January 2008. Retrieved February 11, 2008 from http://secretservice.tpaq.treasury.gov/ntac/final_it_sector_2008_0109.pdf.

Levoy, T. E. (2006, May). *Development of a Methodology for Customizing Insider Threat Auditing on Microsoft Windows XP Operating System*. Master of Science. Graduate School of Engineering and Management, Air Force Institute of Technology, Wright-Patterson AFB, OH.

Levoy, T. E., Grimaila, M. R., & Mills, R. F. (2006). A Methodology for Customizing Security Auditing Templates for Malicious insider Detection. *Proceedings of the 8th International Symposium on System and Information Security.* San Paulo, Brazil.

Lok, C. (2004). Fighting Infections with Data. *Technology Review.* October 2004.

MacDonald, C., & Ounis, I. (2006). *The TREC Blogs06 Collection: Creating and analyzing a blog test collection.* Technical Report (dcs), Department of Computing Science, University of Glasgow.

Martinez-Moyano, I., Rich, E., Conrad, S., & Anderson, D. (2006). Modeling the Emergence of Insider Threat Vulnerabilities. *Proceedings of the 2006 Winter Simulation Conference.* Retrieved June 11, 2008 from http://www.dis.anl.gov/publications/articles/Martinez-Moyano_et_al_2006_WSC.pdf.

Martinez-Moyano, I., Rich, E., Conrad, S., Anderson, D., & Stewart, T. (2008). A Behavioral Theory of Insider-Threat Risks: A System Dynamics Approach. *ACM Transactions on Modeling and Computer Simulation, 18*(2), 7.

Mauw, S., & Oostdijk, M. (2005). Foundations of Attack Trees. *Proceedings of the Eighth Annual International Conference on Information Security and Cryptology,* (pp. 186-198). Seoul, Korea.

Maybury, M., et al. (2005). *Analysis and Detection of Malicious insiders.* 2005 International Conference on Intelligence Analysis, McLean VA. Retrieved December 18, 2007 from https://analysis.mitre.org/proceedings/Final_Papers_Files/280_Camera_Ready_Paper.pdf.

Maybury, M. (2006). *Detecting Malicious Insiders in Military Networks.* MITRE Corporation, Bedford, MA.

McKnight, D. H., Cummings, L. L., & Chervany, N. L. (1998). Initial Trust Formation in New Organizational Relationships. *Academy of Management Review, 23*(3), 473-490.

National Infrastructure Protection Center (NIPC). *Special Technologies and Applications Unit (STAU): Insiders and Information Technology.* Retrieved on April 3, 2008 from http://www.hpcc-usa.org/pics/02-pres/wright.ppt.

Okolica, J., Peterson, G. L., & Mills, R. F. (2008). Using PLSI-U to Detect Insider Threats by Datamining Email. *International Journal of Security and Networks, 3*(2), 114-121.

Paolillo, J. C., & Wright, E. (2005). Social network analysis on the semantic web: Techniques and challenges for visualizing FOAF. In V. Geroimenko & C. Chen (Eds.), *Visualizing the Semantic Web* (pp. 229-242).

Pipkin, D. L. (2001). *Information Security: Protecting the Global Enterprise.* Hewlett-Packard Company.

Randazzo, M., et al. (2004). *Insider Threat Study: Illicit Cyber Activity in the Banking and Finance Sector.* Technical Report, U.S. Secret Service and Software Engineering Institute, Carnegie Mellon University, August 2004. Retrieved from http://secretservice.tpaq.treasury.gov/ntac/its_report_040820.pdf.

Richardson, R. (2007). *2007 CSI/FBI Computer Crime and Security Survey.* Computer Security Institute. Retrieved January 5, 2008 from http://i.cmpnet.com/v2.gocsi.com/pdf/CSISurvey2007.pdf.

Robb, D. (2004). Taming Text. *Computerworld, 38,* 40-41.

Rosen-Zvi, M., Griffiths, T., Steyvers, M., & Smyth, P. (2004). The Author-Topic Model for Authors and Documents. *Proceedings of the 20th Conference on Uncertainty in Artificial Intelligence,* (pp. 487–494).

Schneier, B. (1999). Modeling Security Threats. *Dr. Dobbs Journal*. Retrieved February 8, 2008 from http://www.schneier.com/paper-attacktrees-ddj-ft.html.

Schultz, E.E. (2002). A Framework for Understanding and Predicting Insider Attacks. *Computers and Security, 21*(6), 526-531.

Shaw, E., Ruby, K., & Post, J. (September 1998). The insider threat to information systems. *Security Awareness Bulletin* No. 2-98, Department of Defense Security Institute. Retrieved January 8, 2008, from http://www.pol-psych.com/sab.pdf.

Shi, X., Bonner, M., Adamic, L., & Gilbert. A. C. (2008). *The Very Small World of the Well-connected*, HyperText 2008, Pittsburgh, PA, June 19-21.

Stanton, J. M., Stam, K. R., Mastrangelo, P., & Jolton, J. (2004). Analysis of End User Security Behaviors. *Computers and Security*, (pp. 1-10).

Stoneburner, G., Goguen, A., et al. (2002). *Risk Management Guide for Information Technology Systems*. National Institute of Standards and Technology Special Publication 800-30. Retrieved December 12, 2007, from http://csrc.nist.gov/publications/nistpubs/800-30/sp800-30.pdf.

Theoharidou, M., Kokolakis, S., Karyda, M., & Kiountouzis, E. (2005). The Insider Threat to Information Systems and the Effectiveness of ISO17799. *Computers and Security, 24*, 472-484.

Trends in Proprietary Information Loss: Survey Report, August 2007. Sponsored by Sponsored by National Counterintelligence Executive and American Society of Industrial Security (ASIS) Foundation. Retrieved on April 3, 2008 from http://www.asisonline.org/newsroom/surveys/spi2.pdf.

Turvey, B. (1999). *Criminal Profiling: An Introduction to Behavioral Evidence Analysis*. London: Academic Press.

USDOJ (2008). *Computer Intrusion Cases*. United States Department of Justice, Computer Crime and Intellectual Property Section. Retrieved on February 3, 2008 from http://www.usdoj.gov/criminal/cybercrime/cccases.html.

USDOJ/OIG (2003). *A Review of the FBI's Performance in Deterring, Detecting, and Investigating the Espionage Activities of Robert Philip Hanssen*. United States Department of Justice: Office of the Inspector General. Retrieved 12 February 2008 from http://www.usdoj.gov/oig/special/0308/index.htm.

Wise, D. (1995). *Nightmover: How Aldrich Ames Sold the CIA to the KGB*. New York: Harper-Collins, 1995.

Zhen, J. (2005). *The war on leaked intellectual property*. Retrieved February 11, 2008, from http://www.computerworld.com/securitytopics/security/story/0,10801,98724,00.html.

Chapter IV
An Autocorrelation Methodology for the Assessment of Security Assurance

Richard T. Gordon
Bridging The Gap, Inc., USA

Allison S. Gehrke
University of Colorado, Denver, USA

ABSTRACT

This chapter describes a methodology for assessing security infrastructure effectiveness utilizing formal mathematical models. The goal of this methodology is to determine the relatedness of effects on security operations from independent security events; determine the relatedness of effects on security operations from security event categories; identify opportunities for increased efficiency in the security infrastructure yielding time savings in the security operations; and identification of combinations of security events which compromise the security infrastructure. We focus on evaluating and describing a novel security assurance measure that governments and corporations can use to evaluate the strength and readiness of their security infrastructure. An additional use is as a before and after measure in a security services engagement to quantify infrastructure improvement that can serve as a basis for continuous security assurance.

INTRODUCTION

This chapter presents a novel security assurance methodology organizations can use to quantify their global security posture across the enterprise. The information security industry is addressing many challenges; specifically, how to collect data, often from heterogeneous, non-automated and non-standard sources, and how to properly analyze and act on the data. Before the autocorrelation methodology is described, relevant terms are defined to facilitate discussion.

Security assurance has several variations and definitions in the literature but generally refers to the ability of an organization to protect information and system resources with respect to vulnerability, confidentiality, integrity, and authentication. Security assurance is one broad category of security intelligence that security practitioners and managers are keenly interested in measuring and quantifying. *Vulnerability* is a weakness in the security system that might be exploited to cause loss or harm and an *attack* is when a person or another system exploits vulnerability (Pfleeger & Pfleeger, 2006). This chapter presents an autocorrelation methodology to evaluate security assurance processes, technologies, applications, and practices through a novel security metric. Security metrics are tools that support decision making (NIST, SP800-100, 2006).

The ability to extract actionable information automatically through security metrics is crucial to the success of any security infrastructure. Information security metrics in general should be defined, developed, analyzed, maintained, and reported within a broader information security program with a stated mission and clear and concise goals. Within such a framework, security metrics can be linked back to specific program goals which can be leveraged for managerial decision making.

Data drives intelligence across all industries and data is generated from events. Events happen all around us as messages (or "events") that flow across networks in support of commercial, government, and military operations. *Event driven* is defined as follows:

Event driven means simply that whatever tools and applications are used to automate business and enterprise management processes, those tools and applications rely on receiving events to monitor the progress of a process and issuing events to initiate its next stages. This is becoming universal for all business processing. (Luckham, 2002, pp. 29)

Processing security information is no exception as information security has become an essential business function (NIST, SP800-80, 2006). Within the context of security, the SANS Institute defines an *event* as "an observable occurrence in a system or network" (see glossary at: http://www.sans.org/resources/glossary.php). It follows that a *security event* is a single or collection of "observable occurrence(s) in a system or network" that violate the security policy of an organization. Two related concepts are *event aggregation* and *security event management. Event aggregation* is defined by Luckham (2002, pp. 17) as "recognizing or detecting a significant group of lower-level events from among all the enterprise event traffic, and creating a single event that summarizes in its data their significance". *Security event management software* is "software that imports security event information from multiple data sources, normalizes the data, and correlates events among the data sources" (NIST, 2006, C-3).

For our purposes, we will define a security *incident* as a specific type of security event; one that has been identified and classified by the organization as of sufficient priority to require the response of security personnel and whose time to resolve will be measured and tracked. The terms *security event* and *incident* are often used interchangeably; the distinction becomes important in the *Metrics Development and Implementation Approach* section which describes how to develop and implement the metric used in the autocorrelation methodology within a security event management framework.

Autocorrelation Methodology

Correlation is a mathematical tool used frequently for analyzing series of values, such as a time series, and measures the degree to which two or more quantities are linearly associated (Weisstein, 2008). A *time series* is a set of observations generated sequentially in time (Box & Jenkins, 1976). The autocorrelation methodology presented in this chapter examines the time series generated from incident daily total times to resolve (DTTR). Every day, incident resolution times are summed together and compared to each other over time. Autocorrelation is the correlation of a data set with itself. Autocorrelation enables serial dependence of data to be analyzed; That is, knowing the total time to resolve events today, what can we infer about the time to resolve events tomorrow? Correlation time is useful for analyzing security infrastructure because understanding relationships between incidents helps analysts uncover hidden patterns in the data that in this case provide important information on the problems in security operations. Trends are often more valuable than individual snapshots since baselines can be established to determine if operations are improving or declining across a wide range of categories.

Security infrastructures can be expressed as mathematical objects, utilizing formal methods based on mathematics and logic to model, analyze, and construct them. One indication of security infrastructure effectiveness is the length of time a problem lingers within the environment. A quantity that embodies this effect is the correlation time, which provides insight into the average amount of time needed to recover from an incident. This measure expresses the relationship between the amounts of overlap in security events after removing fluctuations for weekly and/or daily trends, as well as for any periodic trends that may become apparent over longer time periods.

In principle, one would expect that a more effective security infrastructure would have a shorter correlation time. That is, once an event occurs it will be quickly resolved and both the business and security operations brought back to health without recurring effects. On the other hand, a long correlation time suggests that a significant amount of the impact on security capabilities and business operations is due to remaining effects of older events rather than to new ones. Correlation time is relative to the organizations current baseline, or to performance last month versus this month, or as compared to the target correlation time an organization establishes.

By measuring the strength in the coupling of effects at different points in time, the autocorrelation function provides information, which relates to the future performance of the security infrastructure. If the correlation is positive and if today's resolve time is above the mean value, then we would expect that tomorrow would also be a day with a high amount of security capability and business operation impacting effects. This is due to the fact that the occurrence of a number of security events will first, weaken the security infrastructure's ability to handle additional events and to respond to the effects, and second will increase the workload of security systems and personnel.

For security infrastructures that are expected to have a high degree of operations oversight, this measure is particularly important. If a minor event occurs in the business environment and if the security infrastructure is built with appropriate functionality, both the business and security environments can continue operating normally and functionality is not impacted. However, if a serious event or a large number of minor events occurs, a large correlation time would indicate severe impact on business operations and security functionality. Viewed in this way, the correlation time can be thought of as a security assurance measure and a business risk index for extreme or multiple events.

The goal of the methodology presented in this chapter is to:

- Determine the relatedness of effects on security operations from independent security events.

- Determine the relatedness of effects on security operations from security event categories.
- Identify opportunities for increased efficiency in the security infrastructure yielding time savings in the security operations.
- Identification of combinations of security events which place the security infrastructure in an undesired state.

BACKGROUND

Assessing security assurance is a recently established discipline that is rapidly gaining momentum as government agencies and organizations realize the limitations in their ability to measure the effectiveness of their security infrastructure. A central tenet of business management is if it can't be measured, it can't be managed effectively and measuring security strength is no exception. The field is beginning to think of security in the same way other well-established disciplines do; as a process whose efficiencies can and must be measured with key indicators (Jaquith, 2007). Measurement of security assurance requires that metrics be identified and quantified. Quantification is driven by the need for provable security and accountability. What follows in this section is a summary of the challenges inherent in quantifying security system assurance.

Nascent Field with Growing Pains

Assessing security assurance is a rapidly developing field. As such, it lacks standards and broad consensus (Applied Computer Security Associates [ACSA], 2002); it has a strong demand for skilled information security professionals (Theoharidou & Gritazalis, 2007); and its methodologies are not based on the scientific and mathematical rigor that sustains other disciplines (Jaquith, 2007; Skroch, McHugh, & Williams, 2000).

A historic lack of consensus exists about security measures and metrics in everything from what questions to ask to what to measure. Standards and a common vocabulary have not been defined and accepted yet. Considerable controversy still exists regarding terms such as metrics, measure, score, rating, rank, or assessment result (ACSA, 2002). For our purposes we will use and define metrics as a group of measurements that produce a quantitative picture of something over a period of time, as defined by Lowans (2002). The key distinction between metrics and measurement is that metrics utilize a baseline for comparison in order to answer questions like, is my security better this month?

The International Standards Organization (ISO) 17799 framework is a standard for security taxonomy that categorizes the security domain but it lacks sufficient detail on measurement and criteria for success (Jaquith, 2007). In practice, security metrics are often divided into subcategories and used without consensus which makes measuring the effectiveness of security programs across enterprises difficult. For example, the National Institute of Standards and Technology (NIST, 2003) define three types of metrics in its special publication 800-55: implementation metrics, effectiveness/efficiency metrics, and impact metrics. ACSA (2002) describes technical, organizational, and operational "metrics". The quotations around metrics are because ACSA didn't actually use this term but instead opted to use an asterisk as a placeholder that was explicitly defined because of the lack of agreement for the term 'metric'. The ISO/IEC 27004 is a new ISO standard on information security management measurements whose goal is to help organizations measure and report the effectiveness of their information security management systems (See http://www.iso27001security.com/html/27004.html) that will hopefully help address some of these issues.

The second symptom of the discipline's relative youth is its tools and practitioners are often inexperienced. A plethora of diverse and specialized tools are flooding the market, all clamoring for the security manager's attention. The sheer numbers of choices available without expert guidance to make decisions are making security management very difficult. Established baselines, best practices, and tools with proven results are rare. In addition, data collection, analysis, and reporting are often not automated (Robert Frances Group [RFG], 2004; Richardson, 2007). Automation facilitates several key characteristics of a good metric by reducing cost, and ensuring consistency and repeatability (NIST, 2003; Jaquith, 2007).

Often, individuals with no or little background in security practices are tasked with managing security metrics and reporting (RFG, 2004). Practitioners are not well-trained and often don't understand how to interpret data correctly. For example, an increase in the number of viruses detected doesn't necessarily provide any information about a company's security posture. Virus detection statistics are a measure of anti-virus engine activity and will naturally rise and fall as virus release rates change (RFG, 2004). Practitioners must be able to do individual analysis on each metric, correlate different metrics, and understand relationships between them which require a number of different skill sets. The result is often confusion and a prevailing sense that existing measurement practices are ineffective.

The lack of strong methodologies based on scientific rigor is the third manifestation of a burgeoning discipline. Jaquith (2007) describes the use of "scientific method" and "security" in the same sentence as cause for the "giggles". During a panel workshop at the National Information Systems Security Conference (NISSC) in 2000, information assurance is described as a "black art" and one of four perspectives presented by the panel was "the perspective of information assurance metrics being attainable in the near term, if a disciplined, scientific approach is applied to the problem" (Skroch, McHugh, & Williams, 2000). This weak foundation is one

reason for inadequate upper-management support of strong security metrics programs. Another is that typically arguments for investment in IT security lack detail and specificity, and fails to adequately mitigate specific system risk (NIST, 2003). Information assurance assessment is beginning to draw on experience from established disciplines in science and engineering in terms of how metrics are defined, collected, analyzed, and reported. This approach will facilitate rapid growth and, more importantly, an ability to accurately characterize the strength or weakness of security infrastructures.

Metrics Generation is Difficult

The challenge in metrics generation may be easier to discuss if you understand the characteristics of a good security metric. According to Payne (2006), metrics should be SMART: specific, measureable, attainable, repeatable, and time-dependent. Jaquith (2007) defines a good metric as one that can be consistently measured, cheap to gather, expressed as a number or percentage, expressed using at least one unit of measure, and is contextually specific (p. 23-25). NIST (2003) reflects growing consensus and advises the following in considering a security metrics program:

- Metrics must yield quantifiable information (percentages, averages, and numbers)
- Data supporting metrics needs to be readily obtainable
- Only repeatable processes should be considered for measurement
- Metrics must be useful for tracking performance and directing resources

To quantify security assessment, metrics must be based on well-defined performance goals and objectives (NIST, 2003) and mean something to those using them. However, metrics are often ill-defined and not well understood. In addition, metric definition and evaluation often become distanced from the ultimate use and are used outside of contexts for which they were originally intended (ACSA, 2002). There has been some progress in measuring vulnerabilities which are relatively easy to quantify, especially for certain hardware (Payne, 2006), through the use of log audits and event reporting. For example, most organizations count the number of intrusions and virus outbreaks.

Many critical elements of the security infrastructure remain difficult to quantify. One reason is security events tend to be low frequency and high severity which makes them difficult to model (Jaquith, 2007). Another is many metrics require data that is inherently difficult to collect even if they are generated from repeatable and stable processes. For example, how do you quantify a security "attack"? Security vendors approach it by filtering security information or events from intrusion detection software into three levels of criticality which can be counted (Jaquith, 2007). This alone is useful but would be even more powerful if organizations would share security information data to establish comparative baselines.

Complexity of Systems

An organization's information infrastructure is typically a complex system of inter-connected software and hardware components communicating over a network. Connectivity and interdependence of those components continue to increase unabated. The phrase "you're only as strong as your weakest link" is particularly applicable to security environments. Yet, no universally accepted metrics exist for measuring how components relate to each other let alone the security infrastructure as a whole.

System complexity makes it difficult to generate consensus on what exactly should be measured. Metrics can and are defined in many categories often with inconsistent properties for assessing security protocols, security awareness training programs, processes, operational readiness, policies, applications, software, and hardware, to name but a few. The Common Criteria (CC) is an international standard that defines a set of ratings for particular products so, for example, like products from different vendors can be compared. The CC is making progress in this domain but little attention has been given to how to measure any complex system as a distinct entity in its own right.

No one metric can completely capture the effectiveness of a security infrastructure. Useful metrics help improve the overall security program, drive resource allocation, and recommend specific improvements. Security assurance assessment needs a metric that quantifies IT infrastructure from a global perspective to complement localized approaches. The autocorrelation methodology is one global approach that is based on a standard statistical tool inherent to many processes including chemical, services and manufacturing (Keller & Pyzdek, 2005).

METRICS DEVELOPMENT AND IMPLEMENTATION APPROACH

The following introduction to metrics development and implementation is necessarily brief but will cover the major activities an organization needs to employ to get the autocorrelation methodology operational. For more extensive treatment on building a security metrics program the reader is encouraged to review this chapter's references (e.g. Payne, 2006; Jaquith, 2007; NIST, 2003; NIST, SP800-80, 2006; NIST, SP800-100, 2006).

NIST identifies two major activities for the information security metrics development process:

1. Identifying and defining the current information security program; and
2. Developing and selecting specific metrics to measure implementation, efficiency,

effectiveness, and the impact of security controls. (NIST, SP800-100, pp. 61)

We assume the organization has addressed step 1 with, at a minimum, a mission statement and detailed goals that support the mission. We address step 2 with a metrics development and implementation strategy.

Metrics Development

Metrics should be selected and defined to reflect the organization's security priorities. "Devoting sufficient time to establishing information security performance metrics is critical to deriving the maximum value from measuring information security performance" (NIST, SP800-80 Draft,

2006, pp. 21). This is analogous to application security where the importance of design-time metrics are derived from the fact that significantly more resources are spent correcting an error after deployment than if the problem was detected early in the application's life cycle (Nichols & Gunnar, 2007).

We consider sample metrics for a simple network security metrics program since measuring vulnerabilities for network components (web servers, routers, etc) are relatively easy to quantify. The DTTR metric is included within this program and will be analyzed with an autocorrelation function. This example helps illustrate operational details for using the DTTR metric in practice.

We define our metrics using a modified version of the metrics development templates

Table 1. Sample metrics development template

Control Family	Access Control, Identification and Authentication
Metric(s)	Percentage of user logins from HTTP account
	Percentage of unsuccessful logins
Metric Type(s)	Implementation
Frequency(ies)	Organization defined (example: hourly, daily)
	Organization defined (example: hourly)
Formula(s)	(Number of HTTP user logins / total user logins) * 100
	(Number of unsuccessful logins / total logins) * 100

Control Family	Systems and Communications Protection
Metric(s)	Percentage of outbound FTP connections
Metric Type(s)	Implementation
Frequency(ies)	Organization defined (example: hourly, daily)
Formula(s)	(Number of outbound FTP connections / total outbound connections) * 100

Control Family	Incident Response
Metric(s)	Daily total time to resolve (DTTR).
	Percentage of open incidents.
Metric Type(s)	Effectiveness
Frequency(ies)	Organization defined (example: daily)
	Organization defined (example: daily)
Formula(s)	Sum all incidents over the frequency
	(Number of open incidents / total number of incidents) * 100.

NIST provides to ensure repeatability of metrics development (NIST, SP800-80 Draft, 2006). NIST specifies 17 control families to help link organizational strategies to security activities (NIST, 2007). Additional fields can be added or deleted as appropriate to organizational goals. One field (not shown) that should be associated with every metric is a uniquely identifiable metric ID to facilitate automated event management. The metric type is important for enumerating categories that can be compared and contrasted and to help organizations organize their metrics by different frameworks defined within their security program.

Implementation Strategy

One goal of the autocorrelation methodology is to assess the security infrastructure across all systems and policies. Gathering DTTR data depends on a relatively mature information security program that has lower-level event collection automated, managed in a central repository, and policies in place for categorizing specific event(s) as an incident that requires the response of security personnel.

How do you collect the data you need for the defined metrics? First, identify sources of data and configure hardware, applications, and OSs to audit and record relevant events in log files. The SANS Institute provides the "Top 5 Essential Log Reports" that can be used as a guide for what to prioritize and log first. Our network security metrics program requires OSs to log user account activity since unusual user logons and failed authentication can indicate malicious attempts to gain access and to log network traffic in order to characterize suspicious traffic patterns (Brenton, Bird, & Ranum, 2008). Defining normal traffic patterns and triggering incident events if unusual patterns are detected is a strong defense against attacks that are designed to 'fly under the radar' and not raise alarm on the compromised system itself.

An automated centralized security event management system (SEMS) is necessary to handle the millions of events any medium-big security infrastructure will generate. A common problem with log management is applications with the same purpose, like web servers from different vendors, log the same event using different fields, definitions, and formatting. In addition, it is very difficult for security personnel to efficiently locate and analyze logs across all systems that may be necessary for their purpose. All relevant events captured in logs across the enterprise need to be normalized into a consistent format and pushed to a central location as close to real-time as possible. Real time event management has a real cost associated with it as it increases the complexity of the system. Organizations must evaluate how quickly they need data available for analysis and prioritize what must be processed in real-time and which logs can be processed at intervals throughout the day.

Centralized log management facilitates security forensics because attackers often try to tamper with evidence of their crime by erasing log files (Garfinkel, Spafford, & Schwartz, 2003). These attempts are usually in vein if the information is also located on a remote system. Figure 1 is a high-level illustration of this framework. On the left are security personnel or management who may access or generate data, and on the right are the enterprise systems that generate events.

Options for SEMS deployment include commercial products, open-source products or developing a custom system. Until recently, it was

Figure 1. Security event management system (modified from Chuvakin, 2008)

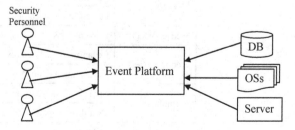

difficult to find commercial vendors that offer centralized metrics collection but now there are many including EventTracker from Prism Microsystems, Inc., Foundstone, Inc., IBM Corp., NetScreen Technologies, Inc., and SecurityMetrics, Inc. (RFG, 2004). Custom systems require some type of database as the central repository and software to parse the logs into the database. Databases are routinely configured to trigger actions automatically when certain conditions in the data are met.

An important requirement for any event management framework is automation. A significant control enhancement recognized by NIST and included in many of their example metrics is the employment of automated mechanisms (NIST, SP800-80 Draft, 2006). A phased automation plan can help balance the pressures on budget and resource availability.

Implementation is an iterative process which includes identifying priority metrics to baseline and adding additional metrics as the data becomes available. With a set of established baselines, analysis techniques can be used to alarm security personnel if defined thresholds are exceeded. For example, the network security metrics program defined before includes three metrics generated from low-level events: percentage of user log-ins from HTTP account, percentage of unsuccessful log-ins, and percentage of outbound FTP connections. Suppose that the percentage of http user log-ins and the percentage of outbound FTP connections both exceed threshold (as they would have in two break-in case studies profiled in Garfinkel, Spafford, & Schwartz, 2003). The SEMS is triggered to automatically create two new incident events and alerts security personnel.

The incidents are timed from the moment they are created until authorized personnel close them through a user interface to the event management system. Closing the incident includes a documented explanation of the root cause, recommendations for additional action, and categorization of the incident as enumerated by the organization.

Through periodic review, the organization adds, deletes, expands and fine-tunes the metrics they manage and generate more rules for what qualifies as an incident. Incident response time is input data to the DTTR metric.

Categorizing the incidents enables the organization to track their effectiveness by knowing, for example, the number of intrusions and their average response time over defined timeframes. The numbers of the types of incidents can be analyzed against the DTTR over the same time period to see if there is a correlation between certain types of incidents and unusually high response times. This could help an organization focus an investigation to determine weaknesses in the security infrastructure. The increase in response time could be because expert security personnel were on vacation at the time, or it could be that associated data wasn't automated yet and tracking down the source was a more time-consuming manual process. The former indicates a need for training and better personnel coverage, the later could help prioritize what to automate in the next phase.

General Applicability of DTTR

The DTTR metric is applicable within any security metrics framework that can apply deviations from acceptable levels among lower-level metrics to define an incident of interest. What is important is to employ baselines to help define "normal" within the security infrastructure (Geer, Soo Hoo, & Jaquith, 2003; Brenton, Bird, & Ranum, 2008). Here are two examples of how correlations could be investigated among metrics frameworks with very different purposes.

Metrics can be organized by the Top Ten metrics defined by the Open Web Application Security Project (OWASP: www.owasp.org). One of the top ten is "PercentValidatedInput" defined as V/T where T is the count of the amount of input forms or interfaces an application exposes and V is the number of these interfaces that use input validation mechanisms (Nichols & Gunnar, 2007). If PercentValidatedInput falls below a defined level, an incident of type 'application vulnerability' can be created. Automated penetration tests can be used to identify numerous vulnerabilities that are input to application vulnerability type incidents. Analyzing application vulnerability DTTRs enables an organization to track efficiency of security related software maintenance, identify process improvements to reduce known vulnerabilities (for example, mandate the use of standard input validation templates) and to facilitate root cause analysis of attacks that may have had their origin in an application vulnerability.

Metrics can also be organized to measure awareness and training programs. Example metrics are the percentage of system users that have received basic awareness training, percentage of information system security personnel that have received security training, and percentage of users with passwords in compliance with the password security policy. If any fall below targets as established through a baseline, an 'awareness and training' incident is created whose DTTR is measured. Analyzing DTTRs for awareness and training incidents can help drive resource allocation and recommend specific improvements for training programs.

To Learn More

An enormous number of resources are available and no list can be comprehensive. However, here are a few the reader may want to investigate further to assist in the development of an automated, centralized event management system:

- The SANS Institute (https://www.sans.org/) has a Buyers Guide to assist in finding leading IT Security vendors, a collection of white papers, and a list of resources at http://www.sans.org/free_resources.php.
- SANS also has a white paper on "Security Information/Event Management Security Development Life Cycle" (see http://www.sans.org/score/esa_current.pdf) that is a complete treatment of how to get an event management system operational.
- Appendix F of NIST SP800-86, "Guide to Integrating Forensic Techniques into Incident Response" provides a list of online tools in several areas including, organizations supporting forensics, technical resource sites, training resources, and other technical resource documents.

AUTOCORRELATION ANALYSIS

Autocorrelation of the total time to resolve time-series does not provide causal information, or information solely about the event resolution process. It provides more of a "global" view of the whole security environment, both the capacity of the actual operation as well as the event resolution process.

Technical Framework

Without a theoretical construct of an ideal security infrastructure and event resolution, complete interpretation of the autocorrelation of the time-series based on total time to resolve events is not possible. The correlation time is best viewed as a global state variable indicative of the level of assurance of the entire security infrastructure, indicating the need for further investigation. Analogous to human temperature, high correlation times can be indicative of "problems", but are certainly not conclusive. Some of the difficulties here lie with biases (example: infrastructure capacity and usage based biases), de-trending processes and definition of what constitutes an incident. The definition of what constitutes an incident will vary from one security infrastructure to another depending on specific business needs. This will in turn impact what the ideal correlation time is.

For a more systemic approach, the following model is offered: A time-series analysis of the types of incidents versus the frequency of occurrence in time.

By creating multiple time-series of the individual incident classes and of the entire conglomerate security environment, based on some unit time interval, time-series analysis of these series in comparison can give better insight into the systemic issues in the security infrastructure.

For example, suppose event A directly causes event B downstream in time. We would expect to see a strong correlation of B's time-series with A's shifted in time. This strong correlation would provide the evidence of where to focus diagnostic efforts to provide further evidence of this causal relationship, along with providing clues as to why the relationship exists and thus how best to mitigate it. This systemic issue in turn provides the business information of where to concentrate resources spent on improving security performance.

This simple example in no way exhausts the possible information gained about systemic issues in a security infrastructure by this type of analysis. More complicated correlation studies can be done, depending on the quality of data, leading to all sorts of insight into security performance.

One big gain in this approach is a movement away from an individual event management focus and a movement towards understanding the complex event relationships within a security environment. While most organizations currently make mitigation recommendations based upon removal of single event issues, the "non-linear" effects are not taken into account, thus current mitigation recommendations may not have the desired effects and in fact could possibly have opposite effects.

Explanation of Correlation Functions

In statistics, time series models can be usefully described by their mean, variance, and autocorrelation function (Box & Jenkins, 1976). The autocorrelation function (ACF) describes the correlation between processes at different points in time. The process under study here is the daily total time to resolve incidents in the information security infrastructure. This process is stochastic since future values of the time series cannot be exactly determined by some mathematical function. Statistically speaking, security events are assumed to be independent and violations of assumptions in mathematical modeling often lead to problems in analysis. Fortunately, the proposed autocorrelation methodology does not depend on whether security events are independent or not for robust analysis. In fact, we assume that very often security events are not independent and employ the ACF because it is a good tool to check the independence assumption (Keller & Pyzdek, 2005).

The events occurring in a security environment and affecting, for example, customer/transaction throughput, dependent business processes, and IT systems elements, are in general not mutually independent. It is common that if an event of type A occurs, then an event (effect) of type B is likely to also occur. For example, if the number of transactions in the business environment increases, then we would expect to see an increase in load on the security infrastructure. In technical parlance, we say that these two events are correlated. The discovery of a correlation between events is important because it helps in the detection or even prediction of security events. An example of this would be of a failing network intrusion device that starts sending a large number of false positives over the security infrastructure, producing at some time later an overload on security personnel and an impairment of some other aspect of security operations. This kind of example introduces the need to think of a correlation in time that is between events occurring at different times.

One kind of security event can be correlated not only with other kinds of events, but also with itself. This means, for example, that the occurrence of an event at 10:00am can change the security environment so that the probability of an event at 10:30am increases. In our analysis we want to use a quantity that reflects the degree of operational security impairment during a given day. One such measure can be the sum of all the event resolution times in a day; a quantity we have defined as the Daily Total Time to Resolve (DTTR).

The DTTR is expected to show a temporal correlation. Which means that today's DTTR will have an effect on tomorrow's DTTR. There are several good reasons to expect this. The occurrence of anything but a minor security event could produce:

- A weakening of the security infrastructure's ability to provide services and to respond to additional events. If, for example, a facility intrusion system fails or a distributed network penetration occurs, then the rest of the security infrastructure will see an increase in its workload, making the business environment more susceptible to additional events.
- Attempts to resolve the event, can lead to rush changes in security operations or policy configuration, increasing the risk of further events.
- An increased workload on the security personnel can lead to longer times for the resolution of subsequent events.

Now that we expect the DTTR to have an interesting day to day evolution, and to give us some information about the efficacy of security operations:

- How do we extract and interpret this information?
- Why is this information relevant to the security infrastructure management?

We need a measure that will take into account the probabilistic nature of the DTTR. This means that on any particular day the DTTR is not known with certainty. This implies that high DTTR values in consecutive days can just be a chance occurrence. That is why we will not look at just two values separated in general by T days.

To introduce the quantity to be calculated we assume that we have the overall average of the DTTRs; these are the x-bars in equation 1. Take all the DTTRs and subtract from them this average. In this way we obtain numbers that can be positive or negative, with about the same probability. Take two of these numbers separated by T days. A positive (negative) correlation would imply that these numbers are more likely to have the same (different) signs than not. Finally, multiply the numbers and average over all pairs of days separated by T days. If the DTTRs are not correlated, then we expect to obtain as many positives as negative factors, averaging to zero or to a very small number.

The output of this process is a set of numbers indexed by the time lag T. We use these numbers to calculate the autocorrelation function (ACF) of the DTTRs and then interpret the meaning of this function. In general, it is reasonable to expect that events separated by one day will be more strongly correlated than events separated by 10 days. Therefore, the ACF should become smaller as T increases. It is in the nature of this decay that some very subtle information about the security infrastructure is revealed. If strong correlations are detected among temporally distant events, this is of interest also as it may indicate an attack that is designed to progress slowly through the infrastructure to not be detected under standard analysis techniques.

The decay of the ACF would give us some information on the time evolution of events in the security environment. We can also obtain information on the coupling of events. If we have all the DTTRs we could calculate the average and find for example that a typical event is resolved in about 100 minutes. By studying the ACF we might discover that the effects of an event are felt throughout the security infrastructure long after it has been labeled as resolved. The mechanism of this influence can be seen as arising from a chain of events. Let's say we have three events A, B, and C, in that time order. If C happens after A has been closed, it can still feel its effects because A affects B and it in turn affects C. So the influence of an event can be embodied in a kind of domino effect.

We need a measure to quantify the decay of the ACF. The main characteristic is the time that the effects of an event linger in the security infrastructure. Therefore, calculate a time that characterizes the decay in influence of an event. This function is called "the autocorrelation time." This number can be seen as a relaxation time, that is, how long it takes the security infrastructure to recover from the effects of events, or more precisely, the effects of a particular day's events. The actual calculation of this time involves adding the ACF for all the time lags {0, 1, 2,...,T}. This simple summation can be shown to be a good choice of autocorrelation time. It is a global measure of all the very complicated dynamics present in the security infrastructure. Since it is an aggregated quantity it smoothes much of the security infrastructure's inherent fluctuations. At the same time it is able to extract important information contained in these fluctuations.

In principle, we would expect that as security operations improve, the autocorrelation time of the DTTR would become shorter. In a well-run security operation, once an event occurs it is resolved quickly and the security infrastructure is brought to full capacity with no remaining effects. On the other hand, if the correlation time is long, then it is apparent that much of the time that the security infrastructure is impaired, is due not only to new events but also to remaining effects of old ones.

The actual value of the autocorrelation time is that it gives important information on the problems in security operations that produce the correlation of events that weaken the security infrastructure. Since the autocorrelation time is only one number it cannot identify specific problems in the security infrastructure. However, it can help to separate a well managed from a poorly managed security operation. Importantly, it can also be used as a before and after measure in a security services engagement to quantify infrastructure improvement.

Impact of Correlation

Suppose we have a time-series of DTTRs for a large-scale security infrastructure such as from a Fortune 500 company like the one shown in Figure 2. This is example data for illustrative purposes. Here we see that the DTTR fluctuates between a high of 486,969 and a low of 9,669 minutes, with a mean DTTR of 176,511 minutes. This mean DTTR is not meaningful until it is evaluated within the context of an organizationally defined baseline for the DTTR metric. When an organization understands their average DTTR, they can make assessments about root cause investigations and how to improve.

Figure 2. Daily total time to resolve scatter plot

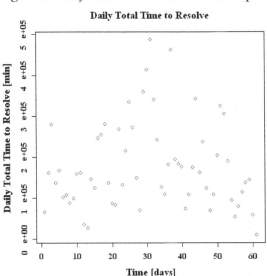

It is difficult to see the time evolution of this series in this plot. So, calculate the ACF for the DTTRs to extract hidden patterns in the data. We have a finite times series $x_1, x_2, \ldots x_n$ of n DTTR observations from which we obtain estimates of the autocorrelations. The ACF is estimated at the given lag (T) as follows (Keller & Pyzdek, 2005):

$$ACF(T) = \sum_{i=1}^{n-T}(x_i - \bar{x})(x_{i+T} - \bar{x})/\sum_{i=1}^{n}(x_i - \bar{x})^2 \quad (1)$$

for $T = 0, 1, 2, \ldots n / 4$, where n is the number of observations, and x-bar is the average of the observations. Estimates at longer lags than n / 4 have been shown to be statistically unreliable (Keller & Pyzdek, 2005).

This function is shown in Figure 3; from this plot we can see that the time-series has a 7-day periodic behavior. This is not unexpected; for example, weekends are often the least busy days of the week for many organizations. Therefore even if the values of the number of events were not correlated, just the fact that this periodicity exists would produce a non-zero correlation.

Figure 3. Correlation function of the daily total time to resolve

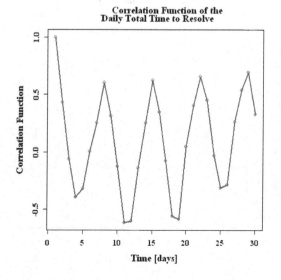

Figure 4. Average daily total time to resolve per day of the week

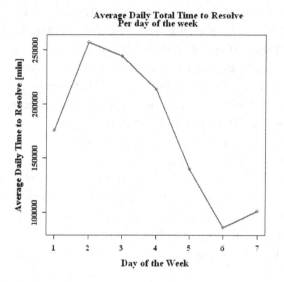

We see that in order to extract more information from this series we need to rescale the values in the series. In order to perform the rescaling of the series we need to know the average DTTR per day of the week and the standard deviation per day of the week; this is show in Figure 4.

In Figure 4, day 1 is a Tuesday. For each Monday we take the actual number for time to resolve and subtract from it the Monday's average, finally we take this number and divide it by the corresponding standard deviation. In general:

AFDW = Average for that day of week   (2)

Rescaled Time = (Actual Time – AFDW) / (std deviation for that day of week)   (3)

Now we have a time-series that has a mean of zero and standard deviation of one and we can calculate its correlation function. We find this result plotted in Figure 5.

This plot seems to have more of a typical look of an autocorrelation function. Notice, that as the time increases in this plot the quality of the calculated function decreases because we have fewer points for the calculation. In characterizing

Figure 5. Autocorrelation function rescaled time to resolve

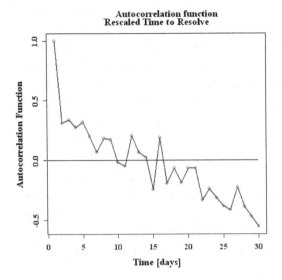

mathematical functions, *decay* refers to a decrease in some quantity. In the ACF function, if the signal decays very rapidly, or exponentially fast, as:

$$ACF(T) \propto exp(-T / \tau) \qquad (4)$$

where τ is the autocorrelation time, then this suggests that using a regression tool on equation (1) would allow us to find τ. There is a better way to do this however. Notice that the integral of $exp(-T / \tau)$ from zero to infinity would give us τ, that is

$$\int_{0}^{\infty} exp(-T/\tau)dt = \tau \qquad (5)$$

On the other hand we have a discrete function, but it can be shown that the following summary does actually play the role of a correlation time:

$$T_{ACF}(L) = \sum_{i=0}^{\infty} ACF(T) \qquad (6)$$

This is not an easy number to calculate due to the fact that the function *ACF(T)* becomes noisy as

T increases. A better way to approach this problem is by plotting the following function

$$T_{ACF}(L) = \sum_{i=0}^{L} ACF(T) \qquad (7)$$

This function is shown in the following plot for the data (Figure 6).

From this figure we can assume that the correlation time for this data is about 3 days. If we remember that a correlation time of 1 in this case means that the events are uncorrelated, then the 3 days means that it takes the security infrastructure about two days to recover from the effects of an event. Notice that this example calculation has been done with only 60 points, therefore caution should be taken in the interpretations of the results.

Linear Approximation

Another way to see the effect of the correlation between consecutive DTTRs is to plot the DTTR for day *(t+1)* as a function of the DTTR for day(t) shown in Figure 7. A straight line obtained us-

Figure 6. Autocorrelation time rescaled time to resolve data

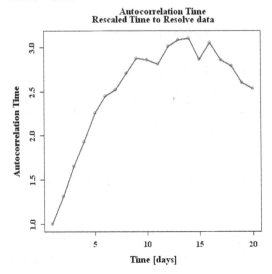

Figure 7. Scatter diagram for lag t = 1, obtained by plotting DTTR for day t against DTTR for day t + 1

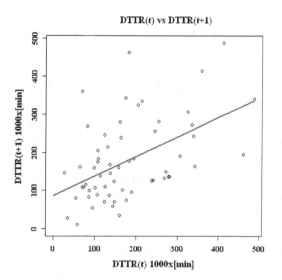

ing a least squares fit to this data is also shown in this picture.

This plot shows clearly that the values of the daily total time to resolve are correlated. Only the correlation between consecutive days can be seen from this plot, and in the rest of this section we will assume that this is enough to account for most of the relevant effects. The straight line in the plot represents the following linear autoregressive model,

$$x(t + 1) = \alpha * x(t) + \beta + \gamma * \varepsilon(t) \qquad (8)$$

where $x(t)$ = DTTR at time t

$\varepsilon(t)$= random error that represents the point's deviation from the straight line

α = slope of the line

β = value of the line's intersection with the vertical axis

γ = amplitude of the fluctuations around the straight line.

Here $\varepsilon(t)$ is scaled so its standard deviation is one. In practice, statisticians commonly use a ran-

dom error to measure uncertainty since you can't expect the data to reveal all sources of variation (Mosteller & Tukey, 1977). One factor that will likely influence the magnitude of this error term is the daily idiosyncrasies of security personnel in terms of how they classify incidents and when they determine an incident should be closed. The bootstrap technique described to follow can also be applied to ensure an appropriately large error is chosen. If the errors are not random, then $\varepsilon(t)$ will pick up systematic mistakes. If a more complex analysis is required, Mosteller & Tukey (1977), discuss techniques for direct assessment and general techniques that are broadly accessible to determine the error term. For this plot α = 0.5136334; β = 86,278 minutes; and γ = 92,738 minutes.

The existence of the correlation between DTTR for day t and the DTTR for day $(t+1)$ is contained in the value of α. If the random variables $\varepsilon(t)$ are distributed according to a normal distribution and are not correlated, then the process described by Equation (8) produces a stationary probability distribution. This distribution is normal with a mean of $\beta / (1 - \alpha)$. This is the fixed point of the deterministic part of Equation (8), with a standard deviation given by $\gamma / (1 - \alpha^2)^{1/2}$. In the case where $\alpha = 0$, Equation (8) would imply the simple case of a normal distribution with mean β and standard deviation γ. Therefore, the existence of a correlation has two main effects. First, it shifts the mean of the distribution, and second it increases the fluctuations around this mean. In particular for the data studies in this example, the location of the mean is nearly doubled, while the standard deviation increases by nearly 20%.

Confidence Interval

The plot in Figure 7 shows a significant amount of noise, this should make us think that the actual value of α = 0.5136334 should also include some account for fluctuations in the distribution of points. We use the bootstrap technique to estimate the confidence interval for α, the slope of the least square fit of Equation (9). The plot in Figure 7 has a series of points, which are located according to a certain probability distribution. This particular sample has 60 points on it. If the distribution was sampled another time, the set of points would change while still retaining a similar shape and the estimated slope of the least square fit would be slightly similar to our value. Here we want to estimate how different these values would be. Since we do not have the actual distribution function that drives the location of these points we will use the next best thing, which is the actual distribution of points in our sample.

The generation of synthetic samples is carried out as follows:

- Choose the number of synthetic samples we want to generate, say 1000 for example.
- Create a sample set by choosing uniformly and with replacement amongst the 60 points in the plot. Uniformly means that the probability of choosing any of the points is 1/60. This replacement means that for each of the 60 points in the synthetic sample we use the same set of actual points to choose from, if point A is chosen as point 10 then while choosing point 11, A will still have a probability 1/60 to be selected.
- For each of the generated synthetic samples calculate the quantity of interest. In this case the slope of the least squares fit to the points.

Once this process is finished we have a series of values for our parameter. With this we can generate its distribution function and extract confidence intervals. The mean of this distribution function would be very close to the parameter estimated from the real sample. Notice here that this technique does not give us a better value of this parameter, but gives us confidence intervals for the location of the actual parameter.

Figure 8. Histogram of the least squares slope using 1000 generated samples

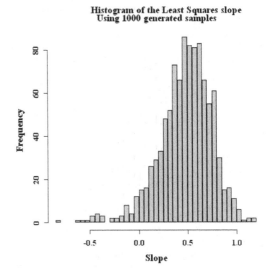

The bootstrap calculation performed to obtain the slope in Figure 7 produces the following histogram.

Not surprisingly we find that the distribution is centered on *α = 0.5*, with a standard deviation of 0.25. This plot shows that the data has a very high probability of being positively correlated, with probability of 95%. The slope has 70% probability of being in the interval [0.25,0.75].

Another quantity of interest is the value of *β*, the intersection of the line with the DTTR = 0 line. This would be the average of the distribution of DTTRs if all the correlations were eliminated, in which case the difference between this number and the actual value of the mean of DTTRs (176,511 minutes) would be the amount of time savings. The following plot shows the histogram for the intersections:

The histogram is centered on β = 88,500 minutes, with a standard deviation of 53,440 minutes. The intersection is clearly positive with a probability of 96%. The intersection has 71% probability of being in the interval [30,000 min, 140,000min]. This means that if the correlation was completely eliminated there is a 71% prob-

Figure 9. Histogram of the least squares intersection using 1000 generated samples

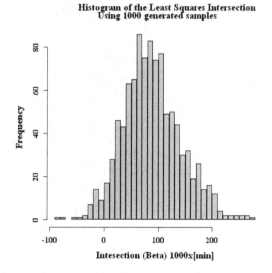

ability of time savings in the interval [36,511 min; 146,511 min].

Further Analysis

Up to this point we have studied the DTTR time-series in two ways:

- First, using a de-trending preprocessing step and calculating the autocorrelation function and time. This is a good way to extract global information from the series in a model-free fashion. The disadvantage of this method is that to obtain meaningful numbers, in a business sense, we need to revert to the rescaling process and treat each day of the week using a different scale. From a technical point of view, this can be done and is not particularly difficult.

- Second, we have used a linear regression model to have a better view, both conceptually as well as graphically, of the meaning of correlated events, and, more importantly, to obtain time savings numbers. The advantage of this analysis is this ability of visualizing

the cloud of points with a fitted line with positive slope and, as already mentioned, the ability to obtain business meaningful numbers. The disadvantage of this analysis are: the use of a linear model, although this is not of great concern since, as seen from Figure 7, the cloud of points does not show many signs of nonlinearity; the fact that the model is Markovian, where again this is not of great concern since further analysis of this assumption can be carried out without much difficulty. The fact is that our aim here is to first obtain general trends and less importantly to discover the "true" underlying phenomena. Another more important problem is the fact that the data used does have the weekly oscillatory behavior. Therefore, the numbers obtained from this analysis have to be taken as gross estimations.

In what follows is an outline of some of the further analyses that can be performed to obtain more consistent numbers. Conceptually and in terms of data manipulation, these analyses are not more complicated than the ones already described. They require the use of the same tools, but with a more restricted data set.

Perform Separated Analysis per Day of the Week

For this analysis, we would split the problem in seven separate but essentially similar problems. So that instead of an aggregated problem we would study the correlation from Monday-to-Tuesday, Tuesday-to-Wednesday, etc. This immediately eliminates the need for rescaling, though we still may need to perform an overall de-trending step. Each of these seven analyses would contribute a different time savings number and the total weekly time savings would just be their sum. This introduces the need to obtain confidence intervals for the aggregated time savings. Again this is not a difficult problem to solve; the strategy here would be a two-step bootstrap process. First, the aforementioned bootstrap procedure is performed in each of the seven problems, generating let's say 100 numbers each. Second, now that we have 7x100 numbers we perform another 100 bootstrap samples, each consisting of choosing randomly one number from each day amongst the 100 generated and finally adding all seven to obtain one total. Seen in this way it would be equivalent to just performing one bootstrap procedure each consisting of adding seven samples. With the two step bootstrap however, we have some freedom in the number of aggregated weekly time savings we calculate, so we can generate more than 100 numbers. While it is true that there is a point where generating more numbers would not improve the estimations, this will help us to obtain a better histogram.

Another advantage of separating the days is that we can study the fluctuation in the correlation during the week. In particular, it may be of interest to look at a plot of correlation versus size of DTTR for the previous day. This is interesting since, as can be seen from Equation (9), the correlation is an intensive quantity. So in principle it could be the same for all days of the week. If we find that the correlation increases with the size of the DTTR this would indicate a deterioration of the security response with increasing loads. In terms of security management, this could help to rearrange some of the security processes during the week, to minimize the total resolution time.

Use of Categorized Time to Resolve

The Daily Total Time to Resolve is typically composed of many events. If these events can be categorized, then we could have a tool to assess the relative importance of different security elements. The categories can be for example:

- Awareness & Training
- Application Vulnerability
- Facilities Intrusion
- System Penetration
- Virus Detection
- Fire/Life/Safety
- Fraud & Theft

Once we have the daily total times for each of N categories $\{x_1(t), x_2(t),..., x_N(t)\}$, then we can model the time-series as a multivariate linear regression:

$$x(t+1) = \alpha_1 * x_1(t) + \alpha_2 * x_2(t) + \ldots + \alpha_n * x_n(t) + \beta + \gamma * \varepsilon(t) \tag{9}$$

$$x(t) = \sum_{i=1}^{N} x_i(t) \tag{10}$$

As in the case of Equation (8), we can obtain values for $\{\alpha_1(t), \alpha_2(t),..., \alpha_N(t); \beta, \gamma\}$ using least-squares regression. Notice that the α's are intensive quantities, that is it gives the effect of each of the categories per unit time, therefore we can use them to make a comparative study.

Calculation of Correlation Matrix

This is not related to the dynamics of resolution times but it could be an interesting quantity to compute. The correlation matrix may prove particularly useful in the diagnosis of combinations of events that place the security infrastructure in an undesired state or "cut sets." The objective here is to identify as many combinations of events as possible that can place a security infrastructure in an undesired state.

If we have the time-series, $\{x_1(t), x_2(t), ...,x_N(t); t = 1, 2,...M\}$ then we can say that we have M points in an N dimensional space. The correlation matrix between these variables is defined as

$$C_{i,j} = \frac{\frac{1}{M-1}\sum_{t=1}^{M}\left(x_i(t)-\overline{x_i}\right)\cdot\left(x_j(t)-\overline{x_j}\right)}{\sigma_i\cdot\sigma_j},$$

$$\sigma_i^2 = \frac{1}{M-1}\sum_{t=1}^{M}\left(x_i(t)-\overline{x_i}\right)^2,$$

$$\overline{x_i} = \frac{1}{M}\sum_{t=1}^{M}x_i(t).$$

(12)

If $C_{2,4}$ is a number close to one, then we expect that if several events of type 2 occur in a particular day, then events of type 4 are also likely to occur. Notice that having a large numerical value does not necessarily imply a cause-effect relationship between 2 and 4, rather both may be caused by the same event in the security infrastructure. In any case the discovery of these kinds of relationships between categories can point to a common solution to both types of events. Once we have calculated the correlation matrix we can think of performing a principal component analysis. Calculating the eigenvectors and eigenvalues of C does this.

The analysis presented in this chapter was carried out on sample data that was created to demonstrate the autocorrelation methodology. Future study needs to be conducted using actual organizational data to help further refine and define systematic analysis techniques to assure robust security across the enterprise.

FUTURE TRENDS

A disciplined, scientific approach is required to realize the full potential of security assurance assessment to minimize risk to critical information resources. Researchers are beginning to define key indicators to quantify security activities using well-established disciplines in science and engineering as guides. To be of most use for benchmarking and certification, organizations need to share and aggregate their data to generate quantifiable measures that facilitate objective analysis and enable comparison of a

security infrastructure to itself as well as to other environments. Additional research is required in systematic methodologies, formal and informal modeling, and in the development of a toolbox of security metrics that cover all important properties of a security infrastructure including global perspectives.

CONCLUSION

This chapter describes a methodology for assessing security infrastructure effectiveness utilizing formal mathematical models. A novel security assurance measure that governments and corporations can use to assess the strength and readiness of their security infrastructure as a whole is described. This methodology can also be used as a before and after measure in a security services engagement to quantify infrastructure improvement and serve as a basis for continuous security assurance.

The major benefits of the autocorrelation methodology include:

- The application of a formal mathematical tool to describe an important security process, the daily total time to resolve security incidents, to quantify improvements in the security infrastructure.
- The global focus of the methodology to describe the strength and effectiveness of security infrastructures as a whole.
- The methodology can be used as a basis for decision-making:
  - If, for example, 'application vulnerability' incidents have longer DTTRs on average it may make sense to implement new policy to address known vulnerabilities, or to change resource allocation.
  - If, for example, the DTTR over all incidents is on an increasing trend (longer than targets or the baseline),

organization's can analyze what has changed and take corrective actions before the infrastructure is compromised.

- o The DTTR average for all incident categories can be compared and used for prioritization of security resources.
- o Systemic issues can be rooted out by correlating across event categories to reveal relationships that may be related to the dynamics of organizational processes.

- The methodology's operational process is designed and implemented within a security program that enforces accuracy, repeatability, and increased measurement frequency. These important characteristics are achieved through automation and the use of well-defined mathematical formulas for lower-level events and for autocorrelation analysis.
- The autocorrelation methodology can help an organization define "normal" across any event category and quantify deviations from normal.
- Increased efficiency in the operation of the security program is achieved through centralized event management and better insight into how events relate to each other.
- Increased effectiveness in the operation of the security program is achieved by defining targets for DTTRs averages across any category of security event and tracking performance with respect to those targets.

This methodology helps address some of the problems in quantifying security assurance assessment and moves the field closer to becoming less of a "black art" and more a discipline based on scientific methods to secure our most valuable resources.

REFERENCES

Applied Computer Security Associates (2002). Workshop on Information Security System Scoring and Ranking. *Proceedings of the 2001 Workshop on Information-Security-System Rating and Ranking*, (pp. 1-70).

Box, G. E. P., & Jenkins, G. M. (1976). *Time Series Analysis forecasting and control*. San Francisco, CA: Holden-Day Inc.

Brenton, C., Bird, T., & Ranum, M. J. (2008). *Top 5 Essential Log Reports*. SANS Institute, Information Security Reading Room.

Chuvakin, A. (2008, June 17). *Six Pitfalls of Logging [Video file]*. Video posted to http://search-security.bitpipe.com/rlist/term/type/multimedia/Security-Event-Management.html

Garfinkel, S., Spafford, G., & Schwartz, A. (2003). *Practical Unix & Internet Security*. Sebastopol, CA: O'Reilly & Associates, Inc.

Jaquith, A. (2007). *Security Metrics: Replacing Fear, Uncertainty, and Doubt*. Upper Saddle River, NJ: Addison-Wesley.

Keller, P. A., & Pyzdek, T. (2005). *Six Sigma Demystified*. New York, NY: McGraw-Hill, Inc.

Lowans, P. (2002). *Implementing a Network Security Metrics Program* (GIAC Administrivia Version Number:2.0). SANS Institute, GIAC practical repository.

Luckham, D. (2002). *The Power of Events*. Addison-Wesley.

Mosteller, F., & Tukey, J. W. (1977). *Data Analysis and Regression: A Second Course in Statistics*. Menlo Park, CA: Addison-Wesley Publishing Company.

National Institute of Standards and Technology. (2003). *Security Metrics Guide for Information Technology Systems* (NIST Special Publication 800-55). Washington, DC: U.S. Government Printing Office.

National Institute of Standards and Technology. (2006). *Guide for Developing Performance Metrics for Information Security* (NIST Special Publication 800-80). Washington, DC: U.S. Government Printing Office.

National Institute of Standards and Technology. (2006). *Guide to Integrating Forensic Techniques into Incident Response* (NIST Special Publication 800-86). Washington, DC: U.S. Government Printing Office.

National Institute of Standards and Technology. (2006). *Information Security Handbook: A Guide for Managers* (NIST Special Publication 800-100). Washington, DC: U.S. Government Printing Office.

National Institute of Standards and Technology. (2007). *Recommended Security Controls for Federal Information Systems* (NIST Special Publication 800-53). Washington, DC: U.S. Government Printing Office.

Nichols, E., & Peterson, G. (2007). A Metrics Framework to Drive Application Security Improvement. *IEEE Security & Privacy*, 5(2), 88-91.

Payne, S. (2006). *A Guide to Security Metrics*. SANS Institute, Information Security Reading Room.

Pfleeger, C. P., & Pfleeger, S. L. (2006). *Security in Computing*. Upper Saddle River, NJ: Prentice Hall.

Richardson, R. (2007). CSI/FIB Computer Crime and Security Survey. *The 12th Annual Computer Crime and Security Survey* (Computer Security Institute).

Robert Frances Group (2004). Collecting Effective Security Metrics. *CSO*. Retrieved March 11, 2008, from http://www.csoonline.com/analyst/report2412.html.

Skroch, M., McHugh, J., & Williams, J. M. (2000). *Information Assurance Metrics: Prophecy, Process, or Pipedream*. Panel Workshop, National Information Systems Security Conference, Baltimore.

Theoharidou, M., & Gritazalis, D. (2007). Common Body of Knowledge for Information Security. *IEEE Security & Privacy*, 5(2), 6.

Chapter V
Security Implications for Management from the Onset of Information Terrorism

Ken Webb
Webb Knowledge Services, Australia

ABSTRACT

This chapter results from a qualitative research study finding that a heightened risk for management has emerged from a new security environment that is increasingly spawning asymmetric forms of Information Warfare. In particular, there is evidence that after recent terrorist events there has been a lift in security across the world and identification of terrorists now able to conduct Information Warfare. Also concerning is that, over the years, there have been many interpretations of what constitutes this threat. Therefore, after extensively reviewing literature mainly on Information Warfare and Terrorism, this chapter defines for readers what the threat of Information Terrorism is and the new dynamic security environment that it has created. Security implications for management have subsequently evolved, as they are now required to think about the philosophical considerations emerging from this increasing threat, and these are outlined and form the basis for future thinking.

INTRODUCTION

The objective of this chapter, so appropriate guidance for future thinking occurs, is to inform readers about Information Terrorism and the adjudged security implications for management from its onset. This occurs by:

1. Defining the Information Terrorism threat;
2. Describing the new security environment and the sub-environments forming it; and
3. Providing a high-level discussion from an information security perspective of the emergent philosophical considerations for management generally.

This is needed because a new set of security dynamics that influence the decision-making process faces society today. For example, at the strategic level, gone is the 20th Century security paradigm that helped form geographically based continental strategy. The traditional international system that links sovereignty to Westphalian-style territorial nation states is under pressure from the new age of globalisation and the 'information revolution' (Evans, 2003).

Some argue that the major strategic change required now is a transition away from a dominant state-centric structure towards that marked by a greater number of non-, sub- and trans-state actors. This influence has devolved down to all levels of society (Hall, 2003).

More specifically, Colarik (2006) confirms that being in this information-dependent age has increased the frequency and potential magnitude of Information Warfare. This is because parties that normally rely upon physical violence, irrespective of their disposition, are now more able to conduct information operations in a myriad of forms. The relative unknown knowledge of this aspect and current perpetrators, alongwith the complexity of information and communications in the global environment, provides a real problem for management.

Also worth considering is that many forms of critical infrastructure assets for society are now information dependent and non-physical. They are invisible to the untrained observer, or difficult to define or harness. Complicating this is that, due to their diversity and complexity, stakeholders throughout the world have not universally accepted a standard definition of critical information infrastructures, let alone standardising the protection of them. This has contributed to government authorities and academia making many attempts to define critical information infrastructures and introducing such issues as technology leadership, quality of service, network centric operations, privacy and other emerging considerations (Barker *et al*, 2006).

Furthermore, Barker *et al* (2006) explain that to date there are no consistent approaches to the forms of reporting and/or evaluation of critical information infrastructures. It means different things to different people, and this perspective issue is part of the described problem.

These observations imply that Information Warfare is now intangible by nature. It impedes the general ability for traditional parties to understand and manage it, as contemporary forces of influence not necessarily contingent on traditional thinking now exist. This means that a clearer understanding for management of the implications from this onset of Information Warfare and the conduct of it by terrorist groups, thus Information Terrorism, is required. Managers dealing with this need to now take a much more expansive and philosophical approach, as there is a range of new environments reflecting these dynamics that are contributing to a new security atmosphere.

Worth considering as part of the managerial approach for dealing with the new security environment, as it applies to Information Terrorism, are three relevant and deep philosophical considerations that congruously interrelate and influence each other. These, as explained later in the chapter, are:

- Change in the direction of thinking,
- Culture, and
- Group dynamics.

They have emerged from the changed Information Warfare environment and form the basis of the implications for management.

BACKGROUND

During the years 2003 to 2007, a doctoral research project conducted by the Author, which used Australia as the case study, investigated how to enhance national security from terrorist groups conducting Information Warfare. This project interviewed 48 academic and industry experts in the area of Information Warfare and Terrorism. Many were Australian but, due to the nature of the threat, a large number were from a variety of nations worldwide.

The findings from the research were considered valuable, as the participants were all generally knowledgeable people well familiar with and/or have a background in national – counter-terrorism, information, intelligence and/or security – operations. Importantly, they had/were/in:

- Researched and lived with current declared terrorist groups, such as Islamic fundamentalists currently involved with the 'Jihad';
- Responsible for designing military strategy and concepts for 'war on terror', and for information operations as it applies to national security;
- Responsible for managing national customs enforcement operations;
- The main national intelligence services and organisations, including Australia's foremost SIGINT collection agency and sub-elements;
- Australian Defence Department's strategic operations and policy divisions, including information strategy and management;
- Australian Defence Force, predominantly Army, responsible for its leadership, manning, communications, and subsidiary elements including NCW, CIS and EW;
- Australian Federal Police's counter-terrorist and high-tech crime elements;
- Heads of and operators for counter-terrorism and international affairs in government Foreign Affairs and Trade both in Australia and UK;
- National security advisors to parliament for terrorism, trans-national crime, international relations and counter-insurgency;
- Academics in information security, intelligence, strategy, international relations, terrorism and politically motivated violence;

- Military special operations headquarters and subsidiary units for counter-terrorism, including SAS, in Australia and the UK, and senior operators in unconventional, guerrilla and special warfare;
- Australia's Protective Security Coordination Centre;
- Audit operations for Australia's main social security agency and other government human services;
- Priest operating in the counter-terrorism area and has operated in countries currently harbouring the alleged major terrorist groups;
- Bureau chief for a national media organisation;
- Responsible for security and management of all the Australian Government's information, as part of the department responsible for communications and information technology;
- Responsible for implementing the Australian national information economy and use of information systems and networks by business for trade;
- Major telecommunication, technology and systems management providers, such as Telstra, Optus, Ericsson, IBM, Siebel and Lucent;
- International security and crisis management firms;
- Government law enforcement, technology, information security and emergency response organisations;
- Forensic psychologist for organised crime and intelligence gathering;
- Australian federal politician;
- Corporate, large, medium and small business people; and
- Basic members of society from various cultural backgrounds.

Figure 1 diagrammatically shows a summary of the interviewees and the authentication of their viewpoint related to their working situation at the time.

The underlying reason for choosing the interview sample was to ensure a complete, as possible, coverage of viewpoints was achieved considering the nature of the research study so strong results would evolve. Rather than just select a specific group of society and global position it was important to broadly cover the spectrum of relevant knowledge, but still with an emphasis on Australia, to ensure the widest amount of viewpoints was examined.

Most of those interviewed expressed that before the 'Information Revolution' Australia was in an advantageous position by being reasonably protected due to its geographical position and means of entry. However, via information networks and globalisation, the rest of the world is now closer. The economy has spread, territorial 'land' has no geographical boundaries anymore and terrorist activity has increased so defence is more than focussing on the continent itself. In effect, Australia's strategic depth has been eroded (Cobb, 2004).

It was found from discussions with the research participants that four dimensions of war – air, land, sea and the Infosphere – exist now. Information operations, which had traditionally been used to shape and influence a target audience in support of the first three dimensions, has lifted its impetus. Components of Information Warfare, such as cyber-warfare, are now getting greater attention.

Clarifying this are Bishop and Goldman (2003) who state:

What makes warfare in the information age a departure from the past is that information as warfare has become as important as information in warfare. Information is no longer just a means to boost the effectiveness of lethal technologies, but opens up the possibility of non-lethal attacks that can incapacitate, defeat, deter or coerce an adversary. (Bishop & Goldman 2003, p.1)

Along with this, a relative to Information Warfare in the domain of asymmetric warfare, being Terrorism, is dominating global security

Figure 1. Summary of interviewees background & viewpoints (Source – Personal)

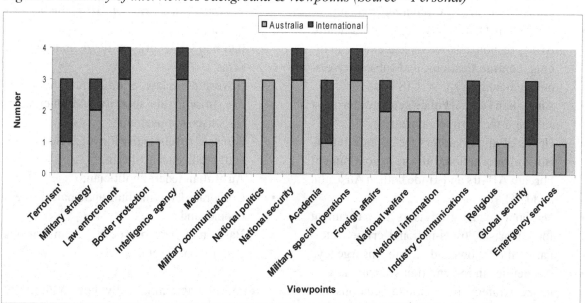

with mass violence by terrorist groups occurring frequently and randomly. Combine Information Warfare with Terrorism and the Infosphere gains greater scope.

Terrorists using information operations to achieve their aims are well served by the Information Revolution. Low entry costs, difficulties in identifying an attack and its origins (anonymity and ambiguity), and the potential for extreme chaos throughout governments, corporations and society in general, all offer rich opportunities to terrorists. They are also attracted to the fact that, in the context of information operations, conventional notions of deterrence are increasingly irrelevant, as counter-targeting becomes difficult when an assault is launched via a multitude of different jurisdictions (Cobb, 1998).

The 'unseen', as in the Infosphere, is a big threat but trying to convince the public of this is hard in the minds of most managers concerned with security.

In essence, due to its prompt evolution, this chapter contends that one is now unable to respond quickly to Information Terrorism. This thereby exacerbates the defensive mode from where it is hard to communicate worldwide and influence large geographical populaces. It highlights a completely new capability/advantage for groups considering the conduct of Information Terrorism and amplifies the dimensions of the security environment. The implications from this introduce a new level of considerations for management.

INFORMATION TERRORISM AND THE NEW SECURITY ENVIRONMENT

Defining Information Terrorism

After reviewing the literature, many interpretations of what constitutes Information Terrorism exist. However, before discussing the implications for management from it, this chapter first defines/clarifies exactly what the threat is and gives an overview of the new security environment caused by it.

Also, worth noting is that an effort has been made when defining it to reflect the various assertions by other authors supporting the scope of the threat. Nevertheless, it should be stated that this list is not exhaustive, and exacerbating it is that the topic of Information Terrorism is diverse and relatively new in its nature.

This has compelled the Author to compose a definition that maximises the possible coverage of all the relevant and salient points derived after reviewing the literature, and much of this is referenced later in this chapter. Based on this rationale, the interpreted conduct of *Information Terrorism* is:

A non-state actor's premeditated and asymmetrical warlike conduct of information activities to fulfil their ethos, foster mass acts of terror and/or affect and disrupt the security and/or well-being of a populace. This is done to:

- Appropriately effect and manage a change in a target audience's perception;
- Market philosophical propaganda so a target public's governance, livelihood and will is influenced through fear;
- Operate advantageously, efficiently, effectively and efficaciously; and
- Protect themselves from activities by allies, competitors and adversaries.

The aim of this definition is to ensure use of the right context when referring to the term. For example, Information Terrorism is not just Cyber-Terrorism, as it is a combination of those activities affecting the security of information generally. Additionally, readers should be cognisant that while a nation/state may sponsor terrorism they are not the actor. Rather, they sponsor actors.

Also, underlying the new situation and threat is that Information Terrorism is a relatively new phenomenon yet to be seen on a massive scale by a declared terrorist group. However, a recent example of Information Terrorism's potential effect, as reported by Davis (2007), is the Estonian event of 2007 where an organised wide-scale cyber attack using 'botnets' of a criminal or, some would argue, warlike nature caused all of Estonia's banks and newspapers to be shut down.

Irrespective of this commentary, Information Terrorism in the new security environment has provided a new dimension and understanding of Terrorism generally. It is further complicated by whether you use information operations or not to counter Terrorism. This threat highlights a dilemma facing not just management in this area but the world in general, and greater detail on the threat can be sourced in a paper by Webb (2007).

The New Security Environment

As stated earlier, the threat of Information Terrorism is contributing to the new security environment. As it relates to Terrorism and Information Warfare, this environment requires strategic review by management to consider its involvement in such and the environment/s that exist within it. This is important so an understanding of the dynamics occurs.

The Author has crafted **Figure 2** to reflect this comment and the following discussion provides the critique of literature explaining this.

As an overview, there are presently three primary global revolutions taking place that are impacting directly on how the world functions. Global society is constantly changing due to the Economic Revolution (Corporatisation), the Information Revolution and a Revolution in Military Affairs. This means the security environment has changed significantly in recent years with groups conducting Terrorism using each of the three revolutions to facilitate their cause (Boni & Kovacich, 2000).

An example of these changes, and their flow on effect to each other, is highlighted by Davis (1996, p.43) when he states:

The Information Revolution is setting in motion forces that challenge the design of many institutions. It disrupts the hierarchies around which modern institutions traditionally have been designed. It diffuses and redistributes power, often to the benefit of those that once may have been considered lesser actors. These changes will inevitably have a profound impact on the means and ends of armed conflict.

Evidence of this observation is made by McPhedran (2005, p.1), almost ten years after the aforementioned statements by Davis, when he noted that "terrorist activities were commonplace in 2003-2005 with attacks in a number of countries; including Indonesia, Saudi Arabia, Morocco, Turkey, the Philippines, Russia, Spain and the UK". This frequency and nature of attacks continues to happen, and demonstrates the global nature of the Terrorism threat and how societies with different positions on international issues have been targeted by terrorists. McPhedran surmises there are surely more attacks to come because asymmetric warfare, particularly in this form, has been around since the beginning of time. However, worth noting when considering the other comments made previously is that the new global environment also enhances the ability to conduct such.

Sub-Environment of Knowledge and Relationships

As it applies to almost every aspect of society, trust is a key element for consideration in the new security environment. Supporting this critique of the literature reviewed are Chatzkel (2002), Covey (1997) and Stewart (1997). They all assert that we are now in a situation where the knowledge of people must be more emphatically shared if relationships are to endure beyond a mere isolated dispute causing great disharmony. They explain that groups and their managers in society now seek a greater share of the knowledge available rather than operate in relative ignorance. This means acquiring more knowledge of others and, hence, the increase in emphasis on Information Warfare and the conduct of Information Terrorism.

Especially since the advent of the Internet, people now have more information available to them than before. They are able to compare one group's set of offerings to those of others (Pottruck & Pearce, 2000). For example, there is the increasing introduction of information sites such as FaceBook, Wikipedia, YouTube and blogs.

Information availability has enabled a shift in almost total power from the group traditionally in control, such as the government, to the people themselves having a greater involvement. This empowers non-state actors pursuing their causes, which means new strategies or those countering them to effectively manage their respective offering to an informed base of people are required (Buzan & Waever, 2003).

Enhancing their strength, groups conducting Terrorism have a 'key relationship' strategic phi-

losophy, which is bringing them to the forefront in global affairs. This strategy usually entails the highly knowledgeable people being allocated the bulk of the attention from the group. In these groups, the people maintaining relationships continually monitor the value of the knowledge being used in terms of stability and future opportunities, and this approach adopts a strengths theory perspective, thereby perplexing management (Buckingham & Clifton, 2001; Buckingham & Coffman, 1999; Howard & Sawyer, 2002).

This implies that it is this knowledge and relationships that are providing terrorist groups with the strength they previously did not have, and new groups with increased capabilities are now more openly pursuing their reason for existence. Bjorgo (2005) espouses this philosophy and claims it is in fact in pursuit of a combination of causes. Although, he says it is important to note that Terrorism is better understood when considering capabilities from a process of interaction between

Figure 2. Outline of the new security environment (source: Personal)

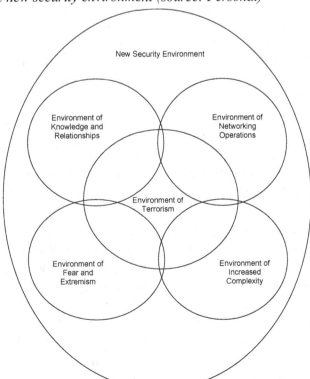

different parties for a relationship, thereby creating knowledge, rather than as a mechanical cause-and-effect relationship.

Sub-Environment of Terrorism

On the subject of what has caused the new security environment, Booth and Dunne (2002) assert that every existing cause has people who follow it. Otherwise, no underlying reason for it exists, as every cause has value and relies on the people pursuing it. Thus, it is said to have a reason to be supported.

Taipan and Tiger (2005) validate this by explaining that due to the direct correlation people have to a religion, ethnic, cultural, ideological and/or political cause, which is the alleged thrust behind terrorist activity; this type of reason is more understandable than direct financial or materialistic ones. However, they further explain that these reasons are gaining greater emphasis today and people opposed are taking exception to it by conducting hostile activities. This may account for the new genre of terrorist group or movement.

Taipan and Tiger further support this by claiming that leaders of the current main terrorist groups and/or movements have spawned and inspired a loose network of fanatical supporters and extremists, with links to groups such as 'Jihads' and with origins worldwide. Notably, they claim that the acquisition of such a large and well networked organisation, with an embedded common purpose, is a capability not previously seen to this extent.

Exacerbating the viewpoints expressed previously is that at present the main terrorist leaders have similar backgrounds in business to their targeted rivals. Examples given by Norton-Taylor (2005) of this are the current alleged leaders of major terrorist groups who have completed major academic accomplishments and sat on many company boards alongside senior people in the places they are targeting. Therefore, as Norton-

Taylor explains, they have a greater understanding and appreciation of their targets, and are also well resourced with millions of dollars deposited in concealed bank accounts at their disposal.

Another worthy observation is made by Buzan & Waever (2003, p.466) who argue that Terrorism now shares the transnational qualities of organised crime, as it has "network structures that penetrate through and around both structures and the patterns of regional and global security". This insinuates the new security environment is global and endearing.

Compounding this observation is Cobb (2004), who attests that terrorists can use Information Warfare, which is much different to the physical acts of terror, to cause a systematic failure that brings a major city to a standstill, invokes mass fear and saps resources for a response. The sophistication of thinking that those parties committing terrorism allegedly have now increased this capability also highlights the frightening aspect of this claim. Of further concern is that under current legislations they can do this so they are relatively immune from prosecution by civil authorities.

Sub-Environment of Fear and Extremism

Terrorism appears to be aimed at undermining the foundations of governments through fear. McPhedran (2005) explains that the 'propaganda of the deed', which is a phrase adopted by many anarchists, is being used to underpin terrorist activities. He claims that this shaping and influencing of the target audience, which is an aim of Information Warfare, is in effect symbolism because it marks the terrorist group as someone to be feared if their cause is not met. Carroll (2002, p.11) provides an example of this, being the terrorist group al-Qaeda, who, before its declared major attacks on the USA in 2001, distributed a video that was aired to the world declaring:

With small capabilities, and with our faith, we can defeat the greatest military power of modern times. America is much weaker than it appears.

Carroll espouses that this and consequent actions have created a whole new security environment in the Western world, which was the declared sought after objective of al-Qaeda. An example of this is outlined by Morgan (2001, p.7):

The US population is living in fear. Airplanes. Tall buildings. Anthrax. Smallpox rumors. Other populations know fear, of course. Terror is the norm for entire peoples trying to survive in acute poverty; or under military, theocratic, or totalitarian rule; or in refugee or displacement circumstances. But this is new to the US. The populace is exhibiting post traumatic stress syndrome. People are sleeping badly; they have nightmares, appetite loss, or irrational hunger; they experience sudden flashbacks, burst into tears for no immediate reason, sink into depression, can't seem to enjoy living, and – despite reassurances from authorities – keep obsessing about violence…We can no longer afford to ignore it, dismiss it, or deal with it piecemeal.

Irrespective whether this opinion is true or not, Rogers (2000, p.6) says that the new threat is inspired by an extreme and militant distortion of doctrine that opposes the values mainly of the West and modernity. He summarises this by stating:

There is an underlying assumption, bordering on an article of faith, that the normal and, indeed, only rational form of political and economic behaviour is the free-market economy overseen by Western democracies. Anything else is frankly irrational and potentially threatening to peace, stability and civilised values.

Rogers (2000) notes that this paradigm provides a possible oversight of the perceived values

being opposed by current terrorist groups. However, it shows little consideration to the security impact of environmental limitations and almost no concern about the widening socio-economic divisions.

The aforementioned comment shows that radical elements are renewing their ideology from extremist forces, and are now using Terrorism as an efficacious and devastating method in pursuit of their cause. This is causing a clash of ideologies and the world is now forced to relearn the ancient lessons of counter rebellion, insurgency and Terrorism. This is supported by Taipan and Tiger (2005, p.16) who cite:

The modern 'over-by-Christmas' impatience has become a feature of western 'have-it-now' political and economic psychology, and this ensures the pain is and will be enormous, as the primarily Christian West washes up in conflict against the almost immovable emotion of reactionary radical Islam.

Additionally, Cobb (2004) argues that the current security environment is not a clash of cultures, as many commentators attest. Rather, he infers it is a clash of ideologies with radical elements again out to challenge, dominate and overturn the Western ideology that is offensive to their fundamental tenets. The main terrorist groups are finding softer targets and their associates are targeting the home bases and populations of Westerners. Cobb further argues that the radical elements are also striving to impose their will against those they consider are apostate rulers in areas formally controlled by their ideological institutions.

Cobb claims this has been the 'propaganda of the deed', which is consistent with McPhedran's (2005) earlier assertion. An example given by Cobb is that when 7 to 12 year old children, who otherwise have little or no opportunity or secular education, are provided with a scapegoat for their fears via propaganda the long term security of the scapegoat is questionable and a few will turn to extremism. He further claims that this is the type of terror that the USA and those supporting its value-set face. He also affirms that the communities where terrorist groups originate from, who have adopted the alleged growing democratic freedoms being espoused by the majority, are included in the USA value-set category.

Sub-Environment of Networking

As explained earlier, current terrorist activity has resulted in a very network-centric and global approach with cells being embedded in the target audience. Laqueur (1999) asserts that this is different to the past though, as the general tendency among terrorists was to embrace centralisation and the leadership principle. He explains that while they have embraced the latter it is the former that has changed. The diversity of nationalities and the location of acts have shown that the threat of Terrorism has shifted from a single centralised body to multiple associated organisations inspired by a symbolic leader and others without necessarily waiting for orders. Rogers (2000) confirms that terrorist groups have become a well-networked movement rather than single group, and this brings a whole new dimension into the terrorist threat. It also fits with the philosophy that terrorist units should be small, because the bigger they are, the more open to infiltration they are.

Using this observation as a basis, and as confirmed by Taipan and Tiger (2005), it is concluded that the networked approach shows terrorists today have increased security from infiltration but also, by maintaining the leadership factor through a movement, have the resources and know-how to conduct major operations. Arquilla and Ronfeldt (2001) amplify this by explaining that the strongest networks will be those where the organisational design is sustained by a winning story and well-defined doctrine, and all this is layered atop advanced communications systems, resting on strong personal and social ties. Each level, and

the overall design, may benefit from redundancy and diversity. All of these characteristics are the hallmarks of present networked terrorist groups (Taipan & Tiger, 2005).

This approach and adoption of Information Warfare brings a range of problems for traditional agencies responsible for countering terrorism, as now there is a widening web of organisations operating in small cells independent of each other but with a common purpose and ability to collaborate through increased communications means. These movements are in a flat but identifiable network so it is clear they exist. However, espionage has traditionally been used to infiltrate them and obtain potentially vital information, and this is now being hindered by the unconventional structure of terrorist groups (Owen, 2002; Segell, 2005).

In addition, this *modus operandi* has been advanced by the Internet, which is one of the primary stimuli for the current transition into a globalised society. While the Internet is a networking creation of the developed world, it is also attractive to terrorists for some of the same reasons it is attractive to society generally. It may be used anonymously so identity is masked; it is global, which allows access to huge audiences around the world; and it is inexpensive and subject to little regulation. Therefore, the Internet **enables** the networked form of global terrorism and terrorist groups appear to be using it to their advantage (Deeks *et al*, 2005; Perl, 2008).

This means that terrorists in their current form are at an advantage, which is confirmed by Arquilla and Ronfeldt (in Clark, 2004, p.12) who contend that "Future conflicts will be fought more by networks than by hierarchies, and whoever masters the network form will gain major advantages".

This is amplified further by Arqilla and Ronfeldt (2001, p.29) who proclaimed several years ago that RAND research has shown that:

Middle East Arab terrorists are on the cutting edge of organizational networking and stand to gain significantly from the information revolution. They can harness information technology to enable less hierarchical more networked designs – enhancing their flexibility, responsiveness and resilience. In turn, information technology can enhance their offensive operational capabilities for the war of ideas as well as for the war of violent acts.

Generally, Truscott (2004) explains it can be difficult to assess intent and capability when terrorists function from cells and use a networked approach. One can look at their own assets and situation but terrorist groups are looking at them also. As this *modus operandi* transfers to other adversarial groups, then this highlights a dramatic consequence for management in the new security environment.

Sub-Environment of Increased Complexity

Consistent with the creation of this networking environment is the generally accepted complexity of society today. This has caused many enabling factors to facilitate terrorism, and the capabilities and myriad of terrorist groups amplifies this. However, deepening the problem are the following global problems from this complexity that are disabling the countering of terrorism:

- The absence of a universal definition of terrorism.
- Disagreement as to the root cause/s of terrorism.
- Religionisation of politics.
- Exploitation of the media.
- Double standards of morality.
- Loss of resolve by governments of all persuasions.
- Weak punishment of terrorists.
- Violation of international law, and promotion of, terrorism by some nations.
- High cost of security in democracies. (Carroll, 2002; Alexander & Alexander, 2003)

The number and nature of these problems provides some scope on the complexity of countering terrorism in the new security environment. Particularly, as it applies to Information Terrorism.

No specific solution is found while reviewing literature but, as Deeks *et al* (2005) attest, a common observation is that the present forms of counter terrorism tend to be reactive, which is a quality shared with civilian law enforcement. The current approach is concerned more with activity threatening social order, which means all actions to counter terrorism are a response to activities or events planned by others. This implies that the approach is reactive and not proactive.

As Alexander and Alexander (2003) claim, if there is enough political will and international cooperation then the problems for countering terrorism could be solved. However, they elaborate that this is unlikely unless the terrorism threat moves onto a greater platform globally due to the complexity of the world today. This increases the current adverse dimensions of national security.

McPhedran (2005) expands on this by explaining that the consistent use of aggressive measures to combat terrorism, which are justifiable and legal to most, is the current *modus operandi*. Frequently, these measures also successfully fulfil a number of important, albeit usually short term, objectives. However, despite this, McPhedran notes that defeating or diminishing the threat of terrorism in the long term is not something that such measures are proficient at doing, as the world is now more complex than ever before. Information Terrorism exacerbates it.

MANAGEMENT IMPLICATIONS FROM INFORMATION TERRORISM

It is clear that key managers are pivotal to the outcome of any enhancement to security. Particularly, in the new security environment described previously. They are the incumbent primary decision-makers who, apart from managing the operational system, are the ones who recruit people. From this point, security improves because people start to have ideas, develop processes, and build knowledge. This allows them to have the necessary understanding and opportunity for operating better.

This concept may help determine whether confidence in the future security outcome in the new dynamic environment exists. Particularly, as various internal and external forces of influence play their role in how leaders and managers shape the direction of their respective element involved with security. This occurs in the way they undertake decisions, form policies, and have those policies and instructions executed.

Complicating the aforementioned thinking is that security operates in a cyclical not linear manner (Rogers, 2000). It means that whatever takes place in terms of security from Information Warfare contributes to another cycle or ongoing cycles indefinitely, which then influences different decisions and actions as the learning emerges.

The aforementioned observations from the onset of Information Terrorism have led to the examination of philosophical considerations that influence the thinking process, such as the new direction in thinking and group dynamics. This is so an understanding of how groups may approach the management of security from Information Warfare transpires.

The underlying premise of this logic is that, in this instance, it includes groups on both sides of the conflict and of whatever disposition. This is because people make the greatest difference to the value of groups, and this is an area requiring consideration when determining, enacting and managing any necessary change.

Amplifying this is that culture, which is a major dynamic in globalisation, appears to exert significant influence over a group and its people. It embraces shared core values, thereby ensuring everyone clearly understands values. It helps those leading and managing to appreciate the extremes of acceptance or resistance to change.

A supposition from these considerations is that countering Information Warfare can possibly guide the future shaping of security management generally. For instance, every time a threat is exposed the receiver applies information in a variety of forms, and the way it does this controls the level of threat.

Supporting this assertion is the fact that there are potentially endless opportunities, in a variety of ways, to apply this information for enhanced success. These opportunities present themselves to management for consideration of information security threats and operating generally but a form of common alignment is required. The supply of a sound management way of thinking can possibly meet this requirement.

Confirming the effect of and need for this requirement is that management must continually come up with new ways to facilitate the information security process. Many elements invest heavily into refining knowledge management systems applicable to security, plus also combining intelligent agents that efficiently target information that is more specific.

Despite this positive effort, management in this new security environment must also keep up to date with the latest developments in the event that it may lead to a new competitive advantage over any actual or potential adversary. This means the dilemma is determining what manner to use for deploying relevant knowledge of information security threats throughout, and to leverage from it to create the balance required for a desired state of harmony, progress and prosperity. This means determining the best way to conduct information operations.

Making this comment more significant is that the ability to review knowledge on information security is crucial. It means that creating and leveraging knowledge is useful only if it confidently improves performance in the specific area in an efficacious way. Success not only depends on the information that one possesses but, rather, how effectively and efficiently this information transforms into relevant, timely and accurate operations; and this supports why a new management way of thinking may be required.

Also, due to the power of knowledge/information in possession of people now and the aforementioned notions, the way that information is used severely affects a group's success. This threatens the traditional models of control and leadership pertaining to management. It infers that the two important factors for value and success in this area are the:

1. Creation of a culture, and
2. Attention to strategy.

This introduces the need for discovery of theory related to cultural and sociological balance, as management now needs to better understand what it takes to build relationships, nurture them and yield positive results. This means the development of a more coherent scheme for analysing social theory may be required.

An examination of communication theory also appears necessary, as communication is one of the most complex and strategic activities of human beings. It may have limited effectiveness through a lack of congruence between the reader and sender, and the acts of formulating and absorbing communications are privately costly (Dewatripont & Tirole, 2005). Any new direction in thinking needs consideration in respect to the sender and receiver's motivations, and abilities to determine the communication mode and transfer of knowledge.

This comment is a worthwhile consideration in society today, as it relates to influence and persuasion, or the power of information. Ergo, it is about controlling the battle for 'hearts and minds', which many (for example, Waltz 1998) claim is a major objective of Information Warfare.

This background means the future creation of more extensive management theory for security from Information Warfare is a priority, as complicating the adoption of any purposeful system

in this regard is the over abundant supply of information. Now posed is the dilemma of sorting and finding the most relevant information, which 'strikes at the heart' of management prowess.

The result from the aforementioned discussion of the implications for management is that the prudent use of information in this 'day and age' is evermore so critical. Particularly, as the adequate presentation of every message must be attractive to the receiver to invoke an appropriate response. As presented earlier, this also happens to be the ultimate aim of any terrorist act.

This comment provides the background behind the basis for countering and conducting Information Terrorism, which has led to the emergence of three philosophical considerations for management in this regard.

Change in the Direction of Thinking

Relevant to and expanding on this overview is a deeper discussion on the change in the direction of thinking, which is one of the emerging philosophical considerations behind the implications to management. Particularly, as it relates to the theory behind the premised problem regarding the onset of Information Terrorism.

As a precursor, Wheatley (1992) argues that scientists have historically tried to apply Newtonian mechanistic principles to analyse human behaviour, under a common belief there exists measurable criteria to teach people how to become better leaders or achieve better performance. However, a major shift in thinking occurred with the discovery of quantum physics where, for example, results from nuclear science experiments started to deviate from previously understood laws of physics and mathematics. Despite this change, groups today still spend an enormous amount of time putting in place various types of controls in the quest to extract creativity - only to find it impedes human potential and the group as a whole adopts a resistance to change (Moser-Wellman, 2001; Rogers, 1995).

Zohar (1997) likens organisations and society to the human brain in that they have the potential for self-organising creativity just waiting to be unleashed within them. He contends that science has provided many of the answers to the world's problems over the years and has made a significant contribution to our present day education systems. Despite this, he asserts that science has now undergone its own metamorphosis since the discovery of the quantum world, and this intimates that a challenge has evolved to not just scientists but every aspect of life itself. Also, it may possibly explain the evolution of Information Warfare.

Confirming this supposition is the fact that the direction of science in recent times has been to move away from absolute truth and absolute perspective toward contextualism (Capra, 1997; Zohar, 1997). Also, the abandonment of the old desire for objective uncertainty has occurred in favour of more the acceptances of ambiguity and complexity (Capra, 1983). This means that, from an information security management perspective, it is interesting to examine the impact that this change in the direction of thinking has had on society. Such direction appears to have offered new means to rethink the structure and leadership of groups, which may also apply to the organisational dynamics of major threats to information security today.

Zohar (1997) further asserts that organisations need to understand that people must appreciate the underlying meanings of things. If they satisfy the meaning (values) then they are more likely to exploit the latent potential that is dormant until the need arises, and this is something that applies across all segments of society. Furthermore, Bohm and Peat (1987) attest that management thinking is about looking at the need of the entire group in context with members' need for personal satisfaction and sense of purpose. A deep-rooted vision encapsulates the purpose whereby shared core values are registered. Zohar (1990) argues repeatedly that creative thinking emerges from a spiritual level (a sense of identity or goals). These comments appear to provide some insight into the religious and ideological aspects of the major terrorist threats today.

In the Newtonian style group (one that employed the scientific management theory of Taylor, 1929) leaders and managers did the thinking, and those below them did the work. Now, in quantum thinking, everyone is a critical participant by having the capacity to be creative (Buckingham & Clifton, 2001). If this is the case, another deliberation for a change in the direction of thinking is that everyone has the ability to invent things when it suits.

An observation of Hamel and Prahalad (1994) may also indicate part of the problem behind the increased onset of Information Warfare, which is a worthy consideration for countering it. They contend that, around the Western capitalistic world, money now forms the basis for measurement of value and success. What started out as the medium of common exchange usurps fundamental values. Their observation bases itself around the corporatisation of the world by profit-biased companies dominating those interested in expressing soft and often moral practices and values, and hence the effect of globalisation towards security.

Another observation from the new direction in thinking and corporatisation of the world is that advertising and marketing companies are growing in numbers (Brown & Bright, 1995). They are utilising the skills of their creative designers to dominate their observer audiences with anticipated subliminal reactions (Kotler *et al*, 1994; Kotler, 1999). This is interesting, as the aim is to motivate people to conduct activities that others would not reasonably feel feasible and/or desirable, which is further something to consider when examining the *modus operandi* of groups conducting Information Warfare.

Gray (1999) explains that major adversarial groups today, irrespective of their disposition, now have creative designers similar to advertising and marketing personnel of the Western world. They seek an artistic effect on a target audience, in the same form as artists, to achieve the sought after demand and even to prompt operatives within them to conduct criminal or warlike acts.

In essence, this and the other observations outlined previously confirm that the increased onset of Information Warfare has resulted in a new direction in thinking amongst potential adversaries and within themselves. It appears to be thinking that has evolved from scientific discovery, which relates the nature of strategy to the character of artistic application and to the relatively unknown context of the 21st century. It displays a change in the direction of thinking for information security management today and is a deep philosophical consideration.

Culture

It is necessary to explain culture in a context that allows its understanding because it appears to be one of the primary dynamics of globalisation and the Information Revolution. This is because culture is an important ingredient to any group because groups by nature are comprised of individuals (Pottruck & Pearce, 2000).

Group members use culture to achieve positive results for themselves and the group, as the inherent values form the basis of meaning (Stewart, 1997; Trompenaars & Hampden-Turner, 1998). This means that culture moulds shared core values into a group context, which creates orderliness and a guiding set of principles for all members (Whiteley, 1995). It binds the history, traditions and beliefs of its people into an overall forward direction for the group, as well as special significance for each person. Despite the group suffering constant change, an embedded and effective culture offers stability for stakeholders in terms of a sense of belonging to a group (Covey, 1997).

Trompenaars and Hampden-Turner (1998) assert that culture provides the basis for engaging new members, and assists existing members to focus on the direction of the group and endorse the values. It is the binding glue of members and

effective if all stakeholders can import the values. Trompenaars and Hampden-Turner also attest that a successful culture will provide a strong sense of desire of belonging to the group. Due to its significant influence over the group and its target audience, evident is the relative importance of culture to any group at conflict with another in today's increasingly competitive environment.

Pottruck and Pearce (2000) say culture, although not conventionally measured, has an effect on performance. They further explain that culture is shaped at the upper end by the leaders and managers who not only espouse the dreams of the group, but act or conduct themselves in a manner supportive of the culture. In other words, this means that unless leaders and managers commit to the culture there is not likely to be support from those following them. Based on this philosophy, leaders and managers must constantly create an atmosphere that induces positive change through reinforcement of the group culture.

Sustaining culture means turning abstract values into something much more tangible and visible as a reality, and Stern (2003) intimates this as a basic philosophy for groups threatening society in this new security environment. Equally important is that it becomes a deep philosophical consideration for generally countering and conducting Information Warfare, as it has become an implication for society from the increased onset of Information Terrorism and dependence on information itself for existence.

Group Dynamics

Given the noticeable effect of the way that adversarial groups operate to conduct Information Warfare in the new security environment, as explained earlier, it is apt to discuss group dynamics as one of the implications for management.

Arquilla and Ronfeldt (2001) explain the potential effectiveness to groups of the networked design compared to traditional hierarchical designs, which attracted the attention of management theorists as early as the 1960s. They claim that heralded today, as effective alternatives to traditional bureaucracies, are virtual or networked groups; due to their inherent flexibility, adaptability and ability to capitalise on the talents of all their members. This intimates the advantage that groups operating in a networked, unconventional and non-traditional way now possess. It also highlights the security dilemma facing society today.

Furthermore, Arquilla and Ronfeldt attest that there is no standard methodology for analysing networked forms of organisations. This means having to determine what holds a network together and what makes it function effectively. To address this, they propose a methodology where design and performance happens across five levels of analysis, which are also levels of practice, being:

- **Organisational level:** Its organisational design;
- **Narrative level:** The story being told;
- **Doctrinal level:** The collaborative strategies and methods;
- **Technological level:** The information systems; and
- **Social level:** The personal ties that assure loyalty and trust.

This alternative approach appears to threaten most of the traditional models that have existed to date, as it would be hard to discover the intricacies at each level and a new style of doing things as a group emerges. In addition, it appears consistent with the change of direction in thinking also discussed previously in this chapter.

It also confirms that this new form of group dynamics has created uncertainty that is contradictory and foreign to modern management philosophies and teachings. This is because, as Hirst (2001) explains, it provides difficulty for formal strategic planning and the provision of rigid guidelines for groups such as the military, which are very prescriptive for consistent repli-

cability. This appears to work to the advantage of different and major adversarial security threat parties, such as terrorist groups.

Placing this line of thought in the context of Information Warfare is Quinn (1992). He says that new information capabilities are emerging so quickly that they are redefining societies, management and governance processes. Complicating this is that binding societies together, both internally and externally, is an intricate web of relationships linked by information (Quinn *et al*, 1998). A further dimension is the emergence of speed and knowledge as a key group dynamic for success, which means embedded knowledge now drives the creation and delivery of management success (Davenport & Prusak 1998; Fine, 1998; Nonaka 1998; Nonaka & Takeuchi 1995).

The aforementioned observations confirm that group dynamics have changed to reflect the nature of groups, such as terrorist groups, operating in an information-based and networked fashion. This deep philosophical consideration further supports the implication to management from the onset of Information Warfare.

FUTURE TRENDS

The research forming the basis for this chapter showed that it is mandatory to enhance security from Information Warfare by terrorist groups and that nations have the capacity to produce a purposeful system to do this. Immediacy and trust were the two paramount factors given and, in regards to the former, it is not whether the required system can be produced but more it is needed straight away.

The other key factor to consider is TRUST; and all research participants expressed more must be done to endear and seal it. This includes reducing the amount of open source information, which is readily accessible to adversaries, to provide a dedicated system sufficiently liquid to change. It also means greater authority and benchmarks, and control of the Internet, which is similar to the media by distributing large amounts of perceptual rather than factual information.

Everyone accepts the 'big picture' outcome of peace, harmony and a high standard of living. However, apart from this, desired is the existence of a much better and smarter information security system that is overwhelmingly successful and managed at all levels. A system where critical information is secure and adversaries cannot use information operations against their targets. This can be translated to a requisite management consideration at all levels of society.

Therefore, it is a robust and safe system, which stops things happening and preservation is paramount. It is fluid because things constantly change, and everything and everywhere is different. Constant situational awareness happens.

Furthermore, some want a system that simplifies the current complex, multi and independent agency approach to the problem, and is orchestrated in the quickest and easiest way. It coordinates and brings together the culture, politics and advantages of each body, with direction and leadership at the highest level. It provides superiority over any 'foe' with an offensive rather than reactive/defensive strategy, which is a critical management consideration to better protect oneself.

Many also believe mutual agreement on items, such as what is the 'war on terror', who is the leader/lead agency and the construction of a purposeful system is required. This is because it removes many constraints and, psychologically, provides the necessary incentive for success.

Other desired outcomes include a greater understanding of the threat fraternity and maintenance of a nation's well-respected reputation. The latter is important because many see a nation's role to be 'neutral' and maintaining, as this allows it to play the 'honest broker' role in any conflict. It allows the country to sit well internationally, which should be a future positive trend/consideration for the management of any organisation in today's new security environment.

However, it is commonly acknowledged that these desired future trends cannot be achieved entirely because the Information Warfare threat cannot be totally removed. However, it is recognised it can be diminished to the point of reasonable safety. Irrespective, everyone considers maintenance of a better situation and enhanced reputation is paramount.

It is also worth noting that, although the future trends identified in the research study used as the basis of this chapter are targeted toward Australia, these trends could possibly be applied across the industrialised world where terrorism is a real threat.

CONCLUSION

This chapter highlights that Information Terrorism in the new security environment has provided a new dimension with implications for management, and this situation complicates overcoming the obstacles facing society to counter this threat. This chapter also implies that the threat of Information Terrorism is relatively new and its impending future use is frightening. Despite whether Information Warfare is used or not to solve this problem, it highlights a dilemma facing the world and organisations generally.

A plethora of commentators reviewed in the literature, many of which are given in this chapter, espouse a whole range of solutions to intervene and counter this threat. However, this observation intimates the complexity and nature of the overall problem of Information Terrorism, which is a major determinant for the new security environment.

Despite this, it is noticeable that a large number of authors argue that, irrespective of what viewpoint they hold, solutions such as a humanitarian convention need to be considered. This infers a preference to just plain aggression and force, which many authors contend is the current approach. It also suggests that, due to the information capacity of the world today, Information Warfare itself be employed to counter Information Terrorism, as it not only addresses the threat holistically but can be done immediately and expediently considering the capacity of those countering and protecting from terrorist acts.

However, both Buzan *et al* (1998) and Rogers (2000) explain that there are two main obstacles to this challenge. The first, and by far the most substantial in their eyes, is that the necessary response will involve considerable limits being placed on wealth and power of the elite global minority, thereby requiring radical economic and political changes that are substantially greater than anything previously experienced. The second is that most thinking and writing on security is deeply ethnocentric and conservative. They imply that, 'unfortunately', management theory today relies heavily on these factors for its basis.

Furthermore, the philosophical considerations given in this chapter; namely a change in the direction of thinking, culture and groups dynamics; provide a basis for the implications to management from the increased onset of Information Warfare. In effect, information now more-so exists at all levels and in a constantly changing global security environment - academia, industry and governments around the world share one fundamental belief - that 'information is power'. This is because there has become an exponential dependence on information to operate and exist successfully.

However, influencing this change is the fact that the culture of a group influences the way information is 'used or abused', and the increased reliance by people on culture from globalisation and the Information Revolution amplifies the effect. Furthermore, it results in a change in the direction of thinking and the way groups operate dynamically.

There is also a strong argument from previous studies (for example, Baird & Henderson, 2001) that it is knowledge not just information that is the

power. However, as shown by the philosophical considerations given in this chapter, the overall major implication for management is that the acquisition of knowledge alone does not constitute power (that is, influence and control), as power also requires the processing of that knowledge by the people. It may also indicate why there has been an increased conduct and countering of Information Warfare generally.

This series of implications pertaining to Information Terrorism deduces that power actually comes from rationally managing the various forms of applicable information that provide knowledge. It comes from *'knowing why, who, what and how'* in an aligned and/or systematic form. It intimates that a more meaningful way of management thinking is required in this new security environment.

REFERENCES

Alexander, D. C., & Alexander, Y. (2003). *Terrorism and Business: The Impact of 11 September 2001*. New York: Transnational.

Arquilla, J., & Ronfeldt, D. (2001). *Networks and Netwars: The Future of Terror, Crime, and Militancy*. Santa Monica: RAND.

Baird, L., & Henderson, J. C. (2001). *The Knowledge Engine, How to Create Fast Cycles of Knowledge-to-Performance and Performance-to-Knowledge*. San Francisco: Berrett-Koehler Publishers, Inc.

Barker, G., Bevis, A., Henderson, G., & McAllister, I. (2006). Where is the Government taking Australia on Counter-Terrorism? *Summit Plenary. 5th Homeland Security Summit 2006*. 7-8.

Bishop, M., & Goldman, E. O. (2003). The Strategy and Tactics of Information Warfare. *Contemporary Security Policy, 24*(1), 113-139.

Bjorgo, T. (ed.) (2005). *Root causes of terrorism: myths, reality, and the ways forward.* Oxon: Routlege.

Bohm, D., & Peat, F. D. (1987). *Science, order and creativity.* New York: Bantam Books.

Boni, W., & Kovacich, G. L. (2000). *Netspionage: The Global Threat to Information.* Boston: Butterworth-Heinemann.

Booth, K., & Dunne, T. (2002). *Worlds in Collision. Terror and the Future of Global Order.* Hampshire: Palgrave Macmillan.

Brown, C., & Bright, D. (1995). *Quality of Life: A powerful yet simple approach for everyone to achieve an enriched, balanced and fulfilled life.* Perth: self published.

Buckingham, M., & Coffman, C. (1999). *First, Break all the Rules, What the World's Greatest Managers Do Differently.* London: Simon & Schuster.

Buckingham, M., & Clifton, D. (2001). *Now, Discover Your Strengths.* New York: The Free Press.

Buzan, B., & Waever, O. (2003). *Regions and Powers. The Structure of International Security.* Cambridge: Cambridge University Press.

Buzan, B., Waever, O., & de Wilde, J. (1998). *Security: a new framework for analysis.* Boulder, Colorado: Lynne Rienner Publishers.

Capra, F. (1983). *The Turning Point: Science, Society and the Rising Culture.* New York: Bantam Books.

Capra, F. (1997). *The Web of Life, A New Synthesis of Mind and Matter.* London: Harper Collins.

Carroll, J. (2002). *Terror: a meditation on the meaning of September 11.* Victoria, Australia: Scribe Publications.

Chatzkel, J. (2002). *Intellectual Capital.* Oxford: Capstone Publishing.

Clark, R. M. (2004). *Intelligence analysis: a target-centric approach.* Washington DC: CQPress.

Cobb, A. (1998). *Thinking about the Unthinkable: Australian Vulnerabilities to High-Tech Risks. Research Paper 18 1997-98.* Canberra: Parliament of Australia.

Cobb, A. (2004). *Counter Terrorism in Australia.* 2004 International Counter Terrorism Conference. Zurich: 1-8.

Colarik, A. M. (2006). *Cyber Terrorism: Political and Economic Implications*, London: Idea Group.

Covey, S. (1997). *Putting principles first" in Rethinking the Future.* London: Nicholas Brealey.

Davenport, T. H., & Prusak, L. (1998). *Working Knowledge, How Organizations Manage What They Know.* Boston: Harvard Business Press.

Davis, J. (2007). Hackers Take Down the Most Wired Country in Europe. *Wired Magazine* 15.09. [On line] Available: http://www.wired.com/wired/issue/15-09 .

Davis, N. (1996). An Information-Based Revolution in Military Affairs. *Strategic Review, 24*(1), 43-53.

Deeks, A. S., Berman, B., Brenner, S. W., & Lewis, J. A. (2005). Combating Terrorist Uses of the Internet. *American Society of International Law. Proceedings of the Annual General Meeting 2005* (pp. 103-115).

Dewatripont, M., & Tirole, J. (2005). Modes of Communication. *The Journal of Political Economy, 113*(6).

Evans, M. (2003). From Kadesh to Kandahar: Military Theory and the Future of War. *Naval War College Review, XVI*(3), 132-150.

Fine, C. (1998). *Clockspeed.* Boston: Perseus Books.

Gray, C. S. (1999). *Modern Strategy.* Oxford: Oxford University Press.

Hall, W. M. (2003). *Stray Voltage: War in the Information Age.* Annapolis MD: Naval Institute Press.

Hamel, G., & Prahalad, C.K. (1994). *Competing for the future.* Boston: Harvard Business School Press.

Hirst, P. (2001). *War and Power in the 21st Century. The State, Military Conflict and the International System.* Cambridge: Polity Press.

Howard, R. D., & Sawyer, R. L. (2004). *Terrorism and Counterterrorism – Understanding the New Security Environment.* Connecticut: McGraw-Hill.

Kotler, P., Chandler, P.,C., Brown, L., & Adam, S. (1994). *Marketing, Australia and New Zealand,* 3rd ed. Sydney: Prentice Hall.

Kotler, P. (1999). *Kotler on Marketing: How to create, win and dominate markets. New York:* The Free Press.

Laqueur, W. (1999). *The New Terrorism: Fanaticism and the Arms of Mass Destruction.* London: Phoenix Press.

McPhedran, I. (2005). *Per. Comm.* Canberra, Australia, 19 September 2005.

Morgan, R. (2001). *The Demon Lover – The Roots of Terrorism.* New York: Washington Square Press.

Moser-Wellman, A. (2001). *The Five Faces of Genius.* New York: Penguin Putnam.

Nonaka, I. (1998). The Knowledge-Creating Company, in *Harvard Business Review on Knowledge Management* (pp. 21-45). Boston: Harvard Business School Press.

Nonaka, I., & Takeuchi, H. (1995). *The Knowledge-Creating Company.* New York: Oxford University Press.

Norton-Taylor, R. (2005). *Asymmetric Warfare.* London: The Guardian.

Owen, D. (2002). *Hidden Secrets: A complete history of espionage and the technology used to support it.* London: Quintet Publishing.

Perl, R. F. (2008). *Terrorist Use of the Internet: Threat, Issues, and Options for International Cooperation.* Presentation by the OSCE at the Second International Forum on Information Security on 7-10 April 2008 at Garmisch-Partenkirchen, Germany.

Pottruck, D. S., & Pearce, T. (2000). *Clicks and Mortar, Passion-Driven Growth in an Internet World.* San Francisco: Jossey-Bass.

Quinn, J. B. (1992). *Intelligent Enterprise.* New York: Free Press.

Quinn, J. B., Anderson, P., & Finkelstein, S. (1998). Managing Professional Intellect: Making the Most of the Best. *Harvard Business Review on Knowledge Management* (pp. 181-205). Boston: Harvard Business School Press.

Rogers, E. M. (1995). *Diffusion of Innovations,* 4th ed. New York: The Free Press.

Rogers, P. (2000). *Losing Control. Global Security in the 21st Century.* London: Pluto Press.

Segell, G.M. (2005). Intelligence Methodologies Applicable to the Madrid Train Bombings, 2004. *International Journal of Intelligence and CounterIntelligence, 18,* 221-238.

Stern, J. (2003). *Terror in the name of God: why religious militants kill.* New York: Harper Collins.

Stewart, T. A. (1997). *Intellectual Capital, The New Wealth of Organizations.* London: Nicholas Brealey.

Taipan & Tiger (2005). In the shadow of the swords. *Rendezvous – Journal of the Australian Special Air Service Association, 30,* 14-16.

Taylor, F. W. (1929). *Principles of Scientific Management.* New York: Harper & Row.

Trompenaars, F., & Hampden-Turner, C. (1998). *Riding the Waves of Culture, Understanding Diversity in Global Business.* New York: McGraw-Hill.

Truscott, J. (2004). *Beyond bin Laden Thinking – The Security Dividend.* 2004 Australian Homeland Security Conference in Sydney: 1-8.

Waltz, E. (1998). *Information Warfare: Principles and Operations.* Norwood: Artech House.

Webb, K. G. (2007). *Information Terrorism in the New Security Environment.* Paper presented at the 2nd International Conference on I-War and Security on 4-5 March 2007 at the Naval Postgraduate School, Monterey California, USA.

Webb, K. G. (2007a). *Managing Asymmetric Threats to National Security – Terrorist Information Operations.* Unpublished Interdisciplinary Doctoral Dissertation, Perth, Western Australia: Edith Cowan University.

Wheatley, M. J. (1992). *Leadership and the New Science, Learning about Organization from an Orderly Universe.* San Fransisco: Berrett-Koehler.

Whiteley, A. (1995). *Managing Change, A Core Values Approach.* South Melbourne: MacMillan Education.

Zohar, D. (1990). *The Quantum Self, Human Nature and Consciousness Defined by the New Physics.* New York: William Morrow & Co.

Zohar, D. (1997). *Rewiring the Corporate Brain, Using the New Science to Rethink How We Structure and Lead Organizations.* San Francisco: Berrett-Koehler.

Section II
Organizational and Human Security

Chapter VI
The Adoption of Information Security Management Standards:
A Literature Review

Yves Barlette
GSCM-Montpellier Business School, France

Vladislav V. Fomin
Vytautas Magnus University, Lithuania

ABSTRACT

This chapter introduces major information security management methods and standards, and particularly ISO/IEC 27001 and 27002 standards. A literature review was conducted in order to understand the reasons for the low level of adoption of information security standards by companies, and to identify the drivers and the success factors in implementation of these standards. Based on the findings of the literature review, we provide recommendations on how to successfully implement and stimulate diffusion of information security standards in the dynamic business market environment, where companies vary in their size and organizational culture. The chapter concludes with an identification of future trends and areas for further research.

INTRODUCTION

In service-oriented, highly industrialized countries, information itself is both a raw material and a product (Castells, 1996). The critical economic role of information and information processing on a firm's productivity may be more important than that from operational efficiency or product innovation (Steinmueller, 2005).

The relevance of information assets to businesses and governments alike can be measured by, for example, the percentage of contributions to gross domestic product (GDP) stemming from information-related processes and services (OECD, 2005). Another argument for the importance of information assets is to see them as *"the 'life-blood' of all businesses"* (Humphreys, 2005, p.15) losing which may bring the business to a dead halt. Louderback (1995) reported in 1995 that one-half of the companies that lose business critical systems for more than 10 days never recover and go out of business. This is increasingly true as companies rely more on their information systems (Kankanhalli et al., 2003). Between 1997 and 2001, U.S. organizations spent $2.5 trillion on information technology, nearly double the amount than the previous five years (Temkin, 2002; Fomin et al., 2005). Informational processes effectively become so critical that private and public institutions alike need to take an active role in ensuring the security of this critical asset (Fomin et al., 2008; GAO, 2004). In order to achieve this task, however, many issues have to be addressed.

With the growing level of interconnectivity between organizations (Barnard & von Solms, 1998), each company is taking its own measures for information security. This leads to the proliferation of different hardware-, software- and processes-based information security measures (von Solms, 1988). The poor security practices of one agent may threaten its partners in the global informational economy (Castells, 1996). This situation calls for a consistent approach to information security management at a company, inter-company, industry, and international levels. Not having proper information security measures in place can be detrimental to a business, while adopting methods for information protection can be a welcomed signal to the business partners that builds trusting relationships with customers, suppliers and stakeholders (Posthumus & von Solms, 2004). The task of adopting proper information security methods is a difficult one. Organizations need to address the task from legal, operational and compliance perspectives; the penalties for

failing to succeed are greater than ever (Myler & Broadbent, 2006).

Inadequate levels of security of information systems (IS) in organizations may result in more than monetary penalties to a company. Top management and board directors can become personally accountable for the security of their IS (OECD, 2004). The leading example is the Sarbanes-Oxley Act (2002) which makes corporate executives legally responsible for the validity of reported financial data and thus responsible for the security of their information systems (Hurley, 2003). Despite the criticality of information assets to business operations and the negative implications of poor security, previous research indicates that the level of information security awareness among many managers is low (Broderick, 2006; Knapp et al., 2006).

It is common for a manager of a contemporary organization to ask questions like these: How does my organization's IS become secure? What are the best practices for establishing IS security management? What is my organization's level of security? Which security level should be appropriate? How much money should I invest?

Information security standards could provide answers to many, if not all of these questions. Nevertheless, there are few research studies that examine the effectiveness of management strategies and tools for information security management (Hong et al., 2003). The suitability of available information security management standards for small and medium enterprises (SMEs) has already been questioned (Barlette & Fomin, 2008) although regardless of the size of a company, implementation of information security standards is not a straightforward process.

Responding to the call for rising awareness on the information security management issues (Barlette & Fomin, 2008; Knapp et al., 2006), in this paper we aim to 1) provide an overview of the major information security standards and discuss their adoption factors, 2) analyze the reasons for the low adoption level of information security standards by companies, and 3) examine various possibilities to foster information security standards adoption in the future.

This chapter is structured as follows. In the first section, we provide the definitions and an overview of information security management methods and standards. In the second section, we review the literature in order to identify the drivers and barriers for the adoption of information security standards by companies and the reasons for their low level of adoption. Then, we discuss various possibilities to foster the adoption of information security standards in the future. We end the paper by suggesting future trends and areas for further research, as well as provide advice to managers.

BACKGROUND

Definitions

Gaston (1996) defines an information security policy as: *"broad guiding statements of goals to be achieved; significantly they define and assign the responsibilities that various departments and individuals have in achieving policy goals"* (p.175). The aspect of responsibility in the definition of information security policy is very important. As Higgins (1999) notes, *"without a policy, security practices will be developed without clear demarcation of objectives and responsibilities"* (p. 217). The objective of an information security policy is *"to provide management direction and support for information security"* (BS 7799). These objectives are consistent with those advocated by many scholars. For example, the information security literature suggests that security policies should be developed from information security management system (ISMS) standards and guidelines (Gaskell, 2000; Janczewski, 2000).

Finally, objectives for companies to adopt an information security management standard vary.

These objectives have been summarized in OECD (2002, p.8) guidelines:

- Promote a culture of security among all participants as a means of protecting information systems and networks;
- Raise awareness about information systems risks; the policies, practices, measures and procedures available to address those risks; and the need for their adoption and implementation;
- Create a general framework in order to help people in charge of elaboration and implementation of coherent policies, practices, measures, and procedures, aiming to ensure information systems security;
- Promote cooperation and information sharing between organizations departments or units to elaborate and implement such security policies, practices, measures and procedures;
- Foster greater confidence among all participants in information systems and networks;
- Promote the consideration of security as an important objective among all participants involved in the development or implementation of standards.

Many methods and standards refer to - or are considered as a set of - "best practices": von Solms & von Solms define them as *"the most broadly effective and efficient means of organizing a system or performing a function"* (2006, p. 495).

In this chapter, we adopt the following definition of information security methods or standards as *"tools that enable to analyze, conceive, evaluate or control, together or separated, the security of information systems"* (DCSSI, 2007). For convenience, we will refer to both methods and standards as standards for the remaining of this paper.

An Overview of Information Security standards

The first attempts to publicize information security standards took place in the 1980's with the publishing of what was called orange and white books by TCSEC in the U.S. and ITSEC in Europe, respectively. After two decades, four waves of information security standards succeeded one another (von Solms, 2000; 2006). During the first wave, information security was treated as a technical issue. The second wave considered the managerial dimension. The third wave or "institutional wave", emphasized standardization, best practices, certification, and information security culture; this wave also addressed the need for measurement and monitoring of information security. The fourth wave embraced information security governance.

The evolution of information security standards through the four waves resulted in over a dozen standards with varying degrees of "representation" of each of the waves. Having analyzed five ISMS overview studies (see Table 1) as the departure point, we conducted a further literature search for the standards that were referred to by at least three of the five sources. We found that some standards offer only technical measures, while others provide comprehensive governance frameworks. In Table 1, we list the major standards that exist in the world today.

ENISA is the European Network and Information Security Agency, created in 2004. In 2006 they published a 167 page report covering 13 standards and methods and the associated tools. The methods considered have been selected by the ENISA's "ad hoc working group", composed of IS security experts from eight EU member states. CLUSIF (2005) is a French information systems security club for medium to large companies. Their study analyzed 26 worldwide standards and methods. Saint-Germain (2005) has compared the scope of 8 security methods with ISO/IEC 17799 (ISO/IEC 27002).

The two following studies have been conducted by scholars. Poggi (2005) is a member of the CASES (Cyberworld Awareness and Security Enhancement Structure) based in Luxemburg. In his report, he has studied 16 of the most widespread information security approaches, while Tomhave (2005) in his paper provided a US-centric overview and analysis of 18 information security frameworks and methodologies.

In the next subsection, we explain why we place the focus on ISO/IEC 27000 set of standards, and we provide a broad description of this international standard.

The Specific Case of ISO/IEC 27000 Set of Standards

Given the global nature of contemporary business operation, and the existence of more than 200 dif-

Table 1. Most widespread standards

	ENISA 06	CLUSIF 05	Poggi 05	Saint Germain 05	Tomhave 05	Citations
COBIT		X	X	X	X	4
EBIOS	X	X	X			3
ISF Methods	X	X			X	3
ISO 13335-2 (ISO 27005)	X	X	X	X		4
ISO 15408 (Common criteria)		X	X	X	X	4
ISO 27001 (BS 7799-2)	X		X		X	3
ISO 27002 (ISO 17799 - BS7799-1)	X	X	X	X		4
ITIL (BS 15000)		X	X	X	X	4
Mehari	X	X	X			3
NIST SP800	X	X	X		X	4
Octave	X	X	X	X	X	5
SSE-CMM (ISO 21827)	X		X		X	3

Sources: ENISA (2006), CLUSIF (2005), Poggi, (2005), Saint Germain, (2005), Tomhave (2005)

ferent information security methods and standards (Poggi, 2005), a need for a single reference point in information security has been recognized by the international business community (Humphreys, 2005). ISO/IEC 27001 and 27002 standards are commonly seen as a response to this need, as they represent the building blocks of the ISO/IEC 27000 integrated and global standard. With the example of ISO/IEC 27000 information security standards, we can see how the issue of information security is taken as a governance issue, as ISO/IEC 27000 can be seen as a series of standards, each complementing the other in some respect.

It is tempting to assume that the ISO/IEC 27000 will soon become the reference among information security standards.

In this section, we will only deal with ISO/IEC 27001 and 27002, we will present further the upcoming extensions of this standard.

ISO/IEC 27001 and 27002 take their roots from BS 7799: In 1995 the British Standard Institution (BSI) established BS 7799-1 standard titled "Information security part I: Code of practice for security management" and added in 1998 a second part, BS 7799-2 "Information security part II: specification for Information Security Management System (ISMS)". BS 7799-2 is a set of requirements for developing an ISMS that encompasses people, processes and IT systems. Both aforementioned BS standards were taken up

by the ISO (International Organization for Standardization) to become global ISMS standards:

- BS 7799-1 was re-published in 2000 as ISO 17799 and renamed ISO/IEC 27002 in 2007;
- BS 7799-2 became ISO/IEC 27001 standard in 2005.

ISO/IEC 27001 can be viewed as an overall program that combines risk management, security management, governance and compliance. It helps an organization ensure that the right people, processes and technologies are in place that are appropriate to the business model and facilitate a proactive approach to managing security and risk (Brenner, 2007). The standard promotes strong values concerning the protection of client and business information. ISO/IEC 27001 responds to business needs in establishing comprehensive ISMS policy, which allows not only harmonization of IS-related organizational processes, but also certification, thus establishing a common reference point for the certified company in the global market.

ISO/IEC 27002 *"established guidelines and general principles for initiating, implementing, maintaining, and improving information security management within an organization"*. The actual controls listed in ISO/IEC 27002 are intended to

Table 2. Overview of methods and standards

Name	Originator's type	Creation date	Compulsory
BS 7799 1 & 2	UK Agency : British Standards Institution (BSI)	1995	No
COBIT	International association: ISACA	1996	No
EBIOS	French government (DCSSI)	1995	For governmental organisations
ISF	USA : ISF (Information security forum)	1996	No
ITIL / BS 15000	International (itSM – BSI)	1989	No
MEHARI	French Users club (CLUSIF)	1996	No
NIST SP 800-30	USA : NIST	2002	No
OCTAVE	USA : Academic (Carnegie Mellon)	1999	No
OSSTMM	Association: ISECOM + Open Source	2001	No
SSE-CMM (ISO 21827)	International association: ISSEA	1996	No
ISO standards			
ISO 13335-2 (ISO 27005)	GMITS (Guidelines for the Management of IT Security)	1996	Standard only
ISO 15408	Common criteria (1999)	1996	Certification
ISO 27001	Evolution of BS 7799-2	2005	Certification
ISO 27002	Evolution of 17799 / BS 7799-1	2007	Standard only

address the specific requirements identified via a formal risk assessment. The standard is also intended to provide a guide for the development of *"organizational security standards and effective security management practices and to help build confidence in inter-organizational activities"*.

Table 2 shows the various methods and standards existing worldwide, their originator, their compulsoriness and their creation date. We can notice that the majority of the methods and standards still in use were created during the 1990's. First, this means that old standards pertaining to the first wave are not used anymore, and second, today standards of wave two to four are coexisting, being replaced little by little by new standards of the fourth wave.

In the rest of the chapter, we will mostly focus on international/ISO standards, as there is a general trend in business to converge on uses of ISO-published management systems standards, such as the ISO 9001 and the 14001 series (Fomin et al., 2008).

THE ADOPTION OF INFORMATION SECURITY STANDARDS

For a standard which was preceded by two widely used successful global management system standards, ISO 9001 and ISO 14001, the worldwide adoption of ISO/IEC 27001 is surprisingly low (see Figure 1). Two years after its publication, the number of ISO/IEC 27001 certifications is well under that of its two predecessors ISO 9001, quality management, and ISO 14001, environmental management system standards, during the same period (Fomin et al., 2008). What explains so low adoption, given the importance of information security management as compared to that of quality and environmental issues?

In Figure 1, we can also notice the discrepancy between the economic ranking of the countries and the number of certifications. We will discuss this in the end of next section.

Aiming at obtaining insights on the unexpectedly low and surprisingly uneven diffusion of the

Figure 1. Number of ISO/IEC 27001 certifications (ISMS user group, July 2008)

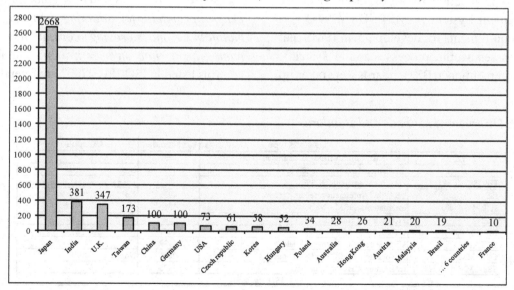

ISO/IEC 27001 standard, in the following section we examine successively the drivers for adoption of information security management standards, the success factors and the specific cases of employees' adoption. Finally, we explore the barriers and the limitations affecting the adoption of ISMS, and solutions and recommendations to foster this adoption.

Drivers and Barriers for Adoption, and Limitations of Information Security Management Standards

Drivers for Adoption

One of the major objectives of information security standards is to provide consistent national and international practices: this is the aim of the standards created by the international standards organization (ISO) such as the ISO/IEC 27000 set of standards. We can also find, for example, the widespread Information Technology Infrastructure Library (ITIL), bringing together IT service management best practices.

Second, the objective of establishing and raising confidence that security is being properly addressed is a recurring preoccupation included in the great majority of information security standards. For organizations, they constitute a mean of demonstrating to their partners' network that they have identified and measured their security risks and implemented a security policy and controls that will mitigate these risks (Saint-Germain, 2005).

The compliance with national and international regulation constitutes a worrying issue, as many international and national regulations were crafted by politicians or lawyers, rarely considered as experts in information security. Consequently, the resulting regulations are often imprecise and open to interpretation (Broderick, 2006). Thus, the main purpose of information security standards is *"to provide executive level management with confidence that the security of corporate manage-*ment is properly managed as required by executive management and/or regulatory requirements and to collect supporting evidence that they are meeting their due diligence and fiduciary responsibilities with respect to information security and their business"* (Broderick, 2006, p. 30).

Standards provide a structured and coherent approach and can be the basis of a comprehensive risk assessment (Hinson, 2008; Hong et al., 2003). Schumacher (2002) considers that security standards can be viewed as an expression of accumulated expertise, thus companies adopting a standard could expect to also adopt best practices. We will question this issue later.

Saint-Germain (2005) argues that standard compliant organizations are exposed to a lower level of risk, and will spend less money recovering from security incidents, which may also translate into lower insurance premiums (von Solms & von Solms, 2001). Therefore, the quantification of ISMS standard adoption benefits remains problematic, as it is not possible to measure the cost of a security failure that has been prevented.

Wiander (2007) conducted the first empirical study concerning the implementation of the ISO 17799 standard. He found that implementing the standard led to an increase in information security understanding, a broadening from technical security to information security management and corporate security. He also noticed improvements in the way organizations practice information security.

Certification corresponds to an independent assessment of compliance with the standard and provides an evaluation of the level of information security. Consequently, it becomes possible to compare the level of information security of two companies that have been certified against the same scheme (von Solms & von Solms, 2001). Certification also serves as a public statement of an organization's ability to manage information security and demonstrates to partners that the organization has implemented adequate information security and business security controls, and is committed to ensuring that its ISMS and security policies continue to evolve and adapt to changes (Saint-Germain, 2005).

However, if security certification is considered as leverage for confidence between companies engaged in business transactions (OECD, 2002), our literature review does not either reveal a significant advantage for adopting companies in business competition or in stock market valuation. Therefore, we can notice that international invitations are beginning to require that organizations be compliant with certain security standards, and security audit demands from financial institutions and insurance companies are increasing (Saint-Germain, 2005). Lichtenstein (1996) identified in his study the driving factors for managers in adopting an information security method. The factors are the low cost, validity and credibility of the method. Credibility means that if managers do not understand why a particular safeguard has been recommended, they will not implement it.

Backhouse et al. (2006) provide a basis for understanding the discrepancy (Figure 1) between countries in ISO/IEC 27001 certification. They used the theoretical framework of 'circuits of power' to better understand the creation and adoption of information security standards.

First, many companies of more developed countries are offshoring or outsourcing activities, or even parts of their information systems, and they require certifications such as BS 7799 and ISO 17799 as a basis for measuring and auditing the security management of their contractors. This explains the high ranking of India (2nd) or Taiwan (4th) for example in Figure 1.

Their paper also explains the advance of U.K. (3rd) and the lateness of other countries and the resistance of some large companies and governments to adopt foreign standards. For instance, American companies (USA ranked 7th) felt that they should use ANSI standards instead of U.K. originated standards. The French government also promoted its own standards (ranked 23rd), such as EBIOS.

Their last explanation resides in the fact that even if some countries did not adopt ISO/IEC 27000 series as a national standard, they nevertheless translated the standard's content into their local language such as Japanese, German or Chinese.

This demonstrates the importance of governments and large companies in fostering information security standards adoption.

Success Factors in Implementing Information Security Standards

The most important success factor in obtaining a certification is management commitment to and support of an ongoing information security management process (Saint-Germain, 2005). The first element of the preparation phase must be top management commitment, as top management carries the ultimate responsibility of backing activities and decisions involved by this approach (Dinnie, 1999; Forcht, 1994). Top management support is also essential for the allocation of resources (Avolio, 2000). Moreover, top management can be considered as a change agent (Lucas, 1981) and a means of gaining employee support for information security. In their study, Knapp et al. (2006) found that top management support positively influences security culture and policy enforcement. Thus, there is a need for managerial involvement (Siponen, 2000) because senior management has authority and leadership to overcome cultural and organizational barriers (Dutta & McCrohan, 2002; Keen, 1981; Markus, 1983).

A second success factor is that information security management should become part of the management structure of the organization and should no longer be regarded as solely an IT issue (Vermeulen & von Solms, 2002). Thus, the implementation approach should be consistent with the organization's culture (Hone & Eloff, 2002; Saint-Germain, 2005) and as stated by von Solms & von Solms, *"one way to ensure that employees actions, behaviors, artifacts and creations are according to company policies is to align these with company culture"* (2004, p. 279). In addition, standards and certifications constitute important drivers as *"an information security culture emerges where specific behavior is encouraged, such as complying with ISO 17799"* (Martins & Eloff, 2002, p. 207).

To foster a better information security culture, it is important to provide a proper training to the employees (Saint-Germain, 2005; von solms & von solms, 2004), which constitutes another success factor. The policies derived from standards must be well aligned with corporate objectives (Rees et al., 2003; Saint-Germain, 2005), tailored to the organizational context of the company (Doherty & Fulford, 2005) and then rigorously enforced (David, 2002).

The third success factor we identified through the literature review corresponds to the use of a governing system that ensures the timely update of security policies as well as organizations-wide collaboration and knowledge-sharing (Saint-Germain, 2005).

We can notice the important role played by the employees in the successful implementation of information security standards. Hence, it becomes necessary to study their behaviors and their adoption of information security practices.

The Adoption of Information Security Practices by Employees

Very few theories are specifically dedicated to information security practices adoption, although we identified many theories and models developed in order to understand employees' behavior in the ICT field. This subsection examines the major theories and discusses their appropriateness to the information security field. We classified them within three main families - behavioral theories, technology and computer acceptance theories, and theories linked to psychology, morals and ethics.

Behavioral theories. The first is the theory of reasoned action (TRA) (Fishbein & Ajzen, 1975; Ajzen & Fishbein, 1980) positing that 1) intention comes from attitude towards behavior, and subjective norms (other's influence), and 2) intention leads to behavior. The theory of planned behavior (TPB) complements TRA by adding the perceived behavioral control (Ajzen, 1991): an employee feels better at ease when s/he has the situation under control. The third theory is the extrinsic (Davis et al., 1992) or intrinsic (Deci, 1975; Deci & Ryan, 1985) motivational model (MM). This model places the focus on the benefits entailed by the adoption and use of information technologies. These three theories have been used in the ICT field to better understand technology adoption and use (Davis et al., 1989; Harrison et al., 1997; Mathieson, 1991, Davis et al., 1992).

Technology and computer acceptance and use theories. Since information security related behaviors can require technical skills, relevant theories in the technology field should be also considered. The technology acceptance model (TAM) is derived from TRA and has been tailored to the IS context to predict ICT acceptance and use (Davis, 1989; Davis et Al, 1989). It is based on perceived usefulness and perceived ease of use. The Model of PC Utilization (MPCU) (Thompson et al., 1991) is more specific and dedicated to "hardware" acceptance.

Psychology, moral and ethical theories. Information security related behaviors can also be linked to morality and ethics: disregarding or circumventing security rules or good practices can lead to security failures. The social bond theory (SBT) postulates that a person commits a crime when the lack of social bonds gives him/her the freedom to act. Researchers measured the effect of social bonds based on four factors: attachment, commitment, involvement and beliefs (Hirschi, 1969; Gottfredson & Hirschi, 1990; Jenkins, 1997; Agnew, 1995).

The Ethical decision-making model (Harrington, 1996) studies the effect of codes of ethics on the intention and opinion of employees in the area of computer abuse. These effects are limited, varying according to different characters of people and are concerned with specific behaviors only. Involved managers can use reminders to reinforce the influence of the codes of ethics on behaviors. Managers can modify the company's moral climate and guide employees in the desired way. Sproul and Kiesler (1991) noticed that users could be unable to identify the consequences of ethical dilemmas in the ICT domain; this is the object of their Domain theory of moral development. Others underline the influence of morality on behaviors (Gattiker & Kelley, 1999; Rest, 1986).

A case study conducted by Barlette (2006) shows that the three aforementioned families of theories are relevant in the security behavioral context and identifies the following major motivational factors:

- Personal motivations or personal convictions;
- Intimacy preservation;
- Motivations linked to the position;
- Motivations linked to the firm;
- Habits (the security behavior issue is solved when a behavior becomes an habit);
- Background (past professional or personal experiences).

The study by Barlette also reveals drawbacks in employees' perception of information security as a needed or desirable asset, exemplified by such quotes of managers as *"15 minutes spent to backup my files equal 15 minutes lost in my work time"* or *"there are no risks"*. These problems mainly correspond to a lack in the security information awareness or training. Barlette suggests remedies to the aforementioned situations. Five solutions were identified:

- Hierarchy influence;
- Computerization (automation of backups, updates, etc.);
- Use of guides / ethical codes;
- Support to the users;
- Awareness / education campaigns.

Top management commitment and support is the most important success factor in implementing information management security standards and it represents the key factor in adopting information security practices (Grover, 1983). Hierarchy influence is also the easier key factor to implement, taking into account the constraints of time and money: managers, for example, should transmit security-related messages to employees.

The other factors identified can complete this: automation could limit the constraints linked to the employees and the effectiveness of ethical codes has been suggested by Harrington (1996).

After examining the drivers and the success factors, we identify the barriers to adoption and the limitations of information security standards as found in the literature.

Barriers to Adoption and Limitations of Information Security Standards

One of the plausible explanations of the low level of information security standards adoption is that some managers are insufficiently concerned about information security (Broderick, 2006). Some of them underestimate the risks that their company has to face; moreover, there is a discrepancy between the risks considered (overestimation of hacker and virus risks) and the reality of security breaches (human error, insider threats, network- and electricity-related downtimes) (Clusif, 2004; Schultz, 2002). Second, managers may be skeptical about information security effectiveness due to the difficulty in evaluating the benefits. Some managers also lack knowledge about the range of controls available to reduce information security abuses (Kankanhalli et al., 2003; Straub, 1990).

Another explanation is the implementation cost. According Hinson (2008), the costs of implementing ISO/IEC 27001 or 27002 stem from:

- Project management and project resources;
- Required organizational change and resources (awareness programs, adaptation, etc.);
- Updating, developing, and testing of processes and controls to be implemented;
- Certification and annual surveillance visits (financial cost, organizational time spent);
- Day to day operation to maintain compliance with the standard.

Beyond the financial costs are the organizational costs, indeed effective security management requires a great deal of time, effort, and money, which many organizations are not prepared to commit (Doherty & Fulford, 2005). Moreover, according Wiander (2007) implementing the standard requires skilled people and this can require higher salary expenses.

However, standards also suffer from many limitations. We identified five types of limitations. The first type of problem refers to organizational specific issues. The second type resides in the complexity of standards while the third is relative to the way of addressing the human factor and the insider threat. Fourth, given the number of SMEs worldwide, an important issue concerns the way information security standards address small companies. The fifth limitation deals with the validity of the standards themselves.

The first limitation of the standards arises precisely from their generality, and thus they fail to pay adequate attention that organizations differ and therefore their security requirements might differ (Baskerville, 1993; Wood, 1999). There is an opposition between the generality of standards, according to Ma & Pearson (2005), and the organization-specific nature of information security management. In addition, as standards are generic, business requirements proposed by the standards may involve conflicts with the organization's normal business requirements (Baskerville & Siponen, 2002).

Hone & Eloff (2002) note that international standards insufficiently address cultural and regional issues, although we stated them as important success factors.

Standards often pay little attention to the fact that organizations are embedded in dynamic business environments (Schweitzer, 2002) and they can become synonymous of "non-agile" organizations. *"Computer security should be understood as fluid, rather than static, to best reflect the constantly changing environments in which they are being deployed"* (Mercuri, 2003, p. 25). At last, information security policies pay little attention to exceptional situations: for example, exploiting sudden business opportunities may require a temporary violation of normative information security policies (Siponen & Iivari, 2006).

The second limitation resides in the complexity of the standards (Arnott, 2002) and the corresponding lack of guidance. According Wiander (2007) standards are difficult to read and implement; Parker (2006) goes further: safeguards provided by today's standards are tricky, context-dependant, and often too complex to be effective against the threats companies have to face with.

The major security standards do not give enough information to help practitioners design and implement information security policies; they often cover the topics in one or two short paragraphs. They describe the various processes and controls needed to successfully implement the policy, but fail to give advice on what the policy should look like (Hone & Eloff, 2002).

According Siponen (2006), they focus on ensuring that some information processes and/or activities exist, but forget "how to" accomplish them. Moreover, they do not give enough advice that could help practitioners. Yet, what matters is how well the job is done, and if you are told to "set up an awareness program", this can be rather vague. Questions remain, such as: "how should users be trained or motivated?" "How should I ensure employees internalize their security mission?" Therefore, ensuring that a set of security processes and activities are in place is not synonymous with satisfying security concerns.

The principles provided by the information security standards are abstract and simplified, and often do not provide advice on how the desired results are to be achieved in practice (Siponen, 2006). For example, ISO 17799 does not suggest how users should be trained or motivated to follow information security procedures, and thus will not ensure employees actually follow or internalize the desired behaviors (Siponen, 2000, 2006).

Inconsistencies with the interpretation of standards by consultants and assessors have been noticed during the implementation of the ISO 9000 quality standard (Brown et al., 1998). We can suggest this could be the same for ISO/IEC 27000 implementation, even if none of the few studies exploring this issue raised the problem.

The third limitation of information security standards is the way of addressing the human factor and the insider threat. Dhillon & Backhouse (2001) criticized security checklists provided by standards, which emphasize the observable events and focus attention on procedure without considering the social nature of the problems. The standards and the related compliance audits are too often dealing with the strategic, operational or technological side of the organization, but do not address correctly the human factor: the results of the employee's behavior are taken into consideration but not the actual behavior itself (Vroom & von Solms, 2004). Thus, it is of utmost importance to take into account the organizational culture. According Vroom & von Solms (2004) *"a utopian security culture would be where the employees of the organization follow the guidelines of the organization voluntarily as part of their second nature".*

Security guidelines are too often not justified in a relevant way, since norms include imperative forms that need argumentation and justification (Siponen, 2000). Warman (1992) highlighted the fact that users often know the guidelines, but fail to apply them correctly. Moreover, if external norms or guidelines become prescriptive states, they can lead to opposite effects in terms of pressure or irritation, thus leading to a lower work efficiency or producing unwanted behaviors such as resistance to change, circumventions, or unethical behaviors (Siponen, 2000). Thus, it is important to give reasons, to foster active participation and to adopt persuasive communication (Fishbein & Ajzen, 1975).

Theoharidou et al. (2005) have studied the deficiencies of the ISO 17799 standard addressing the insider threat; the standard is mainly focused on general deterrence theory, which was first proposed in the early 1960s, though the use of sanction as a deterrent mechanism has been questioned (Lee & Lee, 2002). ISO 17799 does not seem to have been noticeably influenced by any modern theories, however their interest and efficiency has been confirmed in many occasions (Venkatesh et al., 2003). Yet, modern theories recommend informal controls, which are consequently missing in ISO 17799, and very few specific actions and guidance concerning informal controls can be found in the standard.

A fourth important limitation of the standards corresponds to the way they address the specific case of SMEs:

A simple approach designed for small organizations does not exist today, at least not in the form of publicly available guidelines. Some consulting firms have developed good practices for that purpose, but they use them within customer projects. Other approaches, although claiming to be appropriate for SMEs, are still too complex for self-assessments (e.g. OCTAVE). On the other hand, most SMEs cannot afford the cost of fully outsourcing this function to external parties.

European Network and Information Security Agency, (ENISA, 2007, p. 17)

The lower number of countermeasures implemented by SMEs compared to larger companies has been reported as well by surveys (Ernst & Young, 2005) as by scholars (Kankanhalli et al., 2003). Many explanations can be advanced: SMEs lack information security awareness (Chapman & Smalov, 2004; Mitchell et al., 1999) and are challenged more than large companies in evaluating possible IS-related risks (Gupta & Hammond, 2005). Moreover, Gupta & Hammond (2005) report the inability of many SMEs to focus on security due to other business priorities. Additionally, SMEs that have not experienced a security failure are less prepared to invest in security projects (Mitchell et al., 1999).

In Table 3 we notice an assessment of the company size and skills needed to implement the major existing standards.

SMEs generally lack computer experience and do not have sufficient internal IS expertise (De Lone, 1988; Gable, 1991; Spinellis et al., 1999).

This situation is precipitated on difficulties in recruiting and retaining internal IS experts due to scarcity of qualified IS experts and limited career advancement prospects offered by SMEs (Noteboom, 1988; Thong et al., 1996). As a result, SMEs are driven to outsource the necessary competencies (Soh et al., 1992), which they often cannot afford (Gupta & Hammond, 2005; von Solms & Van de Haar, 2000).

The effectiveness of information security controls depends on the competency and dependability of the people who are implementing and using it (Dhillon, 2001). In some cases, this is not harmless: for example, if a SME cannot afford an information security consultant, it will take into account the perceptions and feelings of an internal individual who will not have the adequate role or skills to properly evaluate what needs to be done. This can lead to an inadequacy of preventions and protections implemented compared to those required to reduce actual risks.

Moreover, in SMEs, information security is typically not a full-time job. Consequently, there is a danger that other tasks are seen, by the

Table 3. Issues associated to information security standards

Name	Company size (*)	Skills needed	Language issue
BS 7799 1 & 2	C, L	**	E
COBIT	C, L	**	I
EBIOS	C, L	**	I
ISF Methods	C, L	* to ***	E
ITIL / BS 15000	C, L	N/A	I
MEHARI	C, L	**	E, French
NIST SP 800-30	C, L	**	E
OCTAVE	C, L S (?)	**	E
OSSTMM	C, L S (?)	* to **	E, Spanish
SSE-CMM (ISO 21827)	C, L	** to ***	E
ISO standards			
ISO 13335-2 (ISO 27005)	C, L	**	E
ISO 15408	C, L	N/A	E
ISO 27001 (BS 7799-2)	C, L	**	I
ISO 27002 (ISO 17799 - BS7799-1)	C, L	**	E

(*) C: Civil service, L: Large company, S: Small business

*   : basic level   I: International
**   : standard level   E: English
*** : specialist level

The question marks reflect the questioning of ENISA about the design of approaches for SMEs
Adapted, updated and completed from ENISA, (2006)

person in charge of information security, as more important, because the information security work is often seen as a cost (Wiander, 2007).

Due to the often complex nature of security standards (Arnott, 2002), the lack of skills - and money to buy the skills - for SMEs is further burdened by the lack of time for adoption and certification of standards. Effective security management requires a great deal of time and effort, which most of SMEs are not prepared to commit (Doherty & Fulford, 2005; Moule & Giavara, 1995). For example, security standard's implementation can take more than 5 or 6 months (CNRS, 2002). The language issue can also burden the adoption of IS security standards, particularly in SMEs. We can notice in Table 3 that some methods and standards exist only in English or have not been translated in some specific languages.

The fifth limitation regards that many scholars have questioned the validity of the standards themselves. According Mercuri (2003), standards must be assessed for their appropriateness, Ma & Pearson (2005) notice that very few studies have been conducted to validate standards, particularly ISO 17799, that lead to ISO/IEC 27002. In their study, they confirmed the validity, for information security professionals of only seven of the ten original dimensions in the ISO 17799, and the need for one more dimension, such as business partner security. Doherty & Fulford (2005) studied the relationships between adoption of information security policies and the incidence or severity of security breaches, and they surprisingly found no statistically relationships. They advance some plausible explanations; all of them have already been examined in previous sections:

- Difficulties of raising awareness;
- Difficulties of enforcement;
- Policy standards are too complex;
- Inadequate resourcing (time, money, organizational effort);
- Failure to tailor policies.

The approach to compliance is increasingly evolving from one focused on technical elements to an understanding of compliance as a coherent business process, which intimately involves all aspects of an organization (Saint-Germain, 2005).

Wiander (2007) concludes his study in the implementation of ISO 17799 by stating: *"it is important to understand that the standardization is not necessarily needed for good information security management. And the certificate or standard itself does not guarantee the adequate information security level of an organization"* (p. 99).

Given the variety of the drivers and barriers to the success of implementing information security standards, in the following section we provide managerial recommendations on how to foster their adoption.

General recommendations to foster the adoption of information security standards

Concerning the drivers, we will highlight the importance of government influence and legislation in promoting information security standards. In some cases, companies that have offshore or outsource activities can require standards adoption by other companies thus also promoting information security standards.

The most important success factor in implementing and certifying standards is the top management commitment. Consequently, there is a need for raising their information security awareness, especially in SMEs'. However, how can we assist them if they are not interested? This vicious circle must be broken somehow. Once more, national or international agencies could do something to better inform the firms' managers about the actual risks they face, and help them to assess or at least estimate the value of their information. The financial or time cost would represent lower barriers if they were compared to the potential loss of information. Managerial personnel should also be informed of their critical role in instilling a proper security culture, sometimes simply by setting a good example or even by showing employees their concern about information security.

To help the firms' managerial personnel in their efforts to adopt ISMS standards, developers of these standards should provide more examples with in-depth experience and lessons learned from the standards' implementation and argue their recommendations in a manner which is credible and satisfying to management. A special emphasis should be placed on the social nature and how to address the human factor. Consequently, managers would have more guidance on what to do, and to better assign priorities.

Thus, the three building blocks of managers' and employees' good behaviors would be respected: "what" (what is this security element, what do I need to do?), "why" (what are the relevant reasons for me to perform this behavior?), and "how" (how can I perform this behavior, with what help?) (Barlette, 2006).

In promoting the information security culture, we can notice the importance of auditing compliance with an information security management standard: The compliance audit reinforces strongly the senior management encouragements (Broderick, 2006).

Our last recommendation relies on the necessity to provide guidance on tailoring standards to different organizational cultures, countries or even to technical or cultural groups. This guidance should correspond to specific booklets adapted to the culture of some specific countries or ethnics, designed from lessons learned from previous implementations within this culture. In addition, efforts could be made on the adaptability of the standards and the information security policies related to determine how to deal with exceptional situations and how to review policies in order to avoid in the future the repetition of previous security breaches. Wiander (2007) has identified this need for a more agile framework for implementing the standards.

This subsection presented a number of general solutions and recommendations on fostering information security standards' adoption. As information security standards are evolving, it is important to understand not only the state of art in information security management practice, but also the future trends, as well as identify directions for further research to better understand the adoption of information security management standards.

FUTURE TRENDS

ISO/IEC 27001 and 27002 standards, parts of ISO/IEC 27000 standard will presumably be completed around 2010 with four other parts:

- 27003: implementation guidance (responding to the need of guidance highlighted previously);
- 27004: measures and metrics;
- 27005: risk management (ISO 13335);
- 27006: guidelines for accreditation; this standard meets market demands to better support ISO/IEC 27001.

This global standard will simplify the task of companies aiming to adopt a standard. Companies will have access to a complete and integrated set of complementary standards. We anticipate that this will stimulate the adoption of information security standards.

A specific standard of the ISO/IEC 27000 family dedicated to SMEs (e.g. an 'ISO/IEC 27001 lite') could answer to the complexity and expensiveness criticisms against these standards. However, there is a risk of a dilution of the value of the certification (Casper & Esterle, 2007), and this would add to the naming confusion caused by the numerous name changes that occurred in previous years. Whatever the case, Chapman & Smalov (2004) consider that only a small proportion of the available information security literature will prove relevant to the situation of a SME and consequently call for considerable further study to develop detailed guidance onto pragmatic information security advice relevant to the needs of a specific SME.

Kotulic & Clark have stated that the organizational level of information security is under researched (2004). Further research is thus necessary to explore, for example, the relationships between security objectives and practices (Dhillon & Torkzadeh, 2001). This is important for practitioners to determine the resource allocation and which diagnostics are necessary, and beyond this to implement practices more effectively (Ma & Pearson, 2005). More research is also needed to better identify the success factors of security practices implementation in order to improve the guidance provided by standards. Moreover, case or action research should be performed in companies who are implementing information security standards. Information security standards, beyond the organizational role, should better take into account the socio-organizational role of information security; future empirical studies need to pay attention to this issue.

Identifying the success factors of security practices implementation (executive support, organizational policy, organizational culture, organizational self-efficacy and financial benefit) would prove benefits for information security management (Ma & Pearson, 2005).

Lastly, Siponen & Iivari (2006) propose that information security standards should be designed as agile standards, in order to easier follow the changes in the companies themselves, their environment and industrial sectors they belong to, as well as the evolution of security failures.

CONCLUSION

In this chapter, we provide an overview of the major information security methods and standards in general, and the ISO/IEC 27001 standard specifically. We examine the drivers for adopting information security management standards and the factors for their successful implementation. The most important factor identified is management commitment; without management's visible support, the organizational culture is less tolerant for good security practices, entailing a lower level of enforcement of information security policies (Knapp et al., 2004).

While drivers for information security standards adoption can be identified, there is a surprisingly low adoption of these standards. Through a literature review, we identify the barriers to their adoption, as well as their limitations. The most important issue corresponds to the fact that information security standards insufficiently address human and organizational aspects.

This work has several important contributions to academy and practice. First, we contribute to scholarly domain by providing a comprehensive literature review on ISMS standards and their adoption. Second, we contribute to management practice by providing recommendations for addressing human factors and socio-organizational issues in the deployment of ISMS. Finally, relevant to both scholarly and management domains, we discuss the future trends in ISMS standardization and research.

Responding to the numerous calls for increasing managers' awareness of the issue of information security in our contemporary informational economy, we conclude that firm managers must be aware not only of the information security *per se*, but of the necessity to be committed to information security management. They also have to take into consideration that while the use of ISMS is the foundation of their IS security, they must also *"stay ahead of the curve, outguessing and outsmarting potential incidents and occurrences"* (Myler & Broadbent, 2006, p.52). Adoption of information security management standards will be of vital help to managers in fulfilling this call. However, managers should also remember that, as boldly emphasized by Hone & Eloff (2002), an international standard will not write the information security policy for them. The adapted wording for an information security policy has to come from the organization itself to mold the organizational culture.

REFERENCES

Agnew, R. (1995). Testing the leading crime theories: an alternative strategy focusing on motivational process. *Journal of research in crime and delinquency, 32*(4), 363-398.

Ajzen, I. (1991). The Theory of Planned Behavior. *Organizational Behavior and Human Decision Processes, 50*(2), 179-211.

Ajzen, I., & Fishbein, M. (1980*). Understanding attitudes and predicting social behavior. Prentice Hall, Englewood cliffs, NJ.*

Arnott, S. (2002). *Strategy paper. Computing, February.*

Avolio, F.M. (2000). *Best practices in network security: as the networking landscape changes, so must the policies that govern* its use. Don't be afraid of imperfection when it comes to developing those for your group. *Network Computing, 60*(20), March.

Backhouse, J., Hsu, C. W., & Silva, L. (2006). Circuit of Power in creating de jure Standards: Shaping an International Information Systems Security Standard. *MIS Quarterly, 30*, special issue, 413-438.

Barlette, Y. (2006). *Les comportements sécuritaires des acteurs en entreprise.* (Information security behaviors of companies' actors). PhD thesis. Montpellier University, France.

Barlette, Y., & Fomin, V. V. (2008). Exploring the suitability of IS security management standards for SMEs. *Proceedings of the forty-first annual Hawaii International Conference on System Sciences* (HICSS-41). January 7-10. (10 pages). Computer Society Press, Big Island, Hawaii, USA.

Barnard, L., & von Solms, R. (1998). The evaluation and certification of information security against BS 7799. *Information management and computer security, 6*(2), 72-77.

Baskerville, R. (1993). Information systems security design methods: implications for information systems development. *ACM Computing Surveys, 25*(4), 375-414.

Baskerville, R., & Siponen, M. T. (2002). An information security meta-policy for emergent organizations. *Logistics information management, 15*(5/6), 337-346.

Brenner, J. (2007). ISO 27001: Risk management and compliance. *Risk Management Magazine, 54*(1), 24-29.

Broderick, J. S. (2006). ISMS, security standards and security regulations. *Information security technical report II*, 26-31.

Brown, A., Van der Wiele, T., & Loughton, K. (1998). Smaller enterprises' experiences with ISO 9000. *International journal of Quality & reliability management, 15*(3), 273-285.

BS7799. (1999). *Code of practice for information security management.* UK: British Standards Institute.

Casper, C., & Esterle, A. (2007). *Information security certifications – A primer: product, people, processes.* ENISA deliverable, 18.

Castells, M. (1996). *The Rise of the Network Society.* 2nd edition (2000), Vol. I. Oxford: Blackwell Publishers, Ltd.

Chapman, D., & Smalov, L. (2004). On information security guidelines for small/medium enterprises. *ICEIS 2004 – Information analysis and specification*, 3-9.

CLUSIF. (2004). *Politiques de sécurité des systèmes d'information et sinistralité en France.* Club de la sécurité des informations français, Paris.

CLUSIF. (2005). *Standards et normes en SSI.* October, www.clusif.fr, Paris.

CNRS. (2002). La certification des critères communs: le point de vue du développeur. *Sécurité informatique, 42,* 5-6.

Davis, F. D. (1989). Perceived usefulness, perceived ease of use, and user acceptance of information technology. *MIS Quarterly, 13*(3), 319-339.

Davis, F. D., Bagozzi, R. P., & Warshaw, P. R. (1989). User Acceptance of Computer Technology: A Comparison of Two Theoretical Models. *Management Science, 35*(8), 982-1002.

Davis, F. D., Bagozzi, R. P., & Warshaw, P. R. (1992). Extrinsic and Intrinsic Motivation to Use Computers in the Workplace. *Journal of Applied Social Psychology, 22*(14), 1111-1132.

Deci, E. L. (1975). *Intrinsic Motivation.* Plenum press, NY, USA.

Deci, E. L., & Ryan, R. M. *(1985). Intrinsic motivation and self-determination in human development.* Plenum press, *NY, USA.*

DCSSI. (2007). Direction centrale de la sécurité des systèmes d'information (Information Systems Security Central Agency). http://www.ssi.gouv. fr/fr/dcssi/.

David, J. (2002). Policy enforcement in the workplace. *Computers & Security, 21*(6), 506-513.

DeLone, W. H. (1988). Determinants of success for computer usage in small businesses. *MIS Quarterly, 5*(4), 51-61.

Dhillon, G. (2001). Violation of safeguards by trusted personnel and understanding related information security concerns. *Computers & Security, 20*(2), 165-172.

Dhillon, G., & Backhouse, J. (2001). Current directions in IS security research: towards socio-organizational perspectives. *Information Systems Journal, 11,* 127-153.

Dhillon, G., & Torkzadeh, G. (2001). Value focused assessment of information system security in organizations. *Proceedings of ICIS 2001,* Atlanta, GA.

Dinnie, G. (1999). The second annual global information security survey. *Information management and computer security, 7*(3), 112-120.

Doherty, N. F., & Fulford, H. (2005). Do information security policies reduce the incidence of security breaches: an exploratory analysis. *Information resources management journal, 18*(4), 21-39.

Dutta, A., & McCrohan, K. (2002). Management's role in information security in cyber economy. *California Management review, 45*(1), 67-87.

ENISA. (2006). Risk management implementation principles and inventories for risk management / risk assessment methods and tools, June.

ENISA. (2007). ENISA deliverable: *Information Package for SMEs,* February.

Ernst & Young. (2005). *La gestion des risques dans l'actualité du contrôle interne : pratiques et tendances,* mai 2005.

Fishbein, M., & Ajzen, I. (1975). *Belief, Attitude, Intention and behaviour: An introduction to theory and research.* Addison-Wesley, Reading, MA, USA.

Fomin, V. V., King, J. L., Lyytinen, K., & McGann, S. (2005). Diffusion and Impacts of E-Commerce in the United States of America: Results from an Industry Survey. *The Communications of the Association for Information Systems, 16,* 559-603.

Fomin, V. V., De Vries, H. J., & Barlette, Y. (2008). ISO/IEC 27001 Information Systems Security Management Standard: Exploring the Reasons for Low Adoption. *Proceedings of the third European conference on Management of Technology (EuroMOT) 2008,* Nice, France.

Fomin, V. V., Pedersen, M. K., & De Vries, H. J. (2008). Open Standards and Government Policy: Results of a Delphi Survey. *The Communications of the Association for Information Systems, 22*(April), 459-484.

Forcht, K. A. (1994). *Computer security management.* Boyd & Fraser, MA.

Gable, G. G. (1991). Consultant engagement for first time computerization: A proactive client role in small businesses. *Information & Management, 20,* 83-93.

GAO. (2004). *Technology Assessment. Cyber security for Critical Infrastructure Protection.* Edited by U. S. G. A. Office: United States General Accounting Office.

Gaston, S. J. (1996). *Information security: strategies for successful management.* Toronto, CICA.

Gaskell, G. (2000). Simplifying the onerous task of writing security policies. *Proceedings of first Australian Information Security Management Workshop,* Deakin University, Australia.

Gattiker, U. E., & Kelley, H. (1999). Morality and computers: Attitudes and differences in moral judgments. *Information systems research, 10*(3), 233-254.

Gottfredson, M. R., & Hirschi T. A. (1990). *General Theory of crime.* Stanford University press, Ca, USA.

Grover, V. *(1993).* Empirically derived model for the adoption of customer-based inter-organizational systems. *Decision sciences, 24*(3), 603-639.

Gupta, A., & Hammond, R. (2005). Information systems security issues and decisions for small businesses: an empirical examination. *Information Management and Computer Security, 13*(4), 297-310.

Harrington, S. J. (1996). The effect of codes of ethics and personal denial of responsibility on computer abuse judgments and intentions. *MIS Quarterly, 20*(3), 257-278.

Harrison, D. A., Mykytyn, P. P., & Riemenschneider, C. K. (1997). Executive Decisions about Adoption of Information Technology in Small Business: Theory and Empirical Tests. *Information Systems Research, 8*(2), 171-195.

Higgins, H.N. (1999). Corporate system security: towards an integrated management approach. *Information management and computer security, 7*(5), 217-222.

Hinson, G. (2008). *The financial implications of implementing ISO/IEC 27001 & 27002: a generic cost-benefit model,* IsecT Ltd., 1-4.

Hirschi, T. A. (1969). *Causes of delinquency.* University of California press, Berkeley, Ca, USA.

Hone, K., & Eloff, J. H. P. (2002). Information security policy: what do international security standards say. *Computers & Security, 21*(5), 402-409.

Hong, K. S., Chi, Y. P., Chao, L. R., & Tang, J. H. (2003). An integrated system theory of information security management. *Information Management & Computer Security, 11*(5), 243-248.

Humphreys, T. (2005). State-of-the-art information security management system with ISO/IEC 27001:2005. *ISO Management Systems,* 15-18.

Hurley, E. (2003). Security and Sarbanes-Oxley. *Searchsecurity.*

ISMS User Group. (2008). http://www.iso-27001certificates.com/.

Janczewski, L. (2000). Managing security functions using security standards, in Janczewski, L. (Eds.), *Internet and Intranet Security Management: Risks and Solutions,* (pp. 81-105). Idea Group Publishing, Hershey, PA.

Jenkins, P. H. (1997). School delinquency and the school social bond. *Journal of research in crime and delinquency, 34*(3), 337-367.

Kankanhalli, A., Hock-Hai, T., Bernard, C. Y. T., & Kwok-Kee, W. (2003). An integrative study of information systems security effectiveness. *International journal of information management, 23*, 139-154.

Keen, P. G. W. (1981). Information systems and organizational change. *Communications of the ACM, 24*(1), 24-33.

Knapp, K. J., Marshall, T. E., Rainer, R. K., & Morrow, D. W. (2004). *Top ranked information security issues: the 2004 international information systems security certification consortium (ISC)² survey results,* Auburn university, Auburn AL.

Knapp, K. J., Marshall, T. E., Rainer, R. K., & Ford, N. F. (2006). Information security: management's effect on culture and policy. *Information Management and Computer Security, 14*(16), 24-36.

Kotulic, A., & Clark, J. G. (2004). Why there aren't more information security research studies. *Information and Management, 41*(5), 597-607.

Lee, J., & Lee, Y. (2002). A holistic model of computer abuse within organizations. *Information Management & Computer Security, 10*(2), 57-63.

Lichtenstein, S. (1996). Factors in the selection of a risk assessment method. *Information Management & Computer Security, 4*(4), 20-25.

Louderback, J. (1995). Will You Be Ready When Disaster. Strikes? *PC Week, 12*(5), February 6, 130-131.

Lucas, H. C. Jr. (1981). *Implementation: the key to successful information systems*, McGraw-Hill, N.Y., USA.

Ma, Q., & Pearson, J. M. (2005). ISO 17799:'best practices' in information security management? *Communications of the AIS, 15*, 577-591.

Markus, M. L. (1983). Power, politics, and MIS implementation. *Communications of the ACM, 26*(6), June, 430-444.

Martins, A., & Eloff, J. H. P. (2002). Information security culture. *Proceedings of the IFIP TC11 17th international conference on information security, 214*, 203-214.

Mathieson, K. (1991). Predicting User Intentions: Comparing the Technology Acceptance Model with the Theory of Planned Behavior. *Information Systems Research, 2*(3), 173-191.

Mercuri, R. T. (2003). Standards insecurity. *Communications of the ACM, 46*(12), 21-25.

Mitchell, R. C., Marcella, R., & Baxter, G. *(1999). Corporate information security management.* New Library World, *100*(1150), 213-227, *MCB University press.*

Moule, B., & Giavara, L. (1995). Policies, procedures and standards: an approach for implementation. *Information Management & Computer Security, 3*(3), 7-16.

Myler, E., & Broadbent, G. (2006). ISO 17799: Standard for security. *The information management journal* (pp. 43-52). Nov./Dec.

Noteboom, B. (1988). The facts about small business and the real values of its 'life world'. *American journal of economics and sociology, 47*(3), 299-314.

OECD. (2002). *OECD Guidelines for the Security of Information Systems and Networks, 30.*

OECD. (2004). *Principles of Corporate Governance.* www.oecd.org/dataoecd/32/18/31557724. pdf

OECD. (2005). *Industry, Services & trade, 2005*(30). OECD STI Scoreboard 2005.

Parker, D. B. (2006). Why information security is still a folk art. *Communications of the ACM, 49*(10), 11.

Poggi, F. (2005). *Rapport de veille sur les standards et méthodes en matière de sécurité informatique*, May, www.cases.lu, Luxemburg.

Posthumus, S., & von Solms, R. (2004). A framework for the governance of information security. *Computers & Security, 23*(8), 638-646.

Rees, J., Bandyopadhyay, S., & Spafford, E.H. (2003). PFIRES: A policy framework for information security. *Communications of the ACM, 46*(7), 101-106.

Rest, J. R. (1986). *Moral development: advances in research and theory.* Praeger publishers, New York, USA.

Saint-Germain, R. (2005). Information security management best practice based on ISO/IEC 17799. *Information management journal, 39*(4), 60-66.

Sarbanes-Oxley act. (2002). Sarbanes-Oxley Act of 2002. Ret*rieved April 14, 2008 from* http://fl1.findlaw.com/news.findlaw.com/hdocs/docs/gwbush/sarbanesoxley072302.pdf.

Schultz, E. (2002). A framework for understanding and predicting insider attacks. *Computers and security, 21*(6), 526-531.

Schumacher, M. (2002). Security patterns and security standards. *Proceedings of the 7th European conference on pattern languages of programs (EuroPloP).* Irsee, Germany.

Schweitzer, J. A. (1982). *Managing Information Security: A Program for the Electronic Information Age.* Butterworth-Heinemann, Boston, MA.

Siponen, M. T. (2000). Policies for construction of information systems' security guidelines. *Proceedings of the 15ht information security conference* (IFIP TC11/Sec 2000), Beijing, China, August, 111-120.

Siponen, M. T. (2006). Information security standards focus on the existence of process, not its content. *Communications of the ACM, 49*(8), 97-100.

Siponen, M. T., & Iivari, J. (2006). Six design theories for IS security Policies and Guidelines. *Journal of the Association for Information systems, 7*(7), 445-472.

Soh, C. P. P., Yap, C. S., & Raman, K. S. (1992). Impact of consultants on computerization success in small businesses. *Information and Management, 22,* 309-319.

Spinellis, D., Kokolakis, S., & Gritzalis, S. (1999). Security requirements, risks and recommendations for small enterprise and home-office environments. *Information Management & Computer Security, 7*(3), 121-128.

Sproul, L., & Kiesler S. (1991). *Connections.* MIT press, Boston, USA.

Steinmueller, E. W. (2005). *Technical Compatibility Standards and the Co-Ordination of the Industrial and International Division of Labor.* Advancing Knowledge and the Knowledge Economy, Washington, DC, 2005.

Straub, D. W. (1990). Effective IS security: an empirical study. *Information systems research, 1*(3), 255-276.

Temkin, B. (2002). *The Recovery Update: Coming Of the Bottom.* Forrester Research, March.

Theoaridou, M., Kokolakis, S., Karyda, M., & Kiountouzis, E. (2005). The insider threat to information systems and the effectiveness of ISO 17799. *Computers & Security, 24,* 472-484.

Thong, J. Y. L, Yap, C. S., & Raman, K. S. (1996). Top management support, external expertise and information systems implementation in small businesses. *Information systems research, 7*(2), 248-267.

Tomhave, B. L. (2005). *Alphabet soup: making sense of models, frameworks and methodologies.* Working paper, august, George Washington University.

Thompson, R. L., Higgins, C. A., & Howell, J. M. (1991). Personal Computing: Toward a Conceptual Model of Utilization. *MIS Quarterly, 15*(1), 124-143.

Venkatesh, V., Morris, M. G., Davis, G. B., & Davis, F. D. (2003). User acceptance of information technology: Toward a unified view. *MIS Quarterly, 27*(3), 425-478.

Vermeulen, C., & von Solms, R. (2002). The information security management toolbox: Taking the pain out of security management. *Information management & Computer Security, 10*(3), 119-125.

von Solms, R. (1988). Information security management (1): why information security is so important. *Information management & Computer Security, 6*(4), 174-177.

von Solms, B. (2000). Information security- The third wave? *Computers & Security, 19*(7), 615-620.

von Solms, R., & Van de Haar, H. (2000). From Trusted Information Security Controls to a Trusted Information Security Environment. *Proceedings of the 16th Annual Working Conference on Information Security*, IFIP, August, Beijing, China, contribution n°4/52.

von Solms, B., & von Solms, R. (2001). Incremental information security certification. *Computers & Security, 20*(4), 308-310.

von Solms, R., & von Solms, B. (2006). Information security governance: Due care. *Computers & Security, 25*(7), 494-497.

von Solms, B. (2006). Information security – The fourth wave. *Computers and Security, 5*(3), 165-168.

Vroom, C., & von Solms, R. (2004). Towards information security behavioural compliance. *Computers & Security, 23*, 191-198.

Warman, A. R. (1992). Organizational computer security policy: The reality. *European journal of information systems, 1*(5), 305-310.

Wood, C. C. (1999). *Information Security Policies Made Easy*. Baseline Software, San Rafael, CA.

Wiander, T. (2007). Implementing the ISO/IEC 17799 standard in practice - Findings from small and medium sized software organizations. *Proceedings of the 5th international conference on Standardization, Innovation and Information Technology* (SIIT 2007). 17-19 October, Calgary, Canada.

Chapter VII
Data Smog, Techno Creep and the Hobbling of the Cognitive Dimension

Peter R. Marksteiner
United States Air Force, USA

ABSTRACT

Information overload is an increasingly familiar phenomenon, but evolving United States military doctrine provides a new analytical approach and a unifying taxonomy organizational leaders and academicians may find useful in conducting further study of this subject. The overabundance of information, relentless stream of interruptions, and potent distractive quality of the internet draw knowledge workers away from productive cognitive engagement like an addictive drug, hobbling the quality and timeliness of decisions and causing considerable economic waste. Evolving U.S. military doctrine addressing "Information Operations" applies time tested principles regarding the defense of physical resources to an information age center of gravity—the decision making capacity of people and organizations, or the "cognitive dimension." Using military doctrine and thinking to underscore the potential seriousness of this evolving threat should inspire organizational leaders to recognize the criticality of its impact and motivate them to help clear the data smog, reduce information overload, and communicate for effect.

INTRODUCTION

The instruments of national power come from the diplomatic, informational, military, and economic sectors. . . . They are the tools the United States uses to apply its sources of power, including its culture, human potential, industry, science and technology, academic institutions, geography, and national will. (JP1, p. x)

Prominent voices in business occasionally borrow military vocabulary to describe their strategic plans or business visions. When über capitalist Gordon Gekko (played by Michael Douglas in Oliver Stone's "Wall Street") told his young protégé, Bud (Charlie Sheen) there was much he could learn about making business deals from Sun Tzu's Art of War, aspiring tycoons began pulling the book off shelves in record numbers. Taking advantage of military thinking makes good sense. The U.S. Department of Defense (DoD) is an enormous and complex organization. It manages a budget more than doubling the world's largest corporations and employs more people than a third of the world's countries. Moreover, the U.S. military has a fairly impressive win-loss performance record. In business terms, it's a market leader. The U.S. military has maintained its position by methodically incorporating advances in technology into strategic thinking. From precision weapons, to stealthy invisibility, to space based surveillance the U.S. military, guided by time tested doctrine, has capitalized on technological advance with overwhelming success. Evolving U.S. military doctrine addressing "Information Operations" (IO) applies time tested principles regarding the defense of physical resources to information age centers of gravity—the aggregate decision making capacities of people and organizations. Modern military doctrine defines that center of gravity as the "cognitive dimension" of the information environment. Using that doctrine to underscore the potential seriousness of this evolving threat should inspire organizational leaders to recognize the criticality of its impact and motivate them to help clear the data smog and reduce information overload.

Mission Creep and Fog & Friction

Obviously, not all military principles are useful in the commercial world, but some absolutely are. In business, for example, choices about pursuing one course of action over another are typically based on projected economic returns on investment (ROI). By contrast, choices made by nations about engaging in armed conflict may include considerations of economic ROI, but quite often

also involve other non-economic considerations. Among those military principles particularly well suited to evaluate how organizations produce and manage information are the concepts of "mission creep" and "fog and friction."

Consider the concept of "mission creep." The term is commonly used in defense-related and main stream publications to describe situations wherein a military operation is initiated for a stated purpose but morphs over time into a considerably broader undertaking, often based on early successes (e.g., Stevenson, 1996; Yates, 1997; Siegel, 2000; Hoagland, 1993; Freemon, 2004, Weiland, 2006). More recently, the term is frequently used along side phrases such as "requirements creep" and "scope creep" to describe the tendency of bureaucracies to direct more and more resources to ever expanding and imprecisely defined goals (See e.g., Bennett, 2008; Appelo, 2008).

The phrase "fog and friction" was introduced into the soldier's catechism in the 18th century by Prussian Army officer Carl Von Clausewitz in perhaps the best known work on military thought in modern history, *On War*. "Fog" describes the inherent uncertainty and unpredictability of war. "Friction" describes the proposition that in almost any plan requiring human action, unanticipated variables pop up that not only introduce delays and diversions in their own right, but also often combine with one another to produce entirely unpredictable results, the aggregate effects of which far exceed the sum of their individual impacts.

Mission Creep — Techno Creep

Much of what's happening in businesses and organizations around the world constitutes a very mission creeping approach to the use of Information Technology (IT). In this chapter, the term "IT" is used generally to describe those capabilities that enable knowledge workers to access information or to communicate using a PC or other device. Such capabilities facilitate—even encourage, a sort of bureaucratic mission creep in a way unparalleled in human history. Consider the relationship of e-mail to "Metcalfe's Law." According to the National Science Foundation:

Metcalfe's Law states that the value of a network grows in proportion to the square of the number of users. . . . As a network grows, its value to each individual user increases, and the total value of the network increases much faster than the number of its users. This is also referred to as 'network effects.' Metcalfe's Law explains why the adoption of a technology often increases rapidly once a critical mass of users is reached and the technology becomes increasingly valuable. The internet has been the most dramatic demonstration of Metcalfe's Law. (Metcalfe's Law, 2002)

An emerging information age reality confronts decision and policy makers with a monumental challenge directly related to–actually opposing—Metcalfe's law. That challenge is balancing the opposing needs to control "information overload" (discussed in detail to follow) while at the same time maximizing access to data across organizations and enterprises—expanding the accessible network. Major General Jack Rives, Judge Advocate General, senior uniformed attorney of the USAF, who leads an organization of over 4600 legal professionals—knowledge workers—refers to the changing paradigm as "the new C2. For generations, the military has recognized the essentiality of sound processes and systems for Command and Control—'C2.' In the information age, that term is signaling a new imperative, the need for equally sound processes and systems required to effectively collaborate and communicate—the 'new C2.'"

As organizations scramble to expand their networks and develop new and effective C2 systems, the lure of IT-enabled "organizational flattening," the likes of which Thomas Friedman described in his best selling *The World is Flat* (2007), becomes increasingly potent. In their hurried pursuit of flattening-related efficiencies,

management and leadership teams tend to pursue *IT solutions to problems*, rather than trying to understand problems and their potential solutions, and *then* figuring out how or if IT can help achieve or facilitate those solutions. When the problem solving process gets inverted this way, organizations lose focus on their primary objectives. Militarily speaking, the resulting IT-enabled mission creep—call it "techno creep," begins driving operational philosophy and strategy, resulting in the misutilization of resources to achieve what is possible, instead of what is required. Techno creep diffuses the impact of limited resources and erodes organizational effectiveness.

Business Variants of Fog & Friction: Data Smog and Information Overload

The same sort of imprecision human involvement introduces in the conduct of warfare is endemic in modern communication technology such as e-mail and text or instant messaging. Dozens of books, academic journals, periodicals and commercial consultants in numbers growing by the day advise businesses and organizations how to overcome e-mail's shortcomings as a communication medium. Text only communication, also referred to as "lean media," like e-mail and internet messaging (IM), lack the contextual quality and the communicative effectiveness present in the face-to-face (FTF) transmission of information. A recurrent theme throughout most available commentary on the subject highlights growing frustration associated with how e-mail and other IT tools are used—and misused in workplaces. A growing body of literature also addresses the extent to which the combined impact of all this gadgetry is wreaking substantial unintended costs on businesses and organizations. From emotional and physical health problems to economic waste estimated in the hundreds of billions, the fog and friction of Computer Mediated Communication (CMC) appears to have descended on organizations worldwide (See e.g., Shenk, 1997; Spira, 2007; Schipley, 2007).

Knowledge Work and the Cognitive Dimension

Some management experts refer to them as knowledge workers (Drucker, 1966), others as information workers (Spira, 2007). Though the vocabulary varies, the general meaning of the terms are widely recognized as describing the growing class of knowledge economy workers, the kind Peter Drucker described in 1966 as the employee "who puts to work what he has between his ears rather than the brawn of his muscles or the skill of his hands" (1966, p. 3). Military theorists and business leaders use the term "center of gravity" to describe those physical or virtual assets or aspects of an organization or process that are critical to the product or outcome generated by that organization or process. The zone where knowledge work is performed, the *cognitive dimension,* or "collective mind" (Weick, 1993) is a center of gravity for both public and private organizations. Over 40 years ago, when he wrote *The Effective Executive,* Drucker said "modern society is a society of large organized institutions. In every one of them, including the armed services, the center of gravity has shifted to the knowledge worker" (1966, p. 3). What was an emergent idea in the mid 60s is an axiom in the new millennium; knowledge work is a considerably more ubiquitous common denominator at every level and layer of modern organizations. It is a critical resource—a center of gravity.

Chapter Objectives

Information overload is gaining recognition as an organizational carcinogen, squandering resources in knowledge economy work centers. The crux of the discussion in academic and mainstream media discusses information overload in terms of lost profits, worker health and satisfaction, and gener-alized complaints about organizational efficiency. What follows aggregates those themes around a few core concepts, but suggests considering the problem more holistically. Military vocabulary characterizes threats not in terms of lost profits or productivity, but rather as potential weapons of an enemy. Discussing information overload using the language of the military should help raise awareness of the threat information overload poses to economic prosperity and to more macro level interests such as national sovereignty and security.

While refraining from using the term "information overload," the 9-11 Commission observed "the U.S. government has access to a vast amount of information. . . . But the U.S. Government has a weak system for processing and using what it has" (National Commission on Terrorist Attacks Upon the United States, 2004, p. 416). The report speaks of information that could have been accessed, had the right person asked or known where to look for it. The data smog-9/11 connection illustrates a tragic example of the effect information overload is having on public and private organizations around the world. There's so much information, it's hard to find, focus, and act upon *the right* information.

Military thinking recognizes that technological advances in the tools of warfare, like gunpowder, rifled barrels, airplanes, satellites and now IT, may produce new and evolving vulnerabilities and threats. Strategists and policy makers remain vigilant in order to fortify those vulnerabilities and check those threats as they're identified. The body of military doctrine used to discuss how best to meet evolving IT-related threats is generally found under the subject heading Information Operations (IO). The overarching U.S. military IO doctrine can be found in Joint Publication 3-13, Information Operations.

Information is a strategic resource, vital to national security, and military operations depend on information and information systems for many simultaneous and integrated activities. . . The principle goal [of IO doctrine] is to achieve and maintain information superiority . . . . (JP 3-13, p. ix)

Military doctrine recognizes national power as consisting of not only military, but also diplomatic, economic and informational components (Joint Publication 3-0, Joint Operations, 2006). By borrowing a few IO concepts from U.S. defense thinking, public and private policy makers, elected officials and corporate CIOs will be better equipped to recognize and react to emerging IO threats across their enterprises, and academicians will have a few additional taxonomical tools from which to draw when conducting further study in this area.

BACKGROUND

Information is a strategic resource, vital to national security. . . . The information environment is where humans and automated systems observe, orient, decide, and act upon information, and is therefore the principal environment of decision making. (JP3-13, 2006, pp. ix, I-1)

The Rise of Knowledge Work

The term "knowledge economy' connotes an economic environment where information and its manipulation are the commodity and the activity" (Spira, 2007, p. 1). The transition from an industrial based economy to a knowledge economy marked an important step in the evolution of the tools by which we assess an organization's performance. In the industrial economy, the effectiveness of a given enterprise or organization's output could be measured objectively with a simple piece per hour, or production cost per item formula. By contrast, in the knowledge economy the assessment process is much more intuitive art than objectively quantifiable science. To use Drucker's terms, "for

manual work, we need only efficiency; that is, the ability to do things right rather than the ability to get the right things done" (1966, p. 2).

Importance of Protecting Cognitive Dimension

Making the best possible use of the micro (individual) and macro (collective) cognitive resources and ensuring the "right things" are done are leadership or managerial mandates in the new millennium's knowledge economy. Conserving those cognitive resources and ensuring they are expended judiciously in the furtherance of organizational goals and objectives should be among modern organizations' highest priorities.

The cornerstone of the knowledge economy is the knowledge or information worker. The product rendered by the knowledge worker is cognitive output, most typically in the form of decisions, which in turn lead to one or more organizational courses of action. At the micro level, an accountant may be asked to evaluate two options for taking depreciation on a piece of company equipment or property and then to recommend which option the company should pursue. On a more macro level, entire teams of investment advisors, engineers, analysts and lawyers may spend months or even years evaluating the advisability of risking a company's survival by pursuing a major capital investment. In both cases, the impact of those decisions contributes to the organization's ability to achieve a pre-defined objective—a position of advantage.

Similarly, military doctrine recognizes the criticality of decision making throughout the spectrum of armed conflict—from small scale contingencies to theater-wide operations, in the concept of the "OODA Loop." OODA stands for observe, orient, decide, act. United States military doctrine holds "the forces possessing better information and using that information to more effectively gain understanding have a major advantage over their adversaries" (JP3-13, 2006, pp.

I-5). Military thinking describes this advantage as decision superiority, or decision dominance.

Contemporary Thinking about Information Overload

Whether humanity has completely surrendered its culture and social structures to technology, as Neil Postman suggests in *Technolopy* (1992), is probably a matter of individual perspective. But there is almost seamless uniformity of thinking with regard to information overload, at least by those currently publishing articles on the subject. David Shenk, who coined the term "data smog" in his 1997 book by the same name, set the tone of information overload discussions that would follow for the next decade. "In a very short span of natural history, we have vaulted from a state of information scarcity to one of information surplus—from drought to flood in the geological blink of an eye" (1997, p. 28). The sheer volume of information and the pace at which so much of it is pushed to knowledge workers who use computers in their jobs have outpaced humanity's capacity to keep up. From narrowly focused academic writings, to business and trade journals, to main stream print and television coverage, there's broad consensus that information overload is frustrating information workers and generating inefficiencies for the organizations they serve.

In the last half decade or so, the Pew Internet & American Life Project, appears to be the minority commentator proffering an opposing view. A 2002 Pew report declared "contrary to the perception that wired American workers are buried in e-mail, the large majority of those who use e-mail at work say their experience with e-mail is manageable" (Fallows, 2002, p. 2). A follow up Pew report in 2006 said survey respondents felt the internet was a useful tool upon which they relied when making important life decisions. Further research into the Pew studies' departure from other thinking on this subject is needed to explain or reconcile this apparent divergence of opinion.

DATA SMOG AND TECHNO CREEP ARE CHOKING THE COGNITIVE DIMENSION

While technology makes great quantities of information available to audiences worldwide perception-affecting factors provide the context which individuals use to translate data into information and knowledge. (JP3-13, 2006, pp. I-2)

Careless Production and Management of Information Constitutes A Threat

Threats and risks to the information dimension are typically addressed in terms of security or access issues. Companies are spending billions to control access to their information systems. Indeed the majority of this book is dedicated to addressing the mushrooming vulnerabilities inherent in modern information systems. Our focus here is a more subtle, but no less impactful threat—the growing threat from within. Insufficient attention and resources are being paid to manage internal IT practices. The result constitutes an almost incalculable detriment to productivity, worker health and satisfaction, and ultimately national prosperity and security.

More Aggressive Data Smog: "Information Overload"

In the last 10 years, the smog about which Shenk wrote seems to have taken on a decidedly more aggressive form of information oversaturation than the common understanding of the term "smog" (Webster's definition) conjures up. Whereas smog makes it difficult to find what one is looking for, overload goes one step further by adding an affirmatively disruptive characteristic to the phenomenon being described. Smog is passive; overload is intrusive. Whereas smog is "out there," ready to confound, mislead and frustrate those who venture into it, overload actively and aggressively visits that frustration on every knowledge worker who interacts with a computer as part of his her daily activities. The distinction is subtle, but conceptually noteworthy because the aggressive component of information overload is dramatically on the rise. Nevertheless, for purposes of the discussion that follows, the two terms, data smog and information overload, are treated nearly interchangeably—as Shenk's definition of data smog contemplated.

CAUSES OF DATA SMOG

E-Mail Causes Data Smog and Information Overload

Far and away the most omnipresent component of data smog and information overload is e-mail. All knowledge workers use it—and most that do, use it an awful lot. According to the Radicati Research Group, "approximately 541 million workers worldwide rely on e-mail communications to conduct business. . . . Corporate [e-mail] users send and receive an average of 133 messages per day and this number is expected to reach 160 by 2009. (Radicati Group, Inc., 2005, p. 3). Executive Coach Marsha Egan puts the number at 140 e-mails a day (Gunelius, 2007), and Basex Inc., a leading advisor and consultant to knowledge economy businesses, reports that most people have experienced a 20 fold increase in e-mail they receive from five to ten years ago. Jonathan Spira, researcher and Basex CEO, characterizes sheer e-mail volume as the pre-eminent culprit of information overload in the modern knowledge economy (Spira, 2007, p. 16).

E-Mail is a Suboptimal Means for Much Knowledge Work

The process by which humans convey ideas and thoughts to one another is, when broken down and analyzed, much more complex than one might think. "Over 40 years ago, Ray L. Birdwhistell demonstrated that 'no more than 30-35 percent of the social meaning of a conversation or an interaction is carried by the words.' The rest is communicated with kinesics, non-verbal behavior, commonly called body language, such as facial expression and gestures" (Spira, 2007, p. 5). In 1984, well before e-mail took off as the common communication tool it is today, Professors Richard Daft and Robert Lingel observed that some communication media were more effective than others depending on the purpose and subject matter of the communication. (Daft, 1984). According to their "Rich Media Theory," like the more recently developed "Social Transluscence of Technology" model, a constellation of factors such as facial expression, body language, vocal tone and tenor, as well as others, help to reduce ambiguity in communications (Quan-Hasse, 2005, p. 24). Genrally speaking, communicating complex or potentially ambiguous information requires "rich" media, like telephone or ideally face to face interaction, to communicate the information effectively. Simpler, more straight forward information may be communicated in text only, or "lean" media, with little loss in communicative effectiveness.

The common theme in these and other models and theories is that an array of cues available in face to face (FTF) communication informs the receiver about the importance of the message, the sensitivity of its subject matter, and the immediacy with which the recipient should respond. In the absence of these cues, matching up the sender's intentions and the receiver's understanding, or establishing *coorientation*, becomes considerably more difficult. Consequently, communicative quality and completeness suffer.

Immediate Availability of Almost Limitless Information Generates Data Smog

The U.S. Government Accountability Office, investigative arm of the U.S. Congress, summarized another cause of data smog as follows:

Vast amounts of information are now literally at our fingertips, facilitating research on virtually every topic imaginable; financial and other business transactions can be executed instantaneously, often on a 24-hour-a-day basis; and electronic mail, Internet web sites, and computer bulletin boards allow us to communicate quickly and easily with virtually unlimited number of other individuals and groups. In addition to such benefits, however, this widespread interconnectivity poses significant risks to our computer systems and, more important, to the critical operations and infrastructures they support. (2000, p. 1)

While IT enables unprecedented proficiency at generating information, it has, thus far, produced few tools capable of effectively managing it (Spira, 2007, p. 1). Morever, the ease with which information is produced, distributed, and retrieved have all but eliminated what cyberneticist Francis Heylighen calls the "natural selection' process that would otherwise have kept all but the most important information being published" (Heylighen, 1999). "These hyper-production and hyper-distribution mechanisms," notes Shenk, "have surged ahead of human processing ability, leaving us with a permanent processing deficit, what Finnish sociologist Jaako Lehtonen calls an 'information discrepancy.'" (1997, p. 28).

The overpopulation of the information space has given workers who require access to information to do their jobs far too much of a good thing. A 1996 study commissioned by Reuters, "Dying for Information" evaluated 1300 business people in Britain, the United States, Singapore, Hong Kong and Australia in a variety of industry sectors. "More than 40% [of the study participants] felt that important decisions were delayed and the ability to make choices was hampered by excess information and that the cost of collecting the surplus data exceeded its value" (Bird, 1996, p. 3). A follow on Reuters study one year later, "Glued to the Screen: An investigation into information addiction worldwide" reported similar results;

77 percent of the 1,000 managers in the UK, the US, Germany, Singapore, Hong Kong and Ireland who took part in the survey blamed information overload on the Internet and new sources of published information (Veitch, 1997).

Poorly Designed Programs and Processes Generate Data Smog

David Platt, who teaches systems application development at the Harvard University Extension School, and prolific author on IT-related subjects, suggests the problem of poorly designed IT contributes to the frustration many users feel with modern technology. In *Why Software Sucks: and what we can do about it*, he explains that a common design flaw results from the fact that programmers, as a general proposition, "value control more than ease of use, concentrating on making complex things possible instead of making simple things simple" (2007, p. 13). Because the predominant philosophy says "if some control is good, more control is great," programs tend to become increasingly complex, harder to learn, and harder to use. When that happens, tools that were intended to increase productivity end up having the opposite effect.

The "control over use" design philosophy is a variant of techno creep that frequently leads to what Drucker called "malfunctioning information systems." In *The Effective Executive*, he described how the simple addition of an extra carbon copy of a form in a patient's discharge paperwork provided to the correct office in a timely fashion enabled a hospital to eliminate a nearly 24-hour time lag in identifying vacant bed space for patients. In another example dealing with measuring productivity in a manufacturing process, he described how a company accountant's reports listed averages pertaining to certain processes, when what the shop floor production managers needed was raw total numbers. Accordingly, "to get what they need, they must either spend hours each day adapting the averages or build their own 'secret' accounting organization" (1966, p. 45). What was true in 1966 remains true today: If an IT capability doesn't provide what the knowledge worker needs in a useful, easy to understand format, it's just more smog.

Drucker used the aforementioned examples to illustrate the importance of getting the right information to the right people. Making that determination today is every bit as important as it was in 1966, perhaps more so. The difference is this: today's manager wouldn't need to spend time figuring out who should receive the carbon copy identifying bed vacancies. She could simply send a group e-mail to the entire hospital because e-mail, unlike carbon paper, is free. Similarly, today's manager wouldn't have to figure out whether the shop floor production teams need averages or raw totals. He could—and likely would—simply send them both. The economics of CMC provide few disincentives to discourage rank and file knowledge workers from erring on the side of over-informing.

Data Smog is Difficult to Define and Categorize

Attempt to describe the distinction between data smog and useful information, and you'll quickly find yourself feeling like U.S. Supreme Court Justice Potter Stewart when he tried to specifically define obscenity. Confronted with this most vexing question he said simply, "I'll know it when I see it" (Jacobellis v. Ohio, 378 U.S. 184, 1964). Most knowledge workers can readily differentiate between clearly mission furthering information or communication and patently time wasting materials or endeavors. The vast majority of what constitutes data smog, however, exists between those polar extremes. Neither the tools designed to ferret out data smog or the knowledge workers responsible for generating much of it are more than moderately successful at identifying it—let alone controlling it.

In this respect, military doctrine acknowledges that a multitude of variables makes it difficult to recognize emerging threats to the information environment. "Many of these variables" doctrine notes, "have human dimensions that are difficult to measure, may not be directly observable, and may also be difficult to acquire feedback" (USAF, 2005, p. 28). Consequently, because the threat is so hard to define, formulating a sound defensive strategy is more challenging. For example, if an organization wanted to establish a policy saying e-mail could only be used for official purposes, the rank and file might predictably ask, "what's official? If I need to exchange periodic pleasantries with a client in order to endear myself—and our company—to her, then I must occasionally send materials that might appear impermissibly unofficial to the casual observer." Similarly, experienced leaders understand that levity and good cheer in a workplace have unmistakably positive impacts on organizational performance, so an occasional Dilbert cartoon e-mailed to a team member could also be considered "official." The same rationale applies to internet use. One person's time waster is another's perusal of information that serves—albeit indirectly perhaps, the organizational mission or company bottom line.

Types of Smog and Overload – Those You find, and Those that Find You

At the risk of over generalizing, scholars who study data smog and information overload divvy up the cyber-universe into information that knowledge workers seek out on their own, and information that inserts itself into a worker's functioning consciousness. The nomenclature in the literature varies, but the terms *distractions* and *interruptions* are two phrases commonly used to define the concepts at the introductory level. The distinguishing characteristic is that some smog or overload simply exists *out there* in cyber space, and consumes no time or cognitive energy unless and until someone searches it out. Other smog or overload more affirmatively extracts attention from IT users (Speier, 1999; Spira J. F., 2005).

Clearly Wasteful Smog that Users Seek Out

According to Drs. Cheri Spier, Joseph Valacich, and Iris Vessey, who've studied the impact of interruptions on knowledge workers, distractions people seek out come in two varieties, *internal conscious* and *internal subconscious* (Spier, 1999). Internal conscious distractions, which Spira calls *active interruptions*, are those the worker seeks out knowing full well they aren't work related. "Initiated by the very person who chooses to be interrupted by them," Spira notes, they are "solely the fault of the person who is overcome by the temptation that these interruptions hold" (Spira J. F., 2005, p. 6). Checking on one's personal finances, calendaring weekend movie schedules, or spending time surfing the net in relation to a host of other entertaining but non mission furthering dalliances falls into the category of *internal conscious distractions* or *active interruptions*.

The 1998 Reuters "Glued to the Screen" survey suggests we are witnessing the rise of a new generation of people who are particularly vulnerable to active interruptions—dataholics, a group of people whose defining characteristic is their growing obsession with wading around in all that information. Over half the survey's 1000 respondents, from the UK, US, Ireland, Germany, Singapore and Hong Kong, said they 'crave' information, while an almost equal number declared that if information was recognized as a drug, people they know would be considered addicts (Murray, 1998). Management Professor Jenny Hoobler voices similar concerns, "It can almost amount to sort of obsessive compulsive behavior today with all the things that can tear us away from job tasks. . . . It's almost an addiction for people" (Vivanco, 2007).

The susceptibility of people—dataholics and *other*-holics, to the sort of instant access to enticing materials IT makes available isn't lost on the advertising industry. Spira concluded the most difficult type of distractions to combat are those that entertain the interruptee, perhaps explaining why, according to Comtouch, "in the last three months of 2007, 70% of e-mails offered sexual enhancers, 16 percentage points more than the first three months of the year" (The Economist, 2008). With 30% of peer-to-peer requests related to pornographic downloads (Websense, Inc., 2006), it appears sexual materials are extraordinarily powerful web attractants.

Marginally Wasteful/Suboptimal Smog that Users Seek Out

A second category of user-initiated distractions or interruptions are those involving situations wherein the user spends time working a lower priority project now, deferring a higher priority project for later. The immediate access to limitless information related to every project on a knowledge worker's "to do" list makes it hard for all but the most disciplined workers to know when enough is enough. Spira notes, "knowledge workers may be constantly busy, but that doesn't make them either productive or efficient. It also doesn't mean that what they are doing is aligned with the strategic goals of their employer." John Tang of IBM Research, who studies information overload, calls this the "tyranny of the convenient," explaining that IT enables people to "do the things that are easy to do, rather than the things that are important" (Spira, 2007, p. 17). Platt takes a slightly more cynical view, attributing the inclination of people to use IT to do what's easy over what's required to "Platt's Third Law of the Universe: 'Laziness trumps everything.' If something is easy to do, people will do it whether they should or not, and if it's hard to do, then they'll do it infrequently, whether they should or not" (Platt, 2007, p. 87).

The tyranny of the convenient threatens organizational effectiveness by diverting knowledge workers' cognitive energies from work their employers' require to work they prefer to do. It's difficult to assess the macro impact tyrannical convenience imposes on the knowledge economy, or the percentage of workers susceptible to its distractive nature. What we do know, according to the Reuters, Glued to the Screen study, is that "54 percent of managers say they get a 'high' when they locate information," noting "43 percent say they look for work-related data while on holiday" (Veitch, 1997). Other's report inability to stop looking because they're left wondering if they found the "right information" in the "right place" (Spira, p. 12). It may be a totally new information age challenge caused by the powerfully distracting draw of immediate access to nearly infinite information. Or, it simply may be the product of misplaced good intentions. Whatever the cause, in the absence of policies or protocols designed to fortify human nature's resistance to these sorts of distractions, IT-empowered tyrannical convenience will constitute yet another type of techno creep that sapps the productive capacity of knowledge work organizations.

Smog Users Seek Out is Hard to Prevent Because of Ease of Access and Emerging Cultural Expectations

User initiated distractions, whether clearly wasteful or simply preferable and convenient, are especially hard to prevent or police in the knowledge work center. The very nature of the computer medium places their availability at the worker's desk—right in front of his or her face. One need not loiter at the water cooler to find a social diversion that's preferable to work. All those capabilities and dozens more are incomparably accessible, engageable, mass reproducible, and mass deliverable right there at the worker's finger tips. As Dr. Gloria Mark, who teaches informatics, notes, "the ease of access compounds the distractive potential of the internet for information workers." Reviewing preliminary research she's conducting on internet use, she concludes, "it seems to me that most internet use is a distraction from work . . . It's really the great distracter because it's very easy to get wrapped up in one distraction that leads to another and another" (Mark, 2008).

As the use of information and communication gadgetry becomes increasingly integral to the daily lives of people, it gets harder and harder to cleanly segregate personal conduct from employer-directed work. People are accustomed to immediately accessing all manner of information or communication technologies based on little more than their own impulses. If a person can answer his cell phone or respond to an Instant Message when he's in the produce isle, church pew, or even in bed with his wife (Spira, 2007), the notion of engaging in those same activities "on the clock" doesn't seem at all improper or out of place. People begin to regard information, and the ability to communicate it, as something profoundly personal in nature, irrespective of the fact that the means by which such communication takes place, or the time consumed by such transactions, belongs to their employers. "It is typical for workers to read their personal e-mail, make personal phone calls, and even surf the Web recreationally from their offices," says Spira. "Thanks to the internet, it is taken rather for granted now that a knowledge worker should have access to cartoons games, and an enormous variety of trivial information at any time" (2007, p. 7, 10). Consider these other reported examples:

- In a 2008 survey researchers found Welsh workers spending up to 91% of workplace internet use on social networking sites such as Facebook (Miloudi, 2008).
- According to a U.S. Dept of Treasury investigation, 51 percent of the time IRS employees spent online was for personal use (Arnesen, 2007).

- In a 2006 study, Websense found that 60 percent of employees who spend time online at work do so for non work-related reasons, such as "shopping, banking, checking stocks or watching sports events, playing on-line poker, booking travel, and accessing pornography sites." In fact, the overwhelming majority of access to internet porn sites happens between the hours of 9:00 AM and 5:00PM—during the workday (Websense, Inc., 2006).

- Results from a 2007 AOL survey showed that 60% of people who use e-mail check their personal e-mail while at work three times per day on average (America Online, 2007).

Interruptions Negatively Impact Concentration and Decision Making

The impact of distractions (those the worker seeks) and interruptions (those that insert themselves into the cognitive dimension) on decision making performance has been the subject of academic study since the mid 1970s. "As the number or intensity of the distractions/interruptions increases, the decision maker's cognitive capacity is exceeded, and performance decreases" (Speier, 1999, p. 341). "Informania" (Spira, 2007, p. 17), "data asphyxiation," (Van Winkle) "attentional overload," (Speier, 1999, p. 342), "cyber idigestion" (Horng, 2007) to site just a few descriptors of the commonly recognized problem, lead to a state of "hyperarousal," which undermines performance and makes it harder to think clearly or act rationally (Branegan & Salz-Trautman, 2007, p. 4).

Smog that Seeks Out Users

While both distractions and interruptions contribute to data smog and information overload, interruptions appear to constitute the greater threat to the cognitive dimension. Dr. Spier and her colleagues define *interruption* as "[a]n externally

generated, randomly occurring, discrete event [beyond the control of the individual] that breaks continuity of cognitive focus on a primary task and typically requires immediate attention and insists on action" (Spier, 1999, p. 339). Spira calls them *passive distractions*, explaining they "come from others and arrive via e-mail, the phone, the web, pager, mobile phone, and instant messaging, just to name a few" (Spira., 2005, p. 2).

Dr. Spier and her colleagues found that "increased interruption frequency resulted in both decreased decision accuracy and decreased decision time" (Speier, 1999, p. 350). Moreover, they note that information overload is compounded by interruptions.

More frequent interruptions are likely to place a greater processing load on the decision maker. Each interruption requires a recovery period where reprocessing of some primary task information occurs. Consequently, the number of recovery periods, the recovery time, and likelihood of errors all increase as the frequency of interruption increases. (Speier, 1999, p. 341)

In 2005, Dr. Glenn Wilson of the University of London's Institute of Psychiatry reported a 10 point drop in IQ scores of participants who were constantly being distracted by e-mails and telephone calls. Spira references a similar study that showed smoking marijuana produced only a 4 point drop (Spira, 2007, p. 11).

A substantial part of the problem generated by interruptions is the time and energy required to reorient, and get back to the subject being attended to prior to the interruption; that recovery time also causes a drop in productivity. "People's brains get tired from breaking off from something every few minutes to check e-mails. The more distracted you are. . . then you are going to be more tired and less productive" (Cheng, 2007). Reported objective observations vary, but the theme is fairly consistent.

- Microsoft said "workers took an average of 15 minutes to get back to what they were working on after being interrupted by a phone call, e-mail, or IM" (Cheng, 2007).
- Peter Riley, principal consultant with the IT firm LogicaCMG says "our data suggests it takes 30 seconds to a minute to get back to whatever you were doing before the e-mail came in. And only 40 – 50 percent [of those e-mails] are really relevant" (Elliot, 2007).
- Dr. Gloria Mark found knowledge workers typically spend no more than 11 minutes on a project before being interrupted (Spira, 2007, p. 20).
- Another report says "[a]fter a worker has been interrupted with a message, it generally takes nearly half a hour for him to return to his original task. . . 40 percent of workers moved on to completely new tasks after they were interrupted, leaving their old task behind neglected and unfinished" (Shipley, 2007, p. 26).

More troublingly, the already staggering number of interruptions knowledge workers must endure appears to be on the rise. According to a 2005 Basex Inc., study, the typical knowledge worker spends 20 percent of an average day attending to interruptions, and Basex CEO, Jonathan Spira, observes that if the increase in interruptions continues unchecked—5% a year in 2005, by 2031, interruptions will consume the whole of an eight hour day (Spira J. F., 2005, p. 11).

Experts suggest the interruptive capacity of e-mail may be related to the way many people use e-mail. "E-mail has given us access to more information faster than we've ever had before. Along with that comes the expectation that we're going to process the information" (Mark, 2008). Psychologist Judith Ramsay, statistician Mario Hair and computer science professor Karen Renaud, who studied the e-mail management habits of 177 employees, found that whereas "half of the study's participants report checking their e-mail

once an hour—35 percent reported checking every 15 minutes." Notably, "the researchers found that in reality, people were checking their e-mail far more often: up to 30 or 40 times per hour in some cases" (Cheng, 2007). AOL's "Third Annual E-mail Addiction Survey," conducted in 2007, reported people check e-mail twenty four hours a day; three fifths of portable device users check every time a new e-mail hits their inboxes (America Online, 2007). The AOL results line up with the 2005 Basex survey results, which found "the majority of knowledge workers . . . tend to open new e-mail immediately or shortly after notification, rather than waiting until they have a lull in their work" (Spira, 2007, p. 8).

Interruptions drive a sort of multi task approach to managing activities throughout a given workday, requiring workers to constantly assess incoming information and prioritize and reprioritize response plans. Tang calls this phenomenon a second type of tyranny—the tyranny of the urgent, which results in workers spending their finite time and energies on projects that are urgent instead of those that are important (Spira, 2007, p. 17). All that frenetic cognitive channel changing and multi tasking, with workers typically engaged in 12 projects simultaneously according to Dr. Mark's research, (Mark, 2008) simply is not conducive to the way humans think—at least the way they think productively and solve complex problems.

Paradox – Some Benefits of Distractions and Interruptions

Emerging research suggests not all interruptions render workers less productive. Although stress levels go up when people are chronically interrupted, Dr. Mark's research suggests people may actually work faster to adjust to the hectic pace of inbound information traffic. "People sort of get into 'interruption mode,' where they expect interruptions so they work faster to keep up with them" (Mark, 2008). Similarly, Dr. Spier believes:

Interruptions we choose to take can have positive benefits. . . . I think the type of interruptions where the decision maker or the knowledge worker says, 'I've been working on this really hard, my brain's a little cluttered, let me go out to MSNBC, see what's going on the in the world, or to the water fountain, and then come back on task.' Those types of very self-directed breaks . . . can be positive. (Spier D. C., 2008)

Data Smog and IT Overload are Costly

By hobbling cognitive efficiency, data smog and information overload impose substantial non obvious costs on organizations. They lower concentration levels, making it difficult for people to follow complicated trains of thought. That decrement in concentration dampens an organization's cognitive output. In 2004, the British magazine Precision Marketing reported on average that companies were spending 10K pounds per person annually paying managerial staffs to sift through their e-mail inboxes. One FTSE 100 company estimated the annual cost at 39M pounds, finding much of the correspondence driving that cost unnecessary (Ashton, 2004, p. 14). Robert Ashton, senior consultant at Emphasis Training, reported "[t]he immediacy of e-mail is both its blessing and its curse. It's made it possible for people to communicate badly in great volume" (Management Issues, 2003). Assuming an average salary of $21/hour for a typical knowledge worker, the 2005 Basex study found interruptions consumed 28 billion lost man-hours per year, costing businesses $588 billion (Spira, 2007).

In addition to the financial and cognitive dimension-hobbling costs exacted by data smog and information overload, a growing body of research supports that which seems intuitively obvious to the modern knowledge worker: all this smog and overload causes substantial stress.

- 1996 Reuters study, "[t]wo thirds of those interviewed attributed increased stress to dealing with too much information, said that stress had damaged their personal relationships, increased tension with colleagues at work and contributed to a decline in job satisfaction" (Branegan & Salz-Trautman, 2007, p. 3).
- 1997 Reuters study noted 61 percent of managers feel they receive too much information; 65 percent say their working environment has grown more stressful; 46 percent of managers work longer hours to keep up with data (Veitch, 1997); Spira describes such workers as "day extenders" (Spira, 2007, p. 9).
- "At worst the overload can lead to indigestion, heart problems and hypertension," and "in its mildest form, it sparks irritability and jeopardizes work productivity" (Murray, 1998, p. 1).
- Drs. Michelle Weil and Larry Rosen, authors of *TechnoStress*, echo the observation that technology has outpaced humanity's ability to keep up, observing how such advances have broken down the barriers that used to insulate one's personal life from his or her workaday world (Weil M. M., 1997).
- In a 2007 study by researchers from Glasgow and Paisley Universities, "over a third of the participants report[ed] being stressed by the sheer number of e-mails they receive during the day, and feel even more stress over the obligation to respond to them quickly," (Cheng, 2007), a pheomenon termed by one commentator the "Crackberry effect" (Wailgum, 2008).

Much like prolonged sun exposure damages the skin, the effects of IT induced stress accumulate over time. Technological advancement continues to drive change, and changes of all sorts have long been recognized as stressors. Whereas the initial reaction to change is arousal "as when novelty elicits curiosity, excitement and wonder. . . the longer such arousal is sustained the more likely it is that interest will wear off and fatigue will set in" (Heylighen, 1999). Over prolonged exposure, a person's failed attempts to control change leads to "numbing, apathy, despair and depression, which are all characterized by helplessness" leading to what has become increasingly recognized as "burn-out" syndrome (Heylighen, 1999, p. 5; Mark, 2008).

TECHNO CREEP CONTRIBUTES TO DATA SMOG AND INFORMATION OVERLOAD

Pace of Change and Generational Components

The pace of technological change combined with the undisciplined inclination to assume more technology is better—techno creep—generally exacerbates the effects of data smog and information overload. Ironically, the pace at which technology is driving business process and organizational changes actually makes people more resistant to change. In a 4-year study of 3,129 full time employees from a cross-section of companies in southern California, Drs. Weil and Rosen found business workers—those most likely to be using more IT at work—were actually more hesitant to embrace new technology (Weil & Rozen, 2000, p. 3).

Dr. Mark and her colleagues also suggest there is a generational component to IT adaptation. She observes, "[m]y kids were introduced to the computer when they were two. When they were in first grade they were taking typing classes. It's a way of life for them" (Mark, 2008). According to Spira, younger workers (33 and under—born the year Pong was introduced) appear to be better at multi-tasking (Spira, 2007, p. 3). Consequently, they're more amenable to adapt to technological changes in the way work gets done. If there is a generational component, some of the friction currently slowing the realization of IT-driven improvements in organizational efficiency may disappear. As the people who grew up surrounded by technology ascend to progressively more senior management and leadership positions and replace those more reluctant to adapt, the reluctant adapter problem *may* self correct over time.

Mis-Used IT tools Generate Data Smog and Information Overload

The paradox about IT is that while it puts very powerful analytical tools in the hands of the masses, many of the individuals who make up the masses plainly lack the skill or understanding to use those tools effectively. Applications like Microsoft Excel empower those who can click a mouse to produce very impressive and official looking charts, graphs and statistical proclamations with relative ease. Even if there were no e-mail and no internet, this would be cause for concern, but the smog and overload problem would not be nearly so acute. Today, the same sort of computing power enabling the quick production of lazy math also facilitates its mass distribution. Figuring out how to prevent the creation and dissemination of new data smog is every bit as challenging as navigating that which already exists. Bridget Murray of the American Psychological Association sums up the state of affairs, saying, "the problems stem from people's overuse or misuse of technologies and from technology's ineffective presentation of information" (Murray, 1998, p. 1). Or, more pointedly, as Drucker opined in 1966, "the computer will, of course, no more make decision-makers out of clerks than the slide rule makes a mathematician out of a high school student" (1966, p. 164).

IMPLICATIONS OF DATA SMOG

The focus of Information Operations is on the decision maker and the information environment in order to affect decision making and thinking processes, knowledge, and understanding of the situation. (JP3-13, 2006, pp. I-9)

In 1966, Drucker said that while the computer could do certain things, like performing addition or subtraction, infinitely faster than man, it was not an invention comparable to the wheel or the airplane or the television, which could "actually multiply man's capacity or extend his nature. . . [adding] a new dimension to man" (1966, p. 159). Drucker, like many pre IT revolution commentators, underestimated the breadth and reach of the PC and internet's transformative influence on how people interact with one another. By 1997, Shenk observed that revolution, particularly in communications, was transforming society in ways Drucker hadn't envisioned.

Decision-making is a process, not a rapid binary reaction. Doing it well takes varying amounts of time and focused cognitive energy. As a general proposition, information is a good thing, but too much of it clearly is not. In order for information to be useful, it must be attended to in some fashion and processed by a user to produce situational awareness, or to generate a decision (Boiney, 2007). Drucker punctuated the criticality of human decision making, observing:

The strength of the computer lies in its being a logic machine. It does precisely what it is programmed to do. This makes it fast and precise. It also makes it a total moron; for logic is essentially stupid. It is doing the simple and obvious. The human being, by contrast, is not logical; he is perceptual. This means that he is slow and sloppy. But he is also bright and has insight. (1966, p. 159)

In order to recapture the ability to leverage those irreplacable human qualities, organizations must find a way to clear the data smog currently hobbling the cognitive dimension.

Despite some minor variations from one commentator to the next, the weight of expert opinion strongly suggests the over abundance of raw, poorly organized information is degrading the quality of knowledge work being produced. That degradation portends both near and long term negative impacts for organizations public and private, regarding concerns both financial and and those considerably more serious.

The information revolution is still in its infancy. Based on a LEXIS-NEXIS search of all newspaper and magazine articles, Metcalfe's Law appears to have been first introduced in an article appearing in Forbes magazine in late 1993 (Gilder, 1993). That's the same year the first "web browser" made it possible for twelve scientists to view each other's electronic files over a network, a watershed event in the information revolution (Friedman, 2007). The exception to Metcalfe's law is apparent; "the bigger the network the better" notion originated in a day when the idea of potential "network abuse" was not widespread. The information superhighway was a walking path, e-mail was something most people had never heard of, and few outside hard science academia would have associated the word "web" with anything other than spiders (arachnids, not search engines). Between then and now, amid much fog and friction, techno creep has introduced organizations large and small, private and public, to the inescapable conclusion that Metcalfe's Law has a more sinister cousin-- Marksteiner's corrolary: The *disruptive potential* of a network grows in proportion to the square of the number of *irresponsible and or undisciplined* users.

The left-to-right growth of clouds depicted in Figure 1 is intended to communicate that the addition of new and progressively more prolific elements of data smog present an increasingly impenetrable barrier (more smog) between the decision making centers of gravity of organizations (the "cognitive dimensions of their information environments) and access to useful, relevant, reliable information. Note the arrows, which represent that useful information, decrease from left to right – 16, 9, 4, 1, to visually depict the inverse of Metcalfe's proposition about the

Figure 1. Techno Creep over time

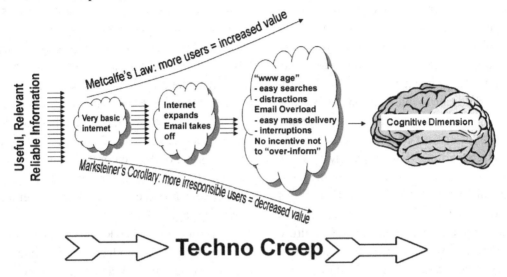

expanding value of a network based on the square of the number of its members.

In every organization, the collective concentration, focus, and intellectual capacity of its knowledge work force is a center of gravity referred to as the cognitive dimension. U.S. military doctrine underscores the importance of protecting how information is managed, processed, and acted upon by decision makers. Most importantly, military doctrine also charges strategists and planners to be constantly on guard for new and emerging threats to the cognitive dimension: "A perceived advantage in information technology (IT) can also be turned into a disadvantage. New technologies introduce new vulnerabilities for exploitation through manipulation or attack" (USAF, 2005). Over saturating one's own information systems or the people who use and rely on them, so as to negatively impact the decision making process, constitutes just such a vulnerability. The overarching objective of IO is "to influence, disrupt, corrupt, or usurp adversarial human and automated decision making while protecting our own" (JP3-13, 2006, p. ix). Data smog and information overload influence, disrupt and corrupt human decision making. The logic is as applicable to business as it is to the battle field.

Plainly speaking, assume for a moment an unfriendly actor introduced a chemical agent into the water supply of London, Paris, Madrid, Berlin, Moscow, or the District of Columbia that rendered everyone in the effected city incapable of making cogent, well thought out decisions for one-to-two hours a day. Such an act would immediately be recognized as an attack with profound national security implications. However, when the same effect is the result of an organization's techno creeping mismanagement of its own information systems and practices, there's less concern. To be clear, much of the problem is not the product of users engaging in behaviors immediately recognizable as counterproductive or inappropriate, like surfing pornographic web sites or sending offensive e-mails. Most public and private sector organizations already have policies in place to address those concerns (The Radicati Group, Inc., 2005; Arnesen D. W., 2007). It's the more benign seeming behaviors that present techno creep's mounting threat.

The warning signs are overwhelming. Mainstream and academic publications speak in numbers about the deleterious impact of interruptions and distractions on the quality of knowledge work. Assuming most experts and surveys are correct, knowledge workers receive 130 – 150 e-mails a day, and the number is climbing. An alarming percentage of those e-mails provide little value to the recipient either because of contextual (lean nature of text only medium) or substantive (not information the recipient really needed) short-comings. In addition to interruptions knowledge workers cannot control, they are also constantly subjected to all manner of distractions they are capable of controlling—but frequently don't, at least not very well. The convenience of the computer, the ubiquity-driven "my stuff" mindset associated with personal communication, and the immediacy expectation endemic to the IT culture entice knowledge workers away from cognitive productivity like an addictive drug. Using the most conservative estimates reported by the experts who've studied the issue, knowledge workers lose at least an hour a day navigating through data smog related to unproductive interruptions and distractions. The figure is likely substantially higher. But even if it's not, the impact is already enormous.

Discussion & Recommendations

The implications of data smog, information over-load, and techno creep are cause for concern. For at least the foreseeable future, the outward expansion of Computer Mediated Communication (CMC) into progressively more corners of the personal and professional daily lives of people is inevitable. Combined with increases in processing power and data transmission speeds, that expansion will require workers to deal with more information, not less. The threat to the cognitive dimension is real, quantifiable, and growing in severity. Military theory lays out a clear, comprehensive framework for recognizing the threat and defend-ing against it.

The basic approach of the military framework for defending against information overload are as follows: Information and the way it's managed should be recognized as a strategic resource.

The cognitive dimension of the information en-vironment, that zone where human analysis and decision making takes place is a critical center of gravity. Organizational success or failure depends on the unhobbled functioning of that center of gravity. The complexity and changing nature of the Information Environment can make threats to the cognitive dimension very hard to identify. Nevertheless, anything that imperils the efficient functioning of that center of gravity constitutes a serious threat. All such threats should be decisively checked before they result in unrecoverable loss of advantage—defeat.

The modern knowledge economy's organi-zational leader must clearly understand that the cognitive dimension is a critical center of gravity, the un-hobbled functioning of which demands constant vigilance and protection. According to the weight of expert opinion and numerous objec-tive measures, techno creep (the undisciplined use of IT resources, primarily e-mail and internet) is influencing, disrupting, corrupting, or usurping human decision making in public and private or-ganizations around the world. Data smog, which is comprised of subtle but powerful forces, causes organizations to surrender advantages otherwise conferred by decision dominance. Data smog and information overload are not simply amorphous, unavoidable overhead costs of doing business in the knowledge economy. Rather, they are products of information age fog and friction brought about by a family of technologies whose advance out-paced humanity's ability effectively to keep up.

Focused training programs will help reduce data smog and halt techno creep. IT users should be trainined early and often on responsible use of e-mail and other IT capabilities. John Montana, General Counsel and consultant with the Pelli Group, a Reston based IT consulting firm, articu-lates that which his contemporaries are painfully aware, "in the absence of training and monitor-ing, it's amazing what a mess people can make of even the most perfectly designed IT solutions" (Montana, 2008). Similarly, Ben Schorr, President and CEO of Roland Schorr & Tower, an IT consultancy based in Honolulu, observed:

I never cease to be amazed at companies who will spend tens of tousands of dollars, sometimes more, on software, but won't spend a thousand dollars to teach its people how to use what they've purchased. . . . Imagine your eagerness to fly on an airline that says, "we don't train our pilots, but we do give them all a copy of 'Big Planes for Dummies.'" (2008)

Organizations should not simply train knowledge workers how to use the IT capabilities at their disposal, they should invest sufficient resouces to refocus knowledge workers' attention on using those capabilities *effectively*. With regard to e-mail and other forms of CMC, the ultimate goal of training and education should be to instill in workers a state of what Send author Shipley calls "digital mindfulness" (McGinn, 2007). People producing and distributing data/information should be held accountable for how well the information they produce and dissiemenate achieves a mission furthering objective of the organization. In military speak, they should be trained to, *target for effect*. Which is to say, they should be conditioned to clearly define the effect or outcome they seek to achieve (by, for example, sending an e-mail), and then consciously and judiciously use the IT tools available (draft an e-mail) to pursue that effect or outcome in as efficient a manner as possible. Moreover, organizational policies should reward employees who *communicate for effect* well, and unambiguously penalize those who do not. There are dozens—probably hundreds of resources describing how people and organizations should more effectively use e-mail. Some discuss e-mail writing, others address setting up alternate e-mail boxes or using e-mail macros or other protocols, but one guide is probably much like the next.

One shortcoming in many such guides, however, is the absence of an exacting "official use only" rule. Squishy terms like "*unreasonable*

use" or "*whenever possible*" or "users *should. . .*" are too ambiguous. They leave room for any use other than the patently unlawful or wildly wasteful to be contorted to fit within the zone of the permissible in the minds of most users. Consequently, they are little help in controlling data smog and information overload.

As described previously, the ideal "official use only" rule would be difficult to precisely define because its enforcement turns on the definition of the word "official." Nevertheless, at the risk of overgeneralizing, the following would be a good start: "Other than situations requiring you to address a personal emergency (health, safety, welfare of you or a family member), neither personal nor company e-mail, IM, or internet communications equipment will be used during working hours for anything other than strictly work-related communications. Exceptions to this rule will be granted on a case by case basis by the supervisor of the employee requesting an exception to this rule." Organizations should enforce the rule by alerting every employee that it will monitor its systems, and that noncompliance is a punishable offense. The ultimate objective of enforcing these sorts of rules would be to change behavior and to more decisively incentivize knowledge workers to communicate for effect. Those who keep abreast of military theory will be aware that military thinkers have very recently begun questioning the utility of effects-based operations (EBO) as model by which to plan and execute objectives in very complex systems, such as those involved in the conduct of warfare. Nevertheless, the basic premise that planners should clearly define the end state they hope to achieve before deciding how to pursue an objective is still a well accepted axiom. To that extent, communicating for effect should be the goal (Mattis, 2008).

Few plans survive first contact with reality, and a rule like the one previously described would be no different. Exceptions and special circumstances would have to be carved out based on the requirements of each user. The point is, there should be at least some feedback mechanism, some factor, that reintroduces the notion that paperless transactions, whether they involve generating correspondence or retrieving information, are not without costs. Creatively leveraging technology to provide that feedback might include monitoring total e-mail traffic, or the frequency with which senders use group mail lists. Similar applications might keep track of where users go on the internet and how long they spend there. Whatever rules are enacted and tools are used to support them, efforts to correct undesirable IT behaviors will succeed only if the policies and rules are unambiguously enforced.

Preliminary indications from organizations that have experimented with "no e-mail Fridays" suggest behavior changing rules have promise. IBM, Intel, and U.S. Cellular, for exmaple, have experimented with rules that either prohibit or strictly limit for some predefined period each week interruptions that would otherwise result from nonessential meetings or excessive e-mail use (Spira, 2007; Goldberg, 2007; Horng, 2007). According to the Wall Street Journal, by October of 2007 "growing numbers of employers [were] imposing or trying out 'no e-mail' Fridays or weekends; such limits aim to encourage more face-to-face and phone contacts with customers and co-workers" (Shellenbarger, 2007). After imposing a no e-mail Friday rule, Georgia-based PBD Worldwide Fulfillment Services reported a 75% drop in total e-mail traffic throughout the work week (Horng, 2007).

The bottom line is this: Organizations should narrowly define and unmistakably enforce rules prophibiting anything other than official, mission-furthering uses of IT resources (zero tolerance policy for personal web surfing or e-mails) during working hours. Existing policies designed to encourage these behaviors should be much more decisively monitored, with appropriate incentives—and disincentives—used to encourage desired practices.

Technological solutions such as e-mail filters, automated data organizers and the like won't clear the data smog. In fact, pursuing IT solutions to behaviorial problems, without instituting unambiguous rules governing those behaviors, would likely generate even more data smog. Ironically the ease with which all sorts of training can be delivered to knowledge workers' desktops presents an additional data smog vulerability—training creep.

The ease with which computer based training (CBT) can be generated and distributed renders it as susceptible to misuse as e-mail. Since e-mail can be mass generated and distributed with relatively zero added expense, no disincentive discourages senders from overinforming. The same is true of CBT. Since generating and distributing CBT is fairly cheap and easy, there's no disincentive discouraging trainors from overtraining. As a prerequisite to directing mandatory CBT, proponents should be required to calculate the nonobvious costs of of doing so. Using the Basex formula (hourly wage X employees X duration of the training) would be a good start. The point is not to discourage training, but simply to ensure those deciding that some sort of training is required is in fact based on an identified need, and to ensure they don't assume it's a no cost proposition. In summary, organizations should ensure they *train for effect*.

CONCLUSION

Drucker predicted that "if properly used . . . [computers] should free senior executives from much of the preoccupation with events inside the organization to which they are now being condemned by the absence or tardiness of reliable information" (1966, p. 163). Ironically, data smog and techno creep are causing precisely the problems Drucker envisioned IT solving. In the new millennium, however, the detrimental impact is not limited to senior executives. Rather, techno creeping data smog siphons off creativity, efficiency, reliability, and worker health and satisfaction at every layer in knowledge economy organizations.

Whether organizations should impose a total ban on personal e-mail and internet traffic over their networks, as the U.S. DoD has considered (UPI Energy, 2008), remains an open—and contentious question. What is certain, however, is that when business enterprises simply stand by and permit the hobbling of their cognitive centers of gravity, they surrender competitive advantage and imperil their economic viability. When governments and their armed forces do so, they risk considerably more.

REFERENCES

America Online. (2007, July 26). *Think You Might Be Addicted to E-mail?* You're Not Alone, Retrieved, October 31, 2007, from http://press.aol.com/article_print.cfm?article_id=1271.

Appelo, J. (2008, June). Progress in Three Dimensions. *Software Quality Professional.* Retrieved from LEXIS, 17 Jul 2008 (search: "scope creep").

Arnesen, D. W. (2007). Developing an Effective Company Policy for Employee Internet and E-mail Use. *Journal of Organizational Culture, Communication & Conflict*, (pp. 53-71).

Ashton, R. (2004, May 28). "Free" e-mails can cost a fortune if the messages aren't efficient. *Precision Marketing*, (p. 14).

Bennet J. T. (2008, June 16). Shift to fixed-price deals urged for DoD. *Federal Times.* June 16, 2008. Retrieved from LEXIS, 17 Jul 2008 (search term: "requirements creep").

Bird, M., Branegan, J., & Salz-Trautman, P. (9 December 1996), System Overload: Excess Information is Clogging the Pipes of Commerce—and Making People Ill, *Time Magazine, International Edition*, (p. 38).

Boiney, L. G. (2007). *More than Information Overload: Supporting Human Attention Allocation.* Paper presented at 12th International Command and Control Research and Technology Symposium.

Cheng, J. (2007, August 14). E-mail stress slowing down workers, say researchers, *ars technica the art of technology,* Retrieved February 17, 2008, from: http://arstechnica.com/news.ars/post/20070814-e-mail-stress-slowing-down-workers-say-researchers.html.

Daft, R. L. (1984). Information Richness: a new approach to managerial behavior and organizational design. *Research in Organizational Behavior*, (pp. 191-233).

Drucker, P. F. (1966). *The Effective Executive.* New York: Harper Collins Publishers, Inc.

Elliot, T. (2007, October 17). *Even superhighways have traffic jams.* Sydney Morning Herald.com, Retrieved October 31, 2007, from www.smh.com.au/news/technology/even-superhighways-have-traffic-jams/2007/10/16/1192300769157.html?page=fullpage.

Fallows, D. (2002). *E-mail at Work: Few Feel Overwhelmed, and Most Are Pleased With the Way E-mail Helps Them Do Their Jobs.* Washington DC: Pew Internet and American Life Project.

Freemon, S. (2004, November 22). Dogwood just the first new mission. *The Times* (p. 28) London.

Gilder, G. (1993, September 13). George Gilder's Telecosm: Metcalfe's Law and Legacy. *Forbes*, (p. 158).

Goldberg, A. (2007, October 18). E-mail backlash takes root in tech heartland. *bankokpost.com.* Retrieved February 17, 2008, from www.indiaenews.com/america/20071018/75796.htm.

Gunelius, S. (2007, October 14). Claiming E-Mail Bankruptcy. *Newstex Web Blogs, ITech Tips.* Retrieved February 21, 2008, from LEXIS. (search term: "E-Mail overload").

Heylighen, F. (1999, February 19). Change and Information Overload. *Principia Cybernetica*

Web, Retrieved November 13, 2007, from http://pcp.lanl.gov/CHINNEG.html.

Hoagland, J. (1993, July 20). Beware 'Mission Creep' in Somalia. *The Washington Post,* (p. A17).

Horng, E. (2007, April 7). No E-Mail Fridays Transform Office, After initial doubts, co-workers learn to deal with each other in person. *abcnews.go.com,* Retrieved October 31, 2007, from: http://abcnews.co.com/print?id+2939232.

Jacobellis v. Ohio, 378 U.S. 184, 378 U.S. 184 (U.S. Supreme Court June 1964, 1964).

JP1, (n.d.). *Joint Publication 1, Doctrine for the Armed Forces of the United States,* U.S. Department of Defense.

JP3-0, (2006, September 17). *Joint Publication 3-0, Joint Operations, Incorporating Change 1.* U.S. Department of Defense.

JP3-13, (2006, February 13). Joint *Publication 3-13, Information Operations.* U.S. Department of Defense.

Management Issues. (2003, July 21). Pointless e-mails costs business billions, *Management Issue,.* Retrieved Febryary 17, 2008, from: www.management-issues.com/2006/8/24/research/pointless-e-mail-costs-business-millions.asp.

Mark, G. (2008, February 18). (P. Marksteiner, Interviewer).

Mattis, James N. (2008, October 1). USJFCOM Commander's Guidance for Effects-based Operations. Parameters 38(1). Retrieved from Westlaw, 8 Jan, 2009 (search term: "Mattis" and "Effects-based operations").

McGinn, D. (2007, April 16). Return to Sender; A new book cautions against overrelying on e-mail. *Newsweek, U.S. Edition,* (p. E16).

Metcalfe's Law. (2002, April). Metcalfe's Law, *National Science Foundation, Division of Science*

Resources Statistics, Science and Engineering Indicators. Retrieved December 15, 2007, from: www.nsf.gov/statistics/seind02/c8/c8s1.htm#metcalfe.

Miloudi, S. (5 February 2008), They come to work... but survey finds that nine-tenths of internet time may be spent chatting at a cost of billions; But sites are useful tools and are good for staff morale, say experts, *The Western Mail,* Retrieved 13 April 2008 from LEXIS, (search term: "personal internet use w/10 workplace").

Montana, J. C. (2008, March 13). Nuts and Bolts of Records Management: Avoiding A Rube Goldberg System. *ABA Tech Show,* Chicago, IL, USA: American Bar Association.

Murray, B. (1998, March 3). Data Smog: newest culprit in brain drain, *American Psyshological Association,* Retrieved November 15, 2007, from: http:www.apa.org/monitor/mar98/smog.htl.

National Commission on Terrorist Attacks Upon the United States. (2004). *The 9/11 Commission Report.* Washington: U.S. Government Printing Office.

Platt, D. S. (2007). *Why Software Sucks: And What We Can Do About It.* Boston: Rolling Thunder Computer, Inc.

Postman, N. (1992). *Technopoly: the surrender of culture to techology.* New York: Random House Inc.

Quan-Hasse, A. C. (2005). Instant messaging for collaboration: A case study of a high-tech firm, *Journal of Computer Mediated Communication,* Retrieved April 6, 2008, from jcmc.indiana.edu/vol10/issue4/quan-hasse.html.

Schorr, B. (2008, March 14). Presentation: "Keeping Up With the Joneses--Upgrading to Office 2007". *ABA Tech Show* . Chicago, IL, USA.

Shellenbarger, S. (2007, October 11). A day without e-mail is like . . . *Wall Street Journal Abstracts* , pp. Section D, Column 2, page 1.

Shenk, D. (1997). *Data Smog: Surviging the Information Glut.* San Francisco: Harper.

Shipley, D. S., & Schwalbe, W. (2007). *Send.* Toronto: Alfred A. Knopf.

Siegel, A. B. (2000). Mission Creep or Mission Misunderstood. *JFQ: Joint Force Quarterly, 112.*

Spier, C. , Valacich, J., & Vessey, I., (1999). The Influence of Task Interruption in Individual Decision Making: An Information Overload Perspective. *Decision Sciences*, (pp. 337-360).

Spier, D. C. (2008, March 27). (P. Marksteiner, Interviewer).

Spira, J. B. (2007). *Information Overload: We have met the enemy and he is us.* Basex Inc.

Spira, J. F. (2005). *The Cost of Not Paying Attention: How Interruptions Impact Kowledge Worker Productivity.* Basex Inc.

The Economist. (2008, February 5). Internet, Sex and shopping, *Economist.com*, Retrieved February 5, 2008, from www.economist.com/daily/chart-gallery/PrinterFriendly.cfm?story_id=10637431.

The Radicati Group, Inc. (2005, March). Taming the Growth of E-mail - An ROI Analysis. Palo Alto, CA, USA: The Radicati Group, Inc.

UPI Energy, (4 February 2008). DoD weighing ban on personal Internet Use, UPI Energy, Retrieved 21 March 2008 from LEXIS (search term: "personal internet use w/10 workplace").

USAF 2-5, (2005, January 11). *Air Force Doctrine Document 2-5, Information Operations.* United States Air Force.

Van Winkle, W. (n.d.). Information Overload. Global *Development Research Center*, Retrieved March 13, 2008, from http://www.gdrc.org/icts/i-overload/infoload.html.

Veitch, M. (1997, December 8). Data Overload Causing Addiction-Reuters, *ZDNet*, Retrieved

March 12, 2008, from http://news.zdnet.co.uk/internet/0,1000000097,2067297,00.htm.

Vivanco, L. (2007, November 12). Masters of multitasking; Doing multiple tasks at once has become second nature for some, but is that a good thing? *Chicago Tribune, RedEye Edition*, 6

Wailgum, T. (2008, January 4). Information Overload is Killing You and Your Productivity, *CIO.com*, Retrieved February 5, 2008, from www.cio.com: www.cio.com/article/print/169200.

Websense, Inc. (2006). Web@work 2006 Employee Computing Trends Surve, *Websense.com*, Retrieved from www.websense.com/global/en/PressRoom/MediaCenter/Research/webatwork/Employee Computing.php.

Weick, K. E., Sutliffe, K, & Ostfeld, D. (1993). Collective Mind in Organizations. *Administrative Science Quarterly*, 357-381.

Weil, M. M. (1997). *TechnoStress.* John Wiley & Sons.

Weil, M. M., & Rozen, L. D. (2000). Four-Year Study Shows More Technology at Work and at Home But More Hesitancy About Trying New Technology. *Human-ware.com*, Retrieved 12 December 2007 from http://www.human-ware.com/BusinessStudy.htm.

Weiland, S. (2006, December 21). *Deployment of German Planes to Afghanistan Sharply Criticized.* Retrieved July 11, 2008, from LEXIS (search term: "mission creep").

Stevenson, C. A. (1996, August). *The Evolving Clinton Doctrine on the Use of Force.* Retrieved July 13, 2008, from EBSCO: web.ebscohost.com (search term: "mission creep").

Yates, L. A. (1997, August). Military stability and support operations: analogies, patterns and recurring themes. *Military Review,* (pp. 51-62). Retrieved July 13, 2008, from EBSCO: web.ebscohost.com (search term: "mission creep").

Chapter VIII
Balancing the Public Policy Drivers in the Tension between Privacy and Security

John W. Bagby
The Pennsylvania State University, USA

ABSTRACT

The public expects that technologies used in electronic commerce and government will enhance security while preserving privacy. These expectations are focused through public policy influences, implemented by law, regulation, and standards emanating from states (provincial governments), federal agencies (central governments) and international law. They are influenced through market pressures set in contracts. This chapter posits that personally identifiable information (PII) is a form of property that flows along an "information supply chain" from collection, through archival and analysis and ultimately to its use in decision-making. The conceptual framework for balancing privacy and security developed here provides a foundation to develop and implement public policies that safeguard individual rights, the economy, critical infrastructures and national security. The illusive resolution of the practical antithesis between privacy and security is explored by developing some tradeoff relationships using exemplars from various fields that identify this quandary while recognizing how privacy and security sometimes harmonize.

INTRODUCTION

Public policy drives private enterprise and public institutional efforts to maintain security. A traditional focus on criminal enforcement and regulatory risks in the protection of physical property fails to adequately protect networked computers and the related impact on the national economy and critical infrastructures. Security failures make confidential-private data more vulnerable. These include vulnerabilities in the electronic transaction processing systems underlying electronic commerce and the systems supporting digital government. National security is imperiled with any substantial weakening of the national economy. Fundamental to information assurance (IA) is regulatory compliance with both security and privacy law, responsibilities that are dispersed among (1) individuals, (2) government at all levels: local, state/provincial, national/federal, regional/international, (3) private-sector entities generally and (4) specifically, private sector organizations in the burgeoning data management industry (e.g., suppliers and users of data, service providers to the "information supply chain"). Public policy must continually draw a balance between individual interests in secrecy or solitude and society's interests in security, order and efficiency. Privacy law in the United States is a fragmented, assortment of rights from various sources: constitutions, federal statutes and regulations, state statutes and regulations, standards, common law precedents and private contracts. This chapter frames the debate over privacy rights and security imperatives, first as a tradeoff, largely in the realms of national security and crimes, but then finds important points of complementarity between individuals' security and their privacy. Analysis using this model reveals insights for public policy makers that contribute to the implementation of technology by attenuating public surprise of privacy intrusions and enabling public support for reasonable security measures.

Confronting the professionals in the information technology (IT) industry who are most intimately engaged in IA, cyber-security and the facilitation of privacy protection, there is an often daunting complexity in public policy imperatives, because they are derived from law, standards, contracts, litigation and regulation and because the sources of these pressures are so varied. This uncertainty is particularly complicated for the control of personally identifiable information (PII) data security risks. A confluence of pressures now focuses on how vulnerabilities of tangible and intangible assets impact the reliability of information systems underlying transaction records.

Internal control systems are the key mechanisms for the maintenance of security over information assets exerted through their influence over decision-making and operations monitoring in private-sector institutions, but with close analogs for public-sector institutions (Sarbanes-Oxley Act, 2002).

This chapter contends that to clarify IA threat reduction duties, IT professionals must more clearly understand public policy imperatives for internal control that emanate from evolving standards of professional practice and ethics, financial reporting standards, corporate governance, privacy law, trade secret intellectual property (IP), technology transfer contractual duties, electronic records management best practices, tort and criminal law and fiduciary duties. These are hugely diverse and complex influences so a comprehensive treatment of their details is well beyond the scope of this chapter. Nevertheless, various exemplars of these sources are examined conceptually to provide insight into how public policy exerts pressure that constitutes a confluence of regulatory and market-based forces influencing the development, implementation, testing, revision and evolution of internal control. These pressures comprise a major component of the public policy environment of IT Governance. In the U.S., privacy laws are apparently distinct regimes, so they may be misinterpreted as limited, "sectoral" silos applicable only narrowly to particular industries or professions. However, this chapter argues that they are increasingly broadening to include internal control pressures impacting service providers, consultants, publicly-traded corporations, closely-held companies, non-governmental organizations (NGOs) and government agencies at all levels (Bagby, 2007-2).

This chapter proposes a supply chain analysis that should apply to the data flows of information but that is not dependant on any supply chain in goods or services. Supply chain concepts and network analysis is adapted to information data flows starting from the acquisition of PII, through the archiving and processing of PII, to analysis and the ultimate use, typically in decision-making. Recognition that information is property permits the development of this information supply chain conceptual framework; in turn, this approach enables the application of supply chain economics, regulatory approaches and cost analysis methods that become useful in participating in the public policy debate and as compliance is necessary with the many specific privacy and security laws.

PUBLIC POLICY BACKGROUND OF PRIVACY AND SECURITY

Conceptual privacy can be misunderstood without an understanding of its historical development including the underlying social expectations (Solove, 2002). There are a number of components to conceptual privacy. Privacy has Biblical origins, initially focusing on the privacy components of shame and modesty. These components persist today through shyness and prudent appearance that attenuate the risks of external predators from harms such as stalking, sexual predation, public contempt and retribution. In Colonial American times, privacy was envisioned as a limitation on despotic government intrusion both as incentive to emigrate and abandon oppression in the American colonists' native lands and again when the American colonists suffered tyranny under the English Crown. Forms of privacy were incorporated by the Founders into the U.S. Constitution as rights: religious freedom, search and seizure limitations, prohibitions on quartering of soldiers, freedom of speech, press and association, due process and equal protection (U.S. Constitution 1791, 1791, 1868). Liberty is fundamental to privacy by separating individuals from interference by government and powerful private interests. Competition is promoted when individuals and firms can economically exploit valuable secrets. With the taming of the American frontier and the industrial revolution privacy concerns shifted

from government intrusions to private party intrusions. In the post 9.11 world of counter-terrorism, a merger of private and government privacy intrusions is becoming the focus of both privacy and security regulation. Privacy is also viewed as a fundamental right and a civil liberty essential to freedom, dignity, and marital privacy (Griswold v. Connecticut, 1965).

Advances in IT heighten public concern over the commoditization and potential for abuse of PII because it is subject to data creep, such as when PII collected for one purpose becomes useful for other purposes. For example, for a long time, social security numbers appeared useful well beyond the original purpose to facilitate payment record-keeping for FICA remittances and Social Security benefit payments. According to Alan F. Westin, the privacy attitudes and expectations of the American public can be segmented into three groups. First, there are "privacy fundamentalists," who comprise about a quarter of the U.S. population. Privacy fundamentalists value privacy highly, summarily reject inquiries by business or government for their PII, are most likely to advocate against PII disclosure and seek to regulate privacy rights most stringently. Second, there is a middle ground of "privacy pragmatists," a group accounting for nearly 2/3 of the population. Pragmatists are generally willing to balance their privacy against society's needs for PII. Pragmatists are likely to consider privacy policies and practices carefully and they will disclose PII when economically rational. They are probably less demanding of stringent government regulation of privacy practices. Some initial empirical research begins to suggest that pragmatists evaluate the security of their PII under a reasonable expectations framework similar to that applied in the courts (Peters, Amato & Hollenbeck, 2007). Third, there are persons unconcerned with privacy, a cohort that has diminished from 1/5 of the U.S. population in 1990 to 1/8 by 2000 (Westin, 2000). The unconcerned would likely disclose PII readily, trust users of their PII or may be oblivious to

PII abuses and seem the least likely to lobby for stringent privacy rights or regulation.

Clarity is elusive in privacy and security discussions, these terms are widely misunderstood. For example, some IT and computer professionals simply define privacy as encryption. Some network administrators define security as encryption. Neither, position can be correct and the two are irreconcilable. Encryption may enhance the security of PII, but encryption is but one of several contemporary security tools to do so. Instead, privacy includes several legal interests derived from individual expectations that often function to define privacy rights (Katz v. U.S., 1967). Privacy rights trigger legal rights and these raise legal duties on various individuals and institutions when engaged in data processing. Synonyms for privacy provide some perspective: seclusion, solitude, retreat from intrusion, intimacy, isolation, secrecy, concealment and separateness. During the 20th century, at least four distinct privacy interests have developed in the U.S. following the influential work of Warren and Brandeis and the prominent tort law scholar Prof. Prosser (Warren & Brandeis, 1890). A privacy taxonomy is now firmly rooted in the tort law of most states recognizing four separate categories of privacy interests: (1) intrusion upon the plaintiffs seclusion or solitude, or into his private affairs; (2) public disclosure of embarrassing private facts about the plaintiff; (3) publicity which places the plaintiff in a false light in the public eye; and (4) appropriation, for the defendant's advantage, of the plaintiff's name or likeness (Prosser, 1960) (Restatement, 1976). Of course, privacy protections are also the product of legislation and regulation, much of which is based on privacy standards.

Privacy Standards

Many features of modern privacy laws and policies throughout the developed world are generally traceable to five "fair information practices," also known as the Fair Information Practice Principles (FIPP). These FIPP originated from a study commissioned by the U.S. Department of Health, Education and Welfare (HEW Report,1973). The FIPP are informal, de jure standards that inspire particular mechanisms, rights and procedures in many privacy statutes, regulations and policies, not only in U.S. governmental privacy regulations but also in self-regulatory programs from the private sector and the privacy public policy of many nations (e.g., EU) (Bagby, 2007-1).

The first FIPP standard is "notice." Subject individuals should be given notice and/or have a clear awareness of the capture, processing and use of their PII, including the purpose for its use. In the notice urged by FIPP, there should be a reasonably adequate, conspicuous and comprehensible notification of the data capture and processing practices and that this be communicated before PII is collected. Subject individuals uninformed of data collection are prevented from making any informed choice. Notice enables subject individuals to take counter-measures for their PII protection. Sufficient details to inform the subject individual's choice are also desirable, including: (i) identity of the PII data collector, (ii) identity of the PII's recipient, (iii) summary of PII use, (iv) description of the PII targeted for collection, (v) description of the means and methods to collect PII, (vi) an acknowledgement when PII collection is a mandatory condition of the subject individual's online access or is required before initiating a relationship with the collector, and (vii) a description of information security controls.

The second FIPP standard is "choice." Subject individuals should be given choice before PII is collected and used. A clear and intentional manifestation of consent should precede any primary PII use for the immediate transaction. Consent to secondary PII uses beyond the immediate needs of the current transaction should also be given. Consent should address expected future "transfers onward" of PII in a sale or barter. Consent may be manifest in various ways, most prevalent currently are either the opt-out or the opt-in method.

The opt-in is generally preferable by the public in EU nations, the opt-out is in general use in the U.S. Opt-in is generally favored by privacy fundamentalists but results in an initially smaller and less valuable database of PII. By contrast, opt-out is generally favored by the data industry, most likely because it reduces transactions costs and the PII databases generally are more valuable initially (Bagby & McCarty, 2003). Clear and unequivocal consent is particularly important in the sensitive developing arena of location-based privacy because insecure, real-time geographical PII exposes the individual to personal and immediate security risks (Petty, 2003).

The third FIPP standard is "access." Review by subject individuals of their PII files in a timely, accurate and inexpensive manner should be enabled. The very considerable experience with credit reporting agencies illustrates how errors can disadvantage subject individuals (FACTA, 2003). Consider the pervasive financial fraud aspects of identity theft. The access right enables subject individuals to avoid damages and this enhances PII database security given the strong incentives that subject individuals have to identify and correct damaging errors. The access right is deployed when subject individuals have simple and effective means to challenge and correct inaccurate PII.

The fourth FIPP standard is "security" and exemplifies when security and privacy are complementary. PII database suppliers, owners, customers and operators have custodial duties to assure data quality, assure quality control of data processing methods and should safeguard the PII from unauthorized alteration or deletion. Security is a set of perpetual IA tasks requiring continuous development and revision of reasonable controls to assure PII accuracy. Administrative and technical security measures are needed to inhibit unauthorized access, destruction, misuse or unauthorized disclosure of PII. Security is preventive when it deters intrusion. Security is reactive when it

responds quickly and effectively to a discovered intrusion. Security is adaptive when it results in improved controls after vulnerabilities are discovered and diagnosed. The security FIPP is the essential aspect of complementarity between security and privacy.

The fifth FIPP standard is "enforcement." Security compliance is costly and intrusion detection is uncertain. The immediate benefits of investments in improved security may not be obvious so this delay may encourage shirking by data processors. Enforcement provides a disincentive to shirking that can encourage persistent and quality performance of security-oriented custodial control. When security is lax, subject individuals risk injury. There exists fairly broad public support, particularly among victims, to require remedies for failure of custodial duties (FTC Report, 2004). Despite tort reformers efforts to eliminate liability for PII custodial failure, a preponderance of political support persists for curative remedies. Liability for money damages for past, unprevented privacy violations is a traditional American enforcement mechanism (Prosser, 1960). Furthermore, in egregious cases, public policy supports punishment to deter negligent data custody or willful privacy intrusion, such as the criminal sanctions for privacy violations in the Health Insurance Portability and Accountability Act (HIPAA, 1996).

A combination of elements is often devised to enforce privacy practices, including, self-regulation, government regulation and/or private rights of action for redress (Rotenberg, 2001). These duties are expanded by professional regulation of data custodian competence, government regulation of security controls and private litigation for damages that would compensate past injuries resulting from data mismanagement (FACTA, 2003). Enforcement in other nations such as the EU generally relies less on U.S.-style private, civil litigation and more on enforcement by regulatory agencies and inquisitorial criminal prosecution.

Data Management as an "Information Supply Chain" Construct

The property rights perspective provides an essential viewpoint on privacy because information is property (Carpenter v. U.S., 1987) (Ruckelshaus v. Monsanto Co., 1984). Thus, the collection, flow and use of PII is actually a flow of property through acquisition, archival, processing, analysis and use of the information. This makes PII data flows susceptible to analysis using supply chain concepts. The information supply chain is a model, structured as an intangible distribution chain, in which valuable information flows. Traditional supply chain analysis focuses on goods and the ancillary information flows necessary to effectively move those goods. However, the information supply chain should be analyzed, at least at first, as unconnected to such goods or services supply chains. This perspective provides insights for public policy influences with analogies to a familiar model of stocks and flows, transactions and bottlenecks. The "information supply chain" conceptualization helps explain efficiencies and losses. A recurring sequence of events is typical in the data management for PII. Privacy regulation efficiency and effectiveness is evident with a clear technical understanding of PII data management as an information supply chain. Controls imposed by various public policies, such as standards, contracts and regulations can discourage insecure activities at any stage along the PII supply chain. There are (at least) four basic steps in the PII information supply chain: (1) data acquisition, (2) data storage, (3) data analysis, and (4) use of data (Bagby & McCarty, 2003).

Data acquisition is the sensing of some activity, a data capture, an observation or other collection of PII. PII is then coded into data storage. PII flows through networks and can be captured during transmission (wireline, wireless, transport of physical storage device). Capture is the interception and storage of data during its creation, entry, discovery, detection or transmission. For example, PII is observed from transactions by vendors, participants in goods supply chains and telecommunications carriers (e.g., TelCos). PII is also supplied by users to queries or surreptitiously using cookies, web bugs, spyware or keyboard capture. New capture and transmission techniques are always under development that provide efficiencies and some enhance stealth in data management operations. Various privacy public policies directly limit or enable such data acquisition under laws authorizing intelligence or investigation as well as in contracts authorizing PII archival.

Information analysis is the next step in the PII information supply chain during which the PII is organized, associated, aggregated and interpreted to create useful information. This requires systematic handling and pragmatic evaluation to enable valid interpretation. Data warehousing is a large scale, automated form of this activity. The real time analysis from multiple data repositories is generally considered data mining (DeRosa, 2004). Analysis techniques are in constant development as innovative discovery techniques are developed and deployed. The more successful of these techniques sometimes reveal insights into important relationships. These methods increasingly require considerable computing power often confronting the challenge of gaining rightful authority to access dispersed, often large data sets. Third party service providers increasingly capture PII from multiple sources, then store and provide the data and/or analysis for clients. Data aggregators (noun, suffix pronounced -gate) is a term that describes service providers that combine numerous partial bits of PII from independent sources and assemble these into profiles or dossiers. Such proprietary reports are sold to decision-makers in marketing, insurance, credit and employment markets and, increasingly, are also useful in security-risk assessments and counter-terrorism to both private sector and government clients. Aggregate data (adjective, suffix pronounced: -git) generally refers to an opposite concept; these are PII practices that anonymize data collections about numerous individuals to enhance compliance with strong privacy rights. Although various practices underlie anonymized aggregate data processing, a common technique permanently removes personal identifiers and then establishes controls that make any re-association difficult.

Information analysis is a multi-disciplinary activity that exploits new methods of data organization, structuring, filtering, aggregation, association and analysis based on theories from social science and natural science fields such as biology, psychology, sociology, social network theory, economics and criminology. However, public policy may intervene to constrain this analysis to the extent that recommendations derived from PII data analysis are based on faulty assumptions, erroneous calculations, premature generalizations (e.g., junk science) or socially unacceptable criteria (e.g., protected demographic classes) (Daubert, 1993). Restrictions on some data analysis methods have been imposed (e.g., lie detector reliability) and other restrictions seem possible (e.g., genetic tissue sampling to deny health care based on disease predisposition inference, inference of potential for dishonesty). It can be expected that privacy advocates will urge public policy to require strong and reliable scientific consensus before permitting conclusions that might be deployed with strong negative impact on individuals based on such PII profiling methods.

The major justification of investment in PII collection, storage, processing and analysis is that there is useful value in such activities. Use is the ultimate step in the PII supply chain. PII has value when it provides knowledge that can be used for decision-making internally or sold to third parties for decision-making. Valuable and accurate knowledge is scarce but can contribute to the avoidance of adverse selection. Public policy serves an important residual function when it focuses incentives or restrictions at this stage of

the PII supply chain such as to prohibit socially unacceptable uses of PII. Indeed, PII collection and analysis may be inevitable; subject individuals may suffer injury only after PII is misused so the least restrictive form of privacy right would impose use restrictions rather than attempt restriction up the information supply chain at some earlier point engaged in collection, storage, processing or analysis and inference. For example, automobile insurance underwriting is sometimes prohibited from considering infractions after a few years pass, prior bankruptcy cannot be considered in making credit decisions once several years elapse, consent is required for the transfer of some financial and health care PII and Miranda warnings are a general prerequisite to the use of certain confessions of guilt. In each of these instances, the privacy restriction is not imposed back up the PII information supply chain, but at the end point where use might cause injury to the subject individual (Tripathi & Nair, 2006).

Strong privacy rights and PII database security duties transform the PII information supply chain into a chain of custody. Custodial duties for PII are analogous to custodial duties for other forms of property: the custodian must use reasonable care to safeguard the property. Applied to PII, privacy law implies custodial duties to secure PII and this likely constrains at least some actions that transfer, transmit, communicate and/or receive PII. A chain of custody perspective focuses on the vulnerability of PII at key points along the information supply chain.

In the U.S. privacy protection is narrowly drawn to particular industry sectors, a "sectoral approach" which contrasts markedly with the European "omnibus approach." The EU now deploys a comprehensive and uniform set of strong privacy rights applicable to most industries and to many government activities. Advocates of strong privacy tend to prefer European omnibus approach while advocates of strong security and laissez-faire markets in PII prefer the U.S.'s sectoral approach (Strauss & Rogerson, 2002). Indeed, debate over this sectoral vs. omnibus model is pervasive in the public policy controversy over privacy rights and security duties in the U.S. (Bagby, 2007-2). So long as considerable differences persist between citizens of different nations or cultures, any standardization of such approaches to privacy will likely remain elusive (Okazaki, 2007).

PRIVACY VS. SECURITY: AN IRRECONCILABLE TRADEOFF?

An economic analysis of PII is a fundamental and useful perspective because it reveals political or market pressures and aids in predicting PII incentives and behaviors of subject individuals, data managers and users. Public policy is often revised to better optimize these perspectives as PII regulations are devised or revised. While privacy law is somewhat stable over time, there is a continuing reset in the balance between personal privacy rights and society's needs for PII (Warren & Brandeis, 1890). Consider these three basic economic principles in the analysis of privacy policy: first, markets malfunction with incomplete information, second, useful information can be costly and is often incomplete, and third, information frequently resists exclusive control, thus it is difficult to maintain secrecy or exert tight, stringent controls on information use or prevent PII misappropriation.

Capitalism presumes markets possess perfect information, indeed, some economists still contend information is sufficiently and freely available to inform all parties in contracts. Under the efficient market theory, there are further presumptions that market transactions are always informed by perfect information and that market participants are rational actors. These stronger presumptions permit efficient market advocates to hypothesize that free markets result in the correct pricing and allocation of products and services and that trading volumes are optimal. Each completed transaction signals consumer

preferences and producers' capacities. Rising demand attracts optimal investment to produce products using the most promising technologies and most efficient methods. Declining demand deters investment from less effective methods to other, more promising alternatives. Adam Smith's "invisible hand" explains how free markets are benefited with perfect information and he argues this produces optimal results for society (Smith, 1776). However, such theoretical optimality does not always prevail in the real world. Indeed, other economists increasingly admit that market anomalies may require public policy intervention. Imperfect information is a well known form of market failure that helps explain huge increases in expenditures to collect information and assure its quality. Policymakers long ago provided for regulation to intervene as society discovers the social harm from secrecy, a form of imperfect information. Persuasive examples include corporate financial reporting, disclosure of toxic chemical use and sex-offender revelations.

Inexhaustible, Non-Rival, and Non-Excludable Information

Information generally, and PII in particular, are seemingly inexhaustible, the original is not used up when copies are made. Inexhaustibility suggests that infinite, multiple-use is feasible. Information products are generally non-rival because consumption by one user does not prevent consumption by another user (Benkler, 2006). This makes finite, multiple-use business models feasible but their design based on non-rival information products can still be problematic. In order for information to satisfy the characteristics of intangible property, it often becomes necessary to limit consumption by some potential users. Preventing consumption is the attribute of excludability. When technologies such as rights management techniques (e.g., DRM) and/or legal remedies enable excludability, economic exploitation becomes more realistic. Absent effective rights management controls, information products are non-exclusive and non-rival so they may appear infinite and inexhaustible. Even inexhaustibility is frequently just an illusion. Information generally, and PII in particular, often enables only brief and narrow profit opportunities. Unless owners can effectively exclude users, their PII, like a trade secret, becomes so useful to competitors after becoming broadly available, that eventually the information's advantages are fully depleted. Privacy regulation is a form of exclusion right.

Derogatory information about wrongdoers, when widely distributed, probably accumulates to improve societal security (Posner, 1978). To complicate matters, "information wants to be free" a maxim recognizing that the strong incentives to learn, acquire and sell information makes information vulnerable to copying, communication and unauthorized or unlawful misappropriation (Brand, 1987). Furthermore, once information is revealed, it is not easily or effectively withdrawn, reclaimed or retrieved. Eventually valuable information becomes widely known and this undercuts its economic exploitability to its owner or to the subject individual.

There is long experience with the challenges arising when IP is non-rival, inexhaustible and non-excludable. Except for effective trade secrets or when reverse engineering is infeasible, IP defies exclusive possession unless public policy intervenes. The traditional method is to establish public policies that create and enforce rights to exclude others' use of the information such as in bringing misappropriation litigation, infringement litigation or the regulation of PII. Tangible property is rival, exhaustible and exclusive so it is rightfully possessed and exploited by just one person at a time. By contrast, the value of intangible property diminishes when these three characteristics are present: non-rivalry, inexhaustibility and non-exclusivity. Adding insult to this injury, an IP owner (or subject individual) may be ignorant that copies were made or their secrets were revealed. Thus, a fourth characteristic com-

plicates exploitation of intangible property rights: the owner may be ignorant that unauthorized copies proliferate. A fifth characteristic exacerbates this, the owner or subject individual may be ignorant that the information was changed, portions deleted or surprises and inaccuracies added. Sixth, the IP owner or subject individual may be further ignorant of exactly who possesses or misuses the unauthorized copies. These three forms of ignorance frustrate the subject individual from undertaking counter-measures to enhance the security of their PII.

The peer to peer content exchange phenomena clearly illustrates an IP owner's proprietary vulnerability. Profit-making opportunities from data, software, music or video are undermined when serious potential buyers obtain illegal copies. The owner loses marginal revenue for the loss of each likely sale. Copies distributed to non-serious buyers is less problematic, the IP owner may actually receive reputational benefits and attract new buyers. However, IP owners prefer strict and constant enforcement of infringement rules without exception because this generally reflects stronger controls. There is an analogous effect when PII is not treated as a personal asset or intangible property, IP under the control of the subject individual. When the subject individual does not consent to use of PII, the subject individual is deprived of personal economic advantage. Furthermore, if outsiders trade in this PII, the subject individual's personal economic advantages are diverted to others who capture the economic benefits, mostly at the subject individual's expense (Shiman, 2006).

Rightful Capture of Information Benefits

There is basic economic conundrum for PII that underlies the debate over privacy vs. security as an irreconcilable tradeoff. The question can be posed this way: who should capture the value of a subject individual's information: the subject individual or some intruder? The European, Hegalian vision is that PII is inalienable, self-expression, a product of each subject individual's right of self-actualization manifest as thought, action and ingenuity. Adherence to this extreme would inspire strong privacy rights. On the other hand, the U.S. Constitution encourages personal expression so that it can have political and social influence on others. The First Amendment therefore suggests that vicarious experience must belong to each person who perceives it and that this must include any lawful observation individuals have of another person's PII (First Amend. 1791). This viewpoint is derived from ancient personal property law defining the finder of property, here PII, as its owner. Perceptual experience is a personal right, perhaps sometimes a property right, to information learned. If individuals are prevented from the rightful use of perception, then important incentives are lost for society to capture, store, analyze and produce highly valuable information triggering suboptimal societal outcomes: lost economic efficiency and dangerous security risks. The privacy-security tradeoff emanates from this puzzle. Both of these extreme positions cannot be accommodated by public policy.

How can this tension be reconciled to the rightful capture of information, including PII? Privacy rights vs. the right to learn and use knowledge must be balanced. As deserving privacy interests are identified, the balance shifts to protect PII. By contrast, as security is significantly enhanced with information learned from various sources, the balance shifts to protect societal security. Accordingly, adjustments are likely to accommodate societal interests in efficient markets, justice, security and social order while continuing to indulge in the individual autonomy of privacy that is fundamental to liberty. Privacy and security can be conflicting in some instances, so the conventional wisdom holds these are irreconcilable, trade-offs. The predicted relationship expects that optimal public policies for both privacy and security are irreconcilable, a zero-sum game. Privacy gains work to weaken security; security gains come at the expense of privacy rights. This conflict appears to pit strong privacy advocates against strong security advocates frequently resulting in these two groups advocating quite opposite public policy prescriptions.

Consider two examples. First, the Chinese "Golden Shield" regulates unlimited access by ordinary Chinese people to "subversive" content, viewed by the Chinese government as threatening to harmony and political stability (Deibert, 2002). The "Great Firewall" directly interferes with Internet governance, a troublesome fragmentation of Internet addressing performed for censorship purposes and national political security. This negatively impacts privacy and ultimately threatens Internet functionality (Bagby & Ruhnka, 2004). Second, the European Union (EU) has a controversial public policy that permits EU national laws to require telecommunications providers to archive certain transaction data (EU Directive, 2002). Such national laws could include requirements that Internet Service Providers (ISP) and telecommunications carriers (TelCos) record, index, and store conveyance of communications data on electronic communications networks including geographic position of mobile phone users (Tripathi & Nair, 2007). In the U.S. this PII is called consumer proprietary network information (CPNI). In the EU, the retention of message contents is not required. This EU Data Retention Directive also implicates the tradeoff and is controversial; compliance by EU nations is incomplete - only Belgium, France, Spain and the UK have enacted valid statutes (European Data Protection Commissioners, 2002). Extrapolating from these examples, the opposing arguments are predictable: strong privacy rights trump society's security needs vs. strong security trumps individual privacy rights. However, most nations have some form of privacy rights so how is the tradeoff reconciled?

Some Benefits of Strong Privacy Outweigh Society's Security Needs

Advocates of strong privacy contend that management of the PII information supply chain is deficient due to market failures in PII markets. Because data managers, not subject individuals, "gain the full benefit of using the information in its own marketing or in the fee it receives when it sells information to third parties" then disclosure of PII does not injure the data industry (Swire & Litan, 1998). Subject individuals seldom understand the full extent of PII archived by the data management industry, its use or the identities of data purchasers or collectors. Secrecy prevents subject individuals from correcting errors or preventing unauthorized PII uses.

Those contending market failure need not argue failure is total to justify some privacy regulation. Indeed, customers of data brokers purchasing inaccurate or misleading PII probably exert some pressure on data managers to improve service quality. However, this mechanism is skewed towards avoidance of errors that risk PII customer losses, they do not avert injury to subject individuals. PII data customers' primary incentive is to avoid inaccurate PII reports that portray subject individuals too favorably so that these customers can avoid making unfavorable underwriting mistakes (e.g., grant credit to the uncreditworthy). Opposite errors, that portray subject individuals too unfavorably, pose risks that the PII customer might miss a potentially favorable relationship (e.g., lost underwriting opportunity). However, PII customers are more concerned with avoiding losses and not so much with capturing every promising business relationship (e.g., passing up a creditworthy subject individual). Of course, lending and financial industry practices leading to the U.S. 2008 mortgage crisis notwithstanding. If the PII vendor's accuracy was more transparent to subject individuals then these lost favorable opportunities, that largely damage the subject individual who has trouble getting credit, might

also be corrected. The subject individual has the stronger, personal and immediate incentive to assure the accuracy of a favorable portrayal.

Markets work well when parties are free to negotiate terms based on perfect information. Despite general recognition that there are many potential terms and conditions in the collection, processing and use of PII, true negotiations between subject individuals and PII data processors occur infrequently providing further evidence of market failure. Indeed, negotiation remains such a remote possibility in the future, given the high transaction costs and typically low value of most PII, that other mechanisms to correct market failure should be explored. Given the three PII market failures in transparency, personal incentives and negotiability, it is not surprising that the data management industry captures most of the benefits of subject individuals' PII while bearing less than optimal responsibility for PII data quality. Since these market failures apparently have not been corrected with more competitive market conditions, then privacy regulations may be the sole remaining market correcting alternative. Regulation is a classic mechanism for the correction of market failure (Evans, 2004).

Subject individuals have personal incentives to preserve confidentiality, generally these are defensive. Subject individuals are motivated to seek legal remedies or deploy self-help measures to protect their privacy by obstructing the collection, archiving and use of PII (Bagby & Gittings, 1999). For example, subject individuals can be expected to thwart the publication or use of false PII or defamatory statements. Some privacy advocates may seek concealment of truthful PII they view as damaging to reputation or solitude. Privacy advocates cite growing evidence that PII archives are insecure (Campbell, Gordon, Loeb & Zhou, 2003). Security vulnerabilities attract misuse by insiders, outside hackers and societal predators imposing such injuries as identity theft, extortion or stalking (U.S. Attorney General Cyberstalking Report, 1999). Therefore, strong privacy is an integral part of IA.

Some Benefits of Strong Security Outweigh Individual Privacy Rights

Advocates of strong security generally argue that PII contributes to more perfect information. Perfect information is needed to inform the evaluation of counter-parties, it informs the negotiation of contract terms, it underlies the prediction of performance quality and it contributes greatly to avoiding societal damage. Strong privacy rights frustrate information symmetry, ultimately leading to adverse selection because privacy conceals relevant PII if its disclosure is blocked (Akerlof, 1970). Parties who are under-informed of key counter-party data (e.g., reputational PII) become unable to accurately predict satisfactory performances. Consider how insurers might underwrite bad risks and creditors might make riskier loans if they were deprived of subject individuals' PII that revealed spotty performance history or doubtful credit-worthiness. This type of PII is derogatory, Judge Posner calls this "deservedly discrediting information" (Posner, 1986). Society will become unable to effectively assess transaction risks and security risks if privacy rights become so strong that PII information asymmetries threaten effective risk assessment. Therefore, strong security is an integral part of IA.

Further inefficiencies are likely when subject individuals have rights to conceal PII that reveals deservedly discrediting information. This market failure has another impact on efficiency because the party with the lowest cost of performing an activity is best suited to perform that activity. Consider when an information supplier is the least-cost provider; this permits society to capture the transaction efficiency. For example, individuals are often in the best position to reveal PII because it is more completely and immediately derived from each subject individual's direct personal knowledge. The least expensive discovery of PII would be extracted directly from the subject individual as well as from other direct observers. However, both have conflicts of interest that may

motivate the reporting of false information. The subject individual prefers favorable characterization while some third parties may prefer disfavorable characterization, such as if they harbor personal animus.

Consider the cumulative reduction of costs for investigations, PII data collection and PII analysis under the last-cost provider analysis discussed previously. An interesting side effect of more perfect least-cost provider conditions is evident when subject individuals more readily reveal discrediting information. Markets for PII investigation intermediaries might be inhibited. Of course, sometimes third party PII collectors are the least-cost providers of profiling and click-stream dossiers or data mining profiles because electronic commerce participants leave data trails in various places. Such profiles are increasingly essential to attain the efficiencies of target marketing (Shiman, 2006). Weak privacy law encourages least-cost providers when they are the subject individuals as well as when third party information intermediaries provide such services. Perfect price discrimination is also dependant on weak privacy law. Variable pricing of goods or services according to each individual customer's ability to pay or their individual perception of the product's usefulness (e.g., utility) could permit more precise customer ranking. More accessible price discrimination could encourage sellers to charge more to customers more intently craving the product and/or those better able to pay higher prices while simultaneously charging less to others. Variable pricing enables the seller to capture more of the benefits in achieving economies of scale (Choi, Stahl & Whinston, 1997).

Users of PII data generally have interests rival to subject individuals. Users will seek to collect any data perceived as useful in decision-making, generally incentivized by the promise of profit potential or utility in enhancing security, such as crime prevention/enforcement or counter-terrorism. The data management industry has incentives to supply users with PII so long as their prospective revenues exceed operational costs. These adversarial interests suggest the data management industry and its best customers, including marketers, underwriting, law enforcement, counter-terrorism and the intelligence communities, are among those most likely to fight against strong privacy rights. Trade associations have traditionally protected their members' access to PII. Credit bureaus and reporting agencies have devised lucrative business models in PII data aggregation.

Rival interests also characterize the private sector data management industry which is expanding its business models beyond PII data sales to private commercial customers to increased provision of PII data to government. Law enforcement at all levels (local, state, federal, regulatory, self-regulation) increasingly use both public and private industry sources of PII through data warehousing. In the post-9.11 world, there has emerged a stronger public policy to protect national security and enhance criminal enforcement resetting the previous balance between security and privacy (USA PATRIOT Act, 2001). Strengthening privacy rights frustrates the business models of PII intermediaries as well as counter-terrorism users. Until the centralization of privacy protection by regulatory agencies in the U.S. fragmented regulation and inconsistent results are inevitable (Rotenberg, 2006).

As a result, it is predictable that those opposing strong privacy rights will lobby for weak privacy regulation, undertake perfunctory industry self-regulation and be slow to invest or innovate in privacy protections (Bagby & Gittings, 1999). Data warehouse service providers and users will likely push aggressively to develop new methods and technologies for collection, archiving, interpretation and use of PII. PII will be sold or bartered whenever profitable. Strong privacy rights appearing in international laws will be opposed because they increasingly erect barriers to cross-border PII data flows and thereby inhibit robust information markets and offshore outsourcing of IT services (Swire & Litan, 1998). The information

management industry and data users have very significant incentives to hide industry practices in PII collection, warehousing, sale and use because publicity attracts stronger privacy regulation. Furthermore, PII users and PII information supply chain participants with growing and profitable business models have strong incentives to oppose arguments made by privacy fundamentalists to regulate privacy rights more stringently.

Balancing Privacy with Security

The tradeoff between strong individual privacy rights and society's security needs implies a balance. This balance considers several factors. First, there are negative externalities on society from strong privacy rights. Privacy compromises security when intruders, criminals or terrorists enjoy anonymity. Privacy protections shield wrongdoers from scrutiny. Second, strong security cannot be achieved without regular, sometimes deeply probing intrusions into privacy. Weak privacy facilitates access to potentially relevant activities of intruders and terrorists. Third, would-be intruders seek to evade detection because their notoriety might trigger countermeasures. Limited privacy rights deter such attacks by limiting concealment. Finally, security is enhanced with limitations on the liberty of intruders, criminals or terrorists. Indeed, weak privacy rights enhance control, thereby discouraging the liberty component of privacy that enables wrongdoing.

There is little practical guidance in how to draw the balance between privacy and security. An understanding of the cultural and historical development of privacy rights and public policy responses to security risks is an essential starting point, but this calculus is highly complex. Unfortunately, there is no deterministic or formulaic balancing methodology. The balancing is generally manifest as a public policy compromise resulting from social, economic and political pressures that are focused through available technology implementations. Long experience with repeated government privacy intrusions and with intrusions by private entities leads society to evaluate two major factors. First, society determines the usefulness of some type of information acquired in an intrusion. Second, society evaluates the repugnance of the intrusion. A balance between these forces is mediated by a cost-benefit analysis that weighs the prospects for success in discovering socially useful information against the costs of the intrusion. This rough calculus inspires various forms of political and social pressure and these generally elicit some legal or regulatory response. Existing mores and society's legitimate needs for information are evaluated and society chooses either to permit, regulate or prohibit the intrusion depending on three factors.

Judge Learned Hand first developed the public policy balancing framework for the imposition of tort law duties (U. S. v. Carroll Towing Co., 1947). This framework was adapted by Judge Richard Posner to the limited context of criminal and intelligence operations in which search and seizure is regulated by the Fourth Amendment (Fourth Amend. 1791) (Posner, 1986). Here, this framework is expanded and further adapted to all forms of privacy rights when the privacy-security tradeoff becomes an issue (Bagby, 2007-2). This model assumes there is a tradeoff between privacy and security, that the relationship is a zero-sum game and that optimal regulation imposes a conundrum. Therefore, the model signals either the protection of privacy or alternatively the enhancement of security depending on a balancing of three factors. First, the model must assess the usefulness to society of PII acquired from an intrusion. Second, the repugnance of the

intrusion must be estimated. Third, the probability of preventing societal losses by permitting or encouraging the privacy intrusion are estimated, as illustrated in Table I.

An optimal public policy balancing of privacy against security or security against privacy is evident in the relationships represented by the inequalities in Table I. The tradeoff theory suggests that a good society will "carefully balance individual rights and social responsibilities, autonomy and the common good, privacy and... public safety" (Etzioni, 1999). The public policy debate in privacy, law enforcement and national security recognizes this fundamental trade-off. The privacy-security tradeoff explains much in the law enforcement, internal private security, counter-terrorism, cyber-security and critical infrastructure protection debates.

PRIVACY AND SECURITY HARMONIZE

Treating privacy and security solely as a tradeoff is overly simplistic. The tradeoff noted before is traditional wisdom that is valid, but only when the subject individual is a likely wrongdoer and only when innocent subject individuals suffer little or no injury from the intrusion into their privacy. Most centrally, the tradeoff characterization ignores the basic public policy underlying the role of IA in privacy protection and the role of privacy in the security of individuals and sectors of society. There are clear security benefits from maintaining privacy, particularly for the subject individuals whose PII is secured.

Table 1. Privacy-security balancing: Impact on public policy through legislation, precedent or regulation

Assume:
B=intrusion costs; P=probability of discovering useful information; L=societal losses
B>P*L: privacy interests outweigh security interests: policy should protect privacy **B<P*L:** security interests outweigh privacy interests: policy should permit intrusion

Consider first how liberty enhances security. For example, an individual's ability to flee averts their personal injury. Liberty is a clear privacy right that can enhance individual security when available to avert injury. Consider how isolation, another form of privacy, is useful to protect prey from predators. For example, self-imposed seclusion or even anonymity is often effective to preempt many external threats. Consider how isolation might be applied to PII. An individual's benefit from privacy is diminished when that subject individual's PII becomes insecure or is revealed publicly. As PII collections become vulnerable to physical and electronic intrusion, the subject individuals whose PII is collected risk injury from the PII misuse. For example, insecure private and public databases are exploited by predators to enable stalking and identity theft. The resulting legislative, regulatory and judicial reactions are privacy regulations expressed as PII security provisions. They are intended precisely to enhance the privacy and therefore the safety of the subject individuals (U.S. Attorney General Cyberstalking Report, 1999) (FTC Report, 2004).

Data security, under the fourth FIPP, is essential to strong and effective individual privacy. Consider the data broker's activities that harvest PII from public records. Pressures for the accountability of government officials lead to open government mechanisms such as the Freedom of Information Act at the federal level and all the states' various open records laws. However, if PII can be easily harvested from court records or other public data sources, subject individuals suffer vulnerability to various threats. Closer regulation of access to court and public records serves to better align privacy rights with the government's custodial duty of security (E-Government Act, 2002) (Coyle, 2006).

Individual security is enhanced with strong privacy protections, privacy rights are one component, strong security over PII is another component. Group security is enhanced with strong privacy protections of their individual and collective PII. The tradeoff is most evident as favoring stronger security when the privacy of likely predators and wrongdoers is too well protected. The complement is most evident as favoring strong privacy when potential victims' privacy is well protected by strong PII security. The real challenge is in granting privacy to potential victims but not to potential predators and recognizing how vague the term security is when applied to national security vs. the security of PII databases. Some people promote public policies that might implement these two axioms with demographic profiling (Bagby, 2008). For example, profiles of frequent victims might be used to offer the benefits of strong privacy to members of such groups. Then profiles of demographic groups best known for predator behavior might be targeted for less privacy protection. Clearly, these approaches are problematic in the U.S. given the fundamental ethic of equal protection. Furthermore, under such a system, predators have the incentive to pose as members of typical victims groups to avoid detection (Fourteenth Amendment, 1868). Unfortunately, this is precisely the evolving profile of modern terrorists.

RECOMMENDATIONS

The following recommendations are based on the critical insights discussed before. This chapter argues that privacy and security are quite durable and fundamental public policies. It does not seem likely that the perceived tradeoff between security and privacy will be abandon anytime soon so long as the primary frame is national security. When strong security advocates can claim that privacy mainly protects predators then public policy will use this approach to protect victims and society. However, this chapter's analysis recognizes that privacy is also the result of security such as when individual victims are benefited. Clearly, there will continue to be public policy pressures to limit privacy or security protections for predators; many will follow the due process rights established in the Constitution as rights for the accused. However, both the privacy and security camps might be more successful if they seek a middle ground, possibly making progress on their separate agendas and without zero sum losses with a better understanding and empathy for the other camp. The key in achieving this would appear to convert some portion of the tradeoff to be seen as complementary. For example, security advocates should become amenable to applying security techniques to the protection of privacy for potential victims, but without anxiety that mainly predators will benefit. Similarly, advocates of strong privacy should consider how to unmask wrongdoers from their privacy protections while lowering the probability of false positives, Type I errors (Neyman & Pearson, 1928).

Privacy advocates are likely to seek public policies that would narrow the legitimate uses of PII. Furthermore, privacy advocates can be expected to support public policies that broaden situations where PII misuses are declared illegitimate and this would result in the imposition of sanctions for PII data misuse. These public policies may be manifest in legal protections for individual privacy under constitutional provisions, through the interpretation of statutes and regulations, and by inclusion of privacy strengthening provisions in private contracts. Finally, the continued publicly exposure of PII misuse as well as the identification of PII custodians' failure to exercise custodial due care, are areas of likely future success for privacy fundamentalists with direct impact on security regulations (Cal.S.B.1386) (Schwartz & Janger, 2007).

A property rights approach is consistent with strong privacy rights but this must give way to the property rights of those rightfully learning from observation, experience and through PII information supply chain transactions. PII under a property rights regime would recognize that individuals have ownership and control rights over their PII. Therefore, PII would be alienable; it could be bought, sold or traded in free market transactions. Effective limitations on the use and reuse of PII exchanged in trade are currently difficult to implement so these limitations would impose both negotiation and implementation expenses. Technical solutions have been proposed that might make such activities feasible. First, technologies could reduce the transactions costs of negotiations, particularly when standard form contracting is adopted. Second, the record-keeping burdens to comply with use limitations might become technically feasible. Digital rights management (DRM) holds promise to implement recordkeeping and preferences implementation. Third, automated negotiations are conceivable to reduce transactions costs.

A PII property rights perspective might be implemented with technical solutions that negotiate PII controls, keep accurate transaction records and/or interrupt prohibited uses mechanically (Cranor, 2002). For example, consider various digital rights management (DRM) systems such as the Platform for Privacy Protections (P3P). A P3P type of regime could be configured to deter and track PII collection, aggregation, use, resale and custody by particular users (Cohen, 2003). Meta-data, digital watermarks and third party web services could also be made available to identify and track PII sources and uses to enforce the subject individual's rights and restrictions on use derived from PII negotiations. This "digital privacy rights management" (DPRM) system could be configured to quickly and cheaply convey a subject individual's profile of privacy preferences, such information could accompany the PII as metadata, and might separately be verified through independent third parties or web services providers. Use of the PII could be controlled with these information controls likely implemented by electronic agents. The P3P could become an interesting prototype for DPRM systems if such technologies can gain acceptance.

It is often hypothesized that PII markets will develop to become responsive to subject individual's privacy concerns. This argument underlies two apparently paradoxical observations: self-regulation of privacy is preferable to costly government regulation or litigation and that competition over privacy has never arisen above the lackluster. This lack of development permits free market theorists to suggest that subject individuals have little interest in privacy. From the demand side, users in the PII information supply chain have clear and immediate incentives to broadly collect and utilize PII. With public policy pressure to deploy more effective security over PII and to respect privacy, at least some data users might respond to these market pressures by strengthening privacy and publicizing this fact to attract subject individuals driven by personal preferences towards a higher privacy consciousness. Genuine attention to privacy self-regulation from the PII data management industry would then be viewed as responsive to market pressures. Such developments might then preempt further pressures for government regulation of privacy.

Pressures will remain to regulate privacy until such time as all participants along the PII information supply chain bargain significantly and effectively with subject individuals over terms and conditions of PII collection and use. In the current market, users sometimes pay outright in a largely wholesale market for large PII databases. Users and data brokers offer discounts or special services and may require subject individuals to register as part of end user license agreements (EULA) for retail information or online services. The EULA is a contemporary and primary method to harvest data at the retail level. As PII markets and the PII information supply chain's operations become visible and competitive, subject individuals might eventually gain choices to purchase products or services from vendors promising privacy or choose alternative vendors that sell products more cheaply if their PII collection and use policies were less privacy protective. Competition over PII practices would result in different contracts for different terms

of service and/or prices depending on subject individuals' privacy level desired. For example, users could be segmented demographically as to the PII information supply chain participants' use of user's PII to enhance location-based marketing practices (Ricker & Porus, 2007). Such market mechanisms are still developing, but competition in terms and conditions of PII collection and use is still embryonic beyond the current take-it-or-leave-it situation.

CONCLUSION

The public policies of privacy and security are widely misunderstood. A better grasp of these public policy pressures could vastly improve the effectiveness of privacy and security regulation while preserving the some of the interests in both camps. Exposure to the conceptual principles of privacy and security are the starting point for a wide array of policy makers, IT professionals, academics, practitioners and designers of systems and software. These public policies drive the deployment of technical solutions, tools and mechanisms. Public policy advocates increasingly recognize that technical solutions have policy impact (Lessig, 2006). These impacts become acceptable or unacceptable as the policy implications of alternative solutions become meaningfully available and are discerned by various political groups. The successful deployment of any technical solution may depend on how quickly the policy implications become widely and thoroughly understood and resolved. There is significant risk of investment loss or the need for costly revisions to privacy and security methods when technologies are unenlightened by likely policy constraints. While privacy and security are generally viewed as tradeoffs, many technologies are adaptable to complement both simultaneously, such as encryption, firewalls, authentication, biometrics, third party certification, and secret codes. However, none of these technologies are synonymous with either privacy or security. Just as any tool the physical world might protect privacy (e.g., door locks/keys, curtains), no tool describes the expectation of privacy itself, nor does any tool adequately impart the condition of achieving security.

This chapter has argued that privacy is largely defined as expectations, met or frustrated. When these expectations are focused through public policy pressures, they create a complex set of rights, sectoral in the U.S., as well as some limitations on countervailing and reciprocal rights of observation or freedom of contract. Of course, technology must continue to play a key role to enable privacy. This chapter argues that for victims, such privacy enhancing technologies will largely be complementary with the protection and enhancement of potential victims' security. An important perspective is the systems engineering approach wherein privacy and security will depend on a coordinated set of technologies deployed along with other effective controls exerted by governmental and regulatory bodies, managerial and supervisory activities, effective monitoring and adequate investment, integrated to achieve satisfactory security protections. Public policy is likely to drive these systems deployments all along the PII information supply chain.

A corollary approach will achieve improvements in security. Technology tools can improve security when integrated into a systems engineering approach. While security tools can destroy privacy, many security tools are also privacy enhancing. There is a complement between privacy and security, if deployed to protect subject individuals. The tools enhancing privacy and security are much more often complementary than is admitted by advocates of either strong privacy or strong security. However, all are frustrated by the challenges in distinguishing potential victims from potential predators.

REFERENCES

Akerlof, G. A. (1970). The market for "lemons:" Quality uncertainty and the market mechanism. *The Quarterly Journal of Economics, 84*(3), 488-500.

Bagby, J. W. (2007a). An Overview of the Public Policy Impact on Standards Development. In S. Bolin (Ed.), *Standards Edge: The Golden Mean*, (pp. 163-84), Seattle WA: The Bolin Group.

Bagby, J. W. (2007b). The Public Policy Environment of the Privacy-Security Conundrum/Complement. In S. Park (Ed.), *Strategies and Policies In Digital Convergence* (pp.195-213). Hershey, PA: Idea Group Reference.

Bagby, J. W. (2008). Book Review: Harcourt, B. E., Against Prediction: Profiling, Policing, and Punishing in an Actuarial Age. *Journal of Law, Economics and Policy, 4*(1).

Bagby, J. W., & Gittings, G. L. (1999). Litigation Risk Management for Intelligent Transportation Systems (Part Two). *ITS-Quarterly, 7*(3) 60-67.

Bagby, J. W., & McCarty, F. W. (2003). *The Legal and Regulatory Environment of e-Business*. St.Paul MN: West Pub.

Bagby, J. W., & Ruhnka, J. C. (2004). Merger of dns Governance into Trademark Law. *Proceedings of the 32nd Telecommunications Policy Research Conference*. Accessible at: http://web.si.umich.edu/tprc/papers/2004/378/TPRC-04-tmDomNaMergerFinal.htm

Benkler, Y. (2006). *The Wealth of Networks: How Social Production Transforms Markets and Freedom*. New Haven CN: Yale University Press.

Brand, S. (1987). *The Media Lab: Inventing the Future at MIT*. NY: Viking Penguin.

Cal. Civ. Code §§ 1798.29, .82, .84 (West Supp. 2006) (California security breach notice statute, S.B.1386).

Campbell, K., Gordon, L. A., Loeb, M. P., & Zhou, L. (2003). The Economic Cost of Publicly Announced Information Security Breaches: Empirical Evidence from the Stock Market. *Journal of Computer Security, 11*, 431-448.

Carpenter v.United States, 484 U. S. 19 (1987).

Choi, S-Y., Stahl, D. O., & Whinston, A. B. (1997). *The Economics of Electronic Commerce*. Indianapolis: MacMillan Technical Pub. P. 344.

Cohen, J. E. (2003). DRM and Privacy. *Berkeley Technological Law Journal, 18*(2), 575-617.

Cranor L. F. (2002). *Web privacy with P3P*. Sebastopol, CA: O'Reilly.

Coyle, M. (2006). Courts balancing privacy, access: U.S. Judiciary must protect 'E-records,'. *National Law Journal, 28*(25).

Cyberstalking: A New Challenge for Law Enforcement and Industry (1999). *Report of the U.S. Attorney General to the Vice President*, accessible at: http://www.justice.gov/criminal/cybercrime/cyberstalking.htm

Daubert v. Merrell Dow Pharmaceuticals, 509 U.S. 579 (1993).

Deibert, R. J. (2002). Dark Guests and Great Firewalls: The Internet and Chinese Security Policy. *Journal of Social Issues, 58*(1), 143-159.

DeRosa, M. (2004). *Data Mining and Data Analysis for Counterterrorism*. Center for Strategic & International Studies.

E-Government Act (2002). Pub. Law 107-347, 44 U.S.C. Ch 36.

Etzioni, A. (1999). *The Limits of Privacy, 184*. Durham: Duke University Press.

Evans, A. W. (2004). Market Failure and Welfare Economics - a Justification for Intervention *Economics and Land Use Planning*, (pp. 13-22). New York: Blackwell Publishing Ltd. P.

EU Directive 2002/58/EC.

Fair and Accurate Credit Transactions Act (FACTA, 2003), 117 STAT. 1954, Pub. Law 108–159, 15 U.S.C. §1601.

Griswold v. Connecticut, 381 U.S. 479 (1965).

Health Insurance Portability and Accountability Act of 1996 (HIPAA), Public Law 104-191 104th Congress.

Katz v. U.S., 389 U.S. 347 (1967).

Lessig, L. (2006). *Code v.2.0*. New York: Basic.

Neyman, J., & Pearson, E. S. (1928). *On the Use and Interpretation of Certain Test Criteria for Purposes of Statistical Inference, Part I*. reprinted at pp.1-66 in Neyman, J. & Pearson, E.S., Joint Statistical Papers, Cambridge University Press, (Cambridge), 1967.

Okazaki, S. (2007). Lessons learned from i-mode: What makes consumers click wireless banner ads. *Computers in Human Behavior, 23,* 1692–1719.

Peters, C. C., Amato, H., & Hollenbeck, C. R. (2007) An Exploratory Investigation Of Consumers' Perceptions Of Wireless Advertising. *Journal of Advertising, 36*(4), 129.

Petty, R. D. (2003). Wireless Advertising Messaging: Legal Analysis and Public Policy Issues. *Journal of Public Policy & Marketing, 22*(1) 71-82.

Posner, R.A. (1978). The Right of Privacy. *Georgia Law Review, 12*(3), 393.

Posner, R. A. (1986). *Economic Analysis of Law* (3d ed.). New York: Little Brown & Co. (pp. 38-39).

Prosser, W. L. (1960). Privacy. *California Law Review, 48*(3), 383.

Report. *National and State Trends in Fraud & Identity Theft: January - December 2003*, Federal Trade Commission (2004).

Restatement (Second) of Torts §652A (1976).

Ricker, Judith and Joseph Porus, (2007) *Mobil Advertising and Marketing USA: Consumer Acceptance Understanding Subscriber Acceptance*, Harris Interactive.

Report: *Records, Computers and the Rights of Citizens Report of the Secretary's Advisory Committee on Automated Personal Data Systems*, Secretary of Health, Education, and Welfare (July, 1973).

Rotenberg, M. (2001). Fair Information Practices and the Architecture of Privacy. *Stanford Technology Law Review 2001*(1), 1.

Rotenberg, M. (2006). *The Sui Generis Privacy Agency: How the United States Institutionalized Privacy Oversight After 9-11*. Available at: http://ssrn.com/abstract=933690

Ruckelshaus v. Monsanto Co., 467 U.S. 986 (1984).

Sarbanes-Oxley Act of 2002, Pub.L. 107-204, 116 Stat. 745.

Schwartz, P. M., & Janger, E. J. (2007). Notification of Data Security Breaches. *Michigan Law Review, 105*(5) 913-984.

Shiman, D. R. (2006). An Economic Approach to the Regulation of Direct Marketing. *Federal Communications Law Journal, 58*, 321.

Smith, A. (1776). *An Inquiry into the Nature and Causes of the Wealth of Nations*. London: Methuen and Co., Ltd. (5th ed. 1904) Book 1, Ch.2.

Solove, D. J. (2002). *Conceptualizing Privacy*. *California Law Review, 90*(4),1087-1155.

Strauss, J., & Rogerson, K. (2002). Policies for Online Privacy in the United States and the European Union. *Telematics and Informatics, 19*(2), 173-192.

Swire, P. P., & Litan, R. E. (1998). *None of Your Business: World Data Flows, Electronic Commerce, and the European Privacy Directive*. Washington: Brookings Institution Press.

Tripathi, A. K., & Suresh, K. N.(2006). Mobile Advertising in Capacitated Wireless Networks. *IEEE Transactions On Knowledge And Data Engineering, 18*(9), 1284–1296.

Tripathi, A. K., & Nair, S. K. (2007). Narrowcasting of wireless advertising in malls. *European Journal of Operational Research, 182*, 1023–1038.

U.S. Const. amend. I (1791).

U.S. Const. amend. IV (1791).

U.S. Const. amend. XIV (1868).

United States v. Carroll Towing Co., 159 F.2d 169, 173 (2d Cir.1947).

Uniting and Strengthening America by Providing Appropriate Tools Required to Intercept and Obstruct Terrorism Act of 2001 (USA PATRIOT Act) Pub. L. 107-56 (2001).

Warren, Samuel & Louis Brandeis (1890). The Right to Privacy. *Harvard Law Review, 4*(5).

Westin, A. F. (2000). *Public Records and the Responsible Use of Information*. Interpretive Essay. Alpharetta, GA: Choicepoint.

Chapter IX
Human Factors in Security:
The Role of Information Security Professionals within Organizations

Indira R. Guzman
TUI University, USA

Kathryn Stam
SUNY Institute of Technology, USA

Shaveta Hans
TUI University, USA

Carole Angolano
TUI University, USA

ABSTRACT

The goal of our study is to contribute to a better understanding of role conflict, skill expectations, and the value of information technology (IT) security professionals in organizations. Previous literature has focused primarily on the role of information professionals in general but has not evaluated the specific role expectations and skills required by IT security professionals in today's organizations. In this chapter, we take into consideration the internal and external factors that affect the security infrastructure of an organization and therefore influence the role expectations and skills required by those who are in charge of the security of network infrastructures in organizations. First, we describe the factors discussed in the literature and support them with quotes gathered from interviews conducted with information security professionals in small organizations in Central New York. Then, we present a set of common themes that expand the understanding of this role and finally we provide practical recommendations that would facilitate the management of these professionals within organizations.

INTRODUCTION

Research in the area of information systems has acknowledged that information technology human capital is a *strategic resource* within organizations and that its "effective management represents a significant organizational capacity" (Ferratt, Agarwal Brown and Moore, 2005, p.237). Most of the research done on human resources management (HRM) within the field of information systems has focused on the role of information technology professionals in general, but little research has been conducted about the role of a more specific group, the information technology security professional. In this book chapter, we will discuss the role, challenges and opportunities of this particular type of job within organizations.

In previous research, Information Technology (IT) professionals in general have been defined as a diverse group of workers trained formally or informally and engaged primarily in the following activities related to information and communication technology systems, components, or applications: conception, selection, acquisition, design, development, adaptation, implementation, deployment, training/education, support, management and documentation (Kaarst-Brown and Guzman, 2005). IT professionals have direct responsibility for the quality of the information available to decision-makers (Prior, Rogerson, and Fairweather 2002). As organizations become more strategically reliant upon information systems, IT professionals' management, recruitment and retention have an increasingly significant impact on the future of their companies. To address these increasing HRM challenges, research has been conducted to improve understanding of the roles and skill requirements of the IT professional. Likewise, it is also important to understand the role of *IT security professionals* because their position within organizations and the importance of their jobs is crucial and has a set of specific challenges that shape this role. In this chapter, we summarize the range of factors that influence the role expectations of IT security professionals, the necessary skills that they should have in order to perform an effective job of securing the network infrastructure of an organization, and the challenges and satisfactions these professionals face in fulfilling this vocation.

ROLES AND RESPONSIBILITIES OF IT SECURITY PROFESSIONALS

The job of IT security professionals is to ensure that the networks, infrastructure, and computer systems within organizations are properly and adequately secure by protecting information assets, such as customer data, financial information and critical network infrastructures. Information security refers to the process of protecting information, specifically its availability, confidentiality and integrity. On the other hand, information technology security refers to the process of controlling the technology that allows access to information making it accessible only to those who are legitimately allowed to do so. As stated by Belsis et al. (2005), IT Security refers to the set of principles, regulations, methodologies, measures, techniques, and tools we use to protect an information system from potential threats. The IT security professionals are the ones in charge of the selection, acquisition, design, development, adaptation, implementation, deployment, training/education, support, management and documentation related to IT security of an information system within the network. All these strategies are now a subsection of the organization's strategic policy (Layton, 2007). This includes, but is not limited to, security threat and risk analysis; security technologies; detection techniques; policies, laws, and regulations governing the procedures used by the IT staff; end user and client user policies for Web access and e-mail; design and implementation of system analysis; and controlling traffic flow through the network. Network security is defined as the protection of networks and their services from unauthorized modification, destruction, or disclosure, and it provides assurance that the network performs its critical functions correctly (Committee on National Security Systems Instruction No. 4009, 2006).

This challenge of protecting the network requires that the IT security professional has both advanced technical knowledge and skills, as well as the ability to work with people at various levels. In many cases, these professionals must have a global and nuanced understanding of IT security needs of the organization and should have the ability to detect cyber attacks and abnormalities, and increase the critical network survivability if an attack is successful. Some of the positions that are fulfilled by IT security professionals within organizations are network security officers, information security engineers, application security engineers, system administrators, network managers, network engineers, Chief Information Officer (CIO), Chief Technology Officer (CTO), Chief Security Officer (CSO), Chief Information Security Officer (CISO), Information Assurance Manager (IAM), and computer operators.

The Importance of IT Security

According to the annual survey of computer crimes and security breaches in early 2007 conducted by the Computer Security Institute (CSI) and the Federal Bureau of Investigation (FBI), the financial losses generated from computer crimes and cyber attacks range from fraud (approx $21 million) down to an exploit of an organization's DNS (Domain Name System) server ($100k). The total losses for 2007 were about $67 thousand, an increase from $52 thousand the previous year. Many of these attacks can be attributed to human errors, such as network operator inefficiencies and clients or end users mistakes at 59% and phishing schemes at 26%. This increase in losses indicates that IT professionals have increased responsibilities in IT security within organizations. It is therefore imperative for managers to have qualified

IT security professionals in order to effectively diagnose and manage attacks remediating damage or losses and preparing for disaster recovery to prevent future security attacks.

A CULTURAL APPROACH TO THE IT SECURITY PROFESSION

According to Guzman, Stam and Stanton (2008), the occupational culture of IT workers is characterized by at least the following elements: high value of technical knowledge; extreme and unusual demands pertaining to long work hours, need for constant self re-education, dealing with unsatisfied users; feelings of superiority relative to the IT user community; and cultural norms manifested in the frequent use of technical jargon and the social stigmatization or stereotyping (e.g., the geek/nerd label). Based on the evaluation of these cultural characteristics, the authors analyzed 110 interviews conducted with managers, employees, and IT professionals about information security issues within small to medium-sized organizations in New York. The respondents represented a wide-range of experience in the field, although the majority of them were seasoned professionals with at least two years in the field. The organizations were participants of an NSF funded study (award SES-0196415 to Stanton) to assess and enhance the behavioral aspects of information security. In each organization, all available IT-related employees complied with requests to be interviewed and surveyed.

In the analysis of these interviews, the cultural characteristics that clearly apply to the information security context and the role expectations of IT security professionals were selected. Following are some indigenous definitions and descriptions of the roles and responsibilities that IT professionals find most salient and complement the general cultural characteristics defined: risk assessment, identification, and prevention of malicious forces from within or outside, cooperation of users and administrators, protection of organizational resources, development and enforcement of security policy, and balancing security needs with convenience and productivity needs.

Value of Technical Knowledge

One of the most important security concerns for organizations is a false sense of security in the field of IT security. Firewalls, anti-virus software, intrusion detection systems, and other technologies are only a small portion of the overall solution to control cyber attacks and abnormalities on a network infrastructure. No single-source technology solution is effective if it is not appropriately configured and used. According to Jenson and Romo (2005), a major weakness in security stems from inadequately trained IT professionals.

The roles and responsibilities of information security professionals vary depending on their level of expertise, the mission of the organization, and the particular niche they fill within the organization. In the most general sense, their role is to secure the organization's information systems and assets, which may include computers, mobile devices, networks, servers, hardware and software and the data they contain. They are responsible for ensuring that the required IT resources are available and appropriate for the myriad of tasks that might be required. Education, risk assessment, and policy-related responsibilities go hand-in-hand as IT professionals must find ways to prevent vulnerability and increase security awareness among employees while at the same time creating, implementing, and evaluating IS policies. Electronic monitoring plays a role in prevention and enforcement as well. All of these occur in an environment that is highly technical and constantly and rapidly changing.

Technical skills must be wide-reaching. This is shown in the following quote of a network administrator who describes his responsibilities in a small company:

Anything having to do with a plug is my responsibility. So, it ranges from the network operations to setting up applications, setting up PC's, arranging the internal and wide area networks, assisting home users with connections, as well as all the telecommunications, the voice mail systems, the PBX's, and the photocopiers. Anything that is network-dependent is my responsibility.

Challenge: Extreme and Unusual Demands in the Field

This characteristic refers to the occupational need to adapt to new problems, new technology, long hours, constant change, and the ability to learn new systems, skills, and programs quickly. Professionals within the IT security arena of an organization have to acquire, share, disseminate, coordinate, store, retrieve, and utilize security knowledge to protect the infrastructure network.

The work of IT security professionals implies a heavy workload. This is expressed in the following quotes of IT staff:

How do you provide support and build the email server, create new user accounts, and create the peripherals around the support and at the same time produce the strategic plan? How do you stay current? It takes time and research. It's never a 40 hour week ever, ever.

Many interruptions are common for IT security professionals. A typical day involves handling the needs of others first, as described:

You get up and start the day and say you are going to accomplish these five things, and it doesn't happen. And it might not happen the next day either, or the next, and that's where the conflict is. You try to set goals and think you are trying to meet them, but it's very difficult.

The role of the information security professional has transformed in recent years from an insignificant position to one of grave importance, significantly due to regulations passed by Congress. A study by the International Information Systems Security Certification Consortium stated, "According to the 2005 Global Information Security Workforce Study, most information security professionals are spending the majority of their time researching and implementing new technologies. In Europe, more than a quarter of respondents indicated that fighting political battles and selling their value to management were their most time-consuming activities, and more than 30% ranked them as their second most time-consuming" (Colley, 2008).

Need for Constant self Re-Education

The demand for IT professionals has increased over the past 15 years, as indicated by a study conducted by Knapp and Boulton (2006) where the need for IT professionals in 1990 moved from "low demand – few certifications" to "higher demand – greater than 35,000 CISSPs" in 2005 (p. 78). Thus, infrastructure network security relies on the training and experience of the IT professionals. Measuring the capabilities of the IT professionals and the technologies they utilize to perform their tasks of securing an infrastructure network is paramount for an organization's survivability in an environment that is evolving with cyber attacks, insider threats, and a host of other vulnerabilities. The constant self re-education includes constant training as well as the acquisition of professional certifications as described:

My agency not only requires the information security personnel to maintain current training, but also they mandate that all employees, regardless of profession, have a working knowledge of security procedures. Each employee must maintain a current certificate of security training on file. Any employee who violates security policies loses network access and is required to successfully repeat the training before access is reinstated".

In terms of the complexity of the job, for example, Rasmussen (2008) describes a specific career path for IT Security Professionals in which one can start as a system administrator with a solid understanding of administration and networking and then pursues certifications such as CISSP and CISM. Next, he moves to an information security auditing role by taking the CISA, followed by information privacy and operational risk positions along with associated certifications (i.e., CIPP and CRP). Appendix A has a definition of all these certifications. After gaining expertise in this field, there are many options, such as moving into management, making a transition into business operations, leaving for another organization, or entering into independent consulting. Appendix A presents a short description and reference links for twenty-five common security certifications available today.

Interacting with Users

Cooperation of users is absolutely essential because users may put the organization at risk in many different ways. Some key issues that employees should know how to deal with in relation to computer security (Rothke, 2004) comprise a long list that includes the following: correct use of passwords, knowledge of protection from viruses and malware, awareness of inappropriateness of using organizational resources for non-work activities, practice of safe data transfer, management of email, safe Web-searching, implementation of back-ups, securing data, responsible use of sensitive information, security of remote access and handheld devices, and the avoidance of tricksters. Securing the workspace and safe disposal of data, as well as knowing who to turn to when things go wrong are also responsibilities of most if not all employees. From this list, it is easy to understand why the IT professional must be a "jack-of-all-trades," and learn how to handle not only the quick pace of technological changes in her field but the many connections IS work has with the smooth management of an organization.

Employees in organizations have great power when it comes to the security of their organization's information systems. Knowingly or inadvertently, skillfully or clumsily, there are many ways in which they can compromise security (Stanton et al, 2003). For example, two categories at either extreme are "intentional destruction", when a behavior requires quite a lot of technical expertise together with a strong intention to do harm, to "basic hygiene" requiring minimal technical expertise and good intentions. The other categories cover various combinations and levels of expertise and intention.

Recent understandings of security have revealed that it is the responsibility of everyone in the organization to take care of security, but this has traditionally not been reinforced in organizations. Learning how to foster widespread motivation and promoting a security-friendly organizational culture is becoming a critical role of the IT security professional.

Also integral to the balancing act that is enacted by security professionals is the need to maintain poise between technical blocks set up to prevent users from doing harmful activities and using education and awareness as a deterrent instead. The following quote from an insurance company describes how tricky this process can be, using the example of passwords:

It's an issue of convenience. It's inconvenient to hide passwords away somewhere. You can't be as productive if you always have to be trying to find where your password is. So there are a lot of trade-offs when you do good security. People are under pressure to produce. That will sometimes tempt them to favor productivity over security. The problem can be dealt with technically by forcing people to choose good passwords, but some of it has to be done with education. Some people just legitimately do not understand, but they can be motivated to do the right thing if they are educated.

Taking care of users is a constant demand, and the IT security professional must decide how much time to spend on the technical aspects and how much on education, as described by the IT manager of a small real estate company:

I have always said that I would have a great job if it wasn't for the users (laughs). But if there has been a complaint of me, it's usually that I have not taken sufficient time to explain the problem. Usually that's because there is a limited amount of time so I did not provide the necessary handholding of the user. There's a careful balance between ignoring the user and just over-coddling the user to make them feel happy. Being me, myself, and I most of the time, I don't have a lot of time to do it.

IT security professionals find satisfaction in helping their coworkers or their organizations choose and learn how to use the most appropriate technology to help accomplish their organizational mission. There is also substantial satisfaction in being the person who can solve coworkers' IT problems, many of which take on crisis proportions.

Helping people in their hour of need is described as a major benefit of working in this profession. But, at the same time these employees feel the need to draw boundaries and protect some of their own time for the technical aspects of the job rather than the time-consuming educational tasks, as described by an IT professional at a utility company:

I am still struggling with learning to say no to people during their hour of need. I have to balance handling the crisis technically and supporting my employees to, which takes a lot of time because their expertise is very limited.

The Influence on Recent Regulations

The Global Information Systems Security study highlights that the information security professional is not only charged with ensuring the organization follows all applicable mandates under the Gramm-Leach-Bliley Act of 1999 (GLB), Health Insurance Portability and Accountability Act of 1996 (HIPAA), and the Sarbanes-Oxley Act of 2002 (SOX), but additionally they must consistently fight battles within the organization for support in protecting the privacy of information gathered by the company. Described to follow, from an IS manager at a private urban hospital, are issues as they affect the privacy of customer health care. Ultimately, the quality of care is expected to precedence over information security rather than being two essential ingredients of care. Employees such as the one quoted to follow take their role as social service providers very seriously:

I have a social conscience. Privacy needs to be maintained, and our customers deserve that. But I recognize the challenge where they need expedited care and the people who are giving the care at that moment need information right away. Somehow you have to rectify that discrepancy. If I allow a weakness in security policy, and gain something in care provision, from a social conscience perspective, I have made the right decision. What people want first is to be well [the mission of the organization]. If that happens first, then we can be concerned about the rest.

The role of the information security professional is one of mediator, manager, technical expert, and legal analyst, among other things. Protection of organizational resources is paired with the development and implementation of information security policy.

In the health care industry, the conflict between secrecy and public "fix" of vulnerabilities can be present. The following quote, also from an IT professional, expresses the difficulty of balancing policy and worker productivity in the field of higher education:

I think that there are policies that make good sense to the IT department but not to the organization. Sometimes the IT department and other security departments get too big for their britches. They forget that they are there to support the organization and not the other way around. When the policies prevent you from performing your job something is going to have to give. I have also seen people publish policy who have no authority to do so. Then they get all bent out of shape when it gets ignored.

Although the regulations put forth by Congress have helped in increasing the security efforts of many organizations, they have a long way to go in order to be successful. According to an article by George Adams, president and CEO of SSH Communications Security Inc, in which he reviews the effectiveness of the SOX Act, more work needs to be done. He states, "True, *SOX* has generated a flurry of activity toward meeting the 'letter of the law' and spawned a new cottage industry for consultants, but it has done little so far about truly enhancing corporate security practices over the long term." In his article, it appears that Adams believes the SOX committee has in some ways hindered progress, and he writes, "under the watchful eye of internal *SOX* Compliance Committees, many already overloaded IT staff have spent more time asking for deadline extensions or been forced to wait until the last minute to meet internal deadlines for implementing *SOX* security measures. And, possibly worse than doing nothing, others have opted to implement minimal *SOX* security requirements without considering the overall security picture" (Adams, 2008).

Desired Non-Technical Skills

In addition to an array of technical skills, IT security professionals are most successful when they have a set of social skills in their repertoire. For example, it is important that they can manage varied people and tasks, have intuition that helps them get a better sense of user needs, and to converse with people regardless of their access to technical vocabulary or occupational conventions. In the following quote, an IT security professional from a manufacturing plant portrays the relevance of all of these non-technical skills as essentially the skills of coordination:

As the IT person, I see myself coordinating and working with the vender [of the proposed new IT system]. I take their implementation plan and coordinate who has to be involved, get the rooms ready, make sure the people are in place, make sure they know what's needed. I have to learn and support all of that myself so as questions arise, I can answer them. Beyond that, I would help the users, one-on-one, to get to a more comfortable place.

Communicating with users can be particularly demanding when users do not share the same knowledge base. IT security professionals often describe ways in which they have learned to express complicated specialized information with non-technical employees. The IT manager at a utility company found innovative ways of communicating with her coworkers about highly technical topics:

I don't have a problem with communicating with non-technical personnel. I try to relate it to something in everyday life. I'll give you an example of trying to explain file structure on a computer to somebody. If I'm talking to a female, I'll use it as a recipe box and use the main folder as the big box and each category underneath as a big folder, and each recipe as a file within that folder. People seem to understand that. If I'm going to explain it to a male, I use a baseball league. I use the National League and each team under the league is a folder and each person on that team is a file, and they get that picture. So I try to relate it to something that they are familiar with, not just files and folders, cause when you do that, people just don't get it.

While the respondent described the need to talk about things with which the user is familiar, there is also a tendency to consider this adjustment as "talking down" to them. Many users are sensitive to this and view this predisposition as a liability, as no one appreciates working with others who are patronizing. In the following quote, an IT security professional describes the intricacy of the use of technical vocabulary in his role:

There is a time to use technical terms and there is a time not to. Being in this job long enough, I know when to use technical terms. The way most organizations work, when you are trying to sell a product, or an idea, you have got to use technical terms so that they will understand that they know you know what you are talking about. If you are trying to correct a problem and explain internally, you have to choose the lowest language level possible, but that is not always easy when there is a complex, technical solution. Today, we were talking about security and used the analogy of a submarine. Instead of putting a brick wall of security around the organization, you need to compartmentalize, so your organization becomes a submarine, so you are a submarine that has a strong outside edge. But then internally, it is also broken up so that if you have a leak somewhere, you can then break it up so that the whole thing doesn't sink. But if you say, 'because of the network address translation and the sonic firewall that is producing the ports and DH CPU, they probably will not understand and will resent you for describing it that way.

Coordination with other departments is fundamental to the work an IT security professional does. Regardless of the content of a planned technical change, other departments may need to be made aware of the purpose and process of change. One IT worker at a university had these related comments:

One of the main areas of concern for me is the adequacy of our backup and storage procedures

I've been working on it for over a year, and the reason that it's taking so long to accomplish is because I've needed to get the attention of some other departments. It's not a priority for them and they're short handed, and I can appreciate that. But it's becoming a much higher priority for our department because we have an upgrade that we'd like to do in 6 months. In order to get that accomplished, we need to come with a totally new methodology for doing our backup so we need their attention.

DISCUSSION

The information gathered in these interviews show the complexity of the job of IT security professionals and its interdependence with other security stakeholders within organizations. In terms of the user interaction, it is important to have educated users and have them sign a user agreement form, understand the guidelines, punishments, proxies and firewalls. IT security professionals emphasized that it is not appropriate to shoot the messenger. For some, the role is seen as especially demanding because they are charged with keeping the organizational network running efficiently, ensuring its protection from intruders, and often times seem to be the bad guys to most of the organization's employees because there is an incorrect perception that their policies and procedures conflict with user productivity.

We know that if a user lacks integrity, no tool in the world will prevent him or her from doing illegitimate tasks on a business network. So, if they are well informed and no bad intention is present, that could only help.

Generally, organizations have rules that are designed with the best interests of all in mind. For what appear to be petty rules that users might complain about, there are generally many sound rules and guidelines that have been put in place to protect some important aspect of business. Communication of this fact is very important,

so that even those who do not understand why will feel compelled to respect the policy. Trust in the organization is important; assuming that even if it may be annoying, they have a reason for setting the policies and being responsible enough to adhere to them.

Organizations that make a habit of reminding employees of the rules will do well, those that explain the reasons and draw connections between the rules and the negative repercussions for not following them will do better.

CONCLUSION AND HRM IMPLICATIONS

In their field research, Belsis et al. (2005) identified three layers of security issues as (1) strategic – corporate IT security policy, (2) tactical – methodologies and practices developed to manage IT security, such as developing an IT security awareness program, and (3) operations – installation and operation of technologies and measures, such as administering firewalls, IDS, IPS, etc. Jenson and Romo (2005) make the following suggestions to handle these IT security issues. Management should (1) know in what areas the IT staff is weak, (2) know where the network/physical security is weak, and (3) make sure IT professionals get the training and experience they require to secure the network. Based on the results of our study, we recommend the following strategies of taking into account the cultural and human dimensions of managing IT security employees:

- Given the importance of technical knowledge for IT security professionals, organizations could implement more formalized approaches to IT security skills identification and recognition in order to promote the acquisition of latest technical security knowledge.
- Organizations need to formally recognize the complexity of the work of IT security

professionals and its direct impact on the normal and secure functioning of information systems. Having a clear distribution of roles, especially in large organizations would facilitate the effective distribution of priorities.

- HRM should provide opportunities for constant update on new security technologies and policies through informal and formal activities. For example, by subscribing to computer magazines and attending training workshops. Being up to date on the latest security attacks and ways of prevention and protection is something that needs to be encouraged all the time by the organization's management.

- HRM should also promote interaction between IT security professionals, users and managers so they could share and coordinate security measures in both informal and formal settings.

REFERENCES

Adams, G. (2008). *Five years and counting: A SOX data security reality check.* scmagazineus.com, retrieved on January 19, 2008 from http://www.scmagazineus.com/Five-years-and-counting-A-SOX-data-security-reality-check/article/104197/

Bayrak, T., & Brabowski, M. R. (2006). Critical infrastructure network evaluation. *The Journal of Computer Information Systems, 46*(3), 67-86.

Belsis, P., Kokolakis, S., & Kiountouzis, E. (2005). Information systems security from a knowledge management perspective. *Information Management & Computer Security, 13*(2/3), 189-202.

Biros, D. P., George, J. F., & Zmud, R. W. (2002). Inducing sensitivity to deception in order to improve decision making performance: A field study. *MIS Quarterly, 26*(2), 119-144.

Bodin, L. D., Gordon, L. A., & Loeb, M. P. (2005). Evaluating information security investments using the analytic hierarchy process. *Communications of the ACM, 48*(2), 79-83.

Chapple, M. (2008). *Don't let trends dictate your network security strategy.* techtarget.com, retrieved on January 16, 2008 from http://searchsecurity.techtarget.com/tip/0,289483,sid14_gci1233918,00.html

Colley, J. (2008). *The information security professional is more than a necessary evil.* out-law.com, retrieved on January 16, 2008 from http://www.out-law.com/page-7614

Committee on National Security Systems (2006). *National Information Assurance Glossary.* CNSS Instruction No. 4009.

Computer Security Institute (2006). *Virus attacks named leading culprit of financial loss by U.S. companies in 2006 CSI/FBI computer crime and security survey.* Retrieved March 15, 2008 from http://gocsi.com/press/20060712.html.

Computer Security Institute Survey 2007: The 12th Annual Computer Crime and Security Survey. (2007). *2007 by Computer Security Institute.*

Ferratt, T. W., Agarwal, R., Brown, C. V., & Moore, J. E. (2005). IT Human Resource Management Configurations and IT Turnover: Theoretical Synthesis and Empirical Analysis. *Information Systems Research, 16*(3), 237-328.

Guzman, I. R., Stam, K. R., & Stanton, J. M. (2008). The Occupational Culture of IS/IT Personnel within Organizations. *The DATA BASE for Advances in Information Systems, 39*(1), 33-50.

ISC: Security Transcends Technology (2008). *Career guide: decoding the information security profession, (isc)2 security transcends technology.* Retrieved June 5, 2008 from www.isc2.org/download/careerguide05.pdf

Issa: Information systems security association (2008). Retrieved June 3, 2008 from www.issa.org/Resources/Industry-Certifications.html

Jenson, B. K., & Romo, J. (2005). The expert opinion. *Journal of information technology case and application research, 7*(2), 49-52.

Kaarst-brown, M. L., & Guzman, I. R. (2005). Who is "the it Workforce"?: Challenges Facing Policy Makers, Management, and Research. *Proceedings of the 2005 ACM SIG MIS CPR*, Atlanta, Georgia, April 14-16.

Knapp, K. J., & Boulton, W. R. (2006). Cyberwarfare threatens corporations: Expansion into commercial environments. *Information Systems Management, 23*(2), 76-87.

Layton, T. P. (2007). *Information Security: Design, Implementation, Measurement, and Compliance*: Auerbach Publications, Taylor & Francis Group.

Prior, M., Rogerson, S., & Fairweather, B. (2002). The Ethical Attitudes of Information Systems Professionals: Outcomes of an initial survey. *Telematics and Informatics, 19*, 21-36.

Rasmussen, G. (2008). *Information Security Professional*. Retrieved, from the World Wide Web: http://www.gideonrasmussen.com

Rothke, B. (2004). *Computer Security: 20 Things Every Employee Should Know.* New York: McGraw Hill.

Stanton, J., & Stam, K. (2006). *The Visible Employee: Using Workplace Monitoring and Surveillance to Protect Information Assets- Without Compromising Employee Privacy and Trust.*

Stanton, J. M., Caldera, C., Isaac, A., Stam, K., & Marcinkowski, S. J. (2003). Behavioral Information Security: Define the criterion space. In P. M. Mastrangelo & W. J. Everton (Eds.),*The Internet at Work or Not: Preventing Computer Deviance. Symposium presentation at the 2003 meeting of the Society for Industrial and Organizational Psychology*, Orlando, FL.

Tittel, E. (2008). Certified Information Systems Security Professional. *SearchSecurity.com and Information Security Magazine.* March 31, 2008. Retrieved June 10, 2008 from www.searchsecurity.techtarget.com

Trice, H. (1993). *Occupational Subcultures in the Workplace.* Ithaca, NY: ILR Press.

APPENDIX A: DESCRIPTION OF SECURITY CERTIFICATIONS

This appendix provides an overview of the more popular information security-related professional certifications. This list demonstrates the extent of offering as well as the specialization of today's certifications. It is not intended to be an exhaustive list of certifications.

1. **Certification and Accreditation Professional (CAP):** Today's vulnerable world calls for an ongoing need for competent, qualified and efficient professionals who can effectively manage complex security issues that threaten the information systems of the organizations. To meet this demand, the U.S. Department of State's Office of Information Assurance and (ISC)[2] have collaborated to develop a credential for the Certification and Accreditation Professional (CAP). The objective of CAP is to prepare the individuals so that they can assess and manage the risks that security threats can pose within an organization, mainly in the government and enterprise sectors (Reference: www.isc2.org).

2. **Certification in Control Self-Assessment (CCSA):** The Certification in Control Self-Assessment (CCSA) is the Institute of Internal Auditor's first specialty certification and second certification to be offered by the Board of Regents in the history of the Institute of Internal Auditors. The program aims to identify the qualified and experienced individuals having the capability and efficiency for CCSA designation and provide guidance so as to successfully complete an exam designed to test an individual's proficiency in control self-assessment (Reference: www.theiia.org).

3. Certified Ethical Hacker (CEH): Certified Ethical Hacker (CEH) is a certification offered by EC Council. The CEH aims to identify the capable security professionals who can work with the same tools and apply the same knowledge as a malicious hacker does while hacking the systems. In this way this certification prepares the skilled professional who understands and knows how to look for the weaknesses and vulnerabilities in target systems and thus helps in finding and detecting vulnerabilities in computer systems and networks. To become a Certified Ethical Hacker, individuals must pass a single exam and prove knowledge of tools as used by hackers and security professionals (Reference: www.eccouncil.org).

4. **Certified Internal Auditor (CIA):** The Institute of Internal Auditors (IIA) offers Certified Internal Auditor (CIA) certification which enhances the candidates' capability to identify risks, examine alternative remedies, and prescribe the best initiatives to control these risks. The CIA exam tests a candidate's knowledge and ability regarding the current practice of internal auditing. The certification is mainly targeted for the financial professionals who are responsible for auditing IT practices and procedures, as well as standard accounting practices and procedures to insure the integrity and correctness of financial records, transaction logs and other records relevant to commercial activities (Reference: www.theiia.org).

5. **Certified Information Privacy Professional (CIPP):** The Certified Information Privacy Professional (CIPP) is the core IAPP privacy certification which provides a strong foundation in a broad range of corporate privacy issues, laws and concepts in force today. The CIPP revolves around the definitions, concepts and applications of U.S. and international privacy laws and information management practices as well as the privacy implications of emerging technologies such as HIPAA, COPPA, GLBA, APEC principles, OECD guidelines, EU Directive, employee records management, workplace monitoring, contingency planning, incident handling, PII, Web forms, cookie files, Spyware, spam and other key items. The CIPP program is targeted for the entry-level

candidates who are interested in learning the essentials of privacy as well as for the intermediate-level privacy professionals who have basic knowledge and understanding of privacy laws and practices (Reference: www.privacyassociation.org).

6. **Certified Information Systems Auditor (CISA):** Certified Information Systems Auditor (CISA) program has grown to be globally recognized and adopted worldwide as a symbol of achievement. Since 1978, the program has measured excellence in the area of IS auditing, control and security. The CISA designation is awarded by the Information Systems Audit and Control Association to those individuals with an interest in information systems auditing, control, and security who have met and continue to meet specific requirements. This certification is mainly targeted for the IT security professionals who are responsible for auditing IT systems, practices and procedures to make sure organizational security policies meet governmental and regulatory requirements, conform to best security practices and principles, and meet or exceed requirements as stated in an organization's security policy (Reference: www.isaca.org).

7. **Certified Information Security Manager (CISM):** The CISM designation is awarded by the Information Systems Audit and Control Association and has been earned by over 9,000 professionals since its introduction in 2003. CISM is business-oriented and focused on information risk management while addressing management, design and technical security issues at the conceptual level. The CISM provides the knowledge and understanding of information security concepts to the IT professionals who manage, design, oversee or assess an enterprise's information security (IS). Thus the certification is of primary interest to IT professionals who are responsible for managing IT systems, networks, policies, practices and procedures to make sure organizational security policies meet governmental and regulatory requirements, conform to best security practices and principles, and meet or exceed requirements as stated in an organization's security policy (Reference: www.isaca.org).

8. **Certified Information Systems Security Professional (CISSP):** The Certified Information Systems Security Professional (CISSP) was developed and is maintained by the International Information Systems Security Certification Consortium (ISC)[2] for the purpose of recognizing individuals who have distinguished themselves as experienced, knowledgeable, and proficient information security practitioners. As the first and only ANSI accredited information security credential under ISO/IEC Standard 17024, the CISSP provides information security professionals with not only an objective measure of competence but a globally recognized standard of achievement through its review of the 10 domains of the information security practice. The CISSP basically revolves around the knowledge of network and system security principles, safeguards and practices and is awarded to those candidates who achieve a prescribed level of information security experience, comply with a professional code of ethics, and pass a rigorous examination on the Common Body of Knowledge of information security. The credential is ideal for mid and senior-level managers who are working toward or have already attained positions as CSOs, CISOs or Senior Security Engineers as well as for the full-time IT security professionals who work in internal security positions or who consult with third parties on security matters (Reference: www.isc2.org).

9. **Certified Identity Theft Risk Management Specialist (CITRMS®):** The Certified Identity Theft Risk Management Specialist (CITRMS®) certification program is the nation's only training program developed by the Institute of Consumer Financial Education (ICFE). The main purpose of this program is to comprehensively prepare and equip law enforcement professionals, financial planners and CPA's, resolution advocates, notaries, lawyers, credit and debt counselors, through

education, testing and computer software training, with the knowledge and skills necessary to help consumers and businesses fully assess and minimize their present risk of credit and identity theft. CITRMS®-qualified professionals are employed by a wide range of organizations including financial institutions; mortgage, real estate, and financial services firms; law enforcement, and other government agencies along with the private practitioners including attorneys, CPAs, financial advisors, counselors, and consultants (Reference: www.financial-education-icfe.org).

10. **Certified Information Technology Professional (CITP):** The AICPA's Certified Information Technology Professional (CITP) Credential recognizes Certified Public Accountants for their technology expertise and unique ability to bridge the gap between business and technology. Unlike other certifications that recognize only a narrow scope of skills, the CITP credential recognizes technical excellence across the wide range of business-technology practice areas. To qualify for the CITP Credential, you must be a full member in good standing of the American Institute of Certified Public Accountants (AICPA) and hold a valid and unrevoked CPA certificate issued by a legally constituted state authority (Reference: www.aicpa.org).

11. **Certified Internet Webmaster Security Professional (CIW-SP):** The Certified Internet Webmaster Security Professional program (CIW-SP) is the recognized job-role certification providing the knowledge of Web and e-commerce-related security principles and practices. A CIW Security Professional implements security policy, identifies security threats, and develops countermeasures using firewall systems and attack-recognition technologies. The certification is mainly targeted to the Web administrators who implement and manage a secure and working web presence including e-commerce capabilities (Reference: www.ciwcertified.com).

12. **CompTIA Security+ Certification:** The CompTIA Security+ certification is recognized by the technology community as a valuable credential that proves competency with information security. It validates knowledge and expertise in information security topics such as communication security, infrastructure security, cryptography, operational security, and general security concepts. It focuses on important security fundamentals related to security concepts and theory, as well as best operational practices. The certification serves as the entry-level information security certification and so is mainly of interest for the IT professionals seeking to pursue further work and knowledge in this area. Although not a prerequisite, it is desirable that candidates have at least two years on-the-job networking experience, with an emphasis on security (Reference: www.certification. comptia.org).

13. **Certified Protection Professional (CPP):** Today's world recognizes the need for qualified and competent professionals who can assess and effectively manage the risks of complex security threats to the people, property and information of corporations, governments, and public and private institutions. To meet this need, the American Society for Industrial Security (ASIS) International administers the Certified Protection Professional (CPP) program which demonstrates a thorough understanding of physical, human and information security principles and practices. This credential is mainly of interest for the professionals who are dedicated to the security profession and recognizes their ability to perform to exemplary standards. Only those who have worked with and around security for some time are able to qualify for this credential (Reference: www. asisonline.org).

14. **Certified Risk Professional (CRP):** Developed by BAI Center for Certifications, the Certified Risk Professional® Program (CRP) is the most extensive and prestigious professional designation which identifies the individuals who are having specialized expertise and strong knowledge of

risk identification, assessment and management in the financial services industry. The certification sets the standards for measuring risk management experience, knowledge and skills of risk management professionals. The CRP designation provides specialization in the areas of Audit, U.S. Regulatory Compliance, Operations & Operational Control, Finance & Accounting and Treasury, Asset/Liability and Balance Sheet Risk Management (Reference: www.bai.org).

15. **EC-Council Certified Security Analyst (ECSA):** Most of the security certifications concentrate on the management or the technical aspects alone but EC-Council Certified Security Analyst (ECSA) helps you bridge the gap to a certain extent by helping you detect the causes of security lapses and what implications it might carry for the management. The objective of ECSA is to add value to experienced security professionals by helping them analyze the symptoms and pin point the causes of those symptoms which reflect the security posture of the network. Candidates must pass exam to achieve this certification (Reference: www.eccouncil.org).

16. **EC-Council Certified Secure Programmer (ECSP):** Certified Secure Programmer (ECSP) developed by EC-Council provides the fundamental skills and knowledge to all application developers and development organizations so that they will be able to produce applications with greater stability and posing lesser security risks to the consumer. This certification targets the programmers who are responsible for the designing of relatively bug-free, stable Windows and Web-based applications with the .NET/Java Framework as well as the developers who have C#, C++ and Java development skills and helps them greatly reducing exploitation by hackers and the incorporation of malicious code. To qualify for this certification, candidates must attend a Writing Secure Code training course and pass a single exam (Reference: www.eccouncil.org).

17. **Global Information Assurance Certification (GIAC):** SANS' GIAC Training and certification program recognizes and develops the candidates so that they will have the knowledge of and the ability to manage and protect important information systems and networks. The program goes beyond theory and terminology and tests the pragmatics of Audit, Security, Operations, Management and Software Security tasks, thus it is designed to be challenging, and accurately measure the candidates' ability to apply knowledge and relate knowledge in specific areas. The standards for the GIAC certification were developed using the highest benchmarks in the industry. Therefore, it provides assurance that a certified individual meets a minimum level of ability and possesses the skills necessary to do the job. Building from the original GSE, GIAC has introduced two additional platinum level certifications, GSE-M and GSE-C. To qualify for this certification, candidates are required to complete three intermediate-level GIAC certifications (GSEC, GCIA and GCIH), with GIAC Gold in at least two of them and pass two proctored exams (Reference: www.giac.org).

18. **NSA INFOSEC Assessment Methodology (IAM):** The IAM consists of a standard set of activities required to perform an on-site Information Security (INFOSEC) Assessment. The course was originally developed by National Security Agency (NSA), a national leader in Information Assurance, to train U.S. Department of Defense (DoD) organizations to perform their own INFOSEC assessments. Today IAM offers a limited number of IAM classes to facilitate the transfer of Government-developed technology into the private sector. Although not a technical certification the IAM "sets the bar" for what needs to be done to conduct a complete comprehensive INFOSEC Assessment as defined by IATRP. To qualify for an IAM certificate, candidates are required to attend the two-day class; demonstrate an understanding of the IAM through group exercises and class discussions; and obtain a passing grade (at least 70 percent) on the IAM test (Reference: www.iatrp.com).

19. **International Systems Security Professional Certification Scheme (ISSPCS):** ISSPCS is a global and open certification scheme for Information and Systems Security professionals based on essential security principles. It was originally developed by the University of Queensland, AusCERT, EWA-Australia and ISSEA (an international administrative authority) in conjunction with a panel of industry experts. ISSPCS offers four certification levels: ISSPCS Practitioner, ISSPCS Professional, ISSPCS Mentor, and ISSPCS Fellow. Applicants must start with the ISSPCS Practitioner level certification before progressing to the Professional level. ISSPCS certifications are valid for 3 years during which candidates must accumulate activity points by attending courses, publishing papers, etc. to ensure that their information security skills remain current (Reference: www.isspcs.org)

20. **Licensed Penetration Tester (LPT):** EC-Council's Licensed Penetration Tester (LPT) program offers the penetration testing professionals the opportunity to develop their skills and standardize their knowledgebase by providing the best practices as followed by the experienced experts in the field. The program identifies and trains the security professionals so that they will be able to effectively analyze the security of a network and thereby provide appropriate corrective measures. The program aims to ensure that each LPT professional licensed by EC-Council must adhere to a strict code of ethics, follows best practices and is conversant with all compliance requirements as mentioned by the industry. To become certified LPT, candidates are required to obtain EC-Council's CEH and ECSA certifications, and complete LPT training criteria which includes submission of an LPT application, background check documentation, detailed resume and an agreement to abide by EC-Council code of ethics. Additionally, candidates are required to attend a three-day LPT workshop through an EC-Council's accredited training center (Reference: www.eccouncil.org).

21. **Professional in Critical Infrastructure Protection (PCIP):** Securing the systems and network environments supporting the critical infrastructure is more important in today's world now more than ever and requires an extended set of specialized skills. In this context, the PCIP certification (formerly the CCISP) maintained by the Critical Infrastructure Institute offers the required skills ranging from highly technical to CIP program management techniques. It is the first and unique certification program which is tailored specifically to the Critical Infrastructure sectors and the Critical Infrastructure Protection Industry (CIP). PCIP certified professionals are able to effectively design, maintain and manage security architectures for critical infrastructure, SCADA, and high-availability environments. The certification consists of three separate classes: CIP Program Course, CIP Technical Course, and CIP Applied Course. To become PCIP certified, candidates are required to complete all these three classes. In addition, they need to recertify every 2 years so as to ensure that they possess current knowledge of security threats and solutions (Reference: www.ci-institute.org).

22 **Qualified Information Security Professional (QISP):** Highly popular with government and industry security heavies, the Security University's QISP program combines coverage of key information security topics, tools and technologies with a hands-on, lab-oriented learning and testing program. Though the program is expensive, as well as time-consuming but it's always worth to invest in this program. It is targeted for IT security professionals, Sys Admins, Security Auditors, Network Auditors, CISO's, or all of the IT personnel who are looking to develop tactical security skills and advance their career opportunities. To attain QISP certification, candidates are required to successfully pass Security University's QISP online 125 questions (Multiple Choice) certification exam (Reference: www.securityuniversity.net)

23. **Sun Certified Security Administrator (SCSECA):** The Sun Certified Security Administrator exam requires an in-depth knowledge and understanding of security topics such as detection and device management, security attacks, file and system resources protection, host and network prevention, and network connection access, authentication, and encryption. The credential is ideal for the system administrators who are having previous experience administering security in a Solaris Operating System. It is desirable that candidates be previously certified as a Sun Certified System Administrator (SCSA) and Sun Certified Network Administrator (SCNA) (Reference: www.sun. com).

24. **Systems Security Certified Practitioner (SSCP):** SSCP Certification was designed to recognize an international standard for practitioners of information security and understanding of a Common Body of Knowledge (CBK). The certification allows network and systems security administrators to achieve recognition as practitioners knowledgeable in the accepted practices, roles and responsibilities of information security. The exam focuses more on operational and administrative issues relevant to information security and less on information policy design, risk assessment details and other business analysis skills that are more germane to senior IT security professional. The credential is ideal for those working toward or who have already attained positions as Senior Network Security Engineers, Senior Security Systems Analysts or Senior Security Administrators (Reference: www.isc2.org).

25. **Security5 Certification:** Identity theft, credit card fraud, online banking Phishing scams, virus and backdoors, email hoaxes, sex offenders lurking online, loss of confidential information and hackers are some of the threats you always afraid of. In this regard, Security5 certification provides you training to take control and secure your information assets. This certification is mainly targeted for non-IT office workers and home users, who understand Internet security terminology, know how to use defense programs such as antivirus and anti spyware applications can implement basic operating system security and follow safe Web and e-mail practices (Reference: www.eccouncil. org).

Chapter X
Diagnosing Misfits, Inducing Requirements, and Delineating Transformations within Computer Network Operations Organizations

Nikolaos Bekatoros HN
Naval Postgraduate School, USA

Jack L. Koons III
Naval Postgraduate School, USA

Mark E. Nissen
Naval Postgraduate School, USA

ABSTRACT

The US Government is moving apace to develop doctrines and capabilities that will allow the Department of Defense (DoD) to exploit Cyberspace for military advantage, and the role of computer networked operations (CNO) has taken on greater importance with the rise of network-centric warfare. Unfortunately, extant CNO organizations are slow to anticipate and react, and as such do not operate well within their highly dynamic environments. Contingency Theory research provides considerable knowledge to guide designing organizational structures that fit well with various mission-environmental contexts, and as such it offers excellent potential to inform leaders and policy makers regarding how to bring their CNO organizations and approaches into better fit, and hence to improve performance. In this chapter, we identify a candidate set of organizational structures that offer potential to fit DoD better as it strives, and struggles, to address the technological advances and risks associated with CNO. Using the Organizational Consultant (OrgCon) expert system to model and diagnose key problems and misfits associated with extant CNO organizations in the DoD, we propose a superior organizational structure for CNO that can also be applied to organizations in the international environment. Results elucidate important insights into CNO organization and management, suitable for immediate policy and operational implementation, and expand the growing empirical basis to guide continued research.

INTRODUCTION

The Internet has become the new frontier where nation states and stateless actors can communicate on a global scale and with a rate of speed and security as never seen before. The Internet has been operational since 1969 in one form or fashion, and over one billion people are said to use the Internet today (*estimated at 1,407,724,920 as of March 2008*, Internet Usage Statistics, 2008). Nation states in particular are becoming increasingly reliant on the Internet and Cyberspace for infrastructure to support economic and security interests.

In addition to nation states, the rise of terrorist groups such as Al Qaeda, and other nefarious groups such as mafia crime families, would have been unable to reach current epic proportions without such modern means of global communications. To counter threats from both nation states and nefarious groups, the US maintains numerous organizations (e.g., National Security Agency, military service network commands) charged with the protection and defense of the communications and network infrastructure enabled by the Internet. Indeed, one can argue that a plethora of different, often non-cooperating organizations (e.g., Federal Bureau of Investigation, Central Intelligence Agency) seek simultaneously and with minimal coordination to accomplish efficiently and effectively computer network operations. This confusion and uncoordination between them serves to slow responses to network attacks and intrusions, particularly where more than one organization strives simultaneously to provide critical infrastructure, expertise and technology.

To reverse this trend in part, the US Government is moving apace to develop doctrines and capabilities that will allow the Department of Defense (DoD) to exploit Cyberspace for military advantage. Within the broad rubric of Information Operations (IO), there is increasing effort devoted to shaping the organizational structures of Computer Network Operations (CNO) at the joint, combatant command, and service levels, and the role of CNO has taken on greater importance with the rise of network-centric warfare. Comprised primarily of defense, attack and exploitation, the technological capabilities are growing exponentially, as is the rate of data exchange, yet the organizational structures supporting CNO are slow to anticipate and react. This presents a serious issue in terms of mission-environmental fit, as such organizations do not operate well within their highly dynamic environments, nor are they suited well to the missions and expectations placed upon them.

A half century of Contingency Theory research (e.g., Burns & Stalker, 1961; Harvey, 1968; Galbraith, 1973) provides considerable knowledge to guide designing organizational structures that fit well with various mission-environmental contexts, and as such it offers excellent potential to inform leaders and policy makers regarding how to bring their CNO organizations and approaches into better fit, and hence to improve performance. The key research question is, which organizational configurations provide the best CNO performance within the network-centric environment?

The purpose of this chapter is to identify a candidate set of organizational structures that offer potential to fit DoD like agencies, and international organizations as they strive, and struggle, to address the technological advances and risks associated with CNO. Using the Organizational Consultant (OrgCon) expert system to model and diagnose key problems and misfits associated with extant CNO organizations in the DoD, we propose a superior organizational structure for CNO, and we outline a three-step transformation plan to guide movement toward such structure.

In the balance of this chapter, we first review key background literature on CNO and the OrgCon expert system. We then describe a grounded CNO organization model specified via OrgCon, and depict such model in two, contrasting, network-centric environments. Results follow to elucidate important insights into CNO organization and management, suitable for immediate policy and operational implementation, and expand the growing empirical basis to guide continued research along these lines. Hence, the potential contribution of this research has both theoretical and real-world implications, and should appeal to both the academic and practitioner communities.

BACKGROUND

In this section we describe a current CNO organization, focusing in particular on Computer Network Defense (CND) to ground our model in current practice for analysis. CND represents a very practical point to begin an investigation such as this: there is little opportunity to conduct computer attacks and exploitations if one's own defenses are weak, and one's own network is vulnerable. We then describe the Organizational Consultant expert system that drives our analysis of such grounded CND organization.

Grounded CND Model

To understand computer network defense as it exists in the field, we survey best practices via published and online references (e.g., see US-CERT, 2008; SANS 2008; University of California

San Francisco Medical Center, 2008; University of Minnesota Office of Information Technology, 2008; The National Strategy to Secure Cyberspace, 2003; DoD IA Strategic Plan Version 1.1, 2004; DoD Net-Centric Data Strategy, 2003 ; CJCSI, 2007; Computer Security Enhancement Act of 2001, 2001; DoD Directive 5200.1-R, 1997), and speak at length with subject matter experts at a major DoD educational institution (to include lecturer and tenured faculty in the Department of Computer Science as well as Network Security Office specialists and administrators). This integrated, online and field research allows us to sample from a wide range of computer network organizational approaches (e.g., educational, governmental, business). We build upon such research to develop a general model, which provides the basis for our OrgCon analysis.

Figure 1 depicts a representative computer network defense approach (e.g., organizational structure, task structure, personnel staffing, technological infrastructure). We ground our depiction of this approach via analysis of the organization structures and workflow processes of a major U. S. West Coast university, and we subject such model to face validation by various DoD CND experts. Our exemplar organization was predicated on the availability of open source material concerning the respective CND effort. In addition, we determined their use of network infrastructure to support research and communication across a large and geographically disperse medical and research facility readily transferable towards any number of international, public, and private network operations. Notice that the CND organization depicted in the figure includes only three levels, and represents a relatively small organization. Clearly, CND comprises only a part of CNO, which in turn comprises only a part of IO, and so forth; hence, we focus on a tangible, front-line organization charged specifically to conduct CND. This provides considerable depth of focus for the study, and enables us to develop a specific, well-understood model for analysis. Nonetheless,

Figure 1. Computer network operations organization diagram & associated workflow

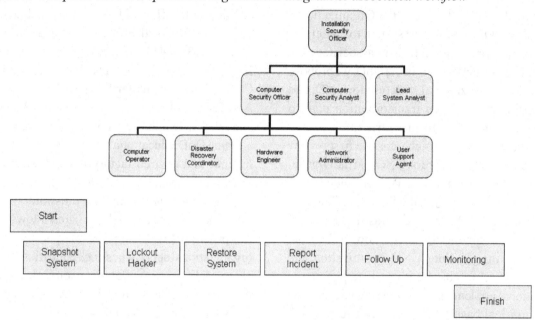

our survey confirms that this organization is quite typical of CND in practice today; hence our results should generalize relatively broadly. To ensure the widest audience, validation of our model was accomplished by tenured faculty and researchers at a major US educational institution as well as relevant subject matter experts. These experts are active in the CNO and CND arena-both in private and public practice.

To focus our modeling and analysis further, we concentrate on a single yet critical and common work process: responding to hacker attacks. This emerges from our survey and fieldwork summarized above as a perennial CND activity, and serves to facilitate the generalizability of this research further. Our model reflects the steps a CERT element (Computer Emergency Response Team) deals with the threat described below (US CERT 2008 & UCSF 2008):

...There are two methods for dealing with an active hacker/cracker incident. The first method is to immediately lock the person out of the system and restore the system to a safe state. The second

method is to allow the hacker/cracker to continue his probe/attack and attempt to gather information that will lead to an identification and possible criminal conviction. The method used to handle a hacker/cracker incident will be determined by the level of understanding of the risks involved. In the case of an active hacker/cracker incident, a decision must be made whether to allow the activity to continue while evidence is gathered or to get the hacker/cracker off the system and then lock the person out. The Director of Infrastructure and Security Officer or the Network Architecture and Security manager must make this decision. The decision will be based on the availability of qualified personnel to monitor and observe the hacker/cracker and the risk involved.

Indeed, responses to hacker attacks typically center on one of three main profiles: 1) unauthorized activity on the host system; 2) unauthorized attempt to gain access to the host system; and 3) anomalies on the host system discovered after the fact (UCSF Medical Center, 2008). The model depicted in the figure also reflects six CND work

Table 1. CND work tasks and activities

Work Task	Activities
Snapshot the System	Make copies of all audit trail information such as system log files, the root history files, and like tasks, and get a listing of all active network connections.
Lockout the Hacker	Kill all active processes for the hacker/cracker, and remove any files or programs that may have been left on the system. Change passwords for any accounts that were accessed by the hacker/cracker.
Restore the System	Restore the system to a normal stage. Restore any data or files that the hacker/cracker may have modified. Install patches or fixes to close any security vulnerabilities that the hacker/cracker may have exploited. Log all actions taken to restore the system to a normal state in a logbook.
Report the Incident	The incident should be reported following the security incident reporting procedures.
Follow Up	After the investigation, a short report describing the incident and actions that were taken should be documented and distributed to the appropriate personnel.
Monitoring	There are no set procedures for monitoring the activity of a hacker. However, monitored information should be reported in a written log. Each incident will be dealt with on a case-by-case basis. The person authorizing the monitoring activity should provide direction to those doing the monitoring. Once the decision has been made to cease monitoring the hacker's activities and have him removed from the system, the steps outlined previously (i.e., Removal of Hacker/Cracker) are followed.

tasks: 1) snapshot the system, 2) lockout hacker, 3) restore system, 4) report incident, 5) follow up, and 6) monitoring. Table 1 summarizes the key activities comprising these six tasks.

Organizational Consultant

In this section, we describe the Organizational Consultant, and indicate its potential for organizational design in the CND domain. DoD in general and the U.S. Air Force specifically, are in the early stages of identifying the basic infrastructure requirements and command and control (C2) mechanisms of CNO (Baddelay, 2008). In particular, the requirement for a CND operator to gain and maintain situational awareness while positioning for proactive response to asymmetrical network threats points to a need for clear C2 lines and organizational structure which supports the dynamic operational environment. Organizational Consultant allows us the ability to use computational modeling to identify those structures best suited for a particular operating environment.

As noted above, the Organization Consultant is a scholarship-based expert system that employs automated inference. A huge formalization and integration of the Contingency Theory literature supports this scholarship-based expert system's knowledgebase. Most such formalization is made in terms of research propositions, expressed via If-Then rules, which are easily intelligible to people as well as machines.

For instance, one proposition reads (Burton and Obel, 2004, p. 19): "If environmental complexity is *simple*, and environmental change is *static*, then the organizational structure should be *functional*." Here the symbols "simple" and "static" represent inputs to the system, and the symbol "functional" represents the output. This formalizes one chunk of organization theory as articulated from above (Duncan, 1979). Other, similar chunks from Duncan's theoretical articulation are formalized similarly in terms of rules. Then theoretical chunks from other authors (e.g., Mintzberg, 1979; Perrow, 1967; Thompson, 1967) are formalized into additional rules, and so forth, until a substantial segment of the Contingency Theory literature is captured in the knowledgebase. For the interested reader this knowledgebase building process is described in Baligh et all (1993). The validation and refinement process used for the Organizational Consultant's knowledgebase relied on information obtained from twenty two case studies, consultation with executives in telecommunications, pharmaceutical, manufacturing, retailing firms and others, dialogue with experts, and finally approximately 150 executive MBA (Master's program in Business Administration) students' assignments in an organizational design course, where the students were asked to apply Organizational Consultant to their organization (Carley and Prietula 1994).

Clearly not all authors from the organization studies literature agree with one another. Hence, many theoretical chunks are mutually inconsistent. The expert system uses the approach *certainty factors* to integrate such diverse and possibly conflicting theoretical chunks. This approach assigns confidence values to various propositions in the knowledgebase, values that are combined algorithmically to determine a composite level of confidence in a particular chunk. For instance, if two authors with propositions in the system agree with one another but a third one disagrees, one might expect to see a certainty factor of 0.67 (i.e., two-thirds) associated with the proposition. The second use of the certainty factors is to refer to the relative strength of the various contingency factors based on the examined organization. For example if the modeler believes that the decentralized structure of the examined organization is more important than its strategic type, different certainty factors can be used to reflect their relative strength. This represents a long-standing and effective approach to knowledge integration in expert systems (Carley and Prietula 1994). In our research, we kept the certainty factors constant (1.00) in order to avoid unnecessary complexity and eliminate any future concerns that the values of the certainty factors have in fact great influence on the output of the expert system. Therefore, the use of a fixed value for the certainty factors eliminates any bias and subjectivity unintentionally introduced by the researcher and any future disagreement among experts about the relative value of specific certainty factors.

Operationally, the Organizational Consultant takes as input description of an organization in terms of six dimensions (i.e., management and leadership style, organizational climate, size, environment, technology, strategy). The expert system asks a number of questions to gather inputs in each area. In the area concerning management style, questions pertain to organizational characteristics such as: top management involvement in data gathering and interpretation; top management control over decision-making; top management preferences in terms of pro-activity, risk-aversion and control; middle management control over budgets, rewards, hiring and unit evaluation; and others. In the area concerning organization climate, questions pertain to characteristics such as: interpersonal trust, sharing and openness; intra-organizational conflict, disagreement and friction; employee morale, confidence and enthusiasm; resistance to change; leader credibility; and others. Inputs such as these involve judgment and interpretation on the part of the person answering the Organizational Consultant's questions.

Size and ownership questions are more objective than those above are. For instance, size is measured principally by the number of employees; the age of the organization is selected from among multiple descriptive categories (e.g., new, mature); and the organization's establishment as a public or private enterprise is input. These represent factual questions. Questions pertaining to technology are similar but require some additional judgment. For instance, the user must determine whether the primary outputs are products or services; whether the technology involves mass production, automation, specialized customization, or some other; how routine (e.g., analyzable, with few exceptions) the technology is; how divisible (e.g., involving decomposable tasks) the work is; the extent of information systems use; and others.

Arguably, questions pertaining to the organizational environment and strategy fall somewhere in between those above in terms of judgment required to answer them. In the area concerning environment, questions pertain to characteristics such as: environmental complexity, uncertainty, equivocally, hostility, and others. In the area concerning strategy, questions pertain to characteristics such as: capital requirements; product and process innovation; concern for quality; relative price level; and others.

The Organizational Consultant uses inputs gathered through such questions and answers to drive a matching process with its myriad propositional rules and confidence factors. Through the analytical lens of Contingency Theory, it uses evaluation criteria (e.g., *effectiveness, efficiency, viability*) to assess the organization's fit in terms of these inputs as well as an overall assessment of appropriateness in terms of its mission and environment. In a natural language format, it associates user inputs with theory through a series of classifications. For instance, it may characterize an organization as "small" or "large" based on the number of employees and the nature of their professionalism. Such classifications are rooted in organization theory. As another instance, it may characterize an organization as having an "internal process climate" or "developmental climate" based on answers to the user's answers provided to questions about organizational climate. As above, such classifications are rooted in organization theory. Theory rooted classifications in the other areas are provided as well in similar fashion.

Where potential misfits are diagnosed, the Organizational Consultant also provides relatively fine-grain, contextualized recommendations for improving fit through different organizational design alternatives. For instance, it may classify the organization as pursuing a "Defender" strategy, but recommend that an alternate strategy such as "Analyzer" appears to be more appropriate. As another instance, it may recommend restructuring a "Machine Bureaucracy" along the lines of an alternate organizational form such as "Functional Configuration," and it may suggest other structural changes such as decreasing the degree

of horizontal differentiation, formalization and centralization. Where multiple recommendations are suggested by the expert system rules and automated inference, it will list each recommendation separately, along with the corresponding certainty factor as an estimate of relative confidence, and explain the characteristics and implications of each. This section on diagnosed misfits and recommendations can be empty or very long, depending upon how well the organizational design appears to be appropriate for its mission and environment. This approach is quite novel in the domain of CNO research.

As with any computer-based system, the Organizational Consultant can be run multiple times for sensitivity analysis. This helps the user to gauge the degree to which one or more particular inputs may be driving the system's classifications, diagnoses and recommendations. To a large extent, this system is relatively robust to small changes in inputs. The inclusion of multiple conclusions and certainty factors augments such robustness. However, as with any computer-based system—particularly one that utilizes automated inference—problematic or erroneous inputs will guarantee problematic or erroneous outputs. Prudent modeling procedure calls for users to validate the accuracy and fidelity of their inputs.

ORGCON CND MODEL

Building upon our discussion above, along with prior research (e.g. see Nissen, 2005), we use the OrgCon expert system environment to represent the structure and behavior of the grounded CND model from above. This analysis takes two steps. We analyze first the current organization in terms of a mission-environmental scenario labeled "Simple Environment." This is used to characterize the environment where largely amateur hacker attacks target known network vulnerabilities, and which can be countered principally via the use of Standard Operating Procedures (SOPs) that exist within the organization. This represents the nature of CND organizations' routine work, and provides an understandable baseline for comparison.

Then we analyze this same, grounded organization in a different scenario labeled "Complex Environment." This is used to characterize an environment where largely professional hacker attacks target unknown network vulnerabilities, which are much less likely to be countered effectively via solely SOPs as above. Although less common than the kinds of amateur attacks corresponding to the simple environment, defending the network effectively in this latter case is critical, as professional hackers can cause crippling damage if left unthwarted.

There is no doubt that there is middle ground between the two extreme cases that have been chosen for our research. There are two main reasons why this approach was followed. The first reason is that by examining the extremes the similarities and the differences are maximized, therefore can be identified and analyzed by the researcher with greater confidence. The second reason is that in order to examine a case that is in fact a hybrid of extreme cases one must first understand and analyze these extremes before examining the middle ground between them.

Simple Environment: Amateur Hacker Attack Scenarios

This scenario conceives of the current CND organization that operates in a simple environment with relatively low levels of uncertainty and hostility. Following our discussion of OrgCon inputs above, six key aspects of the CND organization are addressed to instantiate a model: 1) organization size, 2) climate, 3) management style, 4) strategy, 5) organizational characteristics, and 6) technology. A detailed summary of OrgCon inputs and outputs is included in Appendix A.

Regarding size, the CND organization is modeled via OrgCon as "medium size," reflecting the 25 employees in our grounded model. Also, the

level of professionalism is very high in the CND team. This reflects not only ubiquitous college degrees among organization members but also the considerable formal training received by everyone inside the organization, and is consistent with the highly specialized jobs of people that work within the CND arena.

In terms of climate, the CND team is classified by OrgCon as having "internal process climate." This is consistent with the considerable work formalization, structure, procedure, formality, and policy guidance employed in the CND organization. The employees' morale and the high leader credibility suggest aspects of a "group" climate also, but several attributes of a "group" climate do not appear to match well with our grounded CND organization. The "group" climate is "a friendly place to work where people share a lot of themselves; success is defined in terms of sensitivity to customers and concern for people; and the organization places a premium on teamwork, participation, and consensus." which does not portray the climate of a CND organization.

The management style is classified as one of medium preference for "micro-involvement," because management has both a short-time and long-term horizon when making decisions when countering hacker attacks. The management of CND prefers taking actions on some decisions and being reactive toward others. The fact that management is risk averse and prefers using control to coordinate activities leads it toward a moderate preference for micro-involvement.

The strategy categories derive from Miles and Snow (1978), and include colorful terms such as *Prospector, Defender, Analyzer* and *Reactor* and are summarized in Table 2. An analyzer with innovation strategy appears to fit the CND organization well, and is a combination of the "Defender" and the "Prospector" strategies. A concern for high quality, moderate preference for micro-involvement and influence, and control over current operations all point to the analyzer with innovation strategy.

Table 2. The miles and snow strategy categories (adapted by Burton and Obel 1998)

Strategy Categories	Description
Prospector	An organization that almost continually searches for market opportunities and regularly experiments with potential responses to emerging environmental trends. Thus, the organization often is the creator of change and uncertainty to which its competitors must respond. However, because of its strong concern for product and market innovation, it usually is not completely efficient.
Defender	An organization that has a narrow product market domain. Top managers in this type of organization are highly expert in their organization's limited area of operation but do not tend to search outside their domains for new opportunities. As a result of this narrow focus, these organizations seldom need to make major adjustments in their technology, structure, or methods of operation. Instead, they devote primary attention to improving the efficiency of their existing operations.
Analyzer with innovation	An organization that combines the strategy of the defender and the prospector. It moves into the production of a new product or enters a new market after viability has been shown. But contrary to an analyzer without innovation, it does have innovations that run concurrently with the regular production. It has a dual technology core.
Analyzer without innovation	An organization whose goal is to move into new products or new markets only after their viability has been shown yet maintains an emphasis on its ongoing products. It has limited innovation related to the production process and generally not the product.
Reactor	An organization in which top management frequently perceives change and uncertainty occurring in their organizational environments but are unable to respond effectively. Because this type of organization lacks a consistent strategy or structure relationship, it seldom makes adjustment of any sort until forced to do so by environmental procedures.

Current organizational characteristics are driven by organizational differentiation, centralization and formalization. Differentiation has three components: horizontal, vertical and spatial. These three components of differentiation reflect, respectively: 1) breadth of organizational tasks and jobs, 2) number of hierarchical levels, and 3) geographical distribution of operations. Centralization pertains to information flows and decision rights being concentrated in the leadership at the organization's center. Formalization pertains to the level of standardization of work processes and written procedures to specify and govern work behavior and performance. These descriptors appear to fit the CND organization well.

Finally, technology refers to how the organization transforms inputs into outputs. The CND organization is characterized first as a *service* (i.e., not a product organization). CND does not produce products as manufacturing firms do. Rather it performs valuable services by defending the networks from hacker attacks. The current CND organization technology is characterized also as *standard, high-volume*. This reflects the high degree of standardization in terms of computers, procedures, organizations, training, personnel and other aspects of CND, along with the high volume of attacks experienced by the organization. The CND technology is characterized further as *semi-routine*, reflecting the analyzability of work and predictability of associated outcomes, and is characterized also as *semi-divisible*, which pertains to the decomposability of work tasks into discrete and independent components. CND technology is characterized further as *strong dominant*, which refers to the sophisticated, capital-intensive networks and systems used for CND.

Complex Environment: Professional Hacker Attack Scenarios

This scenario projects the grounded CND organization forward into a highly unstable and unpredictable environment where the organization has to counter professional hackers. As above, a detailed summary of OrgCon inputs and outputs is included in Appendix B.

With this Complex Environment scenario, all inputs to characterize the CND organization are the same as those above in the Simple Environment scenario except for those that refer specifically to the environment. As in a laboratory experiment, we hold constant the grounded CND organization, but vary systematically the nature of its environment. In other words, the same CND organization as described and analyzed above is assessed in a different environmental context.

The inputs *that differ* from above are the four for the environmental category. In the previous scenario: 1) simple environment, 2) with low level of uncertainty 3) and equivocality, 4) within a low hostility environment. In the current scenario: 1) complex environment, 2) with high levels of uncertainty 3) and equivocality, 4) within an extremely hostile environment.

RESULTS

In this section, we present and discuss results of the OrgCon analysis. We begin by summarizing results for the simple and complex environments modeled above, and then proceed to induce a set of organizational design requirements for CND in both environments. We conclude by mapping a preliminary transformation plan for the grounded CND organization to follow.

Table 3. OrgCon diagnosis of CND organization in simple environment

Diagnosis	Misfit	Recommendation
Perceived Misfits	Analyzer with innovation Strategy	Defender or Analyzer without innovation strategy
Configuration	Machine Bureaucracy configuration	Functional configuration
Formalization	High formalization	Medium formalization

Simple Environment

Based upon the model instantiated above, OrgCon draws upon its codified organizational design expertise to diagnose the misfits and recommend transformations to our grounded CND organization. The three such misfits and recommendations are summarized in Table 3.

First, OrgCon summarizes *perceived situation misfits*: aspects of the CND organization that do not appear to fit well with its environment. The analyzer with innovation strategy is questioned first as a possible misfit, because of the few different factors in the environment that affect the CND organization, the low equivocality of CND's environment, and the internal process climate. An analyzer without innovation or a defender strategy is suggested as an alternate approach.

Second, OrgCon recommends that the most likely structure to fit the situation best is a functional configuration. A functional organization reflects unit grouping by functional specialization (e.g., computer operations, network administration, user support). The proposed configuration is functional because the equivocality of CND's environment is not high, the environmental complexity is low, the environment is not highly uncertain, and the organization has an internal process climate. This configuration is feasible for a CND team since units based on functional specialization can counter hacker attacks (i.e. Block Hacker Team, Restore System Team, and Monitoring Team).

Third, OrgCon recommends that organizational formalization should be medium instead of high. It makes this recommendation, because there should be some formalization between the organizational units, but less formalization within the units due to the high professionalization. Medium size organizations and organizations with medium-routine technology should have medium formalization. Medium formalization is consistent with the leadership style when top management's preference for micro-involvement is medium also.

Based upon the diagnosis, we rerun the OrgCon CND Organization – Simple Environment model to reflect the three recommendations summarized in Table 3. This is essentially a test to see whether OrgCon's recommendations are stable; that is, whether OrgCon will diagnose additional misfits even after making its recommended changes. In this situation, the recommendations are stable indeed, and OrgCon diagnoses no additional organizational misfits. For the interested reader, precise variable manipulations are mentioned in Appendix C. Hence, after altering the OrgCon model to reflect its recommendations—and thus obviate its prior misfits—we establish a CND organization reflecting good fit with its simple environment, and the organizational leader or manager has an operationalized set of steps that can be taken to improve the CND organization.

Complex Environment

As for the simple environment, based upon the model instantiated above, OrgCon draws upon its codified organizational design expertise to diagnose the misfits and recommend transformations to our grounded CND organization. The seven such misfits and recommendations are summarized in Table 4.

First, recall from above that we hold constant everything except our four environmental settings. Hence, the same *perceived situation misfits* suggested above (i.e., the analyzer with innovation strategy) obtains in this complex environment also. As above, an analyzer without innovation or a defender strategy is suggested as an alternative solution.

Second, OrgCon recommends that the fittest organizational configuration for this scenario is a simple organization that has a flat hierarchy with a singular head for control and decision making. The primary reason for recommending a simple configuration is that the organization faces extreme environmental hostility, which requires rapid responses to unforeseen challenges. As in the simple environment above, the machine bureaucracy cannot react quickly when unexpected events occur, and is not recommended. Interestingly, *most CND organizations in DoD are Machine Bureaucracies*.

Third, OrgCon recommends also that employees should be loosely supervised with the allowance to deviate from standards; therefore, the organizational formalization should be low. Moreover, the organizational complexity should be low since it is recommended that the number of job titles should be reduced from very many to very few. OrgCon recommends that the managers should get involved more in the data collection

Table 4. OrgCon diagnosis of CND organization in complex environment

Diagnosis	Misfit	Recommendation
Perceived Misfits	Analyzer with innovation Strategy	Defender or Analyzer without innovation strategy
Configuration	Machine Bureaucracy configuration	Simple structure configuration
Formalization	High formalization	Low formalization
Complexity	Many job titles	Few job titles
Centralization	Medium centralization	High centralization
Technology	Routine, high-volume technology	Flexible, adaptable technology
Climate	Internal process climate	Rational goal or development climate

and interpretation; therefore, the centralization should become high. This appears to be in direct conflict with current practice in many DOD like and international organizations and offers further research opportunities in terms of current private and public practice.

Further, CND is in a highly equivocal environment here, and may not be able to react responsively to changes in the environment due to the routine, high-volume nature of its technology. This is a vulnerable situation. A highly equivocal environment requires rapid adjustment to unpredictable environmental shifts, and calls for more flexible and adaptable technology.

In addition, CND's internal process climate is questioned as a misfit, because it may cause problems in a high or moderately high equivocal environment. An internal process climate focuses more on the inside of the organization than on the outside. In an equivocal environment, which is likely to require change and adaptation, the internal process climate may not perceive the shifts or understand the need for change, and may not support adaptation to such needed change. An equivocal environment requires an external orientation, which is found in the rational goal and development climates.

Clearly, OrgCon diagnoses more misfits with the CND organization in the complex environment than in its simple counterpart, and produces correspondingly more recommendations for organizational transformation. As above, the diagnoses are stable, as no additional diagnoses result from rerunning OrgCon after making the recommended changes, and as above, the organizational leader or manager has an operationalized set of steps that can be taken to improve the CND organization.

Design Requirements

In this section, using the OrgCon recommendations from above for guidance, we induce a set of design requirements for a CND organization to

Figure 2. Distribution of incidents and responses (adapted from US-CERT, 2007)

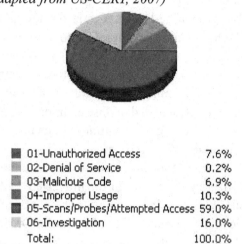

■ 01-Unauthorized Access	7.6%
▨ 02-Denial of Service	0.2%
▨ 03-Malicious Code	6.9%
■ 04-Improper Usage	10.3%
■ 05-Scans/Probes/Attempted Access	59.0%
░ 06-Investigation	16.0%
Total:	100.0%

perform effectively in both simple and complex environmental contexts. The rationale is that our grounded CND organization faces *both simple and complex* environments simultaneously; that is, much of its time and energy are devoted to routine work such as locking out amateur hackers, but considerable time and energy are devoted to thwarting professional attacks as well.

Indeed, we draw from the fourth quarter United States Computer Emergency Response Team (US-CERT *Quarterly Trend Analysis: Cyber Security Trends, Metrics, and Security Indicators,* 2007) data summarized in Figure 2 to estimate that only 16% of hacker/cracker attempts conform to attacks by amateur hackers; the remaining 84% require more extensive organizational responses. Thus, we need to specify requirements for a CND organization that can respond simultaneously to both simple and complex environments. We draw from Tables 3 and 4 above, and integrate the corresponding OrgCon diagnoses and recommendations, to induce such organization design requirements. Clearly, because CND organizations are conservative by default, the integrated organization will tend to reflect the complex-environment recommendations summarized in Table 4 for the most part, but the organization must be efficient as well, and be able to handle routine hacker attempts as such.

In particular, in a complex environment the flat hierarchy with a singular head for control and decision making is suggested, because the organization operates—most of the time—in an extremely hostile environment, one which requires consistently rapid responses to unforeseen challenges. Alternatively, in a simple environment a functional configuration is proposed, because the equivocality of CND's environment is not high—at many times—the environmental complexity is low, not highly uncertain, and the organization needs to operate efficiently in these simple hacking cases. Combining these two results, an integrated approach could include a functional configuration but with a singular head for control and decision making. Where threats are deemed low, the CND organization can rely upon its functional groups and procedures to address amateur attacks, but where threats are high, the leader can still seize control, and take quick actions. The remaining requirements stem directly from recommendations summarized for the complex environment in Table 4.

Preliminary Transformation Plan

Based upon the integrated recommendations above, our CND organization needs to address its strategy (i.e., analyzer with innovation), configuration (i.e., Machine Bureaucracy), formalization (i.e., high), technology (i.e., routine, high-volume), climate (i.e., internal process), complexity (i.e., many job titles) and centralization (i.e., medium). This represents organizational change of considerable scope, and it will be difficult to effect all aspects of such change either quickly or simultaneously. This is the case in particular for the conservative, highly proceduralized, DoD Machine Bureaucracy. Additionally, because all of the various organizational design elements need to fit together—at the same time—it is highly likely that some changing elements will have to *move*

out of fit as others wait for their times to change. This will leave the CND organization in multiple stages of misfit as the leaders and managers work to maneuver it into better overall fit through time. Therefore we are not describing an easy transformation by any means. Nonetheless, the alternative is to accept the status quo: considerable misfit and hence vulnerability. We outline the transformation plan in three, discrete steps.

Step 1: Management Changes. The easiest organizational design changes for management to effect pertain to management itself. Addressing the strategy is something that management can do directly, and adopting a Defender strategy would represent a natural progression for a conservative organization seeking to respond to an increasingly complex environment.

Additionally, management has considerable discretion to re-organize into a functional configuration, simply by revising the organization chart, and shifting people's roles, responsibilities and reporting relationships. Since our grounded CND organization has a relatively small number of people, this should not impact its operations or performance greatly. New, fewer job titles will be required—for jobs that reflect less formalization—and current jobs can be combined to effect this change. This can all take place via written documentation.

Further, along with such re-organization, management can impose stricter policy regarding centralization of information flows and decision making. This will enable the organization to address the complex environment depicted in part by the professional hacker attacks. Where the simple environment depicted in part by the amateur hacker attacks obtains, management can delegate the organizational response via SOPs. These changes will prepare the organization to pursue the next steps.

Step 2: Training and practice. Myriad organizational changes fail to meet objectives, because people are not given adequate training and practice to perform well in different organizational conditions. It is one thing to tell people that they will be organized differently, that they will have new and fewer, less-formalized job titles, and that they will need to adhere to stricter centralization requirements than before; it is another for the people in an organization to adjust to such changes. They need to be trained, and they need to practice. Clearly trial-and-error, on-the-job "training" will provide much of the training and practice necessary, but this approach is both time-consuming and error-prone. Management should seek out professional help with training and practice, and institute fallback procedures for responding to attacks that exceed the CND organization's capabilities while in transition.

Step 3: Climate. The third step involves the most difficult changes: moving to flexible and adaptable technology, and changing to a rational goal or developmental climate. Technological change can be expensive and time-consuming, and each new technology introduced into an organization tends to both disrupt its current operations and require modifications to jobs. Hence technological change will impart feedback on the steps above, and the organization will need to iterate repeatedly through these steps. Such repeated, impacted iteration is challenging.

Moreover, climate change involves culture: long and widely understood to be one of the most difficult aspects of an organization to alter. New managers and/or new employees may be required to accomplish this well, and any cultural change will need to be endorsed by the organizations

superior to our grounded CND unit, but training and practice can help here too. As above, management will need a fallback plan to address the likely cases of slow or stalled climate change, in addition to the repeated disruptions caused by new technology introductions.

In the end, management will have to assess whether the problems associated with its current CND organizational misfits outweigh the problems stemming from organizational change of the magnitude outlined in the three steps above. Perhaps a devastating, professional hacker attack will suffice to convince even the least change-oriented managers, but this would represent an expensive and hazardous way to learn. Counseling on how to convince reluctant managers is beyond the scope of this article, but outlining the three-step path to CND organizational transformation provides such managers with a plan to consider, and with a path to follow. This provides new knowledge to the CND organization manager, and can be used to generate new research questions for other CND researchers to investigate.

DISCUSSION & CONCLUSION

The US Government is moving apace to develop doctrines and capabilities that will allow the DoD to exploit Cyberspace for military advantage, and the role of CNO has taken on greater importance with the rise of network-centric warfare. Comprised primarily of defense, attack and exploitation, the technological capabilities are growing exponentially, as is the rate of data exchange. Unfortunately, many extant CNO organizations are slow to anticipate and react, and as such do not operate well within their highly dynamic environments, nor are they suited well to the missions and expectations placed upon them today.

A half century of Contingency Theory research provides considerable knowledge to guide designing organizational structures that fit well with various mission-environmental contexts, and as such it offers excellent potential to inform leaders and policy makers regarding how to bring their CNO organizations and approaches into better fit, and hence to improve performance. The key research question is, which organizational configurations provide the best CNO performance within the network-centric environment?

In this chapter, we review key background literature on CNO, and describe a current CNO organization. Focusing in particular on Computer Network Defense to ground our model in current practice, we discover how CND represents a very practical point to begin an investigation with the following premise: there is little opportunity for an organization with a specific network infrastructure to conduct computer attacks over time if its own defenses are weak.

We also describe the Organizational Consultant expert system that drives our analysis of such grounded CND organization, and note how this scholarship-based expert system's knowledge-base is supported by a huge formalization and integration of the Contingency Theory literature. Most such formalization is made in terms of research propositions, expressed via If-Then rules, which are easily intelligible to people as well as machines, and we learn how OrgCon diagnoses misfits between organizational structures and mission-environmental contexts.

Further, we use the OrgCon expert system environment to represent the structure and behavior of the grounded CND model from above, and depict such model in two, contrasting, network-centric environments:

1. A relatively simple environment — used to characterize one in which largely amateur hacker attacks target known network vulnerabilities, and which can be countered principally via the use of SOPs that exist within the organization
2. A relatively complex environment — used to characterize one in which largely professional hacker attacks target unknown network vulnerabilities, and which are much less likely to be countered effectively via solely SOPs as above.

Results follow to diagnose three misfits for the grounded CND organization in a simple environment: 1) the analyzer with innovation strategy, 2) the Machine Bureaucracy configuration, and 3) high formalization. OrgCon diagnoses these same three misfits in a complex environment, in addition to four additional ones: 4) routine, high-volume technology, 5) internal process climate, 6) many job titles, and 7) medium centralization. Such diagnoses enable us to induce a set of design requirements for a CND organization to perform effectively in both simple and complex environmental contexts, understanding that such organization must respond to both. Of course, the most costly in terms of time and energy are those devoted to thwarting professional attacks.

This supports our development of a three-step transformation plan: 1) management changes, 2) training and practice, and 3) climate. Such plan constitutes organizational change of considerable magnitude—and that presents substantial challenge—and time to effect well. In the end, management will have to assess whether the problems associated with its current CND organizational misfits outweigh the problems stemming from organizational change of the magnitude outlined via this three-step plan.

Because of our grounded CND model and broadly applicable OrgCon expert system, results also elucidate important insights into CNO organization and management more generally. For instance, most bureaucratically driven CNO organizations (e.g., those organized within the DoD) are likely to suffer from misfit conditions similar to those diagnosed above for our grounded CND organization, and hence to benefit from similar transformational steps as outlined in response.

Further, such results are suitable for immediate policy and operational implementation. For instance, DoD policy makers can and should call to assess all current CNO organizations for signs of misfits like those diagnosed through this study, and consider the relative advantages and disadvantages of undertaking change along the lines of our three-step plan versus leaving such organizations exposed to the risks inherent within misfit organizational structures.

Additionally, our results serve to expand the growing empirical basis of Contingency Theory, and appear to represent the first such results applicable specifically to DoD CNO. Such results can serve well to guide continued research along these lines. For instance, applying OrgCon to assess other, grounded, CND organizations would represent a logical next step, and assessing other aspects of CNO organizations (e.g., exploitation and attack) would follow logically as well. Indeed, this research highlights the promise inherent in the use of OrgCon to assess myriad DoD organizations—that is, well beyond the CNO domain—and calls for a wealth of applied research along these lines to begin. Hence the potential contribution of this research has both theoretical application and real-world implications, and should appeal therefore to both the academic and practitioner/ policy maker communities.

Further, fieldwork is required to validate the model specifications and behaviors described above, as well as to apply and evaluate the kinds of insights and recommendations generated through this research. Such fieldwork can drive additional theoretical insight through induction as well, which can drive in turn further model development, and the subsequent expansion of organizational forms, missions and environments that can be analyzed and emulated. Laboratory research is similar. Indeed, these multiple types of research—theoretical, developmental, computational, field and laboratory—complement one another richly. When integrated into a coherent research stream, they enable the kind of progressive and cumulative accretion of new knowledge that represents a hallmark of science. This represents a relatively novel approach to generating

new knowledge in the CND domain, particularly as it pertains to the hacker attack response team at the group level.

Indeed, the present study provides useful insights regarding organization configuration and the attributes of a CND organization, but as with all studies, it has limitations that should be taken into account. The Organization Consultant is a scholarship-based expert system, which draws from the contingency theory literature to diagnose organizational misfits and to recommend transformations. One important limitation to this approach is that an organization may have some unique attributes that are not reflected well in the OrgCon contingency theory knowledgebase. This does not appear to be the case in the present study, but such limitation is endemic to expert systems, and should be considered by future researchers addressing research questions along the lines of this investigation.

Additionally, the level of analysis in our study is the *group*. Hence, our results apply most directly to group-level CND, and call for caution when making any generalizations the organizational or the inter-organizational levels of analysis. This calls for future research to address different levels of analysis explicitly. Also, the CND organization examined in our research reflects a medium-size organization operating within a DoD environment, and hence our results may not generalize well to either very large or very small organizations outside such environment. Additional research along the lines of this investigation are called for in this regard as well. Moreover, there is clearly substantial room for interpretation of OrgCon results, particularly where composing a set of organizational design requirements and outlining a transformation plan are concerned. The requirements and plan described in this chapter represent one of many approaches and paths that leaders, managers and policy makers can take. Nonetheless, they call for action, and serve to fill a current void in terms of guidance based upon grounded and systematic research.

REFERENCES

Baddelay, A. (2008, April). Systems for Cyber Control. *Military Information Technology, 12*(3). Retrieved May 15,2008 from http://www.military-information-technology.com/article.cfm?DocID=2398

Baligh, H., Burton, R. M., & Obel, B. (1993). *Creating the Theory for a Usable Organization Designing Expert System.* Working Paper, Fuqua School of Business, Duke University, Durham, NC.

Burns, T., & Stalker, G. M. (1961). *The Management of Innovation.* London: Havistock.

Burton, R. M., & Obel, B. (2004). *Strategic Organizational Diagnosis and Design: Developing Theory for Application.* Third Edition, Boston, MA: Kluwer.

Carley, K. M., & Prietula, M. J. (1994). *Computational Organization Theory.* Hillsdale, NJ: Lawrence Erlbaum Associates, Inc.

Chaiman of the Joint Chiefs of Staff Instruction (CJCSI) (2007, Aug 14). *Information Assurance (IA) and Computer Network Defense (CND).* Retrieved May 14, 2008 from http://www.dtic.mil/cjcs_directives/cdata/unlimit/6510_01.pdf

Computer Security Enhancement Act of 2001. (2001, Nov 28). Retrieved May 14, 2008 from http://thomas.loc.gov/cgi-bin/query/D?c107:1:./temp/~c107VdS4Gr::

Department of Defense, (2003). *Information Operations Roadmap (classified).* National Security Archive Electronic Briefing Book No. 177. Unclassified summary retrieved May 14, 2008 from http://www.gwu.edu/~nsarchiv/NSAEBB/NSAEBB177/

DoD Directive 3020.26 (2007, Jan 1). *Defense Continuity Program (DCP).* Retrieved May 14, 2008 from http://www.dtic.mil/whs/directives/corres/html/302026.htm

DoD Directive 5200.1-R. (Jan 17 1997). *Information Security Program.* . Retrieved May 14, 2008 from http://www.dtic.mil/whs/directives/corres/pdf/520001r.pdf

DoD. (2004, Jan). *IA Strategic Plan Version 1.1.* Retrieved May 14, 2008 from http://www.defenselink.mil/cio-nii/docs/DoD_IA_Strategic_Plan.pdf

DoD Chief Information Officer (CIO) (2003, May 9). *DoD Net-Centric Data Strategy.* Retrieved May 14, 2008 from http://www.defenselink.mil/cio-nii/docs/Net-Centric-Data-Strategy-2003-05-092.pdf

Duncan, R.B. (1979). What is the Right Organization Structure?. *Organizational Dynamics, 7*(3), 59-79.

Galbraith, J. R. (1973). *Designing Complex Organizations.* Boston, MA: Addison-Wesley Longman Publishing Co., Inc.

Harvey, E. (1968, April). Technology and the Structure of Organizations. *American Sociology Review, 33*, 247- 259.

Internet Usage Statistics: The Internet Big Picture. (2008, March). Last Retrieved 5/19/2008 from http://www.internetworldstats.com/stats.htm

Miles, R. E., & Snow, C. C. (1978). *Organizational Strategy, Structure, and Process.* New York, NY: McGraw-Hill.

Mintzberg, H. (1979). *The Structuring of Organizations.* Englewood Cliffs, NJ: Prentice-Hall.

Mintzberg, H. (1980). Structure in 5's. A Synthesis of the Research on Organization Design. *Management Science, 26*(3), 322-341.

North American Computational Social and Organization Sciences (NAACSOS). (2007). Retrieved March 13, 2008 from http://www.casos.cs.cmu.edu/naacsos/

Nissen, M. E. (2005, June). A Computational Approach to Diagnosing Misfits, Inducing Requirements, and Delineating Transformations for Edge Organizations. *Proceedings International Command and Control Research and Technology Symposium*, McLean, VA.

Perrow, C. (1967). A Framework for Comparative Analysis of Organizations. *American Sociological Review, 32*, 194-208.

SANS Institute - about SANS. (2008). Retrieved May 14, 2008 from http://www.sans.org/about/sans.php

The National Strategy to Secure Cyberspace Strategy to secure Cyberspace (2003, February). Retrieved May 14, 2008 from http://www.whitehouse.gov/pcipb/

Thompson, J. D. (1967). *Organizations in Action.* New York, McGraw-Hill.

UCSF IT Network Architecture & Security: About us.(2008). Retrieved May 14, 2008 from http://it-nas.ucsfmedicalcenter.org/about_us/

University of Minnesota Office of Information Technology Home Page. (2008). Retrieved May 14, 2008 from http://www1.umn.edu/oit/security/incident/OIT__12654_REGION1.html

US-CERT: United States Computer Emergency Readiness Team. (2008). Retrieved May 14, 2008 from http://www.us-cert.gov/

US-CERT Quarterly Trend Analysis: Cyber Security Trends, Metrics, and Security Indicators. (2007, December). Retrieved May 14, 2008 from http://www.us-cert.gov/press_room/trendsanalysisQ407.pdf

APPENDIX A: ORGCON ANALYSIS AND RECOMMENDATIONS FOR SIMPLE ENVIRONMENTS

Report summary — CND

Input Data Summary

The description below summarizes and interprets your answers to the questions about your organization and its situation. It states your answers concerning the organization's current configuration, complexity, formalization, and centralization. Your responses to the various questions on the contingencies of age, size, technology, environment, management style, cultural climate and strategy factors are also given. The writeup below summarizes the input data for the analysis.

- CND has a machine bureaucracy configuration (cf 100).
- CND has a large number of different jobs (cf 100).
- Of the employees at CND 76 to 100 % have an advanced degree or many years of special training (cf 100).
- CND has 3 to 5 vertical levels separating top management from the bottom level of the organization (cf 100).
- The mean number of vertical levels is 3 to 5 (cf 100).
- CND has 1 or 2 separate geographic locations (cf 100).
- CND's average distance of these separate units from the organization's headquarters is less than 10 miles (cf 100).
- 61 to 90 % of CND's total workforce is located at these separate units (cf 100).
- Job descriptions are available for all employees, including senior management (cf 100).
- Where written job descriptions exist, the employees are supervised closely to ensure compliance with standards set in the job description (cf 100).
- The employees are allowed to deviate very little from the standards (cf 100).
- 81 to 100 % non-managerial employees are given written operating instructions or procedures for their job (cf 100).
- The written instructions or procedures given are followed to a very great extent (cf 100).
- Supervisors and middle managers are to a little extent free from rules, procedures, and policies when they make decisions (cf 100).
- More than 80 % of all the rules and procedures that exist within the organization are in writing (cf 100).
- Top Management is not involved in gathering the information they will use in making decisions (cf 100).
- Top management participates in the interpretation of more than 80 % of the information input (cf 100).
- Top management directly controls 0 to 20 % of the decisions executed (cf 100).
- The typical middle manager has no discretion over establishing his or her budget (cf 100).
- The typical middle manager has some discretion over how his/her unit will be evaluated (cf 100).

- The typical middle manager has great discretion over the hiring and firing of personnel (cf 100).
- The typical middle manager has no discretion over personnel rewards - (ie, salary increases and promotions) (cf 100).
- The typical middle manager has little discretion over purchasing equipment and supplies (cf 100).
- The typical middle manager has some discretion over establishing a new project or program (cf 100).
- The typical middle manager has little discretion over how work exceptions are to be handled (cf 100).
- CND has 25 employees (cf 100).
- CND's age is mature (cf 100).
- CND's ownership status is public (cf 100).
- CND has an undetermined number of different products (cf 100).
- CND has an undetermined number of different markets (cf 100).
- CND only operates in one country (cf 100).
- CND has an undetermined number of different products in the foreign markets (cf 100).
- CND's major activity is categorized as service (cf 100).
- CND has a standard high-volume service technology (cf 100).
- CND has a medium routine technology (cf 100).
- CND's technology is somewhat divisible (cf 100).
- CND's technology dominance is strong (cf 100).
- CND has either planned or already has an advanced information system (cf 100).
- CND's environment is simple (cf 100).
- The uncertainty of CND's environment is low (cf 100).
- The equivocality of the organization's environment is low (cf 100).
- CND's environment has a low hostility (cf 100).
- Top management prefers to make policy and general resource allocation decisions (cf 100).
- Top management primarily prefers to make both long-term and short-time decisions (cf 100).
- Top management has a preference for medium detailed information when making decisions (cf 100).
- Top management has a preference for some proactive actions and some reactive actions (cf 100).
- Top management is risk averse (cf 100).
- Top management has a preference for high control (cf 100).
- CND operates in an industry with an undetermined level of capital requirement (cf 100).
- CND has an undetermined level of product innovation (cf 100).
- CND has a high process innovation (cf 100).
- CND has a high concern for quality (cf 100).
- CND's price level is undetermined relative to its competitors (cf 100).
- The level of trust is medium (cf 100).
- The level of conflict is medium (cf 100).
- The employee morale is medium (cf 100).
- Rewards are given in a inequitably fashion (cf 100).
- The resistance to change is high (cf 100).
- The leader credibility is high (cf 100).
- The level of scapegoating is medium (cf 100).

The Size

The size of the organization - large, medium, or small - is based upon the number of employees, adjusted for their level of education or technical skills.

Based on the answers you provided, it is most likely that your organization's size is medium (cf 50).

More than 75 % of the people employed by CND have a high level of education. Adjustments are made to this effect. The adjusted number of employees is lower than 500 but greater than 100 and CND is categorized as medium. However, for this adjusted number this size does not have a major effect on the organizational structure.

The Climate

The organizational climate effect is the summary measure of people and behavior.

Based on the answers you provided, it is most likely that the organizational climate is a internal process climate (cf 79).

It could also be the that climate is a group (cf 69).

The internal process climate is a formalized and structured place to work. Procedures govern what people do. The leaders pride themselves on being good coordinators and organizers. Maintaining a smooth running organization is important. The long-term concerns are stability, predictability, and efficiency. Formal rules and policies hold the organization together.

Employees with a medium to low morale is frequently one element of an internal process climate. Inequitable rewards in the organization drives the climate towards an internal process climate. High resistance to change is normally present in a internal process climate.

The group climate is characterized as a friendly place to work where people share a lot of themselves. It is like an extended family. The leaders, or head of the organization, are considered to be mentors and, perhaps even parent figures. The organization is held together by loyalty or tradition. Commitment is high. The organization emphasizes the long-term benefit of human resource development with high cohesion and morale being important. Success is defined in terms of sensitivity to customers and concern for people. The organization places a premium on teamwork, participation, and consensus.

Employees with a medium morale can be one element of group climate. High leader credibility characterizes an organization with a group climate.

The Management Style

The level of management's microinvolvement in decision making is the summary measure of management style. Leaders have a low preference for microinvolvement; managers have a high preference for microinvolvement.

Based on the answers you provided, it is most likely that your management profile has a medium preference for microinvolvement (cf 78).

It could also be that your management profile has a high preference (cf 69).

Management has both a short-time and long-term horizon when making decisions, which characterizes a preference for a medium microinvolvement. Since the management has a preference for medium detailed information when making decisions a medium preference for microinvolvement characterization is appropriate. The management of CND has a preference for taking actions on some decisions and being reactive toward others. This will lead toward a medium preference for microinvolvement.

Management is risk averse. This is one of the characteristics of a manager with a high preference for microinvolvement. Management has a preference for using control to coordinate activities, which leads toward a high preference for microinvolvement.

The Strategy

The organization's strategy is categorized as one of either prospector, analyzer with innovation, analyzer without innovation, defender, or reactor. These categories follow Miles and Snow's typology. Based on your answers, the organization has been assigned to a strategy category. This is a statement of the current strategy; it is not an analysis of what is the best or preferred strategy for the organization.

Based on the answers you provided, it is most likely that your organization's strategy is an analyzer with innovation strategy (cf 68).

An organization with an analyzer with innovation strategy is an organization that combines the strategy of the defender and the prospector. It moves into the production of a new product or enters a new market after viability has been shown. But in contrast to an analyzer without innovation, it has innovations that run concurrently with the regular production. It has a dual technology core.

For a medium routine technology, CND has some flexibility. It is consistent with an analyzer with innovation strategy. With a concern for high quality an analyzer with innovation strategy is a likely strategy for CND. With top management preferring a medium level of microinvolvement top management wants some influence. This can be obtained via control over current operations. Product innovation should be less controlled. The strategy is therefore likely to be analyzer with innovation.

The Current Organizational Characteristics

Based on your answers, the organization's complexity, formalization, and centralization have been calculated. This is the current organization. Later in this report, there will be recommendations for the organization.

The current organizational complexity is medium (cf 100).
The current horizontal differentiation is high (cf 100).
The current vertical differentiation is low (cf 100).
The current spatial differentiation is medium (cf 100).
The current centralization is medium (cf 100).
The current formalization is high (cf 100).

The current organization has been categorized with respect to formalization, centralization, and complexity. The categorization is based on the input you gave and does not take missing information into account.

Situation Misfits

A situation misfit is an unbalanced situation among the contingency factors of management style, size, environment, technology, climate, and strategy.

The following misfits are present: (cf 100).

When only few factors in the environment affect CND, the analyzer with innovation strategy may not be a suitable one! With only a few environmental factors, there may be limited need for innovation and adaptation. There are probably limited opportunities to which to adapt. An analyzer without innovation, or a defender strategy that focuses directly on the few environmental factors and meets market needs efficiently will usually yield better results.

When the equivocality of CND's environment is low, the analyzer with innovation strategy may not be a suitable one! With low equivocality, the environment is well known and understood. An innovative strategy works best when the environment offers new opportunities for products and services. Here such opportunities are limited. However, process innovation, which reduces costs, is appropriate.

CND has an internal process climate. This is a mismatch with analyzer with innovation strategy! An internal process climate is internally oriented with a focus on control. Innovation is difficult to achieve with this orientation. More flexibility and a more external orientation are desirable for innovation. An internal process climate supports better an analyzer without innovation and defender strategy.

Orgcon Recommendations

Based on your answers about the organization, its situation, and the conclusions with the greatest certainty factor from the analyses above OrgCon has derived recommendations for the organization's configuration, complexity, formalization, and centralization. There are also recommendations for coordination and control, the appropriate media richness for communications, and incentives. More detailed recommendations for possible changes in the current organization are also provided.

Organizational Configurations

The most likely configuration that best fits the situation has been estimated to be a functional configuration (cf 44).

A functional organization is an organization with unit grouping by functional specialization (production, marketing, etc.).

When the equivocality of CND's environment is not high, the environmental complexity is low, and the environment is not highly uncertain, the configuration should be functional. An organization with an internal process climate could have a functional configuration.

Organizational Characteristics

The recommended degree of organizational complexity is medium (cf 63).

Medium size organizations should have medium organizational complexity. CND has a technology that is somewhat routine, which implies that the organizational complexity should be medium. When the uncertainty of CND's environment is low, the organizational complexity should neither be very low nor very high so that CND will be able to react quickly when the environment changes. Top management of CND has a preference for a medium level of microinvolvement, which drives the organizational complexity towards medium. Because CND has an advanced information system, organizational complexity can be greater than it could otherwise.

The recommended degree of horizontal differentiation is medium (cf 28).

The recommended degree of vertical differentiation is medium (cf 64).

The recommended degree of formalization is medium (cf 55).

There should be some formalization between the organizational units but less formalization within the units due to the high professionalization. Medium size organizations should have medium formalization. Organizations with medium-routine technology should have a medium formalization. Medium formalization is consistent with the leadership style when top management's preference for microinvolvement is neither very great nor very low.

The recommended degree of centralization is medium (cf 55).

CND has an analyzer with innovation strategy. Centralization should be medium. There should be tight control over current activities and looser control over new ventures. CND is of medium size. Such organizations should have medium to high centralization. Medium centralization is recommended when top management has neither a great desire nor very little desire for microinvolvement. Because CND has an advanced information system, centralization can be greater than it could otherwise. An internal process climate in the organization requires a medium to high level of centralization.

CND's span of control should be moderate (cf 62).

Since CND has some technology routineness, it should have a moderate span of control.

CND should use media with medium media richness (cf 70).

The information media that CND uses should provide a small amount of information (cf 70).

Incentives should be based on procedures (cf 85).

CND should use planning as means for coordination and control (cf 87).

When the environment of CND has low equivocality, low uncertainty, and low complexity, the information media need not be rich nor provide a large amount of information. Direct supervision with some planning will be appropriate. Incentives can be procedure based and based on implementation of the rules of formalization. It is appropriate to see that the rules are followed and implemented.

Organizational Misfits

Organizational misfits compares the recommended organization with the current organization.

The following organizational misfits are present: (cf 100).

Current and prescribed configuration do not match.

Current and prescribed formalization do not match.

More Detailed Recommendations

There are a number of more detailed recommendations (cf 100).

You may consider decreasing the number of positions for which job descriptions are available.

You may consider supervising the employees less closely.

You may consider allowing employees more latitude from standards.

You may consider fewer written job descriptions.

Managerial employees may be asked to pay less attention to written instructions and procedures.

You may give supervisors and middle managers fewer rules and procedures.

You may consider having fewer rules and procedures put in writing.

APPENDIX B: ORGCON ANALYSIS AND RECOMMENDATIONS FOR COMPLEX ENVIRONMENTS

Report Summary — CND

Input Data Summary

The description below summarizes and interprets your answers to the questions about your organization and its situation. It states your answers concerning the organization's current configuration, complexity, formalization, and centralization. Your responses to the various questions on the contingencies of age, size, technology, environment, management style, cultural climate and strategy factors are also given. The writeup below summarizes the input data for the analysis.

- CND has a machine bureaucracy configuration (cf 100).
- CND has a large number of different jobs (cf 100).
- Of the employees at CND 76 to 100 % have an advanced degree or many years of special training (cf 100).
- CND has 3 to 5 vertical levels separating top management from the bottom level of the organization (cf 100).
- The mean number of vertical levels is 3 to 5 (cf 100).
- CND has 1 or 2 separate geographic locations (cf 100).
- CND's average distance of these separate units from the organization's headquarters is less than 10 miles (cf 100).
- 61 to 90 % of CND's total workforce is located at these separate units (cf 100).
- Job descriptions are available for all employees, including senior management (cf 100).
- Where written job descriptions exist, the employees are supervised closely to ensure compliance with standards set in the job description (cf 100).
- The employees are allowed to deviate very little from the standards (cf 100).
- 81 to 100 % non-managerial employees are given written operating instructions or procedures for their job (cf 100).
- The written instructions or procedures given are followed to a very great extent (cf 100).
- Supervisors and middle managers are to a little extent free from rules, procedures, and policies when they make decisions (cf 100).
- More than 80 % of all the rules and procedures that exist within the organization are in writing (cf 100).
- Top Management is not involved in gathering the information they will use in making decisions (cf 100).
- Top management participates in the interpretation of less than 20 % of the information input (cf 100).
- Top management directly controls 0 to 20 % of the decisions executed (cf 100).
- The typical middle manager has no discretion over establishing his or her budget (cf 100).
- The typical middle manager has great discretion over how his/her unit will be evaluated (cf 100).

- The typical middle manager has great discretion over the hiring and firing of personnel (cf 100).
- The typical middle manager has no discretion over personnel rewards - (ie, salary increases and promotions) (cf 100).
- The typical middle manager has little discretion over purchasing equipment and supplies (cf 100).
- The typical middle manager has some discretion over establishing a new project or program (cf 100).
- The typical middle manager has little discretion over how work exceptions are to be handled (cf 100).
- CND has 25 employees (cf 100).
- CND's age is mature (cf 100).
- CND's ownership status is public (cf 100).
- CND has an undetermined number of different products (cf 100).
- CND has an undetermined number of different markets (cf 100).
- CND only operates in one country (cf 100).
- CND has an undetermined number of different products in the foreign markets (cf 100).
- CND's major activity is categorized as service (cf 100).
- CND has a standard high-volume service technology (cf 100).
- CND has a medium routine technology (cf 100).
- CND's technology is somewhat divisible (cf 100).
- CND's technology dominance is strong (cf 100).
- CND has either planned or already has an advanced information system (cf 100).
- CND's environment is complex (cf 100).
- The uncertainty of CND's environment is high (cf 100).
- The equivocality of the organization's environment is high (cf 100).
- CND's environment is extremely hostile (cf 100).
- Top management prefers to make policy and general resource allocation decisions (cf 100).
- Top management primarily prefers to make both long-term and short-time decisions (cf 100).
- Top management has a preference for medium detailed information when making decisions (cf 100).
- Top management has a preference for some proactive actions and some reactive actions (cf 100).
- Top management is risk averse (cf 100).
- Top management has a preference for high control (cf 100).
- CND operates in an industry with an undetermined level of capital requirement (cf 100).
- CND has an undetermined level of product innovation (cf 100).
- CND has a high process innovation (cf 100).
- CND has a high concern for quality (cf 100).
- CND's price level is undetermined relative to its competitors (cf 100).
- The level of trust is medium (cf 100).
- The level of conflict is medium (cf 100).
- The employee morale is medium (cf 100).
- Rewards are given in a inequitably fashion (cf 100).
- The resistance to change is high (cf 100).
- The leader credibility is high (cf 100).
- The level of scapegoating is medium (cf 100).

The Size

The size of the organization - large, medium, or small - is based upon the number of employees, adjusted for their level of education or technical skills.

Based on the answers you provided, it is most likely that your organization's size is medium (cf 50).

More than 75 % of the people employed by CND have a high level of education. Adjustments are made to this effect. The adjusted number of employees is lower than 500 but greater than 100 and CND is categorized as medium. However, for this adjusted number this size does not have a major effect on the organizational structure.

The Climate

The organizational climate effect is the summary measure of people and behavior.

Based on the answers you provided, it is most likely that the organizational climate is a internal process climate (cf 79).

It could also be the that climate is a group (cf 69).

The internal process climate is a formalized and structured place to work. Procedures govern what people do. The leaders pride themselves on being good coordinators and organizers. Maintaining a smooth running organization is important. The long-term concerns are stability, predictability, and efficiency. Formal rules and policies hold the organization together.

Employees with a medium to low morale is frequently one element of an internal process climate. Inequitable rewards in the organization drives the climate towards an internal process climate. High resistance to change is normally present in a internal process climate.

The group climate is characterized as a friendly place to work where people share a lot of themselves. It is like an extended family. The leaders, or head of the organization, are considered to be mentors and, perhaps even parent figures. The organization is held together by loyalty or tradition. Commitment is high. The organization emphasizes the long-term benefit of human resource development with high co-hesion and morale being important. Success is defined in terms of sensitivity to customers and concern for people. The organization places a premium on teamwork, participation, and consensus.

Employees with a medium morale can be one element of group climate. High leader credibility characterizes an organization with a group climate.

The Management Style

The level of management's microinvolvement in decision making is the summary measure of management style. Leaders have a low preference for microinvolvement; managers have a high preference for microinvolvement.

Based on the answers you provided, it is most likely that your management profile has a medium preference for microinvolvement (cf 78).

It could also be that your management profile has a high preference (cf 69).

Management has both a short-time and long-term horizon when making decisions, which character-izes a preference for a medium microinvolvement. Since the management has a preference for medium detailed information when making decisions a medium preference for microinvolvement characterization is appropriate. The management of CND has a preference for taking actions on some decisions and being reactive toward others. This will lead toward a medium preference for microinvolvement.

Management is risk averse. This is one of the characteristics of a manager with a high preference for microinvolvement. Management has a preference for using control to coordinate activities, which leads toward a high preference for microinvolvement.

The Strategy

The organization's strategy is categorized as one of either prospector, analyzer with innovation, analyzer without innovation, defender, or reactor. These categories follow Miles and Snow's typology. Based on your answers, the organization has been assigned to a strategy category. This is a statement of the current strategy; it is not an analysis of what is the best or preferred strategy for the organization.

Based on the answers you provided, it is most likely that your organization's strategy is an analyzer with innovation strategy (cf 68).

An organization with an analyzer with innovation strategy is an organization that combines the strategy of the defender and the prospector. It moves into the production of a new product or enters a new market after viability has been shown. But in contrast to an analyzer without innovation, it has innovations that run concurrently with the regular production. It has a dual technology core.

For a medium routine technology, CND has some flexibility. It is consistent with an analyzer with innovation strategy. With a concern for high quality an analyzer with innovation strategy is a likely strategy for CND. With top management preferring a medium level of microinvolvement top management wants some influence. This can be obtained via control over current operations. Product innovation should be less controlled. The strategy is therefore likely to be analyzer with innovation.

The Current Organizational Characteristics

Based on your answers, the organization's complexity, formalization, and centralization have been calculated. This is the current organization. Later in this report, there will be recommendations for the organization.

The current organizational complexity is medium (cf 100).

The current horizontal differentiation is high (cf 100).

The current vertical differentiation is low (cf 100).

The current spatial differentiation is medium (cf 100).

The current centralization is medium (cf 100).

The current formalization is high (cf 100).

The current organization has been categorized with respect to formalization, centralization, and complexity. The categorization is based on the input you gave and does not take missing information into account.

Situation Misfits

A situation misfit is an unbalanced situation among the contingency factors of management style, size, environment, technology, climate, and strategy.

The following misfits are present: (cf 100).

ND is in a highly equivocal environment, but has a mass production technology. CND may not be able to react to changes in the environment. This is a vulnerable situation. Most mass production operations are very limited in capacity to adapt and make different products. Mass production optimizes on the economies of specialization and standardization. A highly equivocal environment requires adjustment to the unknown as that environment becomes clearer. The possibility for mismatch of what the existing mass production can do and what will be required in the new environment is very high and further the economic consequences are likely to be great with low return. A highly equivocal environment calls for a more non routine production capability than most mass production operations have.

CND has an internal process climate. This may cause problems in a high or moderately high equivocal environment! An internal process climate focuses more on the inside of the organization than on the outside. In an equivocal environment which is likely to require change and adaptation, the internal process climate may not either see the shift, understand the need for change and does not have an organization which supports adaptation to such needed change. There is high resistance to change. An equivocal environment requires an external orientation which is found in the rational goal and development climates.

CND has an internal process climate. This is a mismatch with analyzer with innovation strategy! An internal process climate is internally oriented with a focus on control. Innovation is difficult to achieve with this orientation. More flexibility and a more external orientation are desirable for innovation. An internal process climate supports better an analyzer without innovation and defender strategy.

OrgCon Recommendations

Based on your answers about the organization, its situation, and the conclusions with the greatest certainty factor from the analyses above OrgCon has derived recommendations for the organization's configuration, complexity, formalization, and centralization. There are also recommendations for coordination and control, the appropriate media richness for communications, and incentives. More detailed recommendations for possible changes in the current organization are also provided.

Organizational Configurations

The most likely configuration that best fits the situation has been estimated to be a simple configuration (cf 70).

It is certainly not: a machine bureaucracy (cf -100).

A simple organization has a flat hierarchy and a singular head for control and decision making.

The primary reason for recommending a simple configuration is that the organization has extreme environmental hostility. Extreme environmental hostility requires that the organization can respond consistently and rapid to unforeseen challenges. Therefore, it must have a simple configuration.

When the organization is confronted with hostility, it cannot be a machine bureaucracy. A machine bureaucracy cannot act appropriately when unexpected events occur.

Organizational Characteristics

The recommended degree of organizational complexity is low (cf 68).

Not much is known about the environment since both the environmental uncertainty and the environmental equivocality of CND are high. In this situation, the organizational complexity should be low. This allows the organization to adapt quickly. When the environmental hostility of CND is high, organizational complexity should be low.

The recommended degree of horizontal differentiation is low (cf 68).

The recommended degree of vertical differentiation is low (cf 84).

The recommended degree of formalization is low (cf 68).

Since the set of variables in the environment that will be important is not known and since it is not possible to predict what will happen, no efficient rules and procedures can be developed, which implies that CND's formalization should be low. When environmental hostility is high formalization should be low.

The recommended degree of centralization is high (cf 77).

There is evidence against it should be: low (cf -17).

CND is of medium size. Such organizations should have medium to high centralization. When the environment is extremely hostile, top management must take prompt action and centralization must be high. Because CND has an advanced information system, centralization can be greater than it could otherwise. An internal process climate in the organization requires a medium to high level of centralization.

CND's span of control should be moderate (cf 62).

Since CND has some technology routineness, it should have a moderate span of control.

CND should use media with high media richness (cf 70).

The information media that CND uses should provide a large amount of information (cf 70).

Incentives should be based on results (cf 70).

CND should use meetings as means for coordination and control (cf 85).

It should also use planning (cf 75).

It should also use rules (cf 75).

When the environment of CND has high equivocality, high uncertainty, and high complexity, coordination and control should be obtained through integrators and group meetings. The richness of the media should be high with a large amount of information. Incentives must be results based. Top management should play the central role in coordinating and controlling the activities of the organization as well as making strategic and operating decisions.

Top management should make many decisions. However, many individuals should be involved in gathering information and implementing those decisions.

Organizational Misfits

Organizational misfits compares the recommended organization with the current organization.

The following organizational misfits are present: (cf 100).

Current and prescribed configuration do not match.

Current and prescribed complexity do not match.

Current and prescribed centralization do not match.

Current and prescribed formalization do not match.

More Detailed Recommendations

There are a number of more detailed recommendations (cf 100).

You may consider decreasing the number of positions for which job descriptions are available.

You may consider supervising the employees less closely.

You may consider allowing employees more latitude from standards.

You may consider fewer written job descriptions.

Managerial employees may be asked to pay less attention to written instructions and procedures.

You may give supervisors and middle managers fewer rules and procedures.

You may consider having fewer rules and procedures put in writing.

Top management may consider gathering the information needed for decision making themselves.

Top management may interpret and analyze more information itself.

Top management may control the execution of decisions more actively.

The middle managers may be given less discretion over evaluations.

You may give middle managers less discretion on hiring and firing personnel.

APPENDIX C

Complex and Simple Case Detailed Variables

Table 1C.

Categories	Variables	Current Case	Proposed case- Complex Environment	Proposed case- Simple environment
Organizational Configurations		Machine bureaucracy	Simple configuration	Functional Form
Organizational Complexity	Job Titles	Large Number	Very Few	Large Number
	Vertical Levels	3-5	1-2	1-2
Organizational Formalization	Job descriptions	Opera.employees incl. senior managers	Opera. employees and first line supervisors	Opera. employees excl senior managers
	Employee supervision	Close	Loose	Moderately close
	Latitude from standards	Very Little	Large Amount	A Moderate Amount
	Written instructions	81%-100%	41%-60%	61%-80%
	Written procedures followed	A very great deal	Some	Some
	Free from rules to make a decision	Little	A great deal	A great deal
	Procedures in writing	More than 80%	41%-60%	41%-60%
Current Centralization	Managerial data collection	None	A great deal	None
	Managerial data input interpretation	Less than 20%	More than 80%	Less than 20%
	Control of decision execution	0% to 20%	More than 80%	0% to 20%

continued on following page

Table 1C. continued

	Middle manager budget establishment	None	Little	None
	Discretion in hiring and firing personnel	Great	Some	Great
	Middle Manager exception handling	Great	Some	Great
	New project establishment by Middle Managers	Some	Little	Some
Environment	Environmental Complexity	Complex	Complex	Simple
	Level of Uncertainty	High	High	Low
	Environmental Equivocality	High	High	Low
	Competition	Extreme	Extreme	Low

Chapter XI
An Approach to Managing Identity Fraud

Rodger Jamieson
The University of New South Wales, Australia

Stephen Smith
The University of New South Wales, Australia

Greg Stephens
The University of New South Wales, Australia

Donald Winchester
The University of New South Wales, Australia

ABSTRACT

This chapter outlines components of a strategy for government and a conceptual identity fraud enterprise management framework for organizations to manage identity crime occurring via cyberspace. Identity crime, related cybercrimes and information systems security breaches are insidious motivators for governments and organizations to protect and secure their systems, databases and other assets against intrusion and loss. Managing identity crime is a critical step in cyber security and global information assurance. Strategy components and conceptual model elements are constructed through analysis and synthesis of models from academic literature, and reports by industry and government professionals. A comprehensive government strategy with a legislative component reinforces organizational policies to combat identity crimes. Model components used to develop our identity fraud organizational framework were selected from cost of identity fraud, identity risk management, identity fraud profiling, and fraud risk management literature. Our framework is organized into anticipatory, reactionary and remediation phases.

INTRODUCTION

Identity crime and related crimes, cybercrime and information systems security breaches are insidious motivators for governments and organizations to protect and secure their systems, databases and other assets against intrusion and loss. The economic cost to society and more directly to enterprises provides significant impetus for a comprehensive framework for organizations to prevent and combat the growth of identity and related crimes. Table 1 shows the estimated economic impact of identity crime and related crime costs. For example, the accumulated losses caused by identity crime and related crimes, such as money laundering, terrorism, trafficking – drugs, people, weapons, illicit material, etc., globally were estimated at US$221 billion by the end of 2003 and up to US$2 trillion by the end of 2005 (Hurley & Veytsel, 2003). Approximately half of

the estimated global cost could be attributed to money laundering alone (see KPMG, 2007).

These economic costs are so large and pervasive they now reach across whole communities affecting individuals, private organizations, and governments' ability to function smoothly. Cuganesan and Lacey (2003) observe that limited resources for law enforcement to investigate identity crimes, along with the high-level of thresholds for investigation, often results in organizations either writing-off fraud amounts or using alternative methods of third party recovery via mercantile agents. A more appropriate method for enterprises than to 'write-off frauds' or 'outsource the remediation' potentially making the victim pay rather than the perpetrator, would be to combat identity fraud proactively by the implementation of a comprehensive integrated identity fraud enterprise management framework.

Table 1. Summary of identity crime costs (figures are in billions in stated currency)

Country (or Region)	Year	Economic Impact of Identity Crime (billions)	Source
Global	2005	US$2,000.0	*Hurley & Veytsel, 2003, p.1*
	2003	US$221.0	*Hurley & Veytsel, 2003, p.1*
United States	2008	US$45.3	*Kim 2008, p.21**
	2007	US$51.0	*Kim 2008, p.21**
	2006	US$57.7	*Kim 2008, p.21**
	2005	US$57.4	*Kim 2008, p.21*
	2003	US$56.0	*Kim 2008, p.21*
	2002	US$48.0	*Foley & Foley 2003, p.27*
United Kingdom	2006	£1.7	*UK Home Office 2006, p.4*
	2002	£1.3	*The Fraud Advisory Panel, 2003, p.1*
Canada	2002	C$5.0	*Brown & Kourakos 2003, p.12*
Australia	2007	A$1.0[+]	*Australian Bureau of Statistics 2008, p.1*
	2002	A$1.1	*Cuganesan & Lacey 2003, p.55*
South Africa	2007	Rand1.0[#]	*Joseph 2008, p.1*
The Netherlands	2006	Euro5.0	*Model Criminal Law Officers' Committee 2008, p.13*

[#] *Estimate based on first 3 months of 2008 figure of 276 million Rand by Alexander Forbes Insurance.*
[*] *Three-year moving average - original amounts are US$40 (2008), $36 (2007), and $60 (2006) billion.*
[+] *This amount also aggregates costs from lotteries, pyramid schemes, financial advice, and other scams.*
Note there may be gaps in years between estimates gathered for some countries.

The objectives of this chapter are to overview government strategy components and describe elements of an organizational model to manage identity crimes. Implementation by governments of a strategy to manage identity crimes will give confidence to individuals and organizations to transact in cyberspace, enhancing cyber security and contributing to global information assurance. In developing an organizational framework, stages should be functional, complementary, incorporate knowledge innovations that adjust policy statements, and include processes and procedures developed through learning. As well as mitigating legal and regulatory risks and disclosure, implementing an identity fraud enterprise management framework provides significant economic benefits. However, even more important to organizations is reputational damage from identity crime. Implementing identity fraud conceptual frameworks at the organizational level should significantly reduce identity fraud prevalence and reduce identity fraud related reputational losses. Government and organizational level frameworks fill a gap observed in the identity crime and cyber security literature.

The next section explains the background to identity crime, followed by a brief discussion of managing identity crime in cyberspace at the government level. The following section discusses managing identity crime at the organizational level and introduces a comprehensive identity fraud enterprise framework. The second last section considers future trends and research and the final section concludes.

BACKGROUND

Identity crime is a general term covering identity fraud, identity theft, and identity deception (Jamieson, Land, Sarre, Steel, Stephens & Winchester, 2008; Wang, Chen & Aatabakhsh, 2004). *Identity fraud* is "the gaining of money, goods, services or other benefits or the avoidance of obligations through the use of a fabricated identity, a manipulated identity, or a stolen/assumed identity" (Model Criminal Law Officers' Committee, 2008, p.8). *Identity theft* is the theft of an individual's or organization's 'identity' attributes or their personal identifying information (PII) such as personal identifying numbers (PIN), passwords or other authentication details. *Identity deception* is the obtaining of another's identity attributes or authentication details by deception (Jamieson, Land, Sarre, Steel, Stephens & Winchester, 2008). These attributes may be real, lent or fictitious. Identity deception is also known as assumed identity, fabricated identity, false identity, fictitious identity, fraudulent identity, manipulated identity or synthetic identity fraud. Identity theft and identity deception acts are precursors to identity fraud acts.

Identity crimes are facilitated in both off-line and cyberspace or online contexts (Jamieson, Stephens, & Winchester, 2007). As society migrates over time from a paper-based environment to digital, more transactions will occur in cyberspace. This trend in digital storage and means of exchange in cyberspace has encouraged an increasing trend of identity crime perpetrators to seek out victims in cyberspace. *Cybercrime* has been referred to as "criminal activities that specifically target a computer or network for damage or infiltration and also refers to the use of computers as tools to conduct criminal activity" (United States Government Accountability Office, 2007, p.1). A current dilemma facing law enforcement in many countries is that specific identity crime events are not legislated against therefore they are not crimes labeled as identity fraud, identity theft, or identity deception. Such acts are prosecuted under other laws such as credit card fraud, whether committed in an offline or cyberspace environment (see Canadian Internet Policy and Public Interest Clinic, 2007; Paul, 2006).

Current identity crime models have conceptualized identity fraud and related crimes in the context of activity-based costing (Cuganesan & Lacey, 2003), identity risk management (ID Analytics, 2004) and profiling (Jamieson, Land, Stephens & Winchester, 2008; Le Lievre & Jamieson, 2005). More generally, fraud models from an organizations' perspective have developed conceptual and functional models. These models have been tested empirically, and have made important contributions in the areas of general fraud (Samociuk & Iyer, 2003; Wilhelm, 2004), fraud crimes and abuse. As well as across interconnecting fields, such as, computing (Straub & Nance, 1990), auditing and accounting (Stamboulidis, Resnick & Carney, 2005), identity risk management (ID Analytics, 2004), e-fraud (Vasiu, 2004), corporate and internal fraud (Bologna, 1984).

A number of the organizational model components shown in Figure 1 have underlying theoretical foundations across different disciplines. The disciplines vary from criminology e.g., specific and general deterrence (Straub & Nance, 1990; Wilhelm, 2004) and the fraud triangle (see Luijerink, 2006) to sociology. Other disciplines have a management or information systems perspective e.g., policy, and risk assessment (see Bologna, 1984; Brungs & Jamieson, 2005; Vasiu, 2004). Each of these disciplines has strands of theory appropriate to managing identity fraud. Contemporaneous models from the literature on fraud, identity fraud and related crimes and their components facilitated the developed framework shown in Figure 1. Further background literature on the model components will be covered in the discussion of the framework.

MANAGING IDENTITY CRIME: GOVERNMENT LEVEL STRATEGIES

Governments vary in size, resources and responsibilities. At the national level government responsibilities usually cover defense, foreign affairs and trade, telecommunications, currency, and postage. A second level of government (State,

Territory, or Provincial) exists in many countries where they are entrusted with education, health, transport infrastructure, other law enforcement agencies, police and prisons. The lowest level is often local government, which care for libraries, planning, building approvals, and community services. Identity crime perpetrators do not discriminate against any entity, individual or level of government. To mitigate and manage identity crime perpetrator attacks a government should implement an holistic strategy. Components of a strategy should encompass legislation, inter-jurisdictional collaboration, awareness programs, data protection, identity management, appropriate resourcing of justice systems, education programs, reporting transparency, and victim support (Jamieson, Land, Stephens, & Winchester, 2008).

Strategy Components Governments Should Implement to Combat Identity Crime

These strategy components at the national and inter-country level promote collaboration to combat identity crime perpetrators. Within a country the strategy component implementation devolves from a country's executive cascading out to government departments down to customer service providers. Within country inter-jurisdictional issues, for example, national identity theft legislation often takes precedence over state, province, or territory identity theft laws. This is often due to higher national level penalties for offences occurring across jurisdictions within a country. However, the ubiquitous nature of identity crime and cyberspace often means events occur across national borders. These circumstances create enormous jurisdictional problems for nations regarding victim remediation in civil or criminal actions because there is no global identity crime legislation. These circumstances reinforce the need for an holistic government strategy to implement all the components outlined to deter, detect, prevent, and respond to identity crime perpetrator acts on a regional basis, especially at the national level until such global legislation for identity crime in cyberspace is enforceable. At present, some countries or regions do have bilateral or multilateral agreements, directives, conventions or guidelines in place for crimes occurring in cyberspace across country borders. For example, the European Union Directives or the Council of Europe Cybercrime Conventions, may capture some identity crime methods in cyberspace such as data breaches (Commission of the European Communities, 2007, 2004).

In addition to the strategic components listed, government can undertake cyber-attack simulations within and across countries to assess system preparedness for threat analysis and to implement response solutions. The next section briefly describes two such simulations.

Cyber-Attack Simulations

To date there have been two well-publicized international cyber-attack simulations - Cyber Storm (6-10 February 2006) and Cyber Storm II (11-14 March 2008). The first Cyber Storm event involved nine large information technology (IT) firms and critical infrastructure organizations such as, electricity utility firms and major airline carriers. Some of the vendors involved were Cisco, Computer Associates, Computer Sciences Corporation, Microsoft, Symantec, and Verisign.

Cyber Storm II tested the national security of Australia, the US, Canada, the UK and New Zealand. Participants engaged in an international hacking exercise. Cyber Storm divided participants into attackers and defenders over simulations that tested national responsiveness to cyber-attacks on IT systems and transportation, communications, and chemical infrastructure. The event was lead by the US Department of Homeland Security and supported by more than 100 public, private and international organizations. Some of the organizations involved were the FBI, Microsoft, Verizon, McAffee, Australian

Computer Emergency Response Team, Attorney General's department, the Department of Defense, the Australian Federal Police, and Telstra.

Within scenarios of both Cyber Storm simulations, various cyberspace channel identity crime methods were played out e.g., computer virus attacks, worms, purchase of personnel identity data, and malware distribution. These identity crime methods can result in identity details or personnel information identifiers being fraudulently obtained by identity crime perpetrators.

MANAGING IDENTITY CRIME: ORGANIZATIONAL LEVEL STRATEGIES

Individual components of the conceptual model shown in Figure 1 are specified in terms of particular fraud need, business sector, category of fraud, or approach to identity fraud. The increasing use of the Internet, as a medium to perpetrate identity fraud events extended the model search beyond fraud. This facilitated the identification of important components for the proposed framework from a variety of fraud and related disciplines. The importance of this research is due to the omnipresent nature of identity fraud and related crimes even though perpetrators are currently heavily targeting a number of key sectors - for instance financial institutions, retail and utilities organizations. In general, they do not constrain their activity to a sector or a particular location. This section illustrates the development of a comprehensive identity fraud enterprise management framework illustrated in Figure 1.

The framework conceptualizes identity fraud management from an organization's perspective. Policy development personnel are most often the leaders within identity fraud and fraud management teams. Importantly, they must be able to act on board directives to control and allocate resources within the overall identity fraud areas, within and across all stages from policy inception to victim restoration. Each of the phases, stages and steps in the framework are discussed in the following sub-sections.

Anticipatory Phase

The anticipatory phase is proactive in its stance of managing identity fraud. Organizations who implement all the stages of the anticipatory phase should, *ceteris paribus*, encounter less identity fraud losses than those who do not. The stages of the anticipatory phase are integral to protecting an organization against identity fraud perpetrators.

Stage One: Policy

Within the identity fraud management framework, the policy stage must seek to drive the remaining anticipatory stages, and the reactionary and remediation phases, while meeting an organization-wide cost benefit. One of the first steps in formulating policy is to define identity fraud. To date the lack of an appropriate definition and scope has frustrated many organizations (Jamieson, Land, Sarre, Steel, Stephens & Winchester, 2008). Organizations, due in part to not having an appropriate definition of identity fraud, have often just written the fraud losses off as a bad debt (Cuganesan & Lacey, 2003).

Figure 1. Identity fraud enterprise management framework

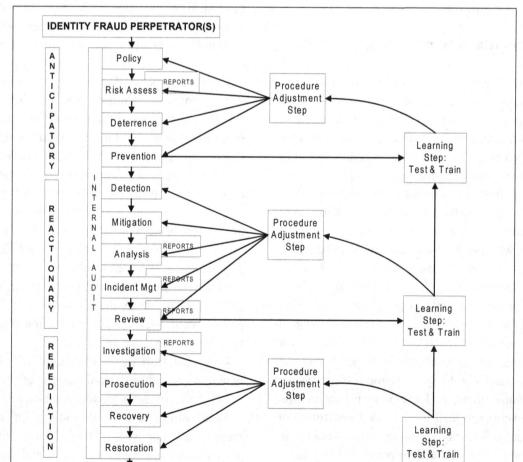

Within the set of related models reviewed, both the e-fraud model by Vasiu (2004) and the fraud model by Wilhelm (2004) specifically name a 'policies' component. However, Samociuk and Iyer's (2003) Fraud Risk Management model, in contrast, includes a component to 'define the objective'. Similarly an internal fraud prevention schema by Bologna (1984) includes 'strategies', 'objectives' and 'assumptions' with choices to 'increase the probability of discovery' or 'decrease the possibility of commission', while Gill and Morrison (2002) also use the term 'strategies'. Other models also use labels similar to policy, such as, 'directive' (Bologna, 1984), 'governance' (Luijerink, 2006), 'devise risk adjusted actions' (ID Analytics, 2004), 'reactive or proactive detective activities' (Straub & Nance, 1990), and 'perpetrator profile' (Le Lievre & Jamieson, 2005).

Due to the diversity of organizations targeted by identity crime perpetrators, developing a set of identity fraud policies within an organization is seen as the necessary first stage in building an integrated approach to identity fraud management. Prudent policy statements and initiatives build the foundation of the following stages in our framework.

Stage Two: Risk Assessment

Risk assessments relate to prioritization and identification of threats both internally and externally for staff and customers. This includes the actual implementation of controls. The dynamic nature of identity fraud means that perpetrators have used new types of identity fraud techniques that risk managers within organizations need to assess on a frequent basis. The real problem is that identity fraud perpetrators hide amongst valued real and potentially real customers.

Cuganesan and Lacey (2003) include risk assessment as the first item in a list of activity related identity fraud costs. Vasiu's (2004) e-fraud model assigns risk assessment to occur between their prevention and audit stages. Samociuk and

Iyer's (2003) fraud risk management model includes 'understand the risk' and 'reduce the risk', which closely relate to risk assessment. Le Lievre and Jamieson (2005) in their model of initial preconception of Identity Fraud profiling, include a step to 'profile the mode of attack'. ID Analytics (2004) pose the question, 'How do you manage ID risk?' and illustrate a solution with a 3-step model of the Identity Fraud Risk Management Process. The first two steps, 'Assess Identity Risk' and 'Devise Risk Adjusted Actions' cover a risk assessment approach. The emphasis on risk assessment across the models investigated underlies its importance.

Stage Three: Deterrence

Successful deterrence stops fraud and identity crime before it happens. Cuganesan and Lacey (2003), refer to deterrence as "activities related to the promotion and communication of disincentives to commit identity fraud acts". Deterrence is an important component of identity fraud control and can be viewed from an anticipatory and reactionary perspective. Cuganesan and Lacey's (2003), meaning adheres to the former. A reactionary position uses threats of past prosecuted perpetrators sentences as a deterrent. However, "fraudsters tend to migrate toward the path of most anonymity and least resistance. Therefore, increasing the difficulty of committing the fraud effectively functions as an incremental increase in deterrence" (Wilhelm, 2004, p.10). Therefore, anticipatory position is preferred for identity fraud.

Stage Four: Prevention

In the general fraud landscape, prevention, detection, and deterrence are sometimes used interchangeably. "The activities in the prevention stage, though closely associated with deterrence and detection, occur after deterrence has failed and before the suspicion or detection of fraud or identity fraud has occurred" (Wilhelm, 2004, p.10). In contrast, according to Cuganesan and Lacey (2003, p.35), prevention "activities are related to strategy, policy and procedural development, and implementation to avoid an identity fraud being perpetrated". Vasiu (2004) uses an integrated supply chain framework for e-fraud that includes policies, implement, and, test and train elements within a prevention approach across suppliers, contractors and customers. Vasiu also includes a risk assessment process within this overall prevention approach. Vasiu (2004, p.5) points out that "prevention should be paramount in any e-fraud control approach". The reason is that "the risk of loss is higher with reactive/detection strategies because either the crime is ongoing or has occurred; hence, the ability to stop or recover the loss is often very limited" (Vasiu, 2004, p.5).

Prevention activities are intended to prevent the identity fraud from occurring or to secure the entity and its processes against internal and external identity fraud. "The ability of prevention to stop losses from occurring versus stopping fraudulent activity from continuing is an important distinction. The latter activities are more appropriately mitigation stage activities" (Wilhelm, 2004, p.11). The United States-Canada Working Group (1997, p.26) corroborates Wilhelm's (2004) point as "the most cost-effective means to control any crime is to prevent it, since this avoids the costs both to victims and society". To complement this, reactionary stages are required.

Reactionary Phase

The reactionary phase has stages that manage the perpetrator attacks while the attack is actually occurring. These stages cover the full range from detection, mitigation, analysis, incident management, to review. Organizations that include all these stages position themselves to better understand identity fraud perpetrator *modus operandi* and therefore better manage any subsequent attacks.

Stage Five: Detection

Wilhelm (2004, p.11) in his fraud management lifecycle framework argues that detection "is characterized by actions and activities intended to identify and locate fraud prior to, during, and subsequent to the completion of the fraudulent activity". According to Wilhelm (2004) 'prior to' refers to "the detection of testing or probing activity used by criminals to facilitate a fraud attempt" (p.11). Detection can be passive and active for indications of identity crime. Vasiu (2004, p.6) suggests, "in the detection function, if e-fraud occurs, it should be rapidly detected, managed to recover or minimize the losses, then effectively investigated to identify the perpetrator(s), and to gather digital evidence for prosecution." Vasiu (2004, p.6) further emphasizes that "adequate audit strategies across the integrated supply chain can be an essential success factor in *a posteriori* fraud detection". Samociuk and Iyer (2003, p.50) divide the emerging science of fraud detection "into two main areas:

- Red flags which provide early warning of a potential problem; and
- Detection tests, which specialists, such as security and audit personnel, can include as part of their normal work programs".

Stage Six: Mitigation

Wilhelm (2004, p.11) states, "mitigation is begun once the presence or a reasonable suspicion of fraudulent activity has been detected. In short, mitigation stops fraud." "Sometimes mitigation activities are referred to as prevention activities, where the prevention is focused on preventing the ongoing fraud from continuing" Wilhelm (2004, p.12). Similarly, detection systems can alert special investigators to the strong likelihood of internal fraud (Bologna, 1984). Before customers and outside agencies become aware of the fraud, the opportunity to mitigate losses, expenses, impact, and exposure will be significantly enhanced.

To mitigate identity fraud losses, organizations should consider using an outside agency to perform a credit check to verify a new client's information such as a business name, address, business tax identification and phone number. For small organizations with less than 100 employees, this may be too high of a cost to incur on a regular basis. However, a bad experience can easily wipe out an organization's annual net profit and the organization could suffer from reputational loss.

Stage Seven: Analysis

The analysis stage collates information regarding outputs and performance from each of the previous stages in our framework and provides feedback through the review stage and learning steps regarding outcomes and performance. Organizations need good systems in place to facilitate accurate analysis that contributes to an organization's competitive advantage, which has a deterrence value. An advantage some organizations have over other organizations is their degree of electronic recording, and that certainly helps the identity crime analysts in tracing perpetrators.

Stage Eight: Incident Management

Incident management implements the activities involved in responding to identity fraud occurrences. The ability for organizations to implement speedy and rigorous incident management processes relies heavily on the quality of internal, external and collaborative systems especially regarding identity information.

Stage Nine: Review

Review is an important feedback loop that incorporates change and innovation into the identity fraud framework. The review stage can also have a forward-looking perspective and therefore the review stage acts as a hub between actions of the past and improvements for the future.

Remediation Phase

The stages within the remediation phase allow the organization to manage the process of compensation from the perpetrator of identity fraud attack. Without the implementation of all the stages in the remediation phase, an organization could miss the opportunity to seek redress as a result of the lack of evidence collected from the attack event. The process to prove the perpetrators' guilt requires meticulous gathering of the facts.

Stage Ten: Investigation

Investigation activities obtain enough evidence and information to stop fraudulent activity, to obtain recovery of assets or restoration, and to provide information and support for the successful prosecution and conviction of the fraudster(s). "A major problem facing investigators and prosecutors is the fact that frauds are often hard to prove, both because of the limited access to evidence and because of the sophistication of the schemes involved" (United Nations, 2004, p.12). Four principal legal elements must be proven in fraud cases:

- A material false statement,
- Reliance by the victim on the false statement,
- Knowledge by the perpetrator that the statement was false at the time it was made, and
- Damage as a result of the false statement.

These elements constitute the needed proof, regardless of the type of fraud. Bank embezzlement, insurance fraud, and con artist schemes are all investigated by essentially the same methods. An organization should ensure that its personnel involved in investigations are familiar with the rules pertaining to securing evidence and the admissibility of evidence in internal hearings as well as criminal trials.

Stage Eleven: Prosecution

There are three main aims of prosecution in the fraud arena, namely punishment, enhancing an organization's reputation for detecting fraud, and recovery or restitution. As Wilhelm (2004, p.14) states the "first is to punish the fraudster in an attempt to prevent further theft. Secondly, prosecution seeks to establish, maintain, and enhance the business enterprise's reputation of deterring fraud. The third goal is to obtain recovery or restitution wherever possible." Another activity relevant at the "prosecution stage is the consistent and visible coordination of supportive legislative and regulatory activities to stop fraudulent activity. This activity frequently falls to senior managers and legal counsel due to their experience, industry contacts, and broad perspective" (Wilhelm 2004, p.15).

Stage Twelve: Recovery

Recovery activities for identity crimes are "related to the recouping of losses/benefits that are directed at the perpetrator and which may be undertaken internally within the organization and/or externally such as through the judicial system or debt collecting agency" (Cuganesan & Lacey, 2003, p.35). Examples include, preparation of evidence briefs, time spent negotiating with the perpetrator and/or in the judicial system, and legal costs. The important process of asset recovery needs to be documented in a professional manner. Given the global nature of identity fraud, the perpetrator can easily transfer assets to other jurisdictions. A major problem in recovering them has been a lack of reciprocity between different global jurisdictions (Brungs & Jamieson, 2005). While mutual legal assistance treaties have been useful in some circumstances, more legal cooperation should be encouraged to help businesses recover assets more efficiently.

Cooperation between the government and private sectors including law enforcement is also an enormous help in the recovery of assets. "A further complicating factor in the recovery of assets has been the issue of bank secrecy. It was also noted that the United Nations Conventions against Transnational Organized Crime and against Corruption include provisions for the recovery of assets" (United Nations, 2004, p.11). Losses should be quantified and attempts should be made to recoup such losses through insurance claims, civil action or compensation orders in criminal courts. Inter-jurisdictional issues frustrate organizations at this stage. This is why government needs an holistic strategy that includes an inter-jurisdictional collaboration component and appropriate legislative backing for identity crime and cybercrime across national boundaries.

Stage Thirteen: Restoration

Restoration involves activities related to attempting to re-establish the victim's position prior to any identity fraud occurrence. While some of these activities are focused on the perpetrator primarily via recovery, other activities are also involved. For example, "media campaigns to reassure stakeholders in response to identity fraud attack, transaction costs associated with hiring new staff for example where staff were involved in identity fraud attack, time spent to re-establish circumstances of the identity" and credit standing restored to that position prior to the identity fraud attack (Cuganesan & Lacey, 2003, p.35).

Audit Stage

The audit stage interfaces with all sequential stages from policy to restoration. Internal audits are ongoing and reporting should be on a regular basis to an audit committee that is part of or reports directly to the board. External audits are periodic in nature often on an annual basis and independent of the organization and report to the chief financial officer or chief executive officer who then report to the board. Both Vasiu (2004) and Samociuk and Iyer (2003) include an auditing function with both internal and external auditors responsibilities within the detection stage. They also argue for the need for proper training, learning and skill base within specific types of frauds.

Auditors are more responsible for detecting different frauds including identity fraud today than in the recent past, and fraudulent transactions are being discovered increasingly in electronic environments. Since a fraud investigation can hinge on electronic evidence, it is now important for the auditing and computer forensics professions to assist one another in collecting and using digital evidence. Without such cooperation, digital data tested during an audit may be forensically unusable and not prosecutable (Brungs & Jamieson, 2005). Audits often pick up errors or anomalies in practices undertaken in systems or processes that cause losses or are fraudulent. Next, we will discuss the learning and procedural adjustment steps in our framework.

Learning Steps

The learning steps include 'test and train' subtasks; we offer two reasons for this. First, within Australian government organizations, personnel in certain fraud roles must have or are required to undertake related training and complete required tests. Second, in normal circumstances there will be learning improvements that will require training with some depth of understanding. All personnel involved need training and associated testing. Within Australian government organizations Regulation 19 of the Financial Management and Accountability Regulations of 1997, guideline 3(7), in part states that, "Risk assessment is a process of continuing improvement. When the risk assessment process begins, agencies must attempt to gain an understanding of the very broad risks of fraud" (Australian Government Attorney General's Department, 2002, p.9).

Learning is carried out by humans or computerized within expert systems or other learning paradigms. There are two different types of computerized learning: supervised and unsupervised. In *supervised learning*, the desired answer is provided by the trainer. Any deviation from the expected response is seen as an error measurement and is used in the correction of network parameters. The error value can be used to modify weights so the other decreases. This learning mode requires a training set of known input and output values (Smith, 2006). *Unsupervised learning* differs because the desired response is largely undefined or vague. Since there is no information available about the correctness of the response, other knowledge must be known to understand the output of the network. These networks must discover any patterns or recognizable properties by themselves. The network is updated using a self-organizing process (Smith, 2006).

Procedure Adjustment Step

In order to implement knowledge innovations from the learning steps, certain procedural adjustments need to occur. These procedural adjustments will be specific to certain individual stages throughout our management framework within the anticipatory, reactionary and recovery phases. The procedure adjustment step is akin to monitoring and assessing the design and operation of the identity fraud stages on a timely basis and making necessary corrective actions to leverage the knowledge innovations.

Reporting Step

Reporting is an essential part of the other phases and stages. Reports are compiled at the Risk Assessment, Analysis, Incident Management, Review, and Investigation stages. Whilst there are differences in purpose, the reports at the various stages are likely to have a similar structure, but will have different functional stages, content and emphasis. There are several reasons for undertaking the reports including auditing, evidence gathering, investigative reports, and facilitating procedure adjustments and future policy implementations. In Australia, Commonwealth organizations should adhere to strict legal guidelines such as the Commonwealth Fraud Control Guidelines. This was issued by the Minister for Justice and Customs as Fraud Control Guidelines under Regulation 19 of the Financial Management and Accountability Regulations 1997 (Australian Government Attorney General's Department, 2002).

Victim (an Individual or Entity)

The high cost to the victims of identity fraud is often due to the delay between when the perpetrator commits the crime against a victim and when the victim realizes they have been victimized. "As many as 85 percent of all identity theft victims find out about the crime only when they are denied credit or employment, contacted by the police, or have to deal with collection agencies, credit cards, and bills" (Pastore, 2004, p.1). The time it takes for a victim to recover from identity theft can be extensive, and while the wounds are not physical, they are psychological and life changing in several ways. For example, a study on identity theft (Foley & Foley, 2003, refer p.4) found that victims spend 600 hours recovering from the crime because they must contact and work with credit cards, banks, credit bureaus, and law enforcement. The time can add up to as much as US$16,000 in lost wages or income.

One-third of the victims of identity theft had their personal information misused for credit card fraud in 2003, according to the Federal Trade Commission, FTC (2004). Phone or utilities fraud was next at 21 percent, 17 percent for bank fraud, and 11 percent for employment-related fraud. Nineteen percent of the instances of identity theft used stolen personal information to open new credit card accounts. Twelve percent used it to commit fraud with existing credit card accounts.

Ten percent of the FTC's cases of identity theft involved opening new wireless phone accounts. The number of victims in the US, measured by the Javelin 2008 Identity Fraud Survey Report in the 12 months prior to the 2008 survey was 8.1 million adults down 300,000 from the 2007 survey estimate (Monahan & Kim, 2008).

The 2005 identity fraud survey (Javelin Research, 2006) found identity theft victims who detected the crime by monitoring accounts online "experienced an average financial loss of US$551", compared "with an average loss of US$4,543 when the crime was detected through paper statements" (Swanson, 2005, p.2). In the UK, in some cases it cost individuals £8,000 or more and took as much as 200 person-hours to fix up what the identity crime perpetrator's acts had created (MyFinances.co.uk, 2006).

FUTURE TRENDS AND RESEARCH

There are mixed views regarding the current and future trend of the cost of identity crime. One view from the US is that the cost of identity fraud has peaked and is now stable or in decline as measured on an annual basis over the last five years (Kim, 2008). Contrary views state that as a greater consensus is reached to defining the phenomenon of identity crime and its component parts of identity fraud, identity theft, and identity deception and more countries undertake sound cost studies, a more accurate picture will appear. Only then could it be stated, with confidence, that identity crime and related crime costs are increasing or otherwise. We take the view that the cost in terms of losses caused by the perpetrators to individuals and organizations through prevention, detection, deterrence, and response expenses is increasing, and will continue into the near future. This will in some part be due to the ubiquitous nature of the internet and mobile technologies offering perpetrators anonymity. Within the enterprise management framework we also have yet to identify and include roles within stages for a coordinated approach within organizations e.g., across audit, security, fraud control, and investigation groups. Future research needs to address these issues. This will then allow in-depth empirical research for studies to test the model's practical implementation. The exclusion of any components or phases and stages could limit implementation in small government agencies or micro-organizations. Future research initiatives include developing a comprehensive understanding of identity fraud in e-commerce and implementing appropriate solutions.

CONCLUSION

Managing identity crime risk is a critical issue for any country, government agency, organization, or individual. This chapter describes a holistic strategy that can be implemented by organizations. Victims can also protect themselves by carefully monitoring their online and offline actions and properly destroying unwanted identity documents or accompanying personal identifying information.

Governments should initiate a holistic identity crime strategy with a specific set of components that helps quarantine the phenomenon as much as practicable. These components include legislation, inter-jurisdictional collaboration, awareness programs, data protection, identity management, appropriate resourcing of justice systems, education programs, reporting transparency, and victim support (Jamieson, Land, Stephens, & Winchester, 2008). Inter-jurisdictional collaboration could include cyber-attack simulations to assess government agency and organizational readiness in terms of threat analysis and ability to implement response solutions. Simulations are important as identity crime perpetrators' innovations continue at an increasing pace.

This research informs theory by presenting a model of identity fraud management, which requires further validation. In practice, this model will aid identity fraud managers to effectively identify identity fraud attacks. Benefits include having a plan of action for each major phase that anticipates, reacts to, and remedies identity fraud incidents. This provides the manager with a ready suite of stages to detect, mitigate, analyze, manage, review, report, and learn from event attacks. Economic benefits derive from the stages incorporated in the remediation phase and designed to remedy any asset or reputational losses.

The proposed identity fraud enterprise management framework identifies three phases: anticipatory, reactionary, and remediation. These phases include 13 sequential stages and an audit stage, which interacts with all other stages. Various reporting, learning and procedural adjustment steps are provided to facilitate innovation tailored to each organization. This framework should be applied to combat the increasing trend of identity fraud and related crimes within an organization. These steps like the internal audit stage interface with the sequential stages from policy to restoration. The internal audit stage is important because it permits the undertaking of rigorous checks and balances on procedures from policies throughout the model's operation. An important contribution of a dedicated internal audit structure includes the mandatory reporting to an organization's executive level that would include the board and should include an independent audit committee.

Our framework provides a useful link between the phases and stages as there are a number of players that traditionally have acted in isolation e.g., auditing, security, recovery, fraud investigation. Our framework facilitates this management integration for organizations.

REFERENCES

Australian Bureau of Statistics. (2008). *Nearly $1 billion dollars lost by Australians to personal fraud: ABS*. Commonwealth of Australia, 26 June, 1.

Australian Government Attorney General's Department. (2002). *Commonwealth Fraud Control Guidelines*. Australia: Issued by the Minister for Justice and Customs.

Bologna, J. (1984). *Corporate Fraud: The Basics of Prevention and Detection*. Boston, U.S.A: Butterworth Publishers.

Brown, D. C. G., & Kourakos, G. (2003). *Public Policy Forum Roundtable on Identity Theft and Identity Fraud*. 26 June, Ottawa, 1-23. Retrieved June 10, 2006, from http://www.ppforum.ca/common/assets/publications/en/identity_theft_fraud.pdf.

Brungs, A., & Jamieson, R. (2005). Identification of Legal Issue for Computer Forensics. *Information Systems Management, 22*(2), 57-66.

Canadian Internet Policy and Public Interest Clinic (CIPPIC). (2007). *Australian, French, and United Kingdom legislation relevant to identity theft: An annotated review*. CIPPIC working paper, March, 3C, 1-49.

Commission of the European Communities. (2007). *Towards a general policy on the fight against cyber crime*. Commission of the European Communities, June, 1-48. Retrieved January 16, 2008, from http://www.coe.int/t/e/legal_affairs/legal_co-operation/combating_economic_crime/6_cybercrime/t-cy/T-CY%20_2007_%2002%20-%20e%20-20Cybercrime%20and%20the%20EU.pdf

Commission of the European Communities. (2004). *Convention on Cybercrime. Commission of the European Communities Online, 185*(1). Retrieved January 16, 2008, from http://conventions.coe.int/Treaty/en/Summaries/ Html/185.htm.

Cuganesan, S., & Lacey, D. (2003). *Identity Fraud in Australia: An evaluation of its nature, cost and extent*. Sydney, Australia: Standards Australia International Ltd.

Federal Trade Commission (FTC). (2004). *National and State Trends in Fraud & Identity Theft*: January-December 2003. January 22.

Foley, L., & Foley, J. (2003). *Identity Theft: The Aftermath 2003. Identity Theft Resource Center*, Summer 2003, September, 1-58. Retrieved April 10, 2008, from www.idtheftcenter.org.

Gill, G., & Morrison, C. (2002). *Diagnosis: Fraud*! Institute of Chartered Accountants of British Columbia, October, 1-6. Retrieved June 27, 2006, from http://www.ica.bc.ca/kb.php3?pageid=1761&term0=gill&term1=gary.

Hurley, J., & Veytsel, A. (2003). *Identity Theft: A $2 Trillion Criminal Industry in 2005*. The Aberdeen Group, 13 May, 1-3.

ID Analytics. (2004). *Identity 2004: The Identity Risk Management Conference*. ID Analytics, 1-10. Retrieved June 1, 2006, from http://www.idanalytics.com/pdf/ ID_2004_Summary.pdf.

Jamieson, R., Land, L., Sarre, R., Steel, A., Stephens, G., and Winchester, D. (2008). Defining Identity Crimes. *ACIS2008 Proceedings of the 19th Australasian Conference on Information Systems,* Christchurch, New Zealand, December 3-5, 1-11.

Jamieson, R., Land, L., Stephens, G., & Winchester, D. (2008). *Identity Crime: The Need for an Appropriate Government Strategy,* Forum on Public Policy Online, Spring 2008 edition, 1-33.

Jamieson, R., Stephens, G., & Winchester, D. (2007). *Identity Fraud: Perpetrator Categories, Channels and Methods of Attack, and their Impact on Target Organisations*. PACIS 2007, Auckland, New Zealand.

Joseph, N. (2008). Identity theft 'costing SA millions'. Originally published in The Mercury, 4 June, 5. http://www.iol.co.za/index.php?set_id=1&click_id=15&art_id=vn20080604060110244C665305.

Kim, R. (2008). *2008 Identity Fraud Survey Report Consumer Version: How Consumers Can Protect Themselves.* Javelin Strategy & Research, February, 1-23.

KPMG. (2007). Global Anti–Money Laundering Survey 2007: How banks are facing up to the challenge. *KPMG International,* (pp. 1-8).

Le Lievre, E., & Jamieson, R. (2005). An Investigation of Identity Fraud in Australian Organizations. *CollECTeR LatAm.* Chile, (pp. 1-10).

Luijerink. D. (2006). The Fraud in Business Club: Effective Fraud Governance. *KPMG,* 2 March, 1-36.

Model Criminal Law Officers' Committee. (2008). *Final Report Identity Crime,* Commonwealth of Australia, March, 1-51.

Monahan, M. T., & Kim, R. (2008). *2008 Identity Fraud Survey Report Excerpts for Card Issuers: Identity Fraud Continues to Decline, But Criminals More Effective at Using All Channels.* Javelin Strategy & Research, Syndicated Report Brochure, March, 1-6.

MyFinances.co.uk, UK. (2006). *ID fraud cost of just cutting up cards.* 27 March. Retrieved June 29, 2006, from http://www.myfinanc es.co.uk/news/credit-cards/identity-fraud/id-fraud-cost-just-cutting-up-cards-$349604.htm.

Pastore, M. (2004). *The Identity Theft Prevention and Recovery Guide.* November 19, Retrieved June 1, 2006, from http://www.in sideid.com/idtheft/article.php/3438261n.

Paul, S. R. (2006). Identity Theft: Outline of Federal Statutes and Bibliography of Selected Resources. *LLRX.com,* February, 1-16.

Samociuk, M., & Iyer, N. (2003). *Fraud Resistance: A Practical Guide.* Strategic Value Management Series. SIRCA. Standards Australia International.

Smith, S. (2006). *An Investigation of IS Security Management in E-Government.* Unpublished doctoral dissertation, University of New South Wales, Australia.

Stamboulidis, G. A., Resnick., L. J., & Carney, J. J. (2005). Expanding The Internal Auditor's Beat. *Internal Auditing,* (20)5, 38-42.

Straub, D. E. Jr. & Nance, W. D. (1990). Discovering and Disciplining Computer Abuse in Organizations: A Field Study. *MIS Quarterly,* March, 45-60.

Swanson, A. (2005). *Most ID theft begins at home.* United Press International, January, 1-4.

The Fraud Advisory Panel. (2003). *Identity theft: do you know the signs*? A guide for businesses and individuals. The Fraud Advisory Panel, July, 1-26.

UK Home Office. (2006). *Updated estimate of the cost of identity fraud to the UK economy.* 2 February, 1-4. Retrieved March 7, 2008, from http://www.identity-theft.org.uk/ID%20fraud%20table.pdf.

United Nations. (2004). *Report on UNCITRAL Colloquium on International Commercial Fraud.* United Nations Commission on International Trade Law, Thirty-seventh session New York, 14 June-2 July, 1-17. Retrieved April 8, 2008, from http://daccessdds.un.org/doc/UNDOC/GEN/V04/539/85/PDF/V0453985.pdf?OpenElement.

United States Government Accountability Office (GAO). (2007). *Cybercrime: Public and Private Entities Face Challenges in Addressing Cyber Threats.* United States Government Accountability Office, Washington, D.C. June, 705, (pp. 1-59).

United States-Canada Working Group. (1997). *United States-Canada Cooperation Against Telemarketing Fraud.* November, 1-28. Retrieved April 8, 2008, from http://www.justice.gov/criminal/fraud/docs/reports/1997/uscwgrtf.htm.

Vasiu, L. (2004). A Conceptual Framework of E-Fraud Control in an Integrated Supply Chain. *Proceedings of the 12th European Conference on Information Systems, Turku School of Economics and Business Administration*, Finland.

Wang, G., Chen, H., & Aatabakhsh, H. (2004). Criminal Identity Deception and Deception Detection in Law Enforcement. *Group Decision and Negotiation*, (13), 111–127, Kluwer Academic Publishers, Netherlands.

Wilhelm, W. K. (2004). The Fraud Management Lifecycle Theory: A Holistic Approach to Fraud Management. *Journal of Economic Crime Management, Spring*, 2(2), 1-38.

Section III
Emergency Response Planning

Chapter XII
A Repeatable Collaboration Process for Incident Response Planning

Alanah Davis
University of Nebraska at Omaha, USA

Gert-Jan de Vreede
University of Nebraska at Omaha, USA

Leah R. Pietron
University of Nebraska at Omaha, USA

ABSTRACT

This chapter presents a repeatable collaboration process as an approach for developing a comprehensive Incident Response Plan for an organization or team. Despite the process of incident response planning being an essential ingredient in security planning procedures in organizations, extensive literature reviews have not yielded any collaborative processes for such a crucial activity. As such, this chapter will discuss the background of incident response planning as well as Collaboration Engineering, which is an approach to design repeatable collaborative work practices. We then present a collaboration process for incident response planning that was designed using Collaboration Engineering principles, followed by a discussion of the application process in three cases. The presented process is applicable across organizations in various sectors and domains, and consist of codified "best facilitation practices" that can be easily transferred to and adopted by security managers. The chapter describes the process in detail and highlights research results obtained during initial applications of the process.

INTRODUCTION

Today, many organizations have connected their systems and networks to the outside world, as is the case of e-business. This brings with it special requirements on computer and information security. Most organizations have to handle security risks such as viruses and worms, theft of proprietary information, financial fraud, system penetration by outsiders, sabotage of data or networks, to mention but a few. Therefore, organizations need to have Incident Response Plans in place to be able to respond efficiently when an incident occurs (Soper, 2003). However, experience shows that creating a high quality Incident Response Plan is a complex task. Creating a comprehensive and useful plan requires the input from many security professionals (Foix, 2004; Sausner, 2007). It is often a time-intensive process as groups of professionals have to share relevant information, deliberate on preventive and reactive measures, and achieve agreement on strategies and policies. To ensure that this collaboration is as efficient and effective as possible, many groups would benefit from a structure, purposeful team process that is guided by an expert facilitator. Yet surprisingly, an extensive literature review did not reveal any reported standard collaborative processes for this critical security activity. Therefore, the goal of this chapter is to present a collaborative team process for the creation of an Incident Response Plan. This process was designed using Collaboration Engineering principles and tested in three case situations. The collaborative Incident Response Plan process consists of codified 'best facilitation practices' that can be easily transferred to and adopted by security managers. Hence, security managers can execute the process by themselves without the support from expensive, expert facilitators. This use of Collaboration Engineering does not suggest that facilitation is easy; however it illustrates how a step-by-step plan using best facilitation practices can be completed by security managers who are novice facilitators.

The chapter begins with a background of incident response planning and Collaboration Engineering. This background provides the basis and information necessary for the design of a collaboration process for incident response planning. Next, the chapter describes the designed process in detail and highlights the research results obtained during initial applications of the process. The chapter then presents a discussion of future trends and research issues which when explored may offer potential for further strengthening these results. The chapter concludes with a discussion of how the presented process can be used across organizations in various sectors and domains.

BACKGROUND

There is a significant amount of research in the area of IT contingency planning and, as a part of that, incident response planning. However, based on our research of existing literature we conclude that no collaborative process has been presented for security practitioners. The background in this chapter will first discuss relevant research related to incident response planning. Then we discuss the Collaboration Engineering approach that was used to design the repeatable incident response planning process.

Incident Response Planning

IT contingency planning supports the development of thorough plans and procedures to recover from an IT service disruption and/or a disaster in an organization. IT comprehensive contingency planning consists of several major planning documents including: (a) Business Impact Analysis (BIA); (b) Incident Response Plan (IRP); (c) Business Contingency Plan (BCP); and (d) Disaster Recovery Plan (DRP) (Swanson et al., 2002). Of specific interest to this chapter is the IRP.

An IRP covers the planning process associated with the definition, identification, classification, response, and recovery from an incident (Poindexter & St. Laurent, 2000). In other words, it describes the practice of detecting a problem, determining its cause, minimizing the damage it causes, resolving the problem and documenting each step of the response for future reference. Traditionally, there are six stages of an IRP, which include 1) preparation, 2) identification, 3) containment, 4) eradication, 5) recovery, and 6) follow-up (Poindexter & St. Laurent, 2000). The basic goals of the six stages include confirmation of whether an incident occurred, determining how the attack was done or the incident happened, minimizing the downtime to business and network services, preventing future attacks or incidents, improving security and incident response, enabling legal and law enforcement to prosecute malicious entities, and finally providing recommendations to senior management. These recommendations are in the form of planning documents, which together comprise a large quantity of documentation.

Typically, documentation does not come naturally to technical individuals. However, documenting the steps taken during an incident response is of paramount importance. Documentation and records of incident responses performed months or years prior have a longer shelf life than an individual's memory. Further, documentation remains when individuals leave the organization to pursue other career opportunities. Planning is also very important to the response because sometimes the investigator may have only one chance to respond correctly. Planning the commands, the order, and what switches will be used on the victim machine will follow hand-in-hand with the documentation (Jones, 2001).

Among the many ways organizations are dealing with incident prevention, reaction, handling, and preparation, is the use of Computer Security Incident Response Teams (CSIRT's). These teams collect all documentation related to any incident occurring in the organization. This documentation could be a text file, a piece of scratch paper, index cards, spreadsheets, databases, and pre-

made forms. All these elements become part of the IRP. The work of a CSIRT is critical for the compilation of documentation. Therefore, it is clear that collaboration is important in an IRP. This type of planning has always been done in a team or with a group of experts (Foix, 2004; Sausner, 2007) and it should only make sense that an efficient process be developed to support this collaboration. To create this process we followed a collaboration process design approach. This approach, known as Collaboration Engineering, is discussed in the next section.

Collaboration Engineering

Collaboration Engineering is an approach to designing, and deploying collaboration processes for recurring high-value collaborative tasks that are executed by practitioners without the ongoing intervention of professional facilitators (Briggs, de Vreede, & Nunamaker Jr., 2003; de Vreede, Koneri, Dean, Fruhling, & Wolcott, 2006). A practitioner is a domain expert within the area supported by the collaboration process (e.g., security), but not a group dynamics expert or facilitator. The main goal of Collaboration Engineering is to enable practitioners to guide group work with minimal cognitive load while providing them with the necessary facilitation skills and knowledge about groups.

In designing a repeatable collaboration process, the key steps or activities in the process are modeled as patterns of collaboration. Patterns of collaboration describe the nature of a group's collaborative process when observed over a period of time as they move from a starting state to some end state. According to Briggs, et al. (2006a), there are six main patterns of collaboration. They include the following:

- **Generate:** To move from having fewer concepts to having more concepts. The goal of generation is for a group to gather or create concepts that have not yet been considered by the group. Brainstorming is an example of a generation process.

- **Reduce:** To move from having many concepts to having a focus on fewer concepts deemed worthy of further attention. The goal of reduction is for a group to decrease their cognitive load by limiting the number of concepts they must address. Reduction can be achieved, for example, by filtering concepts or abstracting a general concept from multiple specific instances.

- **Clarify:** Moving from less to more shared meaning for the concepts under consideration. This is important because people frequently use the same label for different concepts, and use different labels for the same concepts. People on a team also frequently use labels and concepts that are unfamiliar to others on the team.

- **Organize:** To move from less to more understanding of the relationships among the concepts. The goal of organization is to reduce the effort of a follow-on activity. The group might, for example, organize a mixed list of ideas into a number of categories or arrange them into a hierarchical structure.

- **Evaluate:** To move from less to more understanding of the benefit of concepts toward attaining a goal. The goal of evaluation is to focus a discussion or inform a group's choice based on a judgment of the worth of a set of concepts with respect to a set of task-relevant criteria. For example, an evaluation process may involve having a team use a five-point scale to rate the probability of a security risk, or they may conduct a qualitative analysis of the pros and cons of a proposed security policy.

- **Build consensus:** To move from having more disagreement to having less disagreement among stakeholders on proposed courses of action. The goal of consensus building is to let a group of mission-critical stakeholders arrive at mutually acceptable commitments.

For example, a consensus building process might involve seeking policy agreements that are acceptable to each individual security officer involved in a planning session.

To enable the practitioner to create the relevant patterns of collaboration in a group process, Collaboration Engineering advocates the use of collaboration process design patterns. Design patterns were first proposed by Alexander et al. (1977, p. X) "a pattern describes a problem which occurs over and over again and then describes the core of the solution to that problem, in such a way that you can use this solution a million times over, without ever doing it the same way twice." Collaboration Engineering design patterns, called thinkLets, have the same purpose: to provide proven solutions to recurring collaboration problems in terms of techniques, methods, and tools. They are comprised of best practices for collaborative activities, and coded to enable the rapid development of sophisticated, integrated, multi-layered collaboration processes that can improve the productivity and quality of work life for teams (de Vreede et al., 2006). In short, thinkLets are proven, best facilitation practices. The thinkLets represent everything that a practitioner needs to know to create one repeatable, predictable pattern of collaboration among people working toward a goal. Hence, practitioners can use thinkLets during IRP sessions.

The Collaboration Engineering approach has been studied extensively. Research findings indicate that Collaborative Engineering provide practitioners with facilitation skills to support mission-critical tasks (see e.g., Bragge, Merisalo-Rantanen, & Hallikainen, 2005; Briggs et al., 2003; Briggs et al., 2006a; Fruhling & de Vreede, 2005). Using the Collaboration Engineering approach, a repeatable IRP process can be represented as a logical sequence of patterns of collaboration that are in turn created using the appropriate thinkLets. The following section presents the IRP process that was designed using the Collaboration Engineering approach and illustrates how the stages of IRP line up with the patterns of collaboration and the thinkLets.

A COLLABORATION PROCESS FOR INCIDENT RESPONSE PLANNING

The design for the collaborative IRP combines the logical activities in the planning process with the patterns of collaboration and the recommended thinkLets that can be used to create these patterns. A process model representing the logical flow of the process is depicted in Figure 1.

The process model consists of three elements; activities, decisions, and flows. An activity is represented by a rounded rectangle listing the activity name, the pattern of collaboration it aims to create, and the thinkLet that is used for that purpose. A decision is represented by a circle. Arrows represent the flow direction. An arrow can have a label if it is linked to a specific decision outcome. Table 1 summarizes the process

design in terms of the activities necessary for: (a) coming up with an IRP; (b) the deliverables from each activity that is carried out; (c) the patterns of collaboration for each activity, and (d) the related thinkLets. The following subsections discuss each activity in more detail.

Activity 1: Agree on Taxonomy of Incidents

The design process starts by presenting the participants with the taxonomy of incident types that the plan will consider. This taxonomy lists and defines each type of incident that falls within the scope of the plan (or within the scope of the workshop if the plan is to be created in a series of workshops). An incident response taxonomy is, for example, the types of hacker attacks or computer viruses for which a standard response has to be defined. It is important that each participant understands and accepts this taxonomy as it forms the basis for all subsequent group activities. Therefore, the pattern of collaboration that

Figure 1. Process model of the collaborative incident response planning process

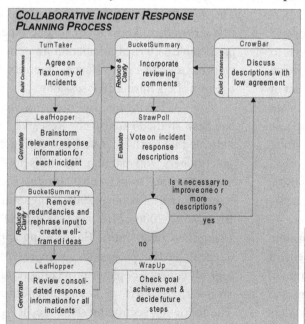

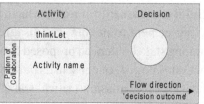

Table 1. Process design

Activity	Deliverables	Pattern of Collaboration	thinkLets
1. Agree on the taxonomy of incidents	Consensus on the list and definitions of incidents	Build Consensus	TurnTaker
2. Brainstorm relevant response information for each incident: a) Course of action b) Team member responsibilities c) Documentation	Information to be considered in each of the response categories	Generate	LeafHopper
3. Clean up the response information in each category	Non-redundant and well-framed ideas in each category	Reduce & Clarify	BucketSummary
4. Review consolidated response information	Reviewed list of incident categories by all session participants	Generate	LeafHopper
5. Incorporate reviewing comments	Categories with feedback incorporated	Reduce & Clarify	BucketSummary
6. Vote on incident response descriptions	An assessment of the acceptability of the response descriptions for all incidents	Evaluate	StrawPoll
7. Discuss incident response descriptions that have low agreement. Continue with step 5 for relevant incidents	A deeper understanding of the reasons why certain description are not yet acceptable	Build Consensus	CrowBar
8. Wrap-up			

the security practitioner has to create is building consensus. The thinkLet employed to accomplish this is called TurnTaker.

TurnTaker is a simple discussion technique. It allows the participants to verbally raise questions or express reservations regarding the concepts on the table. For the IRP workshop, the practitioner instructs the participants as follows: "Please raise your hand if you see any incident for which you do not understand the definition, any incident that is missing from the taxonomy, or any incident that you think falls outside of the scope of this workshop." Each issue that is raised is discussed by the group. This discussion may result in a refinement of the incident definition or the inclusion or exclusion of certain incidents. To make this activity more efficient, the practitioner can circulate the proposed incident taxonomy among the participants before the workshop starts.

Activity 2: Brainstorm Relevant Response Information for Each Incident

The second activity in the process aims to collect relevant response information for each incident that needs to be included in the IRP. To this end, the group needs to perform a pattern of collaboration; in other words, they need to engage in a brainstorming session to generate response information for each incident. To focus this brainstorming activity, the participants are presented with three response information categories for each incident: (1) course of action (i.e., what are the recommended actions that need to be taken once the incident is reported), (2) team member responsibilities (i.e., which members of the security team need to fulfill which responsibilities), and (3) documentation (i.e., what relevant information needs to be recorded each time an incident occurs).

This brainstorming activity is supported with the LeafHopper thinkLet. This technique is useful for groups to brainstorm on a number of topics simultaneously when (a) it is not critical that each participant contributes to each topic or (b) not every participant has sufficient knowledge to contribute to all topics. The security planning practitioner will instruct the participants as follows: "Please contribute relevant response information to the incidents in the taxonomy. You can add response information regarding courses of action, responsibilities of the security team members, and documentation requirements. Please start adding your ideas to the incidents that you know most about or consider most important. Once you are done there, you can add information to other incidents. It is not required to contribute information to all incidents. As a group we will cover all incidents, but as an individual you should first focus on the incidents that you care about most." During the execution of the LeafHopper thinkLet the practitioner can keep an eye on the spread of contributions over the various incidents. If some incidents do not receive any attention, the practitioner/facilitator can redirect the focus of some participants.

Activity 3: Clean Up the Response Information in Each Category

Once the brainstorming activity is over, the group will have to process the results. It is very likely that the response information for each incident contains contributions that are overlapping, poorly formulated, or unclear. The purpose of the third activity in the planning process is to clean up the results so there is a concise description of relevant response information for each incident. This activity requires the group to go through the brainstormed ideas and both reduce and clarify them. With these patterns of collaboration, superfluous information has to be removed and related information has to be combined. The end result of this activity is to arrive at a draft description of the relevant response information that can be included almost verbatim in the final IRP. Table 2 shows an example that can be given to participants as a sample of the expected outcome from this activity.

The thinkLet that the practitioner can use to support this activity is the BucketSummary. With this thinkLet, the practitioner will ask a single participant to clean up the information in one or more incident types and consolidate it into useful response guidelines. Alternatively, the practitioner may request pairs of participants to work together on this activity, which usually yields better results. The instructions given by the practitioner are as follows: "Please consolidate the information for each of the incidents you are assigned. The purpose of this activity is to arrive at a clear and concise description of relevant response information for each incident. The quality of this description has to be such that it can be included in our final response plan. To this end, you can edit, combine, or delete information. Make sure that your final

Table 2. Course of action (COA) clean up example for tornado warnings

Original	Updated
COA for Tornado Warning	COA for Tornado Warning
• Evacuate people to shelters • Sound alarm • Lock doors & windows • Keep people away from windows • People should not panic	At the time of a tornado warning it is imperative to first sound an alarm and start evacuating people in the building to tornado-safe areas. It is also necessary to lock all windows and doors and most importantly keep people from panicking and becoming chaotic.

consolidated text reflects the original ideas and can easily be understood by your team members." This activity can be further clarified by showing an example of an 'acceptable description.' Normally, this activity takes about twice as much time as the brainstorming activity that was used to generate the initial response ideas.

Activity 4: Review Consolidated Response Information

After the participants have produced a consolidated description of the responses for each incident, the next activity includes a peer review of the resulting descriptions. If participants have any issue with the description, a comment should be added to the description. Hence, as needed, the participants generate comments during the peer review for each description. The thinkLet they use for this activity is the LeafHopper. Similar to Activity 2, which uses the same thinkLet, the participants can decide themselves which part of the incident taxonomy they want to review first. The practitioner will start this activity as follows: "Please read the consolidated descriptions that have been created. If you feel any modifications or corrections are required, submit a comment to that description. Start reading the response descriptions for the incidents that you care most about or know most about. Everyone will work in parallel so that we can review all descriptions expeditiously. Please make sure that your reviewing comments are clear and actionable so that the authors of the description can use your feedback to improve it."

Activity 5: Incorporate Reviewing Comments

After all reviewing comments have been collected; the authors of the consolidated response descriptions must revise their descriptions based on the feedback received. In this activity, the participants go through an additional reduce and clarify pattern of collaboration. They read the reviewing comments from their colleagues and modify their response descriptions. The thinkLet used for this activity is the same as for Activity 3: BucketSummary. The practitioner instructs the group as follows: "Please read through the comments your colleagues may have left for you regarding your initial description. Use the reviewing comments to improve your description."

Activity 6: Vote on Incident Response Descriptions

Once the response descriptions for each incident have been revised, the group is ready to take a formal vote on the acceptability of the incident response information for inclusion in the IRP. To perform this evaluate pattern of collaboration, the participants are presented with a voting list of all response descriptions. For every description each participant can vote "Yes" or "No" in response to the question: "Is this description acceptable for inclusion in the IRP?"

This activity of voting translates into an evaluation pattern of collaboration. The related thinkLet in this case is StrawPoll. This thinkLet allows participants to obtain a feeling of the group by casting votes. As a result, the StrawPoll outputs include a tabular and graphical display of the patterns of consensus in the group. Each participant is given a ballot sheet, and asked to read through all the incident categories and record their vote as either a "Yes," suggesting the category is adequately covered, or a "No," suggesting the category is not adequately covered. The voting ballot sheet also has space provided to allow participants to jot down any notes as they read through each incident category for further discussion at a later time. Once each participant has completed reviewing all incident categories, the group is then asked to cast their votes.

Activity 7: Discuss Incident Response Descriptions That Have Low Agreement

Once the votes have been cast, the group needs to take a closer look at the incidents where agreement was low. Therefore, the pattern of collaboration that the security practitioner has to create is building consensus, which is the same as Activity 1. In this activity the thinkLet to accomplish this pattern is called CrowBar. CrowBar allows the group to address the reasons for a lack of consensus on certain issues. This thinkLet enables the participants to engage in a structured discussion of the items that showed the highest percentage of disagreement over the set of scores. The key output from the Crowbar thinkLet is a shared understanding of the reasons disagreement within the group. The security planning practitioner will instruct the participants as follows: "It looks like we have some disagreement on adequately covering one particular incident. Let's go back to Activity 5 and look at it. Would anyone like to comment on why someone would not consider this list complete?" Once this discussion has taken place the practitioner can say: "Let us do a revote on this issue."

Activity 8: Wrap Up

Once all the descriptions have an adequate agreement, the final activity is to wrap up the group work. In this activity the practitioner lets the group know that initial goal of developing an IRP has been successfully achieved.

APPLICATION EXPERIENCES

As aforementioned, the collaborative process design was tested in three cases. The nature of the participants in terms of their background, knowledge and expertise differed among the three cases. The first case included 17 students, including 16 males and one female, enrolled in an undergraduate level information security course. The second case involved ten students, including eight males and two females, enrolled in a graduate level information security course. The final case included a combination of eight computer professionals and information systems professors, including seven males and one female. In all cases the workshop participants had minimal background with technology supported collaboration processes. Each workshop lasted an hour and a half.

For each case the meetings had two participant goals. The primary goal for the meeting participants was to experience how teams come together in order to build an IRP. The secondary goal for the meeting participants was to see how a Group Support System (GSS), a specific collaboration technology can be used to accomplish the main goal. GSS offer a group the ability to work on a shared product in parallel and anonymously. Research suggests that, under certain circumstances, GSS can improve a group's productivity and satisfaction (see e.g., Dennis & Wixom, 2002; Fjermestad & Hiltz, 1998/1999; Fjermestad & Hiltz, 2000/2001; Nunamaker Jr., Briggs, Mittleman, Vogel, & Balthazard, 1997). For Collaboration Engineering efforts GSS has often been the technology of choice to implement the thinkLets that constitute the repeatable collaboration process (see e.g., Bragge et al., 2005; de Vreede et al., 2006; Fruhling & de Vreede, 2005). In our study, we use a specific GSS, *GroupSystems™*, due to easy access by the researchers. However, various other GSS are available in the marketplace with different pricing, equipment, and training options for practitioners to choose from. The purpose of the workshops from the researcher's perspective was to design and evaluate a collaborative enterprise security planning process that is repeatable, predictable and can be executed by practitioners. In each of the three cases, the facilitator was a novice, first-time facilitator. This use of inexperienced facilitators supports the idea that security managers who are also novices could be used as facilitators.

Data was collected through direct observation, online feedback, session data, and informal interviews in order to assess the usefulness of the collaborative process. We then analyzed the process along four constructs including 1) productivity, 2) efficiency, 3) effectiveness, and 4) user satisfaction.

We define productivity as the outcomes achieved in relation to the resources used in a collaborative process in order to arrive at satisfactory results. To measure group productivity, we used the number of total contributions from participants and the uniqueness of these contributions. What we found in terms of productivity was that despite the limited time of 15 to 25 minutes given to each activity, the number of total and unique contributions was substantial and therefore we can conclude that the participants were productive.

In terms of efficiency, we looked at the perceived gain in the collaboration process' efficiency, which we define as the degree to which there is perceived savings of the amount of resources available for attainment of the goal. To measure this construct, we determined how well participants understood the process/task and could easily execute it with minimum effort and time. Our observations in relation to efficiency conclude that the process was fairly efficient. For example, we had about 100 contributions after about 15 minutes in one of the workshops. As aforementioned, in total, it took the participants about an hour and a half in each workshop to execute the process.

In terms of effectiveness we were concerned with the perceived gain in collaboration process' effectiveness which we define as the extent to which participants meet the process goal. To measure this construct, the quality of results in a traditional way of doing things versus quality of results in a new way of doing the same things was established. Specifically, we measured the extent to which participants met the process goal

and from the researcher/developer perspective, the participants managed to arrive at satisfactory results and informal interviews with experts regarding the process outcome showed that the results were satisfactory as well.

Finally, we define satisfaction an affective response with respect to the attainment of goals. In order to judge satisfaction levels, that is, groups' satisfaction of the process outcomes and the process, we determined the extent to which participants arrived at satisfactory results. In order to judge the participants' satisfaction with the process and its outcomes, the General Meeting Assessment Survey questionnaire (Briggs, Reinig, & de Vreede, 2006b) was used. This tool uses 7-point Likert scale questions, ranging from strongly disagree to strongly agree. Based on the survey data and the feedback received, the participants were undoubtedly satisfied and found the workshops to be useful. Additionally, from the researcher/developer perspective, the participants seemed very comfortable with the technology, which made execution easy.

Overall, the case results suggest that the concept of a collaborative IRP process worked. In each of the three cases the groups were able to develop an effective IRP. An example from the third case is included in Appendix A to illustrate this point. Furthermore, we received positive responses from the participants in terms of satisfaction with the process, satisfaction with the outcome and group productivity. Specifically, participants from case 3 made the following comments in relation to what they liked about the process: *"collecting expertise from multiple participants," "using the technology," "it made us sit down and think about the incidents," "anonymity. open forum," "could be iterative to develop other similar plans,"* and *"interesting method for gathering info from a large group of people without participants being interrupted in the process."* These findings are significant for future research in both the areas of IRP and Collaboration Engineering.

FUTURE TRENDS AND RESEARCH ISSUES

In terms of future trends and research issues, the application experiences of this process open various avenues for future research. For example, there are many opportunities to expand and refine this work. First of all, there is a need to determine which thinkLets are the most effective for developing an IRP as well as which order the thinkLets should be in to result in the most efficient use of time and resources. Additionally, while the previous sections present a specific process to address IRP development, there are still several aspects of collaborative security planning that need more study. For example, in terms of future trends, research should address all areas of IT contingency planning, including BIA, BCP, and DRP (Swanson et al., 2002). Because IRP is a part of a larger picture of IT comprehensive contingency planning efforts, the development of collaboration processes in each area may be beneficial. Finally, the idea of using Collaboration Engineering to develop a complete and comprehensive security process that includes such things as vulnerability assessment, BIA, IRP, BCP, and DRP would be another big step in expanding this area. Ultimately, we hope that the process design presented in this chapter ignites a stream of research that needs to be conducted in the enterprise security arena to come up with an all-encompassing collaborative process that will cater to all types of security planning procedures.

CONCLUSION

This chapter has taken a first step toward linking IRP and Collaboration Engineering. Based on the background of IRP and Collaboration Engineering a collaboration process for IRP has been designed. This chapter has described the process in detail and highlighted research results obtained during initial applications of the process.

There are a number of reasons that necessitate firms to have an IRP in place. These include minimizing the impact of a disruptive event, allowing key business processes to move forward in a timely fashion, and to restore normal operations as quickly and as efficiently as possible. Current literature, however, does not provide a process which practitioners can use to develop a plan unique to their needs. The aim of this chapter was to present such a process with the use of Collaboration Engineering. At a high level this process provides value for a number of reasons. First, Collaboration Engineering benefits organizational security stakeholders through designing collaborative IRPs to achieve high-value, yet deploying those designs for incident response practitioners to execute for themselves without ongoing support from professional facilitators (de Vreede & Briggs, 2005). Secondly, Collaboration Engineering focuses on high-value tasks and organizations can derive benefit from improvements to their highest-value tasks (in this case, collaborative IRP) than from improvements to their lower-value tasks (Briggs et al., 2006a). Thirdly, creating IRPs is collaborative work, which may require external support from professional facilitators, and yet they are expensive. Collaboration Engineering seeks to bring the value of facilitated interventions to people who do not have access to facilitation (Briggs et al., 2003). Better still, the designs of recurring processes (i.e., designs of collaborative IRPs) create intellectual capital for organizations (de Vreede & Briggs, 2005). Lastly, when the incident response team collaborates, they strengthen the quality of the plans through having more people "double" checking the results.

REFERENCES

Alexander, C., Ishikawa, S., Silverstein, M., Jacobson, M., Fiksdahl-King, I., & Angel, S. (1977). *A Pattern Language*. Oxford University Press.

Bragge, J., Merisalo-Rantanen, H., & Hallikainen, P. (2005). Gathering Innovative End-User Feedback for Continuous Development of Information Systems: A Repeatable and Transferable E-Collaboration Process. *IEEE Transactions on Professional Communication, 48,* 55-67.

Briggs, R. O., de Vreede, G.-J., & Nunamaker Jr., J. F. (2003). Collaboration engineering with thinkLets to pursue sustained success with group support systems. *Journal of Management Information Systems, 19*(4), 31-64.

Briggs, R. O., Kolfschoten, G. L., de Vreede, G.-J., & Dean, D. L. (2006a, August 4-6). *Defining key concepts for collaboration engineering.* Proceedings of the 12th Americas Conference on Information Systems (AMCIS-12), Acapulco, Mexico

Briggs, R. O., Reinig, B. A., & de Vreede, G.-J. (2006b). Meeting satisfaction for technology-supported groups: An empirical validation of a goal-attainment model. *Small Group Research, 37*(6), 585-611.

de Vreede, G.-J., & Briggs, R. O. (2005). *Collaboration engineering: Designing repeatable processes for high-value collaborative tasks.* Proceedings of the 38th Annual Hawaii International Conference on Systems Science, Los Alamitos.

de Vreede, G. J., Koneri, P. G., Dean, D. L., Fruhling, A. L., & Wolcott, P. (2006). Collaborative Software Code Inspection: The Design and Evaluation of a Repeatable Collaborative Process in the Field. *International Journal of Cooperative Information Systems, 15*(2).

Dennis, A. R., & Wixom, B. H. (2002). Investigating the Moderators of the Group Support Systems Use with Meta-Analysis. *Journal of Management Information Systems, 18*(3), 235-257.

Fjermestad, J., & Hiltz, S. R. (1998/1999). An assessment of group support systems experimental research: Methodology and results. *Journal of Management Information Systems, 15*(3), 7-149.

Fjermestad, J., & Hiltz, S. R. (2000/2001). Group Support Systems: A Descriptive Evaluation of Case and Field Studies. *Journal of Management Information Systems, 17*(3), 115-159.

Foix, R. (2004). Expanding responsibility for incident response. *Computerworld, 38*(40), 28.

Fruhling, A. L., & de Vreede, G.-J. (2005). Collaborative Usability Testing to Facilitate Stakeholder Involvement. In S. Biffl, A. Aurum, B. Boehm, H. Erdogmus & P. Grünbacher (Eds.), *Value Based Software Engineering* (pp. 201-223). Berlin: Springer-Verlag.

Jones, K. (2001, November). Incident Response: Performing Investigations on a Live Host. *The Magazine of Usenix & Sage, 26.*

Nunamaker Jr., J. F., Briggs, R. O., Mittleman, D. D., Vogel, D. R., & Balthazard, P. A. (1997). Lessons from a Dozen Years of Group Support Systems Research: A Discussion of Lab and Field Findings. *Journal of Management Information Systems, 13*(3), 163-207.

Poindexter, D., & St. Laurent, N. (2000). Incident handling at BMDO. *The Information Warfare Site (IWS)* Retrieved October 19, 2006, from http://www.iwar.org.uk/comsec/resources/fasp/BMDOIncHandling.htm

Sausner, R. (2007). There's No Substitute For Good Preparation. *Bank Technology News, 20,* 32.

Soper, T. (2003). *Incident response: Managing security at Microsoft*: Microsoft Technical White Paper.

Swanson, M., Wohl, A., Pope, L., Grance, T., Hash, J., & Thomas, R. (2002). *Contingency Planning Guide for Information Technology Systems.* Washington: National Institute of Standards and Technology

Wack, J. P. (1991). *Establishing a computer security incident response capability.* Gaithersburg, Md: US National Institute of Standards and Technology.

KEY TERMS

Collaboration Engineering: An approach for the design and deployment of collaborative technologies and collaborative processes to support mission-critical tasks (Briggs et al., 2003)

Computer Security Incidents: Any adverse event whereby some aspect of computer security could be threatened; loss of data confidentiality, disruption of data or system integrity, or disruption or denial of availability (Wack, 1991)

Computer Security Incident Response Teams (CSIRTS): Teams that collect all documentation related to any incident occurring in the organization and work together to develop the Incident Response Plan.

E-Business: Organizations that connect their information systems and networks to the outside world.

Incident Response Plan: The documentation or plan which is the outcome or deliverable of incident response planning completed by the computer security incident response team. This documentation could be a text file, a piece of scratch paper, index cards, spreadsheets, databases, and pre-made forms.

Incident Response Planning: The planning process associated with identification, classification, response, and recovery from an incident (Poindexter & St. Laurent, 2000)

Pattern of Collaboration: "The nature of a group's collaborative process when observed over a period of time as they move from a starting state to some end state" (Briggs et al., 2006a).

Practitioner: A domain expert in the area that the collaboration process supports (e.g., security), but not a group dynamics expert or facilitator.

thinkLets: A repeatable collaboration activity that can predictably move a group toward a goal (de Vreede et al., 2006).

APPENDIX A: CASE 3 INITIAL BRAINSTORMING IDEAS AND RESULTING COURSE OF ACTION SECTION OF THE FINAL IRP

Original	Updated
Original COA for Virus Incidents & Worms • At this moment system may generate high traffic and causing bottom neck of the system. It may generate lots of email so that it infects other computers. • Use antivirus vendor and other public sources to determine likely infection and its attributes. • Capture observed state of protective/detective mechanisms (host, gateway, etc). • Using pre-defined template, prepare recovery plan. • Recover the infected system to known good system state. • Identify and make necessary changes to protective mechanisms. • At current state usually system may causes lots network traffic may cause bottomneck (bottleneck?) on the switch. It may be generating lots of emails. • Usually windows computer are more effective with virus. The software we used is MacAfee. • Verify that the antivirus definitions are up-to-date, likely do this out of band from the infected machine • Depend upon the virus the first step is disconnect the computer from the network. Run at least to antivirus software on the safe mode.	**Updated** COA for Virus Incidents & Worms First step is to disconnect the infected host from LAN/WAN to prevent propagation. Second step is to capture system state and observed symptoms. This includes: (1) User-observed symptoms in timeline context (what happened when in connection to what activities); (2) Host system state (O/S version, patches, registry/config-files, ect); antivirus version and signatures); and (3) Network/gateway logs (traffic logs, etc.). This may include scanning the system with other antivirus products and/or updated signatures. Third step: Use the results of step 2 and external sources (like AV vendor, CERT, etc) to characterize the virus/worm/Trojan and its attributes (including recovery methods). Fourth step: Prepare to recover the infected host. This uses pre-determined checklists/templates. Fifth step: Recover the infected host to known good state. Sixth step: Update protective/detective mechanisms at host, antivirus gateway, firewall, ISP filters, etc.. Seventh step: Restore service, including network connectivity, to recovered host. Note: If infection is novel (e.g., 0-day), may need to recreate vulnerable state on a test bed host to determine effectiveness of protective/detective updates before connecting operational hosts to network.
Original COA for Trojan Horses • Same framework specified for virus/worm. • The assumption is you have validated that you have a Trojan horse on the workstation. A couple of things need to happen. The action is somewhat dependant on the evidence at hand. • First you need to accurately determine the program(s) that contain the Trojan horse. This will be easy to hard depending on the basis for the "discovery" of the Trojan horse. If the Trojan horse is discovered or revealed form external sources - the Reader Rabbit - model then it should be a straight forward activity to remove the program from the computer. That activity will be somewhat limited - could be limited - by the degree of dependence you have on that program. If the dependence is minimal then the program could be de-installed and for the incident you are done. If the program is essential, then de-installing and stop will not be a option. For the critical app, you will have to acquire a known clean copy of the program and install it when you de-install the trojaned version. It is likely that you will not - quickly - be able to acquire the clean copy. In that case you might be forced to continue using the trojaned program and take separate action to confine the action of the hidden malware. That, of course depends on your understanding of the actions of the malware component of the Trojan horse. Let's assume the application is critical, and you don't actually know what the malware does and you have no timely way to discover the malware actions. You then must try to isolate the actions of the machine, independently check the output of the program (essentially no trust the program actions and output (all of them)), make a very aggressive effort to acquire the clean version of the code, warn all constituents who might be effected with the output program • replace the first	**Updated** COA for Trojan Horses Same framework specified for virus/worm with the additional tasks of: (1) Identifying what useful function the user perceived from the Trojan (what loss of functionality is associated with the deletion of the Trojan); and (2) Reevaluating trust in other programs from the same source. As necessary, update security awareness training.

Original	Updated
COA for Rootkits	COA for Rootkits
• First I would clarify the definition such that the computer does not "fail" • Determine that the system's problem is root kit-based. • need to identify root kits • Attempt to determine what the system may be infected with. • determine type of root kit • Need to determine if this is an isolated event; e.g., are there others with the same symptoms? • Isolate the system from the network, if it is attached to one. • Obtain logs from surrounding devices • Start a physical log at time of incident. manually logging things like POC's, timelines, first responder, actions taken, individuals notified, etc, etc • Follow the published, upper management approved and possibly industry / government certified incident response plan • Gather logs of the system involved; e.g., system, application, network, etc, save these someplace safe/offline (preferably burned to a CD/DVD) • Determine if the system has been patched properly, check for system updates. • Identify a chain of command for notification and response • Determine classification of the information on the system • Determine if the system had a virus scanner online and running at the time of incident, is it still running? Was it updated? Did it miss the root kit? • Should a virus scanner detect a root kit? • Detail a "chain of custody" for any forensic evidence • Determine impact to company / mission (public face, monetary loss, leaked information, lower assurance of information still on the system)	Follow the published, upper management approved and possibly industry / government certified incident response plan - identify a chain of command for notification and response Start a physical log at time of incident. manually logging things like POC's, timelines, first responder, actions taken, individuals notified, etc, etc - detail a "chain of custody" for any forensic evidence Determine if the system had a virus scanner online and running at the time of incident, is it still running? Was it updated? Did it miss the root kit? - should a virus scanner detect a root kit? Gather logs of the system involved; e.g., system, application, network, etc, save these someplace safe/offline (preferably burned to a CD/DVD) - obtain logs from surrounding devices - Isolate the system from the network, if it is attached to one. Contingency - depends on specifics of incident Determine that the system's problem is root kit-based. Attempt to determine what the system may be infected with. Determine type of root kit - need to identify root kits Need to determine if this is an isolated event; e.g., are there others with the same symptoms? Determine if the system has been patched properly, check for system updates. Determine impact to company / mission (public face, monetary loss, leaked information, lower assurance of information still on the system) - determine classification of the information on the system Are current procedures in place? If yes, then were they followed? If not, where can you get some to aid in future events (it will happen again)?
Original COA for Denial of Service (DOS) attacks	**Updated** COA for Denial of Service (DOS) attacks
• Identify it as a denial of service • Determine if safeguards have been placed in effect • Identify what assets are being affected • Determine where the source of the DoS is • Determine who are the primary/secondary contacts of assets • Is there an IRP plan available to execute • Are their immediate measures that can be taken to eliminate or reduce the impact of the DoS? • Assign one lead as the primary team lead on the incident that is responsible for making all final decisions. • Determine how to get servers back on line • Capture and backup any logs that maybe relevant • Determine level of impact.	1. The assigned lead is responsible for executing IRP plan if it exists. The assigned lead will be the primary contact for all steps involved in this incident and will coordinate all activities with the primary/secondary assets owners. 2. Identify what assets are being affected and what is causing the problems. Is it a DoS? If it is a DoS, then determine the level of impact. The level of impact will determine the response to the incident. 3. Determine where the source of the DoS is coming from and if there are immediate measures that can be taken to reduce or eliminate the DoS impact. Block the source of the attack, get systems back online and backup any relevant system logs.
Original COA for Spyware & Adware Incident	**Updated** COA for Spyware & Adware Incident
• Determine whether or not you have a spam blocker installed on your browser • Run a series of programs to removed spyware and adware • Install adware personal • Review the cookies on the machine and determine whether they are necessary or NOT • May have to review the registry for unknown entries from a program • Blocking of programs through firewalls or other programs • Determine the level of criticality of the asset involved. • Is their confidential information stored on this asset? • Assign primary forensics lead • Use software tools to remove spyware • Determine the level of threat and maliciousness	Assign the primary lead for incident responses, including forensics. Determine the level of criticality and threat. Install appropriate software to block and remove threat. Apply privacy and malicious software policies. If confidential information is stored on this asset, contact appropriate data stewards.

Chapter XIII
Pandemic Influenza, Worker Absenteeism and Impacts on Critical Infrastructures:
Freight Transportation as an Illustration

Dean A. Jones
Sandia National Laboratories, USA

Linda K. Nozick
Cornell University, USA

Mark A. Turnquist
Cornell University, USA

William J. Sawaya
Texas A&M University, USA

ABSTRACT

A pandemic influenza outbreak could cause serious disruption to operations of several critical infrastructures as a result of worker absenteeism. This chapter focuses on freight transportation services, particularly rail and port operations, as an illustration of analyzing performance of critical infrastructures under reduced labor availability. It develops models to assess the likely impacts of varying levels of worker absenteeism on the capacity of these critical systems. Using current data on performance of specific rail and port facilities, we reach some conclusions about the likelihood of severe operational disruption under varying assumptions about the absentee rate. Other infrastructures that are more dependent on information technology and less labor-intensive than transportation might respond to large-scale worker absenteeism in different ways, but the general character of this analysis can be adapted for application in other infrastructures.

INTRODUCTION

Influenza viruses have presented a threat to the health of animal and human populations for centuries. Pandemics occur when a new strain of influenza virus emerges, and develops the ability to infect and be passed between humans. Because humans have little immunity to the new virus, a worldwide epidemic, or pandemic, can ensue.

In 1997, the H5N1 influenza virus emerged in chickens in Hong Kong. The virus has shown the ability to infect multiple species, including migratory birds, pigs, cats and humans (World Health Organization, 2008). While it is impossible to predict whether the H5N1 virus will lead to a pandemic, history suggests that a new influenza virus will emerge at some point and spread quickly through an unprotected human population. The impact of a pandemic is likely to be pervasive, removing essential personnel from the workplace for extended periods. This has significant ramifications for the economy, national security, and the basic functioning of society.

An area of particular concern is the potential effects of worker absenteeism on the functioning of critical infrastructures in our society. In 1997, the report of the U.S. President's Commission on Critical Infrastructure Protection identified eight critical infrastructures, including telecommunications, electric power, oil and natural gas, banking and finance, transportation, water supply, government services and emergency services (President's Commission on Critical Infrastructure Protection, 1997). In subsequent years, this list of critical infrastructures has been expanded and now includes a set of 17 critical infrastructures / key resources (CI/KR) identified in the National Infrastructure Protection Plan (U.S. Department of Homeland Security, 2006).

An important part of government planning for the possibility of a pandemic influenza episode is to understand the potential impacts on the functioning of critical infrastructures. This portion of the government's role in creating a pandemic influenza response plan is part of the homeland security mission. The National Infrastructure Protection Plan lays out an integrated view of physical, cyber and human resources, with a series of iterative activities designed to enhance protection of CI/KR, as illustrated in Figure 1. The volume of which this chapter is a part is focused on cyber security, but a broad view of cyber security should include consideration of the interactions among human and cyber resources, in particular the possible effects of large-scale worker absenteeism resulting from a pandemic event.

The work described here is not focused directly on the cyber infrastructure. It focuses instead on another critical infrastructure – freight transportation. Provision of transportation services is much more labor-intensive than provision of cyber services and one might reasonably question the applicability of this analysis to cyber security concerns. We believe there are two good reasons for inclusion of the work in this volume on cyber security, apart from what we hope are interesting implications for worker absenteeism in the freight transportation sector. First, the analysis illustrates a mechanism for focusing attention on parts of a "flow through" system that may create critical bottlenecks if insufficient resources (in this case, labor) are available. The units of flow through the freight transportation network are containers and railcars, rather than information packets, but the core concepts are transferrable between transportation networks and information networks. Second, the primary focus is on delays and congestion associated with the bottlenecks. This concept of service degradation is also transferrable to information networks. Thus, rather than providing results that are directly reflective of cyber network concerns, this analysis should be viewed as an illustration of an approach that has implications for analysis of cyber systems.

Within the transportation infrastructure, we've chosen to focus on freight services because the demand for freight movements is unlikely to fall very much during a pandemic episode – the basic

Figure 1. Integrated view of physical, cyber and human resources for infrastructure protection (source: U.S. Department of Homeland Security, 2006)

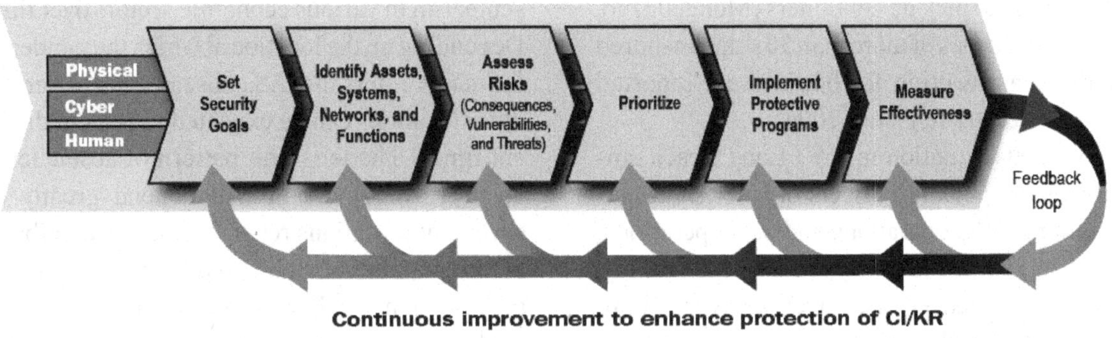

Continuous improvement to enhance protection of CI/KR

needs of people for food and a wide variety of other consumer goods will continue, and this drives movements of all types of materials through the transportation system. Some purchases of consumer durables may be postponed, leading to a slowdown in some parts of related supply chains, but on the whole, the demand for freight movement is likely to change relatively little. Thus, the reduction in capacity resulting from workforce absenteeism may create large disruptions.

Some freight operations are likely to be more susceptible than others. For example, inland waterway (barge) operations are relatively unlikely to suffer serious operational problems, since they are not labor intensive and the barge tow crews are relatively isolated from contact with large numbers of infectious people.

The trucking industry is relatively labor-intensive, but in general the relative isolation of over-the-road drivers may produce a lower infection rate and less absenteeism in this sector than in other parts of the transportation industry. On the whole, we have concluded that the effects in trucking will be "spotty" rather than systemic, and we have chosen to focus our analysis efforts on two other areas where substantial effects of absenteeism are most likely. In this paper, we focus particularly on railroads and container port operations. Both of these portions of the transportation industry are heavily unionized and employees have very specialized skills, making it difficult

to adjust to absenteeism by reallocating people to different tasks. Furthermore, the concentrations of employment in both of these areas are "at the nodes" of the freight system, where substantial numbers of people work in close proximity. This makes it more likely that infections will spread and result in large-scale worker absenteeism.

The effects of insufficient labor that we are analyzing can be illustrated by events at the ports of Los Angeles and Long Beach in 2004. These two ports are operated separately but are physically adjacent. Taken together, they handle about 16 million TEU's (twenty-foot equivalent units) of container traffic per year, and nearly one-half of all U.S. container imports (Port of Long Beach, 2007; Port of Los Angeles, 2007). About 40% of these container imports leave the LA area on intermodal trains operated by the Union Pacific (UP) and the Burlington Northern Santa Fe (BNSF) railroads.

During the summer of 2004, the UP did not have enough trained workers (largely resulting from a change in federal labor law that triggered increased retirements) to handle the level of container traffic coming through Los Angeles / Long Beach and moving east by rail (Machalaba, 2004). The problem was exacerbated by a shortage of longshoremen in the port itself. The rail yards near Los Angeles became clogged; then the congestion reached back into the container storage areas in the port; and eventually ships backed up in the anchorage waiting to unload. By September of that year, truckers were reporting long delays in the terminal to pick up containers (Mongelluzzo, 2004), and queues of more than 30 ships anchored off the coast waiting for berths were reported (*Orange County Register*, 2004).

The 2004 situation in LA / Long Beach emphasizes the potential effects of labor shortages on both railroad operations and port operations, as well as how those two types of operations can be interconnected. For the current analysis, we are concerned with labor shortages that may be caused by pandemic influenza. The period of widespread worker absenteeism in a given location is likely to be of modest duration (a few weeks at most), but the reduction in capacity that results in the transportation sector may create ripples that are felt nationally, and over much longer periods. It is these national-level economic impacts that are of primary concern to the federal government.

The work reported here is related to, although somewhat separate from, the general area of supply chain disruption analysis and management. This is a relatively small, but growing, area of study in the operations management literature. Some recent work in supply chain disruption includes Kleindorfer and Saad (2005), who focus on managing supply chains under risk of disruption; Santoso, *et al.* (2005), who emphasize design of supply chains to better withstand uncertainty; and Blackhurst, *et al.* (2005) who use an empirical survey of companies to understand where important gaps exist in industry's ability to mitigate the effects of disruptions. Our purpose is to assess how localized, but severe, employee absenteeism might affect freight transportation services, in an effort to understand how large a disruption to freight movement might be caused by a pandemic influenza outbreak. However, we are not focused on how the wide variety of shippers might respond to such a disruption in order to mitigate its effects on their own supply chains.

We begin by postulating specific levels of absenteeism. Epidemiological models (e.g., Eubank,

et al., 2004; Ferguson, *et al.*, 2006; Longini, 1988) can be used to estimate likely rates of worker absenteeism in various economic sectors over time. Depending on the location at which the pandemic influenza enters the U.S., absenteeism at various other locations can be expected to peak at different times. The temporal pattern of absenteeism at any given location will depend greatly on several assumptions regarding the susceptibility of the population, transmission parameters for the infection, etc. For the current analysis, we are not focused on the epidemiological modeling, but simply use a series of three scenarios derived from one specific model, corresponding to different levels of peak absenteeism in the transportation sector (5.8%, 13.6% and 28.2%), as shown in Figure 2. This selection of scenarios offers a relatively wide range of possible situations under which to evaluate the performance of sectors of the freight transportation system.

The following two sections describe our analyses of rail and port operations under the various absenteeism scenarios from the epidemiological model and the fourth section of the chapter discusses how these results may relate to other critical infrastructures that are more information-intensive and use labor in a different way. The final section of the chapter offers some general conclusions and suggestions for further research.

ANALYSIS OF RAILROAD OPERATIONS

Portions of the national rail system are operating quite near capacity, and substantial absenteeism would be likely to disrupt freight movements in some important corridors. The major areas where congestion occurs are the large classification yards in the rail network. At these locations, trains are assembled and disassembled, and individual freight cars are sorted as they move through the network. Data in Logan (2006), based on tracing

Figure 2. Possible scenarios for worker absentee rate from epidemiological modeling

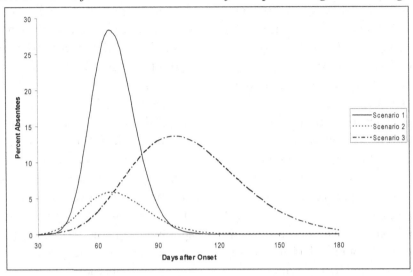

more than 35,000 individual car movement records in 2004, indicate the percentage of total in-transit time that freight cars spend in classification yards. These data are summarized in Figure 3.

Our analysis of the potential effects of absenteeism in the national rail network focuses on 18 of the largest classification yards operated by the four largest Class I railroads. Each of these yards classifies more than 1,200 freight cars daily. Average dwell time statistics for individual yards are reported by the railroads to the Association

of American Railroads (AAR) each week, and published online (Association of American Railroads, 2007). We have used average dwell times published for the month of February 2007 for specific numerical values in this analysis. A different month, or an average over multiple months, could have been used instead, but the values for February 2007 are typical of current operations and the overall conclusions of our analysis are not sensitive to that particular choice.

At each of these major yards, delay functions represent the effects of congestion, and these functions are sensitive to the level of labor present in the yard. A major influenza outbreak and associated absenteeism could cause some of these facilities to be completely overloaded, and some freight traffic normally carried by the railroads could no longer be moved. Identifying when such situations might occur is one of the important elements of the analysis.

Modeling Delay in Rail Classification Yards

Figure 3. Percentage of total in-transit time spent in rail yards (source: Logan, 2006)

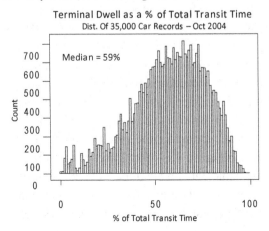

The data from Logan (2006) show that freight cars spend an average of 28.2 hours each yard they pass through, and that 71% of that time (or about 20 hours) is delay waiting for a subsequent operational step. The three largest portions of this delay (comprising about 97% of the total) are waiting for inbound inspection on arrival, waiting to be classified at the "hump" and waiting to be assembled into an outbound train.

In the model developed here, the expected dwell time in a yard for a given car is the sum of three parts: a term (T_1) representing processing time, a delay (T_2) prior to classification (representing waiting for inbound inspection and the hump), and a delay (T_3) waiting for outbound connection. For model calibration, we have used estimated averages of 7 hours, 4 hours and 14 hours, for these three parts, respectively. The sum of these three values is 25 hours, which is consistent with typical reported average yard time values from the railroads (Association of American Railroads, 2007), and their relative values are consistent with the data collected by Logan (2006).

In addition to being dependent on car volume passing through the yard, the elements of dwell time are also sensitive to labor availability. The actual processing steps in car classification within the yard are most directly related to labor availability, so to estimate the effects of absenteeism, we inflate the estimate of 7 hours in direct proportion to the absentee rate. Thus, for example, if the projected absentee rate is 15%, the estimated activity time is $(7)(1.15) = 8.05$ hours. In general:

$$E(T_1) = 7(1 + \beta)\qquad(1)$$

where β is the proportion of workers absent in a given scenario being analyzed. Obviously, equation (1) represents a simple representation of the effects of absentee rate, and should not be used over too wide a range of values for β. For values of β between 0 and 0.3, as used in the analysis here, the simple linear approximation in (1) is likely to be reasonable. However, for much larger values of β (i.e., $\beta \rightarrow 1$), equation (1) would be inadequate because if no people were present, the expected processing time would become infinite. A more complicated version of (1) could have been used, but because additional complication would have little effect over the range of values of β actually used in the analysis, we have opted for simplicity.

The expected delay prior to classification is modeled using a queuing approach, based on previous work by Turnquist & Daskin (1982). Using a bulk-arrival queue, bounds on the expected waiting time for classification can be derived. The difference between these bounds is a factor of two in average waiting time, and as a plausible approximate model, we use a delay time that is halfway between the bounds. This leads to the following expression:

$$E(T_2) = \frac{3(L - 1 + \rho)}{4\mu(1 - \rho)}\qquad(2)$$

where: L = average inbound train length (# cars)

μ = average classification rate (cars/hour)

$\rho = \lambda L/\mu$ (traffic intensity)

λ = average arrival rate of trains (trains/hour).

The quantity λL represents the average flow rate of cars through the yard (measured in cars/hour).

We will assume that the average classification rate depends on the labor available, through a multiplier $\theta(\beta)$ whose value is defined by the relationship shown in Figure 4. Small proportions of absent workers in a yard create a very modest reduction in the service rate, but as the proportion increases the effect is magnified. The function $\theta(\beta)$ is defined for absentee rates up to 0.3 only, because this covers the range to be studied in this analysis. Empirical support for the specific values of $\theta(\beta)$ shown in Figure 4 is quite thin because there is no available data on any recent events of similar character to that being analyzed. The postulated form of $\theta(\beta)$ simply has three linear segments

Pandemic Influenza, Worker Absenteeism and Impacts on Critical Infrastructures

representing increasing marginal reductions of the effective service rate with changes in the absentee rate. This is likely to be the correct general form of the effect, although different specific values could certainly be assumed.

In equation (2), the average classification rate, μ, is replaced by

$$\mu = \mu_0 \theta(\beta) \qquad (3)$$

where μ_0 is the nominal classification rate of a given yard. This change in μ also affects the computation of ρ for a given arrival rate of trains.

A second effect of absenteeism on the classification process is that the average train length is likely to increase. If crews are in short supply, some trains will be cancelled and the ones that run are likely to move more cars, in an effort to maintain overall capacity. We represent the change in average train length as being proportional to the absentee rate, so that L is given by the following expression:

$$L = L_0(1 + \beta) \qquad (4)$$

L_0 is the nominal average train length. For this analysis, we assume $L_0 = 69$ cars, the average train length for the industry as a whole in 2005 (Association of American Railroads, 2006). In the model computations, the input rate to each yard is specified as a number of cars per day (the product

Figure 4. Relation of service rate multiplier to absentee rate

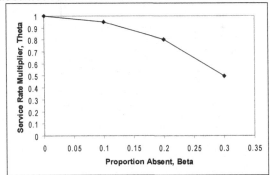

λL in equation (2)), so the effect of the change in L does not directly affect the computation of ρ.

The expected connection delay while cars wait for their outbound connections is determined by the "effective headway" (i.e., time between potential departures) distribution of the outbound connection. We assume a simple discrete distribution based on a "normal" connection to an outbound train that operates once a day. There is a probability, p, that the "effective headway" for a given outbound connection is 48 hours, either because of cancellation of an outbound train, or because of capacity limits that preclude a car from making the first available connection. The remaining probability, $1-p$, is that there is a "normal" 24-hour headway between outbound connections. For this distribution of effective headways, the mean is $E(H) = 24(1 - p) + 48p = 24(1 + p)$ and the variance is $V(H) = 576p(1 - p)$.

When headways between outbound departures are uncertain, the expected waiting time for a car that arrives at a random point in time can be expressed as:

$$E(T_3) = \frac{E(H)}{2} + \frac{V(H)}{2E(H)} \qquad (5)$$

where $E(H)$ and $V(H)$ are the mean and variance of the headway distribution, respectively. This result was first shown in the context of waiting times of passengers at bus stops (Welding, 1957), but the same mathematics can be applied to freight cars in a classification yard.

We can substitute the expressions for $E(H)$ and $V(H)$ for the headway distribution used for the rail yard connections and write the expected connection delay as:

$$E(T_3) = 12\left(\frac{1 + 3p}{1 + p}\right) \qquad (6)$$

With increasing absenteeism, more outbound trains are likely to be cancelled and the probability that an inbound car makes its first scheduled connection decreases (i.e., p increases). A simple reflection of that is the following relationship:

$$p = 0.09 + \beta \qquad (7)$$

The base value of p (0.09) when substituted into (6) results $E(T_3) = 14$ hours. This is the target value based on current observed data. At values of $\beta = 0.1$, 0.2 and 0.3, the values of $E(T_3)$ increase to 15.8 hours, 17.4 hours, and 18.7 hours, respectively.

Substituting (7) into (6), we can rewrite the expression for $E(T_3)$ as:

$$E(T_3) = 12\left(\frac{1.27 + 3\beta}{1.09 + \beta}\right) \qquad (8)$$

Equations (1), (2) and (8) have been used to calibrate overall delay functions for each of the 18 major classification yards at nominal conditions ($\beta = 0$). This calibration has been based on reported average terminal dwell times for February 2007 and reported typical daily classification volumes.

The results of this calibration are summarized in Table 1.

Scenario Analysis

In the lowest impact scenario, absenteeism peaks at 5.8% in the third month after the onset of the pandemic outbreak. Using this 5.8% value as β in equations (1), (3), (4) and (8), we estimate that the effective capacity of the rail yards under consideration will be reduced approximately 3%. Absenteeism also results in additional train cancellations and a modest increase in average train length to 73 cars. If the traffic volume on the rail system is unchanged, the effect of the reduction in yard capacity is to increase the utilization levels of the yards, and hence to increase the delays. In most of the 18 yards analyzed, the increases in average dwell times are between 4 and 17 hours. We could expect origin-destination times for most shipments to increase by 1-3 days, depending on how many yards a specific shipment must pass through. The system-wide average in 2004 was 2.8 reclassifications per shipment (Logan, 2006), so a typical shipment might see an increase in overall travel time of about two days.

Table 1. Estimated characteristics of major rail yards for model calibration

Railyard	Railroad	Reported Average Daily Volume (cars)	Reported Average Dwell Time (hours)	Estimated Base Capacity (cars/day)	Capacity Utilization	Estimated Average Dwell Time (hours)
Argentine-Kansas City, KS	BNSF	1795	29.5	1950	0.92	29.0
Barstow, CA	BNSF	1384	33.5	1480	0.94	33.9
Galesburg, IL	BNSF	1653	40	1720	0.96	39.5
Cincinnati, OH	CSX	1557	32.8	1700	0.92	29.7
Indianapolis, IN	CSX	1494	35.7	1600	0.93	32.7
Nashville, TN	CSX	1695	31	1850	0.92	29.0
Selkirk, NY	CSX	1627	34.4	1750	0.93	31.1
Waycross, GA	CSX	2276	26.8	2500	0.91	26.5
Willard, OH	CSX	1557	36.4	1650	0.94	34.3
Bellevue, OH	NS	N/A	40.4	1500	0.95	38.7
Conway, PA	NS	N/A	28.1	2000	0.91	27.9
Englewood- Houston TX	UP	1500	32.7	1600	0.94	33.4
Fort Worth, TX	UP	1300	37	1380	0.94	36.5
North Platte, NE	UP	2900	30.7	3040	0.95	29.8
North Little Rock, AR	UP	1800	27.6	2000	0.90	27.2
Proviso, Chicago, IL	UP	1600	35.4	1700	0.94	33.4
Roseville, CA	UP	1450	31.1	1600	0.91	29.3
W. Colton, CA	UP	1300	31.1	1450	0.90	29.2

The effects represented in this scenario are noticeable changes in delays for shipments, and the terminals across the rail system would certainly experience an increase in congestion levels, but since the overall duration of the event is limited, this scenario does not create an intolerable level of disruption for the system as a whole.

In the mid-level scenario, absenteeism peaks at 13.6%. The estimated reduction in effective capacity for the major rail yards is approximately 10%, and we might expect the effect of train cancellations to increase the average train length to about 78 cars. If the total volume of shipments is unaffected by absenteeism in other industries, the 10% reduction in effective yard capacity is likely to push all 18 of these major yards to a critical situation, as shown in Table 2. The timing of flu outbreaks will vary at different locations, and not all these points in the national rail network will be severely affected at the same time, but the mid-level scenario is likely to be sufficiently severe to create very substantial problems "rippling" through the rail network.

When the capacity utilization exceeds 1.0, it means that the input rate of cars to be processed every day exceeds the capacity of the yard to handle them, and the delays simply get worse and worse as the days progress. In the terms of the

models used here for analysis, there is no "steady-state" solution at that level of traffic input to the system, and the longer the situation persists, the worse conditions become.

At the level of absenteeism projected in this scenario, it is very likely that shipping and receiving industries that use rail transportation will also be affected, and the level of overall volume being shipped is likely to drop. This may keep the situation in the rail system from becoming as critical as reflected in Table 2, but in this scenario we should expect to see reasonably widespread problems as specific locations are unable to handle volumes coming into them over a 6-8 week period. There are likely to be persistent "waves" of congestion and disruption across the system as various yards become overly congested and adjustments are made, only to move the problem somewhere else. It is also likely that the railroads will embargo shipments to or from areas that are experiencing the worst problems at specific times during the overall event.

In the highest-impact scenario, the peak absentee rate is 28.2%. This absentee rate reduces the effective capacity of the major rail yards by approximately 45%. In the absence of shipment volume reductions, this capacity reduction, combined with train cancellations, reduced maintenance, etc., would likely cause the system to be completely clogged with shipments that are not moving. In this scenario, the demand on the major rail yards is 60-70% above their effective capacity.

Of course, the shipping industries are very likely to be feeling similar absentee rates, and as a result, shipment volumes may be substantially decreased. Nevertheless, at the absentee rates projected in this scenario, there is likely to be an enormous disruption in the rail system over a period of two months or more.

Because the major rail yards considered here are all high-volume facilities that are the focal points in the network, these facilities are likely to experience the congestion worst, but at such a

Table 2. Summary of changes for mid-level absenteeism scenario

Railyard	Railroad	Reported Average Daily Volume (cars)	Nominal Capacity Utilization	Scenario Capacity Utilization
Argentine-Kansas City, KS	BNSF	1795	0.92	1.03
Barstow, CA	BNSF	1384	0.94	1.04
Galesburg, IL	BNSF	1653	0.96	1.07
Cincinnati, OH	CSX	1557	0.92	1.02
Indianapolis, IN	CSX	1494	0.93	1.04
Nashville, TN	CSX	1695	0.92	1.02
Selkirk, NY	CSX	1627	0.93	1.04
Waycross, GA	CSX	2276	0.91	1.02
Willard, OH	CSX	1557	0.94	1.05
Bellevue, OH	NS	N/A	0.95	1.06
Conway, PA	NS	N/A	0.91	1.02
Englewood- Houston TX	UP	1500	0.94	1.05
Fort Worth, TX	UP	1300	0.94	1.05
North Platte, NE	UP	2900	0.95	1.06
North Little Rock, AR	UP	1800	0.90	1.00
Proviso, Chicago, IL	UP	1600	0.94	1.05
Roseville, CA	UP	1450	0.91	1.01
W. Colton, CA	UP	1300	0.90	1.00

high rate of absenteeism over an extended period, the effects will move beyond these major facilities and be felt system-wide.

ANALYSIS OF CONTAINER PORT OPERATIONS

Our approach to analyzing the impact of substantial levels of absenteeism at container ports is to develop a queuing model to represent the process of loading and unloading containers from ships at specific ports. This is an approximation of the true impact of absenteeism because it is limited to dockside activities and therefore does not consider the effects of reductions in capacity caused by absenteeism in the container yards, absenteeism that reduces the ability to transfer containers to and from rail facilities or the impact of reductions in the speed with which truck drivers can pickup and deliver containers to the port. However, dockside operations are frequently a limiting factor in port

throughput and vessel delay represents a critical measure of port performance (Le-Griffin, 2008; Turner, 2000).

The three largest U.S. ports (Los Angeles, Long Beach and New York-New Jersey) handle about 50% of total container traffic (imports and exports) coming through all ports. In 2006, the Port of Los Angeles handled about 8.5 million TEUs (Port of Los Angeles, 2007) and the Port of Long Beach handled about 7.3 million TEUs (Port of Long Beach, 2007). A twenty-foot equivalent unit (TEU) is the standard unit of traffic measurement in container freight shipments. We focus on the Port of Los Angeles to analyze the impacts of substantial absenteeism caused by pandemic influenza on port performance because it is the largest of the seaports and has the best available data. The Port of Los Angeles has 8 terminals operated by various terminal companies. Each terminal has vessel berths, gantry cranes for loading/unloading ships, container yard facilities for staging and storing containers, etc. Different

Table 3. Description of the terminals at the Port of Los Angeles.

Terminal Number	Terminal	Shipping Lines	Number of Cranes	Approximate Number of Vessel Calls in 2005
1	West Basin Container Terminal	China Shipping, Yang Ming, K-Line, Cosco, Hanjin, Sinotrans, Zim	4	*
2	West Basin Container Terminal	China Shipping, Yang Ming, K-Line, Cosco, Hanjin, Sinotrans, Zim	8	*
3	Trans Pacific Container Service Corp.	Mitsui, China Shipping, Norasia, Compania Sudamerica de Vapores, Zim, Wan Hai, APL, Hyundai Merchant Marine Co., CMA-CGM	11	*
4	Port of Los Angeles Container Terminal	N/A	4	75
5	Yusen Terminal	NYK, OOCL, Hapag-Lloyd	10	111
6	Seaside Terminal	Evergreen, Hatsu Marine Ltd., Italia Marittima	8	217
7	APL Terminal/Global Gateway South	APL, Hyundai, MOL, ANZDL, Fresco, HamburgSud, Maersk	12	*
8	APM Terminals/Pier 400	Maersk, Horizon	14	*

* There were 933 total vessel calls among terminals 1, 2, 3, 7 and 8 but because of overlapping usage, data on how many occurred at each terminal individually are unavailable. (Source: Port of Los Angeles, 2007)

sets of ocean carriers have agreements with each terminal operator for use of their facilities. Table 3 summarizes important characteristics of the LA terminals.

The Port of Long Beach is adjacent to the Port of Los Angeles and has 6 terminals. In total, it has the same number of gantry cranes – 71 – as Los Angeles (Port of Long Beach, 2007). Given the similarities in the traffic and terminal capabilities at these two adjacent seaports, we focus on the Port of Los Angeles, with the understanding that similar conclusions are valid for the Port of Long Beach.

The fundamental service process for dockside operations at ports is governed by the rate at which the gantry cranes can unload and then reload the vessels. The key measure of capacity for a crane is the number of lifts per hour (LPH) that it can accomplish. Labor absenteeism reduces the effective capacity of the cranes at dockside. The consequence of reduced effective capacity is increased delay to the vessels, both because unloading and reloading takes longer, and because they must wait longer for an available berth. A reasonable way to represent the impact of absenteeism is to reduce the LPH by the fraction of the workforce that is absent. For example, suppose that a crane under normal operating conditions can lift 25 TEUs per hour, but the absentee rate is 20%. The modified LPH is then 25*(0.8), which equals 20 LPH.

The expected time required to process a ship (i.e., berth the ship, unload the inbound containers, load the outbound containers and have the ship leave the berth) can be estimated based on the total number of inbound and outbound TEUs for that ship (Q), the total number of cranes assigned (N), the processing rate (LPH) of the cranes, the fraction of the containers that are 40 foot containers versus 20 foot containers (ϕ) and the amount of time needed to position the ship at the berth and to move the ship from the berth (τ). The relationship for expected service time, $E[S]$, expressed in hours, is given in equation (9).

$$E[S] = \frac{\left(\dfrac{Q}{1+\phi}\right)}{N * LPH} + \tau \qquad (9)$$

A similar representation of average ship processing time is used by both Turner (2000) and Pachakis & Kiremidjian (2003).

Data for the Port of Los Angeles indicates that about 70% of their containers are 40-foot containers (American Association of Port Authorities, 2007). This statistic is important because it takes about the same amount of time to lift one 20-foot container as to lift one 40-foot container. We assume that the time required to position the ship at the berth and to move it from the berth afterwards is a total of 3 hours. This is consistent with estimates in Turner (2000).

The actual service time for a ship may vary from the value given in equation (9) for a variety of reasons (crane breakdowns, crews not ready on time, other equipment problems, etc.), but the largest source of variation in service times across the processing of many vessels is the variation in the number of TEUs to lift for different ships. We have estimated this variation using data on vessel calls at the Port of Los Angeles for 2005 (U.S. Department of Transportation, 2006).

Using size information for the individual vessels in the Vessel Call data (U.S. Department of Transportation, 2006) and the aggregate number of TEUs handled each month (as reported by the Port), we have estimated the variation in TEUs to lift per ship, and from this, the probability distribution for the service times, using equation (9).

Several previous authors (e.g. Pachakis & Kiremidjian, 2003; Turner, 2000) conclude that the arrival process of ships at seaports can be effectively modeled as a Poisson process where the mean varies by month. We have used this approach, focusing on analysis reflecting both an average month (with approximately 111 vessel arrivals) and a peak month (October).

For a given arrival rate, λ, expressed in vessels/hour, the queuing model formula for the expected vessel time in port, $E[T_p]$, is represented in equation (10) (Nozaki & Ross, 1978) where k is the number of servers, $E[S]$ is the expected service time and $E[S^2]$ is the second moment of the service time, estimated using data on variation in the number of TEUs per ship as indicated before.

To use equation (10) effectively, we must specify the number of servers, k, available to a given stream of arrivals. For the Port of Los Angeles, this means that we need to segregate vessel arrivals by shipping company (or groups of shipping companies), because the ships of a specific company can only use certain terminals, as indicated in Table 3. We note in Table 3 that terminals 4, 5 and 6 can be considered individually, because the set of shipping lines using terminals 5 and 6 is different, and terminal 4 is a common-use terminal. However, terminals 1, 2, 3, 7 and 8 must be considered together because there is overlap in the shipping lines using those terminals and the shipping lines can generally use more than one of those terminals.

In order to calibrate our queuing models of the Port of Los Angeles, we use the Vessel Movement files available from the Maritime Administration (U.S. Department of Transportation, 2007). That dataset records the day of entrance and exit for each vessel call at every U.S. port. The latest year for which that data is available is 2005. Since 2005, all terminals at the Port of Los Angeles have changed to 24 hour-per-day operation, and total volume handled has grown. For analysis of the scenarios, we have used an overall annual demand level of 9.6 million TEUs (slightly above actual reported 2007 volume) and based the terminal service times on 24-hour operation.

Figure 5 summarizes the predicted average vessel times in port for the varying absentee rates represented in the three scenarios of interest – 5.8%, 13.6% and 28.2%. The average time in port with the current volumes and an absentee rate of 0% is also shown for comparison. Terminals other than Terminal 6 could absorb much of the absenteeism associated with the pandemic influenza scenarios. Delays would certainly increase, especially in the 28.3% scenario, where total time in port increases by 40-50% for vessels at most terminals, but if the duration of the events is not excessive, this may be tolerable.

Terminal 6 (the Seaside Terminal, used by Evergreen, Hatsu and Italia Marittima), however, does not have enough capacity to accommodate the high level of absenteeism associated with the 28.3% absentee scenario. At the average monthly volume, the average delay increases to 152 hours (approximately 6.3 days). This would create delays comparable to the situation that existed in the fall of 2004. If the influenza event were to occur in the peak month of October, the delays would be intolerable. The model actually computes a value of nearly 1500 hours (about 63 days), but this value is not shown in Figure 5 because no ship owner would tolerate such a wait. What is important is to note that under high absentee rates there is one terminal that will likely be severely congested. Some vessels from the lines that normally use that terminal may be diverted to the common-use terminal (terminal 4) or be diverted to other ports to unload. Diversion to a common-use terminal is an accepted practice (Imai, 2008), but creates inefficiencies in handling the container transfers to inland transport modes.

Equation 10.

$$E[T_p] = \frac{\lambda^k E[S^2](E[S])^{k-1}}{2(k-1)!(k-\lambda E[S])^2 \left[\sum_{n=0}^{k-1} \frac{(\lambda E[S])^n}{n!} + \frac{(\lambda E[S])^k}{(k-1)!(k-\lambda E[S])} \right]} + E[S] \qquad (10)$$

Figure 5. Summary of average time in port for the LA terminals under various absentee rate scenarios

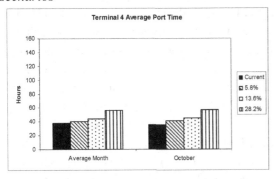

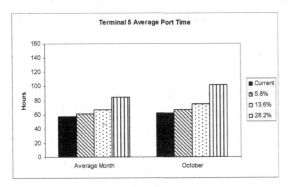

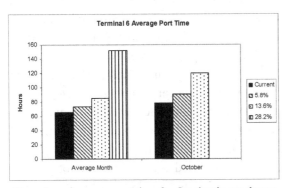

The value of average port time for October is not shown because it is computed at approximately 1500 hours, far larger than would realistically be tolerated

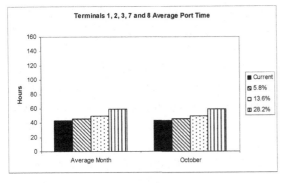

The value of average port time for October is not shown because it is computed at approximately 1500 hours, far larger than would realistically be tolerated.

The Port of Long Beach is similar in many respects to the Port of Los Angeles. It is also experiencing rapid traffic growth and is investing to increase capacity. As in Los Angeles, if the capacity investments keep pace with traffic growth, there should be sufficient capacity to weather an influenza outbreak (and associated worker absenteeism) with noticeable, but tolerable increases in delays. However, with such high growth rates for traffic volume, available "buffer" capacity can disappear very rapidly.

Intermodal Transfers

Beyond the process of unloading and loading containers at the dockside, there is potential concern about the transfer process through which these containers move from the port terminal to truck or rail for delivery across the nation. The severe congestion in Los Angeles / Long Beach that occurred in 2004, for example, had roots in both the rail system and in the port facilities themselves. The inability to move containers through the port and away to their destinations by truck or rail can result from limitations in any step of that overall process.

We have focused on the dockside operations because they are critical to vessel delay, an important performance measure for the port. Over the last two years, the change to 24-hour operations at the dockside in LA / Long Beach has been accompanied by expansion to 24-hour gate operations on the land side of the terminals to help move containers more effectively into and out of the terminal area. Both LA and Long Beach have also increased the proportion of dockside rail loading, so that more containers are placed directly on rail cars at the dock and labor-intensive intermediate handling of the containers is eliminated. These changes help the intermodal transfer process capacity keep pace with the unloading / loading capacity at dockside. However, during a potential pandemic influenza outbreak, the rate of worker absenteeism could exhibit strong local fluctuations and shift the bottleneck in port operations to the container yard or intermodal transfer. In such an event, the delays might be worse than what we have forecast here.

EXTENDING THE CONCEPTS TO OTHER INFRASTRUCTURES

The core idea in our analysis of the potential effects of pandemic influenza on freight transportation systems is that a shortage of available labor reduces the throughput capacity of key facilities, creating congestion, delays and possibly a breakdown of the system. A natural question is then: How does this idea extend to other infrastructures, particularly those that are more information-oriented and less labor-intensive than transportation?

In the IT infrastructures, people are not normally directly involved in the processing of individual transactions (handling individual units of flow). The role of people in the system is more focused on:

- Monitoring system performance and making decisions to respond to abnormalities
- Repairing and/or reconfiguring system elements after failures; and
- Performing routine maintenance and tests to identify problems before failures occur.

The mechanisms through which widespread worker absenteeism might affect system performance are somewhat different from the mechanisms in transportation, and are likely to involve incorrect decisions made by substitute people performing unfamiliar tasks, longer repair times when failures occur, and increased failure rates of equipment and software as a result of deferred tests and maintenance.

For example, consider Supervisory Control and Data Acquisition (SCADA) systems used to monitor and control a wide variety of infrastructure and industrial processes. Considerable attention is being paid to upgrading security in these systems, from both a physical standpoint and a cyber standpoint, because failures have the potential for life-threatening consequences. Lewis (2006) identifies human failures (including operator error) as the most common weaknesses identified in most SCADA systems. Gertman & Blackman (1993), in an analysis of human reliability and system safety, estimated that the error rate of well-trained people responding to correct signals from a semi-automated system is about 2×10^{-5}. However, for people performing even fairly simple tasks rapidly or with reduced attention (as might be the case when operations are short-staffed, or people are pressed into unfamiliar roles), the error rate rises to about .09. This dramatic three-order-of-magnitude increase in human error rate is likely to be one of the main potential effects of worker absenteeism in SCADA systems or other IT infrastructure where people are responsible for monitoring and responding correctly to abnormal operations.

Slower repair/replacement/reconfiguration of system components after failure clearly has capacity implications for an IT system, and in this regard is quite parallel to the analysis of transportation aforementioned system capacity. Degraded or failed components cannot do their normal processing and shift load to other parts of the system, creating congestion and delays. Analysis of this issue would certainly differ in the details from the analysis of freight transportation systems done here, but the underlying concept is similar.

Concern with failed components also raises the issue of network reliability as an important measure of system performance. This is different from measuring delays and congestion, and is likely to be important in IT applications, as it is in the electric power infrastructure. Electric power is not, strictly speaking, a cyber-infrastructure, but it is of interest to note that several recent reports (e.g., Canadian Electricity Association, 2008; North American Electric Reliability Corporation, 2006; U.S. Department of Energy, 2006) have begun to identify an explicit linkage between the "human infrastructure" in the electric power system and overall system reliability. There is a general concern that shortages of skilled labor and engineers among electric utilities will degrade service reliability. While the primary concern in these reports is not with episodic labor shortages, like an influenza epidemic, the connection between insufficient labor and service reliability is important.

Finally, in IT infrastructures, a part of the workload for labor that is likely to be shed first under widespread absenteeism is routine testing and maintenance. Over a period of several weeks (as might be the case in an influenza outbreak), this is likely to result in an increased failure rate of equipment and software. Coupled with a reduced capacity to make repairs after failures occur, this creates a "double effect" of increased failures and reduced repair rate which may be particularly troubling. At present, this must be treated as speculation, but this appears to be an important issue for further assessment.

For many critical infrastructures, including cyber infrastructure, there is an identifiable connection between worker absenteeism and system performance. The National Infrastructure Protection Plan (U.S. Department of Homeland Security, 2006) sets a goal for the federal government that reads, in part, "...to strengthen national preparedness, timely response, and rapid recovery in the event of an attack, natural disaster, or other emergency." The cornerstone of the NIPP is a risk management framework that integrates concerns regarding physical, cyber and human resources. There are many important public concerns surrounding a potential pandemic influenza outbreak – morbidity and mortality risks to the public, the likelihood of overwhelming the health care system, etc. Among these concerns should be placed a concern regarding continued functioning of critical infrastructure systems.

CONCLUSION

The first major conclusion from the analysis here is that at the level of absenteeism projected in the mid-level scenario (13.6% peak absentees), it is very likely that there will be widespread problems in the rail system as specific locations are unable to handle volumes coming into them over a 6-8 week period. There are likely to be persistent "waves" of congestion and disruption across the system as various yards become overly congested and adjustments are made, only to move the problem somewhere else.

In the high-level absentee scenario (28.2% absentees), the effective capacity of the major rail yards is reduced by approximately 45%. In the absence of shipment volume reductions, this capacity reduction, combined with train cancellations, reduced maintenance, etc., would likely cause the system to be completely clogged with shipments that are not moving.

Ortiz, *et al.* (2007) describe the whole national freight system as being "brittle" – i.e., small disruptions can produce large consequences. Under such conditions, the likely unevenness of shipment pattern changes as influenza affects different geographic areas and/or different industries to varying degrees, is likely to create substantial disruptions in freight transportation generally, and among railroads in particular, because there is very little excess capacity to "buffer" the variations across the system.

The second key conclusion is that most of the individual terminals in the Port of Los Angeles could withstand the absenteeism associated with the pandemic influenza scenarios. Delays would certainly increase, especially in the 28.2% absentee scenario, where total time in port increases by about 40-50%, but if the duration of the events is not excessive, this may be tolerable.

Terminal 6 (the Seaside Terminal, used by Evergreen, Hatsu and Italia Marittima) is the likely exception. Under high absentee rates this one terminal will likely be severely congested and some vessels from the lines that normally use that terminal will either have to make temporary arrangements to use other terminals or be diverted to other ports to unload.

The Port of Long Beach is similar in many respects to the Port of Los Angeles. Both ports are experiencing rapid traffic growth and are investing to increase capacity. If the capacity investments keep pace with traffic growth, there should be sufficient capacity to weather an influenza outbreak (and associated worker absenteeism) with noticeable, but tolerable increases in delays. However, with such high growth rates for traffic volume, available "buffer" capacity can disappear very rapidly.

The analysis done here indicates that major breakdowns in the freight transportation sector are likely under the more severe influenza scenarios as a direct result of large-scale worker absenteeism. This may affect distribution and availability of a wide variety of consumer goods as well as availability of raw materials for many other industries. Planning for actions to reduce the rate of infection and to slow the transmission of the disease is very important, and will create benefits in the transportation sector as well as in easing the load on the health care sector.

This analysis is important to cyber security because it raises a set of issues that are not normally considered in assessments of the security of IT systems. There is a connection between labor availability and system performance, and events (like pandemic influenza) that may create large-scale worker absenteeism can expose an IT system vulnerability. The work in this paper illustrates a method of analysis that focuses attention on potential bottlenecks in the system and the effects of labor on the capacity of those bottlenecks. In translating the approach to IT infrastructure, it is likely to be useful to focus attention on failures

of equipment and software within the system and the ability to repair/replace/reconfigure those components. This is particularly important in light of the possibility that reduced maintenance and testing will result in an increased failure rate at the same time that repair capacity is diminished. This appears to be a productive area for further research.

REFERENCES

American Association of Port Authorities (2007). *North American Port Container Traffic 2006*. Retrieved March 15, 2007 from http://www.aapa-ports.org .

Association of American Railroads (2006). *Railroad Facts – 2006 Edition*. Washington, DC.

Association of American Railroads (2007). *Railroad Performance Measures*. Retrieved March 15, 2007 from http://www.railroadpm.org/.

Blackhurst, J., Craighead, C. W., Elkins, D., & Handfield, R. B. (2005). An Empirically Derived Agenda of Critical Research Issues for Managing Supply Chain Disruptions. *International Journal of Production Research, 43*(19), 4067-4081.

Canadian Electricity Association (2008). *Providing Reliable Energy in a Time of Constraints: A North American Concern*, Ottawa, Ontario.

Eubank, S., Guclu, H., Anil Kumar, V.S., Marathe, M., Srivasan, A., & Toroczkal, Z. (2004). Modeling Disease Outbreaks in Realistic Urban Social Networks. *Nature, 429*, 180-182.

Ferguson, N., Cummings, D., Fraser, C., Cajka, J., Cooley, P., & Burke, D. (2006). Strategies for Mitigating an Influenza Pandemic. *Nature, 442*, 448-452.

Gertman, D. I., & Blackman, H. S. (1993). *Human Reliability and Safety Analysis Handbook*. New York, NY: John Wiley.

Kleindorfer, P. R., & Saad, G. H. (2005). Managing Disruption Risks in Supply Chains. *Production and Operations Management*, 14:1, 53-68.

Le-Griffin, H.D. (2008). *Assessing Container Terminal Productivity: Experiences of the Ports of Los Angeles and Long Beach* (Report AR05-06). Los Angeles: University of Southern California, METRANS Transportation Center.

Lewis, T. G. (2006). *Critical Infrastructure Protection in Homeland Security: Defending a Networked Nation*, New York, NY: Wiley-Interscience.

Logan, P. (2006, January). *People, Process and Technology – Unlocking Latent Terminal Capacity*. Paper presented at the Annual Meeting of the Transportation Research Board, Washington, DC.

Longini, I. (1988). A Mathematical Model for Predicting the Geographic Spread of New Infectious Agents. *Mathematical Biosciences*, *90*, 367-383.

Machalaba, D. (2004). Railroad Blues: Woes at Union Pacific Create a Bottleneck for the Economy. *Wall Street Journal*, July 22, 2004, page A1.

Mongelluzzo, B. (2004). From Bad to Worse in LA-Long Beach; Truckers Remain Unhappy about Delays at Southern California Ports. *Journal of Commerce*, September 27, 2004, p. 16.

North American Electric Reliability Corporation (2006). *2006 Long-Term Reliability Assessment*, Princeton, NJ.

Nozaki, S., & Ross, S. (1978). Approximations in Finite-Capacity Multi-Server Queues with Poisson Arrivals. *Journal of Applied Probability*, *14*(4), 826-834.

Orange County Register, In Delays, Their Ship Comes In. Anaheim, CA, September 9, 2004.

Ortiz, D. S., Weatherford, B., Willis, H. H., Collins, M., Mandava, N., & Ordowich, C. (2007). *Increasing the Capacity of Freight Transportation: U.S. and Canadian Perspectives*, RAND Corporation, Santa Monica, CA.

Pachakis, D., & Kiremidjian, A. (2003). Ship Traffic Modeling Methodology for Ports. *Journal of Waterway, Port, Coastal and Ocean Engineering*, *129*(5), 193-202.

Port of Long Beach, data retrieved March 18, 2007 from http://www.polb.com/facilities/cargotenant/containerized/default.asp.

Port of Los Angeles, data retrieved March 18, 2007 from http://www.portoflosangeles.org/facilities_Container.htm.

President's Commission on Critical Infrastructure Protection, *Critical Foundations: Protecting America's Infrastructures*, The White House, Washington, DC, 1997.

Santoso, T., Ahmed, S., Goetschalckx, M., & Shapiro, A. (2005). A Stochastic Programming Approach for Supply Chain Network Design under Uncertainty. *European Journal of Operational Research*, *167*, 96-115.

Turner, H. (2000). Evaluating Seaport Policy Alternatives: A Simulation Study of Terminal Leasing Policy and System Performance. *Maritime Policy and Management*, *27*(3), 283-301.

Turnquist, M. A. & Daskin, M. S. (1982). Queuing Models of Classification and Connection Delay in Railyards. *Transportation Science*, *16*, 207-230.

U.S. Department of Energy (2006). *Workforce Trends in the Electric Utility Industry*, Report to Congress under Section 1101 of the Energy Policy Act of 2005, Washington, DC.

U.S. Department of Homeland Security (2006), *National Infrastructure Protection Plan*, retrieved on March 20, 2008 from http://www.dhs.gov/xlibrary/assets/NIPP_Plan.pdf .

U.S. Department of Transportation (2006). *Vessel Calls at U.S. Ports 2005*, Maritime Administration, Washington, DC.

U.S. Department of Transportation (2007), *Vessel Movement Files for 2005*, Maritime Administration, Washington DC.

Welding, P. I. (1957). The Instability of Close Interval Service. *Operational Research Quarterly*, 8, 133-148.

World Health Organization (2008). "H5N1 Avian Influenza: Timeline of Major Events," retrieved September 7, 2008 from http://www. who.int/csr/disease/avian_influenza/Timeline_ 08_08_20.pdf.

Chapter XIV
Information Sharing:
A Study of Information Attributes and their Relative Significance During Catastrophic Events

Preeti Singh
University at Buffalo, The State University of New York, USA

Pranav Singh
University at Buffalo, The State University of New York, USA

Insu Park
University at Buffalo, The State University of New York, USA

JinKyu Lee
Oklahoma State University, USA

H. Raghav Rao
University at Buffalo, The State University of New York, USA

ABSTRACT

We live in a digital era where the global community relies on Information Systems to conduct all kinds of operations, including averting or responding to unanticipated risks and disasters. This can only happen when there is a robust information exchange facilitation mechanism in place, which can help in taking quick and legitimate steps in dealing with any kind of emergent situation. Prior literature in the field of information assurance has focused on building defense mechanisms to protect assets and reduce vulnerability to foreign attacks. Nevertheless, information assurance does not simply mean building an impermeable membrane and safeguarding information, but also implies letting information be securely shared, if required, among a set of related groups or organizations that serve a common purpose. This chapter will revolve around the central pivot of Information Sharing. Further, to study the relative significance of various information dimensions in different disaster situations, content analyses are conducted. The results hence obtained can be used to develop a prioritization framework for different disaster response activities, thus to increase the mitigation efficiency. We will also explore roles played by few existing organizations and technologies across the globe that are actively involved in Information Sharing to mitigate the impact of disasters and extreme events.

INTRODUCTION

Information assurance is the process of ensuring that the right people get the right information at the right time. This term is sometimes used interchangeably with information security but in a broader connotation, it is a superset of information security and also comprise of managing relevance, integrity, accuracy, authentication, confidentiality and other similar attributes of information (Thomas, Ang, Parbati Ray, & Nof, 2001). The main thrust of this chapter is on Information Sharing, which plays a crucial role in mitigating dire consequences of any disaster or threat to our social/business infrastructure. Here we will be analyzing different attributes of information which will also be referred to as information quality dimensions in the sections ahead and will draw some inference on deciding about their priorities during different kinds of disaster. So we will be studying information assurance through the spectrum of Information Sharing during disasters. It is important to note here that the terms disasters, emergency, crisis, calamity and catastrophe, all may have different meanings in their respective fields. However, as a part of this chapter, all these terms refer to the same context and may appear interchangeably. Similarly, information attributes and information quality dimension are both assumed to mean the same.

Information Sharing is a fundamental component of a successful security program. With the high-level of inter-dependent business operations among business partners and automated control systems, organizations can derive value from accessing and sharing appropriate information. Nevertheless, doing the same in a secure fashion is indeed a daunting challenge, since we have to deal with information content that ranges from the simple to the complex (e.g., travel records, weather information, citizenship records, financial information, intelligence reports, military positions and logistical data, map data, etc.) in an interoperable environment that is constantly changing (Phillips, Ting, & Demurjian, 2002). Therefore, it becomes very important to understand the significance of various information attributes during any disaster management operation, because handling information in a way that can facilitate the special information needs of the particular disaster will expedite the relief operations. Our interest is to help disaster management organizations (DMO) prepare a framework for quick and secure Information Sharing that is required in response to a crisis, e.g., natural disaster (earthquake, hurricane), terrorist attacks (biological warfare or explosions), etc.

Background

In the United States, There are approximately 30,000 local governments, 30,000 local fire departments, 18,000 local police departments, 15,000 school districts, and 3,400 county governments (Pelfrey, 2005). Many organizations collaborate together for responding to a major disaster; for example during the disaster response of 9/11 terrorist attacks in New York City, there were 1,607 governmental and non-governmental organizations involved (Kapucu, 2004). Major international volunteer organizations such as the

Red Cross and Voluntary Organizations Active in Disasters (VOAD) also played an important role in mitigating the disaster impact. Incompatible technology can be a serious concern for all of these organizations. During 9/11 response activity, there was a big communication bottleneck created between responders from different organizations of New York City due to incompatible radio systems. The usage of analog radios by the Fire Department failed in the same way as it happened during 1993 World Trade Center attack (Jaeger, et al., 2007). The following excerpt highlights the technological barrier to the Information Sharing during 9/11 attack:

Firefighters, police, and other emergency personnel at the Pentagon and in New York City could not find common radio frequencies to communicate—cell phone networks flooded frequencies and further hindered information flow in the hours following the 9/11 attacks. (Riley, 2003)

The overall coordination and Information Sharing was even more concerning during the response to Hurricane Katrina. Federal, state and local government agencies and private organizations were very inefficient in coordinating and interrelating their activities, lacked an overall operational concept and had no proper system at place to track and share information (Wise, 2006), Secretary of Homeland Security Michael Chertoff told Congress that the response was "significantly hampered by a lack of information on the ground" (Chertoff, 2005) and the White House report on the failures of the Katrina response mentioned it as "inability to connect multiple communication plans and architectures clearly impeded coordination and communication at the federal, state, and local levels" (WhiteHouse, 2006).

In an emergency, it's generally not possible to know all the answers yourself, but it's quite important to know the resource/entities or collaborating organization that has the answer. Disasters, as we know are mostly unexpected and unavoidable events. Today we are aware of which regions are prone to tornadoes or hurricanes and where the earthquake faults are buried. But what we can never accurately predict, with a comfortable degree of certainty, is what path the hurricane will take, when the earth will shake, how and when terrorists will launch their attack, or where the plane will crash. Yet one thing we surely know is that when a disaster strikes, there will be a pressing need for reliable information exchange to take place. How well we are able to manage that information before, during, and after a disaster can have a direct impact on how well we manage the crisis. So the real essence of Information Sharing is to let the correct information timely reach the appropriate receiver, at the right place and in an understandable format. And this is where the equilibrium gets lost immediately after the disaster. All the information attributes go haywire, unanticipated delays occur, confusion prevails all ultimately resulting in bad emergency response decisions and actions. If a general framework can guide disaster management organizations to focus on more critical information attributes in different types of emergency situations, it will expedite the emergency response operations and will be a boost for disaster management. Previous research in this area focused on describing the emergence and development of the disaster situation under scrutiny, adopting a case study and qualitative analysis approach. While such studies suggest some factors that could influence the performance of disaster management operations in the study context and offer an insight into the particular situation, not many studies have offered objective evidence that certain attributes of information is critical in a disaster response operations.

INFORMATION QUALITY

Intuitively and broadly, "Information Quality" is the degree to which information meets the needs of its users (Gasser & Twidale, 2005). Since different people use information for different purposes, it often happens that information which is high quality for one user is low quality for another. For example, when a large-scale wildfire breaks out, information about weather conditions is more relevant for fire crew and evacuation teams than it is for police and Emergency Medical Service (EMS). That's because fire crew may have to use different attack plan to fight against spreading fire, while evacuation team need to determine the best evacuation path depending on the changing direction and strength of the wind. Similarly the information about approximate casualty level might be more important for Emergency Medical Services since they need to dispatch sufficient medical resources to the disaster site, while preserving as much medical resources as possible for other areas. Yet, it is very important that all information that is sent across from one organization/entity to another is of high quality for a successful emergency response.

Quality Dimensions

Information quality as such, unfortunately, is difficult to observe, capture or measure. Information quality dimensions are the means by which we can measure quality of Information (H. Miller, 1996). Several researchers have identified the dimensions of information quality with as many as 15 dimensions identified by Strong et al. in 2002. In another research project, a literature review was conducted to find out the list of most common information quality dimensions (Parker, 2006). In that study, papers dealing with all quality dimensions and published during the years 1996-2005 were examined and the frequency of each dimension was calculated across those publications. In this chapter, we adopt the nine common information quality dimensions identified by the previous study (Parker, 2006). They are discussed briefly below:

Timeliness

Timeliness is the degree to which information is up-to-date. It can be seen in an objective fashion, meaning that information represents the current state of the real world. Timeliness can also be seen as task-dependent, meaning that the information is timely enough to be used for a specific task. It is one of the most important quality dimensions for handling disasters, because providing new information instantly is a major success factor of preventing a disaster or mitigating its effect. Information must be timely, and not "stale". Stale information is what has become outdated and has been replaced by new information. The implications of untimely/stale information during a disaster can be considerable. Not only does it lead to the expending of valuable time in processing that information, but it also prevents the appropriate response needed by the actual situation. To enable coordination and synchronization of multiple operations, information has to be up to date. Quoting an e-mail sent by a White House Homeland Security Council officer during the Katrina response:

... sending us very stale sit rep info that has already been updated (earlier) by the HSOC is not as helpful. Is there a way to coordinate the info flow so we don't waste time receiving such old data and you folks don't waste time sending us stuff? (Christopher & Robert, 2002)

Also, Timeliness and Accuracy go hand in hand. When a situation changes dynamically, any situational information that is not timely is not accurate.

Security

Security has been identified as another important information quality dimension. If information is not secure, it can be easily intercepted by any intelligent opponent (e.g., terrorists, criminals) and used in a harmful manner. For example, if there is a huge fire that needs to draw police, medical and fire responders from surrounding areas, and if a criminal comes to know this, (s)he can take undue advantage of this information: (S)He can identify which area lacks police force and commit a crime in that area. This information quality dimension is especially important when there exists an active and strategic opponent (e.g., in a terrorist attack situation), as the degree of damage that can be done by information leakage in such cases can be extremely higher. Two aspects of information security include protecting information from intentional and unintentional human acts (information security) and protecting information from disasters (disaster recovery planning). Cyber security relies on logical barriers such as data encryption, passwords and transaction authentication, along with human vigilance. Disaster recovery planning involves protecting information and ensuring appropriate back-up and alternate processing procedures are in place (H. Miller, 1996).

Accessibility

For information to be utilized in an effective manner, it must be accessible. Accessibility implies the degree to which information is available, easily obtainable or quickly retrievable when needed. But this availability of information to the users is generally within the constraints of policy and confidentiality. Knowledge of the existence of information, its availability, and the tools necessary to acquire it are key attributes of access (Fuerth, 1997). It enables Information Sharing, giving an impression as if resources were centralized. When coupled with timeliness, it permits synchronization of interdependent activities. Accessibility is an important issue in a disaster situation as it often happens that all means of communication get disrupted in a disaster. For example, during Hur-

ricane Katrina, the communication infrastructure was completely devastated in many parts of the affected area, and the responders had very tough time in coordinating their emergency response operations (D. R. Miller, 2006).

... It got to the point that people were literally writing messages on paper, putting them in bottles and dropping them from helicopters to other people on the ground. (WhiteHouse, 2006)

The disaster management organizations should identify the technical and other barriers limiting the access to information during disasters and make a cooperative effort to surmount them.

Completeness

Completeness is the degree to which information is not missing. Incomplete information can be hazardous. However, complete information for one person may be incomplete for another. For example, emergency medical services, FBI and Fire crew, all may be interested in the weather conditions around the disaster site, but each may require different levels of detail. Just as information of which precision exceeds a recipient's processing capability may be too accurate, information may also be too complete. During a disaster, it's also an adverse situation that the amount of information generated is so much that processing it all in a timely fashion becomes infeasible. At the same time, in a disaster response, if information is incomplete, it becomes difficult for the responders to accurately assess the situation and hence they are unable to respond effectively. The following excerpt illustrates this situation:

.....Each data set was examined to evaluate the completeness of records as a useful indicator of quality. The mere recording of the occurrence of a disaster with no other information on it makes the record essentially unusable for analyses. (Debarati & Below, 2000)

Accuracy

Accuracy is the degree of correctness and precision with which information in an automated system represents states of the real world. It is a very important quality dimension that on which many early information quality studies have focused (Alexander, 1999; Katerattanakul & Siau, 1999; Strong, Lee, & Wang, 1997). Within information production processes inside organizations, accuracy can be improved by implementing institutional procedures, like having information double checked by two independent people, or by installing technical means, like calibrating sensors or verifying shipping address information received through a website against an address database. The concept of accuracy implies the assumption that information can be captured in an objective fashion. Thus, accuracy is not applicable to subjective information, like destructive impact, public perception or political views. Inaccurate information may be worse than no information at all. Example, if a fire crew does not know the type and extent of situation at a disaster site, they will at least try to extract more information. However, if they have been given inaccurate information, they may respond with inappropriate strategy, which may lead to loss of innocent lives. Similarly, inaccurate information about the death toll in a disaster can lead to pandemonium in public.

Coherence

Coherent information is what "gels" or blends with itself consistently. Incoherent information can lead to confusion and panic during a disaster. This can lead to wastage of valuable time as well as resources. Coherence implies that two or more values do not conflict with each other. Information generated during a disaster is likely to be inconsistent as multiple information providers, which might use different procedures to capture information, have different levels of knowledge and different views of the world. Since most people

are exposed to information through a number of media and from various sources, it must be consistent in order to be credible. Inconsistent information tends to confuse people and allows them to discount some or all of it. For example:

numerous organizations--state agencies, the Red Cross, school authorities, and media outlets--in California met in the immediate aftermath of the Loma Prieta quake just to discuss and agree upon the wording all of them would use for the "Drop, Cover, and Hold!" message. (Sarah et al, 1999)

Relevance

Relevancy is the extent to which information is applicable and helpful for the task at hand. Information must be relevant as per the demands of situation, i.e., it must address the needs of the end user to whom it is being transmitted. For example, when a user calls a 911 operator to tell about an emergency, he might tell irrelevant details out of panic. The operator must analyze what information should be sent across to the responders and ask relevant questions to complete the information. The key component for information quality is whether the information addresses its user's needs. If not, then the user will find the information inadequate regardless of how well the information rates along other dimensions mentioned in this chapter.

Validity

Information should be valid in the sense that it must be true and verified; it must satisfy the set standards related to other dimensions such as accuracy, timeliness, completeness and security. The most common form of information validation is auditing. Auditing can uncover mistakes and is a good way to measure the quality of information (Whitehouse, 2006). Validity is a resultant rather than a causal dimension of information quality.

This means that even though some information may be classified as being highly 'valid', it still may fall under poor quality information if other crucial dimensions like accuracy, timeliness etc. is absent (H. Miller, 1996).

.....When indicators possess high degree of reliability and validity, the data and information they generate is more useful in continuously improving performance. Conversely, indicators that are unreliable and invalid produce confusing, irrelevant and useless data and information while consuming precious resources...... (O'Leary, 2004)

Format

Information must be in such a format that it is uncomplicated and easily understood by the end user. This is especially true in a disaster situation as minimum time must be wasted between information processing and actual response. Information format refers to how the information is presented to the user. Two key components of information format are its underlying form and its context for interpretation, which is sometimes referred to as its frame (H. Miller, 1996). The appropriate format for information depends on the information's recipient and the information's use. For example, while giving demographic details or statistics of any past event, multi-color pie charts may be a better format than putting numbers. Moreover, during disaster management, if there is a commonly agreed upon format for exchange of information between two organizations, say Fire department and 911 operators, it aids understandability and expedites the response. Since there might be huge data to handle, it's always better to keep them formatted instead of letting them go haywire.

For each disaster, too many database and software have been developed and designed and millions of money has been expended. These projects are substantially costly and the main problem are the existing of many parallel sub-systems and activities and repeat labor works in different database format which have to be created for each hazard management systems. Such methodology will be so complicated due to implementation of different platform, different database format, and different program languages and so on. This will make all projects costly and non-efficient. (Assilzadeh & Mansor S.B., 2004)

DISASTER TYPES

Disasters may be natural or man-made. Natural disasters include earthquake, natural fires, volcanoes, tsunami, hurricane, landslide, flood, drought, and so on. Man-made disasters include bio/chemical/radiation/fire emergencies caused by human error or by strategic opponents (e.g., terrorists) and so on. Whatever may be the disaster type, it needs adequate and timely response by several government agencies that interact and exchange information with each other to combat the disaster. In order to make the study more manageable, in current context, we limit our scope to hurricanes, earthquakes, and terrorist attacks.

Disaster Cases Analyzed

We have focused on the below disasters:

1. Katrina Hurricane: It was the third most intense United States (U.S.) land-falling hurricane on record based on central pressure. The catastrophic damage and loss of life inflicted by this hurricane is an estimated 1,353 direct fatalities and 275,000 homes damaged or destroyed. Total economic losses could be greater than $100 billion (Groumann, Houston, & Lawrimore, 2005).

2. Indian Ocean Earthquake (and resulting Tsunami): It originated with an epicenter off the west cost of Sumatra, Indonesia on December 26, 2004. It killed an estimated

350,000 people and caused losses worth US $4.45 billion (Athukorala & Resosudarmo, 2005)

3. 9/11 Attacks: It occurred on September 11, 2001 when a series of suicide bombings using hijacked commercial air-liners hit several strategic US locations. The attacks killed more than 2,600 people (9/11 Commission report, 2005) and caused economic losses in NYC worth US $83-$95 billion (Thompson, 2002).

4. Anthrax Attacks: During the fall of 2001, mail packages containing large numbers of Bacil lus anthracis spores were sent to people at several locations in the US. 22 people got seriously infected and five of them died. As many as 30,000 people in the U.S. Postal Service (USPS) initiated preventive antibiotic treatment (Alibek, Lobanova, & Popov, 2005).

We selected the above mentioned four cases for our research because they not only caused loss of human life and capital, but also grabbed widespread public and media attention in the recent past. Out of these, Tsunami and Hurricane Katrina are natural disasters and 9/11 attacks and Anthrax attacks are man-made. Therefore, our findings will also help in distinguishing the relative significance of information quality dimensions during disaster management in both of these kinds of disasters.

Before we proceed with content analysis, let us make a few statements about expected relationships between the above mentioned information quality dimensions and one or more types of the disasters examined in the content analysis. Security will be obviously more important in the two terrorist attacks (9/11 and Anthrax attacks) than in the other two disasters, because strategic opponents are present. Accessibility will be more important in disasters where communication infrastructure is damaged. Therefore, we can expect that media articles about larger-scale disasters like Katrina and Tsunami would put more weight on the accessibility dimension, compared with other types of disasters of which damages were isolated within a relatively small geographical area (e.g., a city) or did not disrupt telecommunication networks. Timeliness will be more important when the threat situation in a disaster develops dynamically and at a fast phase. Thus, logically, media reports about 9/11 and the Tsunami should emphasize timeliness more than reports about the Anthrax attack.

CONTENT ANALYSIS

In order to be able to quantify the information quality attributes so that they can be compared to determine their relative importance in a disaster situation, we used a semantic content analysis approach. Content analysis is a research method by means of which the presence of certain words or concepts within a given text can be determined (Busch, et al., 2005). Holsti (1969) broadly defines content analysis as, "any technique for making inferences by objectively and systematically identifying specified characteristics of messages". This tool can be used to predict the content and meaning of the text or article under consideration.

In our research, we used CATPAC as content analysis software. CATPAC is a self-organizing artificial neural network computer program that has been optimized to read and analyze large amounts of text (Kim, Song, Braynov, & Rao, 2005). This program identifies the most frequently occurring concepts in a given text which can be interpreted as a measure of importance, attention, or emphasis of that concept (Krippendorff, 1980).

Document Corpus Construction

Since we wanted to predict the importance of information quality dimensions *during* a disaster response, we collected several journal articles and news items relating to emergency response of each disaster event under scrutiny. The articles were collected from comprehensive databases such as Academic Search Premier, MasterFILE Premier, InfoTrac Newspapers, LexisNexis Academic, and Factiva. After a manual inspection to assure relevance, we selected 50 media and journal articles to conduct a semantic content analysis. The list of these articles has been included in Appendix A at the end of this chapter.

Semantic Analysis to Identify Keywords

We created a list of keywords (Table 1) which represent each quality dimension (*semantically equivalent categories*). We included several synonyms while creating the list of keywords for each dimension, considering the fact that authors may use synonyms for stylistic reasons throughout a document – if only a single word is used to do

content analysis, it can lead us to underestimate the importance of a concept (Weber, 1990). For example, an author might use the word 'available' or 'reachable' or 'accessible' while talking about the 'accessibility' aspect of information, and so, we need to consider all three words while doing a content analysis. Similarly, the author might use the word 'inaccessible' or 'unavailable' and still be talking about 'accessibility' (rather, *in*accessibility) aspect of information. As a result, our list of keywords includes both synonyms as well as antonyms to represent a quality dimension. While we understand the limitation that every keyword in each category may not represent that category equally well, there is no well-defined procedure to assign the *weight* of each word (Stemler, 2001). Consequently, we proceeded with our research under the assumption that all keywords for an information quality dimension (i.e., category) are of equal 'weight'.

Table 1. Keywords

Information Quality Dimension	Keywords
Timeliness	timeliness, delay, delays, time, timely, timelines, immediate, immediately, late, early, prompt, slow, fast, speed, waiting, prolonged, expedite, expedited
Security	safe, unsafe, secure, security, threat, threats, threaten, risk, risks, violence, crime, criminal, lawlessness, terrorism, terrorist, protection, protect, protected
Accessibility	accessible, inaccessible, communication, communicate, communicating, reach, reached, coordination, coordinate
Completeness	incomplete, complete, adequate, inadequate, unknown, unaware, insufficient, integrity, wholeness, entirety
Accuracy	accurate, inaccurate, accurately, confirmed, uncertainty, uncertain, rely, reliable, relied, wrong, false
Coherence	coherent, inconsistent, ambiguous, confusion, conflicting, uniform, concrete, consistent
Relevance	relevant, irrelevant, useless, useful, lengthy, redundant, applicable, applicability, cogency, pertinence
Validity	valid, validated, invalid, obsolete, outdated, substantiate, substantiated, unsubstantiated, credible, warrant, warranted, unwarranted
Format	standardized, complex, complexity, complicated, meaningful, unclear

Frequency Analysis

We then conducted a content analysis of the articles using CATPAC and summed up the frequency of words for each dimension, with frequency counts determining the relative concern of each dimension. Also, in order to ensure that we did not miss any high frequency keyword that could possibly represent an information quality dimension, we reviewed all high frequency words in content analysis results. Any word that we found was highly correlated and semantically similar to an existing keyword was added to our list, and then the results were revised accordingly.

Total number of content bearing words for the four disaster cases came out to be:

1. Hurricane Katrina: 4062
2. Tsunami (Indian Ocean Earthquake): 778
3. 9/11 Attacks: 4995
4. Anthrax Attacks: 4082

Since most of the articles analyzed in this study were published in the US, we can see that the total number of content bearing words in Tsunami is relatively less than those in the other cases. Nevertheless, the total word count will not have any impact in determining relative importance because we are measuring the hit density of keywords belonging to different information quality dimensions within a particular disaster.

Filtering Ambiguous Words

Simple frequency of words may not actually represent the importance of each dimension as words can have multiple meanings or appear in multiple contexts. For example the word "uniform" can have a noun meaning "clothing", an adjective meaning "evenly spaced", or an adverb meaning "provide with uniform". In order to resolve the ambiguity in the context in which the words appeared, we used the Key Word In Context (KWIC) search to test for the consistency of word usage. We used HyperRESEARCH to pull up the sentences in which the keywords were used to perform a validation of our results (Stemler, 2001). HyperRESEARCH is a software package that assists collection and analysis of qualitative data. We reduced the word count wherever we found that the context where the word appeared was not 'information' or 'information quality' related.

Hit Density

Since the length of articles varied, the absolute number of keywords appearing in the corpus thus did not represent the actual relevance of each dimension. Therefore, we calculated the 'hit-density' of keywords corresponding to each information attribute. The hit density is a ratio of the number of hits divided by the number of content-bearing words in an article (Efthimiadis, 1993). Here we define the term 'hits' as the number of words corresponding to the quality attribute under consideration, and 'number of content bearing words' as the total number of words that represent *all* quality attributes for a given disaster situation. For example, the number of words associated with the dimension 'accessibility' for the disaster Katrina was 1,431, while the total number of words obtained by summing up word count for *all* dimensions for disaster Katrina was 4062. The hit density is 1,431/4,062, i.e., 35. Accordingly, a hit density index that represents the importance of an information quality dimension can be compared with those of other dimensions within a disaster as well as across all disaster cases. The results of hit density analysis are graphically represented in Figure 1 to facilitate sense making and easy reading of the results.

From the hit density analysis results, we can observe several interesting differences within and across different types of disasters.

1. Security is, by far, the most important issue in terrorist attacks (i.e., Anthrax and 9/11at-

Figure 1. Hit density analysis

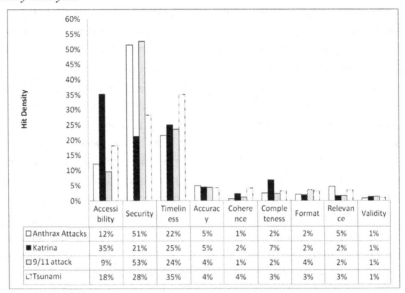

	Accessi bility	Security	Timelin ess	Accurac y	Cohere nce	Comple teness	Format	Relevan ce	Validity
☐ Anthrax Attacks	12%	51%	22%	5%	1%	2%	2%	5%	1%
■ Katrina	35%	21%	25%	5%	2%	7%	2%	2%	1%
☐ 9/11 attack	9%	53%	24%	4%	1%	2%	4%	2%	1%
☐ Tsunami	18%	28%	35%	4%	4%	3%	3%	3%	1%

tacks), while it still remains as the 2nd and 3rd important dimension in Tsunami and Katrina cases respectively. We can induce from this result that existence of an active intelligent opponent (e.g., terrorist) can force stakeholders (e.g., emergency responders, potential victims) to maintain a high-level of information security during emergency response operations. If information is insecure, it could easily be intercepted and misused to spread more terrorism. However, even when there is no immediate threat from intelligent opponents, security seems to remain as an important concern to many stakeholders (e.g., victims, the public, government agencies, non-government relief organizations), because a large-scale disaster will inevitably involves exchange of sensitive information across different organizations with different security requirements.

2. Timeliness was the most important issue in the Tsunami case (35%) and the 2nd most important issue, with almost equal levels (22-25%), for the other cases. It is obvious that if information does not reach the responders in time, they will not be able to

respond before irrevocable and serious damages have already been done. One possible explanation of the relatively high level of the hit density in the Tsunami case may be the time lag between the earthquake and the strikes of tsunami at different regions, because effective and timely warning might allow potential victims to evacuate or minimize the damages. In addition, the extremely higher number of casualty, as the death toll (350,000) suggests, could require timely responses to save valuable, yet perishing lives.

3. Accessibility was the most important issue in Katrina (35%), and the 3rd most important issue in all the other cases (9-18%). However, the gap between Katrina and the other cases are quite obvious, unlike the timeliness dimension. We suspect that the unexpected scale of damages on the once-reliable communication infrastructure could cause the surge of emphasis on accessibility. Also, the number and the variety of organizations involved in the relatively long recovery period, together with the level of bureaucracy imposed by the hierarchical

structure of the US disaster management agencies could result in accessibility issues among different stakeholders.

4. All the other dimensions (i.e., accuracy, coherence, completeness, format, relevance, and validity) are much less emphasized (mostly below 5%), regardless of the types of disaster, than the three most important dimensions (i.e., accessibility, security, timeliness). While it is still much lower than the other dimensions, the hit density of completeness in the Katrina case is distinctively higher than those in the other disasters. This may also result from disruption of communication and transportation systems, as well as reliance on archival systems that became unavailable by the impact of the disaster. One important point to make clear is that the low levels of these dimensions do not necessarily mean these are not important dimensions. We assume that published articles reflect the current issues in the respective context. Therefore, we can consider the three most important dimensions (i.e., accessibility, security, and timeliness) as the ones that became the center of hot discourse because we have misunderstood their impacts, resulting in mis-configured disaster management systems.

From the results of the comparative analyses of information quality dimensions in different disaster situations, we can conclude that these dimensions hold varying significance across different disasters. We can also infer some factors that might influence the differences in the importance levels of the three most important dimensions. Therefore, it is recommended that information be exchanged between different organizations on the basis of the circumstances and resulting relative significance of these information quality dimensions. The prioritization process which can be created utilizing these results will certainly help the emergency response operation to focus

on the information quality dimension which matters the most and thus will reduce the impact of disaster significantly by expediting the relief operations. Moreover, this will save time and resources which get dissipated dealing with less significant dimensions and thus can be utilized in the right direction to respond to the disaster in a better way.

In the previous sections, we discussed the important attributes of information. Taking the information security aspect a step further, let us continue our research to analyze the aspects of information assurance. We will perform content analysis to explore the relative significance of different dimensions of information assurance to provide us with more valuable conclusions which can be utilized to build a prioritization framework in mitigating disaster impacts.

Information Assurance

Information assurance is often used interchangeably with information security. But in specific terms, information assurance can be defined as information operations that protect and defend information and information systems by ensuring their availability, integrity, authentication, confidentiality, and non-repudiation. This includes provision for restoration of information systems by incorporating protection, detection and reaction capabilities (Maconachy, V., Schou, Ragsdale, & Welch, 2001). At the heart of Information assurance is the provisioning of five security services: *Availability, Integrity, Authentication, Confidentiality, and Non-Repudiation* which we are considering as the five important dimensions of information assurance.

1. *Availability* can be defined as timely, reliable access to data and information services for authorized users. It means that the information, the computing systems used to process the information, and the security controls used to protect the information

are all available and functioning correctly when the information is needed. Often it is viewed as a function, which is not entirely security related. Availability is equated with information system operations such as redundant communication channels, back-up power and off-site capabilities to handle crisis. Availability is the utility part of security services. There may be times during the course of operations that demand system availability at the expense of the other security services. The decision to abandon the other security services is a risk mitigation decision often driven by threats and vulnerabilities that fall beyond the system security parameters. Broadcasting a decision or some critical information at the time of disaster, to handle a life-threatening condition may override concerns to do so in a totally secure fashion (Maconachy, et al., 2001).

2. *Integrity* is "the quality of an information system reflecting logical correctness and reliability of an operating system; the logical completeness of the hardware and software implementing the protection mechanisms; and the consistency of the data structures and occurrence of the stored data." (Lohse et al, 2003). It means that data cannot be created, changed, or deleted without authorization. In a formal security mode, integrity is interpreted more narrowly to mean protection against unauthorized modification or destruction of information. Data integrity is a matter of degrees of trust. Integrity must include the elements of accuracy, relevancy, and completeness. Data and system integrity implies robustness.

3. *Authentication* is a security service, "designed to establish the validity of a transmission, message, or originator, or a means of verifying an individual's authorizations to receive specific categories of information" (Maconachy, et al., 2001). Authentication provides a foundation for many security

services by ensuring that data, transactions, communications or documents (electronic or physical) are not exposed to unauthorized entities thereby giving them a chance to tamper or misuse them.

4. *Confidentiality* is "the assurance that information is not disclosed to unauthorized persons, processes or devises" (Maconachy, et al., 2001). The application of this security service implies information labeling and need-to-know imperatives are aspects of the system security policy. Information that is considered to be confidential in nature must only be accessed, used, copied, or disclosed by persons who have been authorized to do so, and only when there is a genuine need to do so. A breach of confidentiality occurs when information that is considered to be confidential in nature has been, or may have been, accessed, used, copied, or disclosed to, or by, someone who was not authorized to have access to the information.

5. *Non-Repudiation* refers to the assurance that "the sender of the data is provided with proof of delivery and the recipient is provided with proof of the sender's identity, so neither can later deny having processed the data" (Fry, 2001). Non-repudiation has ramifications for electronic commerce as well as battlefield orders. Electronic commerce uses technology such as digital signatures and encryption to establish authenticity and non-repudiation.

Now let us do the content analysis of above five mentioned dimensions by using the keywords described below in Table 2, across all the four disasters. Our research approach is the same as we did in the previous content analysis.

After doing content analysis across all the four disasters, we calculated the hit density, as done in the previous section, and plotted them on the bar chart as shown below in Figure 2:

Table 2. Content analysis keywords

Information assurance attributes	Keywords
Availability	Available, accessibility, accessible, inaccessible, communication, communicate, communicating, reach, reached, unavailable, availability, unavailability
Integrity	Completeness, wholeness, relevance, accuracy, incomplete, complete, adequate, inadequate, insufficient, Tamper, tampering, repudiate, manipulate, integrity
Authentication	Valid, genuine, certify, attest, evidence, validity, authenticity, authenticate, authenticated, authenticates, manifest, manifestation, authentication
Confidentiality	Privacy, secret, secrecy, private, classified, confidential, confidentially, conceal, concealed, covert, covertly, unacknowledged, confidentiality
Non-Repudiation	Reject, disown, renounce, repudiate, encryption, decryption, time-stamp, time-stamped, signature, unfair, disclaimer, disclaim, repudiation, non-repudiation

Figure 2. Hit density analysis

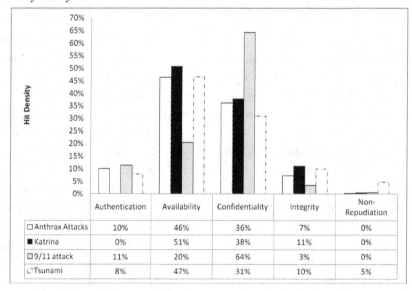

	Authentication	Availability	Confidentiality	Integrity	Non-Repudiation
☐ Anthrax Attacks	10%	46%	36%	7%	0%
■ Katrina	0%	51%	38%	11%	0%
☐ 9/11 attack	11%	20%	64%	3%	0%
☐ Tsunami	8%	47%	31%	10%	5%

From the result of the above content analysis, we can draw the following conclusions:

1. *Confidentiality* was the dominant concern in 9/11 attack (64%), while it was the 2nd most important issue in the other disasters (31-38%). Interestingly, this attribute was not as much emphasized in the other terrorist attack case (i.e., anthrax attacks) as it was

in 9/11. This difference between the two types of terrorist attack cases may come from the nature of attack. In 9/11, the attack was carried within a relatively short period of time, and nothing was clear at the point of attack, from which the US intelligence community had to figure out what really happened and how to handle the situation, before the public is informed of what the public needs to know. On the other hand, the anthrax case involved multiple attacks that aimed at seemingly random targets. Therefore, the public, as a group of individuals who may become a victim of the next attack had to be informed, educated, and mobilized, in order to minimize the impact of the attacks and maximize the chance to catch the attacker by encouraging bottom-up information flow for terrorist investigation tips, in the anthrax case. Therefore, it's very important to assure confidentiality of any information that has a potential to have a negative consequence, should the information fall in the hands of active opponents, while confidentiality should give a way to availability (or some other attributes) if the situation requires cooperation from other relief agencies or the public.

2. In contrast to confidentiality, *Availability* was a more important attribute in the Anthrax attack (46%), Katrina (51%), and Tsunami (47%) cases. It took 20% of the content-bearing words in the 9/11 case, which is a smaller portion, but still the 2nd important dimension. This may reflect issues like inconsistent access control for inter-organizational Information Sharing, lack of redundancy in communication links, absence of good backup practice, and improper business continuity planning for disaster management operations. The results show that confidentiality and availability are two most critical information quality dimensions, together taking a major portion (79-89%) of the content-bearing information security words in the four disaster cases. The hit densities of *Authentication*, *Integrity*, and *Non-Repudiation* were relatively low, suggesting that these dimensions were less of concern in the studied disasters. Non-repudiation appears especially irrelevant to the disaster management situation.

The results obtained can be utilized by government and non-government disaster management organizations to align their relief operations more effectively, by devising special mechanism to take care of every mentioned information attribute as per their significance. There are different organizations which are involved in different types and stages of disaster management operations. Among other information assurance attributes, they tend to focus on availability and confidentiality of information. The results suggest that availability is the most important information assurance dimension in the disaster management context, unless the situation requires confidentiality (e.g., information about the situation may benefit strategic opponents), in which case confidentiality may become the dominant dimension of information assurance quality over the usual golden rule of "availability goes first".

In Appendix B, we will touch upon a few of organizations and technologies that can help disaster management organizations achieve appropriate levels of availability and confidentiality for information assurance, while accommodating relevant information quality dimensions (e.g., accessibility, security, timeliness), in a disaster response situation. By utilizing these organizational and technological supports, relief agencies, esp. those who often participate in large-scale, multi-agency disaster management operations, will be able to better prepare for and improve their performance in different types of disasters.

CONCLUSION

In a disaster, every moment counts. A single minute saved can save a large number of lives, and thus it is very important to utilize time in the most efficient manner during the disaster response operations. Unfortunately, the situation often goes haywire immediately after the disaster, and the relief operations do not necessarily go in the planned manner, giving rise to chaos all around and thus information quality suffers. There exists an urgent need for a prioritization framework on the basis of which information quality dimensions can be weighed and their relative significance used to orient the emergency response operations. In this chapter, we have reviewed nine information quality dimensions, which led us to deduce relative significance of some of the information attributes across different disaster types. Based on the results of our content analyses, this chapter provides empirical evidence that effective disaster management requires a right mix of information quality dimensions to be achieved in their communication, depending on the particular circumstances of the disaster. We also discussed several key organizations and technologies that can promote information assurance in disaster management and improve various aspects of information quality.

The results of our analysis suggest that security is one of the most important information quality dimensions for all types of disaster management, but a much higher level of information security must be provided when an active intelligent opponent (e.g., terrorist) may take advantage of the information about the situation. Timeliness is another very important attribute for all disaster types, but it may gain weight when there is a time lag between a sign of potential damage (e.g., ocean earthquake, request for an ambulance) and actual strike of the disaster (tsunami reaching a coastline, death of a life), during which potential victims or emergency responders can be prepared to minimize the impact. Disaster responders should pay more attention to accessibility if they need to respond to a disaster that affected a large geographical area. Interestingly, all the other dimensions included in our analysis did not receive much attention in the four disaster cases.

The chapter further analyzed 5 sub-dimensions of the information security dimension, one of the three hottest issues in the current disaster management communications. The results that

we have obtained thus can be used by public and private sector disaster management organizations to create an *information dissemination prioritization framework* when responding in an emergency situation. Such a framework will aid decision-making when communicating information across organizations during a disaster. For example, agencies will know when to wait for information to get 'complete' while it is still 'secure,' and when to ensure that information is 'secure' while it is still 'complete,' and so forth.

While mostly in tandem with our predictions, the results of the content analyses also call for more research in this area. For example, a follow-up study may identify different dimensions of disasters (e.g., geographical and time span of the impact/recovery, number of involved responders/relief agencies, changes in the casualty at each phases of the disaster), which will allow more systematic analysis of possible relationships between information attributes and disaster attributes. Similarly, research on organizational attributes of disaster management organizations is highly likely to improve our understanding on the relative importance of information attributes. Also, the importance of various information quality dimensions can be measured on a single reference frame, which will allow direct comparison of the absolute value of the attributes. From a citizen-centric view point, analyzing personal web blogs or comments on first responder websites to understand the relative value of G2C (Government to Citizens) disaster communications will also be a meaningful research avenue. As such, we believe that our findings and discussions in this chapter can provide a fertile ground for future studies in the field of disaster management and information security.

ACKNOWLEDGMENT

This research has been supported by NSF under grant # IIS-0733388 and IIS-0809186. The usual disclaimer applies.

REFERENCES

Alexander, J., & Tate M (1999). *Web wisdom: How to evaluate and create information on the web*. Mahwah, NJ: Erlbaum.

Alibek, K., Lobanova, C., & Popov, S. (2005). *Bioterrorism and Infectious Agents: A New Dilemma for the 21st Century* .

Assilzadeh, H., & Mansor S. B. (2004). *Natural Disaster Data and Information Management System*. Paper presented at the XXth ISPRS Congress, Istanbul, Turkey.

Athukorala, P. C., & Resosudarmo, B. P. (2005). *The Indian Ocean Tsunami: Economic Impact, Disaster Management and Lessons*. Paper presented at the Asian Economic Panel Conference.

Busch, C., Maret, P. S. D., Flynn, T., Kellum, R., Le, S., Meyers, B., et al. (2005). *Content analysis.* : Writing@CSU. Colorado State University Department of English. Retrieved [Date] from http://writing.colostate.edu/guides/research/content/.

Chertoff, M. (2005). *Statement before the Senate Committee on Homeland Security and Governmental Affairs*. Department of Homeland Security: Second Stage Review.

Christopher, C., & Robert, B. (2002). *Disaster: Hurricane Katrina and the Failure of Homeland Security*. Macmillan Publishers.

Debarati, G. S. (2000). *The quality and accuracy of disaster data: A comparative analysis of three global data sets*. A study by the Provention Consortium.

Efthimiadis, E. N. (1993). *A User-Centered Evaluation of Ranking Algorithms for Interactive Query Expansion*. Paper presented at the ACM SIGIR, Pittsburgh, PA.

Fry, S. A. (2001). *Information assurance and Computer Network Defense*. Chairman of Joint Chiefs of Staff Instruction.

Fuerth, L. (1997). *Disaster Information Task Force Report*. The Global Disaster Information Network.

Gasser, L., & Twidale M. (2005). *Information Quality Discussions*. Graduate School of Library and Information Science, University of Illinois at Urbana-Champaign.

Groumann, A., Houston, T., & Lawrimore, J. (2005). *Hurricane Katrina: A climatic perspective*: US Department of commerce

Holsti, O. R. (1969). *Content analysis for the Social Sciences and Humanities*. Reading, MA.

Jaeger, P. T., Fleischmann, K. R., Preece, J., Shneiderman, B., Wu, P. F., & Qu., Y. (2007). *Biosecurity and Bioterrorism: Biodefense Strategy, Practice, and Science, 5*.

Kapucu, N. (2004). Interagency communication networks during emergencies: Boundary spanners in multiagency coordination. *American Review of Public Administration, 36*, 207-225.

Katerattanakul, P., & Siau, K. (1999). *Measuring information quality of web sites: Development of an instrument.* . Paper presented at the the 20th international conference on Information Systems., Charlotte, North Carolina, USA.

Kim, D. J., Song, Y. I., Braynov, S. B., & Rao, H. R. (2005). A multidimensional trust formation model in B-to-C e-commerce: A conceptual framework and content analyses of academia/practitioner perspectives *Decision Support Systems, 40*(2), 143-165.

Krippendorff, K. (1980). *Content analysis: An introduction to its methodology*. Beverly Hills, CA: Sage.

Lohse, E. S., Schou, C., Sammons, D., & Schlader, R. (2003). *Management, Research and Information Distribution in a Confidential, Controlled Environment*. Information Data Archives Idaho State University.

Maconachy, V. W., Schou, C. D., Ragsdale, D., & Welch, D. (2001). *A Model for Information assurance: An Integrated Approach*. Paper presented at the 2nd Annual IEEE Systems, Man and Cybernetics Information assurance Workshop.

Miller, D. R. (2006). *Hurricane Katrina: Communications & Infrastructure impacts, Threats at our threshold*. National Defense University.

Miller, H. (1996). *The Multiple Dimensions of Information Quality Information Systems Management, 13*(2), 79-82.

O'Leary, M. (2004). *Measuring Disaster Preparedness: A Practical Guide to Indicator Development and Application*: iUniverse.

Parker, M. B., Moleshe, V., De la Harpe, R., & Wills, G. B. (2006). *An evaluation of Information quality frameworks for the World Wide Web*. Paper presented at the 8th Annual Conference on WWW Applications, Bloemfontein, Free State Province, South Africa.

Pelfrey, W. V. (2005). The cycle of preparedness: Establishing a framework to prepare for terrorist threats. *Journal of Homeland Security and Emergency Management, 2*(1), 1-21.

Phillips, C. E. Jr., Ting, T. C., & Demurjian, S. A. (2002). *Information Sharing and security in dynamic coalitions*. Paper presented at the Proceedings of the seventh ACM symposium on Access control models and technologies.

Riley, B. (2003). Information Sharing in Homeland Security and Homeland Defense: How the Department of Defense Is Helping. *Journal of Homeland Security*.

Sarah, N., Paula, G., Greene, M., Lemersal, E., & Mileti, D. (1999). *Public Education for Earthquake Hazards*. Natural Hazards informer.

Stemler, S. (2001). An overview of content analysis. Practical Assessment. *Research & Evaluation, 7*(17).

Strong, D., Lee, Y., & Wang, R. (1997). Data Quality in context. *Communications of the ACM, 40*(5), 103-110.

Thomas, B., Ang, C. B., Parbati Ray, & Nof, S. Y. (2001). *Information assurance in Networked Enterprises: Definition, Requirements, and Experimental Results*. CERIAS Tech Report 2001-34.

Thompson, W. J. (2002). *One Year Later: The fiscal impact of 9/11 on New York city*. Comptroller, City of New York.

Weber, R. P. (1990). *Basic Content analysis* (2nd ed.). Newbury Park, CA.

WhiteHouse (2006). *The Federal Response to Hurricane Katrina: Lessons Learned*. Washington, D.C.: White House Report on Katrina,.

Wise, C. R. (2006). Organizing for homeland security after Katrina: Is adaptive management what's missing? *Public Administration Review, 66*, 302-318.

APPENDIX A: DOCUMENT CORPUS

HURRICANE KATRINA:

1. Agency, F. E. M. (2006). *DHS/FEMA Initial Response Hotwash: Hurricane Katrina in Louisiana,* . Baton Rouge, Louisiana: Federal Emergency Management Agency

2. Chua, A., Kaynak, S., Foo S. (2007). An Analysis of the Delayed Response to Hurricane Katrina Through the Lens of Knowledge Management. *Journal Of The American Society For Information Science And Technology, 58*(3), 391-403.

3. Edition, N. M. (Writer) (2004). Report Offers Post-Katrina Emergency response Recommendations: National Public Radio

4. Eosco, G. M., & Hooke, W. H. (2006). Coping with Hurricanes: It's not just about the Emergency response…, . *American Meteorological Society.*

5. In Wikipedia, T. F. E. (2008). Criticism of government response to Hurricane Katrina. , from http://en.wikipedia.org/w/index. php?title=Criticism_of_government_response_to_Hurricane_Katrina&oldid=222561822

6. Marchi, B. D. (2007). Not just a matter of knowledge. The Katrina debacle. *Environmental Hazards, 7*(2), 141-149.

7. Piper, P., & Ramos, M. (2006). A Failure to Communicate: Politics, Scam and Information Flow during Hurricane Katrina, Searcher: . *The magazine for database professionals, www.infotoday.com/searcher/jun.*

8. Representatives, U. S. H. o. (2006). *A failure of Initiative*: the Select Bipartisan Committee to Investigate the Preparation for and Response to Hurricane Katrina.

9. Rojek, J., & Smith, M. R. (2007). Law Enforcement Lessons Learned from Hurricane Katrina, . *Review of Policy Research, 24*(6), 589-608(520).

10. Shane, S., & Shanker, T. (2005). When Storm Hit, National Guard Was Deluged Too. *The New York Times,*

11. Stephan, K. D. (2007). We've got to talk: Emergency Communications and Engineering Ethics. *IEEE Technology and Society Magazine.*

12. Striedl, P., Crosson, J., & Farr, L. (2006). *Observations of Hurricane Katrina: Lessons Learned*: Association of Contingency Planners (ACP)

13. Treaster, J. B., Sontag D. (2005). Despair and Lawlessness Grip New Orleans as Thousands Remain Stranded in Squalor. *The New York Times,*

14. Venkataraman, S., Benger, W., Long, A., Jeong, B., & Renambot, L. (2006). Visualizing Hurricane Katrina: large data management, rendering and display challenges, Conference on Computer Graphics and Interactive Techniques in Australasia and Southeast Asia. *Graphite,* 209-212.

9/11 ATTACKS:

1. Carpenter, T. G. (2005). Missed Opportunities: The 9/11 Commission Report and US Foreign Policy. *Mediterranean Quarterly 16*(1), 52-61.

2. Jenkins-Smith, C., H., & Herron, K. G. (2005). United States Public Response to Terrorism: Fault Lines or Bedrock?, Review of Policy Research, . *22, 5,* 599-623(525).

3. Johnson, C. W. (2005). *Applying the lessons of the attack on the World Trade Center, 11th September 2001, to the design and use of interactive evacuation simulations.* . Paper presented at the *Conference on Human Factors in Computing Systems*, Portland, Oregon.

4. Kwan M-P, L. J. (2005). Emergency response After 9/11: The Potential of Real-Time 3D GIS for Quick Emergency response in Micro-Spatial Environments. *Computers, Environment, and Urban Systems, 29* (93-113).

5. Rashbaum, W. K. (2002). Commissioners Seek Closer Ties For Fire Dept. And the Police. *The New York Times,*

6. Report, T.-C. (2004). *Final Report of the National Commission on Terrorist Attacks Upon the United States* Official Government Edition.

7. Risen, J., & Johnston, D. (2002). F.B.I. Account Outlines Activities Of Hijackers Before 9/11 Attacks. *The New York Times*

8. Shenon, P. (2004). 9/11 Panel Set To Detail Flaws In Air Defenses. *The New York Times,*

9. Shenon, P., & Flynn, K. (2004). 9/11 Panel Has a Question: Why Wasn't the City Prepared? *The New York Times,*

10. Shenon, P., Flynn, K. (2004). Panel Criticizes New York Action In Sept. 11 Attack. *The New York Times,*

11. Staff Statement(2004), The National Commission On Terrorist Attacks Upon The United States, Threats And Responses In 2001

12. Wang, H. M. (2003). *Contingency planning: emergency preparedness for terrorist attacks.* Paper presented at the *Proceedings of IEEE 37th Annual 2003 International Carnahan Conference on Security Technology.*

TSUNAMI DISASTER:

1.   Athukorala, P.-C., & Resosudarmo, B. P. (2005). *The Indian Ocean Tsunami: Economic Impact, Disaster Management and Lessons.* Paper presented at the Asian Economic Panel Conference.

2.   Britton, N. (2007). *Lessons from ADB's Indian Ocean Tsunami Experience.* Paper presented at the Small Group Workshop on Preparing for Large Scale Emergencies.

3.   Darcy, J. (2005). *The Indian Ocean Tsunami Crisis: Humanitarian Dimensions*: Humanitarian Policy Group.

4.   *The December 2004 tsunami* (2007). (No. Online: http://ec.europa.eu/environment/civil/tsunami.htm): European Civil Protection

5.   Dickson, D. (2005). Tsunami Disaster: A Failure in Science Communication. *SciDev.Net News,*

6.   Dorsett, D. J. (2005). *Tsunami! Information Sharing in the wake of destruction.*

7.   Fehr, I. e. a. (2004). Indian Ocean Tsunami Report. *Risk Management Solutions Publications*, Online: www.rms.com/Publications/IndianOceanTsunamiReport.pdf

8.   Fidler, D. P. (2005). Disaster Relief And Governance After The Indian Ocean Tsunami: What Role For International Law? *Melbourne Journal of International Law, 6.*

9.   Grünewald, F., Boyer, B., Maury, H., & Pascal, P. (2007). *Indian Ocean Tsunami 2004 : 10 Lessons Learnt From The Humanitarian Response Funded By The French State*: Groupe URD, French Ministry of Affairs

10.   *IUCN* (2007). *Coastal Ecosystems*: International Union for Conservation of Nature and Natural Resources Newsletter.

11.   Jefferys, A., Simha, V., Samuel, K., Kottegoda, S., & Eskeland, L. (2005). Sharing information for tsunami recovery in South Asia. The International Federation of Red Cross and Red Crescent Societies.

12.   Leoni, B. (2005). *10 lessons learned from the South Asia tsunami of 26*: International Strategy for Disaster Reduction (ISDR).

13.   Wattegama, C. (2007). A Tale of Two Tsunamis: What Went Wrong in Each Case *Daily Mirror,*

ANTHRAX ATTACKS:

1.   Ackerman , G. A., & Moran , K. S. (2006). *Bioterrorism and Threat Assessment.* Sweden The Weapons of Mass Destruction Commission.

2.   Bravata, D. M. e. a. (2002). *Bioterrorism Preparedness and Response: Use of Information Technologies and Decision Support Systems*: Agency for Healthcare Research and Quality Publication.

3.   Chapman, J. (2005). *Countering Bioterrorism: How can Europe and the United States work together?* Paper presented at the the fourth meeting of the New Defence Agenda's Bioterrorism Reporting Group co-organised

4.   Davis, R. (2001). Bioterrorism. *USA Today*

5.   Editor Letters (2003) Bioterrorism Response, Science, Vol 300

6.   Eisenstein, M., & Houghton, B. K. (2000). *Bioterrorism: Homeland Defense: The Next Steps.* Paper presented at the Executive Summary of the Rand Symposium Proceedings

7.   Kaplan, E. H., Craft, D. L., & Wein, L. M. (2003). Analyzing bioterror response logistics: the case of smallpox. *Mathematical Biosciences 185*, 33-72.

8.   Kress, M. (2006). Policies for biodefense revisited: The prioritized vaccination process for smallpox. *Ann Oper Res 148*, 5-23

9.   Kun, L. G., & Bray, D. A. (2002). Information Infrastructure Tools for Bioterrorism Preparedness. *IEEE Engineering In Medicine And Biology*

10.   Lee, B. Y. (2007). The Role of Internists During Epidemics, Outbreaks, and Bioterrorist Attacks. *Society of General Internal Medicine 22*, 131-136

11.   Mackby, J. (2006). *Strategic Study On Bioterrorism*: Center for Strategic and International Studies (CSIS) Publication

12.   Sharp, R. J., & Roberts , A. G. (2006). Review Anthrax: the challenges for decontamination. *Journal of Chemical Technology and Biotechnology, 81*, 1612-1625.

APPENDIX B: ORGANIZATIONAL AND TECHNOLOGICAL RESOURCES

United States Computer Emergency Readiness Team (US-CERT)

A partnership between Department of Homeland Security (DHS) and public and private sector organizations, US-CERT is charged with improving cyber security preparedness and response in the United States. Through US-CERT, companies can access valuable educational resources, find up-to-date security information and receive security alerts. Individual companies are encouraged to register with them to receive alerts, warnings and other cyber security related information that is relevant to company-specific technology.

Cyberspace is a combination of distinct information infrastructures, including government and business operations, emergency preparedness communications, and critical digital and process control systems. Protecting these systems is very important to the resilience and reliability of the Nation's critical infrastructures and key resources and, therefore, to its economic and national security. US-CERT has a very important responsibility to analyze and reduce cyber threats and vulnerabilities, disseminate cyber threat warning information, and coordinate incident response activities. They collaborate with other organizations like Federal agencies, the research community, private sector, state and local governments, and international organizations. By coordinating with different incident response centers using both classified and unclassified systems, US-CERT disseminates reasoned, critical and actionable cyber-security information to the public. (DHS Cyber Security, 2006)

The different collaboration efforts of US-CERT include:

- **US-CERT Web Portal:** Provides a secure web-based collaborative system to share sensitive cyber-related information with government and industry members. And secondly it provides the government, private sector, and public with information needed to improve US-CERT's ability to protect information systems and infrastructures; includes information on current activity, events, resources, publications, and affiliates.
- **National Cyber Alert System:** Delivers targeted, timely, and actionable information to Americans, educating them on how to secure their own computer systems.
- **National Cyber Response Coordination Group:** Established in partnership with the Department of Defense and the Department of Justice; serves as the federal government's principal interagency mechanism to coordinate efforts to respond to and recover from cyber incidents of national significance.
- **Government Forum of Incident Response and Security Teams (GFIRST):** Embodies a community of more than 50 incident response teams from various federal agencies working together to secure the federal government.
- **US-CERT Einstein Program:** Involves an automated process for collecting, correlating, analyzing, and sharing computer security information across the federal government to improve our Nation's cyber situational awareness.
- **Internet Health Service:** Provides information about Internet activity to federal government agencies throughout the GFIRST community.

After the calamity caused by Hurricane Katrina, Department of Homeland Security (DHS) realized that many critical infrastructure control systems were shutdown, damaged, or destroyed. Hence they provided assistance to owners and operators in rebuilding and securely restarting those sensitive control systems. In order to assist control system owners, vendors, operators, and service providers in bringing control systems, and the sensitive processes and functions they monitor and manage, back into operation as safely and as securely as possible under the circumstances, the DHS US-CERT Control Systems Security Center (CSSC) compiled a set of items to consider when restarting and rebuilding control systems. (US-CERT, 2005)

CEO COM LINK for Business Roundtable CEOs

The Critical Emergency Operations Communications Link (CEO COM LINK[SM]) is a secure telephone communications system that will enable the nation's top CEOs to enhance the protection of America's employees, communities and infrastructure by communicating with leading government officials and each other about a threat or during national crises. This communication system links each of the Business Roundtable's 150 CEOS with the federal government to coordinate communication and facilitate effective response in times of crisis. Rapidly linking the private and public sectors during crisis can dramatically improve collaboration and effectiveness in enhancing homeland security.

The CEO COM LINK, developed by Business Roundtable, is an essential tool that enables this collaboration prior to, during, and in the aftermath of a significant national crisis. CEOs are alerted that the system is being activated and dial in to a secure conference call number. Each caller goes through a multi-step authentication process to ensure that only authorized participants are on the call. The calls also would allow CEOs to ask questions or share information with government leaders and with each other. Business rules have been established to govern calls and handle sensitive information (BRT, 2003).

Security is of utmost importance to ensure the confidentiality and integrity of information being shared. A critical security component is authentication. Each CEO is issued a means of authentication (e.g., voiceprints, caller ID), so a caller's identity can be verified. Because the private sector owns or operates 90 percent of our nation's critical infrastructures – including airlines, railroads, financial markets, telecommunications services and information services – CEO leadership in combating terrorist threats is critical to America's security. A timely and effective exchange of information between government and the private sector – and among business leaders – is critical for our nation's ability to detect additional threats, maintain homeland security, and respond effectively to threats or disasters.

Government Emergency Telecommunications Service (GETS)

GETS is a White House directed emergency phone service provided by the National Communications System through the Department of Homeland Security. GETS provides emergency access and priority processing in local and long distance in the Public Switched Telephone Network (PSTN). It provides Federal, State and local government National Security and Emergency Preparedness (NS/EP) users with a ubiquitous switched voice and voice-band data communications service and is used during periods of natural or man-made disasters or emergencies that cause congestion or network outages.

Different imperatives of GETS are:

- *Access Authorization*: GETS access control is accomplished through the use of Personal Identification Numbers (PINs) to ensure only authorized users gain access to GETS features and protect against fraud.

- *Enhanced Routing*: GETS calls use extensive enhancements to the PSTN's robust network of interconnecting paths between switches. With these enhancements to the grid of multiple switch connections, GETS calls can still be connected without any disruptions even when numerous switch failures occur in the PSTN.
- *Priority Treatment*: GETS allows that a high probability call identifier can be carried across the signaling network and used to trigger priority features such as trunk queuing and trunk reservation for designated emergency management communications.

European Network and Information Security Agency (ENISA)

The objective of ENISA is to improve network and information security in the European Union. The agency has to contribute to the development of a culture of network and information security for the benefit of the citizens, consumers, enterprises and public sector organizations of the European Union, and consequently will contribute to the smooth functioning of the EU Internal Market.

Different tasks done by ENISA are:

- Collect appropriate information to analyze current and emerging network and information security risks and provide the results of the analysis to Member States and the Commission;
- Provide advice and, if appropriate, assistance within its objectives to the European Parliament, the Commission and other competent bodies;
- Enhance cooperation between the different players in the sector (e.g., by organizing collaboration links between enterprises and universities) and facilitating cooperation between the Commission and the Member States in the development of common methodologies to prevent security problems;
- Contribute to awareness raising and the availability of rapid, objective and comprehensive information on network and information security issues for all users. This can be achieved by promoting exchanges of best current practice, including methods of alerting users;
- Assist the Commission and the Member States in their dialogue with industry to address security related problems in hardware and software products;
- Track the development of standards for security products and services and promote risk assessment activities;
- Contribute to Community efforts to cooperate with third countries and international organizations to promote a global common approach to security issues.

Chapter XV
An Overview of the Community Cyber Security Maturity Model

Gregory B. White
The University of Texas at San Antonio, USA

Mark L. Huson
The University of Texas at San Antonio, USA

ABSTRACT

The protection of cyberspace is essential to ensure that the critical infrastructures a nation relies on are not corrupted or disrupted. Government efforts generally focus on securing cyberspace at the national level. In the United States, states and communities have not seen the same concentrated effort and are now the weak link in the security chain. Until recently there has been no program for states and communities to follow in order to establish a viable security program. Now, however, the Community Cyber Security Maturity Model has been developed to provide a framework for states and communities to follow to prepare for, prevent, detect, respond to, and recover from potential cyber attacks. This model has a broad applicability and can be adapted to be used in other nations as well.

INTRODUCTION: THE NEED FOR COMMUNITY CYBER SECURITY PROGRAMS

In the introductory letter contained in the National Strategy to Secure Cyberspace, the President of the United States made the following statement concerning the challenge the nation faces in securing cyberspace:

Securing cyberspace is an extraordinarily difficult strategic challenge that requires a coordinated and focused effort from our entire society—the federal government, state and local governments, the private sector, and the American people. (White House, 2003)

The vision embodied in this statement, that securing cyberspace is an effort that an entire society must be part of, is extraordinary. It also, however, is a vision that has often been overlooked by the various federal agencies involved in securing the nation's cyberspace. Entities such as the US-Computer Emergency Readiness Team (US-CERT), part of the Department of Homeland Security (DHS), have been formed to address significant attacks on the nation's Internet infrastructure. The US-CERT and DHS have worked diligently to develop the channels necessary at the national level to address cyber attacks or significant cyber events that could impact the nation's cyber infrastructure. The issues are formidable – what information should be shared between organizations and how? Who is responsible for responding to the various types of threats/attacks that could occur? When does an event change from a criminal activity to a national security event and who makes that decision? Developing a construct that addresses these issues at the national level is difficult but a framework capable of addressing the national-level concerns is slowly evolving.

What has been slower to evolve is the rest of the picture as described in the President's statement. How state and local governments, the private sector (at and below the national level), and the American people participate in securing cyberspace has not been fully addressed (White House, 2003). Organizations, such as the Multi-State Information Sharing and Analysis Center (MS-ISAC), have been created to serve as focal points for the cyber security efforts at the state level but their complete roles in serving states and communities have not been defined. (MS-ISAC, 2008) Alternatively, some states have turned to their fusion centers to help organize their cyber information sharing and incident reporting functions. "A fusion center is an effective and efficient mechanism to exchange information and intelligence, maximize resources, streamline operations, and improve the ability to fight crime and terrorism by merging data from a variety of sources" (DHS, 2008). Fusion centers are generally staffed with individuals who have either a

law enforcement or an intelligence background. Exercises have demonstrated that most states and communities have little to no experience in cyber security and the processes they are to use to fight cyber crime and cyber terrorism are not developed. Local organization to defend against cyber attacks is similarly non-existent in other countries as well. National-level entities exist for incident response (e.g. the AusCERT in Australia (AusCERT, 2008)) but community response capabilities are lacking.

A reasonable question to ask is whether cyberspace, due to its very nature, requires more than a national-level approach to its defense. Thinking in terms of conventional first-responders, the individuals who must react to a disaster or attack are those that are in close proximity to the attack. In cyberspace, however, what is considered close proximity to the attack? Could an attack on computer systems in one area of the nation be addressed by individuals in another since they can have electronic access to the computer system from anywhere in the nation? While there is certainly an element of truth to this, the reality of the situation is that the very nature of cyberspace actually leads to the exact opposite. The element of cyberspace that makes it possible for individuals in one location to respond to attacks on systems at another location, also makes it possible for cyber attackers to assault sites far removed from their physical location and also makes it possible for them to attack many sites at once. The other factor that affects the ability of a single entity being able to respond to attacks anywhere in the nation is the magnitude of what must be monitored. As the number of locations/systems that a single entity wishes to monitor increases, the level of detail that can be monitored decreases.

What then should a nation's response capability consist of? To be effective, the nation requires capabilities at all levels of government. States and communities cannot rely on national level agencies to handle attacks on entities at their level. To accomplish this will require both cyber security incident response and information sharing capabilities. Developing either of these is not a simple endeavor and will require significant time to accomplish. Fortunately, there are many similarities between states and between communities so each does not have to start from scratch but can rely on the lessons learned from others and can borrow heavily from programs that have been developed in other areas of a country.

One approach to developing state and community cyber security programs is outlined in the Community Cyber Security Maturity Model (CCSMM). This model can serve several functions for states and communities. It can be used as a "yardstick" to measure the maturity level of their cyber security program. It can also serve as a roadmap outlining the steps a state or community needs to take to improve their security posture and program. It also serves as a common point of reference for individuals from different areas when discussing their respective programs.

The objective of this chapter is to provide an introduction to the CCSMM so that the reader can understand the need for it as well as what the CCSMM consists of and how it can help states and communities. Prior to 2008, the CCSMM had not been adopted by any state within the United States. In 2008, however, congressional legislation called for the implementation of the model in several states. The goal was to test the effectiveness of the model by evaluating how these states, and the communities within them, performed in the 2010 Cyber Storm III National Cyber Security Exercise sponsored by the Department of Homeland Security (HR 2638, 2008).

Background: Development of the CCSMM

Maturity models are not new to the information technology community. The most famous maturity model is the Capability Maturity Model (CMM) (Humphrey, 1989) which itself has gone through several generations of change. The model was originally designed to evaluate government software development processes but has been more broadly used to evaluate an organization's process capability maturity. Work on various maturity models eventually led to the development of an ISO standard, ISO 15504 Information Technology – Process Assessment. The idea behind a maturity model is to help an organization gain control of and improve its IT-related processes. Different levels (frequently five levels are used) describe the various aspects of the processes as they mature within the organization. These levels can be used as a yardstick with which an organization can measure its improvement as its processes mature. They also provide a framework from which organizations can build their processes. Many aspects of IT can benefit from the application of maturity models, including software development, project management, and risk management. They can also be applied to a security environment where a structured approach to securing a community's computer systems and networks is needed.

The CCSMM was developed by the Center for Infrastructure Assurance and Security (CIAS) at The University of Texas at San Antonio (UTSA). It was the result of efforts by the CIAS to help prepare the nation for a possible cyber terrorist attack on a state or community. The initial event that started the CIAS on this path was a challenge issued by Congressman Ciro Rodriguez (D-TX) to the City of San Antonio to test the ability of San Antonio to prevent, detect, and respond to a cyber terrorist attack. As a result of this challenge, the CIAS led an effort within the city to conduct the first-of-its-kind community cyber security exercise. Called Dark Screen, the exercise was conducted in September 2002. Following this initial exercise, the CIAS received funding from the Department of Defense to continue conducting exercises in communities which had a significant Department of Defense presence. Subsequent exercises were conducted in several communities within Texas as well as communities in other states including Virginia, Ohio, Montana, Hawaii, and Louisiana. In addition, the CIAS conducted several state-level exercises for different states throughout the nation. The exercises were the first cyber only exercises for the participants, who indicated they had learned a lot and that they found the exercises worthwhile (Conklin, 2006).

The exercises were a success in helping to promote awareness of the need to establish community and state cyber security programs. Researchers within the CIAS noted that while communities had the desire to develop cyber security programs, they lacked the understanding of what needed to be done or where to start. In addition, communities had different perceptions of how prepared they actually were and how ready they were to respond to a significant cyber event. As a result, the CIAS began work on a model to provide communities the ability to measure their level of preparedness as well as to help them determine what steps they needed to take. The proposed model became known as the Community Cyber Security Maturity Model (White 2007). It should be noted that a question that is frequently asked about the CCSMM is what exactly does the word "community" refer to in the title. This term can certainly have several meanings – community in a geographical sense or community as in a group of individuals with similar interests. For the purposes of this model, the term is used to refer to a geographical community (e.g. metropolitan area, city, town, village, etc.). The model is equally applicable no matter what the size of the community, though it will generally be easier for a smaller community than a large metropolitan area to attain the higher levels of the model.

The CCSMM

Like other maturity models, the CCSMM utilizes five levels to outline the various aspects of the model. Figure 1 shows the five levels of the CCSMM and the characteristics that indicate where a specific community would fall in the model. There are four major dimensions that the characteristics are focused around and that will be used to measure the level of maturity of the community. The dimensions will be explored following a discussion of the levels.

At Level 1 there is little to no community experience or expertise in this part of the model. At Level 2 community leaders in both the public and private sectors are aware of the issues with cyber security as it relates to this part of the model and are attempting to develop security programs for their area of responsibility to address the issues. Informal programs are implemented at this point. Level 3 sees a formalization of the programs established in Level 2 and an emphasis placed on individual organization components as they play a part in the bigger community picture. Level 4 sees the introduction of both citizens to the picture as well as links to the state and its own security efforts. Finally, at Level 5 it can truly be said that cyber security is fully integrated into all organizations at all levels within the community. The need for cyber security is as accepted as physical security.

The titles for each level also give an indication of the general change in the characteristics at the level. Level 1 is of course the first, or Initial, level. It may at first seem anomalous that Level 2 is referred to as Advanced. This is, after all, a term normally used to describe higher levels in any characterization. It is important to understand why the title Advanced is used so early in this model; it is related to the types of cyber attacks that most organizations are used to dealing with. The vast majority of attacks are unstructured in nature. They include simple scripts run by individuals with no great security or computer expertise and no real target or goal in mind. These "script kiddies" as they are sometimes referred to, can generate an inordinate amount of attack traffic and can also cause a great deal of damage when they find unprotected computer systems and networks. The defenses needed to address this threat, however, are not that sophisticated and are the standard

Figure 1. CCSMM community level characteristics

LEVEL 1 Initial	LEVEL 2 Advanced	LEVEL 3 Self-Assessed	LEVEL 4 Integrated	LEVEL 5 Vanguard
• Minimal cyber awareness • Minimal cyber info sharing • Minimal cyber assessments and policy & procedure evaluations • Little inclusion of cyber into Continuity of Operations Plan (COOP)	• Leadership aware of cyber threats, issues and imperatives for cyber security and community cooperative cyber training • Informal info sharing/ communication in community; working groups established; ad-hoc analysis, little fusion or metrics; professional orgs established or engaged • No assessments, but aware of requirement; initial evaluation of policies & procedures • Aware of need to integrate cyber security into COOP	• Leaders promote org security awareness; formal community cooperative training • Formal local info sharing/cyber analysis, initial cyber-physical fusion; informal external info sharing/ cyber analysis and metrics gathering • Autonomous tabletop cyber exercises with assessments of info sharing, policies & procedures, and fusion; routine audit program; mentor externals on policies & procedures, auditing and training • Include cyber in COOP; formal cyber incident response/recovery	• Leaders and orgs promote awareness; citizens aware of cyber security issues • Formal info sharing/ analysis, internal and external to community; formal local fusion and metrics, initial external efforts • Autonomous cyber exercises with assessments of formal info sharing/local fusion; exercises involve live play/metrics assessments • Integrate cyber in COOP; mentor externals on COOP integration; formal blended incident response and recovery	• Awareness a business imperative • Fully integrated fusion /analysis center, combining all-source physical and cyber info; create and disseminate near real world picture • Accomplish full-scale blended exercises and assess complete fusion capability; involve/ mentor other communities/entities • Continue to integrate cyber in COOP; mentor externals on COOP integration; formal blended incident response and recovery

items found in any "best practice" document on computer security – ensure all security patches are installed, eliminate services that are not needed, lock down which ports are used, install anti-virus and firewall protection software/hardware, etc. While this may be simple to describe, the nation, as a whole, is still far from ensuring that these most basic of steps are implemented and thus the media is replete with stories about computer systems and networks that have been broken into. From the CCSMM perspective, however, these steps should be taken in Level 1 and by Level 2 these basic steps should be in place. This means that the community can then start to concentrate on the more Advanced items that need to be considered if structured (e.g. organized crime) or highly structured (e.g. nation states, terrorist organizations) threats are to be addressed. The rest of the model is concerned with the development of the tools, techniques, processes, and procedures that will allow states and communities to address these more dangerous threats.

The name given to Level 3 is Self-Assessed. At this level the community should be autonomous in terms of its security program. Up until this point, the community may have been relying on outside entities to provide a lot of their security needs. At this level communities are conducting their own exercises and training and taking the steps needed to tailor programs to the specific needs of their area. At Level 4, Integrated, the various components that make up a strong, viable cyber security program capable of dealing with structured and highly structured threats have come together. In particular, cyber information sharing and fusion capabilities are intertwined with other first responder/emergency operations capabilities. Cyber threats and events are not handled through separate channels but are part of the community's incident management operations. Cyber is seen as just another possible threat/event as is fire, natural disasters, or weapons of mass destruction. Finally, at the top is Level 5, Vanguard, which describes a community that is taking all of the steps needed and can be seen as a model for all other communities in terms of their ability to address cyber threats and events. Cyber security is completely woven into all aspects of the community, not just the emergency operations aspects seen in Level 4. As can be imagined, this is not a simple task. In fact, none of the security mechanisms the model encourages are easy, even those at Level 1 that are considered to be part of the industry best practices. Developing a program which will lead to the upper levels of preparedness will take considerable dedication by the leaders within a community and will not be accomplished overnight. Simply reaching the second level can take a community over a year and will take constant vigilance to even maintain this level.

As was previously mentioned, there are four dimensions in each level of the model representing the major thrusts at that level. The first is the awareness or level of understanding in the community of cyber security issues. At the lowest level of the model, a community and its leaders have little to no understanding and awareness of the potential damage that a cyber attack could cause. At Level 2, community leaders are now fully aware of the damage that a cyber attack on or within their community can cause. They understand the community's dependence on various cyber infrastructures and how the loss of cyber assets could adversely impact the various critical infrastructures and degrade the ability of first-responders to do their jobs. At Level 3 community leaders now are promoting security awareness within their communities to the various organizations that make up the community (both public and private). The leaders are now champions for cyber security and are making efforts to ensure that all organizations have viable cyber security programs. A community at Level 4 has extended cyber security awareness past organizations to the citizens of the community. Since the proliferation of high-speed Internet access to many homes has resulted in a tremendous increase in the possible targets adversaries might exploit, everybody in

the community needs to understand their part in protecting the community from a cyber attack. A Level 5 community considers cyber security not just a necessity but instead views it as an imperative that everyone must address.

The progression seen in this first dimension is indicative of similar progressions that exist in the other three dimensions as well. The second deals with information sharing – a vital piece of the model and of any viable security program. There has been considerable discussion since the events of September 11, 2001 on the need for the intelligence community to share information between the various agencies as well as with law enforcement organizations (9/11 Commission, 2004). This need applies equally as well to the cyber community where similar systems (operating systems, hardware platforms, application programs) are used across all of the critical infrastructures. A security flaw in an operating system or application program will affect all sectors that utilize the same platform. Early indications of a problem that is seen in one sector needs to be transmitted to all other sectors as well. This actually is already being accomplished to some degree with the current mechanisms that are in place with the vendors of computer software and organizations such as the Computer Emergency Response Team (CERT) and the US-Computer Emergency Readiness Team (US-CERT). These entities have been dealing with security vulnerabilities found in software for a number of years and have a fairly well defined process to address them when they are discovered. What is not as developed is the information sharing mechanisms necessary to be able to detect pending attacks and the warning mechanisms that can be used to then alert others of the possible attack. If, for example, six communities in one state experienced an increased level of scanning on a specific computer port on systems connected to their water and power utilities, it might indicate a pending attack on those systems, or the communities in general. It would be very useful for all communities in the state to be alerted to this activity. At Level 1 of the model, this type of information sharing is not taking place. At Level 2, informal information sharing mechanisms would be created. These might simply include phone rosters utilized by the IT security professionals in the community so that they can call each other when a security relevant event is occurring. At Level 3 these informal mechanisms have evolved into formal local mechanisms with formalized reporting processes. Level 4 further expands the scope of the information sharing so that all pertinent entities within the community, as well as entities within the state, are sharing information. Level 5 sees a fully integrated information sharing mechanism flowing from the community to the national level. Another important aspect of information sharing that also is further developed at each level of the model is the analysis capability that goes with the sharing of information. Typically, this analysis function takes place in organizations such as the fusion centers that have been prescribed since the attacks on the World Trade Center and the Pentagon.

The third dimension used to measure a community's maturity deals with the ability of the community to assess their cyber security status and general security processes. Initially the community has no ability to assess their status and has not incorporated cyber events into the exercises that all communities perform to evaluate their emergency operations procedures. By the time communities enter Level 2 they will have conducted scenario-driven cyber-only security exercises to examine their understanding of the ways a cyber attack could affect the community and their ability to respond to these attacks. Level 3 communities will not only be conducting exercises to examine their cyber security processes and procedures but they will also be conducting regular audits and assessments of computer systems and networks. The audits are designed to evaluate the systems against prescribed standards and assessments can examine ways that an attacker might attempt to

gain access or disrupt operations. Through Level 3, exercises can be in a tabletop format but starting in Level 4 the tabletop format will be occasionally replaced with live exercises designed to evaluate the community's cyber defenders' ability to detect and follow established procedures to respond to attacks. The assessments conducted in Level 3 should have prepared the community for this sort of live event. In addition, the exercise should provide an opportunity for information sharing and fusion capabilities to be examined. The key to Level 5 is the introduction of cyber into the other exercises that a community performs. A blended attack, one in which the attacker uses both cyber and non-cyber avenues to attack the community, could be particularly damaging to a community as it could severely impact the ability of first-responders to respond to the non-cyber attack. As a result, it is important to address this possibility at the higher levels of the model when structured and highly structured attacks are considered.

The last dimension that is measured is the level of planning and consideration of cyber events in the community's continuity of operations plans (COOP). As in the three other parts of the model, at the initial level there is no inclusion or consideration of cyber in the COOP. At Level 2 cyber is still not included in the COOP but the community is aware of the need to include it and is working on plans to do so. Cyber is included in the COOP in Level 3 and a formal community cyber incident response capability is also developed. In Level 4 the incident response capability integrates cyber into non-cyber incident handling and at Level 5 the community mentors others on this same aspect of cyber security.

Activities at and Between Each Level

The characteristics that define the different levels are not the only elements of the maturity model. There are a number of activities that communities must accomplish at each level in order to meet the characteristics defined for each dimension. These activities include training, collection of metrics by individual organizations and the community, information sharing and analysis, exercises, and the development of processes and procedures. Of these, information sharing and analysis, exercises, and the development of processes and procedures have already been discussed.

Training is something that must take place at every level. The training must be continually reviewed and updated, as cyber security is a constantly changing environment with new vulnerabilities constantly being discovered. Training is not only needed to progress from one level to the next, communities that have reached a specific level must have an on-going training activity to maintain that level. If one were to peruse the Internet looking for security courses, a plethora would be found. Almost all of these, however, are of a technical nature designed to help prepare IT personnel to secure their computer systems and networks. While these are important and should be part of any community's security program, they are not the only courses that are needed. Awareness level courses should be presented to community leaders. Community leaders also need courses which outline their responsibilities in the development and maintenance of a security program. This type of course is not technical in nature, though it is concerned with a very technical issue. Additionally, individual organizations need to know how to respond to an incident and the standard cyber incident response course is applicable to meet this need. A community also needs its leaders to be trained in the nuances of a community handling an incident which stresses information sharing and analysis, the community's fusion capability, and cooperation between various organizations within the community. In addition to more traditional security courses, and the courses that community leaders need, specialized courses are also important for fusion centers (which are generally staffed by individuals with law enforcement or intelligence backgrounds and not an IT background) and law enforcement personnel.

Metrics are important to the model for two major reasons. The first is the need to develop metrics that a community can use in order to measure where in the model it is in terms of its security preparedness. In this regard the metrics are nothing more than a statement of the characteristics for each level. For example, at Level 2 questions such as "Have community leaders participated in a cyber awareness training program?" and "Has the community participated in a community cyber security exercise?" could be used to determine whether the community meets the characteristics at this level. The other type of metric that is important in the maturity model is metrics used in conducting security operations. Metrics of this type include measuring the number of scans and penetration attacks experienced by an organization during a specific period of time. While this type of activity is constant, a drastic increase in the number of attempts or specific unusual attempts might indicate an inordinate interest in the organization and might warn of a pending attack. In addition, if the same activity is seen in several different organizations in the community this might signal a more general attack on the community itself. This type of metric is much more operational in nature and requires constant monitoring throughout the community. At the lower levels of the model, establishment of measurement programs is the key. Once monitoring programs are established, norms can be determined for a variety of measurements which will allow for detection of abnormal activity later.

One final element of the CCSMM that can't be overlooked, and that will be an integral part of any organization, community, or state that attempts to establish its own security program, is the technology that is needed to accomplish the various activities. At the earliest stages and the lower levels of the model, many of the activities are very rudimentary in nature and do not require a lot of technology to be implemented. This is important because most states and communities do not have a large budget for implementing a cyber security program. Many of the initial information sharing initiatives can be accomplished by the creation of informal or ad hoc working groups or advisory boards within the community at minimal cost. At the upper levels of the model, however, when monitoring becomes more essential, specific software/hardware technology will be required along with personnel to conduct the analysis of information as it is obtained. While there is a cost involved with this, there is time from the point when a community embarks on implementing the model to the point when this technology is required for the community to plan and budget for the money that will be required.

The Three-Dimensional Model

The first version of the model was a two-dimensional model as depicted in Figure 1. Further development of the model led researchers to the realization that in order for a community to be prepared for structured and highly structured threats, a portion of their activities requires interaction with individual organizations within the community as well as with state and federal entities. This, however, assumes that individual organizations as well as state and federal agencies

have also embarked on their own computer security programs. Simply put, it is impossible for a community to reach the higher levels of the model without organizations within the community as well as state and federal agencies also reaching a certain level of maturity in cyber security. For this reason it was determined that the two-dimensional model was not adequate and a three-dimensional version was created. The third dimension, which simply adds similar two-dimensional maturity models for individual organizations and the state, is depicted in Figure 2.

The 3-Dimensional CCSMM adds organizational and state elements. For both there is a similar maturity model that they can follow. For each block in the model many elements may exist. Figure 2 shows one block, the awareness training portion of the organizational level, expanded. This is a simple example of what the model includes as it shows several awareness courses that should be conducted by individual organizations to advance from Level 1 to Level 2. The complete model contains many such elements.

For an individual organization, the maturity model includes more technical components at a much lower level of the model. Level 1 and 2 involve the securing of the organization's com-

Figure 2. The 3-Dimensional CCSMM showing activities between levels

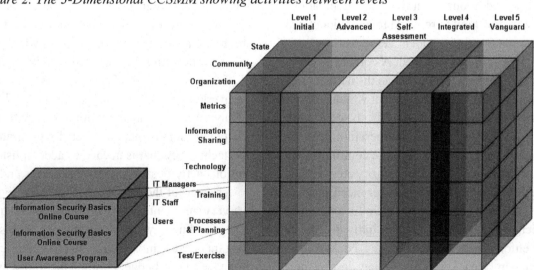

puter and network assets in a manner consistent with industry best practices. For organizations to advance past this level, however, they must realize that they are part of a larger community in both a geographic sense as well as being a member of a larger community of similar organizations (such as the power, water, or the financial services sectors). As such, it is important for them to be an active member within these communities and become involved in active incident information sharing programs.

States have to worry about their maturity from two perspectives. The first views the state as a large organization with assets that it must protect. From this perspective, state agencies must be involved in protecting their own computer and network assets and must conform to state security directives. The other view is the state as the focal point for security efforts within the state involving one or more communities which are experiencing some form of cyber incident. From the first perspective, the state probably has an office or department that is tasked with cyber security initiatives for the other departments/agencies. This is a fairly clear cut responsibility. The second responsibility, however, is more involved and is not really experienced with the state maturity model until Level 3 of that model. In the earliest stages, a separate reporting entity may be used within the state to handle cyber incidents. As the state's capabilities mature, however, this responsibility should be transitioned to the same state office/agency that handles other emergencies within the state. This becomes essential when the community begins to examine its ability to handle a blended attack. Should an attack occur involving both cyber and non-cyber events, it will be important to have a single entity responsible for coordinating the response activities instead of having two separate emergency response infrastructures.

The Use of the Model as a Roadmap or Yardstick

The first thing that most community leaders want to do when considering their community and the CCSMM is to determine where they think their community currently sits in the model. While this is a natural reaction, it is not the real purpose of the model – it is not designed to be a tool for "bragging rights" between communities. Instead, understanding where a community sits within the model provides insight into what level of cyber attack they are currently prepared to address and what the next steps should be to improve their security posture. Roadmaps have been created to go with the model which lay out the transition activities that need to be accomplished to advance from one level to the next. These activities generally consist of exercises, training, and development of certain capabilities, processes, and/or procedures.

Future Efforts

While the CCSMM provides a place for states and communities to start development of their cyber security programs, and while it lays out the initial steps that should be taken, it is a model that is under construction. As the cyber environment changes, the model itself has to evolve. In addition, while the characteristics of communities at the upper levels of the model are understood, the technology that will be required to conduct the information sharing, analysis, and fusion activities at the community and state levels may not yet be developed. There are certainly various vendors that have potential solutions, but none have been implemented to conduct the activities as called for in the model.

The future of CCSMM activities includes the continued development and maintenance of the training modules that are required, the determination of the metrics that will be used to determine when a community is under attack and the technology that will assist in monitoring those metrics, and the continued expansion of the model to additional states and communities throughout the nation. At the time this chapter was developed (in 2008), there were four states involved in the establishment of programs based on the CCSMM.

One area that is lacking currently is in supporting documentation and materials for the model. While there are numerous industry best practices that can be utilized by communities in developing their processes and procedures, none of these best practice documents are written with the model in mind. Efforts are underway to adapt various documents, tools, and training modules to the model but additional materials should be developed and all made available to states and communities as they develop their programs.

Finally, it should be noted that the CCSMM was developed within the United States and therefore refers to states and communities throughout their documents. The underlying issues, however, are equally important to other communities wherever they may be. Whether in Europe, Africa, or Asia, cyber security is increasingly becoming important and the reliance upon cyber infrastructures greater. The Internet is not confined to one country within the world and as such the Internet community is a community without borders. The model, which speaks to communities, states, and the nation can, and needs to, expand to include the world as well. The issues involved with information sharing between nations, however, will not be an easy one and will take significant work to accomplish. There have been initial attempts at expanding cooperation on cyber security issues between various countries. The Cyber Storm II National Cyber Exercise, conducted by DHS in March 2008 included five countries in addition to the several hundred U.S. participants. Examina-

tion of how to expand the CCSMM to other nations is another effort for additional future work.

CONCLUSION

There is no denying that states and communities will need to establish security programs in order to meet the threats they will face in the future. Most early efforts have involved nothing more than ad hoc attempts to organize information sharing/reporting, training of IT personnel, and the technical aspects of securing computer systems and networks. With fifty states in the U.S., and seven territories, unless there is a common approach taken, the result could easily be fifty-seven different approaches to handling information sharing/reporting, analysis, and fusion capabilities at the state level and many times more at the community level. The CCSMM provides an organized approach to address the issue and will lead to states and communities that not only are better prepared to prevent, detect, respond to, and recover from a cyber attack but also states and communities that can interact with other states and communities to create a more prepared nation capable of handling whatever cyber threat it will face. While the model was created for initial implementation within the United States, the issues are common in other nations as well and the model is equally applicable to all.

REFERENCES

9/11 Commission. (2004). *The 9/11 Commission Report - Final Report of the National Commission on Terrorist Attacks Upon the United States (pp.416-419)* (Authorized, First ed.). New York: W. W. Norton & Company.

Australian National Computer Emergency Response Team, http://www.auscert.org.au, July 18, 2008.

Conklin, A., & White, G. (2006). e-Government and Cyber Security: The Role of Cyber Security Exercises. *Proceedings of the 39th Hawaii International Conference on Systems Sciences*, Kauai, Hawaii.

DHS. *Information Technology Initiatives, Fusion Center Guidelines*. Available from http://www.it.ojp.gov/topic.jsp?topic_id=209, April 2, 2008.

HR 2638 (2008). *House Amendment to the DHS Appropriations Act - 2008, Title 3. Protection*

Humphrey, W. (1989). *Managing the Software Process*. Massachusetts: Addison-Wesley.

Multi-State ISAC (2008). http://www.msisac.org, July 18, 2008.

White, G. (2007). The Community Cyber Security Maturity Model. *Proceedings of the 40th Hawaii International Conference on Systems Sciences*, Waikoloa, Hawaii.

The White House (2003). *The National Strategy to Secure Cyberspace*. February 2003, available from http://www.whitehouse.gov/pcipb/, April 2, 2008.

Section IV
Security Technologies

Chapter XVI
Server Hardening Model Development:
A Methodology–Based Approach to Increased System Security

Doug White
Roger Williams University, USA

Alan Rea
Western Michigan University, USA

ABSTRACT

In this chapter the authors present essential server security components and develop a set of logical steps to build hardened servers. The authors outline techniques to examine servers in both the Linux/ UNIX and the Windows Environment for security flaws from both the internal and external perspectives. Ultimately, the chapter builds a complete model which includes advice on tools, tactics, and techniques that system administrators can use to harden a server against compromise and attack.

INTRODUCTION

In a landmark study, Koomey (2007) examines the increased power consumption due to the rapidly growing server population. Using Interactive Data Corporation (IDC) (2008) data, he notes that the number of servers installed between 2000 and 2005 has doubled (Koomey, 2007). With the ever increasing popularity of Web 2.0 services (e.g., Google Applications), social networking Websites (e.g., MySpace), and video sharing (e.g., YouTube), server installations doubled again between 2005 and 2008 (Netcraft, 2008). This trend will continue into the foreseeable future.

The increase in electrical consumption is but one of the side effects of our growing need for Internet-enabled services. Even more pressing to those closely associated with servers is the security of these new machines. Systems administrators are rapidly adding servers to the global interconnected infrastructure known collectively as cyberspace. Without adequate security models for system administrators to follow, we will see increasing numbers of successful attacks as vulnerable systems are put into service (Abu Rajab, Zarfoss, Monrose, & Terzis, 2006; Morphy, 2005).

Moreover, many individuals not familiar with established system administrator security practices are finding it easier to place their powerful desktop machines into service and join the ever-growing digital community. Anyone can transform a small business workstation into a Web server and connect it to the Internet quite easily. This machine has as much potential to wreck havoc on network data flow and communications as a high-end server-class system.

What technology professionals need is a well-designed model, with implementation steps and supporting rubrics, to help them and their organizations implement and maintain secure servers. In this chapter, we provide such a model to assist those who want to implement and maintain secure, hardened servers not only for today's intense demands for server systems but also for the foreseeable future as more servers come online to support new Internet-enabled services.

BACKGROUND

Whether in an international firm with multiple server farms or a non-profit with one or two repurposed desktop workstations as servers, it is a common problem that a server is set up and simply left to run without ensuring security is maintained until new services must be added or a problem occurs.

Server compromise may certainly happen at the inception of the server deployment, but over time additional security flaws are typically uncovered and these revelations are extremely dangerous to established servers that systems administrators have not monitored and audited. On average over 80 attacks happen per day (Moitra & Konda, 2004)

with some days (usually during a new virus outbreak) averaging in the thousands, so hardening a server against attacks is critical to protect an organization's infrastructure and data.

Our discussion focuses on those systems offering external services because they are highly susceptible to compromise, often provide the point of entry for e-commerce transactions, and are typically mission critical systems for an organization. However, servers located on an organization's intranet or a smaller local network can benefit from these approaches as well.

Throughout the discussion, we stress two general concepts that are important to "hardening" the servers in use: 1) monitoring the servers for security flaws, and 2) isolating the servers by task. Because one may approach this differently depending on the server's software architecture, each of these tasks will be discussed in different frameworks—the Microsoft Server and the Linux/UNIX server.

Contemporary Server Models

In today's business environment, most organizations approach server deployment either from a decentralized or centralized model (SEI, 2007). Although there are various permutations of these approaches (e.g., combined Web and file server and a separate mail server), most follow a client/server architecture designed around centralized or decentralized philosophy.

The Client/Server Architecture

Whether researchers look to improve the performance of Web servers (Pariag, Brecht, Buhr, Shukla, & Cheriton, 2007), databases (DeWitt, Futtersack, Maier, & Vélez, 1990), or virtual reality simulations (Ng, Si, Lau, & Li, 2002), they look to the commonly-accepted client/server architecture.

Client/Server architectures comprise the largest segment of organizational computing initiatives. Businesses depend on two-, three-, and multi-tier systems to deliver content, products, and services to clients. These businesses routinely use distributed and collaborative systems in enterprise applications and Web 2.0 services (SEI, 2007). System administrators design a myriad of architectures around either a centralized, decentralized, or a combination of servers from both models.

The Decentralized Server Model (Microsoft)

Microsoft advocates an approach to servers that isolates each server by its purpose. This approach is a natural development in response to server compromise and the demand for uptime. This idea allows servers to function independently for each particular service they are supporting (e.g., file server, print server, database, etc.) and thus not be subject to failure and compromise of another service. This approach to server management also allows system administrators to specialize in their particular environment. The downside is the number of server platforms and administrators rises as organizations add more services.

The Centralized Server Model (UNIX)

The other approach to servers is to consolidate them into a central device. This is similar to the mainframe approach to serving that many UNIX-based servers utilize. The advantage to this approach is the use of limited hardware and administrators. In addition, it centralizes resources to generate economies of scale and control of licensing, updates, etc. A disadvantage in this centralized server model is the single point of failure and the complexity of managing many different products simultaneously. The large scale of this approach (and it certainly may include more than one server) forces administrators to be generalists rather than specialists which creates the need for additional staff simply to monitor the products.

SECURE SERVER MODELING CONCEPTS

An organization can choose to create its server infrastructure around either a centralized or decentralized model. In the contemporary server environment, it is possible to combine these models as well, although this may require more maintenance, personnel, and other support than desired. (Carrera, Beltran, Torres, & Ayguade, 2005). Nevertheless, when system administrators deploy these servers, they must consider certain issues and components necessary for a secure environment.

Key Issues and Components

Chuvakin (2002) details eight key security components that organizations must consider when working to deploy and maintain secure servers.

We have revised these eight components, in some cases simply regrouping them, to form eight key issues system administrators must consider.

We have made subsumed Chuvakin's Component 2 into our Component 1 to provide system administrators with general guidelines and issues they must consider when developing secure environments. In addition, we have separated our Component 2, "Isolating Services and Soft-

Table 1. Chuvakin's eight server hardening security components

Component	Action
1	**Minimize Installed Software**
2	**Patch the System**
3	**Secure Filesystem Permissions**
4	**Improve Login and User Security**
5	**Set Physical and Boot Security Controls**
6	**Secure Daemons via Network Access Controls**
7	**Increase Logging and Auditing**
8	**Use IDS and Firewalls**

Table 2. Revised eight server hardening security components

Component	Issue
1	OS Install and Kernel Hardening
2	Isolating Services and Software Reduction
3	Secure Filesystem Permissions
4	Login and User Security
5	Physical and Boot Security Controls
6	Secure Daemons via Network Access Controls
7	Logging and Auditing
8	Use of IDS and Firewalls

ware Reduction," from Chuvakin's Component 1, "Minimize Installed Software," to reflect the interconnected nature of contemporary network offerings. All other components center around the same areas of concern.

We discuss these issues in the following section. After exploring the general components, we then create the steps, and associated phases, to harden both Microsoft and Linux/UNIX servers.

Operating System (OS) Install and Kernel Hardening

System administrators who want to create a secure, or bastion, server should start with a clean operating system (OS) install. This is particularly important in the case of legacy systems inherited by the system administrator. Administrators should take care during the initial install to avoid installing software and services that the server will not need. Both Linux and Windows products install a variety of daemons (e.g., SMTP, or Simple Mail Transfer Protocol) that can create large security holes if not managed correctly. During the install process, system administrators must review all products they are installing for both their critical need on the server and their security risk.

Many security experts opt for the Decentralized Server Model (DSM) in server environments no matter which OS they select; however, system administrators should develop a template for each OS that describes the services needed on that machine. The template should contain a reference document that lists all services and daemons that administrators will deploy on the server. As an additional security measure, system administrators should include a list of known security risks and affected versions to this document. **Appendix A** contains a sample of the document used to record and monitor this component.

System administrators should note that one of the major challenges of Windows-based products is their proprietary nature. Microsoft controls the kernel of the operating system and therefore the administrator relies on Microsoft to provide security at the kernel level. This is not to say that Linux/UNIX systems are more secure. The Computer Emergency Response Team (CERT) reports Linux systems (and their services) in many of its open source security alerts. These alerts have grown from a handful to almost half the warnings from CERT (Hurley and Hemmendinger, 2002). Moreover, in a review of server-only advisories from US-CERT, the number of advisories was almost equal for Linux (not including Sun and other UNIX variants) and Windows categories (CERT, 2008).

With this in mind, system administrators should be aware that in the Linux environment it is possible to edit and recompile the kernel with only the required drivers to accomplish specific tasks. An administrator using this approach can create a customized system using a kernel with the required drivers; thereby encapsulating the kernel, as well as excluding unnecessary kernel tools. Doing so protects systems from many documented attacks (Kyle & Brustoloni, 2007).

In the Windows environment, the patching of the kernel (service pack updates) is the critical action. The administrator will need to rely on Microsoft updates to correct any problems. Most Windows administrators monitor specific security bulletin lists, such as Microsoft's Security Central (Microsoft, 2008) in addition to US-CERT and other security announcement lists.

Isolating Services and Software Reduction

With the Decentralized Server Model (DSM) an administrator can more easily eliminate unnecessary services from her servers. However, administrators can also accomplish this in a Centralized Server Model (CSM) as well with some effort.

System administrators must remember that most operating system installs automatically include unneeded and sometimes dangerous services (if not managed), such as SMTP or IIS (Internet Information Services) in the default install. When these services are not in use, organizations should not justify installing them, even if they may be needed later. Once a service is running, administrators must monitor it.

Moreover, if an organization later needs a particular service, the system administrator can download and install the most recent version at that time, rather than use the outdated version on the install disks. Thus, we recommend system administrators first identify which services (and these services should include operating system tools) that are needed before beginning an install.

Ideally, in the clean install process one implements the absolute minimum number of services. Rather than accepting all the default installation settings, the system administrator must carefully choose which packages to install and analyze their worth to the system versus the potential security risk they pose. Obviously, a system with no services, or daemons, installed is more secure than a system with a port open to the world. Unfortunately, this makes for a fairly useless server.

During a default server installation, typical daemons on both Windows and Linux/UNIX servers include services, such as SMTP, Web servers (Apache or IIS), Telnet (Telecommunication Network), SSH (Secure Shell), FTP (File Transfer Protocol), and file servers. While some of these services may be needed for basic organizational operations, such as e-mail (e.g., SMTP), there are security risks by simply accepting default install settings without consideration for open ports, documented service vulnerabilities, etc. (Curran, Morrissey, Fagan, Murphy, O'Donnell, Fitzpatrick, & Condit, 2005). System administrators must be careful to install only specific daemons designated for certain purposes and not those whose services may not be entirely evident.

Secure File System Permissions

On both Windows and Linux/UNIX platforms, file systems have security policies that administrators may implement for files or groups of files based on ownership. While Windows and Linux/UNIX use particular variants and different terminology for their file systems, there are similarities (Horowitz, 2007). Essentially, both platforms utilize a series of permissions to determine the level of file access granted to any given system user who is attempting to use that particular system file. This includes both external Web-based users, as well as internal authenticated users on a system.

The Linux/UNIX file system schema implements permissions based on users, groups, and others. Each of these categories has certain levels of permissions which are examined before permitting any sort of access (read, write, and execute) to a file (Sun, 2008). Administrators use groups as a means of managing file permissions in role-based security environments. Normally, this approach advocates determining the role's needs and allocating permissions to the entire role, but administrators should be careful because role-based security is often overused and neglects to address specific access on an individual basis.

A major risk with this schema occurs when users acquire higher levels of permissions by pushing commands into other programs owned by meta-users. For example, a user runs a file as the root user which allows a user to pass arguments. Using this technique, a user may be able to access a database, change passwords, or access restricted files.

Therefore, system administrators must determine and document what applications and daemons not only can be accessed by other users but also have user permissions and ownership assessed to determine the level at which any command might be executed. Without doing so, system administrators open their systems to both malicious and accidental attacks that can hamper services or destroy data (Blunt, 2006).

Common solutions to address this challenge in Linux/UNIX systems are reassigning ownership away from meta-user accounts to heavily restricted accounts (such as nobody or guest) or using other software to reassign control to a "jail," which is a restricted shell environment or other restricted runtime environment that prevents the application user from wantonly executing commands (Kamp & Watson, 2004).

Microsoft implements diverse methods that a system administrator can employ to control user access. Like Linux/UNIX, Microsoft employs users and groups as a means of controlling file and application access. However, unless correctly managed, both Microsoft and Linux/UNIX applications may allow users to execute illegitimate commands via legitimate applications by pushing the commands through as arguments (Christodorescu, Jha, & Kruegel, 2007).

Further complicating the system administrator's task, Microsoft permits various types of software global access to files and drivers on the system; however, Vista is slowly remedying this situation (Russinovich, 2007). Still, these convenient tools have proven to be popular with programmers, but have also led to the creation of many tapeworm viruses and other attack software which rely on the open access to various system components (Stiegler, Karp, Yee, Close, & Miller, 2006). Still, Microsoft allows sharing of files controllable via the same permission system for files, but creates an environment in which files may be viewed and changed by virtually any outsider if administrators do not take steps to manage the access levels.

Ultimately, as a component of server hardening, a system administrator must locate all applications, daemons, services, and clients to determine who may access them and how to minimize the risk that access can cause. Creating groups and permissions is effective only if administrators regularly monitor and manage the groups and permissions. Of course, Windows system administrators can implement the Linux/UNIX method of jailing components by creating users and groups with very limited permissions, and then using these groups to control user access to various services (Kamp & Watson, 2004).

Login and User Security

As with file permissions, administrators need to develop user security by carefully designing the groups in which each user may belong. By creating groups which have appropriate security entitlements, system administrators can effectively manage user access and protect against system abuse. In order to assure the correct user accesses the system, system administrators must first manage user logins.

Users who can log in from unsecured or untrusted networks may be using insecure protocols which could easily result in a system compromise. Services such as Telnet and FTP send packages over unencrypted connections or, in the clear, transmit across unsecure and untrusted networks. Transmissions of this nature will likely result in passwords and usernames being compromised (Lant, 2002). System administrators must enable users to use secure connections, such as SSH or log in via a Virtual Private Network (VPN) tunnel. Making it easy for users to use the system via secure protocols will help maintain system integrity.

Controlling user logins also includes managing user password selection and utilization. Users with insecure and predictable passwords create a risk, particularly those users with high levels of security or meta-user access. Password management is a crucial component of system security. Although not all operating systems integrate system policy methods in a default install to enforce strong passwords, administrators should always create a means to enforce a strong policy.

Both Linux/Unix and Windows administrators need to be aware of login and user security. Without solid practices in this area, no server is truly secure. Although Windows does not support Telnet in a default install, FTP is present. Linux/UNIX servers are notorious for default insecure services, such as Telnet and remote login (rlogin). Newer install protocols are finally turning these off in the default install process (NSA, 2009). As we will discuss later, scanning for these services and shutting them down unless protection precautions are in place is critical for server hardening.

Physical and Boot Security Controls

No matter what other security measures are in place, without physical security, all protection will fail and an attacker will compromise a system. For example, a server connected to a terminal with the superuser (root or administrator) prompt located in an unlocked room is waiting for a compromise. Anyone passing by can make a dramatic or, even worse, a subtle change in the system that may result in severe compromise later. The change may not even be malicious; a well-meaning user may simply turn off the system because she

sees no one around using it. Of course, when an attacker physically removes a system he has as much time as is needed to crack security and extract information.

Boot security closely relates to physical security because most boot/reboot compromises require physical access to the server. When an attacker can reboot the system with his compact disc (CD) or Universal Serial Bus (USB) drive in the server, he will be able to circumvent all security on the system by mounting his own file system and making changes that will allow him additional access (Galligan and White, 2008). Linux/UNIX systems are especially vulnerable to various boot shell attacks and other file mounting attacks. Most of these are the result of physical access, rebooting the server, and then immediately accessing files or installing programs to monitor data and files for later retrieval.

In a similar approach, attackers can modify Microsoft registry entries by booting the system with a DOS (Disk Operating System) diskette or other operating system (such as Linux) off a CD or USB. Attackers commonly use this technique to access the hard drive without the management of the Windows operating system security model. Disabling CD and USB reads on boot, and then locking the system BIOS (Basic Input Output System) with a password, can help prevent this occurrence.

Securing the Daemons via Network Access Controls

Every operating system has its daemons. Daemons provide the services and require open ports to listen for connection attempts, or provide information in response to queries to that port. Most attacks occur via well-known daemon vulnerabilities rather than an actual physical attack on the server equipment (Chari & Cheng, 2003). More often than not an attack occurs because even though administrators have patched the operating system, the actual daemons are out of date, or are beta versions, with known security flaws that make them ripe for an attack (Manadhata, Wing, Flynn, & McQueen, 2006).

Attackers look for these vulnerabilities in all servers because they are easier to find. System administrators know that if a server is to be useful, it must have means of access. What good is a Web server if it cannot deliver content via the default port 80 to users? Finding ways to secure the daemons, yet maintain functionality, is critical.

Besides regularly updating and patching software, system administrators must manage the daemons by controlling access to them in the network. Administrators can actively control systems with firewalling and authentication, or passively implement controls via Intrusion Detection Systems (IDS) to detect compromise attempts from attackers. The active approach is more appropriate, but leads to more administrative overhead and management issues that must be accounted for in terms of staffing support and training, as well as time allocation.

Logging and Auditing

Effective system logs are one of the only ways to not only reveal suspicious activity but also monitor whether the system is running within the expected parameters (Hansteen, 2008). We cannot stress enough the importance of setting up and maintaining effective logs to the hardening process. System administrators who rely on the default system logs, which are familiar to all attackers, will most likely not be able to determine system tampering because attackers remove logs and erase all record of their compromise as a standard procedure.

Moreover, system administrators should carefully audit logging practices and policies to ensure effective log use. Most administrators will ignore logs that are too voluminous or overly complex. Auditing logging practices almost always identifies problematic areas which can then be improved (Schneier & Kelsey, 1999).

Security audits may also reveal new risks and fixes that administrators missed as security processes and procedures are developed. Most organizations fail to understand that security is not a single discreet event, but rather a continuous set of events that system administrators must adjust and revise whenever someone reveals a new security flaw or updates an operating system, and especially when new employees are hired or current employees dismissed. System administrators must treat every one of these events as a critical security factor and assess it.

If administrators do not monitor and account for all events, system security quickly becomes outdated and server hardening becomes an impossible task. Just as a castle with stone walls slowly cracks and crumbles without maintenance, servers without constant upkeep succumb to holes and flaws.

Use of IDS and Firewalls

Although Intrusion Detection Systems (IDS) and firewalls are located external to the server, they are a crucial component of server hardening. When a server supplies services on open ports to external networks, firewalls must be in place to protect data. In cases where services are restricted to ports or users, firewalls maintain this granularity. For example, Web servers often allow anonymous access to the Websites maintained on the system, yet, this opening provides attackers with access to the IP (Internet Protocol) address of the Web server. With an IP in hand, attacker can scan ports and conduct denial of service attempts. A firewall may be the only means to thwart these attacks (Peng, Leckie, & Ramamohanarao, 2007).

System administrators can use an IDS to monitor many levels of activity in a network and to warn when malicious attempts occur. When an IDS detects certain types of activity, such as a port scan or an attempt to connect to a known Trojan portal, the IDS generates a log message, and can also send an e-mail or page, to warn that such activities are occurring (Henders & Opdyke, 2005).

With malicious activity warnings, system administrators can examine the probe's source and determine any necessary action. This type of monitoring is critical to identifying compromised servers. For example, if an IDS detects a connection to a common Trojan virus, SubSeven port 27374 (Petri, 2009), it will request that the system administrator scan the port to determine if it is truly open. If it is open, an attack may have compromised the system. In tandem, the log entry should indicate the source of the probe. Once the system administrator determines the scan origin, she can investigate if other internal compromises have led to this occurrence. If the scan origin is external, she can create firewall entries to block these ports and prevent further probing of the internal networks.

Server Hardening Model Solution

Our revision and expansion of Chuvakin's (2002) components provides system administrators with the rationale behind the concepts needed for a secure, hardened server solution. However, to implement such a system, we need to provide an organized model that promotes a pragmatic approach to apply these concepts.

We use Simon's (1960) model of scientific decision making (Figure 1) as our logical basis for developing hardening techniques. Our server hardening model follows Simon's approach because it has been proven as an effective problem solving model and accepted technique of methodological thought (McHaney & White, 1994) that can be applied to almost any continuous event problem, such as security and server hardening.

By combining Simon's approach with our expansion of Chuvakin's (2002) components we have created a systematic model that any system administrator can use to create a hardened Microsoft or Linux/UNIX server for a plethora of purposes.

Each of the following seven steps includes three phases a system administrator must complete before moving to the next step. This refined process allows administrators to create and manage secure, hardened servers with a proven systematic approach. We organize the following discussion around the seven steps.

Step 1: Initial Planning and OS Installation

The first step includes not only planning and preparing to install the operating system but also the install itself.

Figure 1. Simon's scientific decision making process

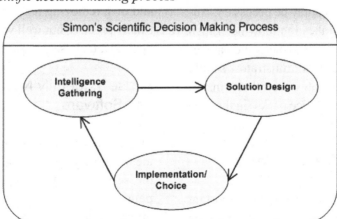

Phase 1: Determine OS Selection

The length spent on this phase can vary greatly. Administrators may quickly make this decision, for example, if an organization has guidelines in place that permit only Windows-based servers or perhaps system administrators are more familiar with a particular Linux/UNIX distribution.

If there are no set parameters for OS decisions, organizations are encouraged to create a matrix of needs to determine if a particular OS or distribution best fits expected requirements. Organizations should also determine if they need consultants, additional staff training, or maintenance contracts. Reaching these decisions is beyond the scope of this discussion. However, experts have created guidelines for these particular decisions (Limoncelli, Hogan, & Chalup, 2007).

Phase 2: Plan OS Install and Updates

After making an OS decision, managers and system administrators must plan for any potential data backups, service downtime if replacing a current system, and other issues that can generally occur during an install. A weekend may be the best time, or perhaps an evening. In any case, a thorough install and potential rollback plan should be in place before proceeding (Limoncelli, et al., 2007).

System administrators should also allot time for the many updates that may be necessary. Administrators should plan ahead and download, then burn to a disk all known OS updates and patches before the install. System administrators should also be sure to have the latest OS release install disks to avoid multiple service packs (in the case of Windows) or service updates.

Phase 3: Install OS and Updates

When the scheduled time arrives, it is important for system administrators to remember that the new server has no security other than the basic operating system security. We recommend that until administrators establish the remaining components in the process, they should protect the server by firewalling it from any public access. Typically, administrators can maintain the server behind a separate firewall to block all access from outside its subnet.

System administrators must take particular care to block not only TCP (Transmission Control Protocol), but also UDP (User Datagram Protocol), ICMP (Internet Control Message Protocol) and other packet types because the server is in a vulnerable state. As recent security compromises have revealed (Register, 2008; Schneier, 2008), even the most supposedly secure operating systems may have dangerous security holes, such as kernel vulnerabilities that allow attackers to gain restricted access. For these reasons, administrators should not expose the new servers publically until taking measures to harden the server against attack. We cover these measures in subsequent steps.

After configuring and patching the server, system administrators can begin hardening the server for implementation.

Step 2: Service and Software Reduction

On a default server install, most systems will have more services running than needed. Identifying and then removing those unneeded services is a timely process, but well worth the investment to operate a truly secure server.

Phase 1: Identify Necessary Services and Software

In this first phase, system administrators must identify every service and piece of software on the server and then judge its usefulness. **Appendix A** is a sample form that administrators might use to conduct this type of audit. System administrators who perform a careful examination will create a list of unused services and default software installed.

Phase 2: Determine a Removal Method

In this phase, system administrators must determine a safe and effective means of uninstalling these services. This may entail preservation of the software for later use. One method is to keep services installed and updated, but not activate them on system boot. Or one might consider archiving the software elsewhere if the organization might need the service or software in the near future. Deciding to disable or remove software services is important especially if the version of the software is significant for compatibility issues and the software may be unavailable in the future.

Phase 3: Remove Unnecessary Software and Services

After administrators remove software, they may vault the original sources for a period of time to insure they will have the software if it is necessary to reinstall it.

System administrators should note that software which appears to be unused may simply be very rarely used. A simple guide for software vaulting is to maintain it for a complete business cycle. If the software involves minimal storage on fixed media, such as optical disks, the storage may be indefinite but a plan should be in place to dispose of old software on a scheduled basis. This prevents large amounts of data storage with no clear indication as to its status, as well as the inadvertent install of old or unnecessary software by technical personnel.

Step 3: Securing File Permissions

System administrators must take the time to examine file permissions and create a policy of access rights. Administrators can audit the files and categorize them as public or private to determine the levels of access to any given group. When working with Web servers, FTP servers, and other systems which involve anonymous use, system administrators must take great care to identify files which are to have public, anonymous access and identify private, protected files. After making the public/private distinction, system administrators should create additional granular controls to set file access permissions according to various user groups.

Phase 1: Audit File Security

Typical audits identify all files that have permissions set for global access, files accessible to various monitored constituents, and meta-user files. System administrators need to focus on the permission structures and identify at-risk files. In Linux/UNIX, system administrators can issue a **<find –perm 777>** command to locate world-writeable and world-readable files. Administrators can find other access settings by changing the three-digit number to reflect the desired file permissions. Windows system administrators can use free tools, such as DumpSec (Somarsoft, 2009) to audit files for this critical information.

Phase 2: Determine Access Needs

Administrators must define permission structures to effectively design and implement groups of users. After organizations determine access needs, system administrators must implement a policy for global, local, and anonymous types of access; however, it may be modified depending on a particular server's purpose (e.g., Web server versus file server) (Etalle & Winsborough, 2007). Although considered a "paranoid" policy, for a truly hardened server, system administrators should exclude all users from any utilities and system files, and then loosen those permissions only as the need arises.

Instead of restricting and slowly allowing access, system administrators may opt for an initial policy that identifies users by groups and assigns access accordingly. For example, programmers may need access to compile tools (e.g., gcc, the GNU Compiler Collection), whereas accountants need access to financial software. If an organization chooses this approach (and most do), system administrators must set up an audit schedule to routinely examine group access. This step is especially critical if administrators implement new user groups or the server offers a new function.

Continual assessments are more manageable in the Decentralized Server Model (DSM) architecture because the server should not change its function or add functions very often. In a Centralized Server Model (CSM) architecture, where many functions are concurrent, system administrators will find it more challenging to determine the needs of all users on the system. They must be careful to maintain functionality as well as security.

Phase 3: Implement File Permission Security Policy

In the final phase, system administrators must set permissions. However, organizations that allot extra time to create tools to either assist or automate this process will save time and resources in future system installs (Limoncelli, et al., 2007). A clear policy must accompany the implementation materials so that system administrators can review all future installs for compliance, as well as evaluate any policy impacts from new groups or services.

Step 4: Login and User Security

In this step, system administrators must concentrate on protecting the system from the users themselves. Weak passwords and insecure connections make it easy for attackers to thwart many of the system security measures (Forget & Biddle,

2008). A hardened server is only as secure as its weakest link. System administrators must audit the system to determine risks, develop policy about user control, and implement and enforce these policies.

Phase 1: Audit User Groups and User Passwords

System administrators should become familiar with attacker tools, such as John the Ripper (Openwall, 2009) because they can use these tools to test their own server security. By running passwords though dictionary attacks as well as brute force attacks, system administrators can identify users with weak passwords, such as "777," "happy," or a variety of pet names. Using this type of audit will expose password weaknesses that allow for quick system cracking attacks (Cisneros, Bliss, & Garcia, 2006).

As a secondary component of this audit, system administrators should test for insecure services, such as Telnet or FTP. If organizations are using these services, no password is safe from an attacker sniffing the network traffic. Administrators must phase out these weak services and replace them with secure versions that supply the same Telnet and FTP functionality, SSH and SFTP (Secure File Transfer Protocol), respectively.

A third audit component requires system administrators to review appropriate user and group login scripts. Default user creation scripts and other implementation scripts (e.g., user-requested software installs) may create path statements that allow dangerous levels of access or cause additional vulnerabilities.

The final audit component is a regular user group assessment. Review user group assignments and determine if users need to be regrouped or new groups created (Meber, 2004). It is possible that roles have changed—an inter-organizational employee transfer, for example—and administrators perhaps overlooked user group updates. Make sure to identify terminated users (e.g., employees who have left the organization).

Phase 2: Plan the Changes

Once the audit is complete, organizations should plan an implementation of the new policies and changes. In addition to the technical implementation, organizations should educate users on how to select appropriate passwords, as well as instruct them on how to use secure connections, such as SSH and SFTP. Administrators must notify users with weak passwords and require the users to change their passwords according to the new guidelines. Review group changes and login script changes, as well as discuss them as part of user training. Periodically remind users of these changes and train all new employees before issuing an account.

Phase 3: Update Policies and Implement Corrections

Once the technical and educational components are in place, organizations should disseminate the policy and schedule training for all users. Steps must be in place to monitor policy adherence. Regular auditing and assessment of passwords is a key mechanism to ensure hardening server compliance and prevent serious security risks.

Step 5: Physical and Boot Security Controls

As we have discussed previously, without strong physical and boot controls, no amount of security can protect a hardened server. An attacker will compromise any server that allows easy physical access, regardless of the amount of hardening to the server's operating system.

Phase 1: Assess Physical Security and Boot Control Security

In the initial phase system administrators must determine the placement of the server and assess its physical location. Organizations must control access so that only authorized users can access the rack or facility which houses the server. In co-location situations, the organization should have assurances as to who will be able to access the machine not only from their organization but also from the hosting company as well.

One method of assessment is to determine which persons have access by listing the groups of users as seen in **Appendix B**. After determining who has access, further restrictions may be necessary to secure the server, such as requiring key card access, biometric scans, or pass codes to the room (Limoncelli, et al., 2007).

A server should typically be in lock down mode at all times unless an administrator is using the system console to administer the server directly. In other words, no one should be able to input information into the server—even inadvertently—via an attached keyboard or console. The server console itself should be password protected or locked with a key. It is not uncommon for attackers to use social engineering techniques to talk their way into server rooms or procure passwords over the telephone. Many techniques to prevent social engineering discuss guarding against such attacks in greater detail (Gragg, 2003; Arthurs, 2001).

In a typical compromise an attacker inserts a diskette or USB key containing another operating system. When the server reboots, the attacker has gained meta-access to the server disks and their data. The attacker can now procure password files, system registries, and other information bypassing the operating system security (Kyle & Brustoloni, 2007).

Even if administrators lock a console with a password, attackers with physical access will attempt to boot the server using an external device. System administrators can prevent this by restricting boots with BIOS password restriction, drive restrictions, or other means to ensure that the server will not boot from system drives, such as removing all CD and DVD drives and turning off USB ports. If attackers compromise the system, administrators will need to take the extra step of entering the BIOS password, reinstalling the CD or DVD drive, and then booting the rescue media. However, the benefits of a secure system outweigh the inconvenience.

Phase 2: Design the Physical and Boot Security

After the physical and boot security risks have been addressed and implemented, the organization must now either place the server in its own server room or lease space from a co-location facility. It is beyond the scope of our discussion to discuss the various requirements for a viable data center, such as power and cooling requirements, network access, etc.; however, many resources are available to organizations wishing to create their own data center or lease space in one (Limoncelli, et al., 2007).

Phase 3: Place the Server and Test the Boot Security

In the last phase of this step, system administrators place the server and connect it to the network. If possible, they should keep the server from the main network segment until completing Step 6. If this is not an option, system administrators must immediately complete the next step to insure network security.

Step 6: Secure Daemons via Network Access Controls

System administrators should know how each of their servers is interacting with the network and other machines. A critical step in the server hardening process is discovering which server ports are listening via running daemons. What many system administrators fail to remember is that a default operating system install enables certain services by default.

In order to identify all active daemons, system administrators should use the Security Administrators Tool for Administering Networks (Porcupine, 2009). SATAN is the acknowledged precursor to many scanning tools used by both security professionals and attackers to probe networked systems for vulnerabilities. One such tool, NMAP (Insecure, 2009), the Network Mapper, provides system administrators with a comprehensive platform for scanning entire networks for vulnerabilities. Monitoring for port scan activity is also important because attackers usually prepare attacks by scanning a system to determine daemons and open ports. Although it is an excellent tool for system and network administrators, system administrators should remove it from Linux images destined for client use.

Phase 1: Port Scan the Server to Assess the Daemons

In the first phase of this step, system administrators should use a tool, such as NMAP, to scan the server's ports. The port scan should include all ports (0-65535) to insure no Trojans, such as SubSeven 2.2 on port 1080 (Petri, 2009), are already in existence on the server. If system administrators have thoroughly assessed the hardened server's software and services in Step 2, nothing more than what they have already identified should surface.

However, we recommend that system administrators perform this test at various distances from the server in the local subnet segment, to an internal scan from a different segment, and ultimately a scan from an external location (intranet or Internet) to identify visible ports and services that may be available to an attacker. At the end of this phase, administrators must identify every listening daemon and provide a clear rationale noted for services viewable from each distance. **Appendix C** contains a form used for recording this information.

Phase 2: Determine Access Policy for Each Service

Once the form in **Appendix C** is completed, system administrators should have identified all services at each distance level. One can assume that, at a given level, potential attackers can also see the services. Because the organization needs the services, yet needs to hide them from attackers, system administrators must create a firewall to prevent an outside attacker from exposing the necessary port.

Create the firewall to filter out any potential port or daemon identification from a distance. This means that the firewall must exist at the outmost edge of the network. For example, if SSH is needed internally it would appear on the server form and a daemon would be listening on port 22. However, if administrators want to filter this service from the outside world, add a rule at the edge router or firewall that would filter any packet to port 22. In this manner, SSH can still be used internally, but an external attacker would have no indication the service exists.

Phase 3: Manage Firewalls and Authentication to Limit Access

The final phase of this step requires system administrators to implement the firewall. After administrators have deployed the firewall and its rules, they should repeat the scans and update the form in order to guarantee casual observers cannot see a particular port. This step allows an organization to harden the server by removing an attacker's ability to communicate with ports that exist, but should not be available to external users. As an additional benefit, this step will also prevent an attacker who attempts to determine the operating system using NMAP fingerprinting (Fyoder, 2002).

Step 7: Maintenance

As with many system development approaches, the final step in the server hardening model is an iterative process. At this point, the system administrator has a well documented, secure, hardened server, but continuously monitors for suspicious events and policy updates.

Phase 1: Monitor Logs for Suspicious Events

In the first phase, system administrators must implement and manage effective logging techniques and mechanisms. A daily task in maintaining a secure, hardened system, most administrators overlook logging until after an attack occurs. By then, it is too late to be of use (GadAllah, 2004).

The single default system log is insufficient to monitor and track system changes. Instead, system administrators need to create logging mechanisms to account for diverse monitoring levels and services, such as the system log, the IDS log, and the firewall log. Streamline each of these logs into an exception report rather than a collector of all events and regularly monitor the report.

IDS tools, such as Snort (SourceFire, 2009), can be set up to generate exception reports of suspicious events. System administrators should also write scripts that will parse the voluminous event logs, or purchase scripts that can be customized (Bombich, 2007). These logs are critical to forensic analysis after attacks occur, and administrators can quickly convert them into concise reports of suspicious activity.

In addition, we strongly recommend automated system scans by NMAP (Insecure, 2009) via scripts to report any daemon changes on the system. Typically, a server should look the same day after day; if a new port suddenly opens, immediately investigate it.

Phase 2: Start an Audit as a Result of an Event

System administrators must carefully review any log or scan that triggers an audit. It is important to review the affected area and evaluate the server's security to determine if an attack was successful. Moreover, administrators must determine if they must implement additional protections. If system administrators determine attackers have compromised a system, they must revisit the entire auditing process to again "harden" the server from attacks.

Phase 3: Update Policies and Impose Corrections

After completing audits, system administrators must impose the new policy conditions on the server. They may simply need to patch a file or may need to revisit the operating system as a whole and start the hardening process anew.

The Completed Model

Organizations that support and promote our server hardening model with their system administrators will discover that their servers, and the data on them, are well protected against the multiple attacks occurring on a daily basis in the Internet-enabled, Web 2.0-infused, global economy.

We cannot guarantee that each step will go as quickly as others. For example, the initial investigations into operating systems in Step 1 may take weeks for an organization exploring its options. For another, it may take less than a minute given that the organization mandates a certain OS. Still, many of the other steps will become ingrained and efficient with practice. Of course, the iterative Step 7 is a continuous process.

The hardened server exists in a state of continuous assessment; any major changes in the server will trigger a recursive process because

system administrators will need to work through Steps 2-6 to assure security. With these notes in mind, one can see the model and its processes as an organic entity (Figure 2). We have also provided an accompanying checklist (**Appendix D**) so system administrators can easily track model implementations in their organization.

FUTURE TRENDS

As we noted in the introduction, the growth of Web 2.0 services in conjunction with the ease at which individuals can connect servers to the vast interconnected Internet requires a greater awareness of security issues. With multiple system attacks occurring globally every minute, a combination of reactive and proactive practices enables those working with servers to address the multitude of security challenges in an efficient manner.

More Reactive Positions

System administrators are in charge of many of the defenses put in place to protect these powerful systems against attack and compromises. They must continue to be vigilant pursuing both pre-deployment hardening of servers, as well as continuous monitoring of the network environment. Any change may signal a potential service disruption or attempted compromise of their servers. By hardening them from the initial steps throughout their development, they will add layers of defense to their systems and the data they hold.

System administrators must contend with the regular release of service packs, as well as almost daily releases of updates reacting to newly-discovered threats. These updates can create both solutions, if the service packs and updates are effective, as well as threats, should they prove to introduce new defects in the hardened server's services. Only through continual monitoring and auditing can system administrators maintain a vigilant posture.

Figure 2. Complete server hardening model

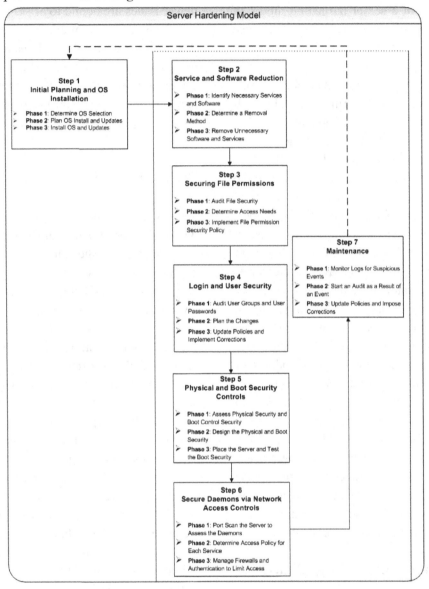

More Proactive Positions

System administrators sometimes view planning against increased system attacks as a greater time commitment than reacting. However, keeping systems, as well as one's knowledge of current security issues, up to date can speed up reaction time when incidents occur. One should develop relevant resources for all pertinent system platforms and stay current on new releases, security issues, and upcoming products. Whether choosing e-mail, blogs, technology review sites, or a combination of various information conduits, system administrators should have a collection of resources at their disposal.

All too often system administrators are reacting to situations, fixing problems, or generally just putting out technology fires. They forget to review or create sound solutions. Instead, system administrators find themselves doing quick fixes, workarounds, or finding other solutions to fix a problem. Without a server hardening model in place, these undocumented solutions will cause additional problems that quickly grow in complexity.

Taking the time to create a set of tools, scripts, and policies will seem daunting at first, but will help system administrators in their daily tasks. For example, if a system administrator finds herself performing a repetitive task with multiple steps, taking the time to write a script to automate the task is in order (Limoncelli, et al., 2007).

Proactively choosing a proven server operating system is a simple technique to assist in the overall server hardening process. Although newer operating systems may have more features, system administrators have deployed and tested many older, and proven server operating systems. Moreover, security experts, programmers, and other technical personnel have found weaknesses and created many security patches and updates for these server operating systems. For example, there are thousands of updates and service patches to a Windows 2003 server even though it has been in its final release since 2005 (Thurrott, 2004). In a similar vein, newer Linux distributions are constantly patched and updated rather than those (e.g., OpenBSD) that have been long in operation and tested by many. Conduct beta testing on test servers, not those destined for production.

One Constant: Technology Changes

In information technology, we continue to see advances in server architectures designed to maximize hardware components. Virtualization allows one machine to run multiple server operating systems independent from one another (Collier, Plassman, & Pegah, 2007). Whether one considers this a decentralized or centralized model, the bottom line is that one machine can now account for multiple servers, including both Windows and Linux/UNIX variants. Meet this challenge with the server hardening model, but newer issues are bound to arise.

Ultimately, system administrators must find the time in their busy schedules to research and review new issues. Thus, the biggest future issue system administrators will need to address is effectively managing their time to allow them to review and update servers in a controlled fashion.

CONCLUSION

Servers are the backbone of today's Internet. Although peer-to-peer computing architectures are growing, the sheer number of client/server implementations used to fuel the growth of Web 2.0, enterprise, and thin computing initiatives dwarfs them by comparison.

Our discussion has revised and expanded on accepted components (Chuvakin, 2002) of system security, such as service identification and reduction, daemon monitoring, auditing, and policy formation. Using these expanded explanations, we put forth a pragmatic set of steps with associated phases to create a solid blueprint for secure, hardening server creation and maintenance.

Although we cannot address all security issues on any given server, we have provided the guidelines to develop policies and procedures for secure server implementations on public networks. Using the secure hardened server model, system administrators can add to their arsenal of tools as they battle the increasing number of attacks on systems.

REFERENCES

Abu Rajab, M., Zarfoss, J., Monrose, F., & Terzis, A. (2006). A Multifaceted Approach to Understanding the Botnet Phenomenon. *Proceedings of the 6th ACM SIGCOMM Conference on Internet Measurement* (Rio de Janeriro, Brazil, October 25-27), IMC '06, 41-52.

Arthurs, W. (2001). A Proactive Defence to Social Engineering. *Sans Reading Room*, Sans Institute. Retrieved October 3, 2003, from http://www.sans.org/rr/paper.php?id=511

Blunt, E. (2006). Delegating Root Authority and Auditing Activities on UNIX/Linux Systems. *ISACA JounalOnline, 2*. Retrieved July 20, 2008 from http://www.isaca.org/Template.cfm?Section=Home&Template=/ContentManagement/ContentDisplay.cfm&ContentID=33441

Bombich, M. (2007). *Mac OS X Management Custom Shell Script Library* [Computer Software]. http://www.bombich.com/mactips/scripts.html

Carrera, D., Beltran, V., Torres, J., & Ayguade, E. (2005). A Hybrid Web Server Architecture for E-Commerce Applications. *Parallel and Distributed Systems Proceedings, 1*(20-22), 182-188.

CERT. (2008). *US-CERT Technical Vulnerabilities*. Retrieved July 20, 2008 from http://www.us-cert.gov/nav/t01/

Chari, S. N., & Cheng, P. (2003). BlueBoX: A Policy-Driven, Host-Based Intrusion Detection System. *ACM Trans. Inf. Syst. Secur., 6*(2), 173-200.

Christodorescu, M., Jha, S., & Kruegel, C. (2007). Mining Specifications of Malicious Behavior. *The 6th Joint Meeting of the European Software Engineering Conference and the ACM SIGSOFT Symposium on the Foundations of Software Engineering* (Dubrovnik, Croatia, September 3-7), ESEC-FSE '07, 5-14.

Chuvakin, A. (2002). *Linux Kernel Hardening*. Retrieved October 3, 2003 from http://www.securityfocus.com/infocus/1539

Cisneros, R., Bliss, D., & Garcia, M. (2006). Password Auditing Applications. *J. Comput. Small Coll., 21*(4), 196-202.

Collier, G., Plassman, D., & Pegah, M. (2007). Virtualization's Next Frontier: Security. *Proceedings of the 35th Annual ACM SIGUCCS Conference on User Services* (Orlando, Florida, October 7-10), SIGUCCS '07, 34-36.

Curran, K., Morrissey, C., Fagan, C., Murphy, C., O'Donnell, B., Fitzpatrick, G., & Condit, S. (2005). Monitoring Hacker Activity with a Honeynet. *Int. J. Netw. Manag., 15*(2), 123-134.

DeWitt, D. J., Futtersack, P., Maier, D., & Vélez, F. (1990). A Study of Three Alternative Workstation-Server Architectures for Object Oriented Database Systems. In D. McLeod, R. Sacks-Davis, & H. Schek, (Eds.), *The 16th International Conference on Very Large Data Bases* (August 13-16)., *Very Large Data Bases* (pp. 107-121). San Francisco, CA: Morgan Kaufmann Publishers.

Etalle, S., & Winsborough, W. H. (2007). A Posteriori Compliance Control. *Proceedings of the 12th ACM Symposium on Access Control Models and Technologies* (pp. 11-20) (Sophia Antipolis, France, June 20-22), SACMAT '07.

Forget, A., & Biddle, R. (2008). Memorability of Persuasive Passwords. *CHI '08 Extended Abstracts on Human Factors in Computing Systems* (Florence, Italy, April 5-10), CHI '08, (pp. 3759-3764).

Fyoder. (2002). *Remote OS detection via TCP/IP Stack Fingerprinting*. Retrieved October 3, 2003 from http://www.insecure.org/nmap/nmap-fingerprinting-article.html

GadAllah, S. (2004). The Importance of Logging and Traffic Monitoring for Information Security. *Sans Reading Room*, Sans Institute. Retrieved July 20, 2008 from http://www.sans.org/reading_room/whitepapers/logging/1379.php

Galligan, W., & White, D. (2008). Examination of the Plausibility of Network Access Compromise Using USB and Live CD Tools. *Proceedings of the Northeast Decision Sciences International Conference* (New York, NY, March 28-30).

Gragg, D. (2003). A Multilevel Defence Against Social Engineering. *Sans Reading Room*, Sans Institute. Retrieved October 3, 2003 from http://www.sans.org/rr/paper.php?id=920

Hansteen, P. (2008). *The Book of PF: A No-Nonsense Guide to the OpenBSD Firewall.* San Francisco, CA: No Starch Press.

Henders, R., & Opdyke, B. (2005). Detecting Intruders on a Campus Network: Might the Threat be Coming from Within?. *Proceedings of the 33rd Annual ACM SIGUCCS Conference on User Services* (pp. 113-117) (Monterey, CA, November 6-9), SIGUCCS '05.

Horowitz, M. (2007). *Linux vs. Windows.* Retrieved July 20, 2008 from http://www.michael-horowitz.com/Linux.vs.Windows.html

Hurley, J., & Hemmendinger, E. (2002). *Open Source and Linux: 2002 Poster Children for Security Problems.* Retrieved October 3, 2003 from http://www.aberdeen.com

Insecure. (2009). *Network Mapper (NMAP)* [Computer Software]. http://nmap.org/

Interactive Data Corporation (IDC). (2008). Retrieved July 20, 2008 from http://www.idc.com/

Kamp, P. & Watson, R. (2004). Building Systems to Be Shared, Securely. *Queue, 2*(5), 42-51.

Koomey, J. (2007). *Estimating Total Power Consumption by Servers in the U.S. and the World.* Retrieved November 21, 2007 from http://enterprise.amd.com/Downloads/svrpwrusecomplete-final.pdf

Kyle, D., & Brustoloni, J.C. (2007). UClinux: A Linux Security Module for Trusted-Computing-Based Usage Controls Enforcement. *Proceedings of the 2007 ACM Workshop on Scalable Trusted Computing* (pp. 63-70) (Alexandria, Virginia, November 2), STC '07,.

Lant, C. (2002). Telnet, You are the Weakest Link! Good-bye. *Berkeley Computing & Com-munications, 12*(1). Retrieved July 20, 2008 from http://istpub.berkeley.edu:4201/bcc/Winter2002/sec.telnet.html

Limoncelli, T., Hogan, C., & Chalup, S. (2007). *The Practice of System and Network Administration, 2ed.* New York, NY: Addison-Wesley.

Manadhata, P., Wing, J., Flynn, M., & McQueen, M. (2006). Measuring the Attack Surfaces of Two FTP Daemons. *Proceedings of the 2nd ACM Workshop on Quality of Protection* (Alexandria, Virginia, October 30), QoP '06, 3-10.

McHaney, R., & White, D. (1994). Development of a Framework for Discrete-Event Simulation. *Proceedings of the 15th Annual Decision Sciences Institute Meeting* (Honolulu, HI).

Meber, D. (2004). *Auditing User Accounts.* Retrieved July 20, 2008 from http://www.windowsecurity.com/articles/Auditing-user-accounts.html

Microsoft. (2008). *Security Central.* Retrieved July 20, 2008 from http://www.microsoft.com/security/default.mspx

Moitra, S., & Konda, S. (2004). An Empirical Investigation of Network Attacks on Computer Systems. *Computers & Security, 23*(1), 43-51. Morphy, E. (2005). *Web Server Attacks, Defacements Increase.* Retrieved July 20, 2008 from http://www.newsfactor.com/story.xhtml?story_id=33523

National Security Agency (NSA). (2009). *Security-Enhanced Linux* [Computer Software]. http://www.nsa.gov/selinux/

Netcraft. (2008). *March 2008 Web Server Survey.* Retrieved July 20, 2008 from http://news.netcraft.com/archives/web_server_survey.html

Ng, B., Si, A., Lau, R. W., & Li, F. W. (2002). A Multi-Server Architecture for Distributed Virtual Walkthrough. *Proceedings of the ACM Symposium on Virtual Reality Software and Technology* (pp. 163-170) (Hong Kong, China, November

11-13), VRST '02.

Openwall. (2009). *John the Ripper* [Computer Software]. http://www.openwall.com/john/

Pariag, D., Brecht, T., Harji, A., Buhr, P., Shukla, A., & Cheriton, D. R. (2007). Comparing the Performance of Web Server Architectures. *SIGOPS Oper. Syst. Rev.*, *41*(3), 231-243.

Peng, T., Leckie, C., & Ramamohanarao, K. (2007). Survey of Network-Based Defense Mechanisms Countering the DoS and DDoS Problems. *ACM Comput. Surv.*, *39*(1), 3.

Petri. (2009). SubSeven 2.2 [Computer Software]. http://www.petri.co.il/trojan_ports_list.htm

Porcupine. (2009). *Security Administrator Tool for Analyzing Networks* (SATAN) [Computer Software] http://www.porcupine.org/satan/

Register. (2008). *Security.* Retrieved July 20, 2008 from http://www.theregister.co.uk/security/

Russinovich, M. (2007). Inside Windows Vista User Account Control. *Microsoft TechNet Magazine*, June. Retrieved July 20, 2008 from http://technet.microsoft.com/en-us/magazine/cc138019.aspx

Schneier, B. (2008). *Schneier on Security.* Retrieved July 20, 2008 from http://www.schneier.com/blog/

Schneier, B., & Kelsey, J. (1999). Secure Audit Logs to Support Computer Forensics. *ACM Trans. Inf. Syst. Secur.*, *2*(2), 159-176.

Simon, H.A. (1960). *The New Science of Management Decision.* New York: Harper and Row.

Software Engineering Institute (SEI) (2007). *Client/Server Software Architectures--An Overview.* Carnegie Mellon University. Retrieved July 20, 2008 from http://www.sei.cmu.edu/str/descriptions/clientserver_body.html

Somarsoft. (2009). *DumpSec* [Computer Software]. http://somarsoft.com/

SourceFire. (2009). *Snort* [Computer Software]. http://www.snort.org/

Stiegler, M., Karp, A. H., Yee, K., Close, T., & Miller, M. S. (2006). Polaris: Virus-Safe Computing for Windows XP. *Commun. ACM, 49*(9), 83-88.

Sun Microsystems. (2008). *File Security Features.* Retrieved July 20, 2008 from http://docs.sun.com/app/docs/doc/806-4078/6jd6cjs2o?a=view

Thurrott, P. (2004). Windows Server 2003 R2 FAQ. Retrieved July 20, 2008 from http://www.winsupersite.com/faq/win2003_r2.asp

APPENDIX A: SERVER SERVICES AND DAEMONS LISTING

Server Machine Name	
Server IP Address	
Server Purpose	
Operating System	
Operating System Patch	

Service	Purpose	Version	Known Risks	Patch Date

APPENDIX B: USER PHYSICAL ACCESS ASSESSMENT FORM

Use this form to assess user access to various areas of the organization and determine necessary user need and restrictions.

Area	User Type	Access Requirement	Identifier

Area	The physical location for this user
User Type	Programmers, Network Administrator, Marketing Executive, etc.
Access Requirement	What does this user need to gain access to the area? A key, keycode, biometric device, etc.
Identifier	How was the user who accessed the area identified? Was it via a video snap, a sign in sheet, a retinal scan, etc.

APPENDIX C: NMAP SCANNING FORM

Use this form to examine the system from different perspectives. Typically, view a system from each perspective adopted by a user of the system. (Web servers have a much wider perspective than a segment-oriented FTP server.)

Service Observed	IP Address	Distance	Need

Service Observed	Which daemon was listening
IP Address	The IP address scanned
Distance	The number of hops: local, subnet, and external

APPENDIX D: SERVER HARDENING MODEL CHECKLIST

Step 1: Initial Planning and OS Installation			
Phase	Completed	Date	Notes
Phase 1: Determine OS Selection			
Phase 2: Plan OS Install and Updates			
Phase 3: Install OS and Updates			

Step 2: Service and Software Reduction			
Phase	Completed	Date	Notes
Phase 1: Identify Necessary Services and Software			
Phase 2: Determine a Removal Method			
Phase 3: Remove Unnecessary Software and Services			

Step 3: Securing File Permissions			
Phase	Completed	Date	Notes
Phase 1: Audit File Security			
Phase 2: Determine Access Needs			
Phase 3: Implement File Permission Security Policy			

Step 4: Login and User Security			
Phase	Completed	Date	Notes
Phase 1: Audit User Groups and User Passwords			
Phase 2: Plan the Changes			
Phase 3: Update Policies and Implement Corrections			

Step 5: Physical and Boot Security Controls			
Phase	Completed	Date	Notes
Phase 1: Assess Physical Security and Boot Control Security			
Phase 2: Design the Physical and Boot Security			
Phase 3: Place the Server and Test the Boot Security			

Step 6: Secure Daemons via Network Access Controls			
Phase	Completed	Date	Notes
Phase 1: Port Scan the Server to Assess the Daemons			
Phase 2: Determine Access Policy for Each Service			
Phase 3: Manage Firewalls and Authentication to Limit Access			

Step 7: Maintenance			
Phase	Completed	Date	Notes
Phase 1: Monitor Logs for Suspicious Events			
Phase 2: Start an Audit as a Result of an Event			
Phase 3: Update Policies and Impose Corrections			

Chapter XVII
Trusted Computing:
Evolution and Direction

Jeff Teo
Montreat College, USA

ABSTRACT

Computer attacks of all sorts are commonplace in today's interconnected, globalized society. A computer worm, written and released in one part of the world, can now traverse cyberspace in mere minutes creating havoc and untold financial hardship and loss. To effectively combat such threats and other novel and sophisticated assaults, our network defenses must be equipped to thwart such attacks. Yet, our software-dominated defenses are woefully inadequate (Bellovin, 2001). The Trusted Computing Group (TCG) has embarked on a mission to use an open standards-based interoperability framework utilizing both hardware and software implementations to defend against computer attacks. Specifically, the TCG uses a trusted hardware called the trusted platform module (TPM) in conjunction with TPM-enhanced software to provide better protection against such attacks. While millions of TPMs have been shipped with more expected annually, adoption of trusted computing technology enabled by the devices has been slow, despite escalating security infractions. This chapter will detail a brief history of trusted computing (TC), the goals of the TCG, and the workings of trusted platforms. The chapter will also look into how the TPM enables roots of trust to afford improved trust and security.

INTRODUCTION

Viruses, unauthorized access, loss of data due to laptop theft, and other computer attacks are common and escalating occurrences in today's open computing platforms. As a result of these invasions, users and companies worldwide have suffered untold losses and negative publicity, and incurred tremendous costs (CSI/FBI, 2004; Deloitte, 2004; CSI/FBI, 2005; Deloitte, 2005; CSI/FBI, 2006; Deloitte, 2006; CSI 2007; Deloitte, 2007). Until recently, the Information Technology (IT) industry's predominant approach to solving security problems was to develop more software-based solutions, even though "most security problems are caused by buggy software" (Bellovin, 2001, p. 131). Because the industry ignored the benefits that hardware implementation could bring (Neumann, 2003), the rampant computer attacks continued unabated.

In response, a group of leading technology companies including IBM, Microsoft, Hewlett Packard (HP), Intel and others formed the Trusted Computing Group (TCG). TCG is working to improve trust and security in today's open computing platforms by utilizing both hardware and software based solutions. They favor vendor neutral, open standards based interoperability frameworks that operate across multiple platforms. TCG is incorporating hardware with a trusted platform module (TPM). This low-cost hardware device has several built-in features that will improve security and trust in today's networked platforms. Beginning in 2006, 50 million TPM-equipped computers were shipped around the world, and TCG is aiming for even wider deployment across all computing platforms with an additional 250 million TPMs to be shipped by 2010 (TCG, 2005). Through this new framework, TCG hopes to enable all computing services to be performed in a more secure and reliable manner.

Even though millions of these TPMs have been embedded in today's enterprise laptops and desktops, widespread adoption of this technology remains slow. What is hindering TPM adoption? Will TCG's vision for improved computer security be realized so that the global community can operate more freely and safely in cyberspace? Can critical information, information systems, and networks be reliably and robustly protected? This chapter will address these questions by examining the concept of trust and the history of trusted computing, and providing an overview of the nature and functionality of trusted computing, trusted platforms, trusted platform module and related issues.

BACKGROUND

Defining Trust

Trust has existed in spoken and written form throughout civilization. This important concept remains a part of daily interactions in personal and business settings. Yet, many academicians have difficulty defining trust in explicit terms (Keen, Balance, Chan, & Schrump, 1999). Trust exists in several domains: anthropology, economics, history, management, marketing, organization theory and behavior, philosophy, politics, psychology, science, sociology, social psychology, and others (Bhattacherjee, 2002; Chopra & Wallace, 2003; Lewicki & Bunker, 1996). Researchers in their respective domains view and define trust according to their disciplines and from their unique perspectives (McKnight, Choudhury, & Kacmar, 2002). For example, according to Rousseau, Sitkin, Burt, and Camerer (1998), economists view trust as either calculative or institutional, whereas psychologists base their assessments of trust on the attributes of the trustees and trustors. Sociologists, on the other hand, look for trust in relationships among people or institutions, while social psychologists define trust as cognition about the trustee (McKnight et al., 2002).

McKnight and Chervany (2002) posit that "there are literally dozens of definitions of trust" (p. 37); naturally this ambiguity results in confusion, contradictions, and even reluctance on the part of some researchers to define this elusive term. According to Mayer, Davis, and Schoorman (1995), there are other reasons as well. These reasons include lack of clarity in the relationship between trust and risk, confusion between trust and its antecedents and outcomes, lack of specificity of trust referents leading to confusion in levels of analysis, and a failure to consider both the trusting party and the party to be trusted (p. 709).

To address these problems, Mayer et al. (1995) propose a trust topology that takes into account the characteristics of both the trustor and trustee. Their extensive review of trust literature contributed to theory building where three characteristics - ability, benevolence, and integrity- were selected and included in this traditional dyadic (one-to-one) trust model.

Ability consists of competencies, skills, and characteristics of the trusted party to have influence over the trustor in a specific domain (Gefen, 2002). Benevolence is the degree to which a trustee is believed to want to do good to the trustor, apart from a legitimate profit motive (Mayer, et al., 1995). Integrity refers to the belief that the trusted party adheres to accepted rules of conduct and that "the trustee makes good faith agreements, tells the truth, acts ethically, and fulfills promises" (Suh & Han, 2003, p. 137).

Luhmann (1979) characterizes trust in broad terms outlining a belief that individuals respond in predictable ways. Fukuyama (1995) further states that for trust to be relevant, it has to occur in a social context in the presence of people. For instance, in a business setting, Gefen and Straub (2003) posit that individuals would trust a bank teller but would not necessarily assign the same trust to an ATM even though the machine would perform exactly the same task. Mayer et al. (1995) define trust as "the willingness of a party to be vulnerable to the actions of another party based on the expectation that the other would perform a particular action important to the trustor, irrespective of the ability to monitor or control that other party" (p. 712).

Trust in E-Commerce

Business and commerce depend on trust. This has become the pivotal issue for e-commerce. According to Keen et al. (1999), trust constitutes the foundation of e-commerce. Quelch and Klein (1996) posit that trust played a critical role in promoting web purchases during the development

stages of the Internet. In fact, trust was found to be more important in electronic markets than in physical ones (Bailey & Bakos, 1997). Hoffman, Novak, and Peralta (1999) report that close to 95% of consumers did not want to provide their personal information to web sites, and that 63% reported that the main reason was "because they do not 'trust' those collecting the data" (p. 82).

McKnight et al. (2002) present an interdisciplinary trust topology related to e-commerce that outlines four high-level constructs: disposition to trust, institutional-based trust, trusting belief, and trusting intention. Disposition to trust is an output of trait psychology that purports that specific childhood events form actions. In institutional-based trust, the environment, rather than the personal aspects of individuals, affects the outcome. Shapiro (1987) further defines institutional-based trust as measures put in place, such as guarantees and safety nets, to assure or influence trust in a party. Trusting beliefs are typically person-specific whereas institutional-based trust is situation-specific. Trusting intention refers to one's willingness to depend on the other party in the absence of any control over that party (McKnight et al., 2002).

Several researchers (Ratnasingam & Pavlou, 2003; Pavlou & Gefen, 2004; McKnight et al. 2002; Zucker, 1986) assert that institutional-based trust is the most important construct. In fact it is the critical component for promoting trust in today's Internet infrastructure, which is devoid of personal, face to face interactions. Pavlou and Gefen (2002) posit that trust could be built if favorable technical, business, regulatory, and legal environments are present online. These structural assurances all work in conjunction to promote the belief that these organizations or entities are bound to act in a trustworthy manner (McKnight et al., 2002). Similarly, Shapiro (1987) and Zucker (1986) stress the importance of guarantees and recommendations from third parties to promote and enhance this form of trust. Zucker adds that institutional-based trust is the dominant trust creation in the business environment, especially when buyers and sellers are unfamiliar with each other and come from diverse ethnic, social, and cultural backgrounds. Within the context of e-commerce, Turban, Lee, King, and Chung (2000) define trust as the psychological status of the involved parties willing to enter into a continuance of activities to achieve a planned outcome or goal.

To facilitate trust in e-commerce, an industry special interest group (SIG), the Trusted Computing Platform Alliance (TCPA) was formed to develop and support vendor neutral, open industry standards specifications for trusted computing across disparate computing platforms. TCPA was reorganized in the spring of 2003 as the Trusted Computing Group (TCG). TCG defines trust as "the expectation that a device will behave in a particular manner for a specific purpose" (TCG, 2008a). The next section will highlight the history of trusted computing as well as TCG's implementation of trust in computing platforms.

TRUSTED COMPUTING: THEN AND NOW

Even though the Trusted Computing Group and vendors like Microsoft and Intel have promoted trusted computing since 1999, these entities did not originate the concept of trusted systems. In the late 1960s, research and development efforts focused on computer security for the United States military which had been the dominant computer user since the 1940s. Also during the sixties, overall computer efficiency increased with the emergence of time-sharing systems that were enabled by multiprogramming and multiprocessing capable mainframes. Users could debug programs interactively to see if their codes had run correctly. In those days of batch processing, it was not unusual to wait several hours for feedback. The move to time-sharing reduced costs especially for the military since it was possible to share computer systems across security levels

where earlier, separate computers had to be used for each security level (Mackenzie & Pottinger, 1997). Mainframes such as the Burroughs B5000 utilized virtual memory, and in 1967, with the IBM CP-40 (one-off research system and predecessor of the IBM System 360-67) became the first computer to demonstrate the use of a Virtual Machine Monitor (VMM) (computerhistory.org). The VMM utilized a hypervisor to implement full virtualization. It was capable of running several instances of client operating systems simultaneously.

Yet, time-sharing systems brought with them other issues. Often individual users with different programs were prevented from interfering with each other. Designers had to figure out how to allocate the computer's main memory to accommodate different users' programs so that one program would not override a memory location being used by another program (Mackenzie & Pottinger, 1997).

Not only did the military utilize time-sharing systems, educational institutions including Dartmouth College, UC-Berkeley, Massachusetts Institute of Technology (MIT) and others also became active users. In a 1960's university setting, computer security was not a dominant issue. Users being able to read each other's data would not be cause for concern. The military, however, viewed this characteristic as a threat and security risk. As more time-sharing systems were purchased and used by other United States government agencies, this threat began to grow. Beginning in 1967, the United States National Security Agency (NSA) implemented a series of initiatives that launched research and development efforts relating to computer security in an attempt to address the issues generated by time-sharing systems in multi-level user (from unclassified to top-secret) environments (Mackenzie & Pottinger, 1997).

One of the earliest works to surface on computer security was by Ware (1967), who articulated the security vulnerabilities of resource-sharing computer systems. Later, he highlighted problems and proposed security controls for computer systems indicating the need for a combination of hardware, software, communication, physical, personnel, and administrative procedure safeguards as foundational to comprehensive security. Ware stressed that software safeguards alone were not sufficient (Ware, 1970). The report also proposed a design using current technology to create a secure system for a closed environment, one where users, cleared to work in contained consoles, were supported by protected communication circuits. Ware warned that this technology would not support a secure system in an open environment, one where uncleared users worked in unprotected consoles with unprotected communication circuits.

During that time, Weissman (1969) performed related research, using a commercial-grade computer (IBM 360 Model 50) in a multi-level environment. Weissman's work was noteworthy as it put into practice some of Ware's report findings. The result was the development of the Adept-50 operating system, built and operated to embody the mathematical model of security.

Another study, underwritten by the United States Air Force, acknowledged the deficiencies of current systems to operate securely in a multi-level mode. To rectify this situation, the report asked for significant research and development funds to investigate the twin concepts of "reference monitor" and "security kernel" (Anderson, 1972). Anderson proposed the concept of a reference monitor to achieve execution control of users programs where

The function of the reference monitor is to validate all references (to programs, data, peripherals, etc.) made by programs in execution against those authorized for the subject (users, etc.). The Reference Monitor not only is responsible to assure that the references are authorized to share resource objects, but also to assure that the reference is the right kind (i.e., read, or read and write, etc)." (p. 17)

The concept of a security kernel was a radical one where, rather than adding controls to enhance or modify the existing operating system, security functions were isolated into primitive operating systems (Mackenzie & Pottinger, 1997). In the area of certification, the development plan stipulated that the security kernel must always be invoked and be tamper-resistant as well as validate each and every reference in the system. In short, the security kernel must demonstrate that "it is complete and performs correctly, and does not perform any function not specified" (Anderson, 1972, p. 48). If security functions were correctly implemented in the kernel, then the design of the rest of the operating system could be relaxed since it was not crucial from a security point of view.

Karger and Schell (1974) recognized the fundamental weaknesses of current computers and their reactive and ineffective approach of using "patches", "fix-ups", "add-ons" and "tiger teams" (p. 6) to deal with computer security. Their work centered on testing the viability of the MULTICS HIS 645 system to operate securely in a multi-level open environment. They supported the use of a reference monitor that was: 1) tamper proof, 2) invoked for every reference to data anywhere in the system, and 3) small enough to be proven correct (p. 7). They also stressed the critical component of certifiability in the development of multi-level secure systems. A notable feature of the MULTICS HIS 645 software security control was the use of the ring mechanism, a protection scheme, numbered from 0-7. These concentric rings denoted access protection privileges, with ring 0 admitting the 'hardcore' supervisor and ring 7 having the least privilege (p. 13).

Building on work performed prior to 1973 and culminating in a report submitted in 1976, the influential work of Bell and LaPadula, which also utilized mathematical modeling to secure computer systems design and operation with a MULTICS system, dramatically changed the landscape of computer security. Their security model was essentially a formal mathematical description using access control to compare or match the subject's cleared status (i.e. top-secret) with the object's classification for proper authorization. Rather than using discretionary access control, the authors used mandatory access control mechanisms to facilitate the rule of 'no write down" which states that if a user with read access to confidential objects has write access to confidential, secret, and top-secret objects, he should not have write access to unclassified objects. This was to prevent, for instance, a malicious agent from using a Trojan horse to write classified data to an unclassified file. The authors also posited the Basic Security Theorem: if the initial state of a system is secure and if all state transitions are secure, then the system will always be secure. Bell and LaPadula's work left an indelible mark on the annals of mathematical applications and the foundations of computer security (Bell & LaPadula 1973; LaPadula & Bell 1973; Bell 1974; Bell & LaPadula 1976).

With the development of formal specifications for secure computers underway, the focus shifted to formal verification. Academic researchers sought to verify that a kernel was in fact a correct implementation of a mathematical model of security. Failure to know that the reference validation took place correctly in all instances would void the certification needed for the system to be deemed secure. The military was keenly interested in the outcome of this research. But legal issues surrounding the definition of kernel, poorly defined requirements for formal specification and verification, coupled with problems encountered by the two entities working on the project, caused a two and half year delay. While certification was finally achieved, an approach favoring cryptographic mechanisms was chosen (Mackenzie & Pottinger, 1997).

According to Tasker (1981) and McCullagh and Caelli (2000), in the early 1980s, the United States Department of Defense (DoD) developed the Computer Security Initiative (CSI) to promote the widespread commercial availability of trusted computer systems which, along with its earlier Rainbow Series Initiative, advanced computer system protection through the construction of a Trusted Computing Base (TCB). Tasker (1981) stated that the DoD defined a trusted computer system as one that would "employ sufficient hardware and software integrity measures to allow its use in processing multiple levels of classified or sensitive information" (p. 1).

In 1985, the DoD defined, codified, and published the definition of trusted systems as Trusted Computer System Evaluation Criteria (TCSEC, CSC-STD-001-83), now commonly referred to as the Orange Book (Walker, 1985). It states the principle of the Trusted Computing Base and defines it as follows (DoD, 1985, p. 66):

The heart of a trusted computer system is the Trusted Computing Base (TCB) which contains all of the elements of the system responsible for supporting the security policy and supporting the isolation of objects (code and data) on which the protection is based. The bounds of the TCB equate to the "security perimeter" referenced in some computer security literature. In the interest of understandable and maintainable protection, a TCB should be as simple as possible consistent with the functions it has to perform. Thus, the TCB includes hardware, firmware, and software critical to protection and must be designed and implemented such that system elements excluded from it need not be trusted to maintain protection.

This set of specifications outlines both design and implementation criteria to judge the degree to which a platform could resist unauthorized attempts to access, alter, or read information in its computers. The Orange Book defines the "trustworthiness" of a computing platform; however, this concept did not become widespread, partly because TCSEC was introduced during the era of mainframe systems.

Irvine et al. (2002, p. 1) state that over the last 10 to 15 years, the IT industry "ignored the requirements to deploy computing systems with the ability to protect data according to its criticality and value to us." In addition, the effects of the U.S. government and military's inclination to utilize commercial-off-the-shelf (COTS) products contributed to the IT industry's lack of incentive to design systems that would "appropriately protect themselves and the data with which they are entrusted" (p. 1). Irvine et al. (2002. p. 1) further state that because the "science and discipline of trusted computing" was neglected, this neglect fostered an erosion of the nation's capability to design and build trusted computers and networks.

The current computing environment is increasingly global and open, fueled by the explosive growth of the Internet, which increased 304% from 360 million users in 2000 to 1.45 billion users in 2008 (Internet World Stats, 2008). Enterprises, governments, academic institutions, and individual users are increasingly interconnected, enabled by an assortment of wired and wireless networks supporting a plethora of computing devices which range from desktops and laptops, to PDAs and smart phones.

Open platforms, prevalent in today's distributed computing environment, are general-purpose computing platforms. Intel (2003a, p. 8) states, "Early PCs were stand-alone devices and therefore easily secured." Modern computers however, are faster and far more connected. A significant advantage of open platforms is the ability to run applications from numerous sources. The openness in today's connected computing environment contributes to worldwide economic growth in many trade sectors. That same openness also created global problems with the onset of computer attacks (Irvine, Levin & Dinolt, 2002). Open platforms suffer from the lack of trust between the hardware of the platform and a third party. As a result, open systems are susceptible to computer attacks and manipulations by unscrupulous entities (TCPA, 2000).

Banking systems and cellular networks currently use closed platforms. They are designed to perform exacting functions that make it difficult to change the operating system or run an unknown or unauthorized application. Closed platforms, equipped with tamper-resistant hardware, allow for end-to-end trust (Garfinkel, Rosenblum, & Boneh, 2003, p. 2), making it easier to ensure data and transaction integrity. Users typically interact with these platforms through a restricted interface (e.g., automated teller machines, game consoles, and satellite and cable receivers). By using a secret key (embedded in the tamper-resistant hardware during manufacture), a closed platform could "authenticate itself as an authorized platform to a remote party." As a result, closed systems that use tamper-resistant hardware are less susceptible to the computer attacks that plague open platforms. According to Challener, Yoder, Catherman, Safford, and Van Doorn (2008), the "Trusted Computing...goal [is] to protect the most sensitive information, such as private and symmetric keys, from theft or use by malicious code" (p. 9).

Even though an extensive network of people, processes, policies, procedures, and technologies are in place to safeguard computers from attacks, computer and online infractions continue unabated (CSI/FBI, 2004; Deloitte, 2004; CSI/FBI, 2005; Deloitte, 2005; CSI/FBI, 2006; Deloitte, 2006; CSI 2007; Deloitte, 2007). It is imperative that current security mechanisms be improved to successfully combat the increasingly inventive ways malicious entities bring about disclosure (when unauthorized users gain access to confidential information), enable alteration (where security mechanisms fail to ensure integrity of data) and facilitate denial (events that prevent authorized individuals from accessing a legitimate resource) of data and information. These attributes, disclosure, alteration, and denial – the DAD Triad – are diametrically opposed to the information security goals of confidentiality, integrity, and availability – the CIA Triad (Solomon & Chapple, 2005).

However, we are seeing the inclusion of hardware as a totality of protection mechanisms, with firmware and software combined to enforce a security policy prescribed by the Trusted Computing Base (TCB) and envisioned by computer security researchers of the late sixties and early seventies. The next section will discuss the efforts of the TCG to integrate hardware and software in platforms to support TCB in an era of open and connected computing environment.

Trusted Platforms

According to Mundie, DeVries, Haynes, and Corwine (2003), "incredibly secure and trustworthy computer systems existed, but they were largely independent, single-purpose systems that [we]re meticulously engineered and then isolated" (p. 7). These high-end physically secure processors, endowed with specialized cryptographic capabilities were used primarily by select industries such as financial institutions and the military that needed to protect sensitive, confidential data, and keys and secrets. They acknowledged the necessity of using secure coprocessors to protect their secrets and assets. They were also among the few who were able and willing to pay the premiums commanded by these high-end systems. For them, costs did not determine value. The IBM 4758 secure coprocessor achieved the highest level of tamper resistance (the FIPS 140-1 level 4 certification) set by the U.S. government, and at two thousand dollars (Anderson, 2008) was considered a "best buy" when compared to its rivals.

Today, however, a more cost-effective option, that is affordable to the masses, and encompasses both hardware and software implementations is needed to combat today's increasingly sophisticated computer attacks. In response to this need, the TCG's mission statement reads, "Through the collaboration of platform, software, and technology vendors develop a specification that delivers an enhanced HW and OS based trusted computing platform that enhances customers' trusted domains" (TCG, 2007b p. 2).

TCG's role in promoting the vision of trusted computing is by far the most prominent to date. Unfortunately, there is no agreement among trusted computing researchers as to what constitutes the functionalities of a trusted platform. For example, Microsoft, via its now defunct Next-Generation Secure Computing Base (NGSCB) initiative, advocated the inclusion of process isolation using a kernel to execute and control simultaneous multiple operating systems. In addition, NGSCB implemented a secure path using hardware extension of user input and output devices.

Other researchers such as Sadeghi and Stuble posit that for trusted platforms to be truly accepted, consumer and software provider requirements must be included (Gallery, 2005). Other entities including Intel, which offers Intel Safer Computing Initiative and Advanced Micro Devices (AMD) with Presidio and Pacifica secure execution technology are focusing on trusted computing. These entities have contributed noteworthy research in the area of trusted platforms. This chapter, however, will highlight TCG's vision of trusted platforms.

TCG's vision of trusted computing is still a relatively new mechanism of assuring security, and the organization believes that security begins with the trusted platform (see Figure 1). So how do you convert a generic platform to a trusted platform? Gallery (2005) states that the TCG requires the following functions to be present in a trusted platform: integrity measurement, storage and reporting functionality, protected capabilities, and platform attestation mechanisms. To facilitate these functions present in a trusted platform, the TCG uses hardware and software mechanisms afforded by a trusted platform module (TPM). A TPM is essentially a tamper-resistant microcontroller affixed to the motherboard and is designed to create, store, and protect cryptographic keys. Specially designed software provides additional functionalities to allow the TPM to be a root of trust for trusted systems.

Integrity measurement, storage and reporting functionality is the process of getting measurements of platform characteristics or the state of the platform affecting the trustworthiness of said platform. This is followed by recording and then storing these measurements in protected registers. Integrity reporting deals with accurately reporting the contents of the integrity storage (Gallery, 2005).

Protected capabilities are commands with exclusive access to data in shielded locations. In a trusted platform, shield locations (memory and register) are protected storage areas designed for sensitive data, integrity metrics or cryptographic keys. Protection of sensitive data and keys is afforded by hardware. Examples of hardware-assisted protected capabilities include random number generation, sealing data to system state, integrity reporting, and key management (Schmidt, 2007b). For the platform to be trusted, protected capabilities and shield locations must first be trusted.

In platform attestation mechanisms, TCG defines attestation as the process by which the accuracy of information may be guaranteed (Gallery, 2005). Simply stated, attestation is the process of reporting already measured data. To facilitate this process, TCG (2007b) uses several forms of attestation mechanisms including (p. 6):

- Attestation by the TPM as an operation that provides proof of data known to the TPM
- Attestation to the TPM as an operation that provides proof that a platform can be trusted to report integrity metrics using platform credentials
- Attestation of the TPM as an operation which provides proof of a set of platform's integrity measurements
- Authentication of the platform which provides evidence of a platform's claim identity

Figure 1. A trusted platform © 2005 Eimear Gallery. used with permission.

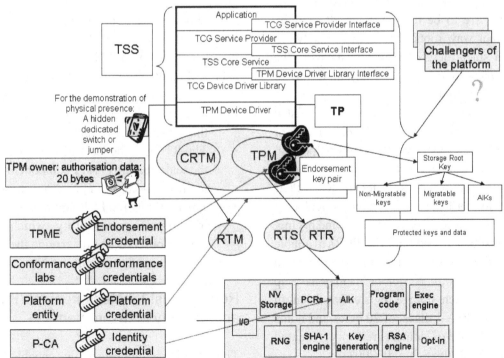

Pearson (2003) states, a "trusted platform is a computing platform that has a trusted component, probably in the form of built-in hardware, and uses this to create a foundation of trust for software processes" (p. 5). To enable this foundation of hardware trust, the TCG's trusted platform relies on the following three fundamental elements (Gallery, 2005 p. 38):

- The Root of Trust for Measurement (RTM)
- The TPM, which is the Root of Trust for Storage (RTS) and the Root of Trust for Reporting (RTR)
- The Trusted Software Stack (TSS), which encompasses the software on the platform that supports the platform's TPM

The RTM, the RTS, and the RTR are defined as the roots of trusts for a TP. These roots of trust work synergistically to gather, store and report evidences or references about the trustworthiness of the software processes running on the platform. A root of trust is defined as a component that must be implicitly trusted if the evidence or the references are to be trusted (Schmidt, 2007b). Put another way, roots of trust must behave as expected since there is no way to measure the roots of trust themselves and any misbehavior cannot be detected.

While these roots of trust are crucial to a trusted platform, there is one key component that links or 'glues' all three root elements. This component, peculiar to TCG's trusted platform, is called a Platform Configuration Register (PCR). A PCR resides within a TPM and is afforded shield location and protection from interference and prying. There must be a minimum of 16 PCRs available for use within a TPM, eight for hardware and the rest for software. Newer TPMs may have up to 24 PCRs. Each storage register has a length equal to the SHA-1 digest of 20 bytes and holds a summary value of all measurements presented to it (Kinney, 2006; Schmidt, 2007c).

According to Pearson (2003, p. 67), PCRs are "possibly the most unusual aspect of a TPM". PCRs store integrity metrics in a way that they prevent misrepresentation of the said values or "of the sequence in which they are presented" (see Figure 1). The results or values of the integrity metrics are not "stored" individually but are extended to a fixed 20 byte size in the PCRs. The term or method that TCG uses is called concatenation. This is the combining of the existing value of the current sequence with the value of the new integrity metric and computing a digest or hashing of the concatenation, and using that new digest as the presentation of the sequence. A PCR is initialized to all zeros during the initial boot but keeps existing values during sleep mode (Pearson, 2003).

A common task that PCRs perform (besides serving as containers for integrity metrics) is that of comparing integrity metric values. In this simple example, a TPM will release a secret only if the current values of said PCR in the platform match the target PCR's values stored with the secret, as in protected storage (to be discussed later).

The remainder of the chapter will show how the roots of trust of RTM, RTS, and RTR, in conjunction with PCRs enable the three functions of a TP and that (Grawrock, 2006, p. 142):

- The RTM provides the measurement values that drive the PCR contents
- The RTS and the PCR combine to provide the seal capability, a key component of a TP to provide long-term protected storage
- The RTR and the PCR combine to provide the attestation capability, which allows outside observers to determine the current platform configuration

Root of Trust for Measurement (RTM) and Integrity Measurement

The RTM is a computing engine capable of making reliable integrity measurements of software and firmware during system boot where it uses a cryptographic mechanism to digitally sign the state of the boot process and store the metrics in PCRs. Once stored in the PCRs, these metrics cannot be tampered with or misrepresented. The RTM is also the root of the chain of transitive trust (TCG 2007b).

For PCs, these calculations are performed by the Core Root of Trust Measurement (CRTM). The CRTM is the BIOS boot block code, and is an extension of normal BIOS. The CRTM and the TPM must exhibit immutability, defined as an object whose state cannot be modified after it is created. According to Piltzecker, Chaffin, Granneman, and Hunter (2007), a key concept in the trusted platform is the Trusted Building Block (TBB) which in PCs, consists of the CRTM and the TPM working conjointly to derive trust in the platform. With these two immutable objects physically present on the motherboard, initial trust is gained and the subsequent code which the platform runs after the TBB is therefore trusted. This establishes the "anchor" for the chain of trust as well as forming the basis for platform integrity metrics (TCG, 2007b). Without the TBB, or if malicious code is present at the start of the chain of execution, anything running after that cannot be trusted.

With the anchor established, the CRTM extends the chain of trust by measuring the BIOS. If the BIOS measurement is deemed trustworthy, control is then passed from the CRTM to the BIOS. The measured value is stored in the Stored Measurement Log (SML) held outside of the TPM. The summary or measurement digest, in the form of a 20-byte SHA-1 hashing function is extended to a platform configuration register (PCR) residing in the TPM and supported by the RTR and RTS functionality (Pearson, 2003; Schmidt, 2007c; TCG, 2007b).

This boot-strapping process continues with the BIOS measuring the OS loader, and if the OS loader's measurement is deemed trustworthy, control is then passed from the BIOS to the OS

loader. Again, the measured value is stored in the SML with a corresponding digest extended to the next PCR, lengthening the chain of trust. This "measure before load" process continues from the OS loader to the OS and then to any applications loaded or software existing on the platform. If along the way measurements taken are not trustworthy, the "undesired" value will be recorded before that untrustworthy entity is able to change the value. When this happens, the chain of trust is 'broken' since the value stored after that point is deemed untrustworthy and the boot-strapping stops. This illustrates that all derived trust in the platform is based on the ability to trust the CRTM and the TPM, the trusted building block, highlighting the importance of their immutability features (Piltzecker et al., 2007).

Root of Trust for Storage (RTS) and Protected Storage

Two important and related features present in a TCG trusted platform are the RTS and protected storage. The RTS is the second root of trust on a trusted platform. It is also another computing engine capable of maintaining an accurate summary of integrity measurements made by the RTM. In protected storage, three operations or aspects support its operation. They are wrapping, binding, and sealing.

To keep the cost of TPMs down, only a limited amount of non-volatile memory is included in the TPM to store data, credentials, and keys, with the rest to be stored in the platform. Since there can be a large number of keys and data to be protected on the platform, the RTS must have the capabilities which "must be trusted if storage of data inside a platform is to be trusted" (Gallery, 2005, p. 39). To undertake this requirement, the RTS utilizes the asymmetric encryption mechanisms provided by protected storage to protect an unlimited amount of data and keys held inside a platform (but outside of the TPM). When the cryptographic operations are completed, the encrypted data is then stored in protected storage.

The RTS has access to a small amount of volatile memory where keys are held while performing both encryption and decryption operations. With the assistance of the Key Cache Manager (KCM), the RTS manages various types of keys necessary for the proper function of a trusted platform. All keys under the supervision of the RTS in a TP have an attribute designation of migratable or non-migratable. A non-migratable key stays within a specific TPM whereas migratable keys may be exchanged between TPM devices. According to the TCG (2007b), there are seven key types (p. 17-18):

- Signing keys are asymmetric general purpose keys used to sign application data and messages. Signing keys can be migratable or non-migratable

- Storage keys are asymmetric general purpose keys used to encrypt data or other keys. Storage keys are used for wrapping keys and data managed externally. They are non-migratable

- Identity Keys (a.k.a. AIK keys) are non-migratable signing keys that are exclusively used to sign data originated by the TPM

- Endorsement Key (EK) is a non-migratable decryption key for the platform. It is used to decrypt owner authorization data at the time a platform owner is established and to decrypt messages associated with AIK creation. It is never used for encryption or signing

- Bind keys may be used to encrypt small amounts of data (such as a symmetric key) on one platform and decrypt it on another. They are by definition migratable

- Legacy keys are keys created outside of the TPM. They are imported to the TPM for use in signing and encryption operations. They are by definition migratable

- Authentication Keys are symmetric keys used to protect transport sessions involving the TPM. They are definition migratable

The only key that is within, protected, and generated by the TPM is the Storage Root Key (SRK). The SRK is a permanently affixed non-migratable key that resides in non-volatile memory in the TPM. The SRK is unique. It sits at the top of the key hierarchy and is the root of all keys in a trusted platform. The SRK's primary role, in conjunction with the RTS and protected storage, is to protect all objects or keys residing outside the TPM. To protect objects created outside a TPM, an operation called binding is used where externally generated objects or data are encrypted by a TPM parent key, in this case by the SRK.

To protect keys generated outside of the TPM, an operation called wrapping is performed where these externally generated keys are encrypted by the TPM-protected SRK key. Wrapping is carried out by using the public portion of the SRK asymmetric key pair to wrap the first layer key outside of the TPM and the corresponding private SRK key is used to unwrap the same key when its use is required (Gallery, 2005).

With the first layer keys now protected by the SRK, further protection can then be extended to the second layer, this time by wrapping (encrypting) a second layer key with the public key belonging to a corresponding first layer key. In turn, successive layers of keys are protected by the layers of keys above it. Given this hierarchical key structure, protection of all keys is possible because the root key, SRK, protected by the TPM and by the wrapping operation, extends protection down the successive layers. It is worthwhile to note that through binding and wrapping, users are assured that the data and keys are secured (even though they are actually stored in the platform and outside of the TPM) simply because the data and keys cannot be decrypted without a key that is stored inside the TPM (Piltzecker et al., 2007).

In addition to wrapping and binding operations, the third operation or aspect of protected storage is sealed storage. Sealing is a powerful operation in the TCG trusted platform. Essentially, sealing is the process of binding data or wrapping a key and linking it to certain PCR platform characteristics. According to Piltzecker et al. (2007, p. 133), "sealing takes it a step further and associates the wrapped key to the state of the platform". Unsealing the data or accessing the key, can only be done when the platform is in a particular platform state and then only under the TPM that created it. If one or more of these conditions are not met, the unsealing process will fail. Therefore, the RTS, in conjunction with the protected storage process of binding, wrapping, and sealing, and utilizing the SRK aided by the KCM, facilitates the protection and storage of data and keys entrusted to the TPM (TCG, 2007b).

Root of Trust for Reporting (RTR), TPM and Attestation

The third root of trust, Root of Trust for Reporting is a computing engine capable of reporting data held by the RTS. There are two functions of the RTR. First, it exposes shield-locations for storage of integrity measurements where it authorizes certain approved functions to access protected areas for updates in PCRs. Second, the RTR attests to the authenticity or correctness of trusted platform identities when challenged by a verifier. Further, Gallery (2005. p. 35) states the "RTR and the RTS together constitute the minimum functionality that should be offered by a TPM". What then is a TPM? The following will describe and discuss the TPM and its role in a trusted platform (see Figure 1).

To facilitate this functionality (RTR and RTS), a TPM uses these discrete components (TCG, 2007b, p. 19-20):

- Input/Output (I/O) component manages information flow over the communications bus. It performs protocol encoding/decoding suitable for communication over external and internal buses. It routes messages to appropriate components. The I/O component enforces access policies associated with the Opt-In component as well as other TPM functions requiring access control

- Non-Volatile Storage is used to store an Endorsement Key (EK), a Storage Root Key (SRK), owner authorization data and persistent flags. Platform Configuration Registers (PCR) can be implemented in either volatile or non-volatile storage. They are reset at system start or whenever the platform loses power. TCG specifies a minimum number of registers to implement (16). Registers 0-7 are reserved for TPM use. Registers 8-15 are available for operating system and application use

- Attestation Identity Keys (AIK) must be persistent, but it is recommended that AIK keys be stored as Blobs in persistent external storage (outside the TPM), rather than stored permanently inside TPM non-volatile storage. TCG hopes TPM implementers will provide ample room for many AIK Blobs to be concurrently loaded into TPM volatile memory as this will speed execution

- Program code contains firmware for measuring platform devices. Logically, this is the Core Root of Trust for Measurement (CRTM). Ideally, the CRTM is contained in the TPM, but implementation decisions may require it be located in other firmware

- Random Number Generator (RNG) is used for key generation, nonce creation and to strengthen pass phrase entropy. The TPM contains a true random-bit generator used to seed random number generation

- SHA-1 Engine is used for computing signatures, creating key Blobs and for general purpose use

- RSA Key Generation engine is used to create signing keys and storage keys. TCG requires a TPM to support RSA keys up to a 2048-bit modulus, and mandates that certain keys (the SRK and AIKs, for example) must have at least a 2048-bit modulus

- RSA Engine is used for signing with signing keys, encryption/decryption with storage keys, and decryption with the EK. The TCG committee anticipates TPM modules containing an RSA engine will not be subject to import/export restrictions
- Opt-In component implements TCG policy requiring TPM modules be shipped in the state the customer desires. This ranges from disabled and deactivated to fully enabled; ready for an owner to take possession. The Opt-In mechanism maintains logic and (if necessary) interfaces to determine physical presence state and ensure disabling operations are applied to other TPM components as needed
- Execution Engine runs program code. It performs TPM initialization and measurement taking

When these "roots of trust" are present in a platform, they enable the platform to be trusted by both local and remote users thereby reducing business risks. The overall computing experience is enhanced when users are not victims of root-kits attacks, for example, since the platform has not been modified without the user's permission or compromised, and that secrets stored in the system are securely protected from adversaries. Without hardware roots of trust, software is vulnerable because it can be compromised by other software. Challener et al. (2008) cited complexity, compatibility, and compromise as the three reasons why software cannot be made completely secure. Experts in information security acknowledge that some security problems cannot be effectively dealt with by software alone and therefore, trusted hardware, anchored by roots of trust, are required as the basis for software security mechanisms (Neumann, 2003; Smith, 2005; Kay, 2007).

Trusted Platform Module (TPM)

As stated earlier, the trusted platform module is an inexpensive computer chip that has two components; hardware and software. The TPM hardware consists of a secure microcontroller that is permanently affixed to a computing platform via the low pin count (LPC) bus on a motherboard. By situating the TPM on the LPC, it becomes a slave device, responding to rather than initiating commands, and does not have access to main system memory (Grawrock, 2006). The second component of the TPM is a set of specially designed software, the TCG Software Stack (TSS), which interfaces between the functions of the microcontroller and security-aware applications. Because of this layer of software, many current and future applications can be written for the TPMs.

Using non-volatile protected storage and its built-in cryptographic engine, a TPM is capable of performing hashing, random number generation, asymmetric key generation and asymmetric encryption/decryption (see Figure 1). TPMs can create, store, and protect encrypted keys, passwords, and digital certificates in a closed hardware environment thereby maintaining data confidentiality and integrity. Within the TPM's non-volatile protected storage reside two persistent keys: the Endorsement Key (EK), and the Storage Root Key (SRK).

The Endorsement Key, protected by the TPM, is cryptographically unique and is only known to that TPM (Gallery, 2005). The EK has a 2048-bit RSA key pair with both private (PRIVEK) and public (PUBEK) keys generated during the manufacture of the TPM. The EK encrypts secrets used to establish a platform owner and once it is activated, cannot be changed. The public Endorsement Key performs encryption while the private EK functions as a decryption key for the platform and is non-migratable, meaning it will never leave, be replaced or be exposed outside of the TPM (Kinney, 2006). To attest that the EK was correctly created and embedded in a valid TPM, two credentials are included to establish its validity and trust.

The first credential is called the Endorsement Credential. This credential is typically issued by the TPM vendor during the fabrication of the TPM. The Endorsement Credential "attests that the EK was properly created and embedded within a valid TPM" (Gallery, 2005, p. 36). The TPM Endorsement Credential usually contains information such as the TPM's manufacturer name, model number, version and public portion of the EK. To vouch for or attest that a TPM is a genuine TPM, a Trusted Platform Module Entity (TPME) embeds the public key of the EK pair into the Endorsement Credential. This credential then binds the public endorsement key to information about the characteristics of the TPM (Pearson, 2003). The resultant Endorsement Credential contains the following (Gallery, 2005, p. 48):

- A statement reflecting the fact that it is an endorsement credential
- The public EK value
- The TPM type and security properties; and
- A reference to the TPME

The credentialing process is further enhanced by the Platform Credential which attests that a platform containing said TPM is linked to the associated EK and is a genuine TP (Gallery, 2005). The Platform Credentials typically contain information about the platform's manufacturer and type, and contain a pointer to the Endorsement Credential. These two credentials work together to enable the EK to validate its role as the root key of the TPM.

The Storage Root Key, also protected by the TPM, is another non-migratable 2048-bit RSA key pair. The function of the SRK in supporting the Root of Trust for Storage (RTS) was discussed earlier but because of its important role, further investigation of its features is warranted. This master key is distinctive in that it is the root of the key hierarchy, providing the template from which all remaining keys are created in the TPM. The Storage Root Key is used primarily to protect keys or other external data and tho store encrypted data in protected storage. The Endorsement Key and the Storage Root Key in the upper level encrypt the lower level which consists of various key types such as migratable and non-migratable storage keys and attestation identification keys (AIKs) (Schmidt, 2007b).

Having discussed what constitutes a TPM, the various discrete components that make up this hardware and the two important persistent keys residing in TPMs, the focus shifts to attestation. As stated earlier, attestation is the process of assuring that the information is accurate (Piltzecker et al., 2007). The following section will highlight the various roles of the EK, platform configuration registers (PCRs), RTR and RTS (which is basically the TPM), and the credentialing processes that will facilitate attestation.

The primary goal of attestation is to vouch for the accuracy of information and/or to reliably communicate measurements of the platform to a remote party or a verifier. This process is carried out in such a way that neither the TPM nor the platform can lie about their settings or modify them without detection when meeting a particular state sought by the third party. Specifically, to preserve privacy, the verifier should only have the ability to determine that some TPM has participated in the transaction but not which TPM has done so.

According to Grawrock (2006), attestation requires roots of trust. For the TCG TP, this requires the RTM, the RTR, and the RTS to come together as a package to enable this process. Due to privacy concerns, the EK is not used as an identity key since repeated use of PUBEK may lead to the discovery of the TPM as Personal Identifiable Information-PII.

To facilitate attestation of the platform, the EK creates attestation identity keys (AIKs). AIKs are 2048-bit RSA key pairs that alias to the EK. In attestation of the platform, three credentials are used: the Endorsement Credential, the Platform Credential and the Conformance Credential (the Endorsement Credential and Platform Credential were discussed previously). In the Conformance Credential, reference to a document attesting that a TPM's design meets the TCG's specifications (in the form of a statement from the manufacturer) is typically warranted. Its logical design has a pointer to the TPM Conformance which is derived from the Endorsement Credential as well as another pointer to the Platform Conformance which is derived from the Platform Credential (TCG, 2007b).

Upon generation of an AIK key pair, the platform owner bundles the public portion of the AIK, Endorsement Credential, Platform Credential, and the Conformance Credential. Next, the platform sends an AIK request to a privacy certificate authority. Upon receipt, the trusted third party verifies the credentials for validity and if it passes, signs the AIK. The process is complete when the trusted third party sends the AIK back to the TPM. EK can create an unlimited number of AIKs, creating several identities based on an EK as the Root of Trust for Reporting (RTR). For example, one AIK can be generated for an online banking transaction while another AIK can be ready for an online shopping transaction.

Attestation to the Platform (commonly referred to as Remote Attestation) involves several entities including a privacy certification authority, a challenger or verifier, and the platform configuration registers (PCRs) whose role in attestation is critical. Remote Attestation is used to prove to a verifier, in a reliable way, the state the platform is in, and provide a way for the challenger to ascertain the platform's trustworthiness using the metrics received from the platform (Schmidt, 2007d). To begin this process, the platform requests service from the privacy CA upon which it creates an AIK credential, sending the AIK public key to the platform, with the AIK private key hidden from interference. Next, the platform requests service from the verifier to start the attestation process. The platform signs or encrypts the PCR's 20 byte SHA-1 hash (note this hash can be thought of as the fingerprint or the state the platform is in) with the AIK public keys received from the privacy CA and sends the attestation response back to the challenger. To decrypt the hash received from the platform, the challenger requests the AIK private key held by the privacy CA which is the cryptographically-related key that can unlock the hash values of the platform. Upon decryption, the challenger evaluates the platform integrity metrics for further action.

Attestation of the TPM is an operation where the TPM provides proof of data known only to it. The process is quite simple. It starts with a privacy CA issuing AIK credentials that vouch for the state of a platform without disclosing the unique values of the EK to a verifier or challenger. The TPM submits the AIK public key with the privacy CA for enrollment. In return, the privacy CA issues a credential certifying the AIK. Since the credential certifying the AIK was created using the TPM AIK public key, only the TPM private key can decrypt the credential.

Authentication of the TPM (commonly referred to as platform authentication) provides evidence of stated platform identity. This process is usually undertaken by using non-migratable signing keys or an AIK which exhibits attestable qualities. With unlimited, non-migratable keys available from TPMs, an unlimited number of platform identities can be authenticated.

Yet, the attestation schemes proposed by TCG presently have limited wide-spread commercial appeal. The current infrastructure, relies on privacy CAs for certification, verification, and accreditation of a trusted platform to enable trusted e-commerce, needs to be built and supported by sustainable business models. According to Van Doorn (2007), TCG's attestation schemes do not scale well in today's open, connected computing environment, lacking in established public key infrastructures (PKI). Synergistic initiatives like Liberty Alliance (projectliberty.org) hold promise for wide-spread trusted computing adoption.

Trusted Computing Group Software Stack (TSS)

According to Grawrock (2008), the TSS specifications define an architecture allowing simple and direct access to the TPM. With the TSS, programmers have an entry point to writing security-enabled applications which take full advantage of all the functionality that the TPM provides (see Figure 1). The TSS is a software specification that provides for standard APIs (Microsoft CryptoAPI, CDSA, and PKCS#11) cryptographic methods for accessing the TPM. TCG (2006) states the TSS architecture is composed of three primary components to support the TPM (p. 38):

- The TSS Service Provider, or TSP, is an object-oriented interface for applications to incorporate the full capabilities of the TCG-enabled platform
- The TSS Core Services, or TCS, which provide all the primitives and functions for key management required to atomically manage the TPM's limited resources
- The TCG Device Driver Library, or TDDL, provides the device driver that abstracts the specific TPM hardware so that all hardware security modules offer the same behavior for TCS

This second component, the software side of the TPM, the TSS, rounds out the three fundamental elements of a TCG TP which are the RTM and the TPM (consisting of the RTS and RTR).

Trusted Computing, Virtualization and Dynamic Roots of Trust (DRTM)

Hardware-assisted virtualization first appeared in 1967 as part of IBM's CP-40 system. Virtualization's role in enabling multiple operating systems to run on mainframes, while beneficial, was diminished by the more efficient timesharing microcomputers, and further eroded by the commoditization of microcomputers.

The advent of x86-based architecture residing in many of today's servers and client-based computers, and the need for server consolidation to improve utilization and reduce operating expenses, brought about renewed interest in virtualization (Figueirdo, Dinda, & Fortes, 2005). But the benefits of virtualization also brought security concerns because the same platform must be designed to support isolated domains.

To enable virtualization, Virtual Machine Monitors (VMMs), also called hypervisors, provide a software layer beneath the operating system to enable a virtual machine, an abstraction that models and emulates a physical machine. The VMM is overarching, controlling the processor and mediating all access to physical resources of any virtual machines present. It provides each virtual machine with a processor abstraction of its resources, physical memory, interrupts, input and output, and communications and notibly, affords isolation between these virtual machines (Berger, Caceres, Goldman, Perez, Sailer, & Van Doorn, 2006).

Work by Berger et al. (2006) combines virtualization and the TPM as the hardware-assisted root of trust. Specifically, they virtualized the TPM exposing all low-level TPM 1.2 commands available to each instance of virtual machines, linking each virtual TPM to its TCB, and laying the foundation for establishing trust in virtualized environments.

Recent work by both Advanced Micro Devices (AMD) and Intel are working to deliver trusted computing and virtualization by developing extensions to today's x86-based architecture. These extensions are necessary to address issues and difficulties in supporting a secure virtual machine monitor under the x86-based architecture. According to Strongin (2005), AMD's supports a trusted computing base is using robust hardware support enabled by "Presidio" (p. 123) which affords:

- Hardware enforced privilege levels
- Strong domain separation
- I/O protection
- Device protection
- Attestable initialization of the TCB software elements and
- TPM support

Specifically, AMD's support for virtualization, code-named "Pacifica," utilizes the first four building blocks shown previously "to make virtualization of the AMD64 architecture easier and to enable increased security through virtualization". The Pacifica extensions can be used by operating system hosted Virtual Machine Monitors (VMMs) and hypervisors to support both native-virtualization and para-virtualization of the complete AMD64 guest machines (Strongin, 2005, p. 123).

Not surprisingly, Intel's contribution of enhancements to the trusted computing base also involves using hardware components to deliver better protection and increase security, under a initiative called "Intel's Safer Computing Initiative". A key component of this vision is a technology code-named "Trusted Execution Technology" (TXT), formerly known as LaGrande Technology. Similar to AMD's, Intel's TXT is a hardware extension to some of Intel's microprocessors, chipsets, keyboard and mouse, graphics and the TPM to deliver the following capabilities (Intel, 2003b, p. 3):

- Protected execution
- Sealed storage
- Protected input
- Protected graphics
- Attestation
- Protected launch

Intel's Virtualization Technology (VT) includes a set of building blocks technologies for hardware-assisted visualization code-named IA-64 (VT-i) and IA-32 (VT-32) for 64 bit and 32 bit platform processing as well as Virtualization Technology for Directed I/O (VT-d), and Virtualization Technology for Connectivity (VT-c). Using the Virtual Machine Manager (VMM), enabled by Intel TXT and VT technologies, allows the Virtual Machine Extensions (VMX) to create one or more protected virtual machines for domain separation and resources protection (Grawrock, 2006).

According to Strongin (2005), the integrity measurement presented earlier using CRTM, is static (SRTM) and exhibits two major weaknesses. The first is the reliance placed on the immutability of the TBB and CRTM. (As noted earlier, an immutable object is one whose state cannot be modified after it is created.) Since attacks are possible against TBB flash-memory firmware, its immutability is questioned. While this weakness can be mitigated, it will require designing a stringent update process that only few platform vendors can handle.

The second and more troubling weakness is "the length and nature of the chain of trust that leads from the beginning of platform initialization to the instantiation of the fully operational TCB" (Strongin, 2005, p. 130). He argues that while the measurement mechanisms may be performing as designed and measuring accurately, he questions whether the measured readings amount to "meaningful information as to the integrity of the initialization process" (p. 130). According to Strongin, 2005, this phenomenon is the outcome of the TGS's substitution of identity for behavior. Van Doorn (2007) stated that the static root of trust measurement is extreme as it measures everything (configuration files and environment variables). In addition, since there are no real isolation boundaries or controlled circumstances, "anything is a potential threat" including scripts, Perl, Shell, Python Scripts, Emacs Macros, Excel spreadsheet and Word files (p. 22). More disappointing is that static root of measurement provides load-time guarantees, not runtime measurements. However, both Strongin and Van Doorn clearly state that while SRTM has limitations, the SRTM mechanism does not invalidate its use but instead calls for its use in specific applications in controlled or static configuration.

To address some of the shortcomings of SRTM, a new dynamic root of trust for measurement (DRTM) was developed in TPM version 1.2. Strongin (2005) stated that under this new scheme, immutable hardware forms the dynamic root of measurement. Instead of starting at the beginning of the BIOS, as in the case of the CRTM/SRTM, secure initialization can start at an arbitrary point in time to platform initialization, commonly called a late launch. Because "uncontrolled software is used to trigger the hardware-endowed secured initialization process", and complemented by the explicit use of hardware-assisted state machines, "the integrity of the process cannot be compromised by software that executes prior to this trigger point" (p. 130). It is worthwhile to note that, similar to SRTM, the DRTM is still prone to DoS attacks but both schemes' weaknesses (when the TCB is not properly initialized) can be mitigated when critical resources are protected by the TPMs sealed storage functionality.

Starting in 2006, AMD, through the implementation of Presidio and Pacifica enhanced platforms, began supporting secure initialization using a new instruction set, SKINIT, to enable the DRTM model. Similarly, in 2007, with Intel's TXT and VT enhanced platforms, a new instruction set, SENTER, was introduced to support the DRTM measurement-and-launch model.

Trusted Computing Issues, Controversies and Misconceptions

To date, the TCG's leadership, coupled with the assistance and contributions of member vendors and OEMs, has actively championed the deployment of embedded TPMs. Major vendors like Dell, HP, Lenovo, Gateway, NEC, Fujitsu and others are selling enterprise laptops equipped with these low-cost chips as standard hardware. Even consumer grade laptops like Dell's Vostro line are expected to have TPMs on board very soon. Yet, in corporate and home settings alike, computer users are generally ignorant of this technology. To exacerbate the situation, those working in the IT industry are also largely unaware that trusted computing can enhance trust and improve security in a significant way.

Network Magazine (2004) indicated a notable lack of awareness and perceived value regarding trusted computing in general and TPMs in specific. When asked, "How will the presence of a TPM affect your purchasing decisions for a laptop?", 47% of respondents preferred not to have a TPM or would not buy one with a TPM. 14% did not know or care. When presented with the statement, "It (TC) will protect my network from spam and viruses", 27% were neutral (didn't know or care), and 54% disagreed – 27% strongly. The responses also indicated a lack of perceived value. "It (TC) will help make my network safer" returned 32% disagreed and 23% didn't know or care. The survey results also indicated fear of the technology. When asked to evaluate this comment, "It sounds useful, but I'm worried about its potential to be abused", 72% agreed, 43% strongly agreed.

To appease privacy concerns, embedded TPMs are shipped deactivated. It takes the conscious effort of a computer user to turn it on. This opt-in functionality, while working against the efforts of TCG and other vested vendors, affords a measure of control and privacy preservation to the end-user. Over the last few years, misconceptions regarding TC have undoubtedly impeded its wide adoption. Residual effects from the ill-fated Intel initiative (embedding unique ID numbers on its processors to limit piracy by tracking users), as well as HP's International Cryptography Framework initiative (claims of impeding electronic communication privacy) may have contributed to this delay.

Several prominent academicians, and respected security practitioners and organizations including Ross Anderson, Bill Arbaugh, Bruce Schneider, Richard Stallman, Lucky Green, and the Electronic Frontier Foundation were, at best, lukewarm in their reception of TC. Concerns regarding possible TC abuses ranged from limiting the use of unlicensed software to being used as pawns by law enforcement and intelligence agencies. Even though the controversies have dissipated, such concerns were initially worrisome and persistent. These misapprehensions were due to inaccurate representations as well as a general resistance to change. Reasoned rebuttals against TC misconceptions from equally well-respected individuals including Sean Smith of Dartmouth College (Smith, 2005) and David Safford of IBM (Safford, 2002) did much to mollify the furor. While TC can enable digital rights management (DRM), it is not a stated goal of the TCG. According to Schmidt (2007, p. 33), false claims against trusted computing include:

- Having a TPM will keep me from using open source software
- Stop the use of open source operation systems, e.g. Linux
- TCG, Palladium/NGSCB, and DRM are all the same
- Loss of Internet Anonymity

Solutions Enhanced by Trusted Computing

There is an array of innovative technologies that have recently been developed to augment trusted computing (TC). While not all of them require TPMs to run, having the TPMs activated and used in conjunction with these technologies will arguably deliver the most valued proposition of improved trust and security. The following are brief descriptions of the technologies. Whenever possible, website information of the vested vendors is provided.

- Network Access Control (NAC): Traditionally, hackers have focused their efforts on attacking the network, and then the servers. Now they are focusing on end points/clients which are typically the weakest links in the network perimeter protection. The marketplace is flooded with a dizzying array of NAC solutions vying for attention. Most of them, however, are software-based with some consideration for hardware to augment the solution.
- In 2007, the TCG benefitted from an overture by Microsoft (it donated pertinent code – Statement of Health, (SOH) client-server protocol) that enabled open standards-based interoperability for NAC. This mutually beneficial arrangement of standards, TCG's Trusted Network Connect, (TNC) and Microsoft Network Access Point (NAP) will ensure improved security for network access without having to be locked into proprietary architectures. Not to be left out, Cisco announced (at the Interop 2008 conference), the company's plan to unite its Network Admission Control (NAC) protocol with TCG's TNC. Having these three entities come together was a major development for improving network security while propelling open standards-based interoperability into a heterogeneous network environment.
- TCG's brainchild, TNC, is based on two concepts. The first is integrity, where the desired state of an endpoint's "health" or configuration metrics is adhered to as defined by IT policies. Second, identity mandates that the network authenticate only authorized users. So, even though TPMs are not needed to participate in NAC per say, network security is vastly improved with their inclusion, since integrity and identity are seamlessly established through hardware (TCG, 2007a).
- Data Protection and Full Disk Encryption (FDE): The disappearance of unencrypted data due to lost or stolen laptops has been reported on numerous occasions in the past

few years, most notably the U. S. Department of Veterans Affairs incident in 2006. (Readers interested in viewing data loss or breaches from 2002 to current can access http://attrition.org/dataloss/). While federal officials insisted that information belonging to 26.5 million veterans and military personnel was not accessed, this embarrassing incident highlighted the vulnerability of data at rest (Lee & Goldfarb, 2006). While this was deemed a contained incident, it resulted in enormous costs (20 million dollars) to U.S taxpayers for postage and paper because two letters were required to inform each person affected. The stakes are now much higher. The State of California (2002 California Information Practices SB-1386) and others, as well as several foreign countries are considering or have already enacted punitive measures to minimize future infractions (California, 2002).

- Bitlocker Drive Encryption: TPMs were utilized in Microsoft Vista operating systems to support Bitlocker Drive Encryption. Specifically, Bitlocker, supported in the Enterprise and Ultimate versions of Vista, encrypts the computer's boot volume and affords integrity authentication facilitating a trusted boot pathway.

- We must distinguish between software-based FDE and hardware-based FDE solutions. According to Hietala (2007), software-based FDE is difficult to use and hardware-based encryption is "far superior to software-based encryption" (p. 16). TCG developed an open specification for access control extending features and properties of storage devices such as hard drives, flash memory drives, dynamic memory, and digital tape drives. The specification extends the root-of-trust from the TPM on host platforms to the storage devices attached to them allowing the storage device to protect itself and the data entrusted to it (Thibadeau, 2006). As a result, hardware-based FDE such as the Seagate Momentus 5400 FDE featured in the Hietala study, coupled with a TPM, will elevate real-time data protection to the next level; all at a reasonable cost. Seagate Momentus 5400 FDEs command only a small premium over traditional hard drives, and other offerings from Seagate, Hitachi, and Fujitsu are forthcoming. Incidentally, this self-encrypting laptop hard drive received certification from the National Security Agency (NSA), the encryption and code-breaking arm of the U.S. government, for having met one of the highest standards for securing sensitive information - NSTISSP #11 (Seagate, 2008).

- Security Solution Areas: Other areas where TC can enhance current security implementations include (Sprague, 2006, p. 17):

  o Data protection: Protects private keys in hardware. Allows workgroup access to encrypted secure drives.

  o Simplified Sign-On: TC protects and automatically supplies passwords and personal information.

  o Strong Network Access: Adds authentication factor to or replaces passwords for network access.

  o Strong Remote Access: Uses TPM as a fixed hardware token for access to VPN.

  o Secure Email: Adds hardware-based encryption.

  o PKI: Protects private keys in hardware.

  o Platform Policy Management: Allows IT management of security policies, TPM keys, and certificates.

  o Platform State or Condition: Allows for granting network access by type or state of PC in addition to user credentials.

Adopters of Trusted Computing

There is a growing list of companies in various industries starting to pilot and adopt TC technologies. Since there are companies which, for security reasons or restrictions in their governing statues, are unwilling to divulge their security implementations, the following is not an exhaustive list (DoD 2007; Kay, 2007; NISC, 2006).

- The NSA adopted a standard for full-disk encryption based on the TPM since it judged that TCG's architecture would foster compatibility among and reliability across heterogeneous PC clients

- U.S. Department of Defense (DoD) issued a mandate requiring all new purchases of computing devices (e.g., servers, desktops, laptops, and PDAs) include a TPM or higher to support DoD enterprises

- The Federal Deposit Insurance Corporation (FDIC) issued a strong recommendation to include trusted platform modules to enable device and user authentication

- The Japanese Ministry of Economy, Trade and Industry (METI) is sponsoring projects (health care and infrastructure) that build upon the capabilities of the TP as the foundation for a new security model

- A large Japanese pharmaceutical company uses the TPM to enable VPN client authentication with multi-factor authentication of biometric fingerprint and password

- A U.S. Pizza chain with more than 340 stores, an automobile rental company, a manufacturing company based in Chicago, Michigan State University, an IT company, as well as a Canadian health care provider all use TPM enhanced software to manage their company's desktops and laptops, to backup keys, to authenticate users, and to encrypt important customer data

FUTURE TRENDS

The confluence of several factors: anticipated increase in internet use here and abroad (especially in the high growth Asian regions of China and India), increasingly sophisticated computer attacks, and continued reliance on software implementation to design, develop, and implement information systems will continue to strain the state of computer security. To stay ahead, innovative security solutions must be developed to advance global information assurance for a more secure future in cyberspace.

Microsoft's End to End Trust is essentially a revamp of its earlier initiative, Next-Generation Secure Computing Base (NGSCB). While Microsoft is primarily a software company, it exerts tremendous influence on the IT industry and demands we pay close attention to its offerings. As mentioned earlier, Microsoft's Bitlocker Drive Encryption uses the TPM to support drive encryption, and End to End Trust will utilize hardware, presumably the TPM, to facilitate "a chain of trust" to reliably authenticate users.

At Interop Las Vegas 2008, the TCG announced a new protocol, IF-MAP (Interface for Metadata Access Point), an extension into network security within the TNC NAC Architecture. IF-MAP allows devices connected on the network to share data in real-time. By being able to respond to threats in real-time, network defense is vastly improved. IF-MAP enables a powerful feature of publish/subscribe/search protocol across a broad range of heterogonous systems with needed and shared data to better protect the network. According to TCG (2008b), an IF-MAP equipped client, such as an intrusion detection system (IDS), can now publish "an alert to an IF-MAP server indicating that a particular endpoint is sending anomalous traffic, and a firewall that subscribes to information involving that endpoint will receive a real-time update from the IF-MAP server, triggering an automatic response" (p.1). IF-MAP takes it one step further, beyond NAC, to real-time post-admission assessment and control. This has never been accomplished until now.

CONCLUSION

Software-dominated solutions to today's increasingly pervasive computer assaults have been woefully inadequate. Computer infractions continue to increase, even as new software applications, web-services, e-commerce transactions, and computer users become part of cyberspace. The failure to act decisively is costing corporations, governments and their citizens billions of dollars. The IT industry must be open to and actively search for creative solutions that can effectively impede the myriad forms of computer attacks and crime.

The efforts of the IT industry have now converged on the use of TPMs to counter these assaults. Through concerted effort, and to its credit, the industry has developed and brought to market millions of TPMs. In a circuitous way, the industry has returned to its hardware roots, ready to reduce its reliance on software. An important ingredient – low cost TPMs – was successfully introduced laying the foundation for TPM acceptance and adoption. The lack of awareness and perceived benefits, coupled with misinformation and resistance to change, create barriers to public acceptance of TPMs. The eventual success of TCG's effort to promote trusted computing and TPMs rests upon its ability to overcome these barriers.

REFERENCES

Aberdeen Group (2008, February). *Trusted Computing: Tune In, Turn it On.* Retrieved July, 2008, from https://www.trustedcomputinggroup. org/news/Industry_Data/Aberdeen_Report_TC_TuneIn_TurnItOn.pdf

Anderson, J. P. (1972). Computer Security Technology Planning Study, ESD-TR-73-51, Vol. II. Bedford, MA: Electronic Systems Division, Air Force Systems Command, Hanscom Field. Retrieved July, 2008, from, from http://csrc.nist. gov/publications/history/ande72.pdf

Anderson, R. (2008). *Security Engineering: A Guide to Building Dependable Distributed Systems.* Indianapolis, IN: Wiley Publishing Inc.

Bailey, J. P., & Bakos, J. Y. (1997). Reducing buyer search costs: Implications for electronic marketplaces. *Management Science, 43*(12), 1676-1692.

Bell, D. E. (1974). *Secure Computer Systems: A Refinement of the Mathematical Model, ESD-TR-73-278, III.* Bedford, MA: ESD/AFSC, Hanscom AFB.

Bell, D. E., & LaPadula, L. J. (1973). *Secure Computer System: Mathematical Foundations, ESD-TR-73-278, I.* Bedford, MA: ESD/AFSC, Hanscom AFB.

Bell, D. E., & LaPadula, L. J. (1976). *Secure Computer System: Unified Exposition and Multics Interpretation*, ESD-TR-75-306. Bedford, MA: ESD/AFSC, Hanscom AFB. Retrieved July, 2008, from http://csrc.nist.gov/publications/history/bell76.pdf

Bellovin, S. M. (2001). Computer security – an end state? *Communications of the ACM, 44*(3), 131-132.

Berger, S., Caceres, R., Goldman, K., Perez, R., Sailer, R., & Van Doorn, L. (2006). *vTPM: Virtualizing the Trusted Platform Module.* Retrieved July, 2008, from http://www.usenix.org/events/sec06/tech/full_papers/berger/berger.pdf

Bhattacherjee, A. (2002). Individual trust in on-line firms: Scale development and initial trust. *Journal of Management Information Systems, 19*(1), 211-241.

Challener, D., Yoder, K., Catherman, R., Safford, D., & Van Doorn, L. (2008). *A Practical Guide to Trusted Computing.* Upper Saddle River, NJ: IBM Press, Pearson plc

Chopra, K., & Wallace, W. A. (2003, January). *Trust in electronic environments.* Paper presented at the Proceedings of the 36th Annual Hawaii International Conference on System Sciences, Big Island, HI.

CSI (2007). *CSI Survey 2007: The 12th Annual Computer Crime and Security Survey.* Retrieved July 31, 2008, from http://i.cmpnet.com/v2.gocsi.com/pdf/CSISurvey2007.pdf

CSI/FBI (2004). *CSI/FBI Computer Crime and Security Survey.* Retrieved July 31, 2008, from http://i.cmpnet.com/gocsi/db_area/pdfs/fbi/FBI2004.pdf

CSI/FBI (2005). *CSI/FBI Computer Crime and Security Survey.* Retrieved July 31, 2008, from http://i.cmpnet.com/gocsi/db_area/pdfs/fbi/FBI2005.pdf

CSI/FBI (2006). *CSI/FBI Computer Crime and Security Survey.* Retrieved July 31, 2008, from http://i.cmpnet.com/gocsi/db_area/pdfs/fbi/FBI2006.pdf

Deloitte (2004). *Global Security Survey.* Retrieved July 31, 2008, from http://www.deloitte.com/dtt/cda/doc/content/dtt_financialservices_Security-Survey2004_051704.pdf

Deloitte (2005). *Global Security Survey.* Retrieved July 31, 2008, from http://www.ladlass.com/ice/archives/files/deliotte%20download.asp.pdf

Deloitte (2006). *Global Security Survey.* Retrieved July 31, 2008, from http://www.deloitte.com/dtt/cda/doc/content/us_fsi_150606globalsecuritysurvey(1).pdf

Deloitte (2007). *Global Security Survey.* Retrieved July 31, 2008, from http://www.deloitte.com/dtt/cda/doc/content/ca_en_Global_Security_Survey.final.en.pdf

Figueiredo, R., Dinda, P. A., & Fortes, J. (2005). Resource virtualization renaissance. *IEEE Computer, 38*(5), 28-31.

Fukuyama, F. (1995). *Trust: The Social Virtues and the Creation of Prosperity.* New York: The Free Press.

Gallery, E. (2005). An overview of trusted computing technology. In C. Mitchell (Ed.), *Trusted Computing* (pp. 29-114). London: The Institution of Electrical Engineers.

Garfinkel, T., Rosenblum, M., & Boneh, D. (2003, May). *Flexible os support and applications for trusted computing.* Paper presented at the USENIX 9th Hot Topics in Operating Systems (HotOS-IX), Lihue, HI.

Gefen, D. (2002). Reflections on the dimensions of trust and trustworthiness among online consumers. *Database for Advances in Information Systems, 33(*3), 38-53.

Gefen, D., & Straub, D. (2003). Managing user trust in B2C e-Services. *E-Service Journal. 2(*2), 7-24.

Grawrock, D. (2006). *The Intel Safer Computing Initiative: Building Blocks for Trusted Computing.* Hillsboro, OR: Intel Press.

Hietala, J. H. (2007, September). *Hardware versus Software: A Usability Comparison of Software-based Encryption with Seagate DriveTrust™ Hardware-Based Encryption – White Paper.* Retrieved July 31, 2008, from http://www.seagate.com/docs/pdf/whitepaper/Seagate-crypto-bake-off.pdf

Hoffman, D. L., Novak, T. P., & Peralta, M. (1999). Building consumer trust online. *Communications of the ACM, 42(*4), 80-85.

Intel Corporation. (2003a, May). *Enterprise Security and the PC Infrastructure – White Paper.* Originally retrieved from Intel Web site, no longer available. On file with the author.

Intel Corporation (2003b). *Intel Trusted Execution Technology Overview*. Retrieved July 31, 2008, from http://www.intel.com/technology/security/downloads/arch-overview.pdf

Internet World Stats (2008). *Internet Usage Statistics: The Internet Big Picture*. Retrieved July 31, 2008, from http://www.internetworldstats.com/stats.htm

Irvine, C. E., Levin, T. E., & Dinolt, G. W. (2002, May). *A National Trusted Computing Strategy* (White Paper NPS-CS-02-003). Monterey, CA: Naval Postgraduate School, the Center for INFOSEC Studies and Research, Computer Science Department.

Karger, P.A., & Schell, R. R. (1974). MULTICS Security Evaluation: Vulnerability Analysis, ESD-TR-74-193, Vol. II. Bedford, MA: ESD/AFSC, Hanscom AFB. Retrieved July 31, 2008, from http://csrc.nist.gov/publications/history/karg74.pdf

Kay, R. (2007, January 29). *Trusted Computing is Real and it's Here*. Retrieved July 31, 2008, from https://www.trustedcomputinggroup.org/news/Industry_Data/Endpoint_Technologies_Associates_TCG_report_Jan_29_2007.pdf

Keen, P. G. W., Balance, C., Chan, S., & Schrump, S. (1999). *Electronic Commerce Relationships: Trust by Design*. Upper Saddle River, NJ: Prentice Hall PTR.

Kinney, S. (2006). *Trusted Platform Basics: Using TPM in Embedded Systems*. Burlington, MA: Elsevier Inc.

LaPadula, L. J., & Bell, D. E. (1973) Secure Computer Systems: A Mathematical Model, ESD-TR-73-278, Vol. II. Bedford, MA: ESD/AFSC, Hanscom AFB.

Lee, C, & Goldfarb, Z. A. (2006, June 30). Stolen VA Laptop and Hard Drive Recovered. *Washington Post*. Retrieved July 31, 2008, from, http://www.washingtonpost.com/wp-dyn/content/article/2006/06/29/AR2006062900352.html

Lewicki, R. J., & Bunker, B. B. (1996). Developing and maintaining trust in work relationships. In R. M. Kramer & T. R. Tyler (Eds.), *Trust in Organizations: Frontiers of Theory and Research* (pp. 114-139). Thousands Oaks, CA: Sage Publications.

Luhmann, N. (1979). *Trust and Power*. New York: John Wiley and Sons.

Mackenzie, D., & Pottinger, G. (1997). Mathematics, technology, and trust: Formal verification, computer security, and the U.S. military. *IEEE Annals of the History of Computing, 19*(3), 41-59.

Mayer, R. C., Davis, J. H., & Schoorman, F. D. (1995). An integrative model of organizational trust. *Academy of Management Review, 20*(3), 709-734.

McCullagh, A., & Caelli, W. (2000). Non-repudiation in the digital environment. *First Monday*. Retrieved July 31, 2008, from http://www.firstmonday.dk/issues/issue5_8/mccullagh/index.html

McKnight, D. H., Choudhury, V., & Kacmar, C. (2002). Developing and validating trust measures for e-commerce: An integrative topology. *Information Systems Research, 13*(3), 334-361.

Mundie, C., DeVries, P., Haynes, P., & Corwine, M. (2002, September 12). *Trustworthy Computing - White Paper*. Retrieved July 31, 2008, from http://download.microsoft.com/download/a/f/2/af22fd56-7f19-47aa-8167-4b1d73cd3c57/twc_mundie.doc

National Information Security Center (NISC). (2006, October). *Japanese Government's Efforts to Address Information Security Issues: Focusing on the Cabinet Secretariat's Efforts*. Retrieved July 31, 2008, from http://unpan1.un.org/intradoc/groups/public/documents/APCITY/UNPAN027267.pdf

Network Magazine. (2004, June 30). *Trusted Computing Survey Results*. Retrieved July 31, 2008, from http://www.techweb.com/news/showArticle.jhtml?articleID=22102893

Neumann, P. G. (2003, Summer). U.S. computer insecurity redux. *Issues in Science and Technology*. Retrieved July 31, 2008, from http://www.nap.edu/issues/19.4/neumann.html

Pavlou, P. A., & Gefen, D. (2004). Building effective online marketplaces with institution-based trust. *Information Systems Research, 15(*1), 37-59.

Pearson, S. (2003). *Trusted Computing Platforms: TCPA Technology in Context.* Upper Saddle River, NJ: Prentice Hall PTR.

Piltzecker, T., Chaffin, L., Granneman, S., & Hunter, L. E. (2007). *Microsoft Vista for IT Security Professionals.* Rockland, MA: Syngress Publishing.

Quelch, J. A., & Klein, L. R. (1996). The Internet and international marketing. *Sloan Management Review, 37(*3), 60-75.

Ratnasingam, P., & Pavlou, P. A. (2003). Technology trust in internet-based interorganization electronic commerce. *Journal of Electronic Commerce in Organizations, 1*(1), 17-41.

Rousseau, D. M., Sitkin, S. B., Burt, R. S., & Camerer, C. (1998). Not so different after all: A cross-discipline view of trust. *Academy of Management Review, 23*(3), 393-404.

Safford, D. (2002, October). *Clarifying Misinformation on TCPA.* Retrieved July 31, 2008, from http://www.research.ibm.com/gsal/tcpa/tcpa_rebuttal.pdf

Schmidt, A. (2007a). *Trusted Computing: Introduction & Applications. Lecture 1: TC History & Intro.* Retrieved July 31, 2008, from http://www.sec.informatik.tu-darmstadt.de/pages/lehre/SS07/tc/folien/tc01.pdf

Schmidt, A. (2007b). *Trusted Computing: Introduction & Applications. Lecture 2: TPM Archi-

tecture, Base Functionality, and Key Hierarchy.* Retrieved July 31, 2008, from http://www.sec.informatik.tu-darmstadt.de/pages/lehre/SS07/tc/folien/tc02.pdf

Schmidt, A. (2007c). *Trusted Computing: Introduction & Applications. Lecture 3: The CRTM and Authenticated boot process.* Retrieved July 31, 2008, from http://www.sec.informatik.tu-darmstadt.de/pages/lehre/SS07/tc/folien/tc03.pdf

Schmidt, A. (2007d). *Trusted Computing: Introduction & Applications. Lecture 5: Remote Attestation, Direct Anonymous Attestation* Retrieved July 31, 2008, from http://www.sec.informatik.tu-darmstadt.de/pages/lehre/SS07/tc/folien/tc05.pdf

Seagate Technology Incorporated. (2008, May 13). Seagate Secure™ Self-Encrypting Laptop Hard Drives Earn National Security Agency Qualification for National Security Systems. Retrieved July 31, 2008, from http://www.seagate.com/ww/v/index.jsp?locale=en-US&name=null&vgnextoid=bd8f322b02fd9110VgnVCM100000f5ee0a0aRCRD

Shapiro, S. P. (1987). The social control of impersonal trust. *American Journal of Sociology, 93,* 623-658.

Smith, S. (2005). *Trusted Computing Platforms: Design and Applications.* New York, NY: Springer Science+Business Media, Inc.

Solomon, M. G., & Chapple, M. (2005). *Information Security Illuminated.* Sudbury, MA: Jones and Bartlett Publisher.

Sprague, S. (2006*). Trusted Computing: Benefiting from the New Standard.* Originally retrieved from Wave Systems Website, no longer available. On file with the author.

State of California, (2002). *California Information Practices.* Retrieved July 31, 2008, from http://www.leginfo.ca.gov/pub/01-02/bill/sen/sb_1351-1400/sb_1386_bill_20020926_chaptered.html

Strongin, G. (2005). Trusted computing using AMD Pacifica and Presidio secure virtual machine technology. *Information Security Technical Report, 10,* 120-132.

Suh, B., & Han, I. (2003). The impact of customer trust and perception of security control on the acceptance of electronic commerce. *International Journal of Electronic Commerce, 7(3)*, 135-161.

Tasker, P. S. (1981, April). *Trusted Computer Systems.* Paper presented at the IEEE Symposium on Security and Privacy, Oakland, CA.

Thibadeau, R. (2006). Trusted computing for disk drives and other peripherals. *IEEE Security and Privacy, 4(1)*, 26-33.

Trusted Computing Group (2005, July). *TCG Newsletter, 1(3)*. Retrieved July 31, 2008, from https://www.trustedcomputinggroup.org/news/newsletter/2005/2005_July/

Trusted Computing Group (2006, January 11). *TCG Software Stack (TSS) Specification Version 1.2*. Retrieved July 31, 2008, from https://www.trustedcomputinggroup.org/specs/TSS/TSS_Version_1.2_Level_1_FINAL.pdf

Trusted Computing Group, (2007a, May). *Trusted Network Connect Frequently Asked Questions.* Retrieved July 31, 2008, from https://www.trustedcomputinggroup.org/faq/TNCFAQ/

Trusted Computing Group, (2007b, August 2nd). *TCG Specification Architecture Overview.* Retrieved July 31, 2008, from https://www.trustedcomputinggroup.org/groups/TCG_1_4_Architecture_Overview.pdf

Trusted Computing Group (2008a). *TCG Glossary of Technical Terms.* Retrieved July 31, 2008, from https://www.trustedcomputinggroup.org/groups/glossary/

Trusted Computing Group (2008b, April 28th). *Trusted Network Connect (TNC) Expands NAC Architecture with Extensions into Network Security, More Products and Proven Interoperability.* Retrieved July 31, 2008, from https://www.trustedcomputinggroup.org/news/events/interop_2008/interop_if_map_tnc_release_april_23_final.pdf

Trusted Computing Platform Alliance. (2000, August). TCPA security and Internet business: Vital issues for IT. Originally retrieved from Trusted Computing Platform Alliance Web site, no longer available. On file with the author.

Turban, E., Lee, J., King, D., & Chung, H. M. (2000). *Electronic Commerce – A Managerial Perspective.* Upper Saddle River, NJ: Prentice Hall PTR.

U.S. Department of Defense. (1985). *Department of Defense Trusted Computing System Evaluation Criteria.* Retrieved July 31, 2008, from http://csrc.nist.gov/publications/history/dod85.pdf

U.S. Department of Defense. (2007, July). *Encryption of Sensitive Unclassified Data at Rest on Mobile Computing Devices and Removable Storage Media.* Retrieved July 31, 2008, from http://iase.disa.mil/policy-guidance/DoD-dar-tpm-decree07-03-07.pdf

Van Doorn, L. (2007, November). *Trusted computing challenges.* Session: Invited talk at the Proceedings of the 2007 ACM workshop on Scalable Trusted Computing, Alexandria, VA.

Walker, S. T. (1985, April). *Network security overview.* Paper presented at the IEEE Symposium on Security and Privacy, Oakland, CA.

Ware, W. H. (1967). Security and privacy in computer systems. *AFIPS Conference Proceeding, Spring Joint Computer Conference,* Vol. 30 (pp. 279-282). Thompson Books.

Ware, W.H. (1970). Security Controls for Computer Systems (U): Report of Defense Science Board Task Force on Computer Security. Santa Monica, CA: The RAND Corporation. Retrieved July 31, 2008, from http://csrc.nist.gov/publications/history/ware70.pdf

Weissman, C. (1969). Security controls in the AD-EPT-50 time-sharing system. Proceedings of the 1969 Fall Joint Computer Conference. Reprinted in L.J. Hoffman (Ed.), *Security and Privacy in Computer Systems (pp. 216-243)*. Los Angeles: Melville Publishing Company, 1973.

Zucker, L. G. (1986). Production of trust: Institution sources of economic structure. In B. M. Staw & L. L. Cummings (Eds.), *Research in Organizational Behavior* (pp. 1840-1920). Greenwich, CT: JAI Press.

Chapter XVIII
Introduction, Classification and Implementation of Honeypots

Miguel Jose Hernandez y Lopez
Universidad de Buenos Aires, Argentina

Carlos Francisco Lerma Resendez
Universidad Autónoma de Tamaulipas, Mexico

ABSTRACT

This chapter discusses the basic aspects of Honeypots, how they are implemented in modern computer networks, as well as their practical uses and implementation in educational environments, providing the reader with the most important points regarding the main characteristics of Honeypots and Honeynets. Honeypots are defined as "closely monitored network decoys" that can be set by network administrators to deal with a wide variety of attacks and interact with users in different levels (Provos, 2004). The implementation of Honeypots provides an answer to a common question posted by the field of information security and forensics: How to dissect the elements that make up an attack against a computer system. The chapter will summarizes the different features and capabilities of Honeypots once they are set up in a production environment to clarify the elements that are needed to be configured in order for a Honeypot to accomplish its main tasks and in order for it to be considered an effective tool. The end of the chapter will shift towards the analysis of virtualization as an important tool that maximizes the practical use of Honeypots in controlled environments that are focused towards the study of attacks, responses and analysis methods.

INTRODUCTION

Historically, the field of Information Security has been focused in a great manner towards defending networks. Firewalls, intrusion detection systems and encryption are tools employed in a defensive way to protect network and Information Technology (IT) resources (Dunsmore, Brown & Cross, 2002). The strategic approach of information security consists in defending the information infrastructure as good as possible, to identify potential failures in the defensive structure and react to those failures as quick as possible, preferably in a proactive way (Roberti & Bonsembiante, 1995). The essence and operation of the entity known as the "information enemy" is purely offensive because that entity is commonly always ready and willing to attack.

Honeypots have proven themselves as valuable research tools in the field of Information Security and also as strong educational tools when it comes to finding potential practical tools in IT classrooms (The Attacker Project, 2005). Honeypots can be defined as "closely monitored network decoys" that "serve several purposes: they can distract adversaries from more valuable machines on a network, provide early warning about new attack and exploitation trends, or allow in-depth examination of adversaries during and after exploitation" (Provos, 2004). Across the globe, researchers and organizations of public and private nature which are part of the information security community, are currently working with trap-style networks to acquire and dissect the tactics, techniques and procedures employed by rogue users to breach information vaults without authorization, vaults that commonly contain potentially sensitive information. Honeypots also provide teachers and students with the means that allow them to dissect security events in a consistent and separate way, which is a well-sought feature in modern Information Security courses.

This chapter attempts to summarize the functions of Honeypots and their inherent features that have evolved into both an important component in a multi-tiered system of security against intruders and also a valuable simulation resource in the learning field.

BACKGROUND

Honeypots are a somewhat new technology that posses an enormous potential for the information technology community. The first references to Honeypots were discussed by some notable icons in the Information Security community, such as those defined by Cliff Stoll (2002) and Bill Cheswick (1997), particularly in the work of the latter that included his experiences tracking down attackers on AT&T's networks and information resources. Ever since, those concepts have been in a process of evolution, changing in a way that has allowed them to become a potent security tool (Riebach, Rathgeb & Tödtmann, 2005). Bill Cheswick's work guides users into the field of intrusion detection systems, offering a solid foundation for people looking to understand the basics of Honeypots. In a more strict sense, a Honeypot possesses the features of both an intrusion detection system (it contains mechanisms that can detect properly when a systems intrusion takes place, as long as the Honeypot is set up to detect and repel such intrusion in real time) and a cyberforensics study aid (providing users with detailed reports that depict the nature of attacks, including the intruder's activities that took place inside a breached computer system) (Schneier, 2000). Even though a Honeypot may display the characteristic form of an intrusion detection system, it should not be regarded as one *per se* because its main purpose is to act simply as a potential target (albeit its ever-present complexity in terms of configuration and place inside a network) for an equally potential rogue user, opposite to being an integral system with a centralized reporting console and agents that run remotely, reporting suspicious activity in real-time (Dalton, King & Osmanoglu, 2001). Even still, both Honeypots and intrusion detection systems share elements in common, such as reporting capabilities (logs and reports), network placement, monitored events and activity alerts. Because of these features, it can also be stated that Honeypots are proactive security tools; they record information that is valuable to properly configure security countermeasures inside a network even before attacks take place and to analyze the network in order to prevent future attacks. They can also be reactive security tools; Honeypots can trigger services that gather information or disguise themselves as a target while the attacker breaches and/or damages the system.

Honeypots are described, in a most basic form, as false information severs that are strategically placed in a network, which are set up with false information disguised as files of important nature. Furthermore, the aforementioned servers are configured in a way that is difficult, but not impossible, to break into by an attacker. This condition is made notable by exposing the servers deliberately and making them highly attractive for a hacker in search of a target (Spitzner, 2002). The final set-up stage of the server consists of loading it with monitoring and tracking tools whose purpose will be to record and report every step and trace of activity left by a hacker, indicating those traces of activity in a detailed manner.

The main objectives of a Honeypot can be described as (Pouget & Holz, 2005):

1. To distract the attention of the attacker from the real network, in such a way that the main information resources are not compromised
2. To capture new viruses or worms for observation

3. To build attacker profiles in order to dissect and study their methods, in a way similar to criminal profiles used by law enforcement agencies in order to identify a criminal's *modus operandi*
4. To pinpoint emergent vulnerabilities and risks of different operating systems, environments and programs which are not thoroughly identified at the moment

Speaking in a more advanced context, a group of Honeypots becomes a Honeynet (Spitzner, 2002). Honeynets are a tool that integrates different types of Honeypots into a single network, providing a wide group of possible threats that has two purposes: to give a rogue user a wider "menu" of options to perform different exploits and to give systems administrators more information for study. It makes the attack more appealing for the rogue user due to the fact that Honeypots can increase the possibilities, targets and exploits.

On Figure 1, a Honeypot is disguised inside of the network and among many systems that make up a server farm. In this scenario, the Honeypot can be placed in the network with the purpose of pinpointing an internal attacker that might be trying to scan the network with the purpose of locating a target containing sensitive information. Since a good amount of attacks come from

Figure 1. A Honeypot placed inside the network

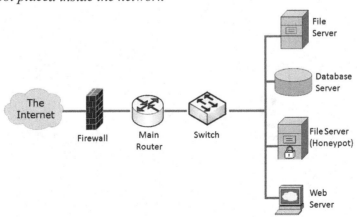

the inside of the network the defensive nature of this Honeypot has to do more with protecting the network against internal attackers. This Honeypot can replicate well-known services that an attacker has already identified and whose access he/she may control through permissions already assigned by the network's administrator. Because of this fact, the Honeypot should be configured so that it may not be used as a launch pad to attack the rest of the internal network due to the location within the protected network.

On Figure 2, a Honeypot has been set up in a more "classic" way, advertising itself as a target on the outside of the protected network and the main firewall or internet router. This is a more aggressive and robust type of Honeypot since it will have to withstand all sorts of attacks from any rogue user that wishes to interact with it. It differs from the example of Figure 1 in that the former example is set up in a network where an administrator or security specialist has already studied the modus operandi from an attacker, while the latter example is focused on analyzing any type of attack that may be directed to the Honeypot. Figure 2 depicts a very good alternative for network administrators and security specialists that wish to study and analyze a wider range of attacks that may even include zero-day methods and attacks that are unknown to them.

CLASSIFICATION OF HONEYPOTS

Honeypots can be classified into two categories: Deployment Scenario and Level of Interaction. This classification criterion makes it easier to understand their operation and uses when it comes to planning an implementation of one of them inside a network.

Classification I: Deployment Scenario

Under this category, we can define two types of Honeypots: Production Honeypots and Research Honeypots.

Production Honeypots

Those used to protect organizations in real production operating environments. They are implemented parallel to data networks or IT Infra-structures and are subject to constant attacks 24/7 (The Attacker Project, 2005). These Honeypots are constantly gathering more importance due to the detection tools they provide and because of the way they can complement network and host protection. Special care should be taken into consideration when configuring production-state Honeypots because they should be able to perform

Figure 2. A Honeypot placed in a perimeter network (DMZ)

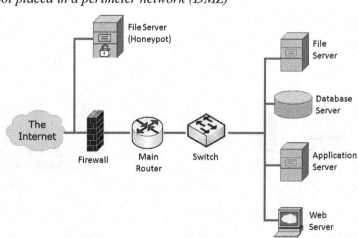

all the functions that administrators set up in them because, once they go online, they become live targets awaiting for real activity (attempts to breach security, attacks, etc.) (Grimes, 2005). Production Honeypots should be able to be recovered quickly in the event of a major attack or catastrophe, since administrators need them to be up and running just like any other system they set up in the network. Also, their level of portability should be fairly high, allowing a system to switch locations within the network and to offer "service modularity" by removing or adding several services inside the system as needed according to the advertised target. Production Honeypots provide the most valuable information for administrators and security professionals because they interact directly with attackers that do not know the undercover identity of the system they are interacting with, thus making this information more valuable when it comes to tracking behavior patterns (attack methods, specific exploits, etc). As stated before, special care should be taken into consideration so that a Honeypot does not become itself a threat to the organization once it has been attacked.

Research Honeypots

These Honeypots are not implemented with the objective of protecting networks. They represent educational resources of demonstrative and research nature whose objective is centered towards the study of all sorts of attack patterns and threats (Lerma, 2007). A great deal of current attention is focused on Research Honeypots, which are used to gather information about the intruders' actions. The Honeynet Project, for example, is a non-profit research organization focused in voluntary security using Honeypots to gather information about threats in cyberspace. While the average user may not consider these type of Honeypots as important as Production Honeypots, they are of high importance because the information originated in and logged by the

Production type can be recreated and analyzed in the Research type. Research Honeypots provide a very stable and isolated platform where security events can be dissected without the fear of making a network vulnerable since they are mostly systems that are used with demonstrative purposes inside of laboratories and research facilities (Grimes, 2005). Even though they are not intended to work directly with attackers, they can provide a solid environment where threats can be re-enacted and where security updates and patches can be tested and released for installation by network administrators before deeming them safe to be deployed. This can be very useful in organizations that possess large amounts of computers and that need to have a degree of assurance that tested updates and patches will not disrupt the normal use of their systems, an event that can yield losses ranging from simple (malfunctions in small number of computers) to extremely catastrophic (disrupting a large-scale server farm intended to provide platform services used as the base of a large business operation).

Classification II: Degree of Interaction

Within this classification criterion, the term "Degree of Interaction" defines the range of attack possibilities that a Honeypot allows an attacker to have. These categories help us understand not just the type of Honeypot which a person works with, but also help define the array of options in relation to the vulnerabilities intended for the attacker to exploit. Those are the most important traits when it comes to starting the construction of an attacker's profile.

Low Interaction Honeypots

Normally, Low Interaction Honeypots work exclusively emulating operating systems and services. The attacker's activities are limited to the Honeypot's level and quality of emulation.

The advantage of a Low Level Honeypot lies upon its simplicity, due to the fact that they tend to be easy to use and maintain, with minimum risks. For example: An emulated File Transfer Protocol (FTP) service, listening on port 21, is probably emulating an FTP login or will possibly support additional FTP commands but it does not represent a target of critical importance due to the fact that it is not possibly linked to a FTP server containing sensitive information.

Generally, the implementation process of a Low Interaction Honeypot consists of installing any kind of operating system emulation software (i.e. VMWare Workstation or Server), choosing the operating system and services to be emulated, establishing a monitoring strategy and let the software operate by itself in a normal manner. This "plug-and-play" type of process makes it extremely easy to use a Low Interaction Honeypot. The emulated services mitigate the risk of penetration, containing the intruder's activities so he/she never gains access to a real operating system that could be used to attack or damage other systems.

The main disadvantage of Low Interaction Honeypots lies in the fact that they only record limited information since they are designed to capture predetermined activity. Because emulated services can only go as far as certain operational thresholds, this feature limits the array of options that can be advertised towards a potential intruder. Likewise, it is relatively simple for an attacker to detect a Low Interaction Honeypot due to the fact that a skilled intruder can detect how good the emulation capabilities are as long as he/she has enough time to verify this.

Effective examples of Low Interaction Honeypots are: Specter, Honeyd and KFSensor (HoneyD, 2007). These tools provide very basic services and features for an attacker to manipulate and are somewhat simple because some of them only emulate a vulnerable service. Also, their ability to change and adapt to threats is somewhat low.

High Interaction Honeypots

These Honeypots constitute a complex solution because they involve the utilization of operating systems and real applications implemented in real hardware, without using emulation software, running in a normal way; many times directly related to services such as databases and shared folders. For example, if a Honeypot needs to be implemented on an actual or non-emulated Linux system running a FTP server, a Linux system needs to be built on an actual computer and a real FTP server will need to be configured.

The aforementioned solution offers two advantages: Initially, there is the possibility of capturing large amounts of information about the modus operandi of attackers because intruders are interacting with a real system. This way, a systems administrator is in a position to study the full extent of the attacker's activities: anything ranging from new rootkits, zero-days up to international IRC sessions. Finally, High Interaction Honeypots do not assume anything about the possible behavior the attacker will display since they only provide an open environment which captures every one of the attacker's moves but they still offer a wide scope of services, applications and information vaults posing as potential targets related to those services which we specifically want to compromise. This allows high interaction solutions to come in contact with unexpected behaviors.

However, the latter capability also increases the risk of attackers using those operating systems as a launch pad for attacks directed at internal systems which are not part of a Honeypot, turning bait into a weapon. As a result of this, there is a need to implement additional technologies which prevent the attacker from damaging non-Honeypot systems that deprives the compromised system of its capabilities of becoming a platform to launch potential attacks.

Currently, the best example of a High Interaction Honeypot is represented by Honeynets (The

Honeynet Project, 2007). A Honeynet provides a wide scope of possible targets and relies on advanced logging, analysis and reporting capabilities, allowing security administrators to dissect attacks in a more granular way. Entire servers can be offered as targets that not only advertise a single service, port or file store, but as whole vulnerable systems.

ADVANTAGES AND LIMITATIONS OF HONEYPOTS

Up to this point in the chapter, we have introduced and provided a general classifications scheme for Honeypots. Now we will point out that honeypots are incredibly simple concepts that offer powerful advantages as well as some limitations. First, we list the advantages:

1. **New tools and tactics:** They are designed to capture anything that interacts with them, including tools or tactics never seen before, better known as "zero-days" (Leita, Dacier & Massicotte, 2006).
2. **Minimal resources:** Resources can be minimal and still enough to operate a powerful platform to operate at full scale. For example: A computer running with a Pentium II Processor with 128 Mb of RAM can easily handle an entire B-class network. This specific feature proves very attractive in a world where many organizations lack the resources to deploy a full-scale, expensive solution. A Honeypot based in open-source software combined with inexpensive hardware can be very attractive to organizations looking for economic solutions that are still reliable and accurate.
3. **Flexible encryption:** Unlike most security technologies, Honeypots also work in IPv6 environments. The Honeypot will detect an IPv6-based attack the same way it does with an IPv4 attack (Man, 2003).

4. **Information gathering:** Honeypots can gather detailed information, unlike other security incident analysis tools. This feature can be very desirable and advantageous if the Honeypot is based in systems that provide tools powerful enough to report a wide range of events and conditions. Most of the time, this capability can be enhanced by creating custom reports and logs that can gather massive amounts of details about certain events as they occur in the system and can also provide filtering and analysis capabilities, which are very desirable once an administrator has to analyze large chunks of reports generated by an attack.
5. **Conceptual simplicity:** Because of their architecture, Honeypots are conceptually simple. There is not a reason why new algorithms, tables or signatures must not be developed or maintained. The configuration of a system meant for Honeypot use is fairly simple and can be brought up in a matter of minutes. Also, alarms and events can be set up in order to gather information in a simple way making it easier to maintain logs and trace files.

Schneier (2000) considers the knowledge of the network layout to be the best advantage that Honeypots offer to security professionals. Administrators who place Honeypots inside a network know exactly the places where no one is supposed to be, the accounts that are not meant to be used, the commands that are supposed to never be issued and so forth. This in-depth knowledge serves as a reference to place Honeypots inside the network in places where it is easy to detect and to expect (as long as there is a previous knowledge of intrusions and/or attempts by the attacker to determine the outline of the network) an attack or breach of security. The explicit nature of the Honeypot is that of a system that is set up to be used by no one except the potential intruder, hence making the Honeypot even more visible when it sounds an alarm indicating activity (whether it might be normal or malicious). Honeypots can also be moved from place to place and reconfigured in order to look like anything we might want to set up for an intruder: it can be moved from subnet to subnet, have its role changed (from an "innocent" file server to a "very important" database server and so forth) and it set of vulnerabilities tailored to lure an attacker into breaching a specific vulnerability. It is stated that these features make a Honeypot look like a "burglar alarm": it is set up specifically to be triggered by no one but an intruder; its placement is based in the knowledge of the layout of a certain place (a clear advantage over the attacker) that a person has (thus enhancing the surreptitiousness of the alarm), and it can be moved to many places as the needs of the user change or the threats evolve.

Just like any other technology, Honeypots also have significant weaknesses inherent to their design and functioning. This is because Honeypots do not replace current technologies, but instead work along with other existing technologies. Here, we list three weaknesses:

1. **Limited scope:** Honeypots can only scan and capture activity destined to interact directly with them. They do not capture information related to attacks destined towards neighboring systems, unless the attacker or the threat interacts with the Honeypot at the same time. This can be a troubling issue when trying to emulate distributed systems in a Honeypot infrastructure (i.e. a portal server or custom application that relies on a complex and separate database system).

2. **Network risk:** Inherently, the use of any security technology implies a potential risk. Honeypots are no different because they are also subject to risks, specifically being hijacked and controlled by the intruder and used as a launch pad for subsequent attacks. Network administrators must be well acquainted with risk management and internal

policies once a Honeypot is to be installed inside a specific network, taking care of not placing an intentionally-compromised system in a strategic place whose integrity cannot be compromised. Administrators should carefully select the services they want to evaluate, the type of systems they wish to test and the way they will offer them to an attacker.

3. **Simulation of large-scale systems:** Certain systems or services can only be mounted on large-scale and very complex pieces of hardware, thus making them practically impossible to offer them to an attacker in an emulated or reduced form. A complex e-mail system housed on large servers with big storage units housing thousands of accounts or a custom-made application that requires special software and hardware requirements are examples of targets that might only be replicated in large and expensive systems that cannot run on emulators and whose costs can be extremely high, thus making them impossible to be set-up as potential Honeypots. Even though Honeypots can vary in size and complexity (accommodating the needs of administrators with ease) one must make sure not to overshoot them in order to make it truly possible to deploy a Honeypot.

PRACTICAL USES IN THE FIELD

The field of Information Security has become a new challenge to investigators when it comes to developing quality material that allows them not just to understand basic concepts (Lerma, 2007), but also to manipulate tools that allow them to dissect the strategies, exploits, tools and methods used by attackers. Moreover, the field of Information Security is based in establishing a set of security guidelines and frameworks that are often tailored according to specific situations and organizations.

When used with productive purposes, Honeypots provide protection to an organization through prevention, detection and response to an attack. When used with research purposes, they gather information related to the context in which the Honeypot was implemented. Some organizations study the tendencies displayed by intrusive actions, while others shift their interest towards prediction and anticipated prevention.

Honeypots can help secure organizational networks by helping to prevent attacks in various forms. In this section, we list four:

- **Defense against automated attacks:** These attacks are based on tools which randomly scan entire networks, searching for vulnerable systems. If a vulnerable system is located, these automated tools will attack and take over the system (with worms that replicate inside the victim). One of the methods to protect a system from the aforementioned attacks is to reduce the speed of their scanning activities in order to stop them later on. Known as "Sticky Honeypots", these solutions monitor unutilized IP space. When systems are analyzed, Sticky Honeypots interact with those systems and reduce the speed of the attack. This is attained by using a variety of TCP tricks, such as setting the Window Size to zero or constantly putting the attacker on hold. This technique is excellent to reduce the speed or prevent the dissemination of worms which have penetrated the internal network.

- **Protection against human intruders:** This concept is known as conning or dissuasion. The idea behind this countermeasure is to confuse the attacker and make him/her waste time and resources while he/she is interacting with the Honeypot. As the process takes place, the attacker's activity can be detected and there is enough time to react and stop the attack.

- **Surgical detection methods:** Traditionally, detection has been an extremely difficult task to carry out. Technologies like Intruder Detection Systems and Logging Systems have been deficient for many reasons: They generate excessive amounts of information, inflated percentages of false positives and do not possess the ability to detect new attacks, work in encrypted mode or work in IPv6 environments. Honeypots excel in the field of intrusion detection by solving many of the problems of classic detection. They reduce false positives; capture small amounts of data of crucial importance like unknown attacks and new methods to exploit vulnerabilities (zero-days), as well as operating in IPv6 environments.

- **Cyber-forensics:** Once a network administrator determines that one of his/her servers was illegally compromised, it is necessary to immediately conduct a forensic analysis in the compromised system in order to produce an assessment of the damages caused by the attacker. However, there are two problems affecting incident response:
  - Frequently, compromised systems cannot be disconnected from the network in order to be analyzed and;
  - The amount of generated information is considerably large, in such a way that it is very difficult to determine what the attacker really did inside the system.

Honeypots help solve both problems due to being excellent incident analysis tools, which can be quickly and easily taken offline to conduct a thorough forensic analysis without impacting daily enterprise operations. The only activity traces stored by a Honeypot are those related to the attacker, because they are not generated by any other user but the attacker. The importance of Honeypots in this setting is the quick delivery of previously-analyzed information in order to respond quickly and efficiently to an incident.

In the educational, investigative and analytical arenas of Information Security, Honeypots provide a safe and manageable environment that can be deployed in a controlled fashion (lab) and can also be implemented in a live production setting (actual network). This capability is also enhanced by the use of virtualization technologies, which allow a Honeypot to be implemented in a matter of minutes and to be stored with particular settings, according to the vulnerability and exploits that will be subjects of study in a particular lesson (Collins, 2006).

According to Wiley (2000), Honeypots fall into the category of Generative-instructional learning objects which are defined as a "combination of objects providing advanced visual and audible capabilities with advanced interactive features, allowing a high level of hands-on experience". Leaving beside the visual and audible capabilities, Honeypots (and specially those mounted on virtualized platforms (Provos, 2004)) allow a high level of interaction between students and the machine. Users can manipulate important elements in Information Security Forensics lessons such as:

- Hardware and software settings (as provided by the virtualization platform)
- Services installed in a **server**
- Operating system logs (especially security and event logs)
- Network settings (including logical network placement of the Honeypot)
- Installed applications (and their respective settings and roles played inside the Honeypot)
- Users and user groups (including group membership and capabilities)
- "Dummy" information inside the server (and its nature)

As stated before, the use of virtualization is a powerful tool when implementing a Honeypot due to the features this technology provides (Border, 2006). Not only do they provide a virtual environment that can replicate a real one in full, but once a Honeypot has been compromised beyond its normal limits or damaged beyond actual recognition, it can be taken offline and brought back to its original settings in a matter of minutes.

Virtualized Honeypots offer a very good feature when it comes to its "level of vulnerability": It can easily be managed and set up according to a particular research topic or field. Due to the modern feature of automatic updating found in most operating systems, vulnerabilities are easily patched and blocked, preventing attackers from exploiting them. When researching specific topics and subjects related to Information Security and Computer Forensics, those vulnerabilities are the true matter of the investigation and they cannot be blocked or patched because that eliminates the subject of study. In this case, virtualized Honeypots can be customized with specific levels of vulnerabilities and once they have been patched or eliminated as a part of a specific laboratory activity, the original virtual image of the Honeypot can be restored with the needed level of vulnerability needed.

FUTURE TRENDS

Like many other security products, the effectiveness of Honeypots will rely on the future development of precise signatures and detection/analysis tools that generate less false positive alarms. Forensic analysis experts rely heavily on true and accurate information that allows them to recreate the actual conditions under which attacks took place on a Honeypot or Honeynet and the presence of false positives tends to clutter valuable reports with information of doubtful origins. While the presence of false positives is almost impossible to eradicate, the fine tuning of a Honeypot will be crucial in order to generate information that is useful to dissect an attack and to determine the modus operandi of an attacker.

Security breaches in the electronic world closely resemble those that occur in real-life, allowing us to detect activity patterns when it comes to a specific modus operandi. Taking this into account, future Honeypot developments will also focus in developing more accurate attack signature databases that document and record events once an attack is taking place. The ability to quickly compare those specific signatures with previous attacks in order to build an "attacker profile" in detail will also be a priority in the future in order to classify and monitor the exploits of recurrent rogue users that look into a network as a potential target for frequent attacks. This capability will enable researchers and system/network administrators to construct more accurate attacker profiles in order to fine tune systems in a matter of minutes or even seconds, depending on how they identify and react to the attack.

Advances in virtualization hardware will also enable Honeypot administrators with capabilities that will offer rogue users with a more "robust" target. This may include virtual capabilities to attack virtual pieces of hardware inside the **server** or to interfere with services not currently available.

CONCLUSION

Honeypots have proven to be valuable tools to gather and analyze information regarding the behavior of network attackers. The greatest advantages provided by Honeypots include the customization of "dummy" network environments in which attackers can make significant modifications to those environments by means of attacks. The information gathered by Honeypots can then be replayed and analyzed in order to discover which methods, tools or exploits the **attacker** used to gain control of the system and perform subsequent activities that can be classified within a wide range.

The effectiveness of the deployment of a Honeypot is strongly linked to the ability of the person who deploys it to understand where the Honeypot will be placed and what kind of services he/she wants the attacker to interact with. The implementation has to include crucial services that the attacker must interact with fully in order to generate information regarding those specific services. When it comes to the physical placement of the Honeypot within the network, the administrator must also perform a careful risk assessment in order to determine the degree to which he is willing to compromise the network. The administrator might choose to establish a semi-isolated demilitarized zone (a zone right before the main firewall where the attacker is able to work without causing damage to the main network) or if the Honeypot will be placed well inside the main protection bastions, right next to real productive servers.

Virtualization is also a very important aspect of Honeypots and one that lately has become essential for people who deploy them in their networks. The use of virtualization software enables administrators with a powerful and cost-saving tool due to the fact that they can recreate several working servers inside the physical hardware of one computer. This fact eliminates the need of several pieces of hardware to run one or more Honeypots and proposes a more economic scheme where administrators need only to provide secondary elements like memory, hard drives and possible secondary processors in order to build a machine that can effectively house a Honeypot. This also enables Honeypot administrators to establish a confined platform that they can easily shut down, update, destroy and bring back to full operational state in almost no time. These are the main reasons why virtualization software is more frequently relied upon when it comes to getting a Honeypot up and running.

REFERENCES

Border, C. (2007). The development and deployment of a multi-user, remote access virtualization system for networking, security, and system administration classes. *In Proceedings of the 38th SIGCSE Technical Symposium on Computer Science Education.* Covington, Kentucky, USA.

Cheswick, W. (1997). *An Evening With Berferd in Which a Cracker is Lured, Endured and Studied.* From Internet Besieged: Countering Internet Scofflaws. ACM Press/Addison-Wesley Publishing Co. New York, NY.

Collins, D. (Apr. 2006). Using VMWare and live CD's to configure a secure, flexible, easy to manage computer lab environment. *J. Comput. Small Coll., 21,* 4 273-277.

Dalton, C. E., King, C. M., & Osmanoglu, T. E. (2001). *Security Architecture: Design, Deployment & Operations.* RSA Press.

Dunsmore, B., Brown, J., & Cross, M. (2002). *Mission Critical!: Internet Security.* Syngress.

Grimes, R. A. (2005) *Honeypots for Windows.* Apress.

Honeynet Project, The. (2005). *Know Your Enemy: Learning about Security Threats.* Addison-Wesley Professional. 2nd Edition.

HoneyD, (2007). Retrieved from http://www.honeyd.org on 9 / October / 2007

Honeynet Project, The. (2007). *Know Your Enemy: GenII Attackers.* Retrieved from http://www.honeynet.org/papers/gen2/ on 2 / September / 2007.

Leita, C., Dacier, M., & Massicotte, F. (2006). Automatic Handling of Protocol Dependencies and Reaction to 0-Day Attacks with ScriptGen Based Honeypots. *RAID 2006, LNCS 4219,* 185–205, 2006. Springer-Verlag Berlin Heidelberg.

Lerma, C. F. (2007). Creating Learning Objects. *Proceedings of the InSITE 2007 Conference.* Ljubljana, Slovenia. June 22-25.

Man, Y. R. (2003). *Internet Security: Cryptographic Principles, Algorithms and Protocols.* Wiley.

Pouget, F., & Holz, T. (2005). A Pointillist Approach for Comparing Honeypots. *In Intrusion and Malware Detection and Vulnerability Assessment.* Springer Berlin / Heidelberg.

Provos, N. (2004). A virtual honeypot framework. *Proceedings from the 12th USENIX Security Symposium.*

Riebach, S., Rathgeb, E. P., & Tödtmann, B. (May, 2005). Efficient Deployment of Honeynets for Statistical and Forensic Analysis of Attacks from the Internet. In proceedings from IFIP-TC6 Networking Conference 2005. Waterloo, Ontario, Canada.

Roberti, R., & Bonsembiante, F. (1995). *Llaneros Solitarios Hackers, Guerrilla.* Espasa Calpa; 1st. Edition.

Schneier, B. (2002). *Secrets and Lies: Digital Security in a Networked World.* 1st Edition. Wiley. New York, NY (2004).

Spitzner, L. (2002). *Honeypots: Tracking Hackers.* 1st Edition. Addison-Wesley, Boston.

Stoll, C. (2002). *The Cuckoo's Egg: Tracking a Spy Through the Maze of Computer Espionage.* 1st edition. Pocket.

Wiley, D. A. (2005). Connecting learning objects to instructional design theory: A definition, a metaphor, and a taxonomy. In D. A. Wiley (Ed.), *The instructional use of learning objects.* Retrieved 2 - 17 - 2005 from: http://reusability.org/read/chapters/wiley.doc

Compilation of References

9/11 Commission. (2004). *The 9/11 Commission Report - Final Report of the National Commission on Terrorist Attacks Upon the United States (pp. 416-419)* (Authorized, First ed.). New York: W. W. Norton & Company.

Aberdeen Group (2008, February). *Trusted Computing: Tune In, Turn it On.* Retrieved July, 2008, from https://www.trustedcomputinggroup.org/news/Industry_Data/Aberdeen_Report_TC_TuneIn_TurnItOn.pdf

Abu Rajab, M., Zarfoss, J., Monrose, F., & Terzis, A. (2006). A Multifaceted Approach to Understanding the Botnet Phenomenon. *Proceedings of the 6th ACM SIG-COMM Conference on Internet Measurement* (Rio de Janeriro, Brazil, October 25-27), IMC '06, 41-52.

Adamic, L., & Adar, E. (2003). Friends and Neighbors on the Web. *Social Networks, 25*(3), 211-230.

Adams, G. (2008). *Five years and counting: A SOX data security reality check.* scmagazineus.com, retrieved on January 19, 2008 from http://www.scmagazineus.com/Five-years-and-counting-A-SOX-data-security-reality-check/article/104197/

Agnew, R. (1995). Testing the leading crime theories: an alternative strategy focusing on motivational process. *Journal of research in crime and delinquency, 32*(4), 363-398.

Ajzen, I. (1991). The Theory of Planned Behavior. *Organizational Behavior and Human Decision Processes, 50*(2), 179-211.

Ajzen, I., & Fishbein, M. (1980*). Understanding attitudes and predicting social behavior. Prentice Hall, Englewood cliffs, NJ.*

Akerlof, G. A. (1970). The market for "lemons:" Quality uncertainty and the market mechanism. *The Quarterly Journal of Economics, 84*(3), 488-500.

Alexander, C., Ishikawa, S., Silverstein, M., Jacobson, M., Fiksdahl-King, I., & Angel, S. (1977). *A Pattern Language.* Oxford University Press.

Alexander, D. C., & Alexander, Y. (2003). *Terrorism and Business: The Impact of 11 September 2001.* New York: Transnational.

Alexander, J., & Tate M (1999). *Web wisdom: How to evaluate and create information on the web.* Mahwah, NJ: Erlbaum.

Alibek, K., Lobanova, C., & Popov, S. (2005). *Bioterrorism and Infectious Agents: A New Dilemma for the 21st Century* .

America Online. (2007, July 26). *Think You Might Be Addicted to E-mail?* You're Not Alone, Retrieved, October 31, 2007, from http://press.aol.com/article_print.cfm?article_id=1271.

American Association of Port Authorities (2007). *North American Port Container Traffic 2006.* Retrieved March 15, 2007 from http://www.aapa-ports.org .

American Heritage (2008). *The American Heritage Dictionary of the English Language.* Fourth Edition. Retrieved April 03, 2008, from Dictionary.com website: http://dictionary.reference.com/browse/threat.

Ammann, P., Pamula, J., Ritchey, R., & Street, J. (2005). A host based approach to network attack chaining analysis. In *21st Annual Computer Security Applications Confer-*

ence (ACSAC '05) (pp. 72-84). IEEE Computer Society, Washington, DC, USA.

Ammann, P., Wijesekera, D., & Kaushik, S. (2002). Scalable, graph-based network vulnerability analysis. In *9th ACM Conference on Computer and Communications Security (CCS)* (pp. 217-224). ACM Press, New York, NY.

Anderson, J. P. (1972). Computer Security Technology Planning Study, ESD-TR-73-51, Vol. II. Bedford, MA: Electronic Systems Division, Air Force Systems Command, Hanscom Field. Retrieved July, 2008, from, from http://csrc.nist.gov/publications/history/ande72.pdf

Anderson, J. P. (1980). *Computer Security Threat Monitoring and Surveillance.* Contract 79F296400," Fort Washington, PA: James P. Anderson Co. Retrieved January 12, 2008 from http://csrc.nist.gov/publications/history/ande80.pdf.

Anderson, R. (2001). *Why information security is hard, an economic perspective.* Paper presented at the 17th Annual Computer Security Applications Conference.

Anderson, R. (2008). *Security Engineering: A Guide to Building Dependable Distributed Systems.* Indianapolis, IN: Wiley Publishing Inc.

Anderson, R. H. (1999). *Research and Development Initiatives Focused on Preventing, Detecting, and Responding to Insider Misuse of Critical Defense Information Systems.* Retrieved April 11, 2008 from http://www.rand.org/publications/CF/CF151/CF151.pdf.

Anderson, R., et al. (2000). *Research on Mitigating the Insider Threat to Information Systems.* Retrieved April 3, 2008, Web site: http://www.rand.org/publications/CF/CF163/.

Anderson, R., & Moore, T. (2006). The economics of information security. *Science, 314,* 610-613.

Appelo, J. (2008, June). Progress in Three Dimensions. *Software Quality Professional.* Retrieved from LEXIS, 17 Jul 2008 (search: "scope creep").

Applied Computer Security Associates (2002). Workshop on Information Security System Scoring and Ranking.

Proceedings of the 2001Workshop on Information-Security-System Rating and Ranking, (pp. 1-70).

Arnesen, D. W. (2007). Developing an Effective Company Policy for Employee Internet and E-mail Use. *Journal of Organizational Culture, Communication & Conflict,* (pp. 53-71).

Arnott, S. (2002). *Strategy paper. Computing, February.*

Arquilla, J., & Ronfeldt, D. (2001). *Networks and Netwars: The Future of Terror, Crime, and Militancy.* Santa Monica: RAND.

Arthurs, W. (2001). A Proactive Defence to Social Engineering. *Sans Reading Room,* Sans Institute. Retrieved October 3, 2003, from http://www.sans.org/rr/paper.php?id=511

Ashton, R. (2004, May 28). "Free" e-mails can cost a fortune if the messages aren't efficient. *Precision Marketing,* (p. 14).

Assilzadeh, H., & Mansor S. B. (2004). *Natural Disaster Data and Information Management System.* Paper presented at the XXth ISPRS Congress, Istanbul, Turkey.

Association of American Railroads (2006). *Railroad Facts – 2006 Edition.* Washington, DC.

Athukorala, P. C., & Resosudarmo, B. P. (2005). *The Indian Ocean Tsunami: Economic Impact, Disaster Management and Lessons.* Paper presented at the Asian Economic Panel Conference.

Australian Bureau of Statistics. (2008). *Nearly $1 billion dollars lost by Australians to personal fraud: ABS.* Commonwealth of Australia, 26 June, 1.

Australian Government Attorney General's Department. (2002). *Commonwealth Fraud Control Guidelines.* Australia: Issued by the Minister for Justice and Customs.

Australian National Computer Emergency Response Team, http://www.auscert.org.au, July 18, 2008.

Avolio, F.M. (2000). *Best practices in network security: as the networking landscape changes, so must the policies that govern its use.* Don't be afraid of imperfection when it comes to developing those for your group. *Network Computing, 60*(20), March.

Backhouse, J., Hsu, C. W., & Silva, L. (2006). Circuit of Power in creating de jure Standards: Shaping an International Information Systems Security Standard. *MIS Quarterly, 30*, special issue, 413-438.

Baddelay, A. (2008, April). Systems for Cyber Control. *Military Information Technology, 12*(3). Retrieved May 15, 2008 from http://www.military-information-technology.com/article.cfm?DocID=2398

Bagby, J. W. (2007). An Overview of the Public Policy Impact on Standards Development. In S. Bolin (Ed.), *Standards Edge: The Golden Mean*, (pp. 163-84), Seattle WA: The Bolin Group.

Bagby, J. W. (2007). The Public Policy Environment of the Privacy-Security Conundrum/ Complement. In S. Park (Ed.), *Strategies and Policies In Digital Convergence* (pp.195-213). Hershey, PA: Idea Group Reference.

Bagby, J. W. (2008). Book Review: Harcourt, B. E., Against Prediction: Profiling, Policing, and Punishing in an Actuarial Age. *Journal of Law, Economics and Policy, 4*(1).

Bagby, J. W., & Gittings, G. L. (1999). Litigation Risk Management for Intelligent Transportation Systems (Part Two). *ITS-Quarterly, 7*(3) 60-67.

Bagby, J. W., & McCarty, F. W. (2003). *The Legal and Regulatory Environment of e-Business*. St.Paul MN: West Pub.

Bagby, J. W., & Ruhnka, J. C. (2004). Merger of dns Governance into Trademark Law. *Proceedings of the 32nd Telecommunications Policy Research Conference*. Accessible at: http://web.si.umich.edu/tprc/papers/2004/378/TPRC-04-tmDomNaMergerFinal.htm

Bailey, J. P., & Bakos, J. Y. (1997). Reducing buyer search costs: Implications for electronic marketplaces. *Management Science, 43*(12), 1676-1692.

Baird, L., & Henderson, J. C. (2001). *The Knowledge Engine, How to Create Fast Cycles of Knowledge-to-Performance and Performance-to-Knowledge*. San Francisco: Berrett-Koehler Publishers, Inc.

Bajada, C., & Schneider, F. (2005). *Size, causes and consequences of the underground economy: An International Perspective*. Ashgate: Aldershot.

Baligh, H., Burton, R. M., & Obel, B. (1993). *Creating the Theory for a Usable Organization Designing Expert System*. Working Paper, Fuqua School of Business, Duke University, Durham, NC.

Barker, G., Bevis, A., Henderson, G., & McAllister, I. (2006). Where is the Government taking Australia on Counter-Terrorism? *Summit Plenary. 5th Homeland Security Summit 2006*. 7-8.

Barlette, Y. (2006). *Les comportements sécuritaires des acteurs en entreprise*. (Information security behaviors of companies' actors). PhD thesis. Montpellier University, France.

Barlette, Y., & Fomin, V. V. (2008). Exploring the suitability of IS security management standards for SMEs. *Proceedings of the forty-first annual Hawaii International Conference on System Sciences* (HICSS-41). January 7-10. (10 pages). Computer Society Press, Big Island, Hawaii, USA.

Barnard, L., & von Solms, R. (1998). The evaluation and certification of information security against BS 7799. *Information management and computer security, 6*(2), 72-77.

Baskerville, R. (1993). Information systems security design methods: implications for information systems development. *ACM Computing Surveys, 25*(4), 375-414.

Baskerville, R., & Siponen, M. T. (2002). An information security meta-policy for emergent organizations. *Logistics information management, 15*(5/6), 337-346.

Bayrak, T., & Brabowski, M. R. (2006). Critical infrastructure network evaluation. *The Journal of Computer Information Systems, 46*(3), 67-86.

Bell, D. E. (1974). *Secure Computer Systems: A Refinement of the Mathematical Model, ESD-TR-73-278, III*. Bedford, MA: ESD/AFSC, Hanscom AFB.

Bell, D. E., & LaPadula, L. J. (1976). *Secure Computer System: Unified Exposition and Multics Interpretation,* ESD-TR-75-306. Bedford, MA: ESD/AFSC, Hanscom AFB. Retrieved July, 2008, from http://csrc.nist.gov/publications/history/bell76.pdf

Bellovin, S. M. (2001). Computer security – an end state? *Communications of the ACM, 44*(3), 131-132.

Belsis, P., Kokolakis, S., & Kiountouzis, E. (2005). Information systems security from a knowledge management perspective. *Information Management & Computer Security, 13*(2/3), 189-202.

Benkler, Y. (2006). *The Wealth of Networks: How Social Production Transforms Markets and Freedom.* New Haven CN: Yale University Press.

Bennet J. T. (2008, June 16). Shift to fixed-price deals urged for DoD. *Federal Times.* June 16, 2008. Retrieved from LEXIS, 17 Jul 2008 (search term: "requirements creep").

Berger, S., Caceres, R., Goldman, K., Perez, R., Sailer, R., & Van Doorn, L. (2006). *vTPM: Virtualizing the Trusted Platform Module.* Retrieved July, 2008, from http://www.usenix.org/events/sec06/tech/full_papers/berger/berger.pdf

Bhattacharya, S., & Ghosh, S. K. (2007). An Artificial Intelligence Based Approach for Risk Management Using Attack Graph. In *International Conference on Computational Intelligence and Security (CIS 2007)* (pp. 794-798). Harbin, China.

Bhattacharya, S., & Ghosh, S. K. (2008), A Decision Model based Security Risk Management Approach. In *International MultiConference of Engineers and Computer Scientists 2008 (IMECS 2008)* (pp. 1194-1200). Hong Kong.

Bhattacherjee, A. (2002). Individual trust in online firms: Scale development and initial trust. *Journal of Management Information Systems, 19(*1), 211-241.

Bird, M., Branegan, J., & Salz-Trautman, P. (9 December 1996), System Overload: Excess Information is Clogging the Pipes of Commerce—and Making People Ill, *Time Magazine, International Edition*, (p. 38).

Biros, D. P., George, J. F., & Zmud, R. W. (2002). Inducing sensitivity to deception in order to improve decision making performance: A field study. *MIS Quarterly, 26*(2), 119-144.

Bishop, M., & Goldman, E. O. (2003). The Strategy and Tactics of Information Warfare. *Contemporary Security Policy, 24*(1), 113-139.

Bistarelli, S., Fioravanti, F., & Peretti, P. (2006). Defense Trees for Economic Evaluation of Security Investments. *Proceedings of the First International Conference on Availability, Reliability and Security (ARES'06).* Vienna, Austria, 2006.

Bjorgo, T. (ed.) (2005). *Root causes of terrorism: myths, reality, and the ways forward.* Oxon: Routlege.

Blackhurst, J., Craighead, C. W., Elkins, D., & Handfield, R. B. (2005). An Empirically Derived Agenda of Critical Research Issues for Managing Supply Chain Disruptions. *International Journal of Production Research, 43*(19), 4067-4081.

Blunt, E. (2006). Delegating Root Authority and Auditing Activities on UNIX/Linux Systems. *ISACA JounalOnline, 2.* Retrieved July 20, 2008 from http://www.isaca.org/Template.cfm?Section=Home&Template=/Content-Management/ContentDisplay.cfm&ContentID=33441

Boddy, M. S., Gohde, J., Haigh, T., & Harp, S. A. (2005). Course of Action Generation for Cyber Security Using Classical Planning. In *International Conference on Automated Planning and Scheduling (ICAPS '05)* (pp. 12-21). California, USA.

Bodin, L. D., Gordon, L. A., & Loeb, M. P. (2005). Evaluating information security investments using the analytic hierarchy process. *Communications of the ACM, 48*(2), 79-83.

Bohm, D., & Peat, F. D. (1987). *Science, order and creativity.* New York: Bantam Books.

Böhme, R. (2006). *A comparison of market approaches to software vulnerability disclosure.* Paper presented at the International Conference, ETRICS 2006, LNCS 3995 Freiburg, Germany.

Boiney, L. G. (2007). *More than Information Overload: Supporting Human Attention Allocation.* Paper presented at 12th International Command and Control Research and Technology Symposium.

Bologna, J. (1984). *Corporate Fraud: The Basics of Prevention and Detection.* Boston, U.S.A: Butterworth Publishers.

Bombich, M. (2007). *Mac OS X Management Custom Shell Script Library* [Computer Software]. http://www.bombich.com/mactips/scripts.html

Boni, W., & Kovacich, G. L. (2000). *Netspionage: The Global Threat to Information.* Boston: Butterworth-Heinemann.

Booth, K., & Dunne, T. (2002). *Worlds in Collision. Terror and the Future of Global Order.* Hampshire: Palgrave Macmillan.

Border, C. (2007). The development and deployment of a multi-user, remote access virtualization system for networking, security, and system administration classes. *In Proceedings of the 38th SIGCSE Technical Symposium on Computer Science Education.* Covington, Kentucky, USA.

Boulding, K. E. (1947). A note on the theory of the black market. *The Canadian Journal of Economics and Political Science / Revue canadienne d'Economique et de Science politique, 13*(1), 115-118.

Box, G. E. P., & Jenkins, G. M. (1976). *Time Series Analysis forecasting and control.* San Francisco, CA: Holden-Day Inc.

Brackney, R., & Anderson, R. (2004). *Understanding the Insider Threat.* CF-196. Santa Monica CA: RAND Corporation, March 2004.

Bragge, J., Merisalo-Rantanen, H., & Hallikainen, P. (2005). Gathering Innovative End-User Feedback for Continuous Development of Information Systems: A Repeatable and Transferable E-Collaboration Process. *IEEE Transactions on Professional Communication, 48*, 55-67.

Brand, S. (1987). *The Media Lab: Inventing the Future at MIT.* NY: Viking Penguin.

Brenner, J. (2007). ISO 27001: Risk management and compliance. *Risk Management Magazine, 54*(1), 24-29.

Brenton, C., Bird, T., & Ranum, M. J. (2008). *Top 5 Essential Log Reports.* SANS Institute, Information Security Reading Room.

Briggs, R. O., de Vreede, G.-J., & Nunamaker Jr., J. F. (2003). Collaboration engineering with thinkLets to pursue sustained success with group support systems. *Journal of Management Information Systems, 19*(4), 31-64.

Briggs, R. O., Kolfschoten, G. L., de Vreede, G.-J., & Dean, D. L. (2006, August 4-6). *Defining key concepts for collaboration engineering.* Proceedings of the 12th Americas Conference on Information Systems (AMCIS-12), Acapulco, Mexico

Briggs, R. O., Reinig, B. A., & de Vreede, G.-J. (2006). Meeting satisfaction for technology-supported groups: An empirical validation of a goal-attainment model. *Small Group Research, 37*(6), 585-611.

Broderick, J. S. (2006). ISMS, security standards and security regulations. *Information security technical report II,* 26-31.

Brown, A., Van der Wiele, T., & Loughton, K. (1998). Smaller enterprises' experiences with ISO 9000. *International journal of Quality & reliability management, 15*(3), 273-285.

Brown, C., & Bright, D. (1995). *Quality of Life: A powerful yet simple approach for everyone to achieve an enriched, balanced and fulfilled life.* Perth: self published.

Brown, D. C. G., & Kourakos, G. (2003). *Public Policy Forum Roundtable on Identity Theft and Identity Fraud.* 26 June, Ottawa, 1-23. Retrieved June 10, 2006, from http://www.ppforum.ca/common/assets/publications/en/identity_theft_fraud.pdf.

Brungs, A., & Jamieson, R. (2005). Identification of Legal Issue for Computer Forensics. *Information Systems Management, 22*(2), 57-66.

BS7799. (1999). *Code of practice for information security management.* UK: British Standards Institute.

Buckingham, M., & Coffman, C. (1999). *First, Break all the Rules, What the World's Greatest Managers Do Differently.* London: Simon & Schuster.

Buckingham, M., & Clifton, D. (2001). *Now, Discover Your Strengths.* New York: The Free Press.

Burns, T., & Stalker, G. M. (1961). *The Management of Innovation.* London: Havistock.

Burton, R. M., & Obel, B. (2004). *Strategic Organizational Diagnosis and Design: Developing Theory for Application.* Third Edition, Boston, MA: Kluwer.

Busch, C., Maret, P. S. D., Flynn, T., Kellum, R., Le, S., Meyers, B., et al. (2005). *Content analysis.* : Writing@CSU. Colorado State University Department of English. Retrieved [Date] from http://writing.colostate. edu/guides/research/content/.

Buzan, B., & Waever, O. (2003). *Regions and Powers. The Structure of International Security.* Cambridge: Cambridge University Press.

Buzan, B., Waever, O., & de Wilde, J. (1998). *Security: a new framework for analysis.* Boulder, Colorado: Lynne Rienner Publishers.

Cal. Civ. Code §§ 1798.29, .82, .84 (West Supp. 2006) (California security breach notice statute, S.B.1386).

Camp, L. J., & Wolfram, C. (2004). Pricing security, a market in vulnerabilities. In L. J. Camp & S. Lewis (Eds.), *Economics of Information Security.* Boston: Kluwer Academic Publishers.

Campbell, K., Gordon, L. A., Loeb, M. P., & Zhou, L. (2003). The Economic Cost of Publicly Announced Information Security Breaches: Empirical Evidence from the Stock Market. *Journal of Computer Security, 11,* 431-448.

Canadian Electricity Association (2008). *Providing Reliable Energy in a Time of Constraints: A North American Concern,* Ottawa, Ontario.

Canadian Internet Policy and Public Interest Clinic (CIPPIC). (2007). *Australian, French, and United Kingdom legislation relevant to identity theft: An annotated review.* CIPPIC working paper, March, 3C, 1-49.

Capelli, D., Moore, A., & Shimeall, T. (2005). *Common Sense Guide to Prevention and Detection of Insider Threats.* United States Computer Emergency Response Team. Retrieved June 11, 2008 from http://www.us-cert. gov/reading_room/prevent_detect_insiderthreat0504. pdf.

Capra, F. (1983). *The Turning Point: Science, Society and the Rising Culture.* New York: Bantam Books.

Capra, F. (1997). *The Web of Life, A New Synthesis of Mind and Matter.* London: Harper Collins.

Carley, K. M., & Prietula, M. J. (1994). *Computational Organization Theory.* Hillsdale, NJ: Lawrence Erlbaum Associates, Inc.

Carpenter v. United States, 484 U. S. 19 (1987).

Carrera, D., Beltran, V., Torres, J., & Ayguade, E. (2005). A Hybrid Web Server Architecture for E-Commerce Applications. *Parallel and Distributed Systems Proceedings, 1*(20-22), 182-188.

Carroll, J. (2002). *Terror: a meditation on the meaning of September 11.* Victoria, Australia: Scribe Publications.

Carroll, M. D. (2006). Information Security: Examining and Managing the Insider Threat. *Proceedings of the 3rd Annual Conference on Information Security Curriculum Development* Kennesaw, GA: ACM, 2006.

Casey, E. (2004). *Digital Evidence and Computer Crime.* London: Academic Press.

Casper, C., & Esterle, A. (2007). *Information security certifications – A primer: product, people, processes.* ENISA deliverable, 18.

Castells, M. (1996). *The Rise of the Network Society.* 2nd edition (2000), Vol. I. Oxford: Blackwell Publishers, Ltd.

Cavusoglu, H., Cavusoglu, H., & Raghunathan, S. (2005). *Emerging issues in responsible vulnerability disclosure.*

Paper presented at the 4th Workshop of Economic and Information Security (WEIS), Cambridge, MA, USA.

Cazemier, J. A., Overbeek, P. L., & Peters, L. M. (2000). Security Management. *IT Infrastructure Library (ITIL) Series*, Stationery Office, UK.

Cerrito, P. (2004). Inside Text Mining. *Health Management Technology*, March 2004.

CERT. (2008). *US-CERT Technical Vulnerabilities.* Retrieved July 20, 2008 from http://www.us-cert.gov/nav/t01/

CERT/CC. (2000). Vulnerability disclosure policy. *CERT Coordination Center.* Retrieved June 10, 2007

Chaiman of the Joint Chiefs of Staff Instruction (CJCSI) (2007, Aug 14). *Information Assurance (IA) and Computer Network Defense (CND).* Retrieved May 14, 2008 from http://www.dtic.mil/cjcs_directives/cdata/unlimit/6510_01.pdf

Challener, D., Yoder, K., Catherman, R., Safford, D., & Van Doorn, L. (2008). *A Practical Guide to Trusted Computing.* Upper Saddle River, NJ: IBM Press, Pearson plc

Chapman, D., & Smalov, L. (2004). On information security guidelines for small/medium enterprises. *ICEIS 2004 – Information analysis and specification*, 3-9.

Chapple, M. (2008). *Don't let trends dictate your network security strategy.* techtarget.com, retrieved on January 16, 2008 from http://searchsecurity.techtarget.com/tip/0,289483,sid14_gci1233918,00.html

Chari, S. N., & Cheng, P. (2003). BlueBoX: A Policy-Driven, Host-Based Intrusion Detection System. *ACM Trans. Inf. Syst. Secur., 6*(2), 173-200.

Chatzkel, J. (2002). *Intellectual Capital.* Oxford: Capstone Publishing.

Cheng, J. (2007, August 14). E-mail stress slowing down workers, say researchers, *ars technica the art of technology,* Retrieved February 17, 2008, from: http://arstechnica.com/news.ars/post/20070814-e-mail-stress-slowing-down-workers-say-researchers.html.

Chertoff, M. (2005). *Statement before the Senate Committee on Homeland Security and Governmental Affairs.* Department of Homeland Security: Second Stage Review.

Cheswick, W. (1997). *An Evening With Berferd in Which a Cracker is Lured, Endured and Studied.* From Internet Besieged: Countering Internet Scofflaws. ACM Press/Addison-Wesley Publishing Co. New York, NY.

Choi, S-Y., Stahl, D. O., & Whinston, A. B. (1997). *The Economics of Electronic Commerce.* Indianapolis: MacMillan Technical Pub. P. 344.

Chopra, K., & Wallace, W. A. (2003, January). *Trust in electronic environments.* Paper presented at the Proceedings of the 36th Annual Hawaii International Conference on System Sciences, Big Island, HI.

Christodorescu, M., Jha, S., & Kruegel, C. (2007). Mining Specifications of Malicious Behavior. *The 6th Joint Meeting of the European Software Engineering Conference and the ACM SIGSOFT Symposium on the Foundations of Software Engineering* (Dubrovnik, Croatia, September 3-7), ESEC-FSE '07, 5-14.

Christopher, C., & Robert, B. (2002). *Disaster: Hurricane Katrina and the Failure of Homeland Security.* Macmillan Publishers.

Chuvakin, A. (2002). *Linux Kernel Hardening.* Retrieved October 3, 2003 from http://www.securityfocus.com/infocus/1539

Chuvakin, A. (2008, June 17). *Six Pitfalls of Logging [Video file].* Video posted to http://searchsecurity.bitpipe.com/rlist/term/type/multimedia/Security-Event-Management.html

Cisneros, R., Bliss, D., & Garcia, M. (2006). Password Auditing Applications. *J. Comput. Small Coll., 21*(4), 196-202.

Clark, K. (2002). From Data to Decisions. *Chain Store Age, 78*, 62.

Clark, R. M. (2004). *Intelligence analysis: a target-centric approach.* Washington DC: CQPress.

Clinard, M. B. (1969). *The Black market: a study of white collar crime*. Montclair, New Jersey: Patterson Smith.

CLUSIF. (2004). *Politiques de sécurité des systèmes d'information et sinistralité en France*. Club de la sécurité des informations français, Paris.

CLUSIF. (2005). *Standards et normes en SSI*. October, www.clusif.fr, Paris.

CNRS. (2002). La certification des critères communs: le point de vue du développeur. *Sécurité informatique, 42*, 5-6.

Coase, R. H. (1988). *The Firm, the market and the law*. Chicago: The University of Chicago.

Cobb, A. (1998). *Thinking about the Unthinkable: Australian Vulnerabilities to High-Tech Risks. Research Paper 18 1997-98*. Canberra: Parliament of Australia.

Cobb, A. (2004). *Counter Terrorism in Australia*. 2004 International Counter Terrorism Conference. Zurich: 1-8.

Coe, K. (2004). Behind the Firewall - The Insider Threat. *eWeek.com*, March 5, 2004. Retrieved January 12, 2008 from http://www.eweek.com/article2/0,1759,1543223,00. asp.

Cohen, J. E. (2003). DRM and Privacy. *Berkeley Technological Law Journal, 18*(2), 575-617.

Colarik, A. M. (2006). *Cyber Terrorism: Political and Economic Implications*, London: Idea Group.

Cole, E. (2006). *Insider Threat: Protecting the Enterprise from Sabotage, Spying and Theft*. Rockland, MA: Syngress Publishing.

Colley, J. (2008).*The information security professional is more than a necessary evil*. out-law.com, retrieved on January 16, 2008 from http://www.out-law.com/page-7614

Collier, G., Plassman, D., & Pegah, M. (2007). Virtualization's Next Frontier: Security. *Proceedings of the 35th Annual ACM SIGUCCS Conference on User Services* (Orlando, Florida, October 7-10), SIGUCCS '07, 34-36.

Collins, D. (Apr. 2006). Using VM Ware and live CD's to configure a secure, flexible, easy to manage computer lab environment. *J. Comput. Small Coll., 21*, 4 273-277.

Commission of the European Communities. (2004). *Convention on Cybercrime. Commission of the European Communities Online, 185*(1). Retrieved January 16, 2008, from http://conventions.coe.int/Treaty/en/Summaries/Html/185.htm.

Commission of the European Communities. (2007). *Towards a general policy on the fight against cyber crime*. Commission of the European Communities, June, 1-48. Retrieved January 16, 2008, from http://www.coe.int/t/e/legal_affairs/legal_co-operation/combating_economic_crime/6_cybercrime/t-cy/T-CY%20_2007_%2002%20-%20e%20-20Cybercrime %20and%20the%20EU.pdf

Committee on National Security Systems (2006). *National Information Assurance Glossary*. CNSS Instruction No. 4009.

Computer Security Enhancement Act of 2001. (2001, Nov 28). Retrieved May 14, 2008 from http://thomas.loc.gov/cgi-bin/query/D?c107:1:./temp/~c107VdS4Gr::

Computer Security Institute (2006). *Virus attacks named leading culprit of financial loss by U.S. companies in 2006 CSI/FBI computer crime and security survey*. Retrieved March 15, 2008 from http://gocsi.com/press/20060712.html.

Computer Security Institute Survey 2007: The 12th Annual Computer Crime and Security Survey. (2007). *2007 by Computer Security Institute*.

Conklin, A., & White, G. (2006). e-Government and Cyber Security: The Role of Cyber Security Exercises. *Proceedings of the 39th Hawaii International Conference on Systems Sciences*, Kauai, Hawaii.

Cormen, T. H., Leiserson, C. E., Rivest, R. L., & Stein, C. (2006). *Introduction to Algorithms*. India: Prentice Hall.

Covey, S. (1997). *Putting principles first" in Rethinking the Future*. London: Nicholas Brealey.

Coyle, M. (2006). Courts balancing privacy, access: U.S. Judiciary must protect 'E-records,'. *National Law Journal, 28*(25).

Cranor L. F. (2002). *Web privacy with P3P*. Sebastopol, CA: O'Reilly.

CSI (2007). *CSI Survey 2007: The 12th Annual Computer Crime and Security Survey*. Retrieved July 31, 2008, from http://i.cmpnet.com/v2.gocsi.com/pdf/CSISurvey2007.pdf

CSI/FBI (2005). *CSI/FBI Computer Crime and Security Survey*. Retrieved July 31, 2008, from http://i.cmpnet.com/gocsi/db_area/pdfs/fbi/FBI2005.pdf

CSI/FBI (2006). *CSI/FBI Computer Crime and Security Survey*. Retrieved July 31, 2008, from http://i.cmpnet.com/gocsi/db_area/pdfs/fbi/FBI2006.pdf

CSO (2007). *2007 E-Crime Watch Survey – Survey Results. CSO magazine*, U.S. Secret Service, CERT® Program, Microsoft Corp. Retrieved March 30, 2008 from http://www.cert.org/archive/pdf/ecrimesummary07.pdf.

Cuganesan, S., & Lacey, D. (2003). *Identity Fraud in Australia: An evaluation of its nature, cost and extent*. Sydney, Australia: Standards Australia International Ltd.

Culotta, A., Bekkerman, R., & McCallum, A. (2004). Extracting social networks and contact information from email and the Web. *First Conference on Email and Anti-Spam (CEAS)*. Mountain View, CA.

Curran, K., Morrissey, C., Fagan, C., Murphy, C., O'Donnell, B., Fitzpatrick, G., & Condit, S. (2005). Monitoring Hacker Activity with a Honeynet. *Int. J. Netw. Manag., 15*(2), 123-134.

CyberEye. (2001). *CERT's full-disclosure policy is responsible, but mistrust remains*. Retrieved April, 15, 2007, from http://www.gcn.com/state/vol7_no1/tech-report/946-1.html

Cyberstalking: A New Challenge for Law Enforcement and Industry (1999). *Report of the U.S. Attorney General to the Vice President*, accessible at: http://www.justice.gov/criminal/cybercrime/cyberstalking.htm

D'Amico, E. (2002). Sorting out the Facts. *Chemical Week, 164*, 22. 16 October 2002.

Daft, R. L. (1984). Information Richness: a new approach to managerial behavior and organizational design. *Research in Organizational Behavior*, (pp. 191-233).

Dalton, C. E., King, C. M., & Osmanoglu, T. E. (2001). *Security Architecture: Design, Deployment & Operations*. RSA Press.

Dantu, R., & Kolan, P. (2005). Risk Management Using Behavior Based Bayesian Networks. In *IEEE International Conference on Intelligence and Security Informatics (ISI '05)* (pp. 115-126). IEEE Computer Society, Washington, DC, USA.

Dantu, R., Loper, K., & Kolan, P. (2004). Risk Management using Behavior based Attack Graphs. In *Information Technology: Coding and Computing (ITCC '04)* (pp. 445-449). IEEE Computer Society, Washington, DC, USA.

Daubert v. Merrell Dow Pharmaceuticals, 509 U.S. 579 (1993).

Davenport, T. H., & Prusak, L. (1998). *Working Knowledge, How Organizations Manage What They Know*. Boston: Harvard Business Press.

David, J. (2002). Policy enforcement in the workplace. *Computers & Security, 21*(6), 506-513.

Davis, F. D. (1989). Perceived usefulness, perceived ease of use, and user acceptance of information technology. *MIS Quarterly, 13*(3), 319-339.

Davis, F. D., Bagozzi, R. P., & Warshaw, P. R. (1989). User Acceptance of Computer Technology: A Comparison of Two Theoretical Models. *Management Science, 35*(8), 982-1002.

Davis, F. D., Bagozzi, R. P., & Warshaw, P. R. (1992). Extrinsic and Intrinsic Motivation to Use Computers in the Workplace. *Journal of Applied Social Psychology, 22*(14), 1111-1132.

Davis, J. (2007). Hackers Take Down the Most Wired Country in Europe. *Wired Magazine* 15.09. [On line] Available: http://www.wired.com/wired/issue/15-09 .

Davis, N. (1996). An Information-Based Revolution in Military Affairs. *Strategic Review, 24*(1), 43-53.

DCID 1/19 (1995). Director of Central Intelligence Directive No. 1/19: Security Policy for Sensitive Compartmented Information and Security Policy Manual. *Director of Central Intelligence*, March 1, 1995.

DCID 6/4 (1998). Director of Central Intelligence Directive No. 6/4: Personnel Security Standards and Procedures Governing Eligibility for Access to Sensitive Compartmented Information. *Director of Central Intelligence*, July 2, 1998.

DCSSI. (2007). Direction centrale de la sécurité des systèmes d'information (Information Systems Security Central Agency). http://www.ssi.gouv.fr/fr/dcssi/.

de Vreede, G. J., Koneri, P. G., Dean, D. L., Fruhling, A. L., & Wolcott, P. (2006). Collaborative Software Code Inspection: The Design and Evaluation of a Repeatable Collaborative Process in the Field. *International Journal of Cooperative Information Systems, 15*(2).

de Vreede, G.-J., & Briggs, R. O. (2005). *Collaboration engineering: Designing repeatable processes for high-value collaborative tasks.* Proceedings of the 38th Annual Hawaii International Conference on Systems Science, Los Alamitos.

Debarati, G. S. (2000). *The quality and accuracy of disaster data: A comparative analysis of three global data sets.* A study by the Provention Consortium.

Deci, E. L. (1975). *Intrinsic Motivation.* Plenum press, NY, USA.

Deci, E. L., & Ryan, R. M. *(1985). Intrinsic motivation and self-determination in human development.* Plenum press, *NY, USA.*

Deeks, A. S., Berman, B., Brenner, S. W., & Lewis, J. A. (2005). Combating Terrorist Uses of the Internet. *American Society of International Law. Proceedings of the Annual General Meeting 2005* (pp. 103-115).

Deibert, R. J. (2002). Dark Guests and Great Firewalls: The Internet and Chinese Security Policy. *Journal of Social Issues, 58*(1), 143-159.

Deloitte (2004). *Global Security Survey.* Retrieved July 31, 2008, from http://www.deloitte.com/dtt/cda/doc/content/dtt_financialservices_SecuritySurvey2004_051704.pdf

Deloitte (2005). *Global Security Survey.* Retrieved July 31, 2008, from http://www.ladlass.com/ice/archives/files/deliotte%20download.asp.pdf

Deloitte (2006). *Global Security Survey.* Retrieved July 31, 2008, from http://www.deloitte.com/dtt/cda/doc/content/us_fsi_150606globalsecuritysurvey(1).pdf

Deloitte (2007). *Global Security Survey.* Retrieved July 31, 2008, from http://www.deloitte.com/dtt/cda/doc/content/ca_en_Global_Security_Survey.final.en.pdf

DeLone, W. H. (1988). Determinants of success for computer usage in small businesses. *MIS Quarterly, 5*(4), 51-61.

DeLong, J. B., & Froomkin, A. M (2000). Speculative microeconomics for tomorrow's Economy. In H. R. Varian (Ed.), *Internet publishing & beyond: The economics of digital information & intellectual.* Cambridge, MA, USA: MIT Press

Denning, D. (1987). An intrusion-detection model. *IEEE Transactions on Software Engineering, SE-13*(2), 222-232.

Denning, D. (1999). *Information Warfare and Security.* New York: Addison-Wesley.

Dennis, A. R., & Wixom, B. H. (2002). Investigating the Moderators of the Group Support Systems Use with Meta-Analysis. *Journal of Management Information Systems, 18*(3), 235-257.

Deo, N. (1974). *Graph Theory with Applications to Engineering and Computer Science.* NJ, USA:Prentice-Hall.

Department of Defense, (2003). *Information Operations Roadmap (classified).* National Security Archive

Electronic Briefing Book No. 177. Unclassified summary retrieved May 14, 2008 from http://www.gwu.edu/~nsarchiv/NSAEBB/NSAEBB177/

DeRosa, M. (2004). *Data Mining and Data Analysis for Counterterrorism*. Center for Strategic & International Studies.

Dewatripont, M., & Tirole, J. (2005). Modes of Communication. *The Journal of Political Economy, 113*(6).

DeWitt, D. J., Futtersack, P., Maier, D., & Vélez, F. (1990). A Study of Three Alternative Workstation-Server Architectures for Object Oriented Database Systems. In D. McLeod, R. Sacks-Davis, & H. Schek, (Eds.), *The 16th International Conference on Very Large Data Bases* (August 13-16)., *Very Large Data Bases* (pp. 107-121). San Francisco, CA: Morgan Kaufmann Publishers.

Dhillon, G. (2001). Violation of safeguards by trusted personnel and understanding related information security concerns. *Computers & Security, 20*(2), 165-172.

Dhillon, G., & Backhouse, J. (2001). Current directions in IS security research: towards socio-organizational perspectives. *Information Systems Journal, 11*, 127-153.

Dhillon, G., & Torkzadeh, G. (2001). Value focused assessment of information system security in organizations. *Proceedings of ICIS 2001*, Atlanta, GA.

DHS. *Information Technology Initiatives, Fusion Center Guidelines*. Available from http://www.it.ojp.gov/topic.jsp?topic_id=209, April 2, 2008.

Dictionary.com (2008). *Dictionary.com Unabridged* (v 1.1). Retrieved April 3, 2008, from Dictionary.com website: http://dictionary.reference.com/browse/insider.

Dinnie, G. (1999). The second annual global information security survey. *Information management and computer security, 7*(3), 112-120.

DoD Chief Information Officer (CIO) (2003, May 9). *DoD Net-Centric Data Strategy*. Retrieved May 14, 2008 from http://www.defenselink.mil/cio-nii/docs/Net-Centric-Data-Strategy-2003-05-092.pdf

DoD Directive 3020.26 (2007, Jan 1). *Defense Continuity Program (DCP)*. Retrieved May 14, 2008 from http://www.dtic.mil/whs/directives/corres/html/302026.htm

DoD Directive 5200.1-R. (Jan 17 1997). *Information Security Program*. . Retrieved May 14, 2008 from http://www.dtic.mil/whs/directives/corres/pdf/520001r.pdf

DoD. (2004, Jan). *IA Strategic Plan Version 1.1*. Retrieved May 14, 2008 from http://www.defenselink.mil/cio-nii/docs/DoD_IA_Strategic_Plan.pdf

Doherty, N. F., & Fulford, H. (2005). Do information security policies reduce the incidence of security breaches: an exploratory analysis. *Information resources management journal, 18*(4), 21-39.

Drucker, P. E. (1995). The Post Capitalistic Executive. In P. E. Drucker (Ed.), *Management in a Time of Great Change*. New York: Penguin.

Drucker, P. F. (1966). *The Effective Executive*. New York: Harper Collins Publishers, Inc.

Du, W., & Mathur, A. P. (1998). *Categorization of software errors that led to security breaches*. Paper presented at the 21st National Information Systems Security Conference, Crystal City, Virginia, VA.

Duncan, R.B. (1979). What is the Right Organization Structure?. *Organizational Dynamics, 7*(3), 59-79.

Dunsmore, B., Brown, J., & Cross, M. (2002). *Mission Critical!: Internet Security*. Syngress.

Dutta, A., & McCrohan, K. (2002). Management's role in information security in cyber economy. *California Management review, 45*(1), 67-87.

Edge, K. (2007). *A Framework for Analyzing and Mitigating the Vulnerabilities of Complex Systems via Attack and Protection Trees*. Doctor of Philosophy. Graduate School of Engineering and Management, Air Force Institute of Technology, Wright-Patterson AFB, OH.

Edge, K., Dalton, G., Raines, R., & Mills, R. (2006). Using Attack and Protection Trees to Analyze Threats and Defenses to Homeland Security. *Proceedings of the*

2006 Military Communications Conference (MILCOM), Washington, D.C.

Edge, K., Raines, R., Grimaila, M.R., Baldwin, R., Reuter, C., & Bennington, B. (2007a). Analyzing Security Measures for Mobile Ad Hoc Networks Using Attack and Protection Trees. *Proceedings of the 2007 International Conference on Information Warfare and Security (ICIW 2007)*. Naval Postgraduate School, Monterey, CA; March 8-9, 2007.

Edge, K., Raines, R., Grimaila, M.R., Baldwin, R., Reuter, C., & Bennington, B. (2007b). The Use of Attack and Protection Trees to Analyze Security for an Online Banking System. *Proceedings of the Fortieth Annual Hawaii International Conference on System Sciences (HICSS)*.

Efthimiadis, E. N. (1993). *A User-Centered Evaluation of Ranking Algorithms for Interactive Query Expansion*. Paper presented at the ACM SIGIR, Pittsburgh, PA.

E-Government Act (2002). Pub. Law 107-347, 44 U.S.C. Ch 36.

Elliot, T. (2007, October 17). *Even superhighways have traffic jams*. Sydney Morning Herald.com, Retrieved October 31, 2007, from www.smh.com.au/news/technology/even-superhighways-have-traffic-jams/2007/10/16/1192300769157.html?page=fullpage.

ENISA. (2006). Risk management implementation principles and inventories for risk management / risk assessment methods and tools, June.

ENISA. (2007). ENISA deliverable: *Information Package for SMEs*, February.

Ernst & Young. (2005). *La gestion des risques dans l'actualité du contrôle interne : pratiques et tendances*, mai 2005.

Etalle, S., & Winsborough, W. H. (2007). A Posteriori Compliance Control. *Proceedings of the 12th ACM Symposium on Access Control Models and Technologies* (pp. 11-20) (Sophia Antipolis, France, June 20-22), SACMAT '07.

Etzioni, A. (1999). *The Limits of Privacy, 184*. Durham: Duke University Press.

EU Directive 2002/58/EC.

Eubank, S., Guclu, H., Anil Kumar, V.S., Marathe, M., Srivasan, A., & Toroczkal, Z. (2004). Modeling Disease Outbreaks in Realistic Urban Social Networks. *Nature, 429*, 180-182.

Evans, A. W. (2004). Market Failure and Welfare Economics - a Justification for Intervention *Economics and Land Use Planning*, (pp. 13-22). New York: Blackwell Publishing Ltd. P.

Evans, M. (2003). From Kadesh to Kandahar: Military Theory and the Future of War. *Naval War College Review, XVI*(3), 132-150.

Evers, J. (2007). *Offering a bounty for security bugs* [Electronic Version], 2007. Retrieved from http://news.com.com/Offering+a+bounty+for+security+bugs/2100-7350_3-5802411.html?tag=sas.email

Fair and Accurate Credit Transactions Act (FACTA, 2003), 117 STAT. 1954, Pub. Law 108–159, 15 U.S.C. §1601.

Fallows, D. (2002). *E-mail at Work: Few Feel Overwhelmed, and Most Are Pleased With the Way E-mail Helps Them Do Their Jobs*. Washington DC: Pew Internet and American Life Project.

Federal Trade Commission (FTC). (2004). *National and State Trends in Fraud & Identity Theft*: January-December 2003. January 22.

Ferguson, N., Cummings, D., Fraser, C., Cajka, J., Cooley, P., & Burke, D. (2006). Strategies for Mitigating an Influenza Pandemic. *Nature, 442*, 448-452.

Ferratt, T. W., Agarwal, R., Brown, C. V., & Moore, J. E. (2005). IT Human Resource Management Configurations and IT Turnover: Theoretical Synthesis and Empirical Analysis. *Information Systems Research, 16*(3), 237-328.

Figueiredo, R., Dinda, P. A., & Fortes, J. (2005). Resource virtualization renaissance. *IEEE Computer, 38*(5), 28-31.

Fine, C. (1998). *Clockspeed.* Boston: Perseus Books.

Finne, T. (2000). Information systems risk management: Key concepts and business processes. *Computers and Security, 19*(3), 234-242.

Fishbein, M., & Ajzen, I. (1975). *Belief, Attitude, Intention and behaviour: An introduction to theory and research.* Addison-Wesley, Reading, MA, USA.

Fishbein, M., & Ajzen, I. (1975). *Beliefs, Attitude, Intention and Behavior: An Introduction to Theory and Research.* Reading, MA: Addison-Wesley.

Fjermestad, J., & Hiltz, S. R. (1998/1999). An assessment of group support systems experimental research: Methodology and results. *Journal of Management Information Systems, 15*(3), 7-149.

Fjermestad, J., & Hiltz, S. R. (2000/2001). Group Support Systems: A Descriptive Evaluation of Case and Field Studies. *Journal of Management Information Systems, 17*(3), 115-159.

Foix, R. (2004). Expanding responsibility for incident response. *Computerworld, 38*(40), 28.

Foley, L., & Foley, J. (2003). *Identity Theft: The Aftermath 2003. Identity Theft Resource Center,* Summer 2003, September, 1-58. Retrieved April 10, 2008, from www.idtheftcenter.org.

Fomin, V. V., De Vries, H. J., & Barlette, Y. (2008). ISO/IEC 27001 Information Systems Security Management Standard: Exploring the Reasons for Low Adoption. *Proceedings of the third European conference on Management of Technology (EuroMOT) 2008,* Nice, France.

Fomin, V. V., King, J. L., Lyytinen, K., & McGann, S. (2005). Diffusion and Impacts of E-Commerce in the United States of America: Results from an Industry Survey. *Communications of the Association for Information Systems (CAIS), 16*, 559-603.

Fomin, V. V., Pedersen, M. K., & De Vries, H. J. (2008). Open Standards and Government Policy: Results of a Delphi Survey. *Communications of the Association for Information Systems, 22*(April), 459-484.

Forcht, K. A. (1994). *Computer security management.* Boyd & Fraser, MA.

Forget, A., & Biddle, R. (2008). Memorability of Persuasive Passwords. *CHI '08 Extended Abstracts on Human Factors in Computing Systems* (Florence, Italy, April 5-10), CHI '08, (pp. 3759-3764).

Francis, B. (2005). *Know thy hacker.* Retrieved April 28, 2007, from http://www.infoworld.com/article/05/01/28/05OPsecadvise_1.html

Franklin, J., Paxson, V., Perrig, A., & Savage, S. (2007). *An inquiry into the nature and causes of the wealth of internet miscreants.* Paper presented at the 14 th ACM Conference on Computer and Communications Security (CCS), Alexandria, VA, USA.

Freemon, S. (2004, November 22). Dogwood just the first new mission. *The Times* (p. 28) London.

Fruhling, A. L., & de Vreede, G.-J. (2005). Collaborative Usability Testing to Facilitate Stakeholder Involvement. In S. Biffl, A. Aurum, B. Boehm, H. Erdogmus & P. Grünbacher (Eds.), *Value Based Software Engineering* (pp. 201-223). Berlin: Springer-Verlag.

Fry, S. A. (2001). *Information assurance and Computer Network Defense.* Chairman of Joint Chiefs of Staff Instruction.

Fuerth, L. (1997). *Disaster Information Task Force Report.* The Global Disaster Information Network.

Fukuyama, F. (1995). *Trust: The Social Virtues and the Creation of Prosperity.* New York: The Free Press.

Fyoder. (2002). *Remote OS detection via TCP/IP Stack Fingerprinting.* Retrieved October 3, 2003 from http://www.insecure.org/nmap/nmap-fingerprinting-article.html

Gable, G. G. (1991). Consultant engagement for first time computerization: A proactive client role in small businesses. *Information & Management, 20*, 83-93.

GadAllah, S. (2004). The Importance of Logging and Traffic Monitoring for Information Security. *Sans Reading Room,* Sans Institute. Retrieved July 20, 2008 from http://www.sans.org/reading_room/whitepapers/logging/1379.php

Galbraith, J. R. (1973). *Designing Complex Organizations.* Boston, MA: Addison-Wesley Longman Publishing Co., Inc.

Gallery, E. (2005). An overview of trusted computing technology. In C. Mitchell (Ed.), *Trusted Computing* (pp. 29-114). London: The Institution of Electrical Engineers.

Galligan, W., & White, D. (2008). Examination of the Plausibility of Network Access Compromise Using USB and Live CD Tools. *Proceedings of the Northeast Decision Sciences International Conference* (New York, NY, March 28-30).

GAO. (2004).*Technology Assessment. Cyber security for Critical Infrastructure Protection.* Edited by U. S. G. A. Office: United States General Accounting Office.

Garfinkel, S., Spafford, G., & Schwartz, A. (2003). *Practical Unix & Internet Security.* Sebastopol, CA: O'Reilly & Associates, Inc.

Garfinkel, T., Rosenblum, M., & Boneh, D. (2003, May). *Flexible os support and applications for trusted computing.* Paper presented at the USENIX 9th Hot Topics in Operating Systems (HotOS-IX), Lihue, HI.

Gaskell, G. (2000). Simplifying the onerous task of writing security policies. *Proceedings of first Australian Information Security Management Workshop*, Deakin University, Australia.

Gasser, L., & Twidale M. (2005). *Information Quality Discussions.* Graduate School of Library and Information Science, University of Illinois at Urbana-Champaign.

Gaston, S. J. (1996). *Information security: strategies for successful management.* Toronto, CICA.

Gattiker, U. E., & Kelley, H. (1999). Morality and computers: Attitudes and differences in moral judgments. *Information systems research, 10*(3), 233-254.

Gefen, D. (2002). Reflections on the dimensions of trust and trustworthiness among online consumers. *Database for Advances in Information Systems, 33(*3), 38-53.

Gefen, D., & Straub, D. (2003). Managing user trust in B2C e-Services. *E-Service Journal. 2(*2), 7-24.

Gertman, D. I., & Blackman, H. S. (1993). *Human Reliability and Safety Analysis Handbook.* New York, NY: John Wiley.

Gilder, G. (1993, September 13). George Gilder's Telecosm: Metcalfe's Law and Legacy. *Forbes*, (p. 158).

Gill, G., & Morrison, C. (2002). *Diagnosis: Fraud!* Institute of Chartered Accountants of British Columbia, October, 1-6. Retrieved June 27, 2006, from http://www.ica.bc.ca/kb.php3? pageid=1761&term0=gill&term1=gary.

Goldberg, A. (2007, October 18). E-mail backlash takes root in tech heartland. *bankokpost.com.* Retrieved February 17, 2008, from www.indiaenews.com/america/20071018/75796.htm.

Golder, S. A., Wilkinson, D., & Huberman, B. A. (2007). Rhythms of social interaction: Messaging within a massive online network. In C. Steinfield, B. Pentland, M. Ackerman, & N. Contractor (Eds.), *Proceedings of Third International Conference on Communities and Technologies* (pp. 41-66).

Gordon, L. A., & Loeb, M. P. (November 2002). The Economics of Information Security Investment. *ACM Transactions on Information and System Security*, 5(4), 438-457.

Gottfredson, M. R., & Hirschi T. A. (1990). *General Theory of crime.* Stanford University press, Ca, USA.

Gragg, D. (2003). A Multilevel Defence Against Social Engineering. *Sans Reading Room*, Sans Institute. Retrieved October 3, 2003 from http://www.sans.org/rr/paper.php?id=920

Gravelle, H., & Rees, R. (1981). *Microeconomics.* London: Longman.

Grawrock, D. (2006). *The Intel Safer Computing Initiative: Building Blocks for Trusted Computing.* Hillsboro, OR: Intel Press.

Gray, C. S. (1999). *Modern Strategy*. Oxford: Oxford University Press.

Grimes, R. A. (2005) *Honeypots for Windows*. Apress.

Grimes, R. A. (2005). *The full disclosure debate*. Retrieved June 19, 2007, from http://www.infoworld.com/article/05/09/30/40OPsecadvise_1.html

Griswold v. Connecticut, 381 U.S. 479 (1965).

Groumann, A., Houston, T., & Lawrimore, J. (2005). *Hurricane Katrina: A climatic perspective*: US Department of commerce

Grover, V. *(1993)*. Empirically derived model for the adoption of customer-based inter-organizational systems. *Decision sciences, 24*(3), 603-639.

Gunelius, S. (2007, October 14). Claiming E-Mail Bankruptcy. *Newstex Web Blogs, ITech Tips.* Retrieved February 21, 2008, from LEXIS. (search term: "E-Mail overload").

Gupta, A., & Hammond, R. (2005). Information systems security issues and decisions for small businesses: an empirical examination. *Information Management and Computer Security, 13*(4), 297-310.

Guzman, I. R., Stam, K. R., & Stanton, J. M. (2008). The Occupational Culture of IS/IT Personnel within Organizations. *The DATA BASE for Advances in Information Systems, 39*(1), 33-50.

Hall, W. M. (2003). *Stray Voltage: War in the Information Age*. Annapolis MD: Naval Institute Press.

Hamel, G., & Prahalad, C.K. (1994). *Competing for the future*. Boston: Harvard Business School Press.

Hansteen, P. (2008). *The Book of PF: A No-Nonsense Guide to the OpenBSD Firewall*. San Francisco, CA: No Starch Press.

Harrington, S. J. (1996). The effect of codes of ethics and personal denial of responsibility on computer abuse judgments and intentions. *MIS Quarterly, 20*(3), 257-278.

Harrison, D. A., Mykytyn, P. P., & Riemenschneider, C. K. (1997). Executive Decisions about Adoption of Information Technology in Small Business: Theory and Empirical Tests. *Information Systems Research, 8*(2), 171-195.

Harvey, E. (1968, April). Technology and the Structure of Organizations. *American Sociology Review, 33*, 247- 259.

Health Insurance Portability and Accountability Act of 1996 (HIPAA), Public Law 104-191 104th Congress.

Heer, J., & Boyd, D. (2005). Vizster: Visualizing online social networks. *Proceedings of Symposium on Information Visualization*, (pp. 33-40).

Henders, R., & Opdyke, B. (2005). Detecting Intruders on a Campus Network: Might the Threat be Coming from Within?. *Proceedings of the 33rd Annual ACM SIGUCCS Conference on User Services* (pp. 113-117) (Monterey, CA, November 6-9), SIGUCCS '05.

Herbig, K., & Wiskoff, M. (2002). *Espionage Against the United States by American Citizens 1947-2001*. Defense Personnel Security Research Center PERSEREC-TR 02-5. Retrieved December 19, 2007 from http://www.ncix.gov/archives/docs/espionageAgainstUSbyCitizens.pdf.

Heylighen, F. (1999, February 19). Change and Information Overload. *Principia Cybernetica Web,* Retrieved November 13, 2007, from http://pcp.lanl.gov/CHINNEG.html.

Hietala, J. H. (2007, September). *Hardware versus Software: A Usability Comparison of Software-based Encryption with Seagate DriveTrust™ Hardware-Based Encryption – White Paper*. Retrieved July 31, 2008, from http://www.seagate.com/docs/pdf/whitepaper/Seagate-crypto-bakeoff.pdf

Higgins, H.N. (1999). Corporate system security: towards an integrated management approach. *Information management and computer security, 7*(5), 217-222.

Hinson, G. (2008). *The financial implications of implementing ISO/IEC 27001 & 27002: a generic cost-benefit model*, IsecT Ltd., 1-4.

Hirschi, T. A. (1969). *Causes of delinquency*. University of California press, Berkeley, Ca, USA.

Hirst, P. (2001). *War and Power in the 21st Century. The State, Military Conflict and the International System.* Cambridge: Polity Press.

Hoagland, J. (1993, July 20). Beware 'Mission Creep' in Somalia. *The Washington Post*, (p. A17).

Hoffman, D. L., Novak, T. P., & Peralta, M. (1999). Building consumer trust online. *Communications of the ACM, 42*(4), 80-85.

Hogg, T., & Adamic, L. (2004). Enhancing reputation mechanisms via online social networks. *Proceedings of the 5th ACM Conference on Electronic Commerce*, (pp. 237-237).

Holsti, O. R. (1969). *Content analysis for the Social Sciences and Humanities.* Reading, MA.

Hone, K., & Eloff, J. H. P. (2002). Information security policy: what do international security standards say. *Computers & Security, 21*(5), 402-409.

HoneyD, (2007). Retrieved from http://www.honeyd.org on 9 / October / 2007

Honeynet Project, The. (2005). *Know Your Enemy: Learning about Security Threats.* Addison-Wesley Professional. 2nd Edition.

Honeynet Project, The. (2007). *Know Your Enemy: GenII Attackers.* Retrieved from http://www.honeynet.org/papers/gen2/ on 2 / September / 2007.

Hong, K. S., Chi, Y. P., Chao, L. R., & Tang, J. H. (2003). An integrated system theory of information security management. *Information Management & Computer Security, 11*(5), 243-248.

Horng, E. (2007, April 7). No E-Mail Fridays Transform Office, After initial doubts, co-workers learn to deal with each other in person. *abcnews.go.com*, Retrieved October 31, 2007, from: http://abcnews.co.com/print?id+2939232.

Horowitz, M. (2007). *Linux vs. Windows.* Retrieved July 20, 2008 from http://www.michaelhorowitz.com/Linux.vs.Windows.html

Howard, M., Pincus, J., & Wing, J. M. (2003). Measuring Relative Attack Surfaces. In *Workshop on Advanced Developments in Software and System Security.*

Howard, M., Pincus, J., & Wing, J.M. (2005). Measuring Relative Attack Surfaces. *Computer Security in the 21st Century.* USA: Springer.

Howard, R. D., & Sawyer, R. L. (2004). *Terrorism and Counterterrorism – Understanding the New Security Environment.* Connecticut: McGraw-Hill.

HR 2638 (2008). *House Amendment to the DHS Appropriations Act - 2008, Title 3. Protection*

Humphrey, W. (1989). *Managing the Software Process.* Massachusetts: Addison-Wesley.

Humphreys, T. (2005). State-of-the-art information security management system with ISO/IEC 27001:2005. *ISO Management Systems*, 15-18.

Hurley, E. (2003). Security and Sarbanes-Oxley. *Searchsecurity.*

Hurley, J., & Hemmendinger, E. (2002). *Open Source and Linux: 2002 Poster Children for Security Problems.* Retrieved October 3, 2003 from http://www.aberdeen.com

Hurley, J., & Veytsel, A. (2003). *Identity Theft: A $2 Trillion Criminal Industry in 2005.* The Aberdeen Group, 13 May, 1-3.

IBM. (2007). *IBM internet security systems X-Force 2006 trend statistics* [Electronic Version]. Retrieved January, from http://www.iss.net/documents/whitepapers/X_Force_Exec_Brief.pdf

ID Analytics. (2004). *Identity 2004: The Identity Risk Management Conference.* ID Analytics, 1-10. Retrieved June 1, 2006, from http://www.idanalytics.com/pdf/ID_2004_Summary.pdf.

Ingols, K., Lippmann, R., & Piowarski, K. (2006). Practical Attack Graph Generation for Network Defense. In *22nd Annual Computer Security Applications Conference (ACSAC' 06)* (pp. 121-130). IEEE Computer Society, Washington, DC, USA.

Insecure. (2009). *Network Mapper (NMAP)* [Computer Software]. http://nmap.org/

Insider Threat IPT (2000). *DoD Insider Threat Mitigation: Final Report of the Insider Threat Integrated Process Team.* Department of Defense, April 24, 2000, Retrieved on March 15, 2008 from https://acc.dau.mil/CommunityBrowser.aspx?id=37478.

Intel Corporation. (2003, May). *Enterprise Security and the PC Infrastructure – White Paper.*Originally retrieved from Intel Web site, no longer available. On file with the author.

Intel Corporation (2003). *Intel Trusted Execution Technology Overview.* Retrieved July 31, 2008, from http://www.intel.com/technology/security/downloads/arch-overview.pdf

Interactive Data Corporation (IDC). (2008). Retrieved July 20, 2008 from http://www.idc.com/

Internet Usage Statistics: The Internet Big Picture. (2008, March). Last Retrieved 5/19/2008 from http://www.internetworldstats.com/stats.htm

Internet World Stats (2008). *Internet Usage Statistics: The Internet Big Picture.* Retrieved July 31, 2008, from http://www.internetworldstats.com/stats.htm

Irvine, C. E., Levin, T. E., & Dinolt, G. W. (2002, May). *A National Trusted Computing Strategy* (White Paper NPS-CS-02-003). Monterey, CA: Naval Postgraduate School, the Center for INFOSEC Studies and Research, Computer Science Department.

ISC: Security Transcends Technology (2008). *Career guide: decoding the information security profession, (isc)2 security transcends technology.* Retrieved June 5, 2008 from www.isc2.org/download/careerguide05.pdf

ISMS User Group. (2008). http://www.iso27001certificates.com/.

Issa: Information systems security association (2008). Retrieved June 3, 2008 from www.issa.org/Resources/Industry-Certifications.html

Jacobellis v. Ohio, 378 U.S. 184, 378 U.S. 184 (U.S. Supreme Court June 1964, 1964).

Jaeger, P. T., Fleischmann, K. R., Preece, J., Shneiderman, B., Wu, P. F., & Qu., Y. (2007). *Biosecurity and Bioterrorism: Biodefense Strategy, Practice, and Science, 5.*

Jajodia, S., Noel, S., & O'Berry, B. (2005). Topological Analysis of Network Attack Vulnerability. In V. Kumar, J. Srivastava, & A. Lazarevic (Ed.), *Managing Cyber Threats: Issues, Approaches and Challenges.* Springer.

Jamieson, R., Land, L., Sarre, R., Steel, A., Stephens, G., and Winchester, D. (2008). Defining Identity Crimes. *ACIS2008 Proceedings of the 19th Australasian Conference on Information Systems,* Christchurch, New Zealand, December 3-5, 1-11.

Jamieson, R., Land, L., Stephens, G., & Winchester, D. (2008). *Identity Crime: The Need for an Appropriate Government Strategy,* Forum on Public Policy Online, Spring 2008 edition, 1-33.

Jamieson, R., Stephens, G., & Winchester, D. (2007). *Identity Fraud: Perpetrator Categories, Channels and Methods of Attack, and their Impact on Target Organisations.* PACIS 2007, Auckland, New Zealand.

Janczewski, L. (2000). Managing security functions using security standards, in Janczewski, L. (Eds.), *Internet and Intranet Security Management: Risks and Solutions,* (pp. 81-105). Idea Group Publishing, Hershey, PA.

Jaquith, A. (2007). *Security Metrics: Replacing Fear, Uncertainty, and Doubt.* Upper Saddle River, NJ: Addison-Wesley.

Jenkins, P. H. (1997). School delinquency and the school social bond. *Journal of research in crime and delinquency, 34*(3), 337-367.

Jenson, B. K., & Romo, J. (2005). The expert opinion. *Journal of information technology case and application research, 7*(2), 49-52.

Jha, S., Sheyner, O., & Wing, J. (2002). Two Formal Analyses of Attack Graphs. In *15th IEEE Computer Security Foundations Workshop (CSFW '02)* (pp.49-63). IEEE Computer Society, Washington, DC, USA.

Jones, K. (2001, November). Incident Response: Performing Investigations on a Live Host. *The Magazine of Usenix & Sage, 26.*

Joseph, N. (2008). Identity theft 'costing SA millions'. Originally published in The Mercury, 4 June, 5. http://www.iol.co.za/index.php?set_id=1&click_id=15&art_id=vn2008060406011 0244C665305.

JP1, (n.d.). *Joint Publication 1, Doctrine for the Armed Forces of the United States*, U.S. Department of Defense.

JP3-0, (2006, September 17). *Joint Publication 3-0, Joint Operations, Incorporating Change 1* . U.S. Department of Defense.

JP3-13, (2006, February 13). Joint *Publication 3-13, Information Operations.* U.S. Department of Defense.

Kaarst-brown, M. L., & Guzman, I. R. (2005). Who is "the it Workforce"?: Challenges Facing Policy Makers, Management, and Research. *Proceedings of the 2005 ACM SIG MIS CPR*, Atlanta, Georgia, April 14-16.

Kamm, G. (2008). Disgruntled Worker Accused of Deleting $2.5 Million of Files. *First Coast News*, January 23, 2008, Retrieved from http://www.firstcoastnews.com/news/local/news-article.aspx?storyid=100625.

Kamp, P. & Watson, R. (2004). Building Systems to Be Shared, Securely. *Queue, 2*(5), 42-51.

Kankanhalli, A., Hock-Hai, T., Bernard, C. Y. T., & Kwok-Kee, W. (2003). An integrative study of information systems security effectiveness. *International journal of information management, 23*, 139-154.

Kannan, K., & Telang, R. (2005). Market for software vulnerabilities? Think again. *Management Science, 51*(5), 726-740.

Kapucu, N. (2004). Interagency communication networks during emergencies: Boundary spanners in multiagency coordination. *American Review of Public Administration, 36*, 207-225.

Karger, P.A., & Schell, R. R. (1974). MULTICS Security Evaluation: Vulnerability Analysis, ESD-TR-74-193, Vol.

II. Bedford, MA: ESD/AFSC, Hanscom AFB. Retrieved July 31, 2008, from http://csrc.nist.gov/publications/history/karg74.pdf

Katerattanakul, P., & Siau, K. (1999). *Measuring information quality of web sites: Development of an instrument. .* Paper presented at the the 20th international conference on Information Systems., Charlotte, North Carolina, USA.

Katz v. U.S., 389 U.S. 347 (1967).

Kautz, H., Selman, B., & Shah, M. (1997). Referral Web: Combining Social Networks and Collaborative Filtering. *Communications of the ACM, 40*(3), 63-65.

Kay, R. (2007, January 29). *Trusted Computing is Real and it's Here.* Retrieved July 31, 2008, from https://www.trustedcomputinggroup.org/news/Industry_Data/Endpoint_Technologies_Associates_TCG_report_Jan_29_2007.pdf

Keen, P. G. W. (1981). Information systems and organizational change. *Communications of the ACM, 24*(1), 24-33.

Keen, P. G. W., Balance, C., Chan, S., & Schrump, S. (1999). *Electronic Commerce Relationships: Trust by Design.* Upper Saddle River, NJ: Prentice Hall PTR.

Keeney, M., et al. (2005). *Insider Threat Study: Computer System Sabotage in Critical Infrastructure Sectors.* Technical Report, U.S. Secret Service and Software Engineering Institute, Carnegie Mellon University, May 2005. Retrieved January 5, 2008 from http://secretservice.tpaq.treasury.gov/ntac/its_report_050516.pdf.

Keller, P. A., & Pyzdek, T. (2005). *Six Sigma Demystified.* New York, NY: McGraw-Hill, Inc.

Kim, D. J., Song, Y. I., Braynov, S. B., & Rao, H. R. (2005). A multidimensional trust formation model in B-to-C e-commerce: A conceptual framework and content analyses of academia/practitioner perspectives *Decision Support Systems, 40*(2), 143-165.

Kim, R. (2008). *2008 Identity Fraud Survey Report Consumer Version: How Consumers Can Protect Themselves.* Javelin Strategy & Research, February, 1-23.

Kinney, S. (2006). *Trusted Platform Basics: Using TPM in Embedded Systems.* Burlington, MA: Elsevier Inc.

Kleindorfer, P. R., & Saad, G. H. (2005). Managing Disruption Risks in Supply Chains. *Production and Operations Management*, 14:1, 53-68.

Knapp, K. J., & Boulton, W. R. (2006). Cyber-warfare threatens corporations: Expansion into commercial environments. *Information Systems Management, 23*(2), 76-87.

Knapp, K. J., Marshall, T. E., Rainer, R. K., & Ford, N. F. (2006). Information security: management's effect on culture and policy. *Information Management and Computer Security, 14*(16), 24-36.

Knapp, K. J., Marshall, T. E., Rainer, R. K., & Morrow, D. W. (2004). *Top ranked information security issues: the 2004 international information systems security certification consortium (ISC)² survey results,* Auburn university, Auburn AL.

Koenig, R. (2004). Beware of Insider Threats to Your Security. *CyberDefense Magazine*. August 2004. Retrieved on January 11, 2008 from http://www.viack.com/download/200408/cdm.pdf.

Kohlenberg, T. (2008). *Intrusion Detection FAQ: How to Make the Business Case for an Intrusion Detection System SANS Institute*. Retrieved March 12, 2008 from http://www.sans.org/resources/idfaq/business_case_ids.php.

Koomey, J. (2007). *Estimating Total Power Consumption by Servers in the U.S. and the World*. Retrieved November 21, 2007 from http://enterprise.amd.com/Downloads/svrpwrusecompletefinal.pdf

Kotler, P. (1999). *Kotler on Marketing: How to create, win and dominate markets. New York:* The Free Press.

Kotler, P., Chandler, P.,C., Brown, L., & Adam, S. (1994). *Marketing, Australia and New Zealand,* 3rd ed. Sydney: Prentice Hall.

Kotulic, A., & Clark, J. G. (2004). Why there aren't more information security research studies. *Information and Management, 41*(5), 597-607.

Kowalski, E., et al. (2008a). *Insider Threat Study: Illicit Cyber Activity in the Government Sector.* Technical Report, U.S. Secret Service and Software Engineering Institute, Carnegie Mellon University, January 2008. Retrieved February 11, 2008 from http://secretservice.tpaq.treasury.gov/ntac/final_government_sector2008_0109.pdf.

Kowalski, E., et al. (2008b). *Insider Threat Study: Illicit Cyber Activity in the Information Technology and Telecommunications Sector.* Technical Report, U.S. Secret Service and Software Engineering Institute, Carnegie Mellon University, January 2008. Retrieved February 11, 2008 from http://secretservice.tpaq.treasury.gov/ntac/final_it_sector_2008_0109.pdf.

KPMG. (2007). Global Anti–Money Laundering Survey 2007: How banks are facing up to the challenge. *KPMG International*, (pp. 1-8).

Krippendorff, K. (1980). *Content analysis: An introduction to its methodology.* Beverly Hills, CA: Sage.

Kyle, D., & Brustoloni, J.C. (2007). UClinux: A Linux Security Module for Trusted-Computing-Based Usage Controls Enforcement. *Proceedings of the 2007 ACM Workshop on Scalable Trusted Computing* (pp. 63-70) (Alexandria, Virginia, November 2), STC '07,.

Landwehr, C. E., Bull, A. R., Mc. Dermott, J. P., & Choi, W. S. (1994). A taxonomy of computer program security flaws, with examples. *ACM Computing Surveys, 26*(3).

Lant, C. (2002). Telnet, You are the Weakest Link! Good-bye. *Berkeley Computing & Communications, 12*(1). Retrieved July 20, 2008 from http://istpub.berkeley.edu:4201/bcc/Winter2002/sec.telnet.html

LaPadula, L. J., & Bell, D. E. (1973) Secure Computer Systems: A Mathematical Model, ESD-TR-73-278, Vol. II. Bedford, MA: ESD/AFSC, Hanscom AFB.

Laqueur, W. (1999). *The New Terrorism: Fanaticism and the Arms of Mass Destruction*. London: Phoenix Press.

Layton, T. P. (2007). *Information Security: Design, Implementation, Measurement, and Compliance*: Auerbach Publications, Taylor & Francis Group.

LeLievre, E., & Jamieson, R. (2005). An Investigation of Identity Fraud in Australian Organizations. *CollECTeR LatAm*. Chile, (pp. 1-10).

Lee, C, & Goldfarb, Z. A. (2006, June 30). Stolen VA Laptop and Hard Drive Recovered. *Washington Post*. Retrieved July 31, 2008, from, http://www.washingtonpost.com/wp-dyn/content/article/2006/06/29/AR2006062900352.html

Lee, J., & Lee, Y. (2002). A holistic model of computer abuse within organizations. *Information Management & Computer Security, 10*(2), 57-63.

Le-Griffin, H.D. (2008). *Assessing Container Terminal Productivity: Experiences of the Ports of Los Angeles and Long Beach* (Report AR05-06). Los Angeles: University of Southern California, METRANS Transportation Center.

Leita, C., Dacier, M., & Massicotte, F. (2006). Automatic Handling of Protocol Dependencies and Reaction to 0-Day Attacks with ScriptGen Based Honeypots. *RAID 2006, LNCS 4219*, 185–205, 2006. Springer-Verlag Berlin Heidelberg.

Lemos, R. (2004). *Mozilla puts bounty on bugs*. Retrieved June 10, 2007, from http://news.com.com/Mozilla+puts+bounty+on+bugs/2100-1002_3-5293659.html

Lerma, C. F. (2007). Creating Learning Objects. *Proceedings of the InSITE 2007 Conference*. Ljubljana, Slovenia. June 22-25.

Lessig, L. (2006). *Code v.2.0*. New York: Basic.

Levoy, T.E. (2006, May). *Development of a Methodology for Customizing Insider Threat Auditing on Microsoft Windows XP Operating System*. Master of Science. Graduate School of Engineering and Management, Air Force Institute of Technology, Wright-Patterson AFB, OH.

Levoy, T. E., Grimaila, M. R., & Mills, R. F. (2006). A Methodology for Customizing Security Auditing Templates for Malicious insider Detection. *Proceedings of the 8th International Symposium on System and Information Security*. San Paulo, Brazil.

Levy, E. (2001). *Full disclosure is a necessary evil*. Retrieved June 10, 2007, from http://www.securityfocus.com/news/238

Lewicki, R. J., & Bunker, B. B. (1996). Developing and maintaining trust in work relationships. In R. M. Kramer & T. R. Tyler (Eds.), *Trust in Organizations: Frontiers of Theory and Research* (pp. 114-139). Thousands Oaks, CA: Sage Publications.

Lewis, T. G. (2006). *Critical Infrastructure Protection in Homeland Security: Defending a Networked Nation*, New York, NY: Wiley-Interscience.

Li, W., & Vaughn, R. B. (2006). Cluster Security Research Involving the Modeling of Network Exploitations Using Exploitation Graphs. In *6th IEEE International Symposium on Cluster Computing and the Grid (CC-GRID'06)* (pp.26). IEEE Computer Society, Washington, DC, USA.

Lichtenstein, S. (1996). Factors in the selection of a risk assessment method. *Information Management & Computer Security, 4*(4), 20-25.

Limoncelli, T., Hogan, C., & Chalup, S. (2007). *The Practice of System and Network Administration, 2ed*. New York, NY: Addison-Wesley.

Lippmann, R. P., & Ingols, K. W. (2005). *An annotated review of past papers on attack graphs* (Tech Rep. No. ESC-TR-2005-054). MIT Lincoln Laboratory, Lexington, MA, 2005. web: www.ll.mit.edu/IST/pubs/0502_Lippmann.pdf.

Logan, P. (2006, January). *People, Process and Technology – Unlocking Latent Terminal Capacity*. Paper presented at the Annual Meeting of the Transportation Research Board, Washington, DC.

Lohse, E. S., Schou, C., Sammons, D., & Schlader, R. (2003). *Management, Research and Information Distribution in a Confidential, Controlled Environment*. Information Data Archives Idaho State University.

Lok, C. (2004). Fighting Infections with Data. *Technology Review*. October 2004.

Longini, I. (1988). A Mathematical Model for Predicting the Geographic Spread of New Infectious Agents. *Mathematical Biosciences, 90,* 367-383.

Louderback, J. (1995). Will You Be Ready When Disaster. Strikes? *PC Week, 12*(5), February 6, 130-131.

Lowans, P. (2002). *Implementing a Network Security Metrics Program* (GIAC Administrivia Version Number:2.0). SANS Institute, GIAC practical repository.

Lucas, H. C. Jr. (1981). *Implementation: the key to successful information systems,* McGraw-Hill, N.Y., USA.

Luckham, D. (2002). *The Power of Events.* Addison-Wesley.

Luhmann, N. (1979). *Trust and Power.* New York: John Wiley and Sons.

Luijerink. D. (2006). The Fraud in Business Club: Effective Fraud Governance. *KPMG,* 2 March, 1-36.

Ma, Q., & Pearson, J. M. (2005). ISO 17799:'best practices' in information security management? *Communications of the AIS, 15,* 577-591.

MacDonald, C., & Ounis, I. (2006). *The TREC Blogs06 Collection: Creating and analyzing a blog test collection.* Technical Report (dcs), Department of Computing Science, University of Glasgow.

Machalaba, D. (2004). Railroad Blues: Woes at Union Pacific Create a Bottleneck for the Economy. *Wall Street Journal,* July 22, 2004, page A1.

Mackenzie, D., & Pottinger, G. (1997). Mathematics, technology, and trust: Formal verification, computer security, and the U.S. military. *IEEE Annals of the History of Computing, 19*(3), 41-59.

Maconachy, V. W., Schou, C. D., Ragsdale, D., & Welch, D. (2001). *A Model for Information assurance: An Integrated Approach.* Paper presented at the 2nd Annual IEEE Systems, Man and Cybernetics Information assurance Workshop.

Malhotra, S., Bhattacharya, S., & Ghosh, S. K. (2008). A Scalable Approach to Attack Path Prediction based on the Attack Surface Measures. In *6th International Conference on Informatics and Systems (INFOS 2008)* (pp. 27-37). Cairo, Egypt.

Man, Y. R. (2003). *Internet Security: Cryptographic Principles, Algorithms and Protocols.* Wiley.

Manadhata, P., Wing, J. M., Fynn, M., & McQueen, M. (2006). Measuring the Attack Surfaces of Two FTP Daemons. In *2nd ACM workshop on Quality of Protection* (pp. 3-10). Alexandria, Virginia, USA.

Manadhata, P., Wing, J., Flynn, M., & McQueen, M. (2006). Measuring the Attack Surfaces of Two FTP Daemons. *Proceedings of the 2nd ACM Workshop on Quality of Protection* (Alexandria, Virginia, October 30), QoP '06, 3-10.

Management Issues. (2003, July 21). Pointless e-mails costs business billions, *Management Issue,.* Retrieved Febryary 17, 2008, from: www.management-issues.com/2006/8/24/research/pointless-e-mail-costs-business-millions.asp.

Mark, G. (2008, February 18). (P. Marksteiner, Interviewer).

Markus, M. L. (1983). Power, politics, and MIS implementation. *Communications of the ACM, 26*(6), June, 430-444.

Martinez-Moyano, I., Rich, E., Conrad, S., & Anderson, D. (2006). Modeling the Emergence of Insider Threat Vulnerabilities. *Proceedings of the 2006 Winter Simulation Conference.* Retrieved June 11, 2008 from http://www.dis.anl.gov/publications/articles/Martinez-Moyano_et_al_2006_WSC.pdf.

Martinez-Moyano, I., Rich, E., Conrad, S., Anderson, D., & Stewart, T. (2008). A Behavioral Theory of Insider-Threat Risks: A System Dynamics Approach. *ACM Transactions on Modeling and Computer Simulation, 18*(2), 7.

Martins, A., & Eloff, J. H. P. (2002). Information security culture. *Proceedings of the IFIP TC11 17th international conference on information security, 214,* 203-214.

Mathieson, K. (1991). Predicting User Intentions: Comparing the Technology Acceptance Model with the Theory of Planned Behavior. *Information Systems Research, 2*(3), 173-191.

Mauw, S., & Oostdijk, M. (2005). Foundations of Attack Trees. *Proceedings of the Eighth Annual International Conference on Information Security and Cryptology,* (pp. 186-198). Seoul, Korea.

Maybury, M. (2006). *Detecting Malicious Insiders in Military Networks.* MITRE Corporation, Bedford, MA.

Maybury, M., et al. (2005). *Analysis and Detection of Malicious insiders.* 2005 International Conference on Intelligence Analysis, McLean VA. Retrieved December 18, 2007 from https://analysis.mitre.org/proceedings/Final_Papers_Files/280_Camera_Ready_Paper.pdf.

Mayer, R. C., Davis, J. H., & Schoorman, F. D. (1995). An integrative model of organizational trust. *Academy of Management Review, 20*(3), 709-734.

McCullagh, A., & Caelli, W. (2000). Non-repudiation in the digital environment. *First Monday.* Retrieved July 31, 2008, from http://www.firstmonday.dk/issues/issue5_8/mccullagh/index.html

McGinn, D. (2007, April 16). Return to Sender; A new book cautions against overrelying on e-mail. *Newsweek, U.S. Edition,* (p. E16).

McHaney, R., & White, D. (1994). Development of a Framework for Discrete-Event Simulation. *Proceedings of the 15th Annual Decision Sciences Institute Meeting* (Honolulu, HI).

McKnight, D. H., Choudhury, V., & Kacmar, C. (2002). Developing and validating trust measures for e-commerce: An integrative topology. *Information Systems Research, 13*(3), 334-361.

McKnight, D. H., Cummings, L. L., & Chervany, N. L. (1998). Initial Trust Formation in New Organizational Relationships. *Academy of Management Review, 23*(3), 473-490.

McPhedran, I. (2005). *Per. Comm.* Canberra, Australia, 19 September 2005.

Meber, D. (2004). *Auditing User Accounts.* Retrieved July 20, 2008 from http://www.windowsecurity.com/articles/Auditing-user-accounts.html

Mell, P., Scarfone, K., & Romanosky, S. (2007). *A Complete Guide to the Common Vulnerability Scoring System Version 2.0.* Retrieved June, 2007, from http://www.first.org/cvss/cvss-guide.html

Mendelson, E. (Ed.) (1997). *Introduction to Mathematical Logic.* Chapman & Hall.

Mercuri, R. T. (2003). Standards insecurity. *Communications of the ACM, 46*(12), 21-25.

Metcalfe's Law. (2002, April). Metcalfe's Law, *National Science Foundation, Division of Science Resources Statistics, Science and Engineering Indicators.* Retrieved December 15, 2007, from: www.nsf.gov/statistics/seind02/c8/c8s1.htm#metcalfe.

Microsoft. (2008). *Security Central.* Retrieved July 20, 2008 from http://www.microsoft.com/security/default.mspx

Middleton, J. (2001). *Coalition condemns full disclosure.* Retrieved April 10 2007, from http://www.vnunet.com/vnunet/news/2116546/coalition-condemns-full-disclosure

Miles, R. E., & Snow, C. C. (1978). *Organizational Strategy, Structure, and Process.* New York, NY: McGraw-Hill.

Miller, D. R. (2006). *Hurricane Katrina: Communications & Infrastructure impacts, Threats at our threshold.* National Defense University.

Miller, H. (1996). *The Multiple Dimensions of Information Quality Information Systems Management, 13*(2), 79-82.

Miloudi, S. (5 February 2008), They come to work... but survey finds that nine-tenths of internet time may be spent chatting at a cost of billions; But sites are useful tools and are good for staff morale, say experts, *The Western Mail,* Retrieved 13 April 2008 from LEXIS, (search term: "personal internet use w/10 workplace").

Mintzberg, H. (1979). *The Structuring of Organizations.* Englewood Cliffs, NJ: Prentice-Hall.

Mintzberg, H. (1980). Structure in 5's. A Synthesis of the Research on Organization Design. *Management Science, 26*(3), 322-341.

Mitchell, R. C., Marcella, R., & Baxter, G. *(1999). Corporate information security management.* New Library World, *100*(1150), 213-227, *MCB University press.*

Model Criminal Law Officers' Committee. (2008). *Final Report Identity Crime,* Commonwealth of Australia, March, 1-51.

Moitra, S., & Konda, S. (2004). An Empirical Investigation of Network Attacks on Computer Systems. *Computers & Security, 23*(1), 43-51. Morphy, E. (2005). *Web Server Attacks, Defacements Increase.* Retrieved July 20, 2008 from http://www.newsfactor.com/story.xhtml?story_id=33523

Monahan, M. T., & Kim, R. (2008). *2008 Identity Fraud Survey Report Excerpts for Card Issuers: Identity Fraud Continues to Decline, But Criminals More Effective at Using All Channels.* Javelin Strategy & Research, Syndicated Report Brochure, March, 1-6.

Mongelluzzo, B. (2004). From Bad to Worse in LA-Long Beach; Truckers Remain Unhappy about Delays at Southern California Ports. *Journal of Commerce,* September 27, 2004, p. 16.

Montana, J. C. (2008, March 13). Nuts and Bolts of Records Management: Avoiding A Rube Goldberg System. *ABA Tech Show,* Chicago, IL, USA: American Bar Association.

Morgan, R. (2001). *The Demon Lover – The Roots of Terrorism.* New York: Washington Square Press.

Moser-Wellman, A. (2001). *The Five Faces of Genius.* New York: Penguin Putnam.

Mosteller, F., & Tukey, J. W. (1977*). Data Analysis and Regression: A Second Course in Statistics.* Menlo Park, CA: Addison-Wesley Publishing Company.

Moule, B., & Giavara, L. (1995). Policies, procedures and standards: an approach for implementation. *Information Management & Computer Security, 3*(3), 7-16.

Multi-State ISAC (2008). http://www.msisac.org, July 18, 2008.

Mundie, C., DeVries, P., Haynes, P., & Corwine, M. (2002, September 12). *Trustworthy Computing - White Paper.* Retrieved July 31, 2008, from http://download.microsoft.com/download/a/f/2/af22fd56-7f19-47aa-8167-4b1d73cd3c57/twc_mundie.doc

Murray, B. (1998, March 3). Data Smog: newest culprit in brain drain, *American Psyshological Association,* Retrieved November 15, 2007, from: http:www.apa.org/monitor/mar98/smog.htl.

MyFinances.co.uk, UK. (2006). *ID fraud cost of just cutting up cards.* 27 March. Retrieved June 29, 2006, from http://www.myfinanc es.co.uk/news/credit-cards/identity-fraud/id-fraud-cost-just-cutting-up-cards-$349604.htm.

Myler, E., & Broadbent, G. (2006). ISO 17799: Standard for security. *The information management journal* (pp. 43-52). Nov./Dec.

National Commission on Terrorist Attacks Upon the United States. (2004). *The 9/11 Commission Report.* Washington: U.S. Government Printing Office.

National Information Security Center (NISC). (2006, October). *Japanese Government's Efforts to Address Information Security Issues: Focusing on the Cabinet Secretariat's Efforts.* Retrieved July 31, 2008, from http://unpan1.un.org/intradoc/groups/public/documents/APCITY/UNPAN027267.pdf

National Infrastructure Protection Center (NIPC). *Special Technologies and Applications Unit (STAU): Insiders and Information Technology.* Retrieved on April 3, 2008 from http://www.hpcc-usa.org/pics/02-pres/wright.ppt.

National Institute of Standards and Technology. (2003). *Security Metrics Guide for Information Technology*

Systems (NIST Special Publication 800-55). Washington, DC: U.S. Government Printing Office.

National Institute of Standards and Technology. (2006). *Guide for Developing Performance Metrics for Information Security* (NIST Special Publication 800-80). Washington, DC: U.S. Government Printing Office.

National Institute of Standards and Technology. (2006). *Guide to Integrating Forensic Techniques into Incident Response* (NIST Special Publication 800-86). Washington, DC: U.S. Government Printing Office.

National Institute of Standards and Technology. (2006). *Information Security Handbook: A Guide for Managers* (NIST Special Publication 800-100). Washington, DC: U.S. Government Printing Office.

National Institute of Standards and Technology. (2007). *Recommended Security Controls for Federal Information Systems* (NIST Special Publication 800-53). Washington, DC: U.S. Government Printing Office.

National Security Agency (NSA). (2009). *Security-Enhanced Linux* [Computer Software]. http://www.nsa.gov/selinux/

Netcraft. (2008). *March 2008 Web Server Survey*. Retrieved July 20, 2008 from http://news.netcraft.com/archives/web_server_survey.html

Network Magazine. (2004, June 30). *Trusted Computing Survey Results*. Retrieved July 31, 2008, from http://www.techweb.com/news/showArticle.jhtml?articleID=22102893

Neumann, P. G. (2003, Summer). U.S. computer insecurity redux. *Issues in Science and Technology*. Retrieved July 31, 2008, from http://www.nap.edu/issues/19.4/neumann.html

Neyman, J., & Pearson, E. S. (1928). *On the Use and Interpretation of Certain Test Criteria for Purposes of Statistical Inference, Part I*. reprinted at pp.1-66 in Neyman, J. & Pearson, E.S., Joint Statistical Papers, Cambridge University Press, (Cambridge), 1967.

Ng, B., Si, A., Lau, R. W., & Li, F. W. (2002). A Multi-Server Architecture for Distributed Virtual Walkthrough.

Proceedings of the ACM Symposium on Virtual Reality Software and Technology (pp. 163-170) (Hong Kong, China, November 11-13), VRST '02.

Nichols, E., & Peterson, G. (2007). A Metrics Framework to Drive Application Security Improvement. *IEEE Security & Privacy, 5*(2), 88-91.

Ning, P., & Xu, D. (2003). Learning Attack Strategies from Intrusion Alerts. In *10ᵗʰ ACM Conference on Computer and Communications Security (CCS '03)* (pp.200-209). ACM Press, New York.

Ning, P., Xu, D., Healey, C., & Amant, R. S. (2004). Building Attack Scenarios through Integration of Complementary Alert Correlation Methods. In *11ᵗʰ Annual Network and Distributed System Security Symposium (NDSS '04)* (pp.97-111). San Diego, California, USA.

Nissen, M. E. (2005, June). A Computational Approach to Diagnosing Misfits, Inducing Requirements, and Delineating Transformations for Edge Organizations. *Proceedings International Command and Control Research and Technology Symposium*, McLean, VA.

Noel, S., & Jajodia, S. (2004). Managing attack graph complexity through visual hierarchical aggregation. In *ACM workshop on Visualization and data mining for computer security (VizSEC/DMSEC '04)* (pp.109-118). ACM Press, New York, NY.

Noel, S., Jajodia, S., O'Berry, B., & Jacobs, M. (2005). Efficient minimum-cost network hardening via exploit dependency graphs. In *19ᵗʰ Annual Computer Security Applications Conference (ACSAC '03)* (pp.86-95). IEEE Computer Society, Washington, DC, USA.

Nonaka, I. (1998). The Knowledge-Creating Company, in *Harvard Business Review on Knowledge Management* (pp. 21-45). Boston: Harvard Business School Press.

Nonaka, I., & Takeuchi, H. (1995). *The Knowledge-Creating Company*. New York: Oxford University Press.

North American Computational Social and Organization Sciences (NAACSOS). (2007). Retrieved March 13, 2008 from http://www.casos.cs.cmu.edu/naacsos/

North American Electric Reliability Corporation (2006). *2006 Long-Term Reliability Assessment*, Princeton, NJ.

Norton-Taylor, R. (2005). *Asymmetric Warfare*. London: The Guardian.

Noteboom, B. (1988). The facts about small business and the real values of its 'life world'. *American journal of economics and sociology, 47*(3), 299-314.

Nozaki, S., & Ross, S. (1978). Approximations in Finite-Capacity Multi-Server Queues with Poisson Arrivals. *Journal of Applied Probability, 14*(4), 826-834.

Nunamaker Jr., J. F., Briggs, R. O., Mittleman, D. D., Vogel, D. R., & Balthazard, P. A. (1997). Lessons from a Dozen Years of Group Support Systems Research: A Discussion of Lab and Field Findings. *Journal of Management Information Systems, 13*(3), 163-207.

O'Leary, M. (2004). *Measuring Disaster Preparedness: A Practical Guide to Indicator Development and Application*: iUniverse.

OECD. (2002). *OECD Guidelines for the Security of Information Systems and Networks, 30.*

OECD. (2004). *Principles of Corporate Governance.* www.oecd.org/dataoecd/32/18/31557724.pdf

OECD. (2005). *Industry, Services & trade, 2005*(30). OECD STI Scoreboard 2005.

OIS. (2004). *Guidelines for security vulnerability reporting and response* [Electronic Version], 2007, from http://www.oisafety.org/guidelines/

Okazaki, S. (2007). Lessons learned from i-mode: What makes consumers click wireless banner ads. *Computers in Human Behavior, 23,* 1692–1719.

Okolica, J., Peterson, G. L., & Mills, R. F. (2008). Using PLSI-U to Detect Insider Threats by Datamining Email. *International Journal of Security and Networks, 3*(2), 114-121.

Openwall. (2009). *John the Ripper* [Computer Software]. http://www.openwall.com/john/

Orange County Register, In Delays, Their Ship Comes In. Anaheim, CA, September 9, 2004.

Ortiz, D. S., Weatherford, B., Willis, H. H., Collins, M., Mandava, N., & Ordowich, C. (2007). *Increasing the Capacity of Freight Transportation: U.S. and Canadian Perspectives,* RAND Corporation, Santa Monica, CA.

Ou, X., Boyer, W. F., & McQueen, M. A.(2006). A Scalable Approach to Attack Graph Generation. In *13th ACM conference on Computer and Communications Security (CCS '06)* (pp.336-345). New York: ACM Press.

Owen, D. (2002). *Hidden Secrets: A complete history of espionage and the technology used to support it.* London: Quintet Publishing.

Ozment, A. (2004). *Bug auctions: vulnerability market reconsidered.* Paper presented at the Workshop of Economics and Information Security (WEIS), Minneapolis, MN.

Ozment, A., & Schechter, S. (2006). *Milk or wine: does software security improve with age?* Paper presented at the The Fifteenth Usenix Security Symposium. July 31 - August 4 2006, Vancouver, BC, Canada.

Pachakis, D., & Kiremidjian, A. (2003). Ship Traffic Modeling Methodology for Ports. *Journal of Waterway, Port, Coastal and Ocean Engineering, 129*(5), 193-202.

PandaLabs. (2007). *Quarterly report PandaLabs* [Electronic Version]. Retrieved July 15, 2007, from http://www.pandasecurity.com/

Paolillo, J. C., & Wright, E. (2005). Social network analysis on the semantic web: Techniques and challenges for visualizing FOAF. In V. Geroimenko & C. Chen (Eds.), *Visualizing the Semantic Web* (pp. 229-242).

Pariag, D., Brecht, T., Harji, A., Buhr, P., Shukla, A., & Cheriton, D. R. (2007). Comparing the Performance of Web Server Architectures. *SIGOPS Oper. Syst. Rev., 41*(3), 231-243.

Parker, D. B. (2006). Why information security is still a folk art. *Communications of the ACM, 49*(10), 11.

Parker, M. B., Moleshe, V., De la Harpe, R., & Wills, G. B. (2006). *An evaluation of Information quality frameworks for the World Wide Web*. Paper presented at the 8th Annual Conference on WWW Applications, Bloemfontein, Free State Province, South Africa.

Parkin, M., Powell, M., & Matthews, K. *Economics*. (2005). Harlow, England: Pearson Addison Wesley.

Pastore, M. (2004). *The Identity Theft Prevention and Recovery Guide*. November 19, Retrieved June 1, 2006, from http://www.in sideid.com/idtheft/article. php/3438261n.

Paul, S. R. (2006). Identity Theft: Outline of Federal Statutes and Bibliography of Selected Resources. *LLRX. com*, February, 1-16.

Pavlou, P. A., & Gefen, D. (2004). Building effective online marketplaces with institution-based trust. *Information Systems Research, 15(1)*, 37-59.

Payne, S. (2006). *A Guide to Security Metrics*. SANS Institute, Information Security Reading Room.

Pearson, S. (2003). *Trusted Computing Platforms: TCPA Technology in Context*. Upper Saddle River, NJ: Prentice Hall PTR.

Pelfrey, W. V. (2005). The cycle of preparedness: Establishing a framework to prepare for terrorist threats. *Journal of Homeland Security and Emergency Management, 2*(1), 1-21.

Peng, T., Leckie, C., & Ramamohanarao, K. (2007). Survey of Network-Based Defense Mechanisms Countering the DoS and DDoS Problems. *ACM Comput. Surv., 39*(1), 3.

Perl, R. F. (2008). *Terrorist Use of the Internet: Threat, Issues, and Options for International Co-operation*. Presentation by the OSCE at the Second International Forum on Information Security on 7-10 April 2008 at Garmisch-Partenkirchen, Germany.

Perloff, J. M. (2007). *Microeconomics* (Fourth Edition ed.). Boston: Pearson, Addison Wesley.

Perrow, C. (1967). A Framework for Comparative Analysis of Organizations. *American Sociological Review, 32*, 194-208.

Peters, C. C., Amato, H., & Hollenbeck, C. R. (2007) An Exploratory Investigation Of Consumers' Perceptions Of Wireless Advertising. *Journal of Advertising, 36*(4), 129.

Petri. (2009). SubSeven 2.2 [Computer Software]. http://www.petri.co.il/trojan_ports_list.htm

Petty, R. D. (2003). Wireless Advertising Messaging: Legal Analysis and Public Policy Issues. *Journal of Public Policy & Marketing, 22*(1) 71-82.

Pfleeger, C. P., & Pfleeger, S. L. (2006). *Security in Computing*. Upper Saddle River, NJ: Prentice Hall.

Phillips, C. E. Jr., Ting, T. C., & Demurjian, S. A. (2002). *Information Sharing and security in dynamic coalitions*. Paper presented at the Proceedings of the seventh ACM symposium on Access control models and technologies.

Phillips, C., & Swiler, L. P. (1998). A graph-based system for network-vulnerability analysis. In *Workshop on New Security paradigms (NSPW '98)* (pp.71-79). ACM Press, New York, NY.

Piltzecker, T., Chaffin, L., Granneman, S., & Hunter, L. E. (2007). *Microsoft Vista for IT Security Professionals*. Rockland, MA: Syngress Publishing.

Pipkin, D. L. (2001). *Information Security: Protecting the Global Enterprise*. Hewlett-Packard Company.

Platt, D. S. (2007). *Why Software Sucks: And What We Can Do About It*. Boston: Rolling Thunder Computer, Inc.

Poggi, F. (2005). *Rapport de veille sur les standards et méthodes en matière de sécurité informatique*, May, www.cases.lu, Luxemburg.

Poindexter, D., & St. Laurent, N. (2000). Incident handling at BMDO. *The Information Warfare Site (IWS)* Retrieved October 19, 2006, from http://www.iwar.org. uk/comsec/resources/fasp/BMDOIncHandling.htm

Porcupine. (2009). *Security Administrator Tool for Analyzing Networks* (SATAN) [Computer Software] http://www.porcupine.org/satan/

Port of Long Beach, data retrieved March 18, 2007 from http://www.polb.com/facilities/cargotenant/container-ized/default.asp.

Port of Los Angeles, data retrieved March 18, 2007 from http://www.portoflosangeles.org/facilities_Container.htm.

Posner, R. A. (1986). *Economic Analysis of Law* (3d ed.). New York: Little Brown & Co. (pp. 38-39).

Posner, R.A. (1978). The Right of Privacy. *Georgia Law Review, 12*(3), 393.

Posthumus, S., & von Solms, R. (2004). A framework for the governance of information security. *Computers & Security, 23*(8), 638-646.

Postman, N. (1992). *Technopoly: the surrender of culture to techology.* New York: Random House Inc.

Pottruck, D. S., & Pearce, T. (2000). *Clicks and Mortar, Passion-Driven Growth in an Internet World.* San Francisco: Jossey-Bass.

Pouget, F., & Holz, T. (2005). A Pointillist Approach for Comparing Honeypots. *In Intrusion and Malware Detection and Vulnerability Assessment.* Springer Berlin / Heidelberg.

President's Commission on Critical Infrastructure Protection, *Critical Foundations: Protecting America's Infrastructures*, The White House, Washington, DC, 1997.

Prior, M., Rogerson, S., & Fairweather, B. (2002). The Ethical Attitudes of Information Systems Professionals: Outcomes of an initial survey. *Telematics and Informatics, 19*, 21-36.

Prosser, W. L. (1960). Privacy. *California Law Review, 48*(3), 383.

Provos, N. (2004). A virtual honeypot framework. *Proceedings from the 12th USENIX Security Symposium.*

Quan-Hasse, A. C. (2005). Instant messaging for collaboration: A case study of a high-tech firm, *Journal of Computer Mediated Communication,* Retrieved April 6, 2008, from jcmc.indiana.edu/vol10/issue4/quan-hasse.html.

Quelch, J. A., & Klein, L. R. (1996). The Internet and international marketing. *Sloan Management Review, 37*(3), 60-75.

Quinn, J. B. (1992). *Intelligent Enterprise.* New York: Free Press.

Quinn, J. B., Anderson, P., & Finkelstein, S. (1998). Managing Professional Intellect: Making the Most of the Best. *Harvard Business Review on Knowledge Management* (pp. 181-205). Boston: Harvard Business School Press.

Radianti, J., & Gonzalez, J. J. (2007). *A preliminary model of the vulnerability black market.* Paper presented at the the 25th International System Dynamics Conference Boston, USA.

Randazzo, M., et al. (2004). *Insider Threat Study: Illicit Cyber Activity in the Banking and Finance Sector.* Technical Report, U.S. Secret Service and Software Engineering Institute, Carnegie Mellon University, August 2004. Retrieved from http://secretservice.tpaq.treasury.gov/ntac/its_report_040820.pdf.

Randers, J. (1980). *Elements of the system dynamics method.* Cambridge, Massachusetts: The MIT Press.

Rasmussen, G. (2008). *Information Security Professional.* Retrieved, from the World Wide Web: http://www.gideonrasmussen.com

Ratnasingam, P., & Pavlou, P. A. (2003). Technology trust in internet-based interorganization electronic commerce. *Journal of Electronic Commerce in Organizations, 1*(1), 17-41.

Rauch, J. (1999). *The Future of vulnerability disclosure?* Retrieved June 19, 2007, from http://www.usenix.org/publications/login/1999-11/features/disclosure.html

Ray, S.K. (1981). *Economics of the black market.* Boulder, Colorado: Westview Press.

Rees, J., Bandyopadhyay, S., & Spafford, E.H. (2003). PFIRES: A policy framework for information security. *Communications of the ACM, 46*(7), 101-106.

Register. (2008). *Security.* Retrieved July 20, 2008 from http://www.theregister.co.uk/security/

Report. *National and State Trends in Fraud & Identity Theft: January - December 2003*, Federal Trade Commission (2004).

Report: *Records, Computers and the Rights of Citizens Report of the Secretary's Advisory Committee on Automated Personal Data Systems*, Secretary of Health, Education, and Welfare (July, 1973).

Rescola, E. (2004). *Is finding security holes a good idea?* Paper presented at the The Third Workshop on the Economics of Information Security, Minneapolis.

Rest, J. R. (1986). *Moral development: advances in research and theory.* Praeger publishers, New York, USA.

Restatement (Second) of Torts §652A (1976).

Richardson, G. P., & Alexander L. Pugh III. (1981). *Introduction to system dynamics modeling.* Portland, Oregon: Productivity Press.

Richardson, R. (2007). *2007 CSI/FBI Computer Crime and Security Survey.* Computer Security Institute. Retrieved January 5, 2008 from http://i.cmpnet.com/v2.gocsi.com/pdf/CSISurvey2007.pdf.

Richardson, R. (2007). CSI/FIB Computer Crime and Security Survey. *The 12th Annual Computer Crime and Security Survey* (Computer Security Institute).

Ricker, Judith and Joseph Porus, (2007) *Mobil Advertising and Marketing USA: Consumer Acceptance Understanding Subscriber Acceptance*, Harris Interactive.

Riebach, S., Rathgeb, E. P., & Tödtmann, B. (May, 2005). Efficient Deployment of Honeynets for Statistical and Forensic Analysis of Attacks from the Internet. In proceedings from IFIP-TC6 Networking Conference 2005. Waterloo, Ontario, Canada.

Riley, B. (2003). Information Sharing in Homeland Security and Homeland Defense: How the Department of Defense Is Helping. *Journal of Homeland Security.*

Robb, D. (2004). Taming Text. *Computerworld, 38,* 40-41.

Robert Frances Group (2004). Collecting Effective Security Metrics. *CSO.* Retrieved March 11, 2008, from http://www.csoonline.com/analyst/report2412.html.

Roberti, R., & Bonsembiante, F. (1995). *Llaneros Solitarios Hackers, Guerrilla.* Espasa Calpa; 1st. Edition.

Rogers, E. M. (1995). *Diffusion of Innovations,* 4th ed. New York: The Free Press.

Rogers, P. (2000). *Losing Control. Global Security in the 21st Century.* London: Pluto Press.

Rosen-Zvi, M., Griffiths, T., Steyvers, M., & Smyth, P. (2004). The Author-Topic Model for Authors and Documents. *Proceedings of the 20th Conference on Uncertainty in Artificial Intelligence*, (pp. 487–494).

Rotenberg, M. (2001). Fair Information Practices and the Architecture of Privacy. *Stanford Technology Law Review 2001*(1), 1.

Rotenberg, M. (2006). *The Sui Generis Privacy Agency: How the United States Institutionalized Privacy Oversight After 9-11.* Available at: http://ssrn.com/abstract=933690

Rothke, B. (2004). *Computer Security: 20 Things Every Employee Should Know.* New York: McGraw Hill.

Rousseau, D. M., Sitkin, S. B., Burt, R. S., & Camerer, C. (1998). Not so different after all: A cross-discipline view of trust. *Academy of Management Review, 23*(3), 393-404.

Ruckelshaus v. Monsanto Co., 467 U.S. 986 (1984).

Russinovich, M. (2007). Inside Windows Vista User Account Control. *Microsoft TechNet Magazine*, June. Retrieved July 20, 2008 from http://technet.microsoft.com/en-us/magazine/cc138019.aspx

Safford, D. (2002, October). *Clarifying Misinformation on TCPA.* Retrieved July 31, 2008, from http://www. research.ibm.com/gsal/tcpa/tcpa_rebuttal.pdf

Saint-Germain, R. (2005). Information security management best practice based on ISO/IEC 17799. *Information management journal, 39*(4), 60-66.

Samociuk, M., & Iyer, N. (2003). *Fraud Resistance: A Practical Guide.* Strategic Value Management Series. SIRCA. Standards Australia International.

SANS Institute - about SANS. (2008). Retrieved May 14, 2008 from http://www.sans.org/about/sans.php

Santoso, T., Ahmed, S., Goetschalckx, M., & Shapiro, A. (2005). A Stochastic Programming Approach for Supply Chain Network Design under Uncertainty. *European Journal of Operational Research, 167*, 96-115.

Sarah, N., Paula, G., Greene, M., Lemersal, E., & Mileti, D. (1999). *Public Education for Earthquake Hazards.* Natural Hazards informer.

Sarbanes-Oxley Act of 2002, Pub.L. 107-204, 116 Stat. 745.

Sarbanes-Oxley act. (2002). Sarbanes-Oxley Act of 2002. Re*trieved April 14, 2008 from* http://fl1.findlaw. com/news.findlaw.com/hdocs/docs/gwbush/sarbanes-oxley072302.pdf.

Sausner, R. (2007). There's No Substitute For Good Preparation. *Bank Technology News, 20*, 32.

Schechter, S. (2002). *How to buy better testing: using competition to get the most security and robustness for your dollar.* Paper presented at the Infrastructures Security Conference, Bristol, UK.

Schmidt, A. (2007a). *Trusted Computing: Introduction & Applications. Lecture 1: TC History & Intro.* Retrieved July 31, 2008, from http://www.sec.informatik.tu-darmstadt.de/pages/lehre/SS07/tc/folien/tc01.pdf

Schmidt, A. (2007b). *Trusted Computing: Introduction & Applications. Lecture 2: TPM Architecture, Base Functionality, and Key Hierarchy.* Retrieved July 31, 2008, from http://www.sec.informatik.tu-darmstadt. de/pages/lehre/SS07/tc/folien/tc02.pdf

Schmidt, A. (2007c). *Trusted Computing: Introduction & Applications. Lecture 3: The CRTM and Authenticated boot process.* Retrieved July 31, 2008, from http://www. sec.informatik.tu-darmstadt.de/pages/lehre/SS07/tc/fo-lien/tc03.pdf

Schmidt, A. (2007d). *Trusted Computing: Introduction & Applications. Lecture 5: Remote Attestation, Direct Anonymous Attestation* Retrieved July 31, 2008, from http://www.sec.informatik.tu-darmstadt.de/pages/lehre/ SS07/tc/folien/tc05.pdf

Schneier, B. (1999). Modeling Security Threats. *Dr. Dobbs Journal.* Retrieved February 8, 2008 from http:// www.schneier.com/paper-attacktrees-ddj-ft.html.

Schneier, B. (2000). *Full disclosure and the window of exposure.* Crypto-Gram Newsletter Retrieved March 10, 2006, from http://www.schneier.com/crypto-gram-0009.html#1

Schneier, B. (2000). *Publicizing vulnerabilities.* Retrieved April 10, 2007, from http://www.schneier.com/ crypto-gram-0002.html

Schneier, B. (2001). *Bug secrecy vs. full disclosure.* Retrieved April 10, 2007, from http://news.zdnet.com/2100-9595_22-531066.html

Schneier, B. (2002). *Secrets and Lies: Digital Security in a Networked World.* 1st Edition. Wiley. New York, NY (2004).

Schneier, B. (2006). *Economics and information security.* Retrieved December 12, 2006, from http://www.schneier. com/blog/archives/2006/06/economics_and_i_1.html

Schneier, B. (2007). *Schneier: full disclosure of security vulnerabilities a 'damned good idea'.* Retrieved June 19, 2007, from http://www.schneier.com/essay-146.html

Schneier, B. (2008). *Schneier on Security.* Retrieved July 20, 2008 from http://www.schneier.com/blog/

Schneier, B., & Kelsey, J. (1999). Secure Audit Logs to Support Computer Forensics. *ACM Trans. Inf. Syst. Secur., 2*(2), 159-176.

Schorr, B. (2008, March 14). Presentation: "Keeping Up With the Joneses--Upgrading to Office 2007". *ABA Tech Show* . Chicago, IL, USA.

Schultz, E. (2002). A framework for understanding and predicting insider attacks. *Computers and security, 21*(6), 526-531.

Schultz, E.E. (2002). A Framework for Understanding and Predicting Insider Attacks. *Computers and Security, 21*(6), 526-531.

Schumacher, M. (2002). Security patterns and security standards. *Proceedings of the 7th European conference on pattern languages of programs (EuroPloP).* Irsee, Germany.

Schwartz, P. M., & Janger, E. J. (2007). Notification of Data Security Breaches. *Michigan Law Review, 105*(5) 913-984.

Schweitzer, J. A. (1982). *Managing Information Security: A Program for the Electronic Information Age.* Butterworth-Heinemann, Boston, MA.

Seacord, R. C., & Householder, A. D. (2005). *A structured approach to classifying security vulnerabilities.* Retrieved December 22, 2005, from http://www.sei.cmu.edu/pub/documents/ 05.reports/pdf/05tn003.pdf

Seagate Technology Incorporated. (2008, May 13). Seagate Secure™ Self-Encrypting Laptop Hard Drives Earn National Security Agency Qualification for National Security Systems. Retrieved July 31, 2008, from http://www.seagate.com/ww/v/index.jsp?locale=en-US&name=null&vgnextoid=bd8f322b02fd9110VgnVCM100000f5ee0a0aRCRD

Segell, G.M. (2005). Intelligence Methodologies Applicable to the Madrid Train Bombings, 2004. *International Journal of Intelligence and CounterIntelligence, 18*, 221-238.

Shapiro, S. P. (1987). The social control of impersonal trust. *American Journal of Sociology, 93,* 623-658.

Shaw, E., Ruby, K., & Post, J. (September 1998). The insider threat to information systems. *Security Awareness Bulletin* No. 2-98, Department of Defense Security

Institute. Retrieved January 8, 2008, from http://www.pol-psych.com/sab.pdf.

Shellenbarger, S. (2007, October 11). A day without e-mail is like . . . *Wall Street Journal Abstracts* , pp. Section D, Column 2, page 1.

Shenk, D. (1997). *Data Smog: Surviging the Information Glut.* San Francisco: Harper.

Sheyner, O., Haines, J., Jha, S., Lippmann, R., & Wing, J. M. (2002). Automated generation and analysis of attack graphs. In *IEEE Symposium on Security and Privacy* (pp.273-284). IEEE Computer Society, Washington, DC, USA.

Shi, X., Bonner, M., Adamic, L., & Gilbert. A. C. (2008). *The Very Small World of the Well-connected*, HyperText 2008, Pittsburgh, PA, June 19-21.

Shiman, D. R. (2006). An Economic Approach to the Regulation of Direct Marketing. *Federal Communications Law Journal, 58*, 321.

Shipley, D. S., & Schwalbe, W. (2007). *Send.* Toronto: Alfred A. Knopf.

Siegel, A. B. (2000). Mission Creep or Mission Misunderstood. *JFQ: Joint Force Quarterly, 112.*

Simon, H.A. (1960). *The New Science of Management Decision.* New York: Harper and Row.

Siponen, M. T. (2000). Policies for construction of information systems' security guidelines. *Proceedings of the 15ht information security conference* (IFIP TC11/Sec 2000), Beijing, China, August, 111-120.

Siponen, M. T. (2006). Information security standards focus on the existence of process, not its content. *Communications of the ACM, 49*(8), 97-100.

Siponen, M. T., & Iivari, J. (2006). Six design theories for IS security Policies and Guidelines. *Journal of the Association for Information systems, 7*(7), 445-472.

Skroch, M., McHugh, J., & Williams, J. M. (2000). *Information Assurance Metrics: Prophecy, Process, or Pipedream.* Panel Workshop, National Information Systems Security Conference, Baltimore.

Smith, A. (1776). *An Inquiry into the Nature and Causes of the Wealth of Nations.* London: Methuen and Co., Ltd. (5th ed. 1904) Book 1, Ch.2.

Smith, S. (2005). *Trusted Computing Platforms: Design and Applications.* New York, NY: Springer Science+Business Media, Inc.

Smith, S. (2006). *An Investigation of IS Security Management in E-Government.* Unpublished doctoral dissertation, University of New South Wales, Australia.

Software Engineering Institute (SEI) (2007). *Client/Server Software Architectures--An Overview.* Carnegie Mellon University. Retrieved July 20, 2008 from http://www. sei.cmu.edu/str/descriptions/clientserver_body.html

Soh, C. P. P., Yap, C. S., & Raman, K. S. (1992). Impact of consultants on computerization success in small businesses. *Information and Management, 22,* 309-319.

Solomon, M. G., & Chapple, M. (2005). *Information Security Illuminated.* Sudbury, MA: Jones and Bartlett Publisher.

Solove, D. J. (2002). *Conceptualizing Privacy. California Law Review, 90*(4),1087-1155.

Somarsoft. (2009). *DumpSec* [Computer Software]. http://somarsoft.com/

Soper, T. (2003). *Incident response: Managing security at Microsoft*: Microsoft Technical White Paper.

SourceFire. (2009). *Snort* [Computer Software]. http://www.snort.org/

Spier, C., Valacich, J., & Vessey, I., (1999). The Influence of Task Interruption in Individual Decision Making: An Information Overload Perspective. *Decision Sciences*, (pp. 337-360).

Spier, D. C. (2008, March 27). (P. Marksteiner, Interviewer).

Spinellis, D., Kokolakis, S., & Gritzalis, S. (1999). Security requirements, risks and recommendations for small enterprise and home-office environments. *Information Management & Computer Security, 7*(3), 121-128.

Spira, J. B. (2007). *Information Overload: We have met the enemy and he is us.* Basex Inc.

Spira, J. F. (2005). *The Cost of Not Paying Attention: How Interruptions Impact Kowledge Worker Productivity.* Basex Inc.

Spitzner, L. (2002). *Honeypots: Tracking Hackers.* 1st Edition. Addison-Wesley, Boston.

Sprague, S. (2006). *Trusted Computing: Benefiting from the New Standard.* Originally retrieved from Wave Systems Website, no longer available. On file with the author.

Sproul, L., & Kiesler S. (1991). *Connections.* MIT press, Boston, USA.

Stamboulidis, G. A., Resnick., L. J., & Carney, J. J. (2005). Expanding The Internal Auditor's Beat. *Internal Auditing,* (20)5, 38-42.

Stanton, J. M., Caldera, C., Isaac, A., Stam, K., & Marcinkowski, S. J. (2003). Behavioral Information Security: Define the criterion space. In P. M. Mastrangelo & W. J. Everton (Eds.),*The Internet at Work or Not: Preventing Computer Deviance. Symposium presentation at the 2003 meeting of the Society for Industrial and Organizational Psychology*, Orlando, FL.

Stanton, J. M., Stam, K. R., Mastrangelo, P., & Jolton, J. (2004). Analysis of End User Security Behaviors. *Computers and Security,* (pp. 1-10).

Stanton, J., & Stam, K. (2006). *The Visible Employee: Using Workplace Monitoring and Surveillance to Protect Information Assets- Without Compromising Employee Privacy and Trust.*

State of California, (2002). *California Information Practices.* Retrieved July 31, 2008, from http://www.leginfo. ca.gov/pub/01-02/bill/sen/sb_1351-1400/sb_1386_bill_ 20020926_chaptered.html

Steinmueller, E. W. (2005). *Technical Compatibility Standards and the Co-Ordination of the Industrial and International Division of Labor.* Advancing Knowledge and the Knowledge Economy, Washington, DC, 2005.

Stemler, S. (2001). An overview of content analysis. Practical Assessment. *Research & Evaluation, 7*(17).

Sterman, J. D. (2000). *Business dynamics: systems thinking and modeling for a complex world.* Boston: Irwin/McGraw-Hill.

Stern, J. (2003). *Terror in the name of God: why religious militants kill.* New York: Harper Collins.

Stevenson, C. A. (1996, August). *The Evolving Clinton Doctrine on the Use of Force.* Retrieved July 13, 2008, from EBSCO: web.ebscohost.com (search term: "mission creep").

Stewart, T. A. (1997). *Intellectual Capital, The New Wealth of Organizations.* London: Nicholas Brealey.

Stiegler, M., Karp, A. H., Yee, K., Close, T., & Miller, M. S. (2006). Polaris: Virus-Safe Computing for Windows XP. *Commun. ACM, 49*(9), 83-88.

Stoll, C. (2002). *The Cuckoo's Egg: Tracking a Spy Through the Maze of Computer Espionage.* 1st edition. Pocket.

Stoneburner, G., Goguen, A., et al. (2002). *Risk Management Guide for Information Technology Systems.* National Institute of Standards and Technology Special Publication 800-30. Retrieved December 12, 2007, from http://csrc.nist.gov/publications/nistpubs/800-30/sp800-30.pdf.

Straub, D. E. Jr. & Nance, W. D. (1990). Discovering and Disciplining Computer Abuse in Organizations: A Field Study. *MIS Quarterly*, March, 45-60.

Straub, D. W. (1990). Effective IS security: an empirical study. *Information systems research, 1*(3), 255-276.

Strauss, J., & Rogerson, K. (2002). Policies for Online Privacy in the United States and the European Union. *Telematics and Informatics, 19*(2), 173-192.

Strong, D., Lee, Y., & Wang, R. (1997). Data Quality in context. *Communications of the ACM, 40*(5), 103-110.

Strongin, G. (2005). Trusted computing using AMD Pacifica and Presidio secure virtual machine technology. *Information Security Technical Report, 10,* 120-132.

Suh, B., & Han, I. (2003). The impact of customer trust and perception of security control on the acceptance of electronic commerce. *International Journal of Electronic Commerce, 7(*3), 135-161.

Sun Microsystems. (2008). *File Security Features.* Retrieved July 20, 2008 from http://docs.sun.com/app/docs/doc/806-4078/6jd6cjs2o?a=view

Sutton, M., & Nagle, F. (2006). *Emerging economic models for vulnerability research.* Paper presented at the The Fifth Workshop on the Economics of Information Security (WEIS), Robinson College, University of Cambridge, England.

Swanson, A. (2005). *Most ID theft begins at home.* United Press International, January, 1-4.

Swanson, M., Wohl, A., Pope, L., Grance, T., Hash, J., & Thomas, R. (2002). *Contingency Planning Guide for Information Technology Systems.* Washington: National Institute of Standards and Technology

Swire, P. P., & Litan, R. E. (1998). *None of Your Business: World Data Flows, Electronic Commerce, and the European Privacy Directive.* Washington: Brookings Institution Press.

Symantec. (2008). *Symantec Global Internet Threat Report: Trend for July - Dec 07,* [Electronic Version]. Retrieved January, from http://eval.symantec.com/mktginfo/enterprise/white_papers/b-whitepaper_internet_security_threat_report_xiii_04-2008.en-us.pdf

Taipan & Tiger (2005). In the shadow of the swords. *Rendezvous – Journal of the Australian Special Air Service Association, 30,* 14-16.

Tasker, P. S. (1981, April). *Trusted Computer Systems.* Paper presented at the IEEE Symposium on Security and Privacy, Oakland, CA.

Taylor, F. W. (1929). *Principles of Scientific Management.* New York: Harper & Row.

Temkin, B. (2002). *The Recovery Update: Coming Of the Bottom.* Forrester Research, March.

The Economist. (2008, February 5). Internet, Sex and shopping, *Economist.com,* Retrieved February 5, 2008, from www.economist.com/daily/chartgallery/Printer-Friendly.cfm?story_id=10637431.

The Fraud Advisory Panel. (2003). *Identity theft: do you know the signs*? A guide for businesses and individuals. The Fraud Advisory Panel, July, 1-26.

The National Strategy to Secure Cyberspace Strategy to secure Cyberspace (2003, February). Retrieved May 14, 2008 from http://www.whitehouse.gov/pcipb/

The Radicati Group, Inc. (2005, March). Taming the Growth of E-mail - An ROI Analysis. Palo Alto, CA, USA: The Radicati Group, Inc.

The White House (2003). *The National Strategy to Secure Cyberspace*. February 2003, available from http://www.whitehouse.gov/pcipb/, April 2, 2008.

Theoaridou, M., Kokolakis, S., Karyda, M., & Kiountouzis, E. (2005). The insider threat to information systems and the effectiveness of ISO 17799. *Computers & Security, 24*, 472-484.

Theoharidou, M., & Gritazalis, D. (2007). Common Body of Knowledge for Information Security. *IEEE Security & Privacy, 5*(2), 6.

Theoharidou, M., Kokolakis, S., Karyda, M., & Kiountouzis, E. (2005). The Insider Threat to Information Systems and the Effectiveness of ISO17799. *Computers and Security, 24*, 472-484.

Thibadeau, R. (2006). Trusted computing for disk drives and other peripherals. *IEEE Security and Privacy, 4*(1), 26-33.

Thomas, B., Ang, C. B., Parbati Ray, & Nof, S. Y. (2001). *Information assurance in Networked Enterprises: Definition, Requirements, and Experimental Results*. CERIAS Tech Report 2001-34.

Thompson, J. D. (1967). *Organizations in Action*. New York, McGraw-Hill.

Thompson, R. L., Higgins, C. A., & Howell, J. M. (1991). Personal Computing: Toward a Conceptual Model of Utilization. *MIS Quarterly, 15*(1), 124-143.

Thompson, W. J. (2002). *One Year Later: The fiscal impact of 9/11 on New York city*. Comptroller, City of New York.

Thong, J. Y. L, Yap, C. S., & Raman, K. S. (1996). Top management support, external expertise and information systems implementation in small businesses. *Information systems research, 7*(2), 248-267.

Thurrott, P. (2004). Windows Server 2003 R2 FAQ. Retrieved July 20, 2008 from http://www.winsupersite.com/faq/win2003_r2.asp

Tittel, E. (2008). Certified Information Systems Security Professional. *SearchSecurity.com and Information Security Magazine.* March 31, 2008. Retrieved June 10, 2008 from www.searchsecurity.techtarget.com

Tomhave, B. L. (2005). *Alphabet soup: making sense of models, frameworks and methodologies*. Working paper, august, George Washington University.

Trends in Proprietary Information Loss: Survey Report, August 2007. Sponsored by Sponsored by National Counterintelligence Executive and American Society of Industrial Security (ASIS) Foundation. Retrieved on April 3, 2008 from http://www.asisonline.org/newsroom/surveys/spi2.pdf.

Trice, H. (1993). *Occupational Subcultures in the Workplace*. Ithaca, NY: ILR Press.

Tripathi, A. K., & Nair, S. K. (2007). Narrowcasting of wireless advertising in malls. *European Journal of Operational Research, 182,* 1023–1038.

Tripathi, A. K., & Suresh, K. N.(2006). Mobile Advertising in Capacitated Wireless Networks. *IEEE Transactions On Knowledge And Data Engineering, 18*(9), 1284–1296.

Trompenaars, F., & Hampden-Turner, C. (1998). *Riding the Waves of Culture, Understanding Diversity in Global Business.* New York: McGraw-Hill.

Truscott, J. (2004). *Beyond bin Laden Thinking – The Security Dividend*. 2004 Australian Homeland Security Conference in Sydney: 1-8.

Trusted Computing Group (2005, July). *TCG Newsletter, 1(3)*. Retrieved July 31, 2008, from https://www.trusted-computinggroup.org/news/newsletter/2005/2005_July/

Trusted Computing Group (2006, January 11). *TCG Software Stack (TSS) Specification Version 1.2*. Retrieved July 31, 2008, from https://www.trustedcomputinggroup.org/specs/TSS/TSS_Version_1.2_Level_1_FINAL.pdf

Trusted Computing Group (2008a). *TCG Glossary of Technical Terms*. Retrieved July 31, 2008, from https://www.trustedcomputinggroup.org/groups/glossary/

Trusted Computing Group (2008b, April 28th). *Trusted Network Connect (TNC) Expands NAC Architecture with Extensions into Network Security, More Products and Proven Interoperability*. Retrieved July 31, 2008, from https://www.trustedcomputinggroup.org/news/events/interop_2008/interop_if_map_tnc_release_april_23_final.pdf

Trusted Computing Group, (2007a, May). *Trusted Network Connect Frequently Asked Questions*. Retrieved July 31, 2008, from https://www.trustedcomputinggroup.org/faq/TNCFAQ/

Trusted Computing Group, (2007b, August 2nd). *TCG Specification Architecture Overview*. Retrieved July 31, 2008, from https://www.trustedcomputinggroup.org/groups/TCG_1_4_Architecture_Overview.pdf

Trusted Computing Platform Alliance. (2000, August). TCPA security and Internet business: Vital issues for IT. Originally retrieved from Trusted Computing Platform Alliance Web site, no longer available. On file with the author.

Turban, E., Lee, J., King, D., & Chung, H. M. (2000). *Electronic Commerce – A Managerial Perspective*. Upper Saddle River, NJ: Prentice Hall PTR.

Turner, H. (2000). Evaluating Seaport Policy Alternatives: A Simulation Study of Terminal Leasing Policy and System Performance. *Maritime Policy and Management, 27*(3), 283-301.

Turnquist, M. A. & Daskin, M. S. (1982). Queuing Models of Classification and Connection Delay in Railyards. *Transportation Science, 16*, 207-230.

Turvey, B. (1999). *Criminal Profiling: An Introduction to Behavioral Evidence Analysis*. London: Academic Press.

U.S. Const. amend. I (1791).

U.S. Const. amend. IV (1791).

U.S. Const. amend. XIV (1868).

U.S. Department of Defense. (1985). *Department of Defense Trusted Computing System Evaluation Criteria*. Retrieved July 31, 2008, from http://csrc.nist.gov/publications/history/dod85.pdf

U.S. Department of Defense. (2007, July). *Encryption of Sensitive Unclassified Data at Rest on Mobile Computing Devices and Removable Storage Media*. Retrieved July 31, 2008, from http://iase.disa.mil/policy-guidance/DoD-dar-tpm-decree07-03-07.pdf

U.S. Department of Energy (2006). *Workforce Trends in the Electric Utility Industry*, Report to Congress under Section 1101 of the Energy Policy Act of 2005, Washington, DC.

U.S. Department of Homeland Security (2006), *National Infrastructure Protection Plan*, retrieved on March 20, 2008 from http://www.dhs.gov/xlibrary/assets/NIPP_Plan.pdf .

U.S. Department of Transportation (2006). *Vessel Calls at U.S. Ports 2005*, Maritime Administration, Washington, DC.

U.S. Department of Transportation (2007), *Vessel Movement Files for 2005*, Maritime Administration, Washington DC.

UCSF IT Network Architecture & Security: About us.(2008). Retrieved May 14, 2008 from http://itnas.ucsfmedicalcenter.org/about_us/

UK Home Office. (2006). *Updated estimate of the cost of identity fraud to the UK economy*. 2 February, 1-4. Retrieved March 7, 2008, from http://www.identity-theft.org.uk/ID%20fraud%20table.pdf.

United Nations. (2004). *Report on UNCITRAL Colloquium on International Commercial Fraud*. United Nations

Commission on International Trade Law, Thirty-seventh session New York, 14 June-2 July, 1-17. Retrieved April 8, 2008, from http://daccessdds.un.org/doc/UNDOC/GEN/V04/539/85/PDF/V0453985.pdf?OpenElement.

United States Government Accountability Office (GAO). (2007). *Cybercrime: Public and Private Entities Face Challenges in Addressing Cyber Threats.* United States Government Accountability Office, Washington, D.C. June, 705, (pp. 1-59).

United States v. Carroll Towing Co., 159 F.2d 169, 173 (2d Cir.1947).

United States-Canada Working Group. (1997). *United States-Canada Cooperation Against Telemarketing Fraud.* November, 1-28. Retrieved April 8, 2008, from http://www.justice.gov/criminal/fraud/docs/reports/1997/uscwgrtf.htm.

Uniting and Strengthening America by Providing Appropriate Tools Required to Intercept and Obstruct Terrorism Act of 2001 (USA PATRIOT Act) Pub. L. 107-56 (2001).

University of Minnesota Office of Information Technology Home Page. (2008). Retrieved May 14, 2008 from http://www1.umn.edu/oit/security/incident/OIT__12654_REGION1.html

UPI Energy, (4 February 2008). DoD weighing ban on personal Internet Use, UPI Energy, Retrieved 21 March 2008 from LEXIS (search term: "personal internet use w/10 workplace").

USAF 2-5, (2005, January 11). *Air Force Doctrine Document 2-5, Information Operations.* United States Air Force.

US-CERT Quarterly Trend Analysis: Cyber Security Trends, Metrics, and Security Indicators. (2007, December). Retrieved May 14, 2008 from http://www.us-cert.gov/press_room/trendsanalysisQ407.pdf

US-CERT: United States Computer Emergency Readiness Team. (2008). Retrieved May 14, 2008 from http://www.us-cert.gov/

USDOJ (2008). *Computer Intrusion Cases.* United States Department of Justice, Computer Crime and Intellectual Property Section. Retrieved on February 3, 2008 from http://www.usdoj.gov/criminal/cybercrime/cccases.html.

USDOJ/OIG (2003). *A Review of the FBI's Performance in Deterring, Detecting, and Investigating the Espionage Activities of Robert Philip Hanssen.* United States Department of Justice: Office of the Inspector General. Retrieved 12 February 2008 from http://www.usdoj.gov/oig/special/0308/index.htm.

Van Doorn, L. (2007, November). *Trusted computing challenges.* Session: Invited talk at the Proceedings of the 2007 ACM workshop on Scalable Trusted Computing, Alexandria, VA.

Van Winkle, W. (n.d.). Information Overload. Global *Development Research Center,* Retrieved March 13, 2008, from http://www.gdrc.org/icts/i-overload/infoload.html.

Varian, H. R. (Ed). (2000). *Internet publishing & beyond: the economics of digital information & intellectual....* Cambridge, MA, USA: MIT Press.

Vasiu, L. (2004). A Conceptual Framework of E-Fraud Control in an Integrated Supply Chain. *Proceedings of the 12th European Conference on Information Systems, Turku School of Economics and Business Administration,* Finland.

Veitch, M. (1997, December 8). Data Overload Causing Addiction-Reuters, *ZDNet,* Retrieved March 12, 2008, from http://news.zdnet.co.uk/internet/0,1000000097,2067297,00.htm.

Venkatesh, V., Morris, M. G., Davis, G. B., & Davis, F. D. (2003). User acceptance of information technology: Toward a unified view. *MIS Quarterly, 27*(3), 425-478.

Vermeulen, C., & von Solms, R. (2002). The information security management toolbox: Taking the pain out of security management. *Information management & Computer Security, 10*(3), 119-125.

Vivanco, L. (2007, November 12). Masters of multitasking; Doing multiple tasks at once has become second nature for some, but is that a good thing? *Chicago Tribune, RedEye Edition,* 6 von Solms, B. (2000). Information security- The third wave? *Computers & Security, 19*(7), 615-620.

von Solms, B. (2006). Information security – The fourth wave. *Computers and Security, 5*(3), 165-168.

von Solms, B., & von Solms, R. (2001). Incremental information security certification. *Computers & Security, 20*(4), 308-310.

von Solms, R. (1988). Information security management (1): why information security is so important. *Information management & Computer Security, 6*(4), 174-177.

von Solms, R., & Van de Haar, H. (2000). From Trusted Information Security Controls to a Trusted Information Security Environment. *Proceedings of the 16th Annual Working Conference on Information Security*, IFIP, August, Beijing, China, contribution n°4/52.

von Solms, R., & von Solms, B. (2006). Information security governance: Due care. *Computers & Security, 25*(7), 494-497.

Vroom, C., & von Solms, R. (2004). Towards information security behavioural compliance. *Computers & Security, 23*, 191-198.

Wack, J. P. (1991). *Establishing a computer security incident response capability.* Gaithersburg, Md: US National Institute of Standards and Technology.

Wailgum, T. (2008, January 4). Information Overload is Killing You and Your Productivity, *CIO.com*, Retrieved February 5, 2008, from www.cio.com: www.cio.com/article/print/169200.

Walker, S. T. (1985, April). *Network security overview.* Paper presented at the IEEE Symposium on Security and Privacy, Oakland, CA.

Waltz, E. (1998). *Information Warfare: Principles and Operations.* Norwood: Artech House.

Wang, G., Chen, H., & Aatabakhsh, H. (2004). Criminal Identity Deception and Deception Detection in Law Enforcement. *Group Decision and Negotiation,* (13), 111–127, Kluwer Academic Publishers, Netherlands.

Wang, L., Noel, S., & Jajodia, S. (2006). Minimum-cost network hardening using attack graphs. *Computer Communications, 29*(18), 3812-3824.

Ware, W. H. (1967). Security and privacy in computer systems. *AFIPS Conference Proceeding, Spring Joint Computer Conference,* Vol. 30 (pp. 279-282). Thompson Books.

Ware, W.H. (1970). Security Controls for Computer Systems (U): Report of Defense Science Board Task Force on Computer Security. Santa Monica, CA: The RAND Corporation. Retrieved July 31, 2008, from http://csrc.nist.gov/publications/history/ware70.pdf

Warman, A. R. (1992). Organizational computer security policy: The reality. *European journal of information systems, 1*(5), 305-310.

Warren, Samuel & Louis Brandeis (1890). The Right to Privacy. *Harvard Law Review, 4*(5).

Webb, K. G. (2007). *Information Terrorism in the New Security Environment.* Paper presented at the 2nd International Conference on I-War and Security on 4-5 March 2007 at the Naval Postgraduate School, Monterey California, USA.

Webb, K. G. (2007a). *Managing Asymmetric Threats to National Security – Terrorist Information Operations.* Unpublished Interdisciplinary Doctoral Dissertation, Perth, Western Australia: Edith Cowan University.

Weber, R. P. (1990). *Basic Content analysis* (2nd ed.). Newbury Park, CA.

Websense, Inc. (2006). Web@work 2006 Employee Computing Trends Surve, *Websense.com,* Retrieved from www.websense.com/global/en/PressRoom/MediaCenter/Research/webatwork/Employee Computing.php.

Weick, K. E., Sutliffe, K, & Ostfeld, D. (1993). Collective Mind in Organizations. *Administrative Science Quarterly,* 357-381.

Weil, M. M. (1997). *TechnoStress.* John Wiley & Sons.

Weil, M. M., & Rozen, L. D. (2000). Four-Year Study Shows More Technology at Work and at Home But More

Hesitancy About Trying New Technology. *Human-ware. com*, Retrieved 12 December 2007 from http://www. human-ware.com/BusinessStudy.htm.

Weiland, S. (2006, December 21). *Deployment of German Planes to Afghanistan Sharply Criticized.* Retrieved July 11, 2008, from LEXIS (search term: "mission creep").

Weissman, C. (1969). Security controls in the ADEPT-50 time-sharing system. Proceedings of the 1969 Fall Joint Computer Conference. Reprinted in L.J. Hoffman (Ed.), *Security and Privacy in Computer Systems (pp. 216-243).* Los Angeles: Melville Publishing Company, 1973.

Welding, P. I. (1957). The Instability of Close Interval Service. *Operational Research Quarterly, 8,* 133-148.

Westin, A. F. (2000). *Public Records and the Responsible Use of Information.* Interpretive Essay. Alpharetta, GA: Choicepoint.

Wheatley, M. J. (1992). *Leadership and the New Science, Learning about Organization from an Orderly Universe.* San Fransisco: Berrett-Koehler.

White, G. (2007). The Community Cyber Security Maturity Model. *Proceedings of the 40th Hawaii International Conference on Systems Sciences*, Waikoloa, Hawaii.

WhiteHouse (2006). *The Federal Response to Hurricane Katrina: Lessons Learned.* Washington, D.C.: White House Report on Katrina,.

Whiteley, A. (1995). *Managing Change, A Core Values Approach.* South Melbourne: MacMillan Education.

Wiander, T. (2007). Implementing the ISO/IEC 17799 standard in practice - Findings from small and medium sized software organizations. *Proceedings of the 5th international conference on Standardization, Innovation and Information Technology* (SIIT 2007). 17-19 October, Calgary, Canada.

Wiley, D. A. (2005). Connecting learning objects to instructional design theory: A definition, a metaphor, and a taxonomy. In D. A. Wiley (Ed.), *The instructional use of learning objects.* Retrieved 2 - 17 - 2005 from: http://reusability.org/read/chapters/wiley.doc

Wilhelm, W. K. (2004). The Fraud Management Lifecycle Theory: A Holistic Approach to Fraud Management. *Journal of Economic Crime Management, Spring,* 2(2), 1-38.

Wise, C. R. (2006). Organizing for homeland security after Katrina: Is adaptive management what's missing? *Public Administration Review, 66,* 302-318.

Wise, D. (1995). *Nightmover: How Aldrich Ames Sold the CIA to the KGB.* New York: Harper-Collins, 1995.

Wood, C. C. (1999). *Information Security Policies Made Easy.* Baseline Software, San Rafael, CA.

World Health Organization (2008). "H5N1 Avian Influenza: Timeline of Major Events," retrieved September 7, 2008 from http://www.who.int/csr/disease/avian_influenza/Timeline_08_08_20.pdf.

Yates, L. A. (1997, August). Military stability and support operations: analogies, patterns and recurring themes. *Military Review,* (pp. 51-62). Retrieved July 13, 2008, from EBSCO: web.ebscohost.com (search term: "mission creep").

Zhen, J. (2005). *The war on leaked intellectual property.* Retrieved February 11, 2008, from http://www. computerworld.com/securitytopics/security/story/0,10801,98724,00.html.

Zhuge, J., Holz, T., Song, C., Guo, J., Han, X., & Zou, W. (2007). *Studying malicious websites and the underground economy on the Chinese website* [Electronic Version]. Honeyblog. Retrieved February 25, 2008, from http://honeyblog.org/archives/2007/12/summary.html

Zohar, D. (1990). *The Quantum Self, Human Nature and Consciousness Defined by the New Physics.* New York: William Morrow & Co.

Zohar, D. (1997). *Rewiring the Corporate Brain, Using the New Science to Rethink How We Structure and Lead Organizations.* San Francisco: Berrett-Koehler.

Zucker, L. G. (1986). Production of trust: Institution sources of economic structure. In B. M. Staw & L. L. Cummings (Eds.), *Research in Organizational Behavior* (pp. 1840-1920). Greenwich, CT: JAI Press.

About the Contributors

Kenneth J. Knapp is the deputy head of the Department of Management at the U.S. Air Force Academy, Colorado. He has over 20 years of experience working with information technology and security in the U. S. Air Force. He earned a bachelor's of science in computer science from DeSales University in Pennsylvania, an MBA from Auburn University at Montgomery and a PhD in the management of information technology from Auburn University, Alabama. Dr. Knapp has published in outlets such as the *International Journal of Information Security & Privacy, Information Management & Computer Security, Communications of the Association for Information Systems, Information Systems Management, Information Systems Security*, and the *Journal of Digital Forensics, Security and Law*. His research has also appeared in numerous chapter books such as the *Information Security Management Handbook*, 2007 and 2008 editions, edited by Hal Tipton and Micki Krause. He has presented his research at numerous conferences to include annual RSA conferences. Dr. Knapp's research results have appeared in online media outlets such as CIO, CSO, Networkworld and Computerworld and he has won numerous research and teaching awards. He recently accepted a tenure-track position in the Information and Technology Management Department at The University of Tampa, Florida.

* * *

Carole C. Angolano is an information technology specialist/LAN manager and information assurance officer at the Department of Defense. She has over 30 years of work experience managing multiple networks and technical quality assurance/information assurance for integrated networks. She is responsible for the development of plans, policies, technical standards, procedures, and WAN security. She holds a degree in computer science and business administration, an MBA, and is a doctoral candidate in business administration at TUI University.

John W. Bagby is professor and co-director of the Institute for Information Policy in the College of Information Sciences and Technology at the Pennsylvania State University. He is sole or co-author of articles in journals and chapters in collective works addressing issues in law, regulation, economics, business, information sciences and technology, and engineering. His interdisciplinary research has been sponsored by various state and federal agencies covering projects on tort and product liability reform, tort data management, technology transfer, intellectual property, information science, security and privacy, open source, and intelligent transportation systems. He is co-author of numerous college texts and has served as special editor for the *American Business Law Journal*'s 2003 Cyberlaw issue. He was a Visiting Fellow at the Intelligent Transportation Society of America, a Visiting Scholar/Professor at the McCombs School: University of Texas-Austin, chaired the ITSAm Legal Issues Committee and the ABA's Task Force on 'Bots (database protections).

Yves Barlette has been an associate professor of information systems in GSCM Montpellier Business School since 1989. He is the head of "IT salesmen and project managers" elective within the framework of a joint master with Montpellier University. He received his Ph.D. degree in management information systems from Montpellier University, France. His research focuses on information systems security and more precisely organizations' actors' security behaviors. He presented a paper related to information security standards for HICSS-41 (2008) and has served as a reviewer for International Conference on Information Systems (ICIS).

Nikolaos Bekatoros is a Lieutenant Junior Grade in the Greek Navy and is currently a PhD student at the Naval Postgraduate School, Department of Information Sciences. His research interests are in team collaboration and decision support systems. He has served for a series of years in various types of ships and commands in the Greek Navy and participated in many multinational exercises and operations.

Somak Bhattacharya, born at West Bengal, India is presently pursuing MS in information technology from School of Information Technology, Indian Institute of Technology (IIT), Kharagpur, India. Prior to his MS, he completed his bachelor's degree from Vidyasagar University, West Bengal, India. His research interests include network and system security.

Alanah Davis is a PhD candidate in the College of Information Science and Technology at the University of Nebraska at Omaha. She holds a master's degree in e-commerce from Creighton University and a bachelor's degree in both computer information systems and marketing from Simpson College. Her research interests include virtual and face-to-face collaboration as well as e-commerce. Her work has been published in *DataBase, Electronic Markets, Journal of Information System Security,* and *American Journal of Business.*

Gert-Jan de Vreede is Kayser distinguished professor at the Department of Information Systems & Quantitative Analysis at the University of Nebraska at Omaha where he is director of the institute for collaboration science. His research focuses on collaboration engineering, field applications of e-collaboration technologies, and the diffusion of collaboration technology. His articles have appeared in journals such as *Journal of Management Information Systems, Journal of the AIS, Communications of the ACM, Small Group Research, DataBase, Group Decision and Negotiation, Journal of Creativity and Innovation Management, International Journal of Technology and Management, Simulation & Gaming, Simulation,* and *Journal of Simulation Practice and Theory.*

Vladislav V. Fomin is associate professor at the faculty of informatics at the Vytautas Magnus University in Kaunas, Lithuania and Visiting Research Fellow at Rotterdam School of Management, Erasmus University in Rotterdam, The Netherlands. His prior positions included associate professor at Montpellier Business School in France (2007), research scientist at the Faculty of Policy, Technology and Management, Delft University of Technology (2006), assistant professor at the department of Informatics, Copenhagen Business School (2004-6), and visiting assistant professor at the School of Information at the University of Michigan (2001-3). Current research interests include standard making processes in the field of information and communication technologies (ICT) and studies of ICT infrastructure development and design.

Allison S. Gehrke is a PhD candidate in computer science from the Department of Computer Science and Engineering at the University of Colorado, Denver. Her research interests include studying how living organisms solve problems and apply those principles in computational methods to solve a wide variety of engineering problems. One of her goals is to design smart engineering solutions that can eventually be transferred into practice. She has one peer-reviewed publication in controlling vulnerabilities in security APIs using a neural network and she is a scholarship recipient from the Society of Women Engineers.

S. K. Ghosh is presently working as assistant professor in the School of Information Technology, Indian Institute of Technology (IIT), Kharagpur, India. He has received PhD degree in computer science & engineering from Department of Computer Science & Engineering, IIT Kharagpur, India. Prior to IIT Kharagpur, he worked for Indian Space Research Organization (ISRO), Department of Space, Government of India, in the field of satellite remote sensing and geographical information system. His research interest includes network security and geospatial database.

Jose J. Gonzalez was born in Spain and received a PhD from the University of Kiel and a PhD from the Norwegian University of Science and Technology. His carrier began in the fields of physics and biophysics with articles in quantum physics, statistical mechanics, critical phenomena and polymer science. Since 1984, he shifted to information science. Starting with system dynamics models of epidemiology, he developed interactive learning environments (ILE's) for prevention of epidemics, and worked on design and evaluation of simulation-based ILE's, instructional design and organizational learning. Since his appointment to the chair of system dynamics at the University of Agder (1999) the research cell (security and quality in organizations) led by Dr Gonzalez focused on security in organizations, critical infrastructure, security culture, organizational learning and security as quality process in organizations. Dr. Gonzalez has business experience as co-founder of Powersim (www.powersim.com).

Richard T. Gordon has a PhD in physics and is a specialist in time-series analysis and the limits of predictability of systems. He has over 20 peer-reviewed research publications including work on cyber security, intelligent systems and encryption. Richard has been quoted or profiled in *Scientific American*, *Fortune Magazine*, *The Scientist* and *The Journal of Commerce*. One of the principals in developing the models used by the financial industry to determine risk and exposure from catastrophes, Dr. Gordon is currently funded by the Risk Foundation to conduct original research on the uncertainty in the prediction of physical systems.

Michael R. Grimaila (CISM, CISSP, NSA IAM/IEM) is an associate professor of information resource management and a member of the Center for Cyberspace Research at the Air Force Institute of Technology. He received a BS and MS degree in electrical engineering, and a PhD in computer engineering at Texas A&M University. He teaches and conducts research in the areas of computer security, information assurance, information operations and warfare, insider threat detection, and mission impact assessment. Dr. Grimaila currently serves on the editorial board of the Information System Security Association (ISSA) Journal and is a member of the Department of Defense Information Assurance

Program (DIAP) Information Assurance Best Practices Group. He is a contributor to the ISO/IEC CD 27004 Security Metrics Standard. He is a member of the ACM, AIS, IRMA, ISACA, ISC2, ISSA, IS-SEA, and is a senior member of the IEEE.

Indira R. Guzman, PhD is a coordinating assistant professor of business administration and information systems and TUI University in Cypress, California, and senior research associate of the NSF funded Information Technology Workforce project at Syracuse University. Her business and teaching experience in the IT field include more than 15 years of work as a network administrator, IT manager, academic and consultant. She received both her PhD in information science and technology and a MS in information management from Syracuse University, and a BS and MS in computer science from Donetsk National Technical University, Ukraine. Her research focuses mostly on human resources in IT, specifically the IT occupational culture, diversity, recruitment and retention in the profession. Her work has been published in journals such as the *ACM DATA BASE for Advances in Information Systems, Human Resource Management, Women's Studies*, and the *Journal of Digital Information*.

Shaveta Hans is a business analyst responsible for analyzing the business needs of her clients to help identify business problems and propose solutions. In the academic area, she holds a MS in information Technology Management from TUI University as well as an MBA with specialized areas of international business and human resource management from the Institute of Management studies and Research (IMSAR) from MDU, India.

Miguel José Hernández y López is a graduate of the School of Business (Unidad Académica Multidisciplinaria de Comercio y Administración – Victoria) at the Universidad Autónoma de Tamaulipas, in Ciudad Victoria, Mexico. Founding member of the Mexican Honeynet Project, he has been a keynote speaker in several information security and open source software events in Mexico and abroad, including a notable participation in the 6th Convention on Open Source Software of the Universidad de Mendoza in Mendoza, Argentina.

Mark L. Huson, CISSP, serves as a senior information security instructor for the Center for Infrastructure Assurance and Security at The University of Texas at San Antonio. He has been involved in computer and network security and system administration since 1986. He served nearly 23 years in the United States Air Force, including a wide range of computer and information technology intensive assignments. He earned his PhD in computer science in 1995 from Arizona State University. His dissertation concentrated on the area of computational complexity and graph coloring. In addition, he has conducted research and published papers in a wide variety of areas including parallel computation, simulation, and computer and network security. He is active in computer and network security research.

Rodger Jamieson is a visiting professor in the School of Information Systems, Technology and Management, University of New South Wales. He holds a PhD as well as honours degrees at both bachelor's and master's of commerce degree level from the University of New South Wales, is a qualified chartered accountant, member of the Australian Computer Society, a former member of the Information Systems Audit & Control Association (USA) serving on their International Academic Liaison Committee. Rodger is co-director of the Security E-Business Assurance Research Group (SEAR) at UNSW. SEAR conducts management and technical research on a range of security, audit, and assurance issues especially in the e-commerce domain. He researches and publishes in the areas of information systems security, audit and assurance with specific emphasis on ecommerce and identity fraud, and disseminates his work in international journals and referred conference proceedings.

Dean A. Jones is a distinguished member of technical staff at Sandia National Laboratories and leader of Sandia's Operations Research and Computational Analysis (ORCA) team. He holds a master's degree in applied mathematics from the University of New Mexico, and has had long experience as both an analyst and project leader on infrastructure and security-related projects for the U.S. Department of Energy and the U.S. Department of Homeland Security. He currently has responsibilities for projects related to the nuclear weapons complex and for modeling work related to national critical infrastructure.

Jack L. Koons III is a Major in the U.S. Army and is currently a PhD student at the Naval Post-graduate School, Department of Information Sciences. Major Koons' current research focuses on how to identify, pattern and disrupt dynamic information and knowledge flows of networked organizations as seen through the larger network-centric operational framework. A U.S. Army Advanced Civil Schooling student, Major Koons has multiple operational tours to include Iraq and Afghanistan in conventional, intelligence, and special operations units as well as tours at the National Security Agency.

JinKyu Lee is an assistant professor of management science and information systems in Spears School of Business, Oklahoma State University. He holds a PhD (2007) in MIS from School of Management, University at Buffalo, master's of information systems (1999) from Griffith University, Australia, and BBA (1996) from Yonsei University, Korea. His current research interest includes development and use of information & communication technologies (ICT) for public/commercial services, information assurance, inter-organizational information sharing, and information security workforce development. He has published research articles in various academic journals and conferences including DSS, CACM, IEEE, ICIS, HICSS, and AMCIS, and has served as a co-guest editor or associate editor for special issues for leading journals including *MISQ* and *Information Systems Frontiers*. He has also been involved in several NSF, NSA, and DoD funded research/educational projects in e-government and information assurance areas.

Carlos Francisco Lerma Reséndez, MSc, is a service engineer heading the area of IT monitoring at the Directorate of Information Technology and Telecommunications (Dirección de Informática y Telecomunicaciones), a service branch of the General Directorate of Technological Innovation (Dirección General de Innovación Tecnológica) at Universidad Autónoma de Tamaulipas in Ciudad Victoria, Mexico. He graduated with a bachelor's degree in public accounting from the School of Business (Unidad Académica Multidisciplinaria de Comercio y Administración – Victoria) at Universidad Autónoma de Tamaulipas and holds a master's of science in telecommunications and network management from Syracuse University in Syracuse, New York.

Samresh Malhotra has completed his post graduation (M.Tech) in information technology from School of Information Technology, Indian Institute of Technology (IIT), Kharagpur, India. Prior to his M.Tech, he completed his bachelor's degree in engineering from Jawaharlal Nehru University where he stood first on the course and also received the Gold Medal for being the best student. He has published couple of research papers in the proceedings of international conferences. His main area of research includes network and system security.

Peter Marksteiner holds an LL.M. in labor and employment law from The Georgetown University Law Center. He has extensive and diverse experience in numerous legal specialties, with a major focus on the law and policy of leading and managing human resources in large organizations. His administrative and judicial litigation experience includes criminal prosecution and defense, and representing the Air Force in federal sector labor & employment, and state workers compensation cases. As the director of legal information services for the judge advocate general's corps, he leads the organization responsible for developing, fielding, and maintaining legal research and knowledge management tools for the USAF's 4600-member legal workforce.

Robert F. Mills is an assistant professor of electrical engineering and a member of the Center for Cyberspace Research at the Air Force Institute of Technology (AFIT), Wright-Patterson AFB OH. He received a BSEE degree from Montana State University, an MSEE degree from AFIT, and a PhD in electrical engineering from the University of Kansas. He teaches and conducts research in communication systems, information warfare, network security, insider threat, and systems engineering. Dr. Mills is a member of Eta Kappa Nu and Tau Beta Pi and is a senior member of IEEE.

Mark Nissen is OASD-NII research chair professor of command & control, and professor of information science and management, at the Naval Postgraduate School. His research focuses on dynamic knowledge and organization for competitive advantage. He views work, technology and organization as an integrated design problem, and has concentrated recently on the design of military organizations for specific mission-environmental contexts. Mark's publications span information systems, project management, organization studies, knowledge management, counterterrorism, command and control, and related fields. In 2000, he received the Menneken Faculty Award for Excellence in Scientific Research, the top research award available to faculty at the Naval Postgraduate School. In 2001, he received a prestigious Young Investigator Grant Award from the Office of Naval Research for work on knowledge-flow theory. In 2002 – 2003 he was visiting professor at Stanford, integrating knowledge-flow theory into agent-based tools for computational modeling. In 2004, he established the Center for Edge Power for multi-university, multidisciplinary research on what the Military terms command & control. Before his information systems doctoral work at the University of Southern California, he acquired over a dozen years' management experience in the aerospace and electronics industries.

Linda K. Nozick is a professor of civil & environmental engineering at Cornell University. She holds a PhD in systems engineering from the University of Pennsylvania, and has been on the faculty at Cornell since 1992. Prof. Nozick specializes in the modeling and analysis of complex systems where uncertainty plays a major role and has worked in areas ranging from defense to product distribution to medical care. She was a winner of a Presidential Early Career Award in Science and Engineering, and has particular interests in infrastructure vulnerability and security.

Insu Park is currently a PhD candidate in management science and systems, School of Management at the State University of New York at Buffalo. His research interests are information security, information privacy, behavioral and economic decision making in the online context.

Gilbert "Bert" Peterson is an assistant professor of computer engineering and a member of the Center for Cyberspace Research at the Air Force Institute of Technology. Dr. Peterson received a BS degree in Architecture, and an MS and PhD in computer science at the University of Texas at Arlington. He teaches and conducts research in digital forensics, insider threat, and artificial intelligence.

Leah R. Pietron, associate professor of information systems, holds a PhD and MS degree from the University of North Dakota; a MBA from Northwest Missouri State University, and BS from Mayville State College. In addition, she has done post-doctoral work at the University of Minnesota and Indiana University. Dr. Pietron's work experience include consulting projects on security policy, cyber defend workshops, security assessments, Sarbanes-Oxley, and ISO 17799 accreditation. Her publications and presentations include information systems development pedagogy, assessment and evaluation, vulnerability assessment methodology, collaboration science, and information assurance and systems development distance education. Her work has been published in *Journal of Information System Security and Journal of Information Systems Education.*

Jaziar Radianti was born in Indonesia. She finished her master's degree from Bandung Institute of Technology in 2000. She joined the "Security and Quality in Organization" Research group at the University of Agder in Grimstad, Norway in 2005 as a PhD fellow. The research group is employing a system dynamics approach to security issues. During her studies in Norway, she has developed an interest in an economic perspective to tackling the software vulnerability problem, and the emerging issue of the vulnerability black markets. Some papers relating to system dynamics modeling and the vulnerability black market have been published in international conferences and workshops. Jaziar is expecting to finish her PhD in 2009.

H. Raghav Rao is a professor at the Management Science and Systems department in the School of Management and an adjunct professor at the Computer Science and Engineering department, University at Buffalo, NY. He holds PhD (1987) degree from Krannert Graduate School, Purdue University, M.B.A. (1981) from University of Delhi, India, and B. Tech.(1979) from Indian Institute of Technology, India. His research interest includes information and decision theory, e-government and e-commerce, information assurance, and economics of information, and has published over 70 refereed research articles in academic conferences and journals. He is a co-editor-in-chief of a new journal by Springer, *Information Systems Frontiers: A Journal of Research and Innovation* and an associate editor of *Decision Support Systems, Information Systems Research, IEEE Transactions on Systems, Man and Cybernetics, Part A.* He has also co-guest edited numerous special issues for leading journals including *Decision Support Systems*, the *Communications of the ACM*, the *Annals of Operations Research.*

Alan Rea is an associate professor of computer information systems at the Haworth College of Business, Western Michigan University in Kalamazoo, MI. At WMU, Alan teaches courses in programming, server administration, and information management. Alan's current research involves a combination of artificial intelligence, computing ethics, security, social engineering, and virtual reality.

William J. Sawaya is an assistant professor of engineering technology and industrial distribution at Texas A&M University. He holds a PhD in management from the University of Minnesota, and previously worked as a post-doctoral research associate at Cornell University. He has particular interests in simulation-based analyses of supply chain systems, as well as in the connections between critical infrastructure and supply chain operations.

Pranav Singh is a well rounded IT professional and is currently working as a product developer at PayPal, an eBay company located in San Jose, CA. He completed his master's degree from State University of New York at Buffalo in June 2008, with a major in management information systems. He has also worked in IBM and Qwest Software Services for two years after completing his bachelor's from computer science and engineering from National Institute of Technology, Durgapur, India. Pranav has profound interest in information technology and project management. He is Sun certified Java developer and IBM certified associate developer for Websphere.

Preeti Singh has recently completed her master's in management information systems from State University of New York at Buffalo. In the past, Preeti has worked for two years at Infosys and Qwest Software Services, Bangalore, India. She cleared prestigious IIT-JEE examination in 2001 and thus went ahead to complete her undergraduation in minerals engineering from Indian School of Mines, Dhanbad, India in 2005. She is very interested in business and data analysis and is currently pursuing her career as a product specialist at Skire Inc, a product development company based in Menlo Park, CA.

Stephen Smith, is the executive officer, emergency management operations in the Office of the Government Chief Information Officer, Department of Commerce, in the New South Wales State Government. He holds a PhD ("An Empirical Study of Information Systems Security, Understanding and Awareness in e-Government") and master's of commerce degrees from the University of New South Wales (UNSW) in Information Systems (IS) and a bachelor's of science/engineering. Stephen is a casual lecturer in IS security at the School of Information Systems, Technology, and Management, UNSW. Publications include: *Information Systems Management Journal*, *The International Journal of Knowledge*, *Culture and Change Management*, and various refereed national and international conference proceedings in IS/information technology (IT).

Kathryn R. Stam, Ph.D. is an Assistant Professor of Anthropology at the SUNY Institute of Technology in Utica, New York. She teaches anthropology and graduate courses in Information Design and Technology. In addition to the book The Visible Employee that she coauthored with IST's Jeffrey Stanton (Information Today, 2006), Dr. Stam has published in a wide range of scholarly journals including the *Journal of Digital Information*, the *Journal of Information Systems Education*, the *ACM SIGMIS Database Journal, Surveillance and Society, Social Science and Medicine*, and the *Heidelberg Journal of Religions on the Internet*. Her current research interests include virtual ethnography, the information technology profession, and e-learning.

Greg Stephens is the associate head of school and a senior lecturer in the School of Information Systems, Technology, and Management, in the Australian School of Business, University of New South Wales (UNSW). Greg earned his PhD titled "Impact of Computer-mediated Communication on Social Networks in Organisations" in 2006 from UNSW. He lectures in information systems security, and data and information management. His research involves group communications and social networks within organizations, expert systems and audit and security concerns. Greg has previously worked as an information systems professional and internal auditor. He is co-director of the Security E-Commerce

Assurance Research Group (SEAR). Greg has published in international journals, book chapters, and refereed conference proceedings.

Jeff Teo is associate professor of computer information systems at Montreat College, USA. His interests include information systems, information security and assurance, computer security, and trusted computing. His doctoral dissertation was titled *A Model of Trusted Computing in Higher Education*. Dr. Teo received funding for his research in developing information assurance curricula and in secure networks from Montreat College and Appalachian College Association. In 2006, he received a Cisco equipment grant to build a computer security lab. Dr. Teo also received funding from the Mellon Foundation for his participation in the Salzburg Global Seminar and is a 2008 Salzburg global fellow.

Mark A. Turnquist is a professor of civil & environmental engineering at Cornell University. He holds a PhD in transportation systems analysis from MIT. He taught at Northwestern University from 1975-79 and has been on the faculty at Cornell since 1979. Prof. Turnquist specializes in large-scale network-based models for use in transportation, logistics and manufacturing systems, as well as in the development of resource planning tools for use critical infrastructure security.

Ken Webb is an independent security advisor from Australia. After graduating from the Royal Military College, Dr. Webb mainly served as a qualified commissioned officer with the SAS and other special operations units. This included commanding strategic counter-terrorist, intelligence-gathering and unconventional warfare elements, where he also focused on special operations in the information warfare area. Upon leaving the military, he worked globally in the information operations field and recently completed an interdisciplinary doctoral level research project for the Government into enhancing national security from the information operations of terrorist groups. Ken was also the counter-terrorism research leader for a Government initiative aimed at identifying and fostering academic, industry and government research into safeguarding Australia. Over the past three years he has consulted with, published papers and/or chaired sessions at over 12 national security related activities around the world. His current interest is the management and collaboration of special operations, information operations, national security, organised crime and counter-terrorism.

Doug White has worked with technology and security for over 20 years. Doug currently works for Roger Williams University in the Security Assurance Studies program and also operates Secure Technology, LLC., a security consulting firm. Doug regularly consults with academic, industry, and law enforcement on forensics, security audit issues, and security infrastructure. He teaches forensics, penetration testing, C++ programming, and Linux as well as being a regular trainer for the CCE certification in forensics.

Gregory White has been involved in computer and network security since 1986. He spent 19 years with the Air Force and is currently in the Air Force Reserves assigned as a mobilization assistant to SAF/XCI in the Pentagon. He obtained his PhD in computer science from Texas A&M University in 1995. His dissertation topic was in the area of computer network intrusion detection and he continues to conduct research in this area today. He serves as the director of the Center for Infrastructure Assurance and Security and is an associate professor of computer science at The University of Texas at San Antonio (UTSA). He has published extensively on the subject of computer security and is active in computer and network security research.

Donald Winchester is a research fellow in security e-commerce Assurance Research Group within the School of Information Systems, Technology and Management, University of New South Wales (UNSW). He is a PhD candidate in the Australian School of Business, UNSW and holds a BCM (Lincoln University), MBA and MBS (Massey University) all in finance. Current research interests are in information systems security, identity crime, risks in financial institutions, risk sharing in IT outsourcing by financial institutions, and international financial flows. His work has been published in international journals, book chapters, symposium (won a best paper award in 2007 – New York), and refereed conference proceedings.

Index

A

adoption 119, 125, 127, 128, 134, 136, 137, 395, 397
anger retaliatory 55
Association of American Railroads (AAR) 269
asymmetric warfare 116, 407
attacker 42, 43, 44, 372, 374
attack graph 23, 37, 45, 46, 386, 398, 407
attack surface 40, 46, 403
attestation 351, 355, 358, 360, 368, 411
auditing 49, 58, 61, 63, 66, 126, 133, 188, 195, 196, 236, 243, 244, 245, 288, 331, 334, 335, 336
autocorrelation function 77, 81, 85, 86, 88, 92
autocorrelation methodology 76, 77, 80, 82, 85, 94, 95
automated attacks 379

B

best practices 48, 50, 61, 79, 120, 121, 122, 125, 138, 165, 199, 203, 253, 311, 315, 316, 403
black market 2, 3, 4, 5, 8, 10, 12, 13, 15, 16, 19, 20, 22, 387, 409
bootstrap 90, 91, 93
bottleneck 263, 278, 285

C

centralized server model 321
climate 211, 214, 221, 227
cognitive dimension 141, 142, 144, 152, 154, 156, 157, 158
collaboration engineering 250, 251, 252, 253, 258, 259, 260, 262
community 9, 11, 16, 17, 123, 186, 197, 236, 283, 296, 303, 307, 308, 309, 310, 311, 312, 313, 314, 315, 316, 320, 344, 372
Computer Network Defense (CND) 203, 217, 389
confidentiality 294, 295, 296
congestion 266, 267, 268, 269, 273, 277, 278, 279, 304
container port operations 267
content analysis 290, 291, 292, 294, 295, 300, 414
contingency theory 201, 202, 205, 207, 214, 215, 216
control analysis 58
control recommendations 60
core root of trust measurement (CRTM) 353
culture 62, 98, 111, 115, 117, 161, 193, 384, 388, 397, 415
cyber-forensics 379

cyber security 50, 235, 266, 280, 303, 307, 308, 309, 233, 309, 308, 309, 310, 311, 312, 313, 314, 315, 316

D

daemons 322, 323, 324, 325, 326, 332
daily total times to resolve (DTTR) 77
data smog 157, 158
decentralized server model 321, 322, 323, 330
digital privacy rights management (DPRM) 179
disaster management organizations (DMO) 284
distraction 151
dummy information 380

E

e-business 251
economics of information security 20, 22, 72, 388, 396, 410, 414
electronic commerce 72, 182, 183, 367, 368, 369, 389, 398, 400, 409, 414, 416
emergency 8, 51, 70, 204, 212, 218, 237, 249, 286, 300, 301, 303, 304, 307, 311, 316, 322, 384, 388, 408, 417
emergency response 99, 285, 286, 287, 291, 293, 294, 298, 315
endorsement key (EK) 354, 355, 356
expert system 217, 385
exploit 29

F

fair information practice principles (FIPP) 167
flexible encryption 377
fog & friction 142, 143
freight transportation 265, 266, 268, 278, 279, 280
full disclosure 8, 9, 11, 21, 22, 397, 404, 411

H

Honeypot 371, 372, 373, 374, 375, 376, 377, 378, 379, 380, 381

honeytokens 68
human resources 61, 185, 266, 267, 279

I

identity keys 354, 355
impact analysis 59, 251
incident response 251, 252, 254, 257, 260, 262, 250, 262, 255, 260, 261, 262, 264, 303, 307, 308, 312, 313, 379, 395, 418
information assurance 79, 96, 165, 186, 193, 195, 198, 217, 233, 235, 283, 284, 294, 297, 298, 364, 389, 390, 412
information operations 117, 141, 142, 144, 155, 162, 163, 202, 217, 392, 400, 417, 418
information overload 146, 147, 155, 161, 163, 387, 397, 413, 417, 418
information quality dimensions 286
information security 9, 10, 20, 21, 22, 55, 70, 72, 73, 75, 76, 78, 80, 81, 82, 85, 95, 96, 97, 99, 108, 110, 111, 113, 116, 119, 120, 121, 122, 123, 124, 125, 126, 127, 128, 129, 130, 131, 132, 133, 134, 135, 136, 137, 138, 139, 140, 167, 182, 184, 186, 187, 188, 189, 190, 193, 194, 195, 196, 197, 198, 199, 200, 217, 251, 258, 284, 287, 293, 294, 297, 298, 305, 337, 349, 356, 367, 368, 369, 371, 372, 378, 380, 384, 385, 386, 387, 388, 389, 390, 393, 395, 396, 398, 399, 401, 402, 403, 404, 405, 406, 407, 408, 409, 410, 411, 412, 413, 414, 415, 417, 418, 419
information sharing 121, 284, 285, 287, 297, 300, 302, 307, 308, 283, 307, 310, 311, 312, 313, 314, 315, 316, 408, 410
information supply chain 169
information terrorism 97, 98, 101, 102, 103, 107, 108, 109, 111, 113, 114, 117, 418

information warfare 71, 97, 98, 99, 100, 101, 102, 103, 104, 106, 108, 109, 110, 111, 112, 113, 114, 117, 261, 386, 392, 394, 408, 418
insider 49, 50, 52, 53, 70, 71, 72, 73, 74, 384, 387, 388, 390, 399, 400, 401, 402, 403, 407, 409, 412, 415
insider attack 53, 58, 60, 62
insider threat 49, 53, 70, 71, 72, 73, 72, 73, 74, 384, 387, 388, 390, 399, 400, 401, 402, 403, 409, 415
integrity measurement, storage and reporting 350
intellectual property 74, 417
internal control 165
intrusion detection system 364, 372
ISO/IEC 27001 119, 123, 124, 125, 126, 129, 133, 134, 136, 137, 395, 397, 398
IT professionals 165, 180, 185, 186, 187, 188, 192, 196, 197

L

lean media 143
likelihood determination 59
linear regression 92, 93

M

malicious insider 73, 402
management 21, 45, 57, 60, 61, 62, 71, 72, 73, 74, 84, 95, 116, 117, 123, 125, 135, 136, 137, 138, 139, 146, 150, 154, 162, 169, 192, 193, 194, 196, 198, 213, 214, 217, 219, 221, 222, 225, 227, 228, 239, 241, 243, 244, 246, 247, 248, 97, 119, 181, 261, 248, 261, 281, 299, 300, 301, 302, 337, 339, 363, 365, 367, 368, 384, 385, 386, 387, 388, 389, 391, 392, 393, 394, 395, 396, 397, 398, 399, 400, 401, 402, 403, 404, 405, 406, 407, 408, 409, 410, 411, 412, 413, 414, 416, 419
Maritime Administration 276, 282, 416

Marksteiner's corrolary 156
maturity model 308, 312, 313, 314, 315
Metcalfe's Law 143, 156, 161, 162, 396, 404
misfits 201, 210, 211, 218, 222, 224, 228, 230, 406
motivation 54, 136, 391, 392

N

National Infrastructure Protection Plan 266, 279, 281, 416
national security 117, 186, 193, 198, 202, 217, 304, 338, 346, 363, 368, 390, 392, 406, 412, 418
new security environment 102, 116, 117, 398, 418

O

observable 50, 64, 65, 68, 76, 130, 149
opportunistic 55
organizational change 129, 138, 213, 214, 215, 400
organizational consultant 205, 206
organization structures 203

P

pandemic influenza 265, 266, 268, 274, 276, 278, 279, 280
personally identifiable information (PII) 164, 165
platform configuration register (PCR) 352
Port of Long Beach 267, 274, 275, 277, 280, 281, 409
Port of Los Angeles 267, 274, 275, 276, 277, 279, 280, 281, 409
power assertive 55
power reassurance 55
privacy rights 175
protected capabilities 350, 351
public policy 164, 166, 181, 182, 246, 385, 387, 399, 408

Q

queuing 270, 274, 276, 305

R

railroad operations 268
reference monitor 347
regulation 174, 183, 243, 244, 412
responsible disclosure 9
results documentation 60
rich media 147
Rich Media Theory 147
risk assessment 57, 243
risk determination 59
risk management 50, 56, 135, 136, 387, 394
risk mitigation 23, 24, 26, 44, 48, 50, 56, 59, 60, 61, 68, 295
role expectations 184, 185, 186

S

secure server 328, 336
security assessment 79
security assurance 75, 76, 77, 78, 94, 95
security assurance assessment 94, 95
security certifications 135, 188, 198, 388
security event 75, 76, 78, 82, 85, 86, 95, 307
security event management 76, 82
security incident 76, 205, 262, 308, 377, 418
security infrastructure 75, 76, 77, 78, 80, 82, 83, 84, 85, 86, 87, 89, 93, 94, 184
security metrics 76, 78, 79, 80, 81, 82, 83, 94
security policy 25, 53, 58, 61, 62, 66, 76, 84, 121, 125, 134, 135, 137, 140, 187, 190, 192, 196, 197, 253, 295, 348, 350, 398, 418
security researchers 6, 7, 8, 9, 11, 350
security standard 135, 385
server hardening 321, 322, 324, 325, 326, 327, 332, 333, 334, 335, 336
server hardening model 327, 333, 334, 335, 336
software vulnerabilities 1, 2, 6, 8, 9, 11, 21, 400
storage root key 354, 355, 356, 357
system audit 66

system characterization 57
system compromise 324
system dynamics 22, 73, 403, 409

T

technical skills 190
techno creep 143
Threat 22, 26, 45, 49, 51, 53, 58, 70, 71, 72, 73, 1, 23, 48, 72, 73, 74, 115, 116, 146, 302, 338, 384, 387, 388, 390, 397, 399, 400, 401, 402, 403, 408, 409, 414, 415
threat identification 26
transformation plan 213
trust 53, 73, 192, 194, 344, 345, 352, 353, 355, 357, 358, 359, 364, 366, 367, 389, 395, 400, 402, 403, 404, 413
trusted computing 338, 343, 344, 346, 348, 349, 350, 359, 361, 362, 364, 365, 366, 367, 368, 367, 369, 343, 367, 368, 369, 383, 389, 396, 399, 400, 401, 406, 408, 411, 413, 416, 417
trusted computing base (TCB) 348, 350
trusted computing group (TCG) 343, 344, 346
trusted platform 343, 344, 350, 351, 352, 353, 354, 355, 356, 358, 364
trusted platform module (TPM) 343, 344, 350
trusted software stack (TSS) 352
tyranny of the convenient 150, 151
tyranny of the urgent 153

U

U.S. Department of Homeland Security 266, 267, 279, 281, 416

V

virtual machine monitor 346
vulnerability 6, 7, 8, 10, 11, 15, 20, 25, 43, 46, 58, 76, 93, 367, 382, 389, 399, 400, 404, 409
vulnerability black markets 3, 5
vulnerability disclosure 8, 9, 10, 11, 20, 22, 386, 388, 409
vulnerability discovery 6

vulnerability identification 58
vulnerability markets 8, 10
vulnerability secrecy 8

W

worker absenteeism 265, 266, 267, 268, 277,
        278, 279, 280

Z

zero-day vulnerability 2